International Business

NINTH EDITION

Thoroughly updated, the 9th edition of this bestselling textbook incorporates global trend and data, supported by an exemplary case selection based on firms from around the world.

The internationally cited author team of Czinkota, Ronkainen, and Gupta balance conceptual understanding of business theory with the day-to-day realities of business practice, preparing students to become successful participants in the global business place.

This edition brings greater focus on Asia and emerging markets, as well as Brexit, the impact of COVID-19 on business, and the importance of technology and the digital space to international business practice. Through its discussion and analysis, the book guides students to a greater understanding of contemporary business issues and helps them to develop new tools of analysis.

Covering all key aspects of international business, the authors emphasize a few key dimensions: international context, role of government in international business, small and medium-sized firms, and social responsibility.

Michael R. Czinkota is Professor Emeritus at Georgetown University, teaching International Business, Trade, and Marketing at Robert McDonough School of Business. He studied law and business at the University of Erlangen-Nüremberg and holds an MBA in international business and a Ph.D. in Logistics from The Ohio State University. He has held professorial appointments at universities in Asia, Australia, Europe, and the Americas. He was listed among the top three contributors to international business research by the Academy of International Business. Widely published in international newspapers, he has been awarded three honorary degrees and gives frequent discourses to business, government, and academic groups.

Ilkka A. Ronkainen is Professor Emeritus of Marketing and International Business at the McDonough School of Business at Georgetown University, where he served as associate director (1981–86) and chairman (1986–87) of the National Center for Export–Import Studies and director of the Hong Kong Program. He holds a Ph.D. and a master's degree from the University of South Carolina and an M.S. (economics) from the Helsinki School of Economics. He was visiting professor and docent of international marketing at the Aalto University School of Business (HSE). He serves on the review boards of the *Journal of Business Research*, *International Marketing Review*, and *Journal of Travel Research*, and has reviewed for the *Journal of International Marketing* and the *Journal of International Business Studies*.

Suraksha Gupta is a Professor of Marketing and Director of Research at Newcastle University, London UK. She holds an M.B.A. from the Institute of Management Technology, India, and a Ph.D. in Marketing from Brunel University, UK. She has been awarded Best Professor in Marketing for her teaching and for Excellence in Academic Research for her work as a marketing scholar. She has served as a member of review boards of journals such as *British Journal of Management*, *Journal of Business Research*, and *Industrial Marketing Management*. Her research has been published in *Journal of World Business*, *British Journal of Management*, *Industrial Marketing Management*, and *Journal of Business Research and Technological Forecasting and Social Change*.

International Business

NINTH EDITION

Michael R. Czinkota
Georgetown University, Washington DC

Ilkka A. Ronkainen
Georgetown University, Washington DC

Suraksha Gupta
Newcastle University, London, UK

CAMBRIDGE
UNIVERSITY PRESS

University Printing House, Cambridge CB2 8BS, United Kingdom

One Liberty Plaza, 20th Floor, New York, NY 10006, USA

477 Williamstown Road, Port Melbourne, VIC 3207, Australia

314–321, 3rd Floor, Plot 3, Splendor Forum, Jasola District Centre, New Delhi – 110025, India

103 Penang Road, #05-06/07, Visioncrest Commercial, Singapore 238467

Cambridge University Press is part of the University of Cambridge.

It furthers the University's mission by disseminating knowledge in the pursuit of education, learning, and research at the highest international levels of excellence.

www.cambridge.org
Information on this title: www.cambridge.org/9781108476744
DOI: 10.1017/9781108667487

First published 2021

Printed in Singapore by Markono Print Media Pte Ltd

A catalogue record for this publication is available from the British Library.

ISBN 978-1-108-47674-4 Hardback
ISBN 978-1-108-70144-0 Paperback

Cambridge University Press has no responsibility for the persistence or accuracy of URLs for external or third-party internet websites referred to in this publication and does not guarantee that any content on such websites is, or will remain, accurate or appropriate.

Contents

Case Studies

Preface

We are grateful for the leadership position you, our market, have awarded to this book. Best-selling status in the international business field imposes an obligation to deliver cutting-edge innovations and improvements in terms of content as well as presentation. We honor your trust by doing our best to delight you through our presentation of conceptually sound, reality-based knowledge and by simplifying your task as students and teachers of international business. In this spirit of innovation, we offer you yet more value through *International Business*, 9th Edition.

Our textbook has gained recognition in its field due to its unique approach to international business. We have hit the refresh button on this 9th Edition to further your understanding of the major changes which the international business field is undergoing – in its concepts, applications, and contents. Governments and international organizations are asserting new roles in the field with the introduction of new regulations, restrictions, and even the use of trade as a weaponized geopolitical tool. Corporate and consumer perceptions are shaped by these factors, as well as by entirely new ways of thinking. Furthermore, the way we process and absorb knowledge in the international business field has changed dramatically. Online debates, internet presentations, and global information reach reshape the international business body of knowledge.

The concepts of risk, competition, profit, private property, and the value of capital are being realigned. Some risks are no longer acceptable or require collaborative actions to be manageable. Recognizing what we do not know – and understanding the resulting uncertainties and the limits to our ability to resolve controversial issues – requires the development of newly creative tools and approaches.

Many players in international business have come to discover that they are but one integral component of society. Politics, security, and religion are other dimensions possibly held in higher esteem than business. Those who argue based on economic principles alone may increasingly find themselves sidelined and on the losing side at that. For example, the level and structure of profits and executive compensation are increasingly expected to reflect a firm's long-term best interests within its overall societal context. The role of capital and its providers may need to be reconsidered, particularly in an era during which the cost of capital is low, if not cheap.

Small and medium-sized firms have – thanks to changes in technology – entirely new opportunities to succeed in new and emerging global markets. At the same time, never before have they been so exposed to unforeseen competition from distant parts of the globe. Fine business school programs without strong reflections of a worldwide context, proportionality, and interaction, sadly are confronted with shortcomings in their teaching, research, and service. Legislators and governments need to appreciate the direct and indirect effects their actions have on international business and also understand how international business affects their plans and decisions. These issues are not always in harmony. Just recall the debates about the opening dates and procedures surrounding the business opening decisions which occurred after the Coronavirus plague.

When we originally decided to write our international business book eight editions ago, we placed our wagers on several dimensions. Some of the key elements were the strong links to government – which we expected to uniquely address due to our ongoing policy exposure in Washington DC. We also offered a strong emphasis on small and medium-sized firms – which to us are significant players in the international field. Driven by the Jesuit education and principles instilled at Georgetown University, we were also aware of the need for moral and social responsibility in the business sector. Our research orientation helped maintain the focus on the truly global nature of actors and activities.

Years later, as we observe news headlines and interact with leaders in the business sector, we can say with confidence that events have moved in our direction like never before. Living in Washington has given us the possibility and the ability to follow, analyze, and incorporate both the role of government in general, and that of the US government, in specific, allowing us to observe and discern change. Having held policy-making positions and being called to advise governments, elected representatives, and international organizations in many nations has given us the insights and the networking capabilities that enable the decisive strategic orientation so necessary for this book. Our experience as founders and leaders of small business ventures, including the first ever university-based, student-run and government certified export-trading company, allows us to understand what the key needs and capabilities of such firms are. Simultaneously, we can render advice on how such firms can thrive. Our advisory work for larger multinational firms in turn permits us to share the realities of the battles in the international marketplace. Our long-term involvement with non-governmental organizations, for example as Chairs of small business foundations, enables us to better understand the not-for-profit world and non-market economies. We have combined our knowledge of business theory with the real-life concerns of governments, industry leaders, and consumers from around the world. Through International Business, 9th Edition, we hope to broaden your horizons and enable you to think more and better about the theories, dynamism, and challenges that international business both offers and faces.

Changes in the Ninth Edition

This most recent edition is truly cutting edge. Theoretical concepts such as investment flows and policies are tackled early on. We thoroughly cover important issues such as the imperative of cultural integration and the potential risks surrounding these aspects. Since publishing our last edition, the digital and online realm has expanded significantly. That is why we have delved into topics such as data knowledge and security, digital contributions, and online thinking, communicating, and researching, all of which permit us to illustrate and highlight the effects the internet has on international business.

Current Coverage

Today, change can happen at breakneck speed. Keeping on top of the evolving world of international issues, identifying trends, and analyzing the future impact on international business can be difficult. This ninth edition of International Business addresses the type of information needs of users, which are not yet addressed by other international business texts.

We have listened closely to our markets, ranging from colleagues to students on a global level, in order to deliver an outstanding product. We begin by presenting the impact of international business on countries, corporations, and individuals. We reflect more fully on some of the controversies in international business today, including the protectionist approaches taken by countries that traditionally were oriented towards trade liberalization such as the United Kingdom and the United States. We discuss why some may be disenchanted with increased globalization. By recognizing how firms and customers are closely connected through technologies around the world, we address how business has to adapt to changing dynamics and policies. That is why we also present areas of friction in international business and development, such as intellectual property rights, and pricing for poor countries. Special attention has also been paid to the strengthening of corporate governance and the tackling of bribery and corruption. We also emphasize the dimensions of ethics, social responsibility, curative marketing, and diversity through case studies, examples, and vignettes.

Our text consistently adopts a truly global approach. Attention is given to topics that may have been overlooked by other international textbooks but are critical to the international manager. This coverage includes chapters on supply chain management, international services trade, digital contributions for international business, changes in ownership, and doing business with emerging market economies.

New and Improved Topic Coverage and Organization

International Business, 9th Edition, is organized into four parts and is presented within 15 chapters. These parts allow the text to flow logically from introductory material to the international macro environment, followed by the micro, including marketing and financial considerations in the international marketplace.

Innovative Learning Tools

Use of Real-Life Examples

Drawing on real-life examples, trends, and data from around the world, rather than limiting ourselves to US-based information only, makes this an international and pragmatic book. As an example, many of our data sets and research insights come from Europe and Asia. In particular, we also emphasize cross-functional thinking, since rarely are actions driven by one dimension alone. A typical example is our simultaneous treatment of international business and terrorism in our research and discussions, which leads to quite unique conclusions.

We also ensure the reality and applications of our content by always addressing "what does this mean for international business?" For example, we explain how to use cultural variables for segmentation purposes in order to create new competitive tools.

Blending Current Theory and Application

Our theory section combines the latest thinking from business researchers and leading economists who regularly contribute to the field of international business. We also present the interdependence between different theories so that students appreciate the diversity of international business logic. All data, tables, figures, and maps were updated to present the most current information.

Technology, E-Commerce, and the Internet

Issues surrounding technology in the international workplace are integrated throughout our text. Discussion questions at the end of each chapter and case studies at the end of the book further emphasize research, so students can keep up with rapid change.

Distinguishing Pedagogic Features

Contemporary Realism

Each chapter offers a number of examples, that describe actual contemporary business situations. These issues include politics, ethics, e-business, culture, and entrepreneurship. Vignettes are intended to stimulate class discussion and aid the students to understand and absorb the text material.

Learning Objectives

Each chapter opens with a list of learning objectives that the student should take away from the text section. These are critical analysis tools and guides which the reader should keep in mind when turning pages. The ability to later on address and define each of the objectives set forth is a key indicator of comprehension.

Chapter Summary, Key Terms, and Discussion Questions

Each chapter closes with a chapter summary which the students should retain. It follows suit with the learning objectives set forth at the beginning. Key terms are those the students should be able to define and apply to a real-life scenario. The discussion questions are a complementary learning tool that will enable students to check their understanding of key dimensions and to think beyond basic concepts and areas that require further study. All these tools help students discriminate between main and supporting points and provide mechanisms for at-home review or class activities.

Take a Stand

These end-of-chapter exercises prompt students to read a short passage outlining a situation and to then make an educated decision about the outcome. They can be used for homework presentation, personal assessment of comprehension, or for classroom discussion.

Internet Exercises

This section found at the end of each chapter, encourages students to explore the various dimensions of the Web for databases and further research topics related to materials covered in each chapter. This hands-on experience helps to develop Internet, research, and business skills.

Exemplary Case Selection

To further link theory and practice, we present 15 case studies, most of which are new or updated. Some cases represent the winning work from the 2019 Cambridge/Czinkota/Kent case competition. Once more, congratulations to our champions. We draw case materials from firms around the world to offer truly global business scenarios, ranging from Germany to Namibia and India to China. The cases deal with the automotive industries such as BMW, aerospace giants such as Boeing, financial technologies such as PayPal, and even an approach to entertainment focused on Bollywood. We present the controversies emanating from the diamond industry, as well as the key drivers for financial institutions to internationalize and enter emerging market economies. Challenging questions accompany each case, to encourage in-depth discussion of the material covered in the chapter and allow students to apply the knowledge they have gained and permit instructors to develop and retain the use of their favorite teaching tool.

Acknowledgments

We are very grateful to Charles Skuba, Professor of the Practice and Senior Associate Dean for Executive Education at Georgetown University. His background as Chief of Staff for Market Access and Compliance in the US Dept. of Commerce, his close linkage with industry, his dedication to students, and his willingness to share all his knowledge and experience have made him a major supporter of this book project. He is always right on track, unfailingly courteous, and deeply insightful. Most importantly, he delivers! Charlie, chapeau! Thanks to Susan Ronkainen who helped pull together the changes in human resources. We thank Professor Suraksha Gupta of Newcastle University, London UK, who went far beyond the duty of a co-author in preparing and analyzing materials so that they are insightful and useful for students and colleagues. Pedagogical materials were suggested by Avdyushka Gupta. Our colleague Peter Dickson of Florida International University provided very valuable momentum when it came to new perspectives on competitiveness. Professor Ruediger Kaufmann of Fachhochschule Mannheim consistently brought new insights to bear when it came to a discussion of global changes. Ms. Katja Bullock, special assistant for personnel to the President of the United States, was instrumental in bringing realism to our thinking. We still believe that she deserves a purple heart medal! Professor Gary Knight of Willamette University shared his academic global thoughts by comparing trade policy shifts between administrations and made very essential contributions based on his personal research, ranging from the effect of terrorism on international business to corporate governance. He also brought the Bolinger insights to us; thank you! Ms. Maureen Smith, Principal Deputy Assistant Secretary of Commerce, was of major help in explaining the policy aspects of negotiations, in which she has taken part for more than 40 years. Our gratitude also goes to Lars Perner of the USC Marshall School who made many far-reaching comments regarding the digitalization of International Business. Substantial input, both for coordination as well as editing, came from three Georgetown University students who assisted both in person as well as online. Thank you Gabrielle M. Irwin (International Business U-2021), Lan H. Nguyen (Public Relations and Corporate Communications G-2020), and Laura M. Newton (Latin American Studies G-2020). You all truly made a difference for this ninth edition and the field of international business!

Kamal M. Abouzeid – Lynchburg College
Jane Adams – Cambridge University Press

Yair Aharoni – Duke University
Zafar U. Ahmed – Minot State University
Riad Ajami – Rensselaer Polytechnic Institute
Joe Anderson – Northern Arizona University
Valerie Appleby – Cambridge University Press
Robert Aubey – University of Wisconsin–Madison
David Aviel – California State University
Josiah Baker – University of Central Florida
Marilynn Baker – University of North Carolina–Greensboro
Bharat B. Bhalla – Fairfield University
Julius M. Blum – University of South Alabama
Sharon Browning – Northwest Missouri State University
Peggy E. Chaudhry – Villanova University
Ellen Cook – University of San Diego
Lauren DeGeorge – University of Central Florida
Luther Trey Denton – Georgia Southern University
Dharma deSilva – Wichita State University
Gary N. Dicer – The University of Tennessee
Peter Dowling – University of Tasmania
Carol Dresden – Coastal Carolina University
Derrick E. Dsouza – University of North Texas
Massoud Farahbaksh – Salem State College
Vivian Faustino-Pulliam – City College of San Francisco
Runar Framnes – Norwegian School of Management
Anne-Marie Francesco – Pace University–New York
Esra F. Gencturk – University of Texas–Austin
Debra Glassman – University of Washington–Seattle
Raul de Gouvea Neto – University of New Mexico
Antonio Grimaldi – Rutgers, the State University of New Jersey
John H. Hallaq – University of Idaho
Daniel Himarios – University of Texas at Arlington
Veronica Horton – Middle Tennessee State University
Basil J. Janavaras – Mankato State University
Michael Kublin – University of New Haven
Diana Lawson – University of Maine
Jan B. Luytjes – Florida International University
John Manley – Iona College
David McCalman – Indiana University–Bloomington
Tom Morris – University of San Diego
James Neelankavil – Hofstra University
V. R. Nemani – Trinity College

Moonsong David Oh – California State University–Los Angeles
Sam C. Okoroafo – University of Toledo
Diana Parente – State University of New York–Fredonia
Rushita Patel – Georgetown University
William Piper – Piedmont College
Jesus Ponce de Leon – Southern Illinois University–Carbondale
Jerry Ralston – University of Washington–Seattle
Peter V. Raven – Eastern Washington University
William Renforth – Florida International University
Martin E. Rosenfeldt – The University of North Texas
Tagi Sagafı-nejad – Loyola College
Rajib N. Sanyal – Trenton State College
Ulrike Schaede – University of California–Berkeley
John Stanbury – Indiana University–Kokomo
John Thanopoulos – University of Akron
Douglas Tseng – Portland State University
Robert G. Vambery – Pace University–New York
C. Alexandra Van Nostrand – Palm Beach Atlantic College
Betty Velthouse – University of Michigan–Flint
Heidi Vernon-Wortzel – Northeastern University
Steven C. Walters – Davenport College
James O. Watson – Millikin University
Mindy West – Arizona State University–Tempe
George A. Westacott – SUNY–Binghamton
Jerry Wheat – Indiana University Southeast
Tim Wilkinson – University of Akron
Bill Wresch – University of Wisconsin–Oshkosh
Kitty Y. H. Young – Chinese University of Hong Kong

Many thanks to those faculty members and students who helped us in sharpening our thinking by cheerfully providing challenging comments and questions. Several individuals had particular long-term impact on our thinking. These are the late Professor Bernard LaLonde of the Ohio State University, a true academic mentor; the late Professor Robert Bartels, also of Ohio State; late Professor Arthur Stonehill of Oregon State University; late Professor James H. Sood of American University; Professor Arch G. Woodside of Tulane University; Professor David Ricks of the University of Missouri-St. Louis; Professor Brian Toyne of St. Mary's University; and late Professor John Darling of Mississippi State University. They are our academic ancestors.

Many colleagues, friends, and business associates graciously gave their time and knowledge to clarify concepts; provide us with ideas, comments, and suggestions; and deepen our understanding of issues. Without the direct links to business and policy that you have provided, this book could not offer its refreshing realism. In particular, we are grateful to Secretaries Malcolm Baldridge, C. William Verity, Clayton Yeutter, and William Brock for the opportunity to gain international business policy experience and to William Morris, Paul Freedenberg, and J. Michael Farrell for enabling its implementation. We also thank William Casselman, Lew Cramer of the Utah World Trade Center, Gregory Unruh of Thunderbird School of Management, and Hannu Seristo of Aalto University. We appreciate all the horse sense shared by Professor Thomas Cooke.

Our elite team of student researchers provided valuable assistance. They made important and substantive contributions to this book. They dug up research information with tenacity and relentlessness; they organized and analyzed research material, prepared drafts of vignettes and cases, and reinforced everyone on the fourth floor of the Hariri Building at Georgetown University with their contagious can-do spirit.

A very special thank you to the people of Cambridge University Press, particularly Valerie Appleby and Jane Adams.

Foremost, we are grateful to our families, who have had to tolerate late-night computer noises, weekend library absences, and emailed vacations. The support and love of Ilona Vigh Czinkota and Margaret Victoria Czinkota and of the Gupta and Ronkainen families gave us the energy, stamina, and inspiration to write this book.

Michael R. Czinkota

June 2020

PART I

1 | The International Business Imperative

LEARNING OBJECTIVES

- To recognize the nature and the historical shifts of international business
- To learn the definition and impact of international business
- To evaluate the impact of international business
- To identify the relationship between international business and emerging markets using theoretical, political, and strategic aspects
- To appreciate the opportunities and challenges offered by social engagement to international business
- To analyze opportunities and challenges of international business

CONTENTS

VIGNETTE 1 Resilience in the face of a global pandemic

Coronavirus is the firing pin for major new innovation in education. To address the need of the hour during the crisis, universities are orienting their staff toward greater use of technology. For faculty members, it is a distance-learning alternative tool. But in many instances the faculty is very much dependent on technology learning from students rather than the traditional reverse flow. For the Higher Education sector, if one could calculate travel time of professors and their students, the time taken by them to travel would be higher than for professors to deliver rapidly while also fulfilling functional aspects of their work. There are still the stepwise rising rows of chairs, the black or white boards to communicate information, and a professor up front, while students take notes or raise their hand. What will happen to office hours, or the distribution of exams?

Any changes to a traditional module delivery model requires consideration of approval by at least four faculty committees, each one of which needs substantial time to investigate the impact and potential repercussions of alterations. Then there are reviews by board members, insights from administrators, and the "Fingerspitzengefuehl," or financial liaison. Woe to the planner of change who is likely to encounter a lead time of what seems like forever. The bottom line: change in education is hard to achieve.

How has the education system performed under virus conditions? Because of the danger emanating from the virus, we can see high degrees of rapidity, focus, transparency, and adaptation, which will lead to significant changes. Students, by the tens of thousands, are moving their main residence within a week. Faculty members have, within the same time, solidified the course materials and are preparing to deliver the content under entirely new conditions. Simultaneously, administrators have to rapidly find ways to work with incensed students and parents.

Also, remember that once the toothpaste has left the tube it won't go back in, and leads to totally different uses and expectations. All these sweeping changes, if considered for long-term contemplations, must be considered within a new kind of framework with an extended term time of about 10 days to 2 weeks. Coronavirus has pushed everyone to look for a way to cope with complexity at an extraordinary speed. The innovative methods of delivery that will finally be accepted are expected to pump new energy and strength into the body of university politic. The best in fusion is yet to come.

It is important to remember here that societies at different time periods have had their own changes, some without much benefit, such as bubonic plague and the great influenza epidemic. Other changes triggered much disruption in society but were very beneficial, such as the printing press of Gutenberg, electricity by Edison, and airplanes by the Wright brothers.

The current virus effect may lead to adjustments which will provide new approaches, unexpected adaptations, and a much wider field of options. There will be new playing fields, new players, and new rules. The post viral times might not necessarily be convenient or tranquil, but there will be many more opportunities for innovation and creativity. Resilience is key in the face of a challenge, and resulting spill-over effects from coronavirus mitigation efforts may well lead Higher Learning into a newly successful future.

Introduction

The nature of business is constantly changing, as the opening vignette shows. Expectations and capabilities adapt to the new business landscape, both with its barriers and opportunities. International business has become the norm for most countries and their companies, as they delight in the new markets discovered away from home. Since the 1950s, the growth of international trade and investment has been substantially larger than the growth of domestic economies. The current landscape for international trade and investment has evolved into a highly dynamic place with changes in global trade architecture, global value chains, and global trade opportunities offered by a digital economy. Technology during the digital era continues to increase the reach and the ease of conducting international business, pointing to even larger growth potential in the future. International business drives the flow of ideas, services, and capital across the world. As a result, innovations can be developed and disseminated more rapidly to firms working as partners in a global value-creation process (Cantwell, 2017; Silva et al., 2017). Although the increase in the development of the digital economy has contributed positively to the context, cybersecurity remains a threat to both buyers and sellers across national boundaries. Simultaneously, a decline in both volumes and prices of products being exported accounts for an increased focus on reforms in operational practices that have changed the priorities from profit making to ethical and coherent management in international supply networks. The priorities, issues, and regulations together have resulted in an increased cost of outsourced manufacturing. The concept of outsourced manufacturing has changed from being a services contract to a governance issue, thereby requiring greater engagement by different stakeholders. Stakeholders expect policy to be beneficial to everyone, including private, public, government, and institutional sectors (Doh et al., 2017). Civil society as a community enforces collaboration between international trade and sustainable development goals. Therefore, the impacts on society at large of investments by foreign companies in another economy have become indicators of performance of international trade. Hence, growth of international business today means an increase in employment, economic diversification, social inclusion, and economic competitiveness, with a reduction in uncertainty related to investment, terrorism, and environmental degradation, and a legitimacy of accelerated sustainable development.

A Definition of International Business

The term "globalization" describes the increased mobility of goods, services, labor, technology, and capital throughout the world. Although globalization is not a new development, its pace has increased with the advent of new technologies that make it easier for people to travel, communicate, and do business internationally, as well as with the recognition of countries around the world that opened trade and implemented investment policies that are beneficial for their economic growth. International business consists of transactions that are devised and carried out across national borders to satisfy the objectives of individuals, companies, and organizations. These transactions take on various interrelated forms. Primary types of international business have been export–import trade and direct foreign investment. International businesses can have varied forms, including wholly owned subsidiaries and joint ventures. Additional types of international business are licensing, franchising, and management contracts. The definition of international business reflects the flow of goods produced by a company to other countries for the sake of making profits and focuses on transactions between two or more countries. It recognizes that doing business internationally is an activity undertaken by a commercial entity to engage in business in multiple countries and not merely as a passive observer. International business refers to trade in the form of imports or exports, foreign direct investment, licensing agreements, franchising, etc. These activities result in innovative business practices, improved access to resources and capital, as well as increases in efficiency. Closely linked to activity is the term "satisfaction." It is crucial that the participants in international business are satisfied. Only if they feel they are better off after the transaction than they were before, will individual business transactions develop into a business relationship. The fact that the transactions are across national borders highlights a key difference between domestic and international business.

The international executive is subject to a new set of macro-environmental factors, to different constraints, and to quite frequent conflicts resulting from different laws, cultures, and societies (Beugelsdijk et al., 2017 and Brannen et al., 2017). The basic principles of business are still relevant, but their application, complexity, and intensity vary substantially. For example, China's gross domestic product

(GDP) heavily depends upon its export figures, whereas, in the case of India's GDP, it is linked with household consumption and the spending of consumers at the bottom of the pyramid (BOP). It is, therefore, important for international managers to focus on the value they wish to offer and norms they wish to follow while evaluating the competition and positioning their product or service. These aspects will enable them to be considerate to other cultures and take appropriate actions while reacting to situations in other countries. Managers of international firms should be aware, reflective, connected, flexible, and pragmatic about the different potentials of different segments in various foreign markets. Subject to constant change, international business is as much an art as a science. Yet success in the art of business depends on a firm grounding in its scientific aspects. Individual consumers, policy makers, and business executives with an understanding of both aspects of business will be able to incorporate international business considerations into their thinking and planning. They will be able to consider international issues and repercussions and make decisions related to questions such as:

- How will our idea, good, or service fit into the international market?
- Should we enter the market through trade or through investment?
- Should supplies be obtained domestically or from abroad?
- What product adjustments are necessary to be responsive to local conditions?
- What threats from global competition should be expected and how can these threats be counteracted?
- Can we serve customers with low incomes, but still maintain reasonable margins?
- Can we penetrate markets that are fragmented and not connected to the mainstream supply channels of distribution?
- Can we help customers with lower levels of literacy to develop their awareness and understanding of the product or service we offer?
- What medium should be used to create demand in the BOP segment (Bork et al., 2010)?

Given the economic dislocations and political challenges that arise with the globalization of business, many agree that globalization has done more harm than good. They believe that governments need to be more involved in managing global market forces to restore and stabilize economic systems and protect domestic jobs. This has led to government "bailouts" of industries and "buy domestic" legislation. Others claim that financial crises occur regularly to correct market imbalances and that extensive government involvement impedes market growth and the benefits that globalization brings. Has globalization gone too far? Should governments enact legislation that protects domestic industries from international competition? When management integrates these issues into the decision-making process, international markets can provide growth, profit, and needs satisfaction not available to those that limit their activities to the domestic marketplace. The purpose of this book is to provide satisfaction and success to companies, consumers, and governments.

International business is typically driven by four key drivers: cost, market, environment, and competition. These factors together created a world economy and have contributed to growth of capitalism that has changed the quality of life for people worldwide and increased their purchasing power. Increases in consumer power pushed companies from different parts of the world to become interdependent not only for profitable production, but also for consumption of their products. Simultaneously, this change also motivated institutional agents and governments in host countries like China and India to promote and facilitate free trade in their country without any restrictions or limitations using technological advancements. Information and communication technology (ICT) helped to create global communication channels that facilitated development of an efficient global value chain. The spillover effects of these developments first led to the creation of trade regions and agreements like the European Union (EU), the Canada–United States–Mexico Agreement (CUSMA), the Association of Southeast Asian Nations (ASEAN), and the Asia-Pacific Countries (APAC). The desire of the emerging middle class in countries like China and India to use innovative products will require flexible and perhaps even new forms of management. Just consider how rapidly major and smaller corporations adopted their production capabilities to respond to newly emerging needs from Coronavirus infections. General Motors (GM) shifted production patterns to bring medical ventilators to patients in need (Boudette & Jacobs, 2020). Prada, the Milanese fashion designer, created masks and hospital gowns for the infected of Italy (Bramley, 2020).

The globalization of business and economic growth has accelerated dramatically since the 1980s. Business and management theories have pushed managers of international firms to consider global expansion in light of challenges like corruption, nepotism, and newly emerging trade restrictions (Cuervo-Cazurra, 2016). Such concerns create a challenge to capitalism in an interconnected world. Firms are best at doing what they set out to do: satisfying customers. Addressing the target market focuses the minds of managers on organizational goals.

Online trade offers many opportunities to all types of firms, including small and medium-sized enterprises (SMEs) and micro, small, and medium enterprises (MSMEs), to serve customers in foreign markets with minimized administrative burdens. International trade through online space is more efficient for both buyers and sellers, as it facilitates efficiency in production, distribution, marketing, sales, and delivery of goods and services. Exhibit 1.1 shows the extent to which business-to-consumer internet marketing has raised its impact.

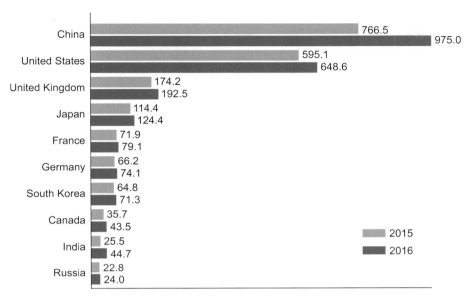

B2C e-commerce turnover in 2015 and 2016 (in billion US dollars)

	2015	2016
China	766.5	975.0
United States	595.1	648.6
United Kingdom	174.2	192.5
Japan	114.4	124.4
France	71.9	79.1
Germany	66.2	74.1
South Korea	64.8	71.3
Canada	35.7	43.5
India	25.5	44.7
Russia	22.8	24.0

Exhibit 1.1 World's largest B2C e-commerce markets
Source: Statista.

However, there may also be difficulties that need to be overcome. Different governments may have different rules for entire business sectors. An example is the case of Antigua and Barbuda offering online gambling services to consumers in the USA and filing a complaint with the World Trade Organization (WTO) because of their belief that the US Government violated international treaties by restricting their online gambling services. The complaint resulted in a $21 million per year judgement, but, so far, the USA has not paid out (Miles, 2018). Other issues that may create conflict situations for international firms include domestic regulation, customs valuation, customs duty payment, import licensing, local standards, nationality of origin, classification, national treatment, favoritism, transparency, competition, and privacy. Three main organizations investigate and adjudicate international business issues: the WTO, which deals with international trade issues in general, the General Agreement on Trade in Services (GATS), which targets complaints in the international services trade area, and the Trade-Related Aspects of Intellectual Property Rights (TRIPS), which deals with disputes related to intellectual property rights.

TRIPS is growing in importance in light of new technologies such as e-commerce and the growing interlinkage and exchange of intellectual capital. Article 1 of the

GATS addresses the financial and fiscal implications of e-commerce for digital products and services delivered electronically. In addition, there are other major concerns, exemplified by cybercrime, cybersecurity, piracy, data protection, and net neutrality, which deals with non-discriminatory monetization of the internet. E-commerce connects societies, governments, and businesses, while facilitating transparency, predictability, and non-discriminatory business practices. Thus, e-commerce adds value to the global supply chain. In addition, e-commerce promotes social inclusion, one of the sustainable development goals of the United Nations. This increases the capacity of small firms to develop economically and access customers across national borders.

The Need for International Business

Firms that have engaged in international business have witnessed an increase in production and consumption, thereby increasing the scope for their own and affiliated businesses. Internationalization helps companies to diversify the risk of failure in one country by expanding their activities to customers in other countries. Free trade between nations has helped develop countries to increase their wealth. Some claim that customers in developing countries have been paying for the growth of international business firms, and have predicted that the outcome may be a monopolistic business environment (Meyer, 2017; Picciotto, 2017).

Scholars find international business to be exciting because it combines the art of business with many other disciplines, such as economics, anthropology, geography, history, language, statistics, technology, and demography. Isolation can be unhealthy for a country's economy. If firms do not become a part of the global economy, they and their country may experience declining economic influence, less profitability, and a deteriorating standard of living for their country's citizens. Successful participation in international business, however, holds the promise of improved quality of life and a society that can offer more diverse alternatives. Many future professional colleagues and competitors will come from different parts of the world. In an era of niche marketing, instant communications, and virtual ways of reaching millions of people, unprecedented opportunities exist for individuals to enter the international business arena. Start-ups can compete with multinational business enterprises by delivering speed, creativity, and innovation. Understanding international business is therefore crucial for firms, both large and small.

Firms are globally linked to each other through supply agreements and joint undertakings in research and development that can have global effects, both positive and negative (Buckley et al., 2017; Cho et al., 2019; Buckley et al., 2018;

Teagarden et al., 2018). For example, high sulfur emissions in one geographical area may cause acid rain in another. Pollution in one country may result in water contamination in another. Service activities can cause cross-national, collateral effects as well. For example, weaknesses in some currencies, due to problems in a country's banking sector, can quickly spill over and reduce the currency values of other nations that heavily depend on trade with the devaluing currency. The deregulation of some service industries, such as air transport or telephony, can thoroughly affect the structure of these industries around the world. All these changes have had an impact on countries' financial positions and ownership of economic activities on a global platform. For example, the USA, after having been a net creditor to the world for many decades, has been a world debtor since 1985. This means that overall, the USA owes more to foreign institutions and individuals than is owed to the USA. China has emerged as the number one US creditor. Research highlights the business potential offered by countries that are the global BOP segment. However, difficulties in accessing these markets have discouraged companies from capturing market share. Lack of rural infrastructure, corruption, and digital illiteracy are some of the shortcomings. However, e-commerce has helped companies to enter markets that were beyond imagination. For example, the penetration of mobile phones has given multinational firms access to information about personal consumption patterns of BOP countries. Such telephony can provide global industry information. Consequently, fishing-ship crews can now see information about the regional catch volume and type. Armed with this information, they can select the port into which they bring their bounty. This of course enables them to obtain higher prices than those they would have obtained had they been uninformed – one of the visible benefits of transparency.

International expansion of companies also assists sustainable development. For example, the creation of green jobs led local entrepreneurial, or not-for-profit firms, to manage the manufacturing, packaging, and processing of waste. International business also offers consumers new choices. It can enable the acquisition of a wider variety of products, both in terms of quantity and quality, and at reduced prices through international competition. International business facilitates the mobility of production elements. As a result, international business activities do not benefit everyone to the same degree. Just like Janus, the two-faced god of the Romans, international business can bring benefits and opportunity to some, while delivering drawbacks and problems to others. The international firm and its managers, as well as the consumers of international products and services, need to understand how to make globalization work for them, as well as think about how to ensure that these benefits are afforded to a wide variety of people and countries.

A Brief History of International Business

Pax Romana

International business is conducted by both nations and individuals. In many instances, international business itself is a major force in shaping borders and changing world history because of its ability to stimulate mass production and efficiency and utilize raw material and natural resources available in the host country. With the advancement of technology and emergence of new techniques, the flow of goods, services, and information has become accessible to SMEs in both the developed and the developing world (Child et al., 2017; Cravino & Levchenko, 2017). As an example, international business played a vital role in the formation and decline of the Roman Empire, whose impact on thought, knowledge, and development can still be felt today. One reads about the marching of the Roman legions, which formed the empire. However, most growth came from the *Pax Romana*, or Roman peace, as a major stimulus from 27 BCE to 180 CE. This ensured that merchants were able to travel safely and rapidly on roads built, maintained, and protected by the Roman legions and their affiliated troops. A second stimulus was the use of common coinage, which simplified business transactions and made them comparable throughout the empire. In addition, Rome developed a systematic law, central market locations through the founding of cities, and an effective communication system, all of which contributed to the functioning of the marketplace and a reduction in business uncertainty.

International business flourished within the empire, and the improved standard of living in the empire became apparent to those outside. Soon city-nations and population groups that were not part of the empire decided to join as allies. They agreed to pay tribute and taxes because the benefits were greater than the drawbacks. Thus, the immense growth of the Roman Empire occurred mainly through the linkages of business. Of course, preserving this favorable environment required substantial effort. When pirates threatened the seaways, for example, Gnaeus Pompeius Magnus (Pompey the Great) sent out a large fleet to subdue them. Once this was accomplished, the cost of international distribution within the empire dropped substantially because fewer shipments were lost at sea. Goods could be made available at lower prices, which in turn translated into larger demand and greater, more widely available benefits. The fact that international business was one of the primary factors that held the empire together can also be seen in the decline of Rome. When "barbaric" tribes overran the empire, it was not mainly through war and prolonged battles that Rome had lost ground. Rather, outside people attacked an empire that was already substantially weakened at its foundations because of infighting and increasing decadence. The Roman peace was no longer enforced, the use and acceptance of the common coinage declined, and communications no longer worked as well. Therefore, affiliation with the empire no longer offered the benefits of the past. Former allies, who no longer saw any benefits in their association with Rome, willingly cooperated with invaders rather than face prolonged battles.

Roman authority and prosperity were firmly established in the Mediterranean, and trade flourished through the Red Sea and Indian Ocean, even as far as China, where the Han Empire provided a similar stability for nearly four centuries. After its beginnings in 202 BCE, Han rulers solidified the unification of China and expanded its borders westward. Under their rule, trade thrived with the development of a system of trade routes to central Asia that became known as the Silk Road. Trade between the Roman and Chinese empires was not direct and occurred through many intermediaries in India, Arabia, and central Asia. Suppliers and recipients may not have even known of each other, even though they became highly dependent on each other. Trading routes and conditions were far more difficult and dangerous in ancient times than today. Travel by sea or land exposed traders to enormous risk of weather, disease, piracy, and the whims of various rulers. A stable political environment encouraged trade. Stable countries are trading countries. When Roman and Han authority collapsed around 200 CE, trade with the East came to an almost complete standstill. Exhibit 1.2 provides an example of Chinese trade reduction policy. Today, broad linkages continue to exist. Many people may not know about the activities of the Deutsche Bundesbank and the European Central Bank – both located in Frankfurt, Germany – or the People's Bank

---

EXHIBIT 1.2 The empress strikes again

The importance of international business has not always prevailed. The Empress Dowager Cixi of China was one of the most powerful women in Chinese history (Encyclopaedia Britannica, 2019). She introduced broad-based education to China, which made the country's population much more competitive internationally. However in 1896, she made significant changes in the budget in order to finance the renovation of her Summer Palace in Beijing. The Empress impounded government funds designated for shipping and the Chinese navy. In consequence, China's participation in world trade almost came to a halt. In the decades that followed, China operated in almost total isolation from world shipping. There was almost no transfer of knowledge from the outside. There also were virtually no major inflows of goods and services. Without the innovation and productivity increases that result from exposure to international business, Chinese industry and policy fell quickly behind its previous world trade partners. Also, the level of well-being of Chinese consumers was substantially affected.

of China in Beijing. These institutions play an important role in the availability of student loans and interest rates.

The stability afforded by the Pax Romana and the Han Empire encouraged the long-range and highly indirect commerce between Rome and China in the first and second centuries after Christ. More recently, the USA developed a world leadership position in trade and investment largely due to its championship of market-based business transactions in the Western world. Also, there is the broad flow of ideas, goods, and services across national borders, and an encouragement of international communication and transportation. The period from 1945 to 1990 for Western countries, and since then for the world, has been characterized by a Pax Americana, an American sponsored and enforced peace.

Earlier economic coercion was used by nations or groups of nations as a political tool. During the Civil War period in the USA, the North consistently pursued a strategy of denying international business opportunities to the South in order to deprive it of needed export revenues. The Smoot–Hawley Tariff Act of 1930 raised import duties to reduce the volume of goods coming into the USA. The Act was passed in the hope that it would restore domestic employment. The result, however, was trade retaliation, global conflict, and cultural disparity.

After WWII, global trade and investment rose to a heretofore unknown level of importance. Since 1945, American peace contributed to rapid growth in international business transactions. Exhibit 1.3 focuses on shifts in foreign direct investment. However, there has been a continuity of shortcomings, in the financial sector as well

EXHIBIT 1.3 FDI volatility

On a global level, annual foreign direct investment (FDI) inflows reached $1.8 trillion in 2007, finally exceeding the previous all-time high set in 2000. The terrorist attacks of September 11, 2001 triggered a major downturn. FDI stock, or accumulated totals, exceeded $15 trillion in 2007. UNCTAD reported a modest rise in FDI by 2019, although the outflow of FDI since 2008 has been very low. Despite the longer-term growth trends in both trade and investment, the financial crisis that began in 2007 resulted in the sharp volume reductions by the end of 2008. By 2009, WTO economists assessed world trade growth as "strongly negative." The major developed economies bore the brunt of this decline. On the other hand, developing economies such as China, India, and Brazil experienced continued growth. Individuals and firms have come to recognize that they are competing in a dynamic global marketplace, characterized by major change. Risk and opportunity must now be examined not only domestically but globally, both in terms of market disruptions and *global supply and sourcing chains*.

as in trade. For example, the global financial crisis of 2008, as well as the Coronavirus outbreak of 2020, had "far-reaching geopolitical consequences, such as less market liberalization and created new periods of government regulation, protectionism, and heightened intervention." (Altman, 2009, Czinkota & Czinkota, 2020).

Current Position of International Business

International business has forged a network of global links that binds all countries, institutions, and individuals much closer than ever before. These links tie together trade, financial markets, technology, and living standards in an unprecedented way. A freeze in Brazil and its effect on coffee and orange juice production are felt around the world. Just as the effects of previous financial crises in Mexico and Asia influenced stock markets, investments, and trade flows in all corners of the globe, the financial crisis that started in 2007 reverberated around the world. Financial institutions and economies throughout the developed and developing world were severely affected, as we can also see with the repercussions of the Coronavirus infections of 2020.

These linkages have also become more intense on an individual level. Communication has built new international bridges, be it through music or the watching of international programs. Overall, culture has brought us many specific products and activities, but it has also delivered new products with international appeal and encouraged similar activities around the world. Specific cultures might lead consumers to purchase similar jeans, dance to the same songs, watch the same movies, and eat burgers, pizzas, and sushi. Transportation links let individuals from different countries see and meet each other with unprecedented ease. Common cultural pressures result in similar social phenomena and behaviors; for example, more dual-income families are emerging around the world, which leads to more frequent but, due to new time constraints, more stressful shopping. Exhibit 1.4 provides some reality check examples.

EXHIBIT 1.4 Make that a caffe latte, please!

If you're hungry in Hong Kong, or in São Paolo or Milan for that matter, you can always find familiar food. However, some cross-cultural developments are initially resisted. For example, in 1999 Jose Bové, a French activist, drove a bulldozer into a McDonald's in Millau, France, to protest against American cultural imperialism and *mal bouffe* (bad food). Despite Bové's sentiments (that being that McDonald's was "bad food"), the French public proved their appreciation for Le Big Mac with their wallets. By 2014, France had become the second most profitable market in the world for McDonald's, ranking only behind the USA.

Since the 1990s, perhaps one of the greatest transformations in daily life has been the global proliferation of chain restaurants and the food choices available to consumers. International business has brought diversity of choice, quality food, clean environments. and fast, efficient service to locations around the world. You can find a California Pizza Kitchen in the Dubai Mall or in Plaza Indonesia in Jakarta. Tim Hortons, a Canadian fast food chain, has brought its famous coffee and Timbits, the bite-sized donut holes, to more than 400 locations in the USA, as well as to locations in at least 13 other countries. However, some criticize restaurant franchise operations for spreading industrialized food processes and junk food to cultures that have a rich cuisine and dining tradition.

The international restaurant business is not only about fast food franchises, coffee, and burgers. International franchising has changed the food culture and eating habits of global audiences with the proliferation of choices available to them. For example, Wolfgang Puck and other celebrity chefs have opened fine dining and more casual restaurants in cities around the world. But sometimes you just want a convenient espresso or cup of coffee. In the café category, Starbucks had coffee shops in 44 countries during 2008. In 2019, Starbucks had a presence in 79 countries through 29,865 coffee shops, out of which 14,758 are in the USA and 3,684 in China.

Shifts in financial flows have had major effects on FDI into plants, which increasingly take the place of trade. All of these developments make us more and more dependent on one another. This interdependence, however, is not stable. On an ongoing basis, realignments take place on both micro and macro levels that make past orientations at least partially obsolete. For example, for its first 200 years the USA looked to Europe for markets and sources of supply. Despite the maintenance of this orientation by many individuals, firms, and policy makers, the reality of trade relationships has changed. During the first two decades of the twenty-first century, entirely new areas for international business activities opened up as Eastern Europe and Russia, and many of the countries of the former Soviet Union have eagerly pursued new trade opportunities. In 2008, Ukraine acceded to the WTO, joining Georgia, Moldova, the Kyrgyz Republic, and Mongolia, which had already become members. As a result, the WTO had 164 members by 2020 (WTO, 2020).

These changes, and the speed with which they come about, significantly affect countries, corporations, and individuals. For example, the relative participation of countries in world trade is shifting. In a world of rapidly growing trade, the market share of Western Europe in trade exports has been declining. The USA's share of global exports has declined while its share of global imports has increased. Some countries, such as China, Germany, and Japan, have become dependent upon exports to drive economic growth. As their economies have grown, the global market shares of China, ASEAN countries, and Brazil have increased. The composition of trade, or the ratio of primary commodities in comparison to manufactured goods in a country's trade, has also been changing. For example, from the 1960s to the 1990s, the trade role of primary commodities declined precipitously while the importance of manufactured goods increased. This meant that countries and workers who had specialized in commodities such as *caoutchouc* (rubber) or mining were likely to fall behind those who had embarked on strengthening their manufacturing sector. Concurrently, a growing regionalization was taking place worldwide along with the development of trading blocs and a proliferation of bilateral trade agreements.

Firms operating in trading blocs must manage and navigate an increasingly complex array of trading arrangements between nations, as well as dealing with international politics, international culture, and international institutions, to construct a dynamic international marketing strategy and minimize the competitive risk they face and costs they incur. They may find that the free flow of goods, services, and capital encounters new impediments as regions become more inward looking and governments become more active, not only because business environment changes, but also because the pace of technological change accelerates. Atari's Pong, one of the earliest arcade video games, was first introduced in the early 1980s. Today action games and movies have computerized "humans," and artificial intelligence (AI) provides consumers with a new experience.

The first office computers emerged in the mid 1980s; today, home computers are commonplace, and notebooks and ultra-portable sub-notebooks are favorites for students in the classrooms of emerging markets. Email was introduced to the mass market in the 1990s; today, many college students reserve "old-fashioned" Facebook and blogs for their parents and professors while using Snapchat and Instagram among themselves. All these shifts allow for a faster and user-intense information exchange, leading to new approaches in advertising, production, and consumption. Companies like Facebook have been sharing social interactions of consumers with companies who use the information to trace the consumer journey for the purpose of predicting a customer's commercial behavior. These initiatives have landed the founder Mark Zuckerberg into antitrust law claims. Some stakeholders do not consider Facebook's practices to be responsible ones. Many of the changes coming about are so new that neither advocates nor adversaries have a full understanding of what regulations need to be implemented. All this demonstrates that activities in the online space are progressing to a new stage, and users, regulatory bodies, and organizations recognize the need for governance and regulations with enforceable mandates.

International business is considered to be the reason for declining world market prices for commodities and rising prices for manufactured goods because producers are increasingly unable to keep up to the volume-based pricing. Some commodity-dependent countries realized temporary windfalls as prices of oil, wheat, and corn rose dramatically in one year, only to watch them evaporate as prices dropped again in the following year. Also, manufacturing has shifted to new nations. In the mid-1800s, manufacturing accounted for about 17% of employment in the USA. This proportion grew to almost 30% in the 1960s, only to decline at a rising rate. By March 2020, US manufacturing experienced the loss of some 18 million manufacturing jobs during the Coronavirus epidemic (Bureau of Labor Statistics, 2020). Still, US manufacturing underwent significant transformation as productivity gains and skills upgrading created a leaner and more skilled manufacturing workforce. Since 2017, German manufacturing employment has risen by 1.6%, while in Japan the increase was 1.8% (McKinsey Global Institute, 2015). All these shifts in employment reflect a transfer of manufacturing away from traditional manufacturers toward the emerging economies. At the end of the second decade of the twenty-first century, employment in developed countries is decreasing. In developing countries, particularly local governments provide support to maintain increases in employment (Perchard et al., 2017).

Substantial shifts are also occurring in the services area. Activities that were confined to specific locales have become mobile. The global transmission of payroll, accountancy, legal document archival, and radiology charts to relevant specialists in India is a portent of shifts in trade composition in the future. From a global perspective, countries like the USA, UK, and those in Europe have gained prominence as a market for the world, but they have lost some of their importance as a supplier to the world. Many new participants have entered the international market. In Europe, firms and countries that had war-torn economies following World War II have reestablished themselves. In Asia, new competitors have aggressively obtained a share of growing world trade. The grouping of countries such as Brazil, Russia, India, China, and South Africa (BRICS) has evolved with unmatchable potential for economic cooperation among businesses and for inclusive growth through shared prosperity. Given the importance of the forum and the opportunity to interact with various stakeholders from government, industry, and leading industry associations, the Confederation of Indian Industry (CII) organized an Indian business delegation to attend the BRICS Business Forum, on the sidelines of the 2018 BRICS Summit in Johannesburg, South Africa.

At the macroeconomic level, where trading relationships affect individual markets, the trade picture is similar in both developed and developing countries with the key focus of local governments on increasing employment. It has been estimated that for the US, $1 billion in exports of manufactured goods supports the creation, on average, of 6,000 jobs. For services exports, the US job effect is 4,500 jobs (USTR, 2020). Imports, in turn, bring a wider variety of products and services into a country. They exert competitive pressure on domestic firms to improve.

Imports, therefore, expand the choices of consumers and improve their standard of living. Exports, in turn, are the crucial factor that makes imports possible and sustainable in the long run.

On the microeconomic level, participation in international business can help firms achieve economies of scale that cannot be achieved in domestic markets. A global market significantly increases the number of potential customers. Increasing production lets firms ride the learning curve more quickly and, therefore, makes goods available more cheaply domestically. Finally, and perhaps most important, international business enables firms to hone their competitive skills abroad by meeting the challenge of foreign products.

By going abroad, firms can learn from their foreign competitors, challenge them on their ground, and translate the absorbed knowledge into productivity improvements at home. Firms that operate only in the domestic market are at risk of being surprised by the onslaught of foreign competition and thus seeing even their domestic market share threatened. Research has shown that US multinationals of all sizes and in all industries outperformed their strictly domestic counterparts. They grow more than twice as fast in sales and earn significantly higher returns on equity and assets. Workers also benefit from exports as, typically, exporting firms of all sizes pay higher wages than non-exporters. Firms that refuse to participate actively are relegated to reacting to the global economy. Many industries have experienced the need for international modifications. As a result of competition, many industries have adjusted, but with great pain. Examples abound in the steel, automotive, and textile sectors of economies such as the USA, the UK, and Germany. In spite of attempts to adjust, entire industries have ceased to exist in their home market and/or have moved manufacturing to other countries. For example, Harley Davidson faced tax penalties from President Donald Trump if they moved production overseas and tried to sell motorcycles back to the USA (Robb, 2018). These developments demonstrate that it has become virtually impossible to disregard the powerful impact that international business has on all of us. Temporary isolation may be possible and delay tactics may work for a while, but the old adage applies: you can run, but you cannot hide.

Participation in the world market has become truly imperative. Globalization has increased mobility of goods, services, labor, technology, and capital worldwide. Global activities offer many additional opportunities to businesses. Market saturation can be delayed by lengthening or rejuvenating the life of products and exporting them to more countries. This is very common for high technology. Often, consumers seek technology but don't have the ability to purchase the latest products. Sourcing policies that once were inflexible have become variable because plants can now be shifted from one country to another and suppliers can be found on almost every continent. Cooperative agreements can be formed that enable each party to bring its major strength to the table and emerge with better goods, services, and ideas than it could have on its own. Consumers worldwide can select from a greater variety of products at lower prices, which enables them to improve their choices and lifestyles.

International business also brings controversy. Consumers are paying much greater attention to product dimensions and implications. E-commerce plays an important role in educating customers about both simple and complex products. Given the general ease of internet access, consumers increasingly have the resources to check whether the firms producing specific goods are exploiting their workers or harming the environment.

All of the intricacies of international opportunities need careful exploration if they are to be realized. What is needed is an awareness of global issues, native understanding of sustainable development goals, and an attitude to adjust to change.

Impact of International Business

The first industrial revolution was in iron and textile industries during the eighteenth century in Europe and the USA, followed by steel, oil, and electricity as a second revolution during the nineteenth century. Advances led to the introduction of the combustion engine in modes of travel, the telephone as a mode of communication, and the light bulb (using electricity) as a mode of illumination. The third revolution was also progressive, with the introduction of personal computers and the Internet, which brought in new verticals, such as robotics, artificial intelligence, the Internet of Things, and 3D printing. Already, there are new challenges, such as increasing poverty and inequality, leading to mistrust, corruption, and terrorism.

Technology has also burdened humanity. A large area in Ukraine and Belarus was rendered uninhabitable by radioactive materials leaked from the Chernobyl reactor in 1986. Improper disposal of waste has seriously harmed land and water resources. In some places, damage can be repaired, but in other locales, restoration may be impossible. Growing concerns about environmental quality have led many people in more economically advanced nations to call for changes in economic systems that harm the natural environment. Concerted efforts are underway, for example, to halt destruction of forests in the Amazon Basin, thereby preserving the vast array of different plant and animal species in the region and saving vegetation that can help moderate the world's climate. Cooperative ventures have been established to promote selective harvesting of nuts, hardwoods, and other products taken from natural forests. Furthermore, an increasing number of restaurants and grocers are refusing to purchase beef raised on pastures that are established by clearing forests.

In some circumstances, stakeholders are blaming the various industrial revolutions and internationalization of industries for the deterioration of the social environment. Disruptive issues, such as climate change, have an impact on humankind. Markets and publics may form different clusters, which might be based on geography, religion, or occupation. Global stakeholders expect different actors and agents of change to collaborate with each other. Governments need to find solutions to previously unforeseen challenges. Gaining stakeholder confidence requires a global strategy of collaboration, where outcomes can be measured not only in financial but also in developmental areas.

Curative Marketing: A New Perspective

A holistic and strategic focus by international business, curative marketing is a vital component integrating a business into the global society (Czinkota et al., 2015). Curative marketing links product branding with personal stewardship. It implements corrective long-term solutions to global social problems. It also makes Extended Producer's Responsibility (EPR) a norm (Tasaki et al., 2019; Gupta, 2019; Hamilton & Webster, 2018; Kourula et al., 2017). Curative marketing strategies require assessment of the actions of all engaged in the global value chain, including the enthusiastic and self-motivated participation of corporations, government, and consumers.

Companies like Stonyfield, a farming school in New Hampshire set up with seven cows 1983 by Samuel Kaymen and Gary Hirshberg, have set good examples of companies focusing on the good of society. The founders aimed to offer healthy foods for healthy people on a healthy planet, with products, such as yogurt, made without the use of any chemical fertilizers or pesticides and in a way that protects the environment – for example, by generating their own renewable energy and developing yogurt cups made of plants instead of petroleum. The company has engaged their local networks and waste management companies at various locations for collection of yogurt cups to be sent back to the head office, where they are recycled and converted into toothbrushes, which after use can be returned to the company by consumers in a post-paid envelope. These efforts have enabled Stonyfield to not only strengthen their customer equity and build their brand equity, but also increase their profits through efficient recycling of raw material. The initiatives of some companies also stem from incidents such as the outbreak of plague in 1994 in Surat, which was due to inefficient solid waste management by the municipal authorities.

Another example of curative marketing comes from the informal recycling sector of India, engaged in managing solid waste. This sector not only helps in reducing and recycling waste, it also provides employment to millions of people who do not have the skills to get into the corporate sector in a structured way. Their delivery chain starts from waste pickers, or thiawalas, progresses to local kabaris, as scrap collectors, then to regional kabaris as scrap traders and reprocessors who are large corporate houses like Aditya Birla Group. The level of efficiency of actors in this case is high and they are competitive in their approach, which makes them profitable. Recycling is a major concern because of the unhygienic working conditions in which people are engaged. Therefore, organizations like the Self-Employed Women's Association (SEWA) have taken the responsibility for communications that create awareness of human dignity and the hazardous aspects of the recycling sector.

The Structure of the Book

This book will help readers understand how participation in the commercial global space helps firms to succeed. Integrating theory with practice will help readers to balance conceptual understanding and knowledge with day-to-day realities. The book, therefore, addresses the international concerns of both organizations starting out on their internationalization and multinational corporations already in existence.. The new international manager will need to know the answers to basic, yet pertinent, questions: How can we find out whether demand for our product exists abroad? What must we do to get ready to market internationally? Can digital space help us start international business? These issues are also relevant for managers in multinational corporations, but the questions they consider are often more specific. Throughout the book, public policy concerns are included in discussions of business activities, since governments are increasingly re-involved in structuring the business environment and conditions. In this way, you are exposed to both the macro- and micro-dimensionality of international business issues.

Chapters 1 and 2 introduce the importance of international business and its global linkages in the digital era. Chapters 3, 4, 5, and 6 present the environment of international business, addressing culture, policies, politics, and law. Chapters 7, 8, and 9 address the startup phase of internationalization. Chapters 10, 11, 12, 13, and 14 target the operational issues surrounding international business, using an implementation-oriented perspective. Chapter 15 concludes by focusing on new horizons for international business and your career. We hope that, once you finish the book, you will not only complete another academic subject but also be well versed in the theoretical, policy, and strategic aspects of international business, and therefore be able to contribute to improved international competitiveness, a better global standard of living, and a more prosperous life for yourself.

SUMMARY

International business has been conducted ever since national borders were formed and has played a major role in shaping world history. Growing in importance since 1980, it has shaped an environment that, due to economic linkages, is today a global marketplace. Over that time, world trade has expanded from $200 billion to more than $19.5 trillion in 2018, while international direct investment reached $1.3 trillion in 2018. The growth of both has been far more rapid than the growth of most domestic economies. As a result, nations are much more affected by international business than in the past. Global links and digital space together have made possible investment strategies and business alternatives that offer tremendous opportunities. Yet these changes and the speed of change can also represent threats to nations, firms, and individuals. New participants in international business compete fiercely for world market share. Individuals, corporations, and policy makers around the globe have awakened to the fact that international business is a major imperative and offers opportunities for future growth and prosperity. International business provides access to new customers, affords economies of scale, and enables the honing of competitive skills. Performing well in global markets is the key to improved standards of living, higher profits, and better wages. International business is not free, and its sometimes localized effects can cause displacement, difficulties, and hardship. Knowledge about international business is therefore important for everyone, whether it is used to compete with foreign firms or simply to understand the world around us.

DISCUSSION QUESTIONS

1. Will future expansion of international business in the digital era emulate past patterns?
2. Does increased international business mean increased risk?
3. Is it beneficial for nations to become dependent on one another?
4. Discuss the reasons for China's increased market share of world trade.
5. Why do more firms from developed countries enter international markets than firms from developing markets?
6. Is it reasonable that curative marketing takes on responsibility for events long past?
7. How can firms and consumers respond to widespread problems such as climate change?

KEY TERMS

artificial intelligence (AI)	17	macroeconomic level	18
composition of trade	17	microeconomic level	19
curative marketing	21	Pax Americana	14
e-commerce	9	Pax Romana	12
foreign direct investment	14	Smoot–Hawley Tariff Act	14
globalization	6	World Trade Organization (WTO)	9
international business	6		

TAKE A STAND

In November 1997, students at Georgetown, Harvard, Duke, and Holy Cross universities began to look at the labels of logo merchandise in their campus bookstores to get an idea of where the clothing was made. Their goal was to find ways to improve the working conditions of people who made their caps and shirts. In April 1998, UNITE, a union of textile workers, sponsored two workers from a Korean-owned apparel factory in the Dominican Republic for a tour of US college campuses. Kenia Rodriguez and Roselio Reyes, both college-aged, described the terrible conditions at the BJ&B factory where goods featuring the logos of major American colleges were made. They explained that workers had to cope with rancid drinking water, locked bathrooms, sweltering conditions, and intimidation. Men and women had unequal pay scales, and workers were fired when they tried to start a union. To help schools monitor factory conditions for themselves, students formed an independent organization called the Workers' Rights Consortium (WRC). Over the next two years, students used tactics such as petitions, faculty and student government resolutions, and rallies to persuade their administrations to sign on to the WRC. At Georgetown, students occupied the office of the university's president for more than 100 hours before the administration agreed to sign on to the WRC and endorse a code of conduct that students felt was stringent enough. In March 2003, the WRC announced a major victory at the factory where Kenia and Roselio had worked. As of 2009, 186 colleges and universities in the USA joined the WRC. In 2017, Georgetown University implemented a new protocol in which coordination between Nike and the WRC was strengthened.

SOURCES:

www.workersrights.org, accessed April 9, 2020; www.georgetown.edu/news/georgetown-advances-workers-rights-through-new-agreement-with-nike-and-worker-rights-consortium/, accessed April 9, 2020; interview with Andrew Milmore, former Solidarity Committee president, April 22, 2003 and April 26,

2003; Steven Greenhouse, "Michigan Is the Latest University to End a Licensing Deal With an Apparel Maker," *New York Times*, February 23, 2009.

INTERNET EXERCISES

1. Using World Bank data for gross domestic product (shown on the Quick Reference Tables of the World Bank's website, www.worldbank.org) and annual revenue information available on the websites of individual corporations, calculate how the largest corporations might rank in relation to countries if their annual corporate revenue were ranked as GDP. Look for ExxonMobil, Walmart, and your choice of three of the largest corporations.
2. Using World Trade Organization data shown on the International Trade page of its website (www.wto.org), determine the following information: (a) the fastest growing traders; (b) the top 10 exporters and importers in world merchandise trade; and (c) the top 10 exporters or importers of commercial services.
3. Using World Bank data for East Asia and Pacific on its website (https://data .worldbank.org/region/east-asia-and-pacific?view=chart), analyze why the region is so attractive for international business, and evaluate the top five countries in the region that are best equipped for successful globalization.

Appendix
A Geographical Excursion
By Thomas J. Baerwald

In the study of international business, an understanding of world geography brings in critical ideas. Simultaneously, information used with an analytic approach based on scientific methods provides answers to questions about the world in which international businesses operate. Geography focuses on gathering, storing, analyzing, and presenting the information necessary to serve consumers in the market at a given location after reviewing valid features such as economic activity and transaction flow. Where are things located and will these locations change? How do different things relate to one another at a specific place? How do different places relate to each other? How do geographic patterns and relationships change over time? These are the questions that take geography beyond mere description and make it a powerful approach for analyzing and explaining geographical aspects of a wide range of different kinds of problems faced by those engaged in international business. It explains why patterns of trade and exchange evolve over time based on analysis of processes that result in different geographic patterns, which provides a means for assessing how patterns might change in the future. Geography has a rich tradition. Classical Greeks, medieval Arabs, enlightened European explorers, and twenty-first-century scholars in the USA and elsewhere have organized geographic knowledge in many different ways.

Natural Features

Goods such as vegetables and dairy products that require more intensive production and are more expensive to ship are produced closer to markets, while less-demanding goods and commodities that can be transported at lower costs come from more remote production areas. A place provides natural resources and influences the types of economic activities in which people engage. Therefore, the population of a place is important because farm production may require intensive labor to be successful, as is true in rice-growing areas of eastern Asia. Variations in soils have a profound impact on agricultural production. The world's great grain-exporting regions, including central USA, the prairie provinces of Canada, the "fertile triangle" stretching from central Ukraine through southern Russia into northern Kazakhstan, and the Pampas of northern Argentina, all have been blessed with mineral-rich soils made even more fertile by humus from natural grasslands that once dominated the landscapes. Soils are less fertile in much of the Amazon Basin of Brazil and in central Africa, where heavy rains leave few nutrients in upper layers of the soil. As a result, few commercial crops are grown in those areas. The interplay between climate and soils is especially evident in the production of wines. Hundreds of varieties of grapes have been bred to take advantage of the different physical characteristics of various places. The wines fermented from these grapes are shipped around the world to consumers, who differentiate among various wines based not only on the grapes but also on the location where they were grown and the conditions during which they matured.

Location

The value of a place based on its location is very important for international business because the characteristics of a place, along with resources and the business potential it offers, have always been important to executives interested in exploring the world for the best places to conduct business outside their local areas. Explorations of the Mediterranean by the Phoenicians, Marco Polo's journey to China, and voyages undertaken by Christopher Columbus, Vasco de Gama, Henry Hudson, and James Cook not only improved general knowledge of the world but also expanded business opportunities by determining locations where certain specific activities take place.

Latitude and longitude are often used to identify the exact location of a place on the Earth's surface, but coordinates provide relatively little information about the place. The city of Singapore, for example, is between 1 and 2 degrees North latitude and is just west of 104 degrees East longitude. Its most pertinent locational characteristics, however, include its being at the southern tip of the Malay Peninsula near the eastern end of the Strait of Malacca, a critical shipping route connecting the Indian Ocean with the South China Sea. For nearly 150 years, this location made Singapore an important center for trade in the British Empire. After attaining independence in 1965, Singapore's leaders diversified its economy by complementing trade in its bustling port with numerous manufacturing plants that could export products internationally. Without clear knowledge of an enterprise's location relative to its suppliers, to its market, and to its competitors, an executive operates like the captain of a fogbound vessel that has lost all navigational instruments and is heading for dangerous shores.

Place

Geologic characteristics, such as presence of critical minerals or energy resources, may make a place a world-renowned supplier of valuable products. Gold and diamonds help make South Africa's economy the most prosperous on that continent. Rich deposits of iron ore in southern parts of the Amazon Basin have made Brazil the world's leading exporter of that commodity, while Chile remains a pre-eminent exporter of copper. Coal deposits provided the foundation for massive industrial development in eastern USA, the Rhine River Basin, western Russia, and north-eastern China. Standards of living in Saudi Arabia and nearby nations have risen rapidly to be among the highest in the world because of abundant pools of petroleum beneath deserts.

Business leaders throughout the centuries have capitalized on the geology of place as it shapes a terrain that plays a critical role in focusing and inhibiting the movement of people and goods. People traditionally have clustered in lower, flatter areas, because valleys and plains have permitted the agricultural development necessary to feed the local population and to generate surpluses that can be traded. Just as feudal masters sought control of mountain passes in order to collect tolls and other duties from traders who traversed an area, modern executives maintain stores and offer services near bridges and at other points where the terrain focuses travel. The terrain of a place is related to its hydrology. Rivers, lakes, and other bodies of water influence the kinds of economic activities that occur in a place. In general, abundant supplies of water boost economic development because water is necessary for the sustenance of people and for both agricultural and industrial production. Locations such as Los Angeles and Saudi Arabia have prospered despite having little local water, because of other features that offer advantages that exceeded the additional costs incurred in delivering water supplies from elsewhere. While sufficient water must be available to meet local needs, overabundance of water may pose serious problems, such as in Orissa in India where development has been inhibited by frequent flooding. Smooth-flowing streams and placid lakes can stimulate transportation within a place and connect it more easily with other places, while waterfalls and rapids can prevent navigation on streams. The rapid drop in elevation of such streams may boost their potential for hydroelectric power generation, however, thereby stimulating development of industries requiring considerable amounts of electricity. Large plants producing aluminum, for example, are found in the Tennessee and Columbia river valleys of the USA and in Quebec and British Columbia in Canada. These plants refine materials that originally were extracted elsewhere, especially bauxite and alumina from Caribbean nations like Jamaica and the Dominican Republic. The presence of abundant and inexpensive electricity in these areas offsets the high cost of delivery of these materials to the plant.

Climate

Another natural feature that has profound impact on economic activity in a particular place is climate. Locales blessed with pleasant climates, such as the Côte d'Azur of France, the Crimean Peninsula of Ukraine, Florida, and the Gold Coast of north-eastern Australia, have become popular recreational havens, attracting tourists whose spending fuels the local economy. Agricultural production is influenced by climate as the average daily and evening temperatures, the amount and timing of precipitation, the timing of frosts and freezing weather, and the variability of weather from one year to the next all influence the kinds of crops grown in an area. Plants producing bananas and sugarcane flourish in moist tropical areas, while cooler climates are more conducive to crops such as wheat and potatoes. Climate influences other industries as well. The aircraft manufacturing industry in the USA developed largely in warmer, drier areas where conditions for test and delivery flights were best throughout the year. In a similar way, major rocket-launching facilities are in locations where climatic conditions and trajectories are most favorable. As a result, the primary launch site of the European Space Agency is not in Europe but rather in the South American part of France, French Guiana. Climate also affects the length of the workday and the length of economic seasons. For example, in some regions of the world, the construction industry can build only during a few months because permafrost makes construction prohibitively expensive the rest of the year. Variations in soils have a profound impact on agricultural production. In addition, concern with climate change has become a matter of key societal preoccupation.

Human Features

Considering human characteristics of a place, such as the skills and qualifications of the population, plays a role in determining how a place fits into global economic affairs. Although blessed with few mineral resources and a terrain and climate that limit agricultural production, the Swiss have emphasized high levels of education and training in order to maintain a labor force that manufactures sophisticated products for export around the world. In recent decades, Japan and smaller nations such as South Korea and Taiwan have increased the productivity of their workers to become major industrial exporters. As people live in a place, they modify it, creating a built environment that can be as, or more, important than the natural environment in economic terms.

The most pronounced areas of human activity and their associated structures are in cities. In nations around the world, cities have grown dramatically during the twentieth century. Much of the growth of cities has resulted from the migration of people from rural areas. This influx of new residents broadens the labor pool and creates a vast new demand for goods and services. As urban populations have grown, residences and other facilities have replaced rural land uses. Executives seeking to conduct business in foreign cities need to be aware that the geographic patterns found in their home cities will not necessarily be the same in many other nations. For example, wealthier residents in the USA generally have moved outward and, as they established their residences, stores and services followed. Residential patterns in the major cities of Latin America and other developing nations tend to be the reverse, with the wealthy remaining close to the city center while poorer residents are consigned to the outskirts. Thus a store location strategy that is successful in the USA may fail miserably if transferred directly to another nation without knowledge of the different geographic patterns of that nation's cities. Therefore, the international business professional seeking to take advantage of opportunities present in different places should learn to view each place separately.

Fortuitous combinations of features can spur a region's economic development. The presence of high-grade supplies of iron ore, coal, and limestone powered the growth of Germany's Ruhr Valley as one of Europe's foremost steel-producing regions, just as the proximity of the fertile Pampas and the deep channel of the Río de la Plata combine to make Buenos Aires the leading economic center in southern South America.

Interaction

How a place functions depends not only on its presence and form with certain characteristics but also on interactions among those characteristics – for example, the establishment of Dubai as a corporate and tourist destination. Interactions among different features change over time within places, and, as they do, so does that place's character and economic activities. Human activities can have profound impacts on natural features. The courses of rivers and streams are changed as dams are erected and meanders are straightened. Soil fertility can be improved through fertilization. Vegetation is changed, with naturally growing plants replaced by crops and other varieties that require careful management. Many such interactions and human modifications have been successful. For centuries the Dutch have constructed dams and drainage systems, slowly creating polder land that once was covered by the North Sea but is now used for agricultural production.

Like so many other geographical relationships, the nature of human–environmental interaction changes over time. With technological advances, people have been able to modify and adapt to natural features in increasingly sophisticated ways. The development of air-conditioning has permitted people to function more effectively in torrid tropical environments, thereby enabling the populations of cities such as Houston, Rio de Janeiro, and Jakarta to multiply many times over in recent decades. Owners of winter resorts now can generate artificial snow to ensure best conditions for skiers. Advanced irrigation systems now enable crops to be grown in places such as southwestern USA, northern Africa, and Israel.

However, the use of new technologies may cause serious problems in the long run. Extensive irrigation in large parts of the USA has seriously depleted groundwater supplies. In central Asia, the diversion of river water to irrigate cotton fields in Kazakhstan and Uzbekistan has reduced the size of the Aral Sea to a fifth of its 1960 surface area (Gaybullaev et al., 2012). In the future, business leaders may need to factor into their decisions the additional costs associated with interactions and their impact on the restoration of environmental quality after they have finished using a place's resources. While the theme of interaction encourages consideration of different characteristics within a place, movement provides a structure for considering how different places relate to each other.

Movement

International business exists because transportation enables the movement of people and goods, along with the communication of information and ideas, to different places. No matter how many people in one place want something found elsewhere, they cannot have it unless transportation systems enable the product to be brought to them. The location and character of transportation, especially with technologically advanced communication systems, has had powerful influences on the economic standing of places. Especially significant are places on which transportation routes have focused. Many ports have become prosperous cities because they channeled the movement of goods and people between ocean and inland waterways. New York became the largest city in North America because its harbor provided sheltered anchorage for ships crossing the Atlantic; the Hudson River provided access leading into the interior of the continent. In eastern Asia, Hong Kong grew under similar circumstances, as British traders used its splendid harbor as an exchange point for goods moving in and out of southern China. Businesses also have succeeded at well-situated places along land routes. The fabled oasis of Tombouctou has been an important trading center for centuries because it has one of the few dependable sources of water in the Sahara. Chicago's ascendancy as the premier city in the US heartland came when its early leaders engineered its selection as the termination point for a dozen railway lines converging from all directions. Not only did much of the rail traffic moving through the region have to pass through Chicago, but passengers and freight passing through the city had to be transferred from one line to another, a process that generated numerous jobs and added considerably to the wealth of many businesses in the city.

Other forms of economic activity have become concentrated at critical points in the transportation network. Places where transfers from one mode of transportation to another often served as sites for manufacturing activities. Global patterns of resource refining also demonstrate the wisdom of careful selection of sites with respect to transportation systems. Some of the world's largest oil refineries are located in places like Bahrain and Houston, where pipelines bring oil to points where it is processed and loaded onto ships in the form of gasoline or other distillates for transport to other locales. Conversely, an absence of good transportation severely limits the potential for firms to succeed in a specific place. Failure to adapt to changing transportation patterns can have deleterious impacts on a place. During the middle of the nineteenth century, business leaders in St. Louis discouraged railroad construction, seeking instead to maintain the supremacy of river transportation. Only after it became clear that rail was the mode of preference did St. Louis officials seek to develop rail connections for the city, but by then it was too late – Chicago had ascended to a dominant position in the region.

Technology

Continuing advances in transportation technology have, in effect, "shrunk" the world, and modern manufacturing techniques have transformed the notion of relationships among suppliers, manufacturers, and markets. Automobile manufacturers, for example, once maintained large stockpiles of parts in assembly plants that were located near the parts plants or close to the places where the cars would be sold. Auto assembly plants now are built in places where labor costs and worker productivity are favorable and where governments offer attractive inducements. The plants keep relatively few parts on hand, calling on suppliers for rapid delivery of parts as they are needed when orders for new cars are received. This "just-in-time" system of production leaves manufacturers subject to disruptions caused by work stoppages at supply plants and to weather-related delays in the transportation system, but losses associated with these infrequent events are more than offset by reduced operating costs under normal conditions.

The role of advanced technology as a factor affecting international business is even more apparent with respect to advances in communications systems. Sophisticated forms of telecommunication that began more than 180 years ago with the telegraph machine have today advanced through the telephone to facsimile transmissions, electronic mail networks, and ultimately cloud services. As a result, distance and physical hardware based infrastructure has practically ceased to be a consideration with respect to the transmission of information. Whereas information once moved only as rapidly as the person carrying the paper on which the information was written, data and ideas now can be sent to and shared with anyone, almost anywhere in the world. These advancements have had a staggering impact on the way that international business is conducted. They have fostered the growth of multinational corporations, which operate in diverse places around the globe while maintaining effective links with headquarters and regional control centers. International financial operations also have been transformed because of communication advances. The increasingly mobile forms of money in the BOP at one end, and stocks in New York, London, Tokyo, and Frankfurt at the other, have enabled modern business executives to engage in activities around the world.

Regions

Economic aspects of movement may help define functional regions by establishing areas where certain types of economic activity are more profitable than others. Regions organize groups of places in meaningful ways. A region is a set of places that share certain characteristics that places in the group have in common. When economic characteristics are used, the delimited regions include places with similar kinds of economic activity. Agricultural regions include areas where certain farm products dominate. Corn is grown throughout the "Corn Belt" of central USA, for example, although many farmers in the region also plant soybeans and many raise hogs. Regions where intensive industrial production is a prominent part of local economic activity include the manufacturing belts of southern Canada, north-western Europe, and southern Japan.

Advances in transportation have dramatically altered regional patterns. Regions can also be defined by patterns of movement. Transportation or communication linkages among places may draw them together into configurations that differentiate them from other locales. Studies by economic geographers of the locational tendencies of modern high-technology industries have identified complex networks of firms that provide products and services to each other. Because of their links, these firms cluster together into well-defined regions. The "Silicon Valley" of northern California, the "Western Crescent" of London, and "Technopolis" of the Tokyo region are all distinguished as much by connections among firms as by the economic landscapes they have established.

Governments have a strong impact on the conduct of business, and the formal borders of government jurisdictions often coincide with the functional boundaries of economic regions. However, the formation of common markets and free trade areas in western Europe and North America has dramatically changed the patterns and flows of economic activity, and similar kinds of formal restructuring of relationships among nations are likely to continue in this century. As a result, business analysts increasingly need to consider regions that cross international boundaries.

Dr. Baerwald is the senior Science Advisor at the National Science Foundation in Alexandria, Virginia. He is co-author of *Prentice Hall World Geography* – A Bestselling Geography Textbook.

2 Trade and Investment Policies

LEARNING OBJECTIVES

- To understand the role of policies in facilitating international trade and investments across borders
- To examine how traditional attitudes toward trade and investment policies have changed over time
- To recognize the role of policy makers and challenges faced by them in their focus on international trade
- To understand that nations must adapt their role to new condition of international business
- To understand what policies are needed to achieve a growing, viable global trade and investment environment for both industrialized and developing nations

CONTENTS

VIGNETTE 2 The US-China trade war and global investment policy

The GDP of the USA and China accounts for two-fifths of global GDP. Little wonder that a trade war between the two nations disrupted global trade and had a lasting influence on the trade policies of many countries. To resolve the conflict between the USA and China, global negotiations resulted in the draft of the Trans-Pacific Partnership Agreement (TPP). This agreement was signed in 2016 by 12 countries and addressed global economic governance, international security, and energy policy. The United Nations Conference on Trade and Development (UNCTAD) reported that the main beneficiary of the agreement would be Europe. The US Government sought from China concessions related to intellectual property, enhanced agricultural purchases, and limited technology transfer. The newly elected Trump administration decided to abandon the TPP, which largely weakened the entire proposal. However, a number of countries, both from Europe and Asia, still sought to create a global trade policy framework with new trade rules to allow progress to be made in a twenty-first-century global marketplace. However, many substantial changes in trade policy were proposed and implemented by the USA, thus increasing complexity and the need for adaptation (Czinkota & Zeneli, 2016).

Introduction

The outbreak of the Coronavirus (COVID-19) pandemic caused many Chinese factories to shut down their production lines with many of their workers under quarantine since January 2020. Their closure has had a ripple effect on the global economy. The disease spread from China to Italy to Spain to the USA. Chinese harbors lost most of their container traffic, and there was major concern about the safety of humans working in the supply chain. The purpose of policy is to regulate, direct, and protect an environment for a government, which typically seeks the betterment of conditions for its national stakeholders. International trade policies also determine foreign investments – not only from a business perspective, but also for national security. Trade policies regulate, stimulate, and protect activities related to imports and exports. Many of the government policies in a country have repercussions on firms and individuals living or operating in other nations. Therefore, they must be considered in the formulation of a nation's trade and investment policies. To develop new markets abroad and increase their sphere of influence, nations may give foreign aid to other countries or make greenfield or brownfield investments. Greenfield investments are foreign direct investments (FDI) that require contributions to overall development of infrastructure in locations that lack basic facilities. The goal is to promote trade, entrepreneurship, and employment. Brownfield investments result in acquisitions of local firms to create or grow opportunities in trade.

Policies of government can have direct or indirect effects on trade and investment. Domestic policies typically aim to increase the standard of living of a nation's citizens. The results of national policies are often linked between countries. For example, if government support makes foreign industries more competitive and allows firms to increase their exports, then employment in the importing countries may suffer. Likewise, if a country accumulates large quantities of debt, which must be repaid, the present and future standard of living will be threatened. Government officials may believe that imports threaten culture, health, or standards of living, which leads them to then develop regulations to protect citizens.

Foreign policy measures are sometimes designed with domestic concerns in mind but explicitly aimed to exercise influence abroad. Another goal of foreign policy may be national security. For example, nations may develop alliances, coalitions, and agreements to protect their borders or their spheres of interest, which may change. Just consider the relationship of the UK with African nations and the USA with Latin American countries. Nations may take measures to enhance their national security preparedness in case of international conflict. Each country has its own agenda. Therefore, policy aims generally differ between nations. Yet closer economic links have made the emergence of conflict less frequent.

An Institutional History of International Trade and Investment

Many months of international negotiations in London, Geneva, and Lake Success (New York) culminated on March 24, 1948, in Havana, Cuba, with the signing of the Havana Charter, creating the International Trade Organization (ITO). ITO was a forward-looking agreement addressing international trade and investment relations. The ITO resulted in the creation of the United Nations Agency and the introduction of the General Agreement on Tariffs and Trade (GATT). GATT has been called a "remarkable success story of a postwar international organization that was never intended to become one" (Graham, 1983). It started as a set of rules to ensure nondiscrimination, transparent procedures, settlement of disputes, and participation of the lesser-developed countries in international trade. To increase trade, GATT used tariff concessions, through which member countries agreed to limit the level of tariffs they would impose on imports from other GATT members. An important tool is the most-favored nations (MFN) clause, which calls for each member country to grant other member countries the same favorable treatment

Exhibit 2.1 A 2017 plenary session of the IMF in Washington, DC during the IMF/World Bank spring meetings
Source: Stephen Jaffe/IMF via Getty Images.

with respect to imports and exports. MFN provides for equal, rather than special, treatment. The GATT initiated promotion of international trade with rules for discrimination, transparency procedures, settlement of disputes, and participation of less-developed countries. On January 1, 1995, the World Trade Organization (WTO) supplanted the GATT. The WTO was an intergovernmental organization created for administering international trade and regulating international investment accords. There are currently 164 member nations.

Various governments have reacted to the strength of international institutions. They have imposed trade barriers, tariffs, and trade regulations to weaken the influence of the WTO. This in turn has also affected the capability of the International Monetary Fund (IMF), an agency established by the United Nations in 1944. Simultaneously, the World Bank was created in 1944 to facilitate world trade. As a result, many less-developed nations gradually emerged as developing nations (Exhibit 2.1). Formation of the European Union aimed to strengthen trade between European economies, improve local standards of living, and achieve a meaningful defense against the then Soviet Bloc. Since 1989, the world, along with its opportunities and threats, and the usefulness of policy tools, has changed.

At the national level, strategic application of international trade theories changes not only the positioning but also the future of countries. For example, India has abundant natural resources, appropriate professions, a cultural heritage of an open society, and dignified relationships between men and women. Historically, women were of equal stature with men in the fields of education, science, and innovation. After the advent of British traders in India, a wealthy nation became a poor country of beggars and snake charmers.

In the contemporary world, comparative advantage is offered by the business environment of a country. When combined with competitive advantage developed by firms, both become the foundation of internationalization. A country can attract foreign investments based on the comparative advantage it offers. Product and production leadership demonstrated by South Korean firms such as Samsung, innovativeness of design and customer experience by American firms such as Apple, and marketing strength required for remote penetration by firms such as Procter and Gamble are some of the firm-level competitive advantages that competitors find hard to imitate. Additional examples of comparative advantages offered by different countries are formerly low-cost labor in China, successful IT professionals from India, and abundant availability of oil from Saudi Arabia. They all enable firms to decide destinations for trade and investments.

The principle of mercantilism makes governments focus on their domestic industrial environment to promote domestic businesses through international trade policies that discourage imports and encourage stability of its reserves. This concept involves restriction of imports through barriers created by host countries. Examples are increased tariffs, changes in government-driven prices for, say, oil, or the creation of quotas. The objective is the accumulation of reserves in the form of foreign currency: gold or silver. Governments also use quotas to restrict the number of foreign products that can be imported. Non-tariff barriers consist of a variety of measures such as testing, certification, or simply bureaucratic hurdles with the effect of restricting imports. These measures tend to raise the price of imported goods and reduce the choices of consumers. Governments can manage tariffs and other trade barriers or delay implementation of agreed-upon reductions of barriers.

Worldwide, most countries maintain at least a surface-level conformity with international principles. Many nations still exert substantial restraints on free trade through import controls and barriers. Countries that suffer from major trade deficits or major infrastructure problems tend to enter into voluntary restraint agreements with trading partners, or selectively apply trade-restricting measures not covered by WTO rules, in order to help domestic industries reorganize, restructure, and recapture production prominence. Due to their "voluntary" nature, the agreements are not subject to any previously negotiated bilateral or multilateral trade accords. Companies comply to avoid the threat of even tougher measures between trading countries. Many countries use antidumping laws as a route to impose tariffs on imports. Antidumping helps domestic industries injured by competition from abroad. The claim here is that goods are sold abroad at prices lower than those in the exporter's home market or at a price below the cost of production. Large domestic firms often use the antidumping process to obtain strategic, administrative shelter from foreign competitors. Other ways to build barriers for exporting firms are:

- requirements for special import authorization or advance import deposits or taxes on foreign exchange deals
- licensing applications, excise duties, or licensing fees.

Historically, mercantilism has resulted in the creation of competitive advantage for local firms through practices supported by subsidies offered by local government. Such strategies create comparative advantage for the country and competitive advantage for the domestic industry based on state monopolies granted to firms actively engaged in international trade. An important example of these practices can be noticed in the formation of the British Empire that used the England Navigation Act of 1651 to restrict its colonies such as India to utilize products of its own domestic industry and to force them to import those products from the UK. A revolt of the Indian population towards the British Tax on Salt is recorded in history as a public march known as the "Dandi March" or "Salt March," led by Mohandas Karamchand Gandhi. China has been accused of imposing mercantilism onto its industrial production policies. To protect local firms during such events, importing countries tend to increase tariffs on Chinese products, thereby under-valuing their currency.

Tariffs used by governments to restrict imports can be bound tariffs, which are the highest permissible tariffs that can be imposed after negotiations with the WTO. There are also the applied tariffs, which is what actually has to be paid at a country's borders. Often, countries have, over time, reduced their applied tariffs substantially below the bound tariffs that they are allowed to charge. In times of economic stress, however, many countries raise their applied tariffs to a level much closer to the bound tariffs. As long as the increase does not carry the charges beyond the bound tariff level, there is no violation of WTO rules.

Non-tariff barriers can consist of buy-domestic campaigns, preferential treatment for domestic bidders compared to foreign bidders, national standards that are non-compatible with international standards, and an emphasis on the design rather than the performance of products. Such non-tariff barriers are often the most insidious obstacles to free trade because they are difficult to detect, hard to quantify, and demands for their removal are often blocked by references to a nation's cultural and historical heritage. With tariffs, nations run the risk of sliding down a slippery slope. Mahatma Gandhi said, "An eye for an eye makes the whole world blind." An inquiry made by Adam Smith, generally considered the father of economics, on the wealth of nations in the year 1776 was based on a belief that mercantilism is a zero-sum game. It provides a benefit to one at the cost of the other and is unhealthy for the economy of a country. Therefore, Adam Smith concluded that free trade could increase global growth, address global problems, and should be promoted.

The concept of free trade led to the opening of new markets and the participation of more countries' globalization as equal partners. This resulted in the growth of companies outside of their home country and pushed them to adopt new concepts, such as economies of scale. Free trade was further supported by the theory of **comparative advantage**, which stated that a country in which opportunity cost is lower in comparison to other countries would be a preferred destination for business and trade. Although benefits of comparative advantage sometimes get lost because of costs of trade, free trade encourages imports with a reduction in tariffs and allows firms to improve strategic management of the life cycles of its products. Companies benefit from the strategic combination of product life cycle management with price leadership, cost leadership, and/or innovation leadership. Countries with comparative advantage benefit from international trade by increased utilization of local resources or availability of goods produced at cheaper costs.

Policy makers in the past have been faced with several problems when trying to administer import controls. They may restrict the most efficient sources of supply into a country leading to supply of second-best products at higher costs, which in turn causes quality and customer service standards to drop. The social cost of trade controls may be damaging to the economy.

Challenges Faced by Policy Makers in a Global Trade Environment

The word *policy* conjures up an image of a well-coordinated set of governmental activities. Unfortunately, in the trade and investment sector, as in most of the domestic policy areas, this is rarely the case. Policy makers too often need to respond to short-term problems, to worry too much about what is politically salable to multiple constituencies, and, in some countries, are in office too short a time to formulate a guiding set of long-term strategies. All too often, because of public and media pressures, policy makers must be concerned with current events such as monthly trade deficit numbers and investment flow figures that may not be very meaningful in the larger picture. In such an environment, actions may lead to extraordinarily good tactical steps but fail to achieve long-term success.

Another major problem that confronts the policy maker is that of efficiency. Import controls designed to provide breathing room to a domestic industry so it can either grow or recapture its competitive position, often do not work. Rather than improve the productivity of an industry, such controls may provide it with a level of safety and security. A cushion of increased income can subsequently cause a lag in technological advancement.

One must also be aware of possible responses to import restrictions by others. In order to protect their industries, governments may retaliate against restrictions by erecting similar barriers at home. The result can be a gradually escalating set of trade obstacles. Corporations can also strategically use such barriers by incorporating them into their business plans and exploiting them in order to gain market share. For example, some multinational corporations have pressed governments to initiate antidumping actions against their competitors when faced with low-priced imports. In such instances, corporations substitute administrative shelter obtained through adroit handling of government relations for innovation and competitiveness.

Finally, corporations also can circumvent import restrictions by shifting their activities. For example, instead of conducting trade, corporations can shift to FDI. The result may be a drop in trade inflow, yet the domestic industry may still be under strong pressure from foreign firms. The investments of Japanese car producers substituting domestic production for imports in the USA is an example. However, due to the job-creation effects of such investment, such shifts may have been the driving desire on the part of the policy makers who implemented the import controls. Retaliation is the way international trading corporations or investment policy makers respond to national trade actions or restrictions, in order to demonstrate displeasure or to seek retribution and change. Exhibit 2.2 discusses such a situation between the USA and China.

EXHIBIT 2.2 A report on the US–China trade war

"In July 2018, America announced a series of tariffs aimed at China. The USA imposed three rounds of tariffs on Chinese goods, totaling more than $250 billion and impacting a wide variety of industries, from consumer goods to railway equipment. China fired back, first imposing tariffs on $50 billion of US goods, and later retaliating with tariffs on an additional $60 billion, including agricultural goods such as soybeans. The latest 10% tariff means that roughly half of the products that China sells to the USA each year will be hit by American tariffs."

Tariffs can have both dire and supportive effects globally.

Impact on Business Operations

How are these combined tariffs impacting your business operations in China? (Check all that apply)

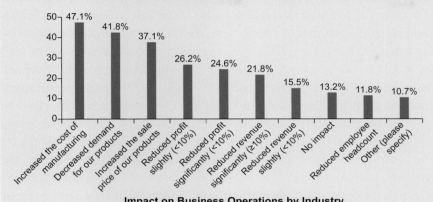

Impact on Business Operations by Industry

Reduced profit		Increased cost of manufacturing		Increased sale price of product	
Healthcare products	82.1%	Machinery	77.9%	Retail & distribution	69.2%
Electronics	75.0%	Chemicals	73.1%	Agribusiness	66.7%
Chemicals	65.4%	Aerospace	72.7%	Aerospace	63.6%
Machinery	63.2%	Electronics	68.8%	Machinery	55.9%
Automotive	61.1%	Automotive	63.9%	Chemicals	53.8%

Impact on Business Strategy

How are tariffs and US-China trade tensions impacting your business strategy? (Check all that apply)

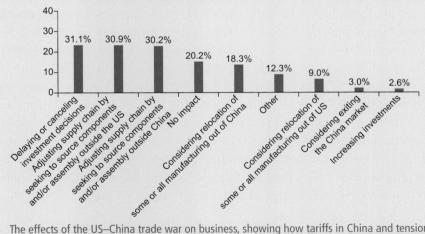

The effects of the US–China trade war on business, showing how tariffs in China and tensions stemming from the US–China trade war are affecting business operations and strategy
Source: Sokolowski, 2020.

Policy Responses to Changing Conditions

Nations have come to accept that they must generate sufficient outgoing export and incoming investment activities to compensate for the inflow of imports and outgoing investment. In the medium and long term, the balance of payments should be reasonably balanced. For some periods of time, gold or capital transfers can be used to finance a deficit. Such financing, however, can only continue while gold and foreign assets last or while foreign countries will accept the IOUs of the deficit countries, permitting them to pile up foreign liabilities. This willingness will vary and depend on responsibilities and forecasts. Governments also find that domestic policy decisions have major international repercussions. Legislators around the world are continually confronted with the effects of international links. In some countries, the implications are understood, and new legislation is devised with an understanding of its international consequences. In other nations, legislators often ignore the international repercussions and side effects of their actions. Yet, given the links among economies, this is an unwarranted and sometimes even dangerous view. It threatens to place firms at a competitive disadvantage in the international marketplace or may make it easier for foreign firms to compete in the domestic market. Even when policy makers want to take decisive steps, they are often unable to do so.

Policy makers find themselves with increasing responsibilities, yet with fewer and less-effective tools to carry them out. More segments of the domestic economy are vulnerable to international shifts at the same time that they are becoming less controllable. To regain some power to influence policies, some governments have sought to restrict the influence of world trade by erecting barriers, charging tariffs, and implementing import regulations. However, these measures too have been restrained by international agreements forged through institutions such as the WTO or bilateral negotiations. World trade has changed many previously held notions about the sovereignty of nation-states and extraterritoriality. Simultaneously, the interdependence that made us all more affluent has also left us more vulnerable. The concentration of supplies with a few large companies is moving the global market towards monopolistic practices. The intense links among nations, the new economic environment resulting from the financial crisis, and the growing influence of developing economies have all brought into question the role that traditional international institutions should play.

Disputes and Conflicts in International Trade and Investment Policies

The increased use of WTO as a dispute settlement mechanism is one sign of the important strategy that it uses for its 164 members. However, the organization is also confronted with many difficulties. A profound challenge to the WTO is the future of the overall multilateral trading system. With regional agreements multiplying, analysts are concerned about the future of multilateral trade liberalization and the role and focus of the WTO.

With some of its members urging that the WTO introduces "social causes" into trade decisions, reducing barriers to trade would become commingled with issues such as poverty reduction, labor laws, competition, emigration freedoms, food security, provision of health care, freedom of religion, and the safety of animals. Member governments have diverse perspectives, histories, relations, economies, and ambitions. There is a fear that social causes can be used to devise new rules of protectionism against their exports. There is also the question of how much companies – which, after all, are the ones doing the trading and investing – should be burdened with concerns outside their scope. Therefore, to succeed, the WTO needs to be able to focus on its core mission, which is the support of international trade and investment.

The addition of social causes may appear politically expedient, but it will be a cause for divisiveness and dissent and thus will inhibit progress on further liberalization of trade and investment. Similar problems confront international financial institutions, which have been even more the focus of criticism and reform efforts. The IMF, as an international financial institution with some power over national authorities, deals with conflicts related to balance of payment and oversees the international monetary system by providing macroeconomic and financial policy advice to its members. Many of the developing and least-developed economies believe that its lending policies are too austere and inflexible, and that the IMF does not fully understand and appreciate their situations and needs.

The IMF now strives "to reform and modernize the international financial institutions to ensure they can assist members and shareholders effectively in the new challenges they face" (Gur, 2015). The World Bank successfully met its goal of aiding the reconstruction of Europe but has been less successful in furthering the economic goals of the developing world and the newly emerging market economies in the former Soviet Bloc. Some even claim that instead of alleviating poverty, misguided bank policies may have been the cause of an increase in poverty (Weisbrot, 2019).

In the 1960s and 1970s, it was hoped that the developmental gap between the industrialized nations and many countries in the less-developed world would gradually be closed. This goal was to be achieved with the transfer of technology and the major infusion of funds. During the 1970s, vast quantities of petrodollars were available for recycling and major growth in borrowing for some developing nations. Yet the results have not been as expected. Many developing nations had become highly indebted, a burden that impeded new policies and economic development. Even with substantial debt forgiveness, the subsequent global financial crisis caused many developing nations to become increasingly aggressive in reshaping trade and investment ground rules. Both the IMF and the World Bank initiated what was termed the Washington Consensus, which required economic liberalization, financial austerity, and privatization of national industries. In addition, an increase in environmental awareness has contributed to further disagreements. Developing nations, with urgent investment needs, may have a different perspective of environmental protection than their developed counterparts. If they are to take measures that will assist the industrialized nations in their environmental goals, they expect to be assisted and rewarded for these efforts. Yet many in the industrialized world view environmental issues as a global obligation.

Promoting International Trade and Investment

The desire to increase participation in international trade and investment has led nations to implement export promotion programs. They are to help domestic firms enter and maintain their position in international markets and to match or counteract similar export promotion efforts by other nations. Governments have developed various approaches toward export promotion. One focus is on knowledge transfer to enable greater competence within firms. Market development programs provide sales leads to local firms.

A second export-promotion approach deals with direct or indirect subsidization of export activities. For example, low-cost export financing can produce an attractive and competitive offer, particularly for large sales that are paid over time, such as airplanes or power plants. Exports are also supported by lower tax rates for export earnings and favorable insurance rates. The overall focus of these subsidized activities is to increase the profitability of exporting to the firm, either by reducing the risks or by increasing the rewards.

A third approach consists of reducing governmental red tape for exporters. For instance, the reduction of multiple export licenses can increase exports.

What also helps, can be increased export financing. In response to actions by foreign competitors, banks can offer mixed aid credits at rates composed partially of commercial interest rates and partially of highly subsidized developmental interest rates. Such credits can result in very low interest rates to exporters.

Any export promotion raises several questions. One concerns the justification of the expenditure of public funds for what is essentially an activity that should be driven by profits. A second question focuses on the capability of the government to provide such support. Both for the selection and reach of firms as well as the distribution of support, the government is not necessarily better equipped to do a better job than the private sector. A third issue focuses on the evaluation of the effectiveness and competitive impact of export promotion activities. Such promotion can be particularly beneficial when it addresses market gaps. Typically, export promotion will only comprise a small fraction of any national budget and directly support only a limited portion of exports. Perhaps one should characterize export promotion funds as the venture capital of international economic activity. Such a step may also create room for the development of import promotion measures.

The discussion of policy actions has focused thus far on merchandise trade. Similar actions can also apply to investment flows and, by extension, to international trade in services. In order to protect ownership, control, and development of domestic industries, many countries influence investment capital flows. Investment-screening agencies decide on the merits of foreign investment projects. India, for example, has "Invest India," a national investment promotion and facilitation agency as the face of India to potential investors. Many nations, such as the US, China, and India, require special government permission for investment projects. There are requirements as to levels of ownership permitted, dividends that can be repatriated, numbers of jobs that must be created, or the extent to which management can be carried out by individuals from abroad.

Impact of FDI

Foreign direct investment (FDI) has contributed greatly to world development in the past 40 years. Several countries, such as Brazil, have imposed export requirements as a precondition for FDI. On the capital account side, FDI may have a short-term impact in lowering a deficit and long-term impact in keeping capital at home. Measurement is difficult because significant portions of investment flows may not be detected (see Exhibit 2.3). The host country sees the various contributions, especially economic, that FDI will make. On the other hand, fears of dominance, interference, and dependence are often voiced and acted on.

FDI can diversify the industrial base and reduce the country's dependence on a sector. At the company level, FDI may intensify competition and result in benefits to the economy as a whole. The major impact of such investment on the balance of payments is long term. FDI is closely linked to knowledge transfer, particularly industries where the role of intellectual property is substantial, such as pharmaceuticals, software development, or managerial skills. Jobs are often the most obvious reason to cheer for FDI. Multinational corporations pay higher salaries than those usually paid by domestic firms.

Threats of multinational corporations and FDI can be stunted economic development, lowered levels of research and development, and poor treatment of local employees. FDI is most often concentrated in technology-intensive industries. With its knowledge transfer, a multinational corporation can assist the host country's economic development. Multinational firms may also contribute to the brain drain by attracting scientists from host countries to the firm's home.

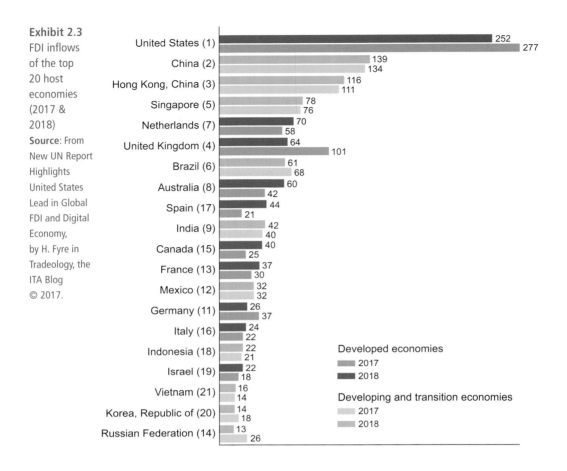

Exhibit 2.3
FDI inflows of the top 20 host economies (2017 & 2018)

Source: From New UN Report Highlights United States Lead in Global FDI and Digital Economy, by H. Fyre in Tradeology, the ITA Blog © 2017.

Many countries have found that, even if available, multinational companies do not necessarily want to rely on international supply of raw materials, components, capital equipment, or sensitive products such as pharmaceuticals or healthcare equipment. Governments may also see multinationals as a disruption to their economic planning, both outbound and inbound. Canada, Switzerland, and the USA, for example, use foreign investment review to determine whether foreign-owned companies will be good corporate citizens.

Restrictions on FDI

To restrict capital flight, (i.e., rapid flow of private funds abroad because investors believe that the return on investment or the safety of capital is not sufficiently ensured in their own countries), many nations restrict the export of capital. Particularly in situations where countries lack necessary foreign exchange reserves,

EXHIBIT 2.4　Effects of FDI

FDI for the home country means increases in the gross domestic product (GDP) from profits, royalties, and fees remitted by affiliates with stimulated economic growth that would expand export markets and serve other goals, such as political motives for gaining preferential access to resources and raw materials. A major negative issue centers on employment. Most controversial have been investments in plants in developing countries that export back to the home countries. Multinationals such as electronics manufacturers who have moved plants to Southeast Asia and Mexico have justified this as a necessary cost-cutting competitive measure. Another critical issue is that of knowledge advantage. By establishing plants abroad or forming joint ventures with foreign entities, the country may be giving away its competitive position in the world marketplace.

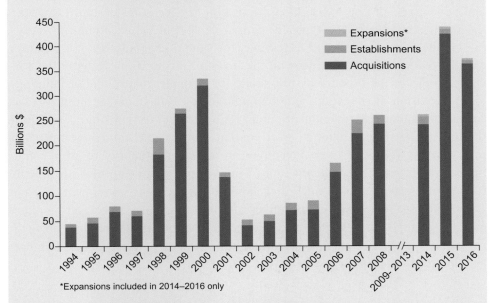

*Expansions included in 2014–2016 only

New investment by foreign direct investors by type, 1994–2016

Source: U.S. Bureau of Economic Analysis, Expenditures by Foreign Direct Investors for New Investment in the United States, 2014–2016 [www.bea.gov/news/2017/expenditures-foreign-direct-investors-new-investment-united-states-2014–2016] (accessed 2019).

governments are likely to place restrictions on capital outflow in order to have payment reserves. Exhibit 2.4 explains the various levels of impact of foreign direct investment. In essence, government claims to have higher priorities for capital than its citizens. They, in turn, often believe that the return on investment or the safety of the capital is not sufficiently ensured in their own countries. The reason may be governmental measures or domestic economic factors, such as inflation. These holders of capital want to invest abroad. By doing so, however, they deprive their domestic economy of much-needed investment funds. Once governments impose restrictions on the export of funds, the desire to transfer capital abroad only increases. Because companies and individuals are ingenious in their efforts to circumvent governmental rules, their governments miss out on internationally accepted capital. In addition, few new outside investors will enter the country because they fear that dividends and profits will not be remitted easily.

Investment Promotion

Investment promotion efforts are often undertaken by governments as incentives on investments. Such encouragement is mainly of three types: fiscal, financial, and non-financial. Fiscal incentives are specific tax measures designed to attract the foreign investor. They typically consist of special depreciation allowances, tax credits or rebates, special deductions for capital expenditures, tax holidays, and the reduction of tax burdens on the investor. Financial incentives offer special funding for the investor by providing, for example, roads, land or buildings, loans, provision of education, and loan guarantees. Non-financial incentives can consist of guaranteed government purchases, special protection from competition through tariffs, import quotas, local content requirements, and investments in infrastructure facilities. These incentives are designed primarily to attract more industry and therefore create more jobs. For example, when countries compete for foreign investment, several may offer more or less the same investment package. The slight advantage that the incentives of one country may have over another's package generally makes little difference in the investment site selected. However, particularly in the cultural and educational infrastructure offers, major differences may attract certain investors.

Management of Policy Relationships

In most cases, the relationship between the parties engaged in FDI is not necessarily based on logic, fairness, or equity, but rather on the relative bargaining power of each. The multinational corporation can maintain its bargaining strength by developing a local support system through local financing, procurement, and business contracts as well as by maintaining control over access to technology and markets. The first approach attempts to gain support from local market entities. A second approach aims to assure the value of ongoing local contributions by the parent. However, bargaining power may change over time as departure or retrenchment becomes uneconomical given large "sunk" investments.

Host countries, on the other hand, try to enhance their role by instituting control policies and performance requirements. Governments attempt to prevent the integration of activities among affiliates and control by the parent. In this effort, they exclude or limit foreign participation in certain sectors of the economy and require local participation in the ownership and management of the entities established. For example, for many years, the USA did not permit foreign ownership of local airlines, or the foreign control of computer aided design.

The extent of government interference will depend on the industry, its national importance, and the investment needed by the host economy. Typical performance requirements are programs aimed at established foreign investors in an economy. There are often local content requirements, export requirements, limits on foreign payments (especially profit repatriation), and demands concerning the type of technology transferred or the sophistication of operations.

In some cases, demands of this type have led to firms packing their bags. For example, Coca-Cola left India when the government demanded access to what the firm considered confidential intellectual property. Only India's free-market reforms have brought Coca-Cola and many other investors back to the country. On their part, governments can, as a last resort, expropriate the affiliate, especially if they believe that the benefits are greater than the cost. Host-country policies on **intellectual property rights (IPR)** can also have an important influence on the foreign investment decisions by other companies. For example, global pharmaceutical firms approach investments in China cautiously because of IPR risks.

SUMMARY

Policy makers must be willing to trade off short-term achievements for long-term goals. All too often, measures that would be beneficial in the long term are sacrificed on the altar of short-term expediency to avoid temporary pain and the resulting political cost. New mechanisms to evaluate restraint measures will also need to be designed. The beneficiaries of trade and investment restraints are usually clearly defined and have much to gain, whereas the losers are much less visible. The voices of retailers, consumers, wholesalers, and manufacturers all need to be heard. Only then will policy makers set policy objectives that increase opportunities for firms and choices for consumers.

DISCUSSION QUESTIONS

1. Discuss the different types of incentives used by policy makers to attract FDI.
2. Discuss the effect of FDI on the home country and the host country.
3. Discuss the impact of import restrictions on consumers.
4. Why would policy makers sacrifice major international progress for minor domestic policy gains?
5. Discuss the role of tariffs and quotas in international trade.
6. What is meant by capital flight?
7. Do investment promotion programs of state (or provincial) governments make sense from a national perspective?

KEY TERMS

bilateral negotiations	44	intellectual property rights (IPR)	51
capital flight	48	International Monetary Fund	
comparative advantage	41	(IMF)	38
competitive advantage	40	international trade	36
foreign direct investments (FDI)	36	mercantilism	39
General Agreement on Tariffs		most-favored nations (MFN)	37
and Trade (GATT)	37	World Bank	38

TAKE A STAND

In 1893, the US Supreme Court grappled with an international legal question that continues to confound to this day – does a tomato qualify as a vegetable or a fruit?

Though many associate the tomato with the stews, salads, and sandwiches that are typically the domain of vegetables, any botanist will tell you that the plant meets the scientific definition of a fruit: a seed-bearing structure that develops from the ovary of a flowering plant.

But in the US Supreme Court case *Nix* v. *Hedden*, the judges unanimously arrived at a different definition. They ruled that imported tomatoes should be taxed as vegetables, which had a 10 percent tariff when they arrived on American shores, rather than as fruit, which carried no tariff.

INTERNET EXERCISES

1. Go to the website of the Indian Economy (www.indianeconomy.net) to write a critical review of the pharmaceutical industry's relation to greenfield and brownfield investments and write a report for executives on key issues related to two types of investments in a developing market of your choice. Also,

explain how the local government promotes FDI and what its key promotional initiatives are for exporters in the local market.

2. Analyze FDI inflows from 2000–2018 on OECD's website (https://data.oecd .org/fdi/fdi-flows.htm#indicator-chart). Paying special attention to the world trendline, identify at least five factors discussed in the chapter and develop a report to explain the trendline.

3. Using the same OECD website, analyze why, with further global economic involvement of developing countries, FDI has decreased so drastically? Add an assessment of two industries of your choice to pinpoint their specific FDI inflows. If they do not correspond with overall FDI inflow levels, why?

FURTHER RESOURCES

Bellora, C. and Fontagné, L. (2019). Shooting oneself in the foot? Trade war and global value chains. Presented at the 22nd Annual Conference on Global Economic Analysis, Warsaw, Poland. Available at www.gtap.agecon.purdue.edu/resources/ res_display.asp?RecordID=5733 (Accessed on April 8, 2020).

Berthou, A., Jardet, C., Siena, D., and Szczerbowicz, U. (2018). Quantifying the losses from a global trade war. Banque de France ECO Notepad, 19.

Colton, C. (2017). Contestability 'theory', its links with Australia's competition policy, and recent international trade and investment agreements. Australian Journal of International Affairs, 71(3), 315–334.

Downie, C. (2017). Business actors, political resistance, and strategies for policymakers. *Energy Policy*, 108, 583–592.

De Ville, F. and Siles-Brügge, G. (2018). The role of ideas in legitimating EU trade policy: from the Single Market Programme to the Transatlantic Trade and Investment Partnership. In S. Khorana and M. García (eds.), Handbook on the EU and International Trade. Cheltenham, UK: Edward Elgar Publishing.

George, C. C. and Rengamani, J. (2018). International trade Importance trends and Approaches. Indian Journal of Public Health Research & Development, 9(3), 886–895.

Handley, K. and Limao, N. (2015). Trade and investment under policy uncertainty: theory and firm evidence. American Economic Journal: Economic Policy, 7(4), 189–222.

Ley, D. (2017). Global China and the making of Vancouver's residential property market. International Journal of Housing Policy, 17(1), 15–34.

Li, C., He, C., and Lin, C. (2018). Economic impacts of the possible China–US trade war. Emerging Markets Finance and Trade, 54(7), 1557–1577

Liu, K. (2018). Chinese manufacturing in the shadow of the China–US trade war. Economic Affairs, 38(3), 307–324.

Liu, T. and Woo, W. T. (2018). Understanding the US-China trade war. China Economic Journal, 11(3), 319–340.

Lodefalk, M. (2017). Servicification of firms and trade policy implications. World Trade Review, 16(1), 59–83.

Niepmann, F. and Schmidt-Eisenlohr, T. (2017). International trade, risk and the role of banks. Journal of International Economics, 107, 111–126.

Petri, P. (2019). The interdependence of trade and investment in the Pacific. In E. Chen (ed.), Corporate links and foreign direct investment in Asia and the Pacific, 1st ed. Abingdon-on-Thames, UK: Routledge, pp. 29–55.

Picciotto, S. (2017). Rights, responsibilities and regulation of international business. Globalization and International Investment. Routledge, pp. 177–198.

Roy, M. (2019). Elevating services: Services trade policy, WTO commitments, and their role in economic development and trade integration. Journal of World Trade, 53(6), 923–950.

Schram, A., Ruckert, A., VanDuzer, J. A., Friel, S., Gleeson, D., Thow, A. M., ... and Labonte, R. (2018). A conceptual framework for investigating the impacts of international trade and investment agreements on noncommunicable disease risk factors. Health Policy and Planning, 33(1), 123–136.

Thow et al. (2017). Food trade and investment in South Africa: Improving coherence between economic policy, nutrition and food security. Working Paper 50. Cape Town: PLAAS, UWC.

Visvizi, A., Lytras, M. D., Damiani, E., and Mathkour, H. (2018). Policy making for smart cities: Innovation and social inclusive economic growth for sustainability. Journal of Science and Technology Policy Management, 9(2), 126-133.

Zadek, S. (2017). Third-generation corporate citizenship: public policy and business in society. Tomorrow's History Routledge, (pp. 294–305).

3 | The Essence of Culture

LEARNING OBJECTIVES

- To define and demonstrate the effect of culture on business
- To examine how cultural knowledge can be acquired for cross-cultural interaction
- To illustrate how cultural risk can challenge the conduct of business
- To convey businesses' role as a change agent
- To demonstrate the linkage between business skills and business performance of their employees
- To highlight how cultural knowledge helps international business expansion
- To recognize the strength of trust-based culture linked with the soul of business

CONTENTS

VIGNETTE 3 Crossing cultures: Balancing the global with the local

The influence of culture on international business has been described as the unspoken differences and truth and meaning of similar gestures recognized across the world. Gaining knowledge of local culture through an understanding of local languages in different markets has been one of the important features of international business management techniques (von Glinow et al., 2004). Language in different spoken and non-spoken forms reflects on the multidimensionality of the culture in ways meaningful for international business managers. Nonverbal behaviors such as friendly gestures, body position, or eye contact act as nonverbal cues and reveal hidden notions and intentions, which spark the business conversations between people from different cultures and countries (Ferraro & Briody, 2017). International managers use nonverbal behaviors as cues to gain the understanding required to position their business and make an offer for cross-border dealings. Understanding of time management and commitment helps them understand the flexibility required to operate in a given market. For example, in Mexico it is not unusual to show up at 1:45 p.m. for a 1:00 p.m. appointment. In some of the other parts of the world, keeping up to the time committed is considered to be respectful of the other person or the potential business partner, individual, or firm. But understanding of traffic-related delays in countries like Hong Kong or cities like Calcutta or Mumbai can enable managers of international firms to acknowledge that a delay is not a cue for lack of respect, but an operational factor. Another example would be an afternoon siesta in cities like Pune in India, which helps people stay at their desks until 10 p.m., which, in turn, could be seen as a lack of work–life balance by people in the UK. Similar would be the tendency toward resentment to impatience in countries like the UK, which is contrary to behaviors of people in Asia or Latin America. The similarity in the approach to developing long-term relationships in Asia and Europe is contrary to those in Americans who believe in short-term dealings and/ or relationships. Other cues could be preferences of people at the individual level, for example, preferences related to personal spaces. Individuals in Arab countries and countries in Latin America like to stand close to the person they are conversing with, whereas an American would not be comfortable with such closeness and might move slightly away, resulting in offending the Arab person who may perceive the movement negatively. Therefore, international managers should adapt localized thinking to their international strategies to overcome cultural barriers.

Kraft Foods learned that Chinese consumers thought the Oreo sandwich cookie was too sweet and the package size was too big. Kraft tinkered with the recipe of the cookies and repackaged Oreos in small and economy sizes. China is now the brand's second largest market.
Credit: Visual China Group via Getty Images.

Introduction

Business across borders is complex for managers who negotiate in multiple countries within a short period of time. Business initiatives differ from each other because culture causes how people have been brought up to think, behave and communicate in a given situation. Cultures vary not only between but also within national boundaries. Even if firms and their employees live close together, they may still insist on finely-honed cultural differences, ranging from religion to singing and language. The clashes between Greece and Turkey because of mass migration from Syria pose widespread threats to national security. The local economy is also affected, as local people lose jobs and migrants do not easily integrate into the local culture. Such conditions affect diversity at the micro level within Europe. Resolution of these issues requires efforts from both international relations and intercultural relationships. International relations address issues of integration at the macro level such as trying to manage conflicts between nations, companies, or people across borders. Intercultural relationships deal with a post-conflict phase of establishing harmony, such as activating communication and synergy through intercultural dialogue. An aligned function between the two can lead to treatment of culture as a tool for promoting economic growth and inclusiveness.

Culture Defined

Managers should be aware of the culture and societies in which their business operates because the socio-cultural aspect of a region gives an anchoring point, an identity, as well as codes of conduct that make businesses and their products relevant to their stakeholders. Cultures change with time and the changes influence decisions (Kavanagh & Ashkanasy, 2006). For example, McDonalds does not serve its signature product, the Big Mac, in India because the cow is a sacred animal for Hindus. Similarly, the alliance between Qantas, an Australian airline, and Emirates, a Dubai based airline, resulted in the decision to not serve pork and alcohol on flights operating in Europe in reverence to Muslim travelers. Religion, customs, traditions, and norms are important factors that require businesses operating internationally to address changing preferences and customer needs.

Scholars and practitioners have defined the term "culture" differently. Kroeber and Kluckhohn reviewed more than 164 definitions of culture. Such variety of definitions was also described by Cohen and Fulkner et al. Some are conceived as separating humans from nonhumans, some define it as communicable knowledge, and some as the sum of historical achievements produced by human beings' social life. All of the definitions have common elements: culture is learned, shared, and transmitted from one generation to the next. Culture is primarily passed on from parents to their children but also transmitted by social organizations, religious institutions, special interest groups, the government, and schools. Common ways of thinking and behaving are developed and then reinforced through social pressure. Geert Hofstede calls this the "collective programming of the mind" (Hofstede, 2003; Beugelsdijk et al., 2016). Culture is also multidimensional, consisting of a number of common elements that are interdependent. Changes in one dimension will affect the others (Beugelsdijk et al., 2016).

We define culture as an integrated system of learned behavioral patterns that are characteristic of the members in their given society. It includes everything that a group member thinks, says, does, and makes – based on customs, language, material artifacts, and shared systems of attitudes and feelings. The definition encompasses a wide variety of elements from the materialistic to the spiritual. Culture is inherently conservative, resisting change and fostering continuity. Every person is acculturated into a particular environment, learning the "right way" of doing things. Problems may arise when a person acculturated in one culture has to adjust to another. The process of successful acculturation, which requires adjusting and adapting to a culture other than one's own, is one of the keys to success in international operations.

Edward T. Hall studied the effects of culture on business, and distinguished between high- and low-context cultures. In high-context cultures, such as Japan and Saudi Arabia, context of communication is at least as important as what is actually said. The speaker and the listener rely on a common understanding of that context and what is not being said can carry more meaning than what is said. In low-context cultures, however, most of the information is contained explicitly in the words. North American cultures engage in low-context communications. Unless one is aware of this basic difference, messages and intentions can easily be misunderstood. As an example, performance appraisals are typically a human resources function. If they are to be centrally guided or conducted in a multinational corporation, those involved must be acutely aware and reflective of cultural nuances. Interestingly, the US system emphasizes individual development, whereas the Japanese system focuses on the group within which the individual works. In the USA, criticism is more direct and recorded formally, whereas in Japan, it is more subtle and verbal. The international manager's task is to distinguish relevant cross-cultural and intra-cultural differences and then to isolate potential opportunities and problems for the firm. Brands like McDonald's, KFC, Coca-Cola, Disney, and Pepsi, for example, have all been demonstrators or even icons of globalization and cultural integration. In markets such as Taiwan, McDonald's and other fast-food entities dramatically changed eating habits, especially those of the younger generation. The international business entity can act as a change agent by introducing new products, ideas, and practices. Although this may only shift consumption from one product brand to another, it may also lead to massive social change in the manner of consumption, the type of products consumed, and the location of consumption (see Exhibit 3.1).

EXHIBIT 3.1 Context cultures from low to high

The differences between high and low context cultures should be understood and applied not only at a cross-regional level but within a region as well. For example, north Europeans tend to be reserved in nature and maintain their personal space during conversations compared to south Europeans, whose beliefs about maintaining personal space are not as strong. Similarly, the use of a finger-and-thumb as a sign to communicate "okay" by an American manager can reflect worthlessness to people in Southern France or request for a bribe in Japanese culture and insulting gesture to Brazilians, thereby undermining international negotiations. Eastern and Chinese negotiators use body language such as leaning back with frequent eye contact in order to project a negative or indifferent approach, which is contrary to the meaning of similar position and gaze by Western country-based negotiators. Therefore, an understanding of nonverbal cues to establish appropriate personal rapport is important for managing international business relationships and conducting business internationally across different cultures.

Recognizing the cognitive requirements of a potential business partner before initiating negotiations can help business transactions sail smoothly beyond handshakes into complex agreements. The ever-increasing level of world trade, the opening of new markets, and intensifying competition have allowed – and sometimes forced – businesses to expand their operations. The challenge for managers is to handle the different values, attitudes, and behaviors that govern human interaction. First, managers must ensure smooth interaction of the business with its different constituents and, second, they must assist others in implementing programs within and across markets. It is no longer feasible to think of markets and operations in terms of domestic and international. Because the separation is no longer distinguishable, the necessity of culturally sensitive management and personnel becomes paramount when a firm expands its operations across borders and acquires new customers and new partners in new environments. Two distinct tasks become necessary during **internationalization:** first, to understand cultural differences and the ways they manifest and, second, to determine similarities across cultures and exploit them in strategy formulation. Success in new markets is very much a function of cultural adaptability: patience, flexibility, and appreciation of others' beliefs (see Vignette 3). Recognition of different approaches may lead to establishing best practices; that is, a new way of doing things applicable throughout the firm. Ideally, this means that successful ideas can be transferred across borders for efficiency and adjusted to local conditions for effectiveness.

Food Names and Their Locale

Local conditions can have an impact in a variety of ways: the climate, the way the product is grown or made, culture, and tradition. As a result, a food's name may mean different things to different people. To some, it's as simple as a food or wine that hails from specific regions; to others, it requires that the products be made using high standards or traditional methods. The European Union identifies the following three kinds of *terroir* for wines, olive oils, butters, cheeses, meats, honeys, and breads:

- Protected designation of origin products (PDOs), such as pecorino Romano cheese and kalamata olives, are associated with a specific location and made in a traditional way.

- Protected geographic indication products (PGIs), such as Alsatian honey and bresaola (air-dried beef), have a geographic connection for at least one stage of production, but not all.
- Traditional specialty guaranteed products (TSGs), such as mozzarella cheese and Lambic beers, have traditional ingredients or production methods, but are not linked to a specific region.

The European Commission summarized the European viewpoint in this way: Indications of production locale links a product and its source location tightly together. Europeans fear that the prolonged use of named products may undermine producers of goods in selling these goods themselves (Exhibit 3.2). A company in Canada, for example, could trademark a product named for a European place, preventing the rightful European originator from selling its goods in that market.

EXHIBIT 3.2 Is location everything when it comes to food?

If European negotiators in the World Trade Organization get their way, food names associated with specific regions – Tikka and Curry Masala from India, Parma ham from Italy, Stilton cheese from the United Kingdom, and Feta cheese from Greece – would be reserved solely for companies located in the respective regions. EU officials argue that mozzarella, for example, is made according to exacting standards only in that particular part of Italy, and, similarly, Stilton cheese can only be produced in the three English counties of Derbyshire, Leicestershire, and Nottinghamshire.

The Elements of Culture

The study of culture has led to generalizations that may apply to all cultures. Such characteristics are called cultural universals, which are manifestations of the total way of life of any group of people (Jameson, 2007). These include such elements as bodily adornment, courtship rituals, etiquette, the concept of family, gestures, joking, mealtime customs, music, personal names, status differentiation, and trade customs. These activities occur across cultures, but they may be uniquely manifested in a particular society, bringing about cultural diversity. Common denominators can indeed be found across cultures, but cultures may vary dramatically in how they perform the same activities. Even when a segment may be perceived to be similar across borders, as in the case of teenagers, cultural differences make dealing with them challenging. Cultural elements are both material (such as tools) and abstract (such as attitudes). The sensitivity and adaptation to cultural elements by an international firm depend on the firm's level of involvement in the market – for example, licensing versus direct investment – and the good or service marketed. While some goods and services or management practices require little adjustment, others may have to be adapted dramatically.

Language

A total of 6,912 known living languages exist in the world, with 311 being spoken in the USA, 297 in Mexico, 241 in China, and 13 in Finland. The European Union has 23 official languages for its bureaucracy. Interestingly, 96% of the world's languages are spoken by just 4% of the world's population (Gravier, 2013). Language has been described as the mirror of culture.

Language itself is multidimensional by nature. This is true not only of the spoken word but also of what can be called the nonverbal language of international business. Messages are conveyed by the words used, by how the words are spoken (e.g., tone of voice), and through nonverbal means such as gestures, body position, and eye contact. Often, mastery of the language is required before acculturation is achieved. Language mastery must go beyond technical competency because every language has words and phrases that can be readily understood only in context. Such phrases are carriers of culture; they represent special ways a culture has developed to view some aspect of human existence. Language capability serves four distinct roles in international business.

1. Language aids in information gathering and evaluation. Rather than rely completely on the opinions of others, the manager is personally able to see and hear what is going on. People are far more comfortable speaking their own language, and this should be treated as an advantage.
2. Language provides access to local society. Although French may be widely spoken and may even be the official company language, speaking the local language may make a dramatic difference.
3. Language capability is increasingly important in company communications, whether within the corporate family or with channel members. Imagine the difficulties encountered by a country manager who must communicate with employees through an interpreter.
4. Language provides more than the ability to communicate. It extends beyond mechanics to the interpretation of contexts that may influence business operations.

The manager's command of the national language(s) in a market must be greater than simple word recognition (Ang & Inkpen, 2008). Consider, for example, how dramatically different English terms can be when used in the UK or the USA. In negotiations, for US delegates, "tabling a proposal" means that they want to delay a decision, while their British counterparts understand the expression to mean that immediate attention is to be given to it. Languages are not immune to this phenomenon either. Goodyear identified five different terms for the word "tires" in the Spanish-speaking Americas: *cauchos* in Venezuela, *cubiertas* in Argentina, *gomas* in Puerto Rico, *neumaticos* in Chile, and *llantas* in most of the other countries in the region, and it adjusts its communications messages accordingly.

The role of language extends beyond that of a communication medium. Linguistic diversity is often an indicator of other types of diversity (Maffi, 2005). In Quebec, the French language has always been a major consideration of most francophone governments because it is one of the clear manifestations of the province's identity vis-à-vis the English-speaking provinces. Germans have founded a society for the protection of the German language from the spread of "Denglish." Poland has directed that all companies selling or advertising foreign products use Polish in their advertisements. In Hong Kong, the Chinese Government is promoting the use of Cantonese rather than English as the language of commerce, while some people in India – with its 800 dialects – scorn the use of English as a lingua franca since it is a reminder of British colonialism. Although English is encountered daily by those on the Internet, the "e" in e-business does not necessarily translate into "English." A truly global portal works only if the online functions are provided in a multilingual and multicultural format.

Dealing with language invariably requires local assistance (Putsch, 1985). A good local advertising agency and a good local market research firm can prevent many problems (Suharyanti et al., 2016). When translation is required, such as when communicating with suppliers or customers, care should be taken in selecting the translator. To make sure, the simplest method of control is back translation – translating a foreign language version back to the original language by a different person than the one who made the first translation. This approach may be able to detect omissions and blunders. Language also has to be understood in the historical context. Nokia launched an advertising campaign in Germany for the interchangeable covers for its portable phones using a theme "*Jedem das Seine*" ("to each his own"). The campaign was withdrawn after the American Jewish Congress pointed out that the same slogan was found on the entry portal to Buchenwald, a Nazi-era concentration camp.

Nonverbal Language

International body language must be included in the nonverbal language of international business. An interesting exercise is to compare and contrast the conversation styles of different nationalities. Northern Europeans are quite reserved in using their hands and maintain a good amount of personal space, whereas southern Europeans involve their bodies to a far greater degree in making a point. Individuals vary in the amount of space they want, separating them from others. Arabs and Latin Americans like to stand close to people when they talk. If an American, who may not be comfortable at such close range, backs away from an Arab, this might incorrectly be taken as a negative reaction. Also, Westerners are often taken aback by the more physical nature of affection between Slavs – for example, being kissed squarely on the lips by a business partner, regardless of gender.

Managers also must analyze and become familiar with the hidden language of foreign cultures (Exhibit 3.3). Five key topics – time, space, material possessions, friendship patterns, and business agreements – offer a starting point from which managers can begin to acquire the understanding necessary to do business in foreign countries. In many parts of the world, time is flexible and not seen as a limited commodity; people come late to appointments or may not come at all. In Hong Kong, for example, it is futile to set exact meeting times because getting from one place to another may take minutes or hours depending on the traffic situation. Showing indignation or impatience at such behavior would astonish an Arab, Latin American, or Asian.

In some countries, extended social acquaintance and the establishment of appropriate personal rapport are essential to conducting business. The feeling is that

Exhibit 3.3 Prior to any meeting international managers must exercise due diligence and work to understand nonverbal cultural language
Credit: Rawpixel/iStock / Getty Images Plus.

one should know one's business partner on a personal level before transactions can occur. Therefore, rushing straight to business will not be rewarded, because deals are made on the basis of not only the best product or price but also the entity or person deemed most trustworthy. Contracts may be bound on handshakes, not lengthy and complex agreements – a fact that makes some, especially Western, businesspeople uneasy.

Religion

Religion affects international business that is seen in a culture's values and attitudes toward entrepreneurship, consumption, and social organization. The impact will vary depending on the strength of the dominant religious tenets. While religion's impact may be indirect in Protestant northern Europe, its impact in countries where Islamic fundamentalism is on the rise (such as Algeria) may be profound. Religion provides the basis for transcultural similarities under shared beliefs and behavior. The impact of these similarities will be assessed in terms of the dominant religions of the world: Christianity, Islam, Judaism, Hinduism, Buddhism, and Confucianism. Other religions may have smaller numbers of followers, but their impact is still significant due to the centuries they have influenced world history. While some countries may officially have secularism, such as Marxism-Leninism as a state belief (e.g., China, Vietnam, and Cuba), traditional religious beliefs still remain a powerful force in shaping behavior.

In most cultures, people find in religion a reason for being and legitimacy in the belief that they are of a larger context (Smith, 2003). To define religion requires the inclusion of the supernatural and the existence of a higher power. Religion defines the ideals for life, which in turn are reflected in the values and attitudes of societies and individuals. Such values and attitudes shape the behavior and practices of institutions and members of cultures and are the most challenging for the marketer to adjust to. When Procter & Gamble launched its Biomat laundry detergent in Israel, it found reaching Orthodox Jews (15% of the population) a challenge because they do not own traditional media such as television sets. The solution was to focus on the segment's core belief that they should aid those less fortunate (Vranica, 2005). A Biomat truck equipped with washing machines traveled around key towns. People would donate their clothing, and Biomat would wash and distribute it to the needy. As a result, the brand's share has grown 50% among the segment.

International managers must be aware of the differences not only among the major religions but also within them. The impact of these divisions may range from hostility, as in Sri Lanka, to barely perceptible historic suspicion, as in many European countries where Protestant and Catholic are the main divisions. With some religions, such as Hinduism, people may be divided into groups, which determines their status and, to a large extent, their ability to consume. Christianity has the largest following among world religions, with more than 2 billion people. While there are many subgroups within Christianity, the major division is between Catholicism and Protestantism. A prominent difference between the two is the attitude toward making money. While Catholicism has questioned it, the Protestant ethic has emphasized the importance of work and accumulation of wealth for the glory of God. At the same time, frugality was emphasized, and the residual of wealth from hard work formed the basis for investment. It has been proposed that the work ethic is responsible for the development of capitalism in the Western world and the rise of predominantly Protestant countries into world economic leadership in the twentieth century.

Major holidays are often tied to religion. Holidays are observed differently from one culture to the next, to the extent that the same holiday may have different connotations. Christian cultures observe Christmas and exchange gifts on either December 24 or December 25, with the exception of the Dutch, who exchange gifts on St. Nicholas Day, December 6. Tandy Corporation, in its first year in the Netherlands, targeted its major Christmas promotion for the third week of December with less than satisfactory results. The international manager must see to it that local holidays, such as Mexico's Día de los Muertos (October 31 to November 2), are taken into account in scheduling events ranging from fact-finding missions to marketing programs and in preparing local work schedules.

Values and Attitudes

Values are shared beliefs or group norms that have been internalized by individuals (Zhen, 2012). Attitudes are evaluations of alternatives based on these values. Differences in cultural values affect the way planning is executed, decisions are made, strategy is implemented, and personnel is evaluated. The cultural values have to be accommodated or used in the management of business functions. The more rooted values and attitudes are in central beliefs (such as religion), the more cautiously one has to move. Attitude toward change is basically positive in industrialized countries, as is one's ability to improve one's lot in life; in tradition-bound societies, however, change is viewed with suspicion – especially when it comes from a foreign entity. The Japanese culture raises an almost invisible – yet often unscalable – wall against all *gaijin* (foreigners). Many middle-aged bureaucrats and company officials believe that buying foreign products is downright unpatriotic. The resistance is not so much to foreign products as to those who produce and market them. Similarly, foreign-based corporations have had difficulty hiring university graduates or mid-career personnel because of bias against foreign employers. Even under such adverse conditions, the race can be run and won through tenacity, patience, and drive.

Cultural attitudes are not always a deterrent to foreign business practices or foreign goods (Hovav & D'Arcy, 2012). Japanese youth, for instance, display extremely positive attitudes toward Western goods, from popular music to Nike sneakers to Louis Vuitton haute couture to Starbucks lattes. Global brands are able to charge premium prices if they tap into cultural attitudes that revere imported goods. Similarly, attitudes of US youth toward Japanese "cool" have increased the popularity of authentic Japanese "manga" comics and animated cartoons. Pokémon cards, and Hello Kitty, are examples of Japanese products that caught on in the USA almost as quickly as in Japan. Working in China and with the Chinese, the international manager will have to realize that making deals has more to do with cooperation than competition. The Chinese believe that one should build the relationship first and, if successful, transactions will follow. The relationship, or *guanxi,* is a set of favor exchanges to establish trust (Dunfee & Warren, 2001). A manager must be careful not to assume that success in one market using the cultural extension ensures success somewhere else. For example, while the Disneyland concept worked well in Tokyo, it had a tougher time in Paris. One of the main reasons was that while the Japanese are fond of American pop culture, the Europeans are quite content with their own cultural heritage.

Manners and Customs

Changes in manners and **customs** must be carefully monitored, especially in cases that seem to indicate a narrowing of cultural differences among peoples. Offerings such as McDonald's and Coke have met with success around the world, but this does not mean that the world is becoming Westernized. Modernization and Westernization are not at all the same (Exhibit 3.4). Understanding manners and customs is especially important in negotiations because interpretations based on one's own frame of reference may lead to a totally incorrect conclusion. To effectively negotiate abroad, all types of communication should be read correctly. Americans often interpret inaction and silence as negative signs. As a result, Japanese executives tend to expect that their silence can get Americans to lower prices or sweeten a deal. Even a simple agreement may take days to negotiate in the Middle East because the Arab party may want to talk about unrelated issues or do something else for a while. The aggressive style of Russian negotiators and their usual last-minute change requests may cause astonishment and concern on the part of ill-prepared negotiators. Some of the potential ways negotiators may not be prepared include:

1. insufficient understanding of different ways of thinking
2. insufficient attention to the necessity to save face
3. insufficient knowledge and appreciation of the host country – its history, culture, government, and image of foreigners
4. insufficient recognition of the decision-making process and the role of personal relations and personalities
5. insufficient allocation of time for negotiations.

Exhibit 3.4 McDonald's succeeds internationally by working to be part of the local culture
Credit: Barry Cronin / Hulton Archive/Getty Images

One area where preparation and sensitivity are called for is gift-giving with an understanding of what and when to give. An ideal gift represents the giver's own culture while being sensitive to the recipient's. For example, a Finn may gift a Suunto compass to a Saudi business partner (to help him determine the direction for daily prayers). Giving gifts that are easily available in that country (e.g., chocolates to a Swiss) is not advisable. Some gifts are not suitable; clocks or other timepieces are symbols of death in China, while handkerchiefs symbolize tears in Latin America and Korea. Care should be taken with the way the gift is wrapped; for example, it should be in appropriately colored paper. Always wrap the gifts you present but remember to avoid white and brightly colored wrapping paper in Japan. If delivered in person, the actual giving has to be executed correctly; in China, extending the gift to the recipient using both hands does this. It should be noted, however, that many of the international companies such as Intel and Coca-Cola have policies that do not allow the giving and receiving of gifts.

Managers must be concerned with differences in the ways products are used. The questions that the international manager has to ask are "what are we selling?", "what are the benefits we are providing?" and "who or what are we competing against?" Care should be taken not to assume cross-border similarities even if many of the indicators converge. For example, a jam producer noted that the Brazilian market seemed to hold significant potential because per capita jelly and jam consumption was one-tenth that of Argentina, clearly a difference not justified by obvious factors. However, Argentines consume jam at teatime, a custom that does not exist in Brazil. Furthermore, Argentina's climate and soil favor growing wheat, leading it to consume three times the bread Brazil does. Therefore, meticulous research plays a major role in avoiding these types of problems. Concept tests determine the potential acceptance and proper understanding of a proposed new product. As explained in Chapter 8, focus groups can be instrumental in learning about one's audience. The adjustment to the cultural nuances of the marketplace has to be viewed as long term and may even be accomplished through trial and error.

Technological advances have been the major cause of cultural change in many countries. Increasingly, consumers are seeking more diverse products as a way of satisfying their demand for a higher quality of life and more leisure time. For example, Chinese consumers want more than just function. If a company wants to sell vacuums or washing machines in China, it better pay attention to emotional needs as well as physical ones.

Aesthetics

Each culture makes a clear statement about good taste, as expressed in the arts and in the particular symbolism of colors, form, and music. Color is often used as a mechanism for brand identification, feature reinforcement, and differentiation. In international markets, colors have more symbolic value than in domestic markets. Black, for instance, is considered the color of mourning in the USA and Europe, whereas white has the same symbolic meaning in Japan and most of the Far East.

A British bank was interested in expanding its operations to Singapore and wanted to use blue and green as its identification colors. A consulting firm was quick to tell the client that green may be associated with death in that country. Although the bank insisted on its original choice of colors, the green was changed to an acceptable shade. International firms have to consider local tastes and concerns in designing their outlets. They may have a general policy of uniformity in building or office space design, but local tastes often warrant modifications. Respecting local cultural traditions may also generate goodwill toward the international marketer.

Education

Education, either formal or informal, plays a major role in the passing on and sharing of culture (Bruner, 1996). Educational levels of a culture can be assessed using literacy rates, enrollment in secondary education, or enrollment in higher education available from secondary data sources. International firms also need to know about the qualitative aspects of education, namely, varying emphases on particular skills and the overall level of the education provided. Japan and South

Korea, for example, emphasize the sciences, especially engineering, to a greater degree than do Western countries. Educational levels also affect various business functions. For example, a high level of illiteracy suggests the use of visual aids rather than printed manuals. Local recruiting for sales jobs is affected by the availability of suitably trained personnel. In some cases, international firms routinely send locally recruited personnel to headquarters for training. The international manager may also need to overcome obstacles in recruiting a suitable sales force or support personnel. For example, the Japanese culture places a premium on loyalty, and employees consider themselves members of the corporate family. If a foreign firm decides to leave Japan, its employees may find themselves stranded in mid-career, unable to find their place in the Japanese business system. Therefore, university graduates are reluctant to join any but the largest and most well-known foreign firms. If technology is marketed, the product's sophistication will depend on the educational level of future users. Product adaptation decisions are often influenced by the extent to which targeted customers are able to use the good or service properly.

Social Institutions

Social institutions affect the ways people relate to each other. The family unit, which in Western industrialized countries consists of parents and children, is extended to include grandparents and other relatives in a number of cultures. This affects consumption patterns and must be taken into account, for example, when conducting market research. The concept of kinship, or blood relations between individuals, is defined in a very broad way in societies such as those in sub-Saharan Africa. Family relations and a strong obligation to family are important factors to consider in human resource management in those regions. Understanding tribal politics in countries such as Nigeria may help the manager avoid unnecessary complications in executing business transactions. The division of a particular population into classes is termed **social stratification**. Stratification ranges from the situation in northern Europe, where most people are members of the middle class, to highly stratified societies in which the higher strata control most of the buying power and decision-making positions. An important part of the socialization process of consumers worldwide is **reference groups**. These groups provide the values and attitudes that influence behavior. Primary reference groups include the family and coworkers and other intimate acquaintances, and secondary groups are social organizations where less-continuous interaction takes place, such as professional associations and trade organizations. In addition to providing socialization, reference groups develop a person's concept of self, which is manifested by the choice of products used. Reference groups also provide a baseline for compliance with group norms, giving the individual the option of conforming to or avoiding certain behaviors.

Social organization also determines the roles of managers and subordinates and how they relate to one another. In some cultures, managers and subordinates are separated explicitly and implicitly by various boundaries ranging from social class differences to separate office facilities. In others, cooperation is elicited through equality (Miroshnik, 2002). Fitting an organizational culture to the larger context of a national culture has to be executed with care. Changes that are too dramatic may disrupt productivity or, at the minimum, arouse suspicion. Although Western business has impersonal structures for channeling power and influence – primarily through reliance on laws and contracts – the Chinese emphasize personal relationships to obtain clout, typically referred to as *guanxi*. For the Chinese, contracts form a useful agenda and a symbol of progress, but obligations come from relationships. McDonald's found this out in Beijing, where it was evicted from a central building after only two years despite having a 20-year contract. The incoming business had a strong *guanxi*, whereas McDonald's had not kept its in good repair (Luo, 2007).

Sources of Cultural Knowledge

The concept of cultural knowledge is broad and multifaceted. Cultural knowledge can be defined by the way it is acquired. Objective or factual information is obtained from others through communication, research, and education (Sue, 2001). Experiential knowledge, on the other hand, can be acquired only by being involved in a culture other than one's own. Both factual and experiential information can be general or country specific. Market-specific knowledge does not necessarily travel well; however, the general variables on which the information is based, do travel. From the corporate point of view, global capability is developed in painstaking ways: foreign assignments, networking across borders, and using multi-country, multicultural teams to develop strategies and programs. There is a variety of sources and methods to extend knowledge of specific cultures. Many of them provide factual information. In addition, governmental organizations are offering more specific business advice. The US Department of Commerce's *Country Commercial Guides* cover more than 153 countries, while the Economist Intelligence Unit's *Country Reports* cover 188 countries. *Culturegrams*, which detail the customs of people of 206 countries, is published by the Center for International and Area Studies at Brigham Young University. Many facilitating agencies – such as advertising agencies, banks, consulting firms, and transportation companies – provide background information on the markets they serve for their clients. These range from AIRINC international reports on-site selections and cost of living for 125 countries; the Hong Kong Shanghai Banking Corporation's *Business Profile Series* (Dubai, Hong Kong, Singapore, South Africa, United Kingdom); to *World*

Trade magazine's "Put Your Best Foot Forward" series, which covers Europe, Asia, Mexico/Canada, and Russia.

Specialists who advise clients on the cultural dimensions of business not only help avoid mistakes but also add culture as an ingredient of success in country- or region-specific programs. Blunders in foreign markets that could have been avoided with factual information are generally inexcusable. A manager who travels to Taipei without first obtaining a visa and is therefore turned back, has no one else to blame. Other oversights may lead to more costly mistakes. For example, Brazilians are several inches shorter than the average American, but this was not taken into account when Sears erected American-height shelves that block Brazilian shoppers' view of the rest of the store. Over the long run, culture can become a factor in the firm's overall success.

Cultural Analysis

To try to understand and explain differences among and across cultures, researchers have developed checklists and models showing pertinent variables and their interaction. Multinational corporations introduce management practices, as well as goods and services, from one country to others, where they are perceived to be new and different. Although many question the usefulness of such models, they do bring together all or most of the relevant variables on how consumers in different cultures may perceive, evaluate, and adopt new behaviors. However, any manager using such a tool should periodically cross-check its results against reality and experience. The key variable of the model is a propensity to change, which is a function of three constructs:

1. cultural lifestyle of individuals in terms of how deeply held their traditional beliefs and attitudes are, and also which elements of culture are dominant
2. change agents (such as multinational corporations and their practices) and strategic-opinion leaders (for example, social elites)
3. communication about the innovation from commercial sources, neutral sources (such as government), and social sources, such as friends and relatives.

It has been argued that differences in cultural lifestyle can be explained by four dimensions of culture:

1. individualism ("I" consciousness versus "we" consciousness)
2. power distance (levels of equality in society)
3. uncertainty avoidance (need for formal rules and regulations)
4. masculinity (attitude toward achievement, roles of men and women).

A fifth dimension has also been added to distinguish cultural differences: long-term versus short-term orientation. All of the long-term countries are Asian (e.g., China, India, Hong Kong, Taiwan, Japan, and South Korea), while most Western countries (such as the USA States and the UK) are thinking short-term. Some have argued that this cultural dimension may explain the Japanese marketing success based on market share (rather than short-term profit) motivation in market development.

Knowledge of similarities along these four dimensions allows the clustering of countries and regions and the establishment of regional and national marketing programs. It is important to position products as a continuous innovation that does not require radical changes in consumption patterns. Understanding the implications of the dimensions helps businesspeople prepare for international business encounters. For example, when negotiating in Germany, one can expect a counterpart who is thorough, systematic, and very well prepared, but also rather dogmatic and, therefore, less flexible and willing to compromise. Efficiency is emphasized. In Mexico, however, the counterpart may prefer to address problems on a personal and private basis rather than on a business level. This means more emphasis on socializing and conveying one's humanity, sincerity, loyalty, and friendship. Also, differences in the pace and business practices of a region have to be accepted. Boeing Airplane Company found that accumulation of personal individualism and power distances had accident rates 2.6 times greater than those at the other end of the scale (Philips, 1994). A result which is important in the preparation of the training and service operations.

Communication about innovation takes place through the physical product itself (samples) or through experiencing a new company policy. If a new personnel practice, such as quality circles or flextime, is being investigated, the participating employees may communicate in reports or through word of mouth results. Communication content depends on the following factors: the good's or policy's relative advantage over existing alternatives; compatibility with established behavioral patterns; complexity, or the degree to which the good or process is perceived as difficult to understand and use; taste-testing, or experimentation without incurring major risk; and observability, which is the extent to which the consequences of the innovation are visible. Before a good or policy is evaluated, information should be gathered about existing beliefs and circumstances. Distortion of data may occur as a result of selective attention, exposure, and retention. As examples, anything foreign may be seen in a negative light, another multinational company's efforts may have failed, or the government may discourage the proposed activity. Additional information may then be sought from any of the sources or from opinion leaders in the market. Adoption tendency refers to the likelihood that the product or process will be accepted. Individualism has a significant positive relationship and uncertainty avoidance, a negative relationship with acceptance and diffusion rates of new products. Similar findings have been reached on the penetration of e-commerce in different markets. If an innovation clears the hurdles, it may be adopted and slowly diffused into the entire market. An international manager has two basic choices: to adapt company offerings and methods to those in the market or to try to change market conditions to fit company programs. Adjusting to differences requires putting one's own cultural values aside. However, the self-reference criterion i.e., the unconscious reference to one's own cultural values, has been recognized as cultural bias and the root of most international business problems. Analytical procedures enable constant monitoring of changes caused by outside events as well as the changes caused by the business entity itself. Ethnocentrism, the tendency to consider one's own culture superior to those of other, can be controlled only by acknowledging it and properly adjusting to its possible effects in managerial decision-making. The international manager needs to be prepared and able to put that preparedness to effective use.

The Cultural Sensitivity

International managers face a dilemma in terms of international and intercultural competence. The lack of adequate foreign language and international business skills has led to firms losing contracts, weakened negotiations, and ineffectual management. The increase in the overall international activity of firms increases the need for cultural sensitivity training at all levels of the organization. Further, today's training must encompass not only outsiders to the firm but interaction within the corporate family as well. However inconsequential the degree of interaction may seem, it can still cause problems if proper understanding is lacking. Some companies try to avoid the training problem by hiring only nationals or well-traveled individuals for their international operations. This makes sense for the management of overseas operations but will not solve the training need, especially if transfers to a culture unfamiliar to the manager are likely. To foster cultural sensitivity and acceptance of new ways of doing things within the organization, management must institute internal education programs that may include:

1. culture-specific information
2. general cultural information
3. self-specific information.

The objective of formal training programs is to foster the four critical characteristics of preparedness, sensitivity, patience, and flexibility in managers and other personnel. Programs vary dramatically in terms of their rigor, involvement, and cost. Environmental briefings and cultural-orientation programs provide factual preparation for a manager to operate in, or work with people from, a particular country. Area studies should be a basic prerequisite for other types of training programs. Alone, area studies serve little practical purpose because they do not get the manager's feet wet. Other, more involved, assimilator-based programs contribute context in which to put facts so that they can be properly understood. The cultural assimilator is a program in which trainees must respond to scenarios of specific situations in a particular country. The programs have been developed for the Arab countries, Iran, Thailand, Central America, and Greece. A panel of judges evaluates the results of the trainees' assimilator experience. This type of program has been used most frequently in cases of transfers abroad on short notice.

When more time is available, managers can be trained extensively in language. This may be required if an exotic language is involved. Sensitivity training focuses on enhancing a manager's flexibility in situations that are quite different from those at home. The approach is based on the assumption that understanding and accepting oneself is critical to understanding a person from another culture. While most of the methods discussed are best delivered in face-to-face settings, web-based training is becoming more popular. Finally, training may involve field experience, which exposes a manager to a different cultural environment for a limited amount of time. Although the expense of placing and maintaining an expatriate is high (and, therefore, the cost of failure is high), field experience is rarely used in training. One field experience technique that has been suggested when the training process needs to be rigorous is the host-family surrogate. This technique places a trainee (and possibly his or her family) in a domestically located family of the nationality to which they are assigned. Regardless of the degree of training, preparation, and positive personal characteristics, a manager will always remain foreign. A manager should never rely on his or her own judgment when local managers can be consulted. In many instances, a manager should have an interpreter present at negotiations, especially if the manager is not completely bilingual. Overconfidence in one's language capabilities can create problems.

Making Culture Work for Business Success

Culture should not be viewed as a challenge, but rather it should be considered as an opportunity that can be exploited through an understanding of differences and their fundamental determinants amongst different cultures. Differences can easily be dismissed as indicators of inferiority or viewed as approaches to be changed; however, the opposite may actually be the case. Best practice knows no one particular origin, nor should it acknowledge boundaries. The following rules serve as a summary of how culture and its appreciation may serve as a tool to ensure success.

Embrace local culture: Many corporate credos include a promise to be the best possible corporate citizens in every community operated in. The Walt Disney

Company has made it a priority to build its international business in television, movies, retail, and theme parks. Disney's theme park in Hong Kong, which opened in 2005, suffered largely due to a limited appeal to mainland Chinese audiences (Exhibit 3.5). The first big opportunity to reverse the trend was a stroke of astrological fortune: the year 2008 was the Year of the Rat, allowing Disney to proclaim it the "Year of the Mouse." The Disneyland Chinese New Year campaign featured a logo with the Chinese character for luck flipped upside down (a New Year tradition), with mouse ears added on top. Inside the park, dumplings and turnip cakes were featured on the menus. The parade down Main Street USA was joined by the "Rhythm of Life Procession," featuring a dragon dance and puppets of birds, flowers and fish, set to traditional Chinese music reflecting on the cultural integration of Chinese culture into American culture.

Build relationships: Each country-market has its own unique set of constituents who need to be identified and nurtured. Establishing and nurturing local ties at the various stages of the market-development cycle develops relationships that can be invaluable in expansion and countering political risk.

Employ locals in order to gain cultural knowledge: Disney undertook major efforts to give its Hong Kong park a more Chinese character. Research was conducted in the homes of Chinese consumers, who were asked about their knowledge of the Disney brand and their lifestyles. As a result, for example, Disneyland ads now feature only one child (Chinese Government rules limit most couples to just one child), two parents, and two grandparents (many households are extended ones) sharing branded Disney activities, such as watching a movie or giving a plush version of the mouse as a gift.

Help employees understand you: Employing locals will give a marketer a valuable asset in market development (i.e., acculturation). However, these employees also need their own process of adjustment (i.e., "corporatization") in order to be effective. Disney has given more power to local managers to develop completely local approaches, to adapt US franchises and make local versions of them, or to build interest in the US shows such as *Hannah Montana* and *Kim Possible*. It is also important to help employees understand the firm better. Chinese executives and staff benefit from visits to Burbank, California, and interaction with Disney executives from around the world to combine Disney and Chinese values.

Adapting products and processes to local markets: Nowhere is a commitment to local markets as evident as in product offerings. The gods of wealth, longevity, and happiness have been added to the Hong Kong Disneyland gang. To support the marketing efforts of the theme park, Disney has expanded its TV, online, and film businesses in China. The *Secret of the Magic Gourd* (2007) was the first-ever movie made just for Chinese audiences. The movie also meant a departure from Disney's obsession with going it alone because it joined local experts (including the state-run China Film Group) to produce the culturally customized product.

Culture of Trust and the Soul of Business

The role of trust in business relationships and alliances is an established concept, but the soul of business is a relatively new concept. The need for considering businesses having souls became imperative because of growing competition in the home country and the need for firms to go international, looking for new markets. For firms operating internationally, trust helps them to create a binding with stakeholders in the target market and bring people together. In the case of international firms aiming to enter a developing market, their managers may find it challenging to fight corruption due to a lack of transparency in local regulations and governance.

When the global economy is being driven by constant technology-based communication and connectivity, international firms must follow standards that will create trust among global stakeholders. Development of an international business must adopt to the core dimensions of truthfulness, simplicity, expanded participation, and personal responsibility.

SUMMARY

Culture is one of the most challenging aspects for any firm operating internationally or planning to expand out of the home country. Learned behavioral patterns help managers of international firms to characterize the culture practiced by the members of a given society. In a technologically advanced world, the approach to culture can change and be shaped by a set of dynamic elements such as language, religion, values and attitudes, manners and customs, aesthetics, technology, education, and social institutions. To cope with these changes in the system, an international manager needs both actual and interpretive knowledge of culture to be able to link it with the soul of the business. To some extent, the factual knowledge about culture for creating linkages can be learned as its interpretation comes only through experience. The most complicated problems in dealing with the cultural environment stem from the fact that to truly become part of a culture, it has to be lived. In some cases, globalization is a fact of life; however, cultural differences are still far from converging. Two schools of thought that exist in the business world help us learn how to deal with cultural diversity. One is that business is business the world around, following the model of Pepsi and McDonald's. The other school proposes that companies must tailor business approaches to individual cultures. Setting up policies and procedures in each country has been compared to an organ transplant, the critical question centers around acceptance or rejection. The major challenge to the international manager is to make sure that rejection is not a result of cultural myopia or blindness. The internationally successful companies all share an important quality: patiently focusing on building the soul of their business. They have not rushed into situations but rather built their operations carefully by following key business principles with recognition of adversaries to all stakeholders.

DISCUSSION QUESTIONS

1. Comment on the assumption "If people are serious about doing business with you, they will speak your language."
2. You are on your first business visit to Germany. You feel confident about your ability to speak the language (you studied German in school and have taken a

refresher course), and you decide to use it. During introductions, you want to break the ice by asking "Wie geht's?" and insisting that everyone call you by your first name. Speculate as to the reaction.

3. **Q:** *"What do you call a person who can speak two languages?"*
   a) "Bilingual."
   b) "Trilingual."
   Q: *"Excellent. How about one?"*
   A: *"Hmmmm ... American!"*
   Is this joke malicious, or is there something to be learned from it?

4. What can be learned about a culture from reading and attending to factual materials?

5. Provide examples of how the self-reference criterion might manifest itself.

6. How can an international company reflect on the "soul of its business" in different markets globally?

7. Differentiate between multinational and international companies.

KEY TERMS

acculturation	58	field experience	75
area studies	74	high-context cultures	59
back translation	63	internationalization	60
cultural assimilator	75	linguistic diversity	63
cultural sensitivity	74	low-context cultures	59
cultural universals	61	multidimensional	58
culture	58	reference groups	70
customs	67	self-reference criterion	74
ethnocentrism	74	sensitivity training	75
experiential knowledge	71	social stratification	70

TAKE A STAND

Questions for Debate

1. How can companies manage their workplace culture with employees working from home in a technologically driven business environment?

2. Can companies empower their employees and manage employee experiences in a technologically enabled work culture without the personal connections that are important for motivating humans.

3. What kind of boundaryless policies and practices will Human Resources require for managing, motivating, and retaining talent residing in different parts of the world.

INTERNET EXERCISES

1. Many companies, such as Cultural Savvy, provide cross-cultural consulting and coaching, as well as training. Using the company's web site (www.culturalsavvy.com), assess the different services with which consultants can help master cultural competency.
2. In 2009, Burger King pulled an advertising campaign in the UK and Spain promoting its "Texican Whopper" because of complaints from the Mexican Government of cultural insensitivity. View the commercial on YouTube, using keyword Burger King Texican Whopper ad, and relate your perspective of the commercial. Should the advertisement be discontinued?

FURTHER RESOURCES

Magnusson, P. and Westjohn, S. (2019). Advancing global consumer culture research. International Marketing Review, 36(4), 593–597.

Rohlfer, S. and Zhang, Y. (2016). Culture studies in international business: paradigmatic shifts. European Business Review, 28(1), 39–62.

Stahl, G. and Tung, R. (2014). Towards a more balanced treatment of culture in international business studies: The need for positive cross-cultural scholarship. Journal of International Business Studies, 46(4), 391–414.

Zhou, L. and Zhang, Q. (2012). Cultural adaptation pattern analysis of McDonald's and KFC in the Chinese market.

4 Politics and Laws

CONTENTS

VIGNETTE 4 International trade and elephants

This headline tends to make readers think of ivory and trade in elephant tusks. International trade in such products has ground to a halt. In order to protect elephants from poachers, governments around the world support restrictive measures in ivory trade.

But elephants have been an important part of international trade for millennia. Mostly, however, the trade did not focus on elephant parts, but on the entire beast itself. In many instances, elephants defined the strength of nations. In the frequent international conflicts of ancient times, elephants were the "tanks" of war. Those generals who had larger and more elephants typically won the battles. Even disciplined Roman legionnaires took flight when confronted with the giant pachyderms from Africa. For hundreds of years, Roman mothers tried to threaten their children into obedience by calling out that "Hannibal ante portas esse" ("Hannibal at the gates"). This was a reference to Roman archenemy Hannibal, from the key trading opposition city of Carthage, who had introduced elephants into warfare against the Romans and had virtually arrived at the front doors of Rome. He and his elephant tanks had devastated multiple legions during the second Punic War (218–201 BC) and might have taken Rome itself, had he not been ordered back home by the leaders of Carthage.

Even earlier, the Egyptians were very active in international elephant trade. Their key trade priority was to acquire elephants from Ethiopia, which they transported using specially constructed boats, called *elefantegos*. After completing their training in Egypt, these elephants were then used quite successfully to attack the Greek Empire in Persia.

Though elephants no longer feature in most military conflicts today, the impact of trade in new and strong weapons continues to be with us. Millennia after Hannibal, international discussions and negotiations are ongoing, trying to assess whether nations with advanced military technology should be using the new weapons and selling weapons systems to the world. Such sales can dramatically affect not only the trade and capital accounts of nations but also their politics and the freedom of their citizens.

Sources: Bernstein, 2008; Livius, 2006; Walbank, 2003.

Introduction

The political and legal environment in both the home and host countries constitutes an important context that affects the operations and activities of international firms. Governments in the home country devise laws, regulations, and policies that affect as to how the firm can operate abroad. At the same time, each foreign country establishes its own laws and political systems that strongly influence business. Even though legislative action may strictly be aimed at domestic or at international firms, collateral damage affecting non-targeted concern is quite frequent. Indeed, the foreign environment may pose substantial political and legal risk. Managers must be able to navigate the political and legal environment, at home and abroad. Firms must obey laws, regulations, and practices, and avoid unethical or questionable conduct. Success means learning about the foreign context and managing company operations accordingly. In this chapter, we examine the political and legal environment in both the home and host countries. We highlight as to how well-managed companies go about minimizing risk. We highlight the critical role of international relations and laws.

The Home-Country Perspective

No manager can afford to ignore the rules and regulations of the country from which he or she conducts international business transactions. Many laws and regulations may not specifically address international business issues, yet they can have a major impact on a firm's opportunities abroad. Minimum-wage legislation, for example, has a bearing on the international competitiveness of a firm using production, significantly affecting the pricing policies of firms. For example, US chemical firms must pay into mitigation funds based on their production volume, regardless of whether the production is sold domestically or exported. As a result, these firms are at a disadvantage internationally when exporting their commodity-type products. They are required to compete against firms that have a cost advantage because their home countries do not have to pay into an environmental fund.

Often, governments also have specific rules and regulations that restrict international business. Such regulations are frequently political in nature and are based on governmental objectives that override commercial concerns. The restrictions are particularly sensitive when they address activities outside the country. Such measures challenge the territorial sovereignty of other governments and raise the issue of extraterritoriality – meaning a nation's attempt to set policy outside its territorial limits. Yet actions implying such extraterritorial reach are common because nations often argue that their citizens and products maintain their nationality wherever they may be, and they therefore continue to follow the rules and laws of their home country.

Three main areas of governmental activity are of major concern to the international business manager. They are embargoes or trade sanctions, export controls, and the regulation of international business behavior.

Embargoes

Trade embargoes have been used frequently and successfully in times of war or to address specific grievances. For example, in 1284, the Hansa, an association of north German merchants, believed that its members were suffering from several injustices by Norway. On learning that one of its ships had been attacked and pillaged by the Norwegians, the Hansa called an assembly of its members and resolved an economic blockade of Norway. The export of grain, flour, vegetables, and beer was prohibited on pain of fines and confiscation of the goods. The blockade was a complete success. Deprived of grain from Germany, the Norwegians were unable to obtain it from England or elsewhere. As a contemporary chronicler reports: "then there broke out a famine so great that they were forced to make atonement." Norway was forced to pay indemnities for the financial losses that had been caused and to grant the Hansa extensive trade privileges (Dollinger, 1999).

Over time, economic sanctions and embargoes have become a principal tool of foreign policy for many countries (Exhibit 4.1). Often, they are imposed unilaterally in the hope of changing a country's government or at least changing its

Exhibit 4.1 A US trade embargo against Cuba, imposed in 1962, continues to deprive Americans of cigars and Cubans of export income
Credit: Holger Leue/The Image Bank Unreleased/Getty Images.

policies. Reasons for the impositions range from the upholding of human rights to promotion of nuclear nonproliferation or antiterrorism.

For applied conditions of an embargo, see Take a Stand: Iran Embargoes, at the end of this chapter.

Sanctions

Multilateral use of economic sanctions was incorporated into international law under the charter of the United Nations, but greater emphasis was placed on the enforcement process. United Nations sanctions decided on, are mandatory for member compliance. Each permanent member of the Security Council can veto efforts to impose them. The charter also allows for sanctions as enforcement actions by regional agencies, such as the Organization of American States, the Arab League and the Organizations of African Unity, but only with the Security Council's authorization.

One problem with sanctions is that frequently their unilateral imposition does not produce the desired result. Sanctions may make it more difficult or expensive for the sanctioned country to obtain goods, yet their purported objective is almost never achieved. In order to work, sanctions need to be imposed multilaterally and affect goods that are vital to the sanctioned country – goals that are clear, yet difficult to implement

Sanctions usually mean a significant loss of business to firms. Many claim that the economic sanctions held in place by the USA cost the country and its firms billions of dollars in lost exports annually. Due to these costs, the issue of compensating the domestic firms and industries affected by these sanctions need to be considered. Yet trying to impose sanctions slowly, or making them less expensive to ease the burden on these firms, undercuts their ultimate chance for success; the international business manager is often caught in this political web and loses business as a result. However, the reputation of a supplier unable to fulfill a contractual obligation will be damaged much more seriously than that of an exporter who anticipates sanctions and realizes it cannot offer a transaction in the first place (Erickson, 1997; USTR, 2020).

The terms sanction and embargo, as used here, refer to governmental actions that distort free flows of trade in goods, services, or ideas for decidedly adversarial and political, rather than economic, purposes. Sanctions tend to consist of specific coercive trade measures such as the cancellation of trade financing or the prohibition of high-technology trade, while embargoes are usually much broader in that they prohibit trade entirely. For example, the USA imposed sanctions against some countries by prohibiting the export of weapons to them.

Export Controls

Export-control systems are designed to deny or at least delay the acquisition of strategically important goods by adversaries. The legal basis for export controls varies by nation. For example, in Germany, armament exports are covered in the so-called War Weapons list, which is a part of the War Weapon Control law. The exports of other goods are covered by the German Export List. **Dual-use items**, which are goods useful for both military and civilian purposes, and are therefore controversial, are then controlled by the Joint List of the European Union. (European Commission, 2018; USTR, 2020).

US legislation to control exports focus on **national security** controls – that is, the control of weapons exports or high-technology exports that might adversely affect the safety of nations. In addition, exports can be controlled for reasons of foreign policy and short supply. These controls restrict the international business opportunities of firms if a government believes that such a restriction would send a necessary foreign policy message to another country.

The US export control system is based on the Export Administration Act and the Munitions Control Act. The determinants for controls are national security, foreign policy, short supply, and nuclear nonproliferation. For example, in addition to the comprehensive sanctions on Iran, the Departments of State and Commerce imposed strict export control restrictions on Iran. Exporting information or commodities that may be controlled, individuals and companies should analyze whether such exports are exempt or whether authorization from the government must be secured.

An **export license** in the USA permits the export of sensitive goods and services. It is issued by the US Department of Commerce. In consultation with other government agencies – particularly the Departments of State, Defense, and Energy – the Commerce Department has drawn up the **critical commodities list,** which is the governmental information about products that are either sensitive to national security or controlled for other purposes. In addition, a list of countries differentiates nations according to their political relationship with the USA. Finally, a list of individual firms considered to be unreliable trading partners because of past trade-diversion activities exists for each country. If no concerns regarding any of the three exist, an export license is issued. Control determinants and the steps in the decision process are summarized in Exhibit 4.2.

This process does not apply in equal measure to all exports. Most international business activities can be carried out under "no license required (NLR)" conditions. NLR provides blanket permission to export to most trading partners, provided that neither the end-user nor the end-use is considered sensitive. It, therefore, pays to check out the denied persons list published by the US

Decision Steps in the Export Licensing Process

Exhibit 4.2 US export control system

Determinants of Export Controls

• National security

• Foreign policy

• Short supply

• Nuclear nonproliferation

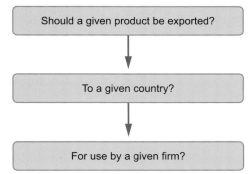

Should a given product be exported?

To a given country?

For use by a given firm?

government (www.bis.doc.gov) to ensure that one's trading partner is not a sanctioned trading party. The process becomes more complicated and cumbersome when products incorporating high-level technologies and countries not friendly to the USA, are involved. The exporter must then apply for an export license, which consists of written authorization to send a product abroad. However, even in most of these cases, license forms can be downloaded from, and license applications submitted via, the Internet.

The international business repercussions of export controls are important. One needs an export control system that is effective, and that restricts international business activities subject to national security. However, caution is required when one country's firms are at a competitive disadvantage with firms in other countries whose control systems are less extensive.

Export control concerns a key debate focus on what constitutes military-use products, civilian use products, and dual-use items. Increasingly, goods are of a dual-use nature, typically commercial products that have potential military applications. For example, a pesticide factory might be redeployed as a poison gas factory (Bade, 2015). It is difficult enough to define weapons clearly. It is even more problematic to achieve consensus among nations regarding dual-use goods. For example, what about harmless screws if they are to be installed in rockets or telecommunications equipment used by the military? The problem becomes even greater with attempts to classify and list subcomponents and regulate their export. The very task of drawing up any restrictive list is fraught with difficulty when it comes to components that are assembled. For example, the Patriot missile consists, according to German law, only of simple parts whose individual export is permissible.

The transfer of knowledge and technology is of equal or great importance. Weapons relevant to information can be exported easily via the Web, periodicals, and memory sticks. Therefore, their content also would have to be controlled. Foreigners would need to be prevented from gaining access to such sources during visits or from making use of data networks across borders. Attendance at conferences and symposia would have to be regulated, the flow of data across national borders would have to be controlled, and today's communication systems such as the Internet would have to be scrutinized. All these concerns have led to an emerging focus of controls of **deemed exports**. These controls address people rather than products when knowledge transfer could lead to a breach of export restrictions. More information is available at www.bis.doc.gov.

Conflicts can also result from the desire of nations to safeguard their own economic interests. Due to different industrial structures, these interests vary between nations. For example, Germany, with a strong world market position in machine tools, motors, and chemical raw materials, will think differently about manufacturing equipment controls than a country such as the USA, which sees computers as an area of its competitive advantage.

Regulating International Business Behavior

A firm's home country may implement laws and regulations to ensure that the international business behavior of firms headquartered in them is conducted within moral and ethical boundaries. The definition of appropriateness may vary between countries. Therefore, the content, enforcement, and impact of such regulations may vary substantially among nations. As a result, the international manager must balance the expectations held in different countries.

One major area in which nations attempt to govern international business activities involves **boycotts**. As an example, Arab nations developed a blacklist of companies that deal with Israel. The US Government adopted antiboycott laws to prevent US firms from complying with the boycott. US firms that comply with the boycott are subject to heavy fines and to denial of export privileges. See www.bis .doc.gov/index.php/enforcement/oac.

Caught in a web of governmental activity, firms may be forced either to lose business or to pay substantial fines. The problem increases if a firm's products are competitive, yet not unique, so that the customers can opt to purchase them elsewhere.

Another key area of business regulatory activity is **antitrust laws**. In many countries, antitrust agencies watch closely when a firm buys a company, engages in a joint venture with a foreign firm, or makes an agreement abroad with a competing firm (see Exhibit 4.3).

EXHIBIT 4.3 *EU v. Google*

When a company controls a large portion of the market, there is both a likelihood that its products or services have a strong customer appeal and that its competitive practices will attract the attention of governments. Such was the case in 2009 when the European Commission fined US computer chip manufacturer Intel a record $1.06 billion for unfair business practices that violated European Union antitrust laws.

A decade later, a similar fate befell a tech giant – Google. On June 7, 2017, Google was charged a record fine of $1.7 billion from the EU. This verdict involved Google AdSense and its operating system, Android. Although Google denies the EU's accusations against them, the EU found Google guilty of favoring their services over their competition's services in the two cases. In 2018, the European Union fined Google itself a record $ 5 billion.

Sources: Wielaard, 2009; Romm, 2018.

Given the increase in worldwide cooperation among companies, however, the wisdom of extending antitrust legislation to international activities is being questioned.

Corruption

Firms operating abroad are also affected by laws against bribery and corruption. In many countries, payments or favors are a way of life, and "a greasing of the wheels" is expected in return for government services. As a result, many companies doing business internationally are routinely forced to pay bribes or do favors for foreign officials in order to gain contracts. Every year, businesses pay huge amounts of money in bribes to win friends, influence, and contracts.

Businesses and individuals pay an estimated $1.5 trillion in bribes each year, which is about 2% of global GDP and 10 times the value of overseas development assistance. In 2019, about 18 percent of all firms worldwide reported experiencing at least one bribe payment request. (OECD, 2016; World Bank, 2018 and 2020). Transparency International defines corruption as "the misuse of public power for private benefit." According to their Corruption Perceptions Index 2019, corruption is a significant feature of public sector activity in more than 120 countries (Transparency International, 2020).

Corruption is particularly widespread in nations where the administrative apparatus enjoys excessive and discretionary power, where there is a lack of transparency of laws and processes. Poverty, insufficient salaries of government servants, and income inequalities also tend to increase corruption (Dimant & Tosato,

2018). Fighting corruption is therefore not only an issue of laws and ethics, but also of creating an environment that makes honesty possible and desirable.

In the 1970s, a major national debate erupted in the USA about these business practices, led by arguments that US firms have an ethical and moral leadership obligation and that contracts won through bribes do not reflect competitive market activity. As a result, the Foreign Corrupt Practices Act (FCPA) was passed in 1977, making it a crime for US executives of publicly traded firms to bribe a foreign official in order to obtain business.

Many business executives believe that the USA should not apply its moral principles to other societies and cultures in which bribery and corruption are endemic. To compete internationally, executives argue, they must be free to use the most common methods of competition in the host country.

On the other hand, applying different standards to executives and firms based on whether they do business abroad or domestically is difficult to do. Also, bribes may open the way for shoddy performance and loose moral standards among executives and employees and may result in a spreading of general unethical business practices that hurt domestic consumers. Typically, international businesses that use bribery fall into three categories: those who bribe to counterbalance the poor quality of their products or their high price; those who bribe to create a market for their unneeded goods; and, in the bulk of cases, those who bribe to stay competitive with other firms that bribe (World Bank, 2018; US Department of Justice, 2017). In all three of these instances, the customer is served poorly, the prices increase, and the transaction does not reflect economic competitiveness.

The international manager must carefully distinguish between reasonable ways of doing business internationally – that is, complying with foreign expectations – and out-right bribery and corruption. To assist the manager in this task, the 1988 Trade Act clarifies the applicability of the Foreign Corrupt Practices legislation. The revisions outline when a manager is expected to know about violation of the act, and they draw a distinction between the facilitation of routine governmental actions and governmental policy decisions. Routine actions are issues such as the obtaining of permits and licenses, the processing of governmental papers (such as visas and work orders), the providing of mail and phone service, and the loading and unloading of cargo.

Policy decisions refer mainly to situations in which the obtaining or retaining of a contract is at stake. While the facilitation of routine actions is not prohibited, the illegal influencing of policy decisions can result in the imposition of severe fines and penalties. The risks inherent in bribery have grown since 1999, when the Organization for Economic Cooperation and Development (OECD) adopted a treaty criminalizing the bribery of foreign public officials, moving well beyond its previous discussions, which only sought to outlaw the tax-deductibility of improper payments. The Organization of American States (OAS) has also officially condemned bribery. Similarly, the World Trade Organization has placed bribery rules on its agenda. In addition, nongovernmental organizations such as Transparency International are conducting widely publicized efforts to highlight corruption and bribery and even to rank countries on a Corruption Perceptions Index (www .transparency.de). In 2018, Panasonic, a Japan-based company, agreed to pay more than $143 million to resolve FCPA charges involving a lucrative consulting position it offered to a government official at a state-owned airline to induce the official to help its US subsidiary in obtaining and retaining business from the airline (Smith, 2018).

These issues place managers in the position of having to choose between home-country regulations and foreign business practices. This choice is made even more difficult because diverging standards of behavior are applied to businesses in different countries. However, the gradually emerging consensus among international organizations may eventually level the playing field.

A major issue that is critical for international business managers is that of general standards of behavior and ethics. Increasingly, public concerns are raised about such issues as environmental protection, global warming, pollution, and moral behavior. However, these issues are not of the same importance in every country. What may be frowned upon or even illegal in one nation may be customary or at least acceptable in others. For example, the cutting down of the Brazilian rainforest may be acceptable to the Government of Brazil, but scientists and concerned consumers may object vehemently because of the effect on global warming and other climatic changes. The export of US tobacco products may be legal but results in accusations of exporting death to developing nations. China may use prison labor in producing products for export, but US law prohibits the importation of such products. Mexico may permit the use of low safety standards for workers, but the buyers of Mexican products may object to the resulting dangers.

International firms must understand the conflicts in standards. Not everything that is legally possible should be exploited for profit. By acting on existing, leading-edge knowledge and standards, firms will be able to benefit in the long term through consumer goodwill and the avoidance of later recriminations.

International executives are "selling" the world on two key issues: the benefit of market forces that result in the interplay of supply and demand, and international marketers will do their best to identify market niches and bring their products and services to customers around the globe. Key underlying dimensions of both of these issues are managerial and corporate virtue, vision, and veracity. The world should believe in what executives say and do, and trust their global activities. It is of vital interest for executives to ensure that corruption, bribery, lack of transparency, and the misleading of consumers, investors, and employees are systematically relegated to the history books – where they belong. It will be the extent of openness, responsiveness, long-term thinking, and truthfulness that will determine the degrees of freedom of international business (Czinkota et al., 2004).

Host-Country Political and Legal Environment

Politics and laws of a host country affect international business operations in a variety of ways. The good manager will understand these dimensions of the countries in which the firm operates so he or she can work within existing parameters and can anticipate and plan for changes that may occur.

Political Action and Risk

Firms usually prefer to conduct business in a country with a stable and friendly government, but such governments are not always easy to find. Managers must, therefore, continually monitor the government, its policies, and its stability to determine the potential for political change that could adversely affect corporate operations.

There is political risk in every nation, but the range of risks varies widely from country to country. In general, political risk is lowest in countries that have a history of stability and consistency. Political risk tends to be highest in nations characterized by instability and frequent change in the political and legal environments. In a number of countries, however, consistency and stability that were apparent on the surface have been quickly swept away by major popular movements that drew on the bottled-up frustrations of the population. Three major types of political risk can be encountered: ownership risk, which exposes property and life; operating risk, which refers to interference with approach operations of a firm; and transfer risk, which is mainly encountered when attempts are made to shift funds between countries. Firms can be exposed to political risk due to government actions or even actions outside the control of governments. The type of actions and their effects are classified in Exhibit 4.4

A major risk in many countries is that of conflict and violent change. A manager will want to think twice before conducting business in a country in which the likelihood of such change is high (Exhibit 4.5). To begin with, if conflict breaks out, violence directed toward the firm's property and employees is a strong possibility. Guerrilla warfare, civil disturbances, and terrorism often take an anti-industry bent, making companies and their employees potential targets. International corporations are often subject to major threats, even in countries that boast great political stability. Terrorist attacks around the world have increased greatly in recent decades, average of 21,000 deaths annually and over 26,000 fatalities in 2017 alone (Ritchie et al., 2019). Most attacks are directed at civilians, businesses, and business-related infrastructure. The five countries most exposed to terrorist attacks

EXHIBIT 4.4 Political action and its effects

	Loss may be the result of:	
Contingencies may include:	The actions of legitimate government authorities	Events caused by factors outside the control of government
The involuntary loss of control over specific assets without adequate compensation	• Total or partial expropriation • Forced divestiture • Confiscation • Cancellation or unfair calling of performance bonds	• War • Revolution • Strikes • Extortion
A reduction in the value of a stream of benefits expected from the foreign-controlled affiliate	• Nonapplicability of "national treatment" • Restriction in access to financial, labor, or material markets • Control on prices, outputs, or activities • Currency and remittance restrictions • Value-added and export performance requirements	• Nationalistic buyers or suppliers • Threats and disruption to operations by hostile groups • Externally induced financial constraints • Externally imposed limits on imports or exports

Source: Adapted from Jose, de la Torre and David H. Neckar, "Forecasting Political Risks for International Operations," in H. Vernon-Wortzel and L. Wortzel, 2nd ed. (New York: John Wiley and Sons, 1990), 195.

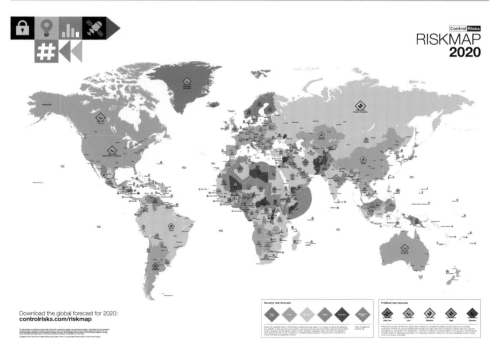

Exhibit 4.5
Political risk
Source:
RiskMap
2020, Control
Risks Group
Limited.
Available at:
https://www
.controlrisks.
com/riskmap.

in 2016 are Iraq (2965), Afghanistan (1340), India (927), Pakistan (734), and the Philippines (482) (US Department of State, 2017).

International terrorists frequently target US facilities, operations, and personnel abroad. US firms, by their open nature, cannot have the elaborate security and restricted access of US diplomatic offices and military bases. As a result, US businesses remain vulnerable to terrorists worldwide (Miller, 2013). Ironically enough, in many instances, the businesses attacked or burned are the franchisees of US business concepts. Therefore, the ones suffering most from such attacks are the local owners and local employees.

The methods used by terrorists against business facilities include bombing, arson, hijacking, and sabotage. To obtain funds, the terrorists resort to kidnapping executives, armed robbery, and extortion (Laqueur, 2016). To reduce international terrorism, recent experience has demonstrated that international collaboration is imperative to identify and track terrorist groups and to reduce their safe havens and financial support systematically. However, perpetrators have observed that relatively low-cost terrorist operations can inflict extensive damage and profound disruption. Consequently, attacks are likely to persist.

As a consequence, governments are likely to continue imposing new regulations and restrictions intended to avert terrorist acts. For example, increasingly complex customs clearance and international logistical requirements, or specific requirements imposed to enhance security systems, all combine to increase the cost of doing business internationally. Moreover, these security measures will also tend to lessen the efficiency with which international business channels can function.

Less drastic, but still worrisome, are changes in government policies that are not caused by changes in the government itself. These occur when, for one reason or another, a government feels pressured to change its policies toward foreign businesses. The pressure may be the result of nationalist or religious factions or widespread anti-foreign feelings.

A broad range of policy changes is possible as a result of political unrest. The changes can affect the company's international operations, but not all of them are equal in weight. Except for extreme cases, companies do not usually have to fear violence against their employees, although violence against company property is common. Also common are changes in policy that result from a new government or a strong new stance that is nationalist and opposed to foreign investment. The most drastic public steps resulting from such policy changes are usually expropriation and confiscation. Exhibit 4.6 discusses the impact of terrorism on international business.

Expropriation is the transfer of ownership by the host government to a domestic entity with payment of compensation. Expropriation was an appealing action to many countries because it demonstrated their nationalism and transferred a certain amount of wealth and resources from foreign companies to the host country

EXHIBIT 4.6 The impact of terrorism on international business

There is limited empirical research on terrorism effects on firms, government, and people. We conducted qualitative interviews with internationally active firms on terrorism to develop a broad understanding of what companies and managers see as the key salient issues. We also conducted discussions, generally 45 to 60 minutes in length, via telephone and at company sites, with senior managers of nine firms with extensive international operations. These interviews provided a clearer picture of managers' concerns about and response to terrorism, and facilitated the creation of a survey used in the second phase of our research.

Respondents worried about interruptions of supply chains, distribution channels, and logistics due to terrorism. Concerns also focused on the trustworthiness and reliability of foreign suppliers and intermediaries exposed to terrorism. Attention also rested on corporate capabilities, which allow firms to prepare for disruptions and delays due to terrorism.

The second phase of our research was an online survey of a sample of international firms headquartered in the USA but active in many countries around the world. The survey aimed to validate earlier findings, to better understand perceptions about terrorism, and to assist with the planning and responses that managers are undertaking when confronted with terrorism.

The unit of analysis was the firm. For standardization purposes, company resources were assessed as "annual revenues per employee." We used 5-point Likert scales.

In internationalizing firms, it appears that the threat or occurrence of terrorism is associated with immediate increases in international marketing costs and with disruptions in international supply chains. Management becomes likely to include terrorism as a detrimental factor in international marketing planning, and in the design of global distribution channels.

Finally, the more resources held by the firm, the more willingly terrorism and its repercussions will be recognized. The trend appears to be that, particularly among informed and wealthy firms, a terrorism presence creates early and significant corporate responses. Terrorism seems to be a key causal factor in fomenting poverty much more so than poverty creating terrorism.

Source: Czinkota, 2019.

immediately. It did have costs to the host country, however, to the extent that it made other firms more hesitant to invest there. Expropriation does not relieve the host government of providing compensation to the former owners. However, these compensation negotiations are often protracted and frequently result in settlements that are unsatisfactory to the owners. For example, governments may offer compensation in the form of local, nontransferable currency or may base compensation on the book value of the firm. Even though firms that are expropriated may deplore the low levels of payment obtained, they frequently accept them in the absence of better alternatives.

In the mid-1970s, when more than 83 expropriations took place in a single year, expropriation was a serious policy tool by some governments. In 2017, General Motors Co., the world's third-largest carmaker, announced it had stopped operating in Venezuela, because Venezuelan authorities had taken over GM's plant in the central Carabobo state, seizing production facilities and car stock, and the company had been forced to lay off its 2,700 workers (Exhibit 4.7) (Kurmanaev & Vyas, 2017).

Confiscation is similar to expropriation in that it results in a transfer of ownership from the firm to the host country. It differs in that it does not involve compensation for the firm. Some industries are more vulnerable than others to confiscation and expropriation because of their importance to the host country's economy and their lack of ability to shift operations. For this reason, such sectors

Exhibit 4.7 General Motors had been fostering a relationship with Venezuela for over 90 years when they were forced to close their factory in 2017
Credit: Underwood Archives/Getty Images.

as mining, energy, public utilities, and banking have frequently been targets of such government actions.

Confiscation and expropriation constitute major political risks for foreign investors. Other government actions, however, are equally detrimental to foreign firms. Many countries are turning from confiscation and expropriation to more subtle forms of control, such as domestication. The goal of domestication is the same – that is, to gain control over foreign investment – but the method is different. Through domestication, the government demands transfer of ownership and management responsibility. It can impose local content regulations to ensure that a large share of the product is locally produced or demand that a larger share of the profit is retained in the country.

Changes in labor laws, patent protection, and tax regulations are also used for purposes of domestication. In Bolivia, President Evo Morales nationalized the oil and natural gas industry, taking over control from companies like the Spanish/Argentine venture Repsol-YPF and Brazil's Petroleo Brasileiro. Rather than outright expropriation, the nationalization took the form of renegotiated contracts and higher taxes on petroleum companies. Consequently, the private companies chose to stay in the country and continue operations, but Bolivia's government income from the oil and gas industry increased dramatically (Prada, 2006).

Domestication can have profound effects on an international business operation for a number of reasons. If a firm is forced to hire nationals as managers, poor cooperation and communication can result. If domestication is imposed within a very short time span, corporate operations overseas may have to be headed by poorly trained and inexperienced local managers. Domestic content requirements may force a firm to purchase its supplies and parts locally. This can result in increased costs, less efficiency, and lower-quality products. Export requirements imposed on companies may create havoc for their international distribution plans and force them to change or even shut down operations in third countries.

Finally, domestication usually will shield an industry within one country from foreign competition. As a result, inefficiencies will be allowed to thrive due to a lack of market discipline. This will affect the long-run international competitiveness of an operation abroad and may turn into a major problem when, years later, domestication is discontinued by the government.

Intellectual Property

For leading-edge companies, intellectual property is the key asset. If government action consists of weakening or not enforcing intellectual property right (IPR) protection, companies run the risk of losing their core competitive edge. This may cause domestic firms to become quick imitators. Yet, in the longer term, they will not only discourage the appropriate transfer of technology and knowledge by multinational firms, but also reduce the incentive for local firms to invest in innovation and progress.

Poor IPR legislation and enforcement in the otherwise lucrative markets of Asia illustrate a clash between international business interests and developing nations' political and legal environments. Businesses attempting to enter the markets of China, India, Indonesia, Russia, and Venezuela face considerable risk as these countries have poor records for copyright piracy and intellectual property infringements (Radu, 2019). But these emerging market countries argue that IPR laws discriminate against them because they impede the diffusion of technology and artificially inflate prices. They also point to the fact that industrialized nations such as the USA and Japan violated IPR laws during earlier stages of development. In fact, the USA became a signatory to the Berne Convention on copyrights only in 1989 – around one hundred years after its introduction – and Japan disregarded IPR laws in adapting Western technologies during the 1950s. Although newly industrialized nations are learning that strong IPR protection will encourage technology transfer and foreign investment, the weak nature of these countries' court structures and the slow pace of legislation often fail to keep pace with the needs of their rapidly transforming economies (Deng et al., 1996).

Due to successful international negotiations in the Uruguay Round, the World Trade Organization (www.wto.org) reached agreement on significant dimensions of the trade-related aspects of intellectual property rights (TRIPS). The agreement set minimum standards of protection to be provided by each member country for copyrights, trademarks, geographical indications, industrial designs, patents, layout designs of integrated circuits, and undisclosed information such as trade secrets and test data (World Trade Organization, 2020). While not all-encompassing, these standards provide substantial assurances of protection, which, after an implementation delay for the poorest countries, will apply to virtually all parts of the world.

World Trade Organization rules do allow countries to get around intellectual property rights for medical emergencies, which has had serious implications for pharmaceutical companies. In 2007, for example, Thailand and Brazil issued compulsory licenses for certain anti-retroviral drugs used in treating HIV/AIDS, bypassing patents held by companies including Abbott Laboratories and Merck. This allowed the countries, both afflicted by AIDS epidemics, to purchase the drugs at cheaper prices for free distribution to their citizens (Dugger, 2007). Such special pricing was also brought to bear in the COVID-19 situation. All this certainly seems like a humane and moral action on the part of governments. From the companies' point of view, however, this affects their ability to realize the profits that allow further research and development for advancement in medical research.

Economic Risk

Nations that face a shortage of foreign currency will sometimes impose controls on the movement of capital into and out of the country. Such controls may make it difficult for a firm to remove its profits or investments from the host country. Sometimes **exchange controls** are also levied selectively against certain products or companies in an effort to reduce the importation of goods that are considered to be luxuries or to be sufficiently available through domestic production. Such regulations often affect the importation of parts, components, or supplies that are vital to production operations in the country.

Countries also use **tax policy** toward foreign investors to control multinational corporations and their capital. Tax increases may raise much-needed revenue for the host country, but they can severely damage the operations of foreign investors. This damage, in turn, will frequently result in decreased income for the host country in the long run. The raising of tax rates needs to be carefully differentiated from increased tax scrutiny of foreign investors.

The international executive also has to worry about **price controls**. In many countries, domestic political pressures can force governments to control the prices of imported products or services, particularly in sectors considered highly sensitive from a political perspective, such as food or healthcare. A foreign firm involved in these areas is vulnerable to price controls because the government can play on citizens' nationalistic tendencies to enforce the controls. Particularly in countries that suffer from high inflation, frequent devaluations, or sharply rising costs, the international executive may be forced to choose between shutting down the operation or continuing production at a loss in the hope of recouping profits when the government loosens or removes its price restrictions. Price controls can also be administered to prevent prices from being too low.

Managing the Risk

Managers face the risk of confiscation, expropriation, domestication, or other government interference whenever they conduct business overseas. But there are ways to lessen the risk. If a host country's citizens feel exploited by foreign investors, government officials are more likely to take antiforeign action. To reduce the risk of government intervention, the international firm needs to demonstrate that it is concerned with the host country's society and that it considers itself an integral part of the host country, rather than simply an exploitative foreign corporation. Ways of doing this include intensive local hiring and training practices, better pay, contributions to charity, and societally useful investments. In addition, the company can form joint ventures with local partners to demonstrate that it is willing to share its gains with nationals. Although such actions will not guarantee freedom from political risk, they will certainly lessen the exposure. Another action that can be taken by corporations to protect against political risk is the close monitoring of political developments. Increasingly, private sector firms offer such monitoring assistance, permitting the overseas corporation to discover potential trouble spots as early as possible and to react quickly to prevent major losses.

Firms can also take out insurance to cover losses due to political and economic risk. Most industrialized countries offer insurance programs for their firms doing business abroad. In Germany, for example, Euler Hermes (www.eulerhermes .com/) is a world-leading credit agency that provides exporters with insurance. In the USA, the Development Finance Corporation (DFC) (www.dfc.gov) provides various types of risk insurance, including currency inconvertibility insurance, which covers the inability to convert profits, debt service, and other remittances from local currency into US dollars; expropriation insurance, which covers the loss of an investment due to expropriation, nationalization, or confiscation by a foreign government; and political violence insurance, which covers the loss of assets or income due to war, revolution, insurrection, or politically motivated civil strife, terrorism, and sabotage. The cost of coverage varies by country and type of activity, but for manufacturers, it averages $0.35 for $100 of coverage per year to protect against inconvertibility, $0.68 to protect against expropriation, and $0.50 to compensate for damage to business income and assets from political violence (USIDFC, 2020). Usually, the policies do not cover commercial risks and, in the event of a claim, cover only the actual loss – not lost profits. In the event of a major political upheaval, however, risk insurance can be critical to a firm's survival.

Legal Differences and Restraints

Over the millennia of civilization, many different laws and legal systems have emerged. King Hammurabi of Babylon codified a series of decisions by judges into a body of laws. Legal issues in many African tribes were settled through the verdicts of clansmen. A key legal perspective that survives today is that of **theocracy**. Examples are Hebrew law and Islamic law (the **Sharia**), which are the result of the dictates of God, scripture, prophetic utterances and practices, and scholarly interpretations (Boyett, 2016). These legal systems have faith and belief as their key focus and are a mix of societal, legal, and spiritual guidelines.

While legal systems are important to society, from an international business perspective, the two major legal systems worldwide can be categorized into common law and code law. **Common law** is based on tradition and depends less on written statutes and codes than on precedent and custom. Common law originated in England and is the system of law in the USA. **Code law,** on the other hand, is based on a comprehensive set of written statutes. Countries with code law try to spell out all possible legal rules explicitly. Code law is based on Roman law and is found in the majority of the nations of the world.

In general, countries with the code law system have much more rigid laws than those with the common law system. In the latter, courts adopt precedents and customs to fit cases, allowing a better idea of basic judgment likely to be rendered in new situations. The differences between code law and common law and their impact on international business, while wide in theory, are not as broad in practice. One reason is that many common-law countries, including the USA, have adopted commercial codes to govern the conduct of business.

Host countries may adopt a number of laws that affect the firm's ability to do business. Tariffs and quotas, for example, can affect the entry of goods. Special licenses for foreign goods may be required. Sometimes, as shown in Exhibit 4.8, these different ideas of laws can cause some cultural conflict.

Other laws may restrict entrepreneurial activities. In Europe, for example, 11 EU member states restrict nonpharmacists from holding a majority stake in pharmacies. Spanish laws restrict pharmacy ownership to pharmacists with a limit of one

EXHIBIT 4.8 The Archbishop of Canterbury

Rowan Williams is the former archbishop of Canterbury and the spiritual leader of the Anglican Church, which has approximately 80 million members globally. He stirred up controversy when he examined the role of Sharia in British life. Sharia is the body of Islamic religious law that is based on the Koran, the words and actions of the Prophet Mohammad, and the rulings of Islamic scholars. It typically finds its application mainly in Muslim countries.

The archbishop suggested that, with a population of more than 2 million Muslims in the UK, Sharia already figures prominently in the lives of many. For example, informal neighborhood councils provide ruling on family issues such as divorce; and banks, such as HSBC already market mortgages that comply with Sharia rules of lending. Perhaps Muslims in the UK would be more comfortable and willing to build a more constructive relationship with their fellow citizens if they could choose Sharia for the setting of civil disputes, suggested Williams.

Many commentators, which included former British Prime Minister Gordon Brown, strongly opposed such thinking. There was the feeling that such a move would undermine British values and laws and substantially weaken the position of women. Perhaps not since Thomas Becket ran afoul of King Henry II in 1170 (and was murdered for his disagreement about the rights of church and state) was there such controversy surrounding the archbishop and the law.

Sources: Adam, 2008; Matthew, 2008

location, while German laws allow a licensed pharmacist to own up to four stores. The European Court of Justice (ECJ) has upheld pharmacy ownership requirements on the grounds that its member-states should be able to take protective measures to minimize risks to human health (European Medicines Agency, 2016; USTR, 2020).

Specific legislation may also exist regulating what does and does not constitute deceptive advertising. Many countries prohibit specific claims that compare products to the competition, or they restrict the use of promotional devices. Even when no laws exist, regulations may hamper business operations. For example, in some countries, firms are required to join the local chamber of commerce or become a member of the national trade association. These institutions, in turn, may have internal sets of rules that specify standards for the conduct of business that may be quite confining.

Seemingly innocuous local regulations that may easily be overlooked can have a major impact on the international firm's success. For example, Japan had an intricate process regulating the building of new department stores or supermarkets. The government's desire to protect smaller merchants brought the opening of new, large stores to a virtual standstill. Because department stores and supermarkets serve as the major conduit for the sale of imported consumer products, the lack of new stores severely affected opportunities for market penetration of imported merchandise (Czinkota & Woronoff, 1991; JETRO, 2012). Only after intense pressure from the outside did the Japanese Government reconsider the regulations.

Other laws may be designed to protect domestic industries and reduce imports. For example, Russia assesses high excise taxes on goods such as cigarettes, automobiles, and alcoholic beverages, and provides a burdensome import licensing regime for alcohol to depress Russian demand for imports (USTR, 2020). In 2018, President Trump announced tariffs against steel and aluminum imports to help industries long-suffering from import pressure (Czinkota, 2018). A further example of the use of tariffs can be seen in Exhibit 4.9.

EXHIBIT 4.9 China trade war

In the summer of 2018, a trade war between the world's two largest economies officially began as the USA imposed sweeping tariffs on $34 billion worth of imports from China goods, including flat-screen televisions, aircraft parts, and medical devices. China immediately responded by imposing 25% tariffs on $34 billion worth of US imports into China. These include soybeans, automobiles, and lobsters, and China accused the USA of starting "the largest trade war in economic history to date." The USA threatened to slap a 25% tariff on $200 billion worth of Chinese goods, while China threatened tariffs on another $60 billion worth of US goods.

The USA claimed it was safeguarding national security and the intellectual property of US businesses. American campaign manager and political adviser, Sarah Huckabee Sanders, stated that the measures would cause "short-term pain" but bring "long-term success."

Teng Jianqun, head of US research at the China Institute of International Studies in Beijing – a think tank affiliated with the Ministry of Foreign Affairs – said, "China has never experienced such aggressive challenges" and needed a sustainable strategy for the long run. The trade war also would force China to seek reforms to allow it to move up the manufacturing value chain.

Sources: Swanson, 2018; Aleem, 2018; The White House, 2018; Smith, 2020; Wu, 2018.

Finally, the interpretation and enforcement of laws and regulations may have a major effect on international business activities. For example, in deciding what product can be called a "Swiss" Army knife or "French" wine, the interpretation given by courts to the meaning of a name can affect consumer perceptions and sales of products.

The Influencing of Politics and Laws

To succeed in a market, the international manager needs much more than business know-how. He or she must also deal with the intricacies of national politics and laws. Although to fully understand another country's legal political system is rarely possible, the good manager will be aware of its importance and will work with people who do understand how to operate within the system. To do so is particularly important for multinational corporations. These firms work in many countries and must manage relationships with a large number of governments. Often, these governments have a variety of ideologies that may require different corporate responses. To be strategically successful, the firm must therefore be able to formulate and implement political activities on a global scale (Blumentritt & Nigh, 2002; Cannizzaro, 2019).

Many areas of politics and law are not immutable. Viewpoints can be modified, or even reversed, and new laws can supersede old ones. Therefore, existing political and legal restraints do not always need to be accepted.

The international manager has various options. One is to simply ignore prevailing rules and expect to get away with it. Pursuing this option is a high-risk strategy because the possibility of objection and even prosecution exists. A second, traditional option is to provide input to trade negotiators and expect any problem areas to be resolved in multilateral negotiations. The drawbacks to this option are, of course, the quite time-consuming process involved and the lack of control by the firm.

A third option involves the development of coalitions and constituencies that can motivate legislators and politicians to consider and ultimately implement change. This option can be pursued in various ways. One direction can be the re-casting or redefinition of issues. Often, specific terminology leads to conditioned, though inappropriate, responses. For example, before China's accession to the World Trade Organization in 2001 (Exhibit 4.10), the country's trade status with the USA was highly controversial for many years. The US Congress had to decide annually whether or not to grant "most-favored-nation" (MFN) status to China. The debate on this decision was always very contentious and acerbic, and often framed around the question as to why China deserved to be treated the "most favored way." Lost in the debate was often the fact that the term "most favored" was simply taken from WTO terminology, and only indicated that trade with China would be treated like that with any other country. Only in late 1999 was the terminology changed from MFN to NTR, or "normal trade relations." Even though there was still considerable debate regarding China, at least the controversy about special treatment had been eliminated (Czinkota, 2000; Pierce & Schott, 2018).

Exhibit 4.10 China's accession to the WTO in 2001, being celebrated here, was not without controversies on the world stage
Credit: Alain BUU/Gamma-Rapho via Getty Images.

Beyond terminology, firms can also highlight the direct links and their costs and benefits to legislators and politicians. For example, a manager can explain the employment and economic effects of certain laws and regulations and demonstrate the benefits of change. The picture can be enlarged by including indirect links. In addition, the public at large can be involved through public statements or advertisements.

Developing such coalitions is not an easy task. Lobbying usually works best when narrow economic objectives or single-issue campaigns are involved. Typically, lobbyists provide this assistance. Usually, there are well-connected individuals and firms that can provide access to policy makers and legislators in order to communicate new and pertinent information.

Many US firms have representatives in Washington, DC, as well as in-state capitals and are quite successful at influencing domestic policies. Often, however, they are less adept at ensuring proper representation abroad even though, for example, the European Commission in Brussels wields far-reaching economic power. A survey of US international marketing executives found that knowledge and information about foreign trade and government officials was ranked lowest among critical international business information needs. This low ranking appears to reflect the fact that many US firms are far less successful in their interactions with governments abroad and far less intensive in their lobbying efforts than are foreign entities in the United States (Czinkota, 1991; Czinkota & Ronkainen, 2014).

Political influence can be useful when it comes to general issues applicable to a wide variety of firms or industries, or when long-term policy directions are at stake. In such instances, the collaboration and power of many market actors can help sway the direction of policy.

Although representation of the firm's interests to government decision-makers and legislators is entirely appropriate, the international manager must also consider any potential side effects. Major questions can be raised if such representation becomes overt. Short-term gains may be far outweighed by long-term negative repercussions if the international firm is perceived as exerting too much political influence.

International Relations and Laws

In addition to understanding the politics and laws of both home and host countries, the international manager must also consider the overall international political and legal environment. This is important because policies and events occurring among countries can have a profound impact on firms trying to do business internationally.

International Politics

The effect of politics on international business is determined by both the bilateral political relations between home and host countries and by multilateral agreements governing the relations among groups of countries.

The government-to-government relationship can have a profound influence in a number of ways, particularly if it becomes hostile. President Trump's threat to withdraw from the World Trade Organization, and his aggressive posture toward China, have tended to aggravate political relationships and to set back negotiations by US companies to secure important business deals in Asia and elsewhere (Noland, 2018). In another example, although the internal political changes in the aftermath of the Iranian Revolution certainly would have affected any foreign firm doing business in Iran, the deterioration in US–Iranian political relations that resulted had a significant additional impact on US firms, which were injured not only by the physical damage caused by the violence, but also by the anti-American feelings of the Iranian people and their government. The resulting clashes between the two governments subsequently destroyed business relationships, regardless of corporate feelings or agreements on either side.

International political relations do not always have harmful effects. If bilateral political relations between countries improve, business can benefit. One example is the improvement in Western relations with central Europe following the official end of the Cold War. The political warming opened the potentially lucrative former Eastern Bloc markets to Western firms.

The overall international political environment has effects, whether good or bad, on international business. For this reason, the manager must strive to remain aware of political currents and relations worldwide and will attempt to anticipate changes in the international political environment so that his or her firm can plan for them.

International Law

International law plays an important role in the conduct of international business. Although no enforceable body of international law exists, certain treaties and agreements are respected by a number of countries and profoundly influence international business operations. For example, the World Trade Organization (WTO) defines internationally acceptable economic practices for its member nations. Although it does not directly deal with individual firms, it does affect them indirectly by providing some predictability in the international environment.

The **Patent Cooperation Treaty (PCT)** provides procedures for filing a single international application designating countries in which a patent is sought, which has the same effect as filing national applications in each of those countries. Similarly, the European Patent Office examines applications and issues national patents in any of its member countries. Other regional offices include the African

Industrial Property Office (ARIPO), the French-speaking African Intellectual Property Organization (OAPI), and one in Saudi Arabia for six countries in the Gulf region. Negotiations for the Anti-Counterfeiting Trade Agreement are continuing among many nations, including the USA, the European Union, Japan, Korea, and Australia, to create new legal standards in the global fight against counterfeiting and piracy.

International organizations such as the United Nations and the Organization for Economic Cooperation and Development have also undertaken efforts to develop codes and guidelines that affect international business. These include the Code on International Marketing of Breast-Milk Substitutes, which was developed by the World Health Organization (WHO) (www.who.int/en), and the UN Code of Conduct for Transnational Corporations. Even though there are many such codes in existence, the lack of enforcement ability often hampers their full implementation.

In addition to multilateral agreements, firms are affected by bilateral treaties and conventions between the countries in which they do business. For example, a number of countries have signed bilateral Treaties of Friendship, Commerce, and Navigation (FCN). The agreements generally define the rights of firms doing business in the host country. They normally guarantee that firms will be treated by the host country in the same manner in which domestic firms are treated. While these treaties provide for some stability, they can also be canceled when relations worsen.

The international legal environment also affects the manager to the extent that firms must concern themselves with jurisdictional disputes. Because no single body of international law exists, firms usually are restricted by both home and host country laws. If a conflict occurs between contracting parties in two different countries, a question arises concerning which country's laws are to be used and in which court the dispute is to be settled. Sometimes the contract will contain a jurisdictional clause that settles the matter with little problem. If the contract does not contain such a clause, however, the parties to the dispute have a few choices. They can settle the dispute by following the laws of the country in which the agreement was made, or they can resolve it by obeying the laws of the country in which the contract will have to be fulfilled. Which laws to use and in which location to settle the dispute are two different decisions. As a result, a dispute between a US exporter and a French importer could be resolved in Paris but based on New York State law. The importance of such provisions was highlighted by the lengthy jurisdictional disputes surrounding the Bhopal incident in India, in which an explosion of chemicals killed and maimed thousands.

In cases of disagreement, the parties can choose either arbitration or litigation. Litigation is usually avoided for several reasons. It often involves extensive delays and is very costly. In addition, firms may fear discrimination in foreign countries. Therefore, companies tend to prefer conciliation and arbitration, because they result in much quicker decisions. Arbitration procedures are often spelled out in the original contract and usually provide for an intermediary who is judged to be impartial by both parties. Intermediaries can be representatives of chambers of commerce, trade associations, or third-country institutions.

One key nongovernmental organization handling international commercial disputes is the International Court of Arbitration, founded in 1923 by the International Chamber of Commerce (www.iccwbo.org). ICC announced that a total of 810 new cases were filed in 2017 and involved 2,316 parties from a record 142 countries (International Chamber of Commerce, 2018).

Arbitration usually is faster and less expensive than litigation in the courts. In addition, the limited judicial recourse available against arbitral awards, as compared with court judgments, offers a clear advantage. Parties that use arbitration rather than litigation know that they will not have to face a prolonged and costly series of appeals. Finally, arbitration offers the parties the flexibility to set up a proceeding that can be conducted as quickly and economically as the circumstances allow (International Chamber of Commerce, 2020).

SUMMARY

The political and legal environment in the home and host countries and the laws and agreements governing relationships among nations are important to the international business executive. Compliance is mandatory in order to do business successfully abroad. To avoid the problems that can result from changes in the political and legal environment, it is essential to anticipate changes and to develop strategies for coping with them. Whenever possible, the manager must avoid being taken by surprise and letting events control business decisions.

Governments affect international business through legislation and regulations, which can support or hinder business transactions. An example is when export sanctions or embargoes are imposed to enhance foreign policy objectives. Similarly, export controls are used to preserve national security. Nations also regulate the international business behavior of firms by setting standards that relate to bribery and corruption, boycotts, and restraint of competition.

Through political actions such as expropriation, confiscation, or domestication, countries expose firms to international risk. Management, therefore, needs to be aware of the possibility of such risk and alert to new developments. Many private-sector services are available to track international risk situations. In the event of a loss, firms may rely on insurance for political risk, or they may seek redress in court. International legal action, however, may be quite slow and may compensate for only part of the loss.

Managers need to be aware that different countries have different laws. One clearly pronounced difference is between code law countries, where all possible legal rules are spelled out, and common law countries such as the USA, where the law is based on tradition, precedent, and custom.

Executives must also pay attention to international political relations, agreements, and treaties. Changes in relations or rules can mean major new opportunities and occasional threats to international business. Even though conflict in international business may sometimes lead to litigation, the manager needs to be aware of the alternative of arbitration, which may resolve the pending matter more quickly and at a lower cost.

DISCUSSION QUESTIONS

1. Do you think economic sanctions could force countries to behave peacefully in the international community?
2. What are the problems that could happen if each country put more and more tariffs on one another?
3. If you are an international manager in China, how will you help your company eliminate risk in a trade war?

KEY TERMS

antitrust laws	88	international competitiveness	83
boycotts	88	international law	106
code law	100	local content	97
common law	100	national security	86
confiscation	96	operating risk	92
critical commodities list	86	ownership risk	92
deemed exports	88	Patent Cooperation Treaty (PCT)	106
domestication	97	political risk	92
dual-use items	86	price controls	99
embargo	85	sanction	85
exchange controls	99	sharia	100
export license	86	tax policy	99
export-control systems	86	terrorism	92
expropriation	94	theocracy	100
extraterritoriality	83	transfer risk	92
Foreign Corrupt Practices Act (FCPA)	90		

TAKE A STAND

In May of 2018, the USA withdrew from the Joint Comprehensive Plan of Action (JCPOA) with Iran, which is known commonly as the Iran nuclear deal, and revived sanctions on Iran. According to the abandoned framework, Iran wanted to redesign, convert, and reduce its nuclear facilities. In exchange, the USA would lift all nuclear-related economic sanctions, freeing up tens of billions of dollars in Iranian oil revenue and frozen assets. The US Treasury gave businesses and individuals time – up to 180 days – for an "orderly wind-down of activities."

SOURCES:

The White House (2018). President Donald J. Trump is Ending United States Participation in an Unacceptable Iran Deal. Washington DC; Gladstone, R. and Chinoy, S. (2018). What Changes and What Remains in the Iran Nuclear Deal. *The New York Times.*

QUESTIONS FOR DEBATE

1. Should international political dimensions be used to reduce business transactions?
2. Are 180 days sufficient time to rescind business relations?
3. Does the largest party always win?

INTERNET EXERCISES

1. Suppose you work for a firm that is considering exporting to two countries: Indonesia and Nigeria. However, company knowledge about the trade policies of these countries is limited. Conduct online research to identify current import restrictions and policies in these countries. Prepare a brief report on the most salient restrictions and policies affecting firms. Useful sites include the World Trade Organization (www.wto.org; enter country name in the search engine) and the US Commercial Service (www.buyusa.gov).
2. Transparency International is a nonprofit organization that monitors the state of corruption worldwide. It publishes an annual Corruption Perceptions Index, which you can view at www.transparency.org/en/cpi. The Index scores and ranks countries based on how corrupt a country's public sector is perceived to be by experts and business executives. Visit the site, and answer the following questions. (a) How does corruption affect international business? (b) What can governments in affected countries do to reduce the prevalence of corruption? (c) What are the implications of the rankings for firms doing international business?

FURTHER RESOURCES

Bade, Donna. (2015). *Export Import: Procedures and Documentation.* New York: American Management Association.

Rickard, Stephanie. (2018). *Spending to Win: Political Institutions*, Economic Geography, and Government Subsidies. Cambridge, UK: Cambridge University Press.

UNCTAD. (2019). *World Investment Report.* New York: United Nations. www.unctad.org.

US Department of Commerce. 2020. *Country commercial guides.* www.export.gov/ccg.

World Bank, *Doing Business: Equal Opportunity for All* 2017, www.doingbusiness.org.

PART II

Financial Management

CONTENTS

VIGNETTE 5 Balancing culture with financial goals

The European Union (EU) created the Economic and Monetary Union (EMU) in 1992 and established a common currency, the euro, for use by 19 EU member countries. Using a common currency reduces currency risk – the problem of fluctuating exchange rates – and facilitates trade among EMU member nations.

The United Kingdom (UK) joined the EU in 1973, but decided not to join the EMU, and kept the pound as its national currency. Over time, many British citizens came to resent perceived interference by the EU Central Government in the UK's economic, political, and immigration affairs. In 2016, the UK voted to withdraw from the EU, in a referendum known as "Brexit." The event triggered fears in European currency markets, and the pound lost value relative to the euro. The weaker pound hurt consumer confidence and increased prices of parts, components, and finished goods imported into the UK.

Brexit supporters campaigning for the UK to leave the EU
Credit: Kiran Ridley/Getty Images News/Getty Images Europe.

By 2016, many multinational enterprises (MNEs) from Asia had established European operations in the UK. Following Brexit, numerous such firms moved their operations to EU member countries on the European continent. For example, Japan's Panasonic moved its European headquarters from London to the Netherlands, and Toyota shifted some of its UK manufacturing to Eastern Europe. The goals of such moves were to minimize currency risk, avoid potential tax issues related to Brexit, and circumvent cost competitiveness in the face of growing uncertainty.

Management at Asian MNEs understood that a weakening pound would result in higher operational costs for their UK-based operations that sourced inputs from euro-based suppliers in continental Europe. Management at Panasonic and Toyota had to manage currency risk – such as transaction, translation, and economic exposures – arising from the weaker pound.

Panasonic and Toyota also undertook much currency hedging – using financial contracts to minimize currency risk. And because such firms have many ongoing transactions among their subsidiaries in Europe, they took steps to strategically reduce cash transfers, bank fees, and transaction costs by eliminating offsetting cash flows between headquarters and local country subsidiaries.

Panasonic and Toyota established centralized depositories for accounts receivable and accounts payable in cross-national European operations to optimize receipt and spending of cash and reduce the costs of moving funds across national borders. The firms also hedge against currency risk by taking positions in "forward contracts." Such instruments allow financial managers to buy or sell currency at a specific future date at an agreed-upon exchange rate. For example, if Panasonic managers in the Netherlands felt uncertain about the value of future pound-denominated receivables from the UK, the firm could guarantee a fixed exchange rate and minimize currency risk by locking in a specific exchange rate through a futures contract. Large banks facilitate currency hedging, and MNEs pay banks fees and other costs for such services.

Sources: Bartram, 2015; BBC News, 2018; Buckland and Du 2018; Dhingra, Machin, and Overman, 2017; Fidler, 2018; Sampson, 2017; Shane, 2018.

Introduction

What exactly is the leadership of the multinational firm attempting to achieve? *Profit maximization* – the first words that leap from the lips – is the simplest answer. But as is the case with much of global business, it is not quite that simple. Should leadership be maximizing the profits in the short run, the long run, for stockholders alone, or for all of the stakeholders of the multinational organization?

The Goal of Financial Management

The Anglo-American markets, primarily the USA and the UK, are characterized by many publicly traded companies that seek to maximize shareholder wealth – so-called stockholder wealth maximization. This dictates that company management should actively seek to maximize the returns to stockholders by working to push the share prices up and raising the dividends paid out. This can imply that management is not seeking to build value or wealth for the other stakeholders in the multinational enterprise: the creditors, management itself, employees, suppliers, the communities in which these firms reside, and government. The concept of free-market capitalism long has focused on building wealth for stockholders. Conditions sometimes change; for example, for some managers, wealth creation comes with a short-term focus, also, since the early 2000, the leading role of capital has been substantially diminished.

There are a few universally accepted truths in global business. Continental European and Japanese firms have long pursued a wider definition of wealth maximization that considers the financial and social health of all stakeholders, and does not focus on the financial returns of the multinational firm alone. The firm aims to maximize its profitability, but also considers a balance of short-term financial goals and long-term societal goals, such as continued employment, community citizenship, and public welfare needs.

Different philosophies are not necessarily exclusive, and many firms attempt to find a balance. Although, in many ways, a kinder and gentler philosophy, corporate maximization of social wealth attempts to meet the desires of multiple stakeholders. Decision-making can become slower, less decisive, and frequently results in organizations unable to meet the constant pressures of a global marketplace that seeks and rewards innovation, speed, and lower costs. The concerns of social impacts, environmental responsibility, and sustainable development may impress readers of press releases but they impose heavy burdens on organizations trying to compete globally. Successful enterprises will be those that learn to balance between financial objectives and corporate culture (Gerber, 2018; Daniels & VanHoose, 2018). As highlighted in Exhibit 5.1, this includes being profitable while not causing harm to society.

EXHIBIT 5.1 Corruption at Siemens

Siemens is one of the world's largest industrial engineering and electronics firms. It makes and sells industrial controls, lighting products, and power generation equipment, and operates in 190 countries. In the pursuit of profits around the world, Siemens found itself accused of bribery by governments in numerous countries. One former executive was accused of handling more than $70 million in bribes. A court found that Siemens had paid millions to bribe government officials in Nigeria and Russia.

Eventually, however, the firm had to confront the corruption in its operations. Authorities in the USA ordered Siemens to pay $800 million in fines in a ruling under the Foreign Corrupt Practices Act. The USA found that, in order to win various business contracts, Siemens allegedly had spent more than $1 billion to bribe officials around the world. Bribes were offered to obtain contracts to supply medical devices in Russia, transit systems in Venezuela, power equipment in Iraq, and telecommunications equipment in Asia.

Numerous customers halted orders with the firm in response to the scandals, and the firm's profits declined. The World Bank forced Siemens to forego bidding on Bank development projects for an extensive period. In the end, several Siemens' senior executives lost their jobs.

Subsequently, Siemens' senior management took steps to eliminate the firm's bribery culture. The company appointed a law firm to review its compliance system and uncover improper operational procedures. Siemens strengthened its business-conduct code and established a task force to improve internal financial controls. Management sought to create an ethical culture that would avoid sacrificing ethical behavior in the pursuit of profits.

Sources: Choudhary, 2013; Verschoor, 2007; Crawford and Esterl, 2007c; Milne and Scheele, 2007; Crawford and Esterl, 2007b; Crawford and Esterl, 2007a; Esterl and Crawford, 2008.

Global Financial Objectives

Because multinational corporations operate in many economic environments, they must determine the proper balance between three primary financial objectives:

1. Maximization of consolidated, after-tax, income
2. Minimization of the firm's effective global tax burden
3. Correct positioning of the firm's income, cash flows, and available funds.

These goals are frequently inconsistent, in that the pursuit of one goal may result in a less desirable outcome for another goal. Management must make trade-offs between goals about the future (which is why people are employed as managers, not computers).

In general, firms prefer to minimize their income taxes. This motivation tends to influence how company operations are structured around the work. For example, MNEs often will avoid generating very high profits in high income tax countries, while simultaneously maximizing profits in low tax countries. Many MNEs with extensive international operations devise methods to transfer profits among their subsidiaries and affiliates in order to minimize the firm's overall tax burden (Asquith & Weiss, 2016).

Currency Management

MNEs face currency risk because they typically receive funds and incur obligations in currencies other than their own. Managers must constantly monitor exchange rates and devise strategies to maintain company performance in light of changing currency values. The firm will manage the risk associated with fluctuating currency values with a view to responsively adjusting currency flows. Customers typically prefer to pay for purchases in the currency of the country where they reside. Consequently, exporting firms face currency risk as exchange rates fluctuate over time. Risk varies with exposure, particularly when all inputs are paid for in one currency while all outputs are paid for in another currency.

Exposure to currency fluctuations can produce positive results when exchange rates change favorably for the firm. In general, managers are more concerned about fluctuations that harm the firm. Such problems help explain why most countries in Europe use a single currency, the euro. Using a single medium of exchange helps eliminate currency risk for trade among the countries that use the euro. For international firms that operate outside the euro zone, however, currency risk can remain a problem (Kumar & Muniraju, 2014).

Multinational Management

Some helpful reminders about multinational companies aid in describing the financial management issues confronting the typical multinational firm:

- The primary goal of the firm, domestic or multinational, is the maximization of consolidated profits, after tax.
- *Consolidated profits* are the profits of all the individual units of the firm originating in many different currencies, but expressed in the currency of the parent company. Consolidated profits are not limited to those earnings that have been brought back to the parent company (repatriated), and in fact, may never be removed from the country in which they were earned.
- Each of the incorporated units of the firm (the parent company and the foreign subsidiaries) has its own set of traditional financial statements: statement of income, balance sheet, and statement of cash flows. These financial statements are expressed in the local currency of the unit for tax and reporting purposes.

Multinational financial management is not a separate set of issues from domestic or traditional financial management, but the additional levels of risk and complexity introduced by the conduct of business across borders. This introduces different laws, different methods, different markets, different interest rates, and most of all, different currencies (Kapadia, 2012; Aliber, 1979). All combined to new playing fields, new players, new rule books, and new referees, often even entirely new games. What a challenge!

The many dimensions of multinational financial management are most easily explained in the context of a firm's financial decision-making process in evaluating a potential foreign investment. Such an evaluation includes:

- Capital budgeting, which is the process of evaluating the financial feasibility of an individual investment, whether it be the purchase of a stock, real estate, or a firm
- Capital structure, which is the determination of the relative quantities of debt capital and equity capital that will constitute the funding of the investment (cultural differences heavily affect the portion to which capital should be part of the corporation or merely borrowed.)
- Working capital and cash flow management, which is the management of operating and financial cash flows passing in and out of a specific investment project.

Changes in interest and exchange rates will affect each of the above steps in the international investment process. All firms, no matter how "domestic" they may seem in structure, are influenced by exchange rate changes. The financial managers of a firm that has any dimension of international activity, imports or exports, or foreign subsidiaries or affiliates, must pay special attention to these issues if the firm is to succeed in its international endeavors. The discussion begins with the difficulties of simply getting paid for international sales: import-export financing (Aliber, 1979; Adelaja, 2016).

Export Trade Financing

Unlike most domestic business, international business often occurs between two parties that do not know each other well. Conducting business, however, necessitates substantial trust between the parties. This financial trust is basically the trust that the buyer of a product will actually pay for it on or after delivery. For example, if a furniture manufacturer in South Carolina receives an order from a distributor located in Cleveland, Ohio, the furniture maker will ordinarily fill the order, ship the furniture, and await payment. Payment terms are usually 30 to 60 days after shipment. This is trade on an "open account basis." The furniture manufacturer has placed a considerable amount of financial trust in the buyer but normally is paid with little problem.

Internationally, however, financial trust is pushed to its limit. An order from a foreign buyer may constitute a degree of credit risk (the risk of not being paid) that the producer (the exporter) does not wish to take. The exporter needs some guarantee that the importer will pay for the goods. Other factors that tend to intensify this problem include the increased lag times necessary for international

Exhibit 5.2 Export trade financing requires a degree of trust
Credit: STR/AFP via Getty Images.

shipments and the potential risks of payments in different currencies (Exhibit 5.2). For this reason, arrangements that provide guarantees for exports are important to countries and companies wanting to expand international sales. This can be accomplished through a sequence of documents surrounding the letter of credit (Sukar & Hassan, 2001; Seyoum, 2013).

Trade Financing Using a Letter of Credit

A lumber manufacturer in the USA, Atlas, receives a large order from a Japanese construction company, Takagi, for a shipment of old-growth cedar lumber. Atlas has not worked with Takagi before and therefore seeks some assurance that payment for the lumber will actually be made. Atlas ordinarily does not require any assurance of the buyer's ability to pay (sometimes a small down payment or deposit is made as a sign of good faith), but an international sale of this size is too large a risk. If Takagi could not or would not pay, the cost of returning the lumber products to the USA would be prohibitive. Exhibit 5.3 illustrates the following sequence of events that will complete the transaction.

1. Takagi Construction requests a letter of credit (L/C) be issued by its bank, Tokyo Bank.
2. Tokyo Bank determines that Takagi is financially sound and capable of making the payments as required.

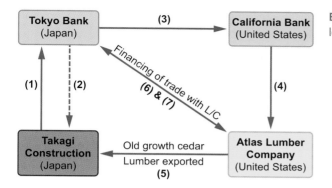

Exhibit 5.3 Trade financing using a letter of credit (L/C)

3. Tokyo Bank, once satisfied with Takagi's application, issues the L/C to the exporter's bank, California Bank. The L/C guarantees payment for the merchandise if the goods are shipped as stipulated in accompanying documents, such as the commercial invoice, packing list, and bill of lading.

4. The exporter's bank, California, assures Atlas that payment will be made after evaluating the letter of credit. At this point, the credit standing of Tokyo Bank has been substituted for the credit standing of the importer itself, Takagi Construction.

5. When the lumber order is ready, it is shipped to the importer with a contract which is the receipt that the shipper has obtained the goods, termed a bill of lading.

6. Atlas draws a draft against Tokyo Bank for payment. The draft is the document used in international trade to effect payment and explicitly requests payment for the merchandise, which is now shown to be shipped and insured consistent with all requirements of the previously issued L/C. (If the draft is issued to Tokyo Bank, the bank issuing the L/C, it is termed a bank draft. If the draft is issued against the importer, Takagi Construction, it is a trade draft.) The draft, L/C, and other appropriate documents are presented to California Bank for payment.

7. California Bank (USA) confirms the letter of credit from Tokyo Bank and immediately pays Atlas for the lumber and then collects from the issuing bank, Tokyo.

Regardless, with the letter of credit as the financial assurance, the exporter or the exporter's bank is collecting payment from the importer's bank, not from the importer itself. It is up to the specific arrangements between the importer (Takagi) and the importer's bank (Tokyo) to arrange the final settlement at that end of the purchase. For its work on the letter of credit, the participating bank will of course charge a fee. If the trade relationship continues over time, both parties will gain faith and confidence in the other, and the fee structure may even improve. With this strengthening of financial trust, the trade financing relationship will improve. Sustained buyer–seller relations across borders eventually end up operating on an open account basis similar to domestic commerce (Seyoum, 2013; Cottrell, 2006).

Multinational Investing

Any investment, whether it be the purchase of stock, the acquisition of real estate, or the construction of a manufacturing facility in another country, is financially justified if the present value of expected cash inflows is greater than the present value of expected cash outflows; in other words, if it has a positive **net present value (NPV)**. The construction of a capital budget is the process of projecting the net operating cash flows of the potential investment to determine if it is indeed a good investment (Asquith & Wiess, 2016; Melvin & Norrbin, 2017). Of course, the NPV depends on the ongoing economic and social environment and may change over time, for example, due to the sudden emergence of an epidemic.

Capital Budgeting

A **capital budget** is the financial evaluation of a proposed investment to determine whether the expected returns are sufficient to justify the investment expenses. All capital budgets are only as good as the accuracy of the cost and revenue assumptions. Adequately anticipating all of the incremental expenses that the individual project imposes on the firm is critical to a proper analysis.

A capital budget is composed of three primary cash flow components:

1. **Initial expenses and capital outlays.** The initial capital outlays are normally the largest net cash outflow occurring over the life of a proposed investment. Because the cash flows occur up front, they have a substantial impact on the net present value of the project.
2. **Operating cash flows.** The operating cash flows are the net cash flows the project is expected to yield once production is underway. The primary positive net cash flows of the project are realized in this stage; net operating cash flows will determine the success or failure of the proposed investment.
3. **Terminal cash flows.** The final component of the capital budget is composed of the salvage value or resale value of the project at its end. The terminal value will include whatever working capital balances can be recaptured once the project is no longer in operation (at least by this owner).

The financial decision criterion for an individual investment is whether the net present value of the project is positive or negative. The net cash flows in the

EXHIBIT 5.4 Complicating factors that MNEs face in capital budgeting

Capital budgeting in the multinational firm is complicated by four factors:

- Cash flows may be received or paid out in a currency that differs from that of the parent firm's operating currency.
- Taxation and tax law vary substantially around the world.
- Governments sometimes place restrictions on the transfer of funds from the project to the home of the parent firm.
- Risk can be substantial in individual countries, requiring a higher rate of return for current or proposed projects.

future are discounted by the average cost of capital for the firm (the average of debt and equity costs). The purpose of discounting is to capture the fact that the firm has acquired investment capital at a cost (interest). The same capital could have been used for other projects or other investments. It is therefore necessary to discount the future cash flows to account for this foregone income of the capital, its opportunity cost. If NPV is positive, then the project is an acceptable investment. If the project's NPV is negative, then the cash flows expected to result from the investment are insufficient to provide an acceptable rate of return, and the project should be rejected (Seyoum, 2013; Asquith & Wiess, 2016; Melvin & Norrbin, 2017). Computations will also be affected by the declining value of capital to society. As shown in Exhibit 5.4, capital budgeting faces various complications in international business.

Risks in International Investments

Risks associated with international investments are substantial, but here we will focus on two – exchange rate risk and interest rate risk – and how they are viewed by investors. Compared to domestic ventures, international ventures are relatively risky because of different countries, their laws, regulations, potential for interference with the normal operations of the investment project, and variations of currencies – all of which are unique to international investment.

Governments have the ability to pass new laws, including the potential nationalization of the entire project. Other problems that may arise are foreign tax laws, restrictions placed on when or how much in profits may be repatriated to the parent company, and restrictions that hinder the free movement of merchandise, services, and capital between the project and the parent. The other major distinction between a domestic investment and a foreign investment is that the viewpoint or perspective of the parent and the project are no longer the same. The two perspectives differ because the parent only values cash flows it derives from the project (Melvin & Norrbin, 2017).

Combining Interest-Rate and Exchange-Rate Risks

If there is one mistake made more often than any other in international financial management, it is the understanding of what borrowing or investing in a foreign currency really means. For example, many companies and investors borrow money in Japan for many years because Japanese yen interest rates are amongst the lowest in the world. This practice, called the *Japanese Carry Trade*, relies on being able to borrow cheaply and reinvest somewhere else in the world to make a greater return. So what could go wrong? Consider an international investor who borrows ¥10 million at 1.00 percent interest per annum, which is a very low rate. At the end of one year, the investor will need to repay the loan in full, principal and interest, of ¥10.1 million. The money borrowed is exchanged for US dollars at the current spot rate of, say, ¥100/$, yielding $100,000. This $100,000 is then invested in US dollar securities earning 5.00 percent interest for one year. At the end of one year the investor has $105,000 and has earned 5 percent while borrowing the funds at 1 percent. All that is left is to repay the loan and calculate the profits. But that's where things can go wrong.

The entire investment's return is dependent on what the exchange rate is at the end of the period. If the spot rate is still ¥100/$, then the investor exchanges dollars for yen and locks in a profit of ¥400,000 on the investment. This is shown in Exhibit 5.5. But if the Japanese yen's value has risen against the dollar over that year, to, say, ¥95/$, the $105,000 yields only ¥9,975,000, which is not enough to even repay the loan. Of course, if the yen depreciates in value against the dollar, to, say, ¥105/$, the investor's return is even greater. It all depends on the ending spot rate of exchange.

Exhibit 5.5 The Japanese yen carry trade

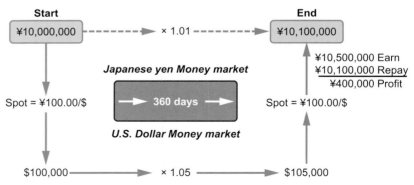

Investors borrow yen at 1.00% per annum

Invest dollars at 5.00% per annum

This type of international investment or debt is extremely common in global business. A few examples:

- A Norwegian citizen is buying a new home. She can acquire a mortgage for the home's purchase in Norwegian krone for 7.00 percent, or in euros for 5.00 percent. Although the euro is obviously a lower interest rate, she has no real idea of what the rate of exchange between the Norwegian krone and the euro will be in the coming years. The mortgage payments may end up being either higher, lower, or the same.
- A Thailand-based company needs to borrow $20 million or the Thai baht equivalent in order to make a new acquisition. US dollar interest rates offered the company are 8 percent, while the corresponding loan in Thai baht is 18 percent. The Thai company, although it knows it is taking a currency risk, borrows dollars at 8 percent because the difference between interest rates appears so great. Recently, however, the Thai baht lost value, going from B25/$ to B40/$. The effective interest rate ended up being 72.85 percent, not 8 percent.

Borrowing or investing in foreign currencies includes foreign exchange risk. Unless the borrower or the investor knows with certainty what the exchange rate will be at all future dates of repayment or returns, the currency risk is always present (World Economic Forum, 2018; Black & Webb, 2017; Seyoum, 2013).

International Cash Flow Management

Cash flow management is the financing of short-term or current assets, but the term is used here to describe all short-term financing and financial management of the firm. Even a small multinational firm will have a number of different cash quantities moving throughout its system at one time. The maintenance of proper liquidity, the monitoring of payments, and the change of capital positions – all of these require a great degree of organization and planning in international operations.

Firms possess both operating cash flows and financing cash flows. Operating cash flows arise from the everyday business activities of the firm, such as paying for materials or resources (accounts payable) or receiving payments for items sold (accounts receivable). In addition to the direct cost and revenue cash flows from operations, there are a number of indirect cash flows. These may be paid to the owners of particular technological processes and royalties to the holders of patents or copyrights. There may also be deposits from product sales to the public, particularly for consumer goods.

Financing cash flows are the cash flows of a firm related to the funding of its operations, especially debt and equity-related flows. The servicing of existing funding sources, interest on existing debt, and dividend payments to shareholders constitute potentially large and frequent cash flows. Periodic additions to debt or equity through new bank loans, new bond issuances, or supplemental stock sales may also add to the volume of financing cash flows in the multinational firm (O'Malley, 2016).

Operational and financial cash flows can be quite complex in the typical multinational firm. In addition to generating export sales, most MNEs also import parts, components, and services from various countries. Sales and purchases by the parent and its subsidiaries give rise to a continuing series of accounts receivable and accounts payable, which may be denominated in various currencies. Simultaneously, the firm may make various international payments related to its foreign direct investment activities.

One of the most difficult pricing decisions many multinational firms must make concerns the price at which they sell their products to members of the same corporate family. These are transfer prices, which are the prices at which a firm sells its products to its own subsidiaries and affiliates. Transfer prices theoretically are equivalent to what the same product would cost if purchased on the open market. However, it is often impossible to find such a product on the open market; which may be unique to the firm and its product line. The result is a price that is set internally and may result in the subsidiary being more or less profitable. This, in turn, has impacts on taxes paid in host countries.

The foreign subsidiary may also be using techniques, machinery, or processes that are owned or patented by the parent firm and so must pay royalties and license fees. The cash flows are usually calculated as a percentage of the sales price. Many multinational firms also spread the overhead and management expenses incurred at the parent over their foreign affiliates and subsidiaries that are using the parent's administrative services (Seyoum, 2013; Asquith & Weiss, 2016; Melvin & Norrbin, 2017; Czinkota & Ronen, 1983).

Cash Management

The structure of the firm dictates how cash flows and financial resources can be managed. The trend in the past decade has been for the increasing centralization of most financial and treasury operations. The centralized treasury often is responsible for both funding operations and cash flow management. It also may enjoy significant economies of scale, offering more services and expertise to the various units of the firm worldwide than the individual units themselves could support.

Netting

Suppose an MNE's subsidiary in Mexico owes the equivalent of $1,000,000 to the firm's subsidiary in France, and the French subsidiary, in turn, owes $300,000 to the subsidiary in Mexico. If each firm pays its debts as indicated, the cash flows between the two units are two-way and will result in unneeded transfer costs and transaction expenses. Coordination between units simply requires planning and budgeting of intrafirm cash flows so that two-way flows are "netted" against one another, with only one smaller cash flow as opposed to two having to be undertaken. Thus, by using a **netting** strategy, the Mexican subsidiary need make only one payment of $700,000 to the French subsidiary ($1,000,000 minus $300,000) and the total debt will be resolved with only one transaction. Such netting can occur between each subsidiary and the parent, and between the subsidiaries themselves. Netting is particularly helpful if the two-way flow is in two different currencies because exchanging currencies inherently gives rise to fees.

Cash Pooling

A large firm with a number of units operating both within an individual country and across countries may be able to economize on the amount of firm assets needed in cash if one central pool is used for cash pooling. With one pool of capital and up-to-date information on the cash flows in and out of the various units, the firm spends much less in terms of foregone interest on cash balances, which are held in safekeeping against unforeseen cash flow shortfalls.

A typical MNE would consolidate all cash management and resources in one place, usually at headquarters. One cash manager for all units is charged with planning intercompany payments, including controlling the currency exposures of the individual units. A single large pool also may allow the firm to negotiate better financial service rates with banking institutions for cash-clearing purposes. In the event that the cash manager would need to be closer to the individual units (both proximity and time zone), the corporate units could combine to run cash between themselves.

Internal Banks

Some multinational firms have found that their financial resources and needs are becoming either too large or too sophisticated for the financial services that are available in many of their local subsidiary markets. One solution to this has been the establishment of an internal bank within the firm. The internal bank actually buys and sells payables and receivables from the various units, which frees them from struggling for continued working capital financing and lets them focus on their primary business activities (Doupnik & Perera, 2015; Seyoum, 2013; Melvin & Norrbin, 2017).

Foreign Exchange Exposure

Companies today know the risks of international operations. They are aware of the substantial risks to balance sheet values and annual earnings that interest rates and exchange rates may inflict on any firm at any time. Financial managers, international treasurers, and financial officers of all kinds are expected to protect the firm from such risks. As highlighted in Exhibit 5.6, exchange rates can fluctuate substantially in the wake of events that arise in firms' external environments. Companies experience, to varying degrees, three types of foreign currency exposure:

1. Transaction exposure. This is the risk associated with a contractual payment of foreign currency. For example, a US firm that exports products to France will receive a guaranteed (by contract) payment in euros in the future. Firms that buy or sell internationally have transaction exposure if any of their cash flows are denominated in foreign currency.

2. Economic exposure. This is the risk to the firm that its long-term cash flows will be affected, positively or negatively, by unexpected future exchange rate changes. Although many firms that consider themselves to be purely domestic may not realize it, most firms have some degree of economic exposure. Just think of your candy bar, which is made largely with foreign sugar.

3. Translation exposure. This risk arises from the legal requirement that all firms consolidate their financial statements (balance sheets and income statements) of all worldwide operations annually. Therefore, any firm with operations outside its home country – operations that will be either earning foreign currency or valued in foreign currency– has translation exposure.

Transaction exposure and economic exposure are "true exposures" in the financial sense. This means they both present potential threats to the value of a firm's cash flows over time. The third exposure, translation, is a problem that arises from accounting.

Transaction exposure is the most commonly observed type of exchange rate risk. Only two conditions are necessary for a transaction exposure to exist: (1) a cash flow that is denominated in a foreign currency and (2) the cash flow that will occur at a future date. Any contract, agreement, purchase, or sale that is denominated in a foreign currency that will be settled in the future constitutes a transaction exposure.

The risk of a transaction exposure is that the exchange rate might change between the present date and the settlement date. The change may be for the better or for the worse. For example, suppose that an American firm signs a contract to purchase heavy rolled-steel pipe from a South Korean steel producer for 21,000,000 Korean won. The payment is due in 30 days upon delivery. The 30-day account payable, so typical of international trade and commerce, is a transaction exposure for the US firm. Suppose the spot exchange rate on the contract date is Won 700/$. The exchange rate likely will fluctuate over the 30-day period. If the spot rate at the end of 30 days is Won 720/$, the US firm would actually pay less. The payment would then be $29,167. If, however, the exchange rate changed in the opposite direction, for example, to Won 650/$, the payment could just as easily increase to $32,308. This type of price risk, transaction exposure, is a major problem for international commerce.

MNEs engage in transaction exposure management to mitigate such risks. The most common approach is hedging, wherein the firm uses financial contracts to hedge the transaction exposure. The most common foreign currency contractual hedge is the forward contract, although other financial instruments and derivatives, such as currency futures and options, are also used. A forward contract allows the firm to be assured a fixed rate of exchange between the desired two currencies at the precise future date. The forward contract would also be for the exact amount of the exposure.

A hedge is an asset or a position whose value moves in the equal but opposite direction of the exposure. This means that if an exposure experienced a loss in value of $50, the hedge asset would offset the loss with a gain in value of $50. The total value of the position would not change (Doupnik & Perera, 2015; Seyoum, 2013; Melvin & Norrbin, 2017). Of course, protective payment needs to be made to the financial market player who designs and offers hedges.

EXHIBIT 5.6 Politics and currencies turbulence following Russia's military intervention in Ukraine

In 2014, Russia made various military incursions into the nation of Ukraine. Russian soldiers also took control of key infrastructure and institutions in the Ukrainian territory of Crimea. Russia then annexed Crimea in a referendum. The event escalated into an armed conflict between the Ukrainian Government and Russia-backed forces. Russia also had attempted to silence human rights workers who were attempting to reduce the damage arising from the incursion.

Numerous governments, including those of the USA and the European Union, condemned Russia for its actions in Ukraine, accusing the Russian Government of violating international law and Ukrainian sovereignty. In the wake of the crisis, many countries implemented economic sanctions against Russia, and Russia responded in kind, which worsened economic conditions in Europe. In 2015, Russia redeployed some of its elite units from Ukraine to Syria to support Syrian President Bashar al-Assad, in an already troubled region.

The intervention into Ukraine gave rise to turbulence in world financial markets. The average valuation of numerous stock markets around the world fell significantly due to perceptions about rising instability in Ukraine and nearby areas. Following the incursion, Russia's currency, the ruble, fell substantially in value relative to the US dollar and the European euro. The decline resulted partly from a plunge in the demand for rubles. Investor sentiment was influenced by the perception of a cooling of relations between East and West. In addition, the Russian stock market declined by more than 10 percent. In response, the Russian central bank raised interest rates and intervened in foreign exchange markets in an effort to stabilize its currency. For the time being, investors who had counted on a firm value of the rubles were disappointed, as were their bankers.

Sources: Adamyk, 2016; Sakwa, 2016; Wilson, 2014.

Russia's 2014 invasion of the Ukrainian territory of Crimea set off a series of sanctions between the international community and Russia that has had a continuing wave of effects across Europe
Credit: Alexander Aksakov/Getty Images.

Currency Risk Sharing

Firms that import and export on a continuing basis have constant transaction exposures. If a firm is interested in maintaining a good business relationship with one of its suppliers, it must work with that supplier to assure it that it will not force all currency risk or exposure off on the other party on a continual basis. Exchange rate movements are inherently random; therefore, some type of risk-sharing arrangement may prove useful.

If Ford (USA) imports automotive parts from Mazda (Japan) every month, year after year, major swings in exchange rates can benefit one party at the expense of the other. One solution would be for Ford and Mazda to agree that all purchases by Ford will be made in Japanese yen as long as the spot rate on the payment date is between ¥120/$ and ¥130/$. If the exchange rate is between these values on the payment dates, Ford agrees to accept whatever transaction exposure exists (because it is paying in a foreign currency). If, however, the exchange rate falls outside of this range on the payment date, Ford and Mazda will "share" the difference. If the spot rate on the settlement date is ¥110/$, the Japanese yen would have appreciated versus the dollar, causing Ford's costs of purchasing automotive parts to rise. Because this rate falls outside the contractual range, Mazda would agree to accept a total payment in Japanese yen that would result from a "shared" difference of ¥10. Thus, Ford's total payment in Japanese yen would be calculated using an exchange rate of ¥115/$.

Risk-sharing agreements like these have been in use for nearly 50 years on world markets. They became something of a rarity during the 1950s and 1960s, when exchange rates were relatively stable (under the Bretton Woods Agreement). But with the return to floating exchange rates in the 1970s, firms with long-term customer–supplier relationships across borders returned to some old ways of keeping old friends. And sometimes old ways work very well.

Economic Exposure

Economic exposure, also called operating exposure, is the change in the value of a firm arising from unexpected changes in exchange rates. Economic exposure emphasizes that there is a limit to a firm's ability to predict either cash flows or exchange rate changes in the medium to long term.

It is customary to think only of firms that actively trade internationally as having any type of currency exposure. But actually, all firms that operate in economies affected by international financial events, such as exchange rate changes, are affected. A barber in Dahlewitz, Germany, seemingly isolated from exchange rate chaos, is still affected when the euro rises in value. If German products become increasingly expensive to foreign buyers, manufacturers with factories in Germany, such as Rolls-Royce Aerospace in Dahlewitz, will be forced to cut back production and lay off workers, and businesses of all types decline – even the business of barbers. The impacts are real, and they affect all firms, domestic and international alike.

How susceptible is an individual firm to economic exposure? It is impossible to predict with accuracy. Such measurements are subjective – and, for the most part, dependent on the degree of internationalization present in the firm's cost and revenue structure. Just because it is difficult to measure does not mean that management cannot take some steps to prepare the firm for the unexpected.

Impact of Economic Exposure

The impacts of economic exposure are as diverse as the firms in their international structure. Take the case of a US corporation with a successful British subsidiary.

The British subsidiary manufactured and then distributed the firm's products in the UK, Germany, and France. The profits of the British subsidiary are paid out annually to the American parent corporation. What would be the impact on the profitability of the British subsidiary and the entire US firm if the British pound suddenly fell in value against all other major currencies (as it did in 2016)?

If the British firm had been facing competition in Germany, France, and its own home market, it would now be more competitive. If the British pound is cheaper, so are the products sold internationally by British-based firms. The British subsidiary of the American firm would, in all likelihood, see rising profits from increased sales.

But what of the value of the British subsidiary to the US parent corporations? The same fall in the British pound that allowed the British subsidiary to gain profits would also result in substantially fewer US dollars when the British pound earnings are converted to US dollars at the end of the year. It seems that it is nearly impossible to win in this situation. Actually, from the perspective of economic exposure management, the fact that the firm's total value, subsidiary and parent together, is roughly a wash. Sound financial management assumes that a firm will profit and bear risk in its line of business, not in the process of settling payments on business already completed.

Economic Exposure Management

Management of economic exposure is being prepared for the unexpected. A firm such as Hewlett-Packard (HP), which is highly dependent on its ability to remain cost competitive in markets both at home and abroad, may choose to take actions now that would allow it to passively withstand any sudden unexpected rise of the dollar. This could be accomplished through diversification of operations and of financing.

Diversification of operations would allow the firm to be desensitized to the impacts of any one pair of exchange rate changes. For example, a multinational firm such as Hewlett-Packard may produce the same product in manufacturing facilities in Singapore, the USA, Puerto Rico, and Europe. If a sudden and prolonged rise in the dollar made production in the USA prohibitively expensive and uncompetitive, HP is already positioned to shift production to a relatively cheaper currency environment. Although firms rarely diversify production location for the sole purpose of currency diversification, it is a substantial additional benefit from such global expansion.

Diversification of financing serves to hedge economic exposure much in the same way as it did with transaction exposures. A firm with debt denominated in many different currencies is sensitive to many different interest rates. If one country or currency experiences rapidly rising inflation rates and interest rates, a firm with diversified debt will not be subject to the full impact of such movements.

Purely domestic firms, however, are actually somewhat captive to the local conditions and are unable to ride out such interest rate storms as easily.

It should be noted that, in both cases, diversification is a passive solution to the exposure problem. This means that without knowing when or where or what the problem may be, the firm that simply spreads its operations and financial structure out over a variety of countries and currencies is prepared (Doupnik & Perera, 2015; Seyoum, 2013; Melvin & Norrbin, 2017; Lund et al., 2017; Daniels & VanHoose, 2018).

Countertrade

General Motors exchanged automobiles for a trainload of strawberries. Control Data swapped a computer for a package of Polish furniture, Hungarian carpet backing, and Russian greeting cards. Boeing has exchanged aircraft for petroleum. These are all examples of countertrade activities carried out around the world.

Countertrade is a sale in international trade that involves the exchange of goods for other goods, rather than goods for cash. In effect, countertrade amounts to barter, the exchange of products for other products without using money. As illustrated in Exhibit 5.7, countertrade has become more salient in recent years.

EXHIBIT 5.7 Countertrade's rising global influence

International trade in goods and services is typically conducted with currencies, the value of which is settled by the four legs of trust, demand, supply, and risk. If any of these legs weaken, substitute exchange methods emerge, based on precious metals, commodities, or even cigarettes. In the wake of economic and financial volatility in the global economy, such substitutions are rising again in the global market.

As a result of all various instabilities in global economies, barter and other forms of countertrade are re-appearing in the global market, offering new efficiencies in the conduct of trade. Companies need to understand how such international shifts will affect them and learn to adjust their marketing and financing approaches to these new opportunities.

Countertrade is the use of goods, services, and other non-monetary resources as payment. For example, in order to help pay for the acquisition of military airplanes, a country may demand that the seller of the planes encourages tourism to the country – as done by Egypt. Zaire and Italy exchanged scrap iron for 12 locomotives. China traded Russia 212 railway trucks full of mango juice in exchange for a passenger jet.

Countertrade agreements have shown that an exchange of goods for goods can overcome problems that may arise with national currencies. Historically, countertrade was used by soft currency countries. Its use has risen since the 2008–2009 financial crisis, bridging currency gaps and providing MNEs with a competitive edge. It keeps transactions alive and reduces the fear of high currency volatility. Many firms just want to carry on their business, rather than become currency speculators.

Economic hardship is not the only incentive to countertrade. Bilateralism plays a large role in the acceptance of a countertrade offer. A country may encourage its companies to accede to barter requests from foreign trade partners and allies. The link between business and politics encourages such accommodation, even though doing so may be inconvenient. In a world of economic hardship and currency uncertainty, countertrade is a viable solution for market and political shortcomings.

Source: Czinkota, 2016.

Historically, countertrade was mainly conducted in the form of barter, which is a direct exchange of goods of approximately equal value between parties, with no money involved. Such transactions were the very essence of business at times during which no money – that is, no common medium of exchange – existed or was available. Over time, money emerged as a convenient medium that unlinked transactions from individual parties and their joint timing and therefore permitted greater flexibility in trading activities. Repeatedly, however, we can see returns to the barter system as a result of environmental circumstances. For example, during periods of high inflation in Europe in the 1920s, goods such as bread, meat, and gold were seen as much more useful and secure than paper money, which decreased in real value by the minute. In the late 1940s, American cigarettes were an acceptable medium of exchange in most European countries, much more so than any particular currency except for the dollar.

Countertrade transactions have therefore always arisen when economic circumstances made it more acceptable to exchange goods directly rather than use money as an intermediary. Conditions that encourage such business activities are lack of money, lack of value of or faith in money, lack of acceptability of money as an exchange medium, or greater ease of transaction by using goods.

Increasingly, countries and companies are deciding that, sometimes, countertrade transactions are more beneficial to them than transactions based on financial exchange alone. One reason is that the recent world financial crisis has made ordinary trade financing very risky. Many countries, particularly in the developing world, simply cannot obtain the trade credit or financial assistance necessary to pay for desired imports. Heavily indebted countries, faced with the possibility of not being able to afford imports at all, hasten to use countertrade to maintain at least some product inflow. However, it should be recognized that countertrade does not reduce commercial risk. Countertrade transactions will, therefore, be encouraged by stability and economic progress. Research has shown that countertrade appears to increase with a country's creditworthiness because good credit encourages traders to participate in unconventional trading practices (Claessens et al., 2014).

The use of countertrade permits the covert reduction of prices and therefore allows the circumvention of price and exchange controls. Particularly in commodity markets with cartel arrangements, such as oil or agriculture, this benefit may be very useful to a producer. For example, by using oil as a countertraded product for industrial equipment, a surreptitious discount (by using a higher price for the acquired products) may expand market share.

Countertrade is also often viewed by firms and nations alike as an excellent mechanism to gain entry into new markets. When a producer believes that marketing is not its strong suit, the producer often hopes that the party receiving the goods will serve as a new distributor, opening up new international marketing channels and ultimately expanding the original market.

Because countertrade is highly sought after in many large markets such as China and Russia, the former Eastern bloc countries, as well as South America, engaging in such transactions can provide major growth opportunities for firms. In increasingly competitive world markets, countertrade can be a good way to attract new buyers. By providing countertrade services, the seller is in effect differentiating its product from those of its competitors.

Countertrade also can provide stability for long-term sales. For example, if a firm is tied to a countertrade agreement, it will need to source the product from a particular supplier, whether or not it wants to do so. This stability is often valued very highly because it eliminates, or at least reduces, vast swings in demand and thus allows for better planning. Countertrade, therefore, can serve as a major mechanism to shift risk from the producer to another party. In that sense, one can argue that countertrade offers a substitute for the missing forward markets. Finally, under certain conditions, countertrade can ensure the quality of an international transaction. In instances where the seller of technology is paid in output produced by the technology delivered, the seller's revenue depends on the success of the technology transfer and maintenance services in production. Therefore, the seller is more likely to be concerned about providing services, maintenance, and general technology transfer.

In spite of all the apparent benefits of countertrade, there are strong economic arguments against the activity. The arguments are based mainly on efficiency grounds. But countries and companies increasingly view countertrade as an alternative that may be flawed but worthwhile to undertake, since some trade is preferable to no trade. Both industrialized and developing countries exchange a wide variety of goods via countertrade (Martin, 2014; Sanders, 2017).

International Taxation

Governments alone have the power to tax. Each government wants to tax all companies within its jurisdiction without placing burdens on domestic or foreign companies that would restrain trade. Each country will state its jurisdictional approach formally in the tax treaties that it signs with other countries. One of the primary purposes of tax treaties is to establish the bounds of each country's jurisdiction to prevent double taxation of international income.

Nations usually follow one of two basic approaches to international taxation: a residential approach or a territorial or source approach. The residential approach to international taxation taxes the international income of its residents without regard to where the income is earned. The territorial approach to transnational income taxes all parties, regardless of country of residency, within its territorial jurisdiction.

Most countries in practice must combine the two approaches to tax foreign and domestic firms equally. For example, the USA and Japan both apply the residential approach to their own resident corporations and the territorial approach to income earned by nonresidents within their territorial jurisdictions. Other countries, such as Germany, apply the territorial approach to dividends paid to domestic firms from their foreign subsidiaries; such dividends are assumed to be taxed abroad and are exempt from further taxation.

Within the territorial jurisdiction of tax authorities, a foreign corporation is typically defined as any business that earns income within the host country's borders but is incorporated under the laws of another country. The foreign corporation usually must surpass some minimum level of activity (gross income) before the host country assumes primary tax jurisdiction. However, if the foreign corporation owns income-producing assets or a permanent establishment, the threshold is automatically surpassed (Mankiw, 2017; Contractor, 2016).

Types of Taxes

Taxes are generally classified as direct and indirect. **Direct taxes** are calculated on actual income, either individual or firm income. Exhibit 5.8 describes how the level of income taxes can affect nations' attractiveness for business and investment.

> ### EXHIBIT 5.8 Low corporate taxes make the USA competitive
>
> One of the biggest challenges facing the US economy in past years was the nation's very high corporate income tax rates. However, this situation changed in 2017 when the USA passed legislation to lower the rate to 21%. Thus, the average corporate US tax rate is now considerably lower than the average rate in numerous other prominent countries, including Australia, Brazil, Canada, China, Germany, India, and Japan. This lower tax rate helped make the USA an attractive country in which to invest. Foreign corporations from around the globe increasingly invest in businesses in the USA where they will pay a lower tax rate than that same business would, if it were formed in numerous other countries. The new tax law follows the lead of several other countries that have lowered their corporate income tax rate, including Ireland, Russia, and the UK. Formerly, the USA had been tied with Japan for having the highest corporate income tax rate in the world.
>
> Many proponents of lower taxes argue that foreign companies will now prefer to invest their capital in the USA. The change will help stimulate foreign investment into the USA, provide added stimulus to both US economic growth and its expanding productivity. As foreign investment grows, the US economy should start to gain added global competitiveness. In addition, many USA-based companies have moved foreign profits, long held in accounts overseas, back to the USA to benefit from the lower corporate tax rate. This shift has freed up capital for such firms to reinvest in new projects and innovation, all of which benefits the US economy. US corporations generally do not have to pay US taxes on profits made outside the USA unless they bring the profits back to the USA.
>
> **Source:** Hendrie, 2019; Keen and Konrad, 2013.

Indirect taxes, such as sales taxes, severance taxes, tariffs, and value-added taxes, are applied to purchase prices, material costs, quantities of natural resources mined, and so forth. Although most countries still rely on income taxes as the primary method of raising revenue, tax structures vary widely across countries.

The value-added tax (VAT) is the primary revenue source for the European Union. A value-added tax is applied to the amount of product value added by the production process. The tax is calculated as a percentage of the product price less the cost of materials and inputs used in its manufacture, which have been taxed previously. Through this process, tax revenues are collected literally on the value added by that specific stage of the production process. Under the existing General Agreement on Tariffs and Trade (GATT), the legal framework under which international trade operates, value-added taxes may be levied on imports into a country or group of countries (such as the European Union) in order to treat foreign

producers entering the domestic markets equally with firms within the country paying the VAT (Exhibit 5.9). Similarly, the VAT may be refunded on export sales or sales to tourists who purchase products for consumption outside the country or community. For example, an American tourist leaving London may collect a refund on all value-added taxes paid on goods purchased within the UK. The refunding usually requires documentation of the actual purchase price and the amount of tax paid (Cohn & Caminiti, 2011; Kemme et al., 2017).

Income Categories and Taxation

There are three primary methods used for the transfer of funds across tax jurisdictions: royalties, interest, and dividends. Royalties are under license for the use of intangible assets such as patents, designs, trademarks, techniques, or copyrights. Interest is the payment for the use of capital lent for the financing of normal business activity. Dividends are income paid or deemed paid to the shareholders of the corporation from the residual earnings of operations. When a corporation declares the percentage of residual earnings that is to go to shareholders, the dividend is declared and distributed.

Taxation of corporate income differs substantially across countries. Exhibit 5.10 provides a summary of corporate tax rates around the world. The exhibit reveals top marginal and effective corporate tax rates for a collection of countries. The top marginal rate is the maximum tax rate that corporations pay in each country by law. In most countries, income taxes are charged in multi-tiered brackets, which rise in increments as the amount of income earned rises. In the exhibit, the effective rate is an estimate of the rate that companies actually pay. It is the rate calculated by dividing total taxes paid by total taxable income. Tax rates affect international

EXHIBIT 5.10 Corporate tax rates for various countries

Country	Top marginal corporate tax rate	Effective corporate tax rate
Ireland	12.5	12
Russia	20	20
UK	20	20
Italy	24	21
China	25	19
Canada	26.5	16
USA	21	21
South Africa	28	20
Australia	30	20
Germany	30	15
Japan	31	24
Brazil	34	22
India	35	28

Sources: Based on Congressional Budget Office, 2017; KPMG, 2018; Mankiw, 2017; PwC, 2017.

business because managers tend to organize and locate business activities in ways that minimize taxation. Companies may be able to reduce their tax burden by taking deductions and allowances specified by national laws. MNEs employ various tax avoidance strategies, which translates into lower overall tax burdens.

Royalty and interest payments to nonresidents are normally subject to withholding taxes. Corporate profits are typically double taxed in most countries, through corporate and personal taxes. Corporate income is first taxed at the business level with corporate taxes, then a second time when the income of distributed earnings is taxed through personal income taxes. Withholding tax rates also differ by the degree of ownership that the corporation possesses in the foreign corporation. Minor ownership is termed portfolio, while major or controlling influence is categorized as substantial holdings. In the case of dividends, interest, or royalties paid to nonresidents, governments routinely apply withholding taxes to their payment in the reasonable expectation that the nonresidents will not report and declare such income with the host-country tax authorities. Withholding taxes are specified by income category in all bilateral tax treaties (Cohn & Caminiti, 2011; Kemme et al., 2017).

SUMMARY

Multinational financial management is both complex and critical to the multinational firm. Beginning with the very objective of management, stockholder wealth maximization or corporate wealth maximization, all traditional functional areas of financial management are affected by the internationalization of the firm. Capital budgeting, firm financing, capital structure, and working capital and cash flow management, all traditional functions, are made more difficult by business activities that cross borders and oceans, not to mention currencies and markets.

In addition to the traditional areas of financial management, international financial management must deal with the three types of currency exposure: (1) transaction exposure, (2) economic exposure, and (3) translation exposure. Each type of currency risk confronts a firm with serious choices regarding its exposure analysis and its degree of willingness to manage the inherent risks.

This chapter not only described the basic types of risk, but also outlined a number of the key strategies employed in the management of the exposures. Some of the solutions available today have arisen only with the development of new types of international financial markets and instruments, such as the currency swap. Others, such as currency risk-sharing agreements, are as old as exchange rates themselves.

DISCUSSION QUESTIONS

1. What are the pros and cons of the theories of wealth maximization?
2. Why is it important to identify the cash flows of a foreign investment from the perspective of the parent rather than from just the project?
3. Is currency risk unique to international firms? Is currency risk good or bad for the potential profitability of the multinational?
4. Which type of currency risk is the least important to the multinational firm? Should resources be spent to manage this risk?
5. Are firms with no direct international business (imports and exports) subject to economic exposure?
6. What is the purpose of hedging? Under what circumstances would a firm employ a hedging strategy?
7. What are some of the causes of the resurgence of countertrade?
8. What forms of countertrade exist and how do they differ? What are their relative advantages and drawbacks?
9. How consistent is countertrade with the international trade framework?
10. How do differences in corporate income tax rates across countries affect investment by multinational companies?

KEY TERMS

TAKE A STAND

Many multinational companies believe that hedging is really nothing other than formalized speculation. Since many firms use the same complex financial instruments and derivatives that arbitragers and speculators use, they argue that companies are endangering their own future by allowing individuals within the organization to gamble with the company's own funds – for profit. And the profit only arises from the ability of the individual to "beat the market." Do you see such consistent performance as likely?

Questions for Debate

1. Multinationals should accept foreign currency risks as part of doing business internationally, and therefore should not spend precious resources and take unnecessary risks related to the use of financial derivatives for hedging. The cure is more harmful than the disease. Why do managers purchase international financial coverage?

2. Multinationals must protect all of their stakeholders – stockholders, creditors, employees, and community – from the risks associated with conducting business in a global marketplace using currencies that bounce up and down in value. Although some hedging techniques may introduce new types of risks for the firm, is it in the entire firm's interest that it hedge significant cash flow risks and add certainty to the conduct of the firm's total business?

INTERNET EXERCISES

1. Although major currencies like the US dollar and the Chinese renminbi dominate the headlines, there are nearly as many currencies as countries in the world. Many of these currencies are traded in extremely thin and highly

regulated markets, making their convertibility suspect. Finding quotations for these currencies is sometimes very difficult. Using some of the web pages listed below, see how many African currency quotes you can find. See Emerging Markets at http://emgmkts.com.

2. Use the *Economist*'s website to find the latest version of the Big Max Index of Currency over and under-valuation. See www.economist.com.

3. The single unobservable variable in currency option pricing is the volatility since volatility inputs are an expected standard deviation of the daily spot rate for the coming period of the option's maturity. Using the following website, pick one currency volatility and research how its value has changed in recent periods over historical periods. See the Philadelphia Stock Exchange at www.phlx.com.

4. Using the following major periodicals as starting points, find a current example of a firm with a substantial operating exposure problem. To aid in your search, you might focus on businesses having major operations in countries with recent currency crises, either through devaluation or major home currency appreciation. Sources are the *Financial Times* at www.ft.com; *the Economist* at www.economist.com; the *Wall Street Journal* at www.wsj.com.

5. In the World Trade Organization's Agreement on Government Procurement, how are offsets defined and what stance is taken toward them (refer to the government procurement page on the website www.wto.org)?

FURTHER RESOURCES

Bekaert, Geert and Hodrick, Robert. (2018). *International Financial Management*, 3rd ed. New York: Cambridge University Press.

Broner, Fernando and Ventura, Jaume. (2016). Rethinking the Effects of Financial Globalization. *The Quarterly Journal of Economics*, 131(3): 1497–1542.

Lewis, Robin J., Villasenor, John D., and West, Darrell M. (2017). *The 2017 Brookings Financial and Digital Inclusion Project Report: Building a Secure and Inclusive Global Financial Ecosystem*. Washington, DC: Center for Technology Innovation, Brookings Institution.

6 Developing and Emerging Markets and Their Integration

LEARNING OBJECTIVES

- To review types of economic integration among countries as industrial trade clusters
- To compare the costs and benefits to advancing economic integration
- To examine how an organization tries to control the price and quantity supplied of a particular commodity
- To evaluate impact of infrastructural challenges in emerging markets on their economic integration as a potential player in the global trade
- To recognize the shift in the approach of developing markets from being free markets to planned economies

CONTENTS

VIGNETTE 6 Organizing trade in Southeast Asia

Economic integration is a liberalization approach that promotes international trade amongst countries by bringing them together regionally for the efficient flow of products, people, and investments. The Commonwealth Preference System, a preferential trade regime of the British Empire, established an economic integration between 48 countries in 1932. Today, international trade organizations like the WTO play an important role in promoting free trade between countries from different regions of the world and reducing barriers to international trade through new trade agreements established during its international conferences known as "rounds" such as the "Doha Round". The creation of various regional clusters like the Association of Southeast Asian Nations (ASEAN) has resulted in free trade between member states with restrictions for the rest of the world (Jones, 2019). Similarly, the European Union (EU) is an example of economic integration that has progressed beyond free trade to the creation of an **economic union** between countries. The EU's use of a common currency with a common monetary and fiscal policy facilitates a common marketplace. This, in turn, increases accessibility and reduces costs to consumers by either reducing or removing trade barriers such as tariffs, non-tariffs, and quotas for companies. Disruptions in supply chain and food supplies amid COVID-19 will create major food shortages, and across all markets prices will differ. However, a number of arguments surround economic integration. The trade creation and diversion of trade post COVID-19 will affect integration on import prices, competition, economies of scale, and factor productivity – and the benefits of regionalism versus nationalism.

Introduction

Growth of transition economies was reported at 5.1% for the period 2000–2009 by the United Nations in 2011. This growth rate was much higher when compared to the average GDP of developed countries, which were growing at 1.3%. Transition economies have been growing since 2009, demonstrating the business potential they offer. These economies include not only Asian countries such as India, China, and Nepal, but also East European countries such as Albania, Kyrgyzstan, and Tajikistan. Branding philosophies, combined with marketing and selling capabilities, help companies from developed markets to build a competitive advantage with superior positioning. This chapter introduces the opportunities and challenges of doing business in emerging, developing, and transitioning economies.

Levels of Economic Integration

The integration of nations into regional economic clusters for trade is generally based on commonalities in culture, history, or politics (Perraton, 2019). Economic cooperation enables policy makers to take advantage of their geography and promote trade across borders with mutual support (Siles-Brügge, 2019). Economic integration of nations eases trade barriers imposed individually by nations and creates new opportunities of trade across their national borders and within the regional cluster. In the Americas, the USA continued its success with NAFTA by implementing CUSMA, or the Canada–United States–Mexico Agreement. MERCOSUR eliminates barriers among Brazil, Argentina, Paraguay, and Uruguay (Veiga & Rios, 2019). ASEAN is increasingly successful in Asia (Jones & Mei, 2019).

Industrial Trade Clusters for Worldwide Free Trade

The **cluster of five** (the USA, UK, France, Germany, and Japan), are the five industrialized nations that meet periodically to achieve a cooperative effort on international economic and monetary issues. The Cluster of Seven, the Cluster of Ten, and the Cluster of Twenty are forums for member nations, created to discuss key issues related to their business in the global economy (Exhibit 6.1). It can also be expanded to encompass the members of the Organization for Economic Cooperation and Development, OECD, which is comprised of 30 countries.

The Cluster of Twenty was prominent in dealing with the economic crisis during 2009. Today, important among the middle-income developing countries are the newly industrialized countries (NICs), which include Singapore, Taiwan, Korea, Hong Kong, Brazil, and Mexico (some propose adding Malaysia and the Philippines to the list as well). Over time, some of these NICs will earn a new acronym, RIC (rapidly industrializing country).

EXHIBIT 6.1 Industrial trade clusters

Trade cluster	Member countries
Cluster of Five	USA, UK, France, Germany, and Japan
The Cluster of Seven	USA, UK, France, Germany, Japan, Italy, and Canada
The Cluster of Ten	USA, UK, France, Germany, Japan, Italy, Canada, Sweden, Netherlands, and Belgium
The Cluster of Twenty	The Cluster of Seven plus Argentina, Australia, Brazil, China, India, Indonesia, Mexico, Russia, Saudi Arabia, South Africa, South Korea, and Turkey

Arguments Surrounding Economic Integration

The creation of regional trade clusters enables companies to achieve greater economies of scale with standardization of products and improve the efficiency of procurement, production, marketing, and sales (Ronquillo, 2017). Opening national borders to businesses from other countries increases competition, making it difficult for local suppliers to charge a premium. Consumers benefit from regional economic integration due to a larger product offering at competitive prices. But companies face ever-intensifying competition within these blocs even as they take advantage of emerging opportunities provided by governments allowing global companies to enter their local competition.

Today, there are an estimated thirty-two economic clusters (i.e., three in Europe, four in the Middle East, five in Asia, and ten each in Africa and the Americas). Regional economic integration in Asia has been driven more by market forces and a need to maintain balance in negotiations with Europe and North America than by treaties (Esty et al., 2017). Broader formal agreements are in formative stages; for example, the Asia Pacific Economic Cooperation (APEC) initiated in 1989 has brought together partners from multiple continents and blocs. APEC members are economic powerhouses, such as China, Japan, South Korea, Taiwan, and the USA. These Pacific Rim countries have successfully created a large free trade zone. Over the past 20 years, Singapore has served as a hub for APEC members, providing critical financial and managerial services to the Southeast Asian markets. Singapore has successfully attracted foreign investment and has served as one of the main gateways for Asian trade. Its exports have reached well over 300% of GDP.

The major oil-exporting countries – the eleven members of the Organization of Petroleum Exporting Countries (OPEC) and countries such as Russia in particular – are dependent on the price of oil for their world market participation. Singapore and BRIC countries (i.e., Brazil, Russia, India, and China) have successfully attracted foreign investments with the establishment of mostly regional corporate headquarters of knowledge-intensive industries. China has been the world's largest exporter of textiles since the 1980s. India's nearly 300 million middle-class consumers may provide the biggest potential market opportunity for marketers in the twenty-first century. The "Next 11" countries like Bangladesh, Egypt, Indonesia, Iran, Korea, Mexico, Nigeria, Pakistan, the Philippines, Turkey, and Vietnam can rival the G7 in time, although they lack the scale of the BRIC countries. Khari Baoli, Asia's largest wholesale food market in India, was devastated in April 2020, when the migrant population from other cities left for their homes due to lockdown over COVID-19 because they feared uncertainty of access to essentials during the lockdown.

In less-developed countries, debt problems and falling commodity prices make market development difficult (Buffie et al., 2018). Africa, the poorest continent, owes the rest of the world $200 billion, an amount equal to three-quarters of its gross domestic product (GDP) and nearly four times its annual exports. Another factor contributing to the challenging situation is that only 1% of the world's private investment goes to sub-Saharan Africa (Africa: The Good News, 2011).

In the former centrally planned economies, capital inflows have been the key to modernizing the newly emerging democracies. Western technology, management, and marketing know-how provide better jobs and put more consumer goods in the shops.

Prospects vary: the future for countries such as Hungary, the Baltics, the Czech Republic, and Poland looks far better than it does for Russia, as they reap the benefits of membership in the EU. The EU Parliament, with 751 members elected by popular vote in their home nations, has the power to veto membership applications and trade agreements with non-EU countries. Clusters of countries may give preferential treatment to other countries on the basis of historical ties or political motivations. Examples include the EU granting preferential access for selected products from their former colonies under the Cotonou Agreement, or similar treatment by the United States of Caribbean nations through the **Caribbean Basin Trade Partnership Act (CBTPA)**, which extended trade preferences to Caribbean countries up to 2020 (US Trade Representative, 2020). Since the benefits are unidirectional, these arrangements are not considered to be part of economic integration.

Regional Clusters

Every regional cluster provides a free trade area, which is the least restrictive and loosest form of economic integration among countries (Baldwin & Venables, 1995). In a **free trade area,** all barriers to trade among member countries are removed. Goods and services are freely traded among member countries of a regional cluster in much the same way that they flow freely between, for example, South Carolina and New York. No discriminatory taxes, quotas, tariffs, or other trade barriers are allowed. Sometimes a free trade area is formed only for certain classes of goods and services. An agricultural free trade area implies the absence of restrictions on the trade of agricultural products only.

The most notable feature of a free trade area is that each country continues to set its own policies in relation to nonmembers. In other words, each member in the regional cluster is free to set any tariffs, quotas, or other restrictions it chooses on trade with countries outside the free trade area. Among such free trade areas, the most notable are the European Free Trade Area (EFTA) and the Canada–United States–Mexico Agreement (CUSMA).

As an example of the freedom members have in terms of their policies toward nonmembers, Mexico has signed a number of bilateral free trade agreements with other blocs (the EU) and nations (Chile) to both improve trade and to attract foreign direct investment. The USA has 14 free trade agreements with 20 countries (Australia, Bahrain, Canada, Chile, Colombia, Costa Rica, Dominican Republic, El Salvador, Guatemala, Honduras, Israel, Jordan, Mexico, Morocco, Nicaragua, Oman, Panama, Peru, Singapore and South Korea) (US Department of State, 2020).

Customs Union

Collaboration among trading countries in which members of a regional cluster dismantle trade barriers among members and establish a common trade policy with respect to nonmembers is called a **customs union**. A customs union is one step further along the spectrum of economic integration, where members dismantle barriers to trade in goods and services among themselves. In addition, a customs union establishes a common trade policy with respect to nonmembers. Typically, this takes the form of a common external tariff, where imports from nonmembers are subject to the same tariff when sold to any member country. Tariff revenues are then shared among members according to a pre-specified formula. The Southern African Customs Union is the oldest (1910) and most successful example of economic integration in Africa.

Common Market

Further along the spectrum of economic integrations is the **common market**, which is a regional cluster of countries that removes all trade barriers among members, establishes a common trade policy with respect to nonmembers, and allows mobility for factors of production: land, labor, capital, and technology. Thus, restrictions on immigration, emigration, and cross-border investment are abolished. The importance of **factor mobility** for economic growth is major. Such mobility can provide very productive uses. Members of a common market must be prepared to cooperate closely in monetary, fiscal, and employment policies. While often beneficial, not all common markets have created wealth.

Economic Union

A true economic union requires integration of economic policies. Member nations surrender their national sovereignty to community-wide institutions like the European Parliament to harmonize monetary policies, taxation, and government spending. Economic integration of the EU has moved beyond the four freedoms and entails today:

- Closer coordination of economic policies to promote exchange rate stability and convergence of inflation and growth rates

- The creation of a European central bank
- The replacement of national monetary authorities by the European Central Bank
- The adoption of the euro as the European (mostly) common currency (even though nations such as Denmark, Hungary, Sweden, and Croatia have not yet adopted the euro).

The Treaty of Nice (February 1, 2003) reformed the institutional structure of the EU to withstand eastward expansion. In addition, moves were made toward a political union with common foreign and security policy, and judicial cooperation. The Lisbon Treaty (December 1, 2009) made an attempt to streamline EU institutions to make the enlarged bloc of 28 states function better (of course, since then, the UK has diminished that number to 27 with its Brexit).

Trade Creation and Trade Diversion

Trade creation is a benefit of economic integration to a particular country when a cluster of countries trade a product freely among themselves, but maintain common barriers to trade with nonmembers. Trade diversion is the cost of economic integration to a particular country when a cluster of countries trade a product freely among themselves, but maintain common barriers to trade with nonmembers. Either negative or positive effects may result when a cluster of countries trade freely among themselves but maintain common barriers to trade with nonmembers. Countries like the USA, Canada, and Japan trade with the EU and suffer the common external tariff.

For example, imports of agricultural products from Spain or the USA had the same tariff of 20% applied to their products. The USA is a lower-cost producer of wheat compared to Spain. US exports to EU members may cost $3.00 per bushel, plus a 20% tariff of $0.60, for a total of $3.60 per bushel. If Spain at the same time produced wheat at $3.20 per bushel, plus a 20% tariff of $0.64 for a total cost to EU customers of $3.84 per bushel, its wheat is more expensive and, therefore, less competitive. However, when Spain joined the EU as a member in 1986, its products were no longer subject to the common external tariffs; Spain had become a member of the "club" and therefore enjoyed its benefits. Now Spain was the low-cost producer of wheat at $3.20 per bushel, compared to the price of $3.60 from the USA. As a result, trade flows changed. The increased export of wheat and other products by Spain to the EU as a result of its membership is termed trade creation. Eliminating the tariff created more trade between Spain and the EU. At the same time, because the USA was outside of the EU, its products suffered a higher price as a result of tariff application. US exports to the EU fell.

When trade creation is distinctly positive – moving toward freer trade and the lower prices for consumers within the EU – the impact of trade diversion becomes negative due to the shift in competitive advantage from the low-cost producer to the high-cost producer. The two major benefits of Spain's membership are that Spanish farmers enjoy greater export sales while EU consumers enjoy lower prices. The two major costs are reduced tariff revenues collected and costs borne by the USA as a result of lost sales. In such cases, the injured party may seek compensation based on global trade rules. On expansion of the EU in 2004, when the Japanese Government argued that its exporters would lose sales of $22 million in the new member countries in product categories such as automobiles and consumer electronics, the EU argued that the Union's expansion would benefit Japanese companies in the long term.

From the perspective of nonmembers, the formation or expansion of a customs union is obviously negative. Most damage goes to countries that rely on trade to build their economies, such as countries of the Third World. From the perspective of members of the customs union, the formation or expansion is only beneficial if the trade creation benefits exceed trade diversion costs.

Import Prices, Competition, Economies of Scale, and Factor Productivity

When a small country imposes a tariff on imports, the price of the goods will typically rise because someone needs to cover the cost of the tariff. This increase in price, in turn, will result in lower demand for imported goods. If a bloc of countries imposes the tariff, the fall in demand for the imported goods will be substantial. The exporting country may then be forced to reduce the price of the goods and cover the tariff. The possibility of lower prices for imports results from the greater market power of the bloc relative to that of a single country. This may result in an improvement in the trade position of the bloc countries. Any gain in the trade position of bloc members, however, is offset by a deteriorating trade position for the exporting country. Unlike the win–win situation resulting from free trade, the scenario involving a trade bloc is instead win–lose. Integration increases market size and therefore may cause a lower degree of monopoly in the production of certain goods and services. This is because a larger market will tend to increase the number of competing firms, resulting in greater efficiency and lower prices for consumers.

Many industries, such as steel and automobiles, require large-scale production to obtain economies of scale in production (Sorge & Streeck, 2018). Therefore, such industries may simply not be economically viable in smaller, trade-protected countries. The formation of a trading bloc enlarges the market so that large-scale production is justified. The lower per-unit costs resulting from scale economies may then be obtained, and are called **internal economies of scale**. This is evident if the region adopts common standards, thus not only allowing for bigger markets for companies but also enabling them to become global powerhouses (see Exhibit 6.2). Ericsson and Nokia both benefited from the EU adopting the Global System for Mobile (GSM) standard for wireless communication to build scale beyond their small domestic markets. The increased usage of new technology, artificial intelligence, and 3D printing capabilities may reduce the importance of economies of scale.

In a common market, external economies of scale with lower production costs resulting from the free mobility of factors of production may also be present. Firms then have access to cheaper capital, more highly skilled labor, and superior technology. These factors can improve the quality of the firm's goods or services, lower costs, or achieve both. In addition to the economic gains from factor mobility, there are other benefits not so easily quantified. Communication across cultures can lead to a higher degree of cross-cultural understanding.

For poor countries, factor mobility may cause the loss of needed investment capital to a richer country, with more profitable opportunities. They also may suffer from loss of capable human resources through brain-drain. Nokia's decision to close a major production facility for mobile devices in Bochum, Germany, and to move its manufacturing to more cost-competitive regions in Europe (such as Cluj in Romania) met with a hailstorm of protests from the German Government and individual citizens.

EXHIBIT: 6.2 List of regional clusters

Cluster	Full name	Member countries
ASEAN	Association of South East Asian Nations	Brunei-Darussalam, Indonesia, Malaysia, Philippines, Singapore, Thailand, Vietnam, Myanmar Laos (Cambodia)
SAARC	South Asian Association for Regional Co-operation	Bangladesh, Bhutan, India, Maldives, Nepal, Pakistan, Sri Lanka
ECO	Economic Co-operation Organisation	Afghanistan, Iran, Kazakhstan, Kyrgyzstan, Pakistan, Tajikistan, Turkmenistan, Uzbekistan, Azerbaijan, Turkey
Baltics	The Baltic States	Estonia, Latvia, Lithuania
GCC	Gulf Co-operation Council	Bahrain, Kuwait, Oman, Qatar, Saudi Arabia, UAE
UMA	Union de Maghreb Arabe	Morocco, Tunisia, Algeria, Libya, Mauritania
ECOWAS	Economic Community of West African States	Benin, Burkina Faso, Cape Verde, Côte d'Ivoire, Gambia, Ghana, Guinea, Guinea-Bissau, Liberia, Mali, Mauritania, Niger, Nigeria, Senegal, Sierra Leone, Togo
ECOWAS	Lake Chad Basin + Nigeria	Central African Republic, Chad, Niger, Zaire

EXHIBIT: 6.2 (Cont.)

Cluster	Full name	Member countries
IGAD	Inter-Governmental Authority on Development	Ethiopia, Kenya, Uganda, Djibouti, Somalia, Eritrea, Sudan
EAC	East African Community	Uganda, Kenya, Tanzania,
SADC	Southern African Development Community	Angola, Botswana, Lesotho, Malawi, Mozambique, Namibia, South Africa, Swaziland, Tanzania, Zambia, Zimbabwe, Mauritius
SEE	South-Eastern Europe	Albania, Greece, Romania, Macedonia, Bosnia-Herzegovina, Croatia, Yugoslavia, Slovenia.
ANDEAN	ANDEAN Community	Bolivia, Columbia, Ecuador, Peru
CARICOM	Caribbean Community	Antigua and Barbuda, Belize, Dominica, Gernada, Haiti, Montserrat, St. Kitts and Nevis, St. Lucia, St. Vincent and the Grenadines, Bahamas, Barbados, Guyana, Jamaica, Suriname, Trinidad and Tobago
MERCOSUR	Mercado Comun del Sur	Argentina, Brazil, Paraguay, Uruguay, Venezuela

Several cooperative treaties and coalitions, such as The European Coal and Steel Community (Montan Union) in 1951 and the European Economic Community (EEC) established by the Treaty of Rome in 1957, contributed to the development of regional clusters. The EEC envisioned that the successful integration of the European economies would result in an economic power to rival that of the USA. Some countries were reluctant to embrace the ambitious integrative efforts of the Treaty of Rome. In 1960, a looser, less integrated philosophy was endorsed with the formation of the European Free Trade Association (EFTA) by eight countries: the United Kingdom, Norway, Denmark, Sweden, Austria, Finland, Portugal, and Switzerland. Barriers to trade among member countries were dismantled, although each country maintained its own policies with nonmember states. Because all but Norway, Switzerland, and newer members Iceland and Liechtenstein have joined or plan to join the EU, EFTA has lost much of its significance. Since 1994, the European Economic Area (EEA) agreement between the EU and three EFTA countries allows these EFTA countries to participate in the European Single Market without joining the EU. Swiss–EU bilateral agreements link Switzerland to the EU with its own special content.

The most important benefit of the four freedoms anticipated for Europe was regional economic growth resulting from the elimination of border-crossing transaction costs. Second, economic growth in the region was to benefit from economies of scale. Third, there were to be gains from more intense competition among EU companies. The Euro was expected to add efficiency as well.

These expectations in general have worked out. Today, countries in Europe enjoy cheaper transaction costs, reduced currency risks, growing price transparency, and increased price-based competition. Today, there is a substantial benefit to firms already operating in Europe. They gain from integration because operating in one country lets them expand freely into others. A borderless Europe gives its firms access to 505 million consumers. The free movement of capital allows the firms to sell securities, raise capital, and recruit labor throughout Europe.

Progress toward the goal of free movement was largely achieved through the shift from a "common standards approach" to a "mutual recognition approach" between different member nations (see Exhibit 6.2). Under the common standards approach, EU members negotiated specifications for literally thousands of products, often unsuccessfully. For example, because of differences in tastes, an agreement was never reached on specifications for beer, sausage, or mayonnaise. Under the mutual recognition approach, the laborious quest for common standards is, in most cases, no longer necessary. Instead, as long as a product meets legal and specification requirements in one member country, it may be freely exported to any other, and customers serve as the final arbiters of success.

The primary difficulty that EU members have faced is being unable to agree on a common immigration policy. Some countries – notably Germany – have had relatively lax immigration policies, while others – especially those with higher unemployment rates – favor strict controls. A second issue concerning the free movement of people between different member nations is the acceptability of professional certifications across countries. Since 1993, workers' professional qualifications are recognized throughout the EU, guaranteeing them equal treatment in terms of employment, working conditions, and social protection in the host country.

Attaining free movement of capital requires that citizens be free to trade in EU currencies without restrictions. Second, the regulations governing banks and other financial institutions were harmonized. In addition, mergers and acquisitions are regulated by the EU rather than by national governments. Finally, securities would be freely tradable across countries. A key aspect of free trade in services is the right to compete fairly to obtain government contracts. Under the guidelines, a government should not give preference to its own citizens in awarding government contracts. Little progress has been made in this regard. Public procurement accounts for 10 to 25% of world trade but is mostly restricted to national companies.

Another source of difficulty that intensified in the 1980s and continues today is the administration of the community's common agricultural policy (CAP). Most industrialized countries, including the USA, Canada, and Japan, have adopted wide-scale government intervention and subsidization schemes for agriculture. The EU, however, has implemented these policies on a community-wide, rather than national, level. The CAP includes (1) a price-support system, whereby EU agriculture officials intervene in the market to keep farm product prices within a specified range; (2) direct subsidies to farmers; and (3) provides rebates to farmers who export or agree to store farm products rather than sell them within the community. The implementation of these policies absorbed about 34.5% of the annual EU budget in 2020 (European Parliament, 2020). The CAP has caused problems both within the EU and in relationships with nonmembers. Within the EU, the richer, more industrialized countries resent the extensive subsidization of the more agrarian economies. Outside trading partners, especially the USA, have repeatedly charged the EU with unfair trade practices in agriculture. Exhibit 6.3 looks at the Belt and Road initiative that is an effort to fix similar issues along the Silk Road Economic Belt.

EXHIBIT 6.3 Clusters and their member countries

The Belt and Road Initiative (BRI) is an ambitious effort to improve regional co-operation and connectivity on a trans-continental scale. The initiative aims to strengthen infrastructure, trade, and investment links between China and some 65 other countries that account collectively for over 30% of global GDP, 62% of population, and 75% of known energy reserves. The BRI consists primarily of the Silk Road Economic Belt, linking China to Central and South Asia and onward to Europe, and the New Maritime Silk Road, linking China to the nations of South East Asia, the Gulf Countries, and North Africa. Six other economic corridors have been identified to link other countries to the Belt and the Road. The scope of the initiative is still taking shape – more recently, the initiative has been interpreted to be open to all countries as well as international and regional organizations. The Belt and Road Initiative can transform the economic environment in which economies in the region operate. Regional cooperation on the new and improved transport infrastructure and policy reforms could substantially reduce trade costs and improve connectivity, leading to higher cross-border trade and investment and improved growth in the region.

The Belt and Road Initiative includes 1/3 of world trade and GDP and over 60% of the world's population

Source: World Bank, 2019; World Bank, n.d.

Cartels and Commodity Price Agreements

An important characteristic that distinguishes developing countries from industrialized countries is the nature of their export earnings. While industrialized countries rely heavily on the export of manufactured goods, technology, and services, the developing countries rely chiefly on the export of primary products and raw materials – for example, copper, iron ore, and agricultural products. This distinction is important for several reasons. First, the level of price competition is higher among sellers of primary goods because of the typically larger number of sellers and also because primary goods are homogeneous. For example, there are only three or four countries that are competitive forces in the technology product manufacturing market, whereas there are at least a dozen countries that compete in the sale of copper. Furthermore, while goods differentiation and therefore brand loyalty are likely to exist in the technology products market, buyers of copper are likely to purchase on the basis of price alone. A second distinguishing factor is that supply variability will be greater in the market for primary goods because production often depends on uncontrollable factors such as weather.

Responses to this problem have included cartels and commodity price agreements. A cartel is an association of producers of a particular good, such as

OPEC, which consists of 12 oil producing and exporting countries, such as Iran, Iraq, Saudi Arabia, and United Arab Emirates. This group, together with the USA and Russia, is very important in setting global oil prices and delivery terms.

The objective of a cartel is to suppress market forces to gain greater control over sales revenues. A cartel may accomplish this objective in several ways like price-fixing, which entails an agreement by producers to sell at a certain price, eliminating price competition among sellers. A cartel may allocate sales territories among its members, again suppressing competition. Another tactic calls for members to agree to restrict production, and therefore supplies, resulting in higher prices.

OPEC has had its challenges. Not all oil-producing countries are members of OPEC. Current OPEC members account for about 40 percent of world oil production and about two-thirds of the world's proven oil reserves. The cohesiveness of members in a cartel may vary. Sales have occurred at less-than-agreed-upon prices, and production quotas have been violated. It is also difficult to balance the market's tolerance for high prices, the impact of price changes on suppliers and consumers, and the need for oil revenues to support member-countries' domestic spending programs.

International **commodity price agreements** involve both buyers and sellers in an agreement to manage the price of a commodity (Jacobs & Horster, 2020; Arora, 2017). Often, the free market is allowed to determine the price of the commodity over a predetermined range (Bolling, 2019; Czinkota & Enke, 2014). However, if supply-and-demand pressures cause the commodity's price to move outside that range, a manager will enter the market to buy or sell the commodity to bring the price back into the range. The manager controls the **buffer stock** of the commodity, which is the stock of a commodity kept on hand to prevent a shortage in times of unexpected demand. If prices float downward, the manager purchases the commodity and adds to the buffer stock. Under upward pressure, the manager sells the commodity from the buffer stock. This system is analogous to a managed exchange rate system, in which authorities buy and sell to influence exchange rates. International commodity agreements are currently in effect for sugar, tin, rubber, cocoa, and coffee.

Emerging Markets

Emerging markets are newly industrialized countries with low income but high prospects of growth. Stakeholders in emerging markets attempt to raise the performance of their economy to the level achieved by the world's more advanced nations. Improved economies have witnessed higher income levels and better standards of living, more exports, increased foreign direct investment, and more stable political structures.

The major emerging markets are Africa, the Middle East, Latin America, and the Caribbean. Russia and the countries of the former Soviet Union are often categorized as markets in transition from centrally planned economies to market-oriented economies (Czinkota, 1997). The biggest emerging markets display the factors that make them strategically important: favorable consumer demographics, rising household incomes, increasing availability of credit, and increasing productivity.

When combined with a pattern of accelerated development, large populations make countries strategically attractive to companies. A key group often considered by investors are the so called BRICS nations, referring to Brazil, Russia, China, and South Africa. Today, China and India are the most populous countries in the world, followed by the USA, Indonesia, and Brazil. Businesses are increasingly looking to emerging markets for sources of growth and competitive advantage, as parts of the developing world have outpaced developed countries in economic growth. The growing demand for industrial products that promise quality at a reasonable price to a rising consumer class in countries such as Brazil. Russia, India, China, and Indonesia present opportunities for global businesses to realize more robust, long-term performance than in mature markets.

Serving low-income BOP consumers in emerging markets using international trade models will not only serve their needs with high quality, low priced products but also improve the quality of life of people living with limited means in this segment. The BOP segment within emerging markets is divided into urban and rural categories, of which urban markets are being served successfully, but consumers in rural markets are not. Although spending of consumers in urban versus rural areas differs drastically from country to country, various Fast Moving Consumer Goods (FMCG) companies like Unilever have successfully penetrated the BOP segment in both urban and rural areas using competitive pricing and innovative packaging.

Economic Growth of China

A major key to the phenomenal economic growth of China was its rapid transformation from a largely agrarian socialist state to an export-driven platform for global manufacturing (Exhibit 6.4). When China's leader, Deng Xiao Ping began the liberalization of his country in 1979, he famously said: "Poverty is not socialism" (China Daily, 2014). Deng opened the doors to Chinese participation in capitalism and encouraged international companies to invest in China. Much of the early investment by international firms capitalized on inexpensive factors of production, particularly low-cost labor. Over time, the Chinese production platform increased its attractiveness through improved production facilities, infrastructure, access to ports, and skilled labor. China's huge population has provided companies with a large pool of low-wage workers and a set of new customers, which enables mass-market factories to produce both for the export market and for the growing Chinese market. Rapid economic development and rising standards of living in China, along with the rise of new, lower-cost production platforms in countries like India, Indonesia, Malaysia, Vietnam, and Bangladesh, has made Asia a new international marketplace. Exhibit 6.5 provides some detail.

Economic Growth of India

In the middle of a currency crisis and shortly after the assassination of Prime Minister Rajiv Gandhi in 1991, India initiated a series of economic reform measures

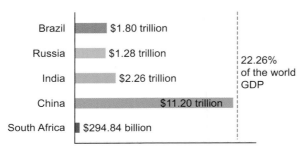

Exhibit 6.4 2016 GDP of BRICS members

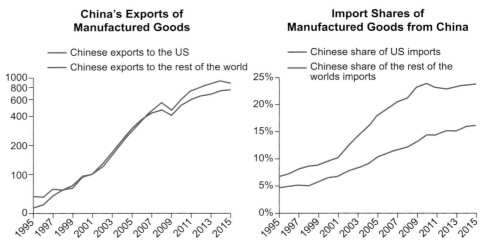

Exhibit 6.5 China's rapid economic growth
Source : Amiti, Dai, Feenstra, and Romalis, 2017.

that propelled India from a long stagnation into sustained economic growth and participation in the global economy. Today, India's economy has grown, but differently from China. Indian economic growth focuses on its domestic economy and the service sector rather than export-oriented manufacturing.

Economic Growth of Brazil

Brazil has not experienced the economic growth rate similar to India and China in the first decade of the twenty-first century. Brazil grew consistently and steadily in the range of 3.9 to 5% due to President Lula da Silva's implementation of economic liberalization policies and the avoidance of inflation problems. Because of its history of alternating between economic disciplines and more interventionist policies, plus a succession of economic crises, many observers have been cautious in assessing Brazil's ability to continue to grow. However, Brazil's economic performance in 2008 demonstrated great resiliency in the midst of the recession, and international companies show increased interest in doing business there. UNCTAD World Investment Prospects Survey identified Brazil as the fourth most attractive country for foreign direct investment. Many Brazilian companies are already competing at the highest level in international business. Embraer, the Brazilian aircraft manufacturer, is one of the largest companies in the world aircraft industry and one of Brazil's leading exporters. Exhibit 6.6 looks deeper into the emergence of BRICs countries.

EXHIBIT 6.6 BRICS

Emerging economies have not only made great contributions to the global economy in terms of growth, but have also been successful in promoting the growth of international trade. According to estimates by the World Trade Organization, from 2000 to 2015, imports from developing countries increased from 27% of world trade to 41%, and exports increased from 30% to 43%. In 2005, developing countries contributed 24% of global service exports. In 2015, this figure was 39.4%. Goldman Sachs predicts that by 2050, the top five economies would be composed of the BRICS countries and the USA.

In recent years, BRICS have taken an ever-increasing share of global economic growth. According to estimates by the International Monetary Fund, the contribution of the BRIC countries to global economic growth was about 60% in 2016. The World Bank reported that GDP of BRICS increased from 11.8 to 22.3% of the world GDP.

Emerging economies have enormous needs for infrastructure, consumption, and services. Emerging economies have better demographics, are more open-minded, are more willing to participate actively in international cooperation, and are more ready to build coordination mechanisms (Kingiri & Fu, 2020).
Source: Yifan, 2018.

Barriers to Business

Despite their attractiveness to business, the large emerging markets are difficult places to conduct business. Internet service companies confront ongoing problems in China, where that country's authorities conduct extensive filtering of content they consider to be objectionable for political, social, or religious reasons. Intellectual property rights protection remains a serious issue in China, Brazil, and India. The problem is so serious that companies must approach these markets very carefully, and some have even chosen not to compete in them.

Foreign companies can sometimes be subject to capricious government actions at the national or local levels. In 2006, India's Kerala province banned Pepsi and Coca-Cola products in state schools, hospitals, and other buildings after a study was released showing that the products contained high levels of pesticides. An Indian court quickly lifted the ban after finding scientific inconsistencies in the study.

Some barriers to entry come in traditional tariff structures. India maintains tariffs on American wine, which, when combined at the federal and provincial levels, can amount to 400% tax. A significant challenge to international companies in emerging markets is the lack of infrastructure (Aksoy et al., 2020). Poor roads, outdated port facilities, the lack of refrigeration capacity, and inefficient distribution systems make it difficult to bring products to the marketplace. Special packaging is required to prevent deterioration of products in situations with high variations in temperature and inadequate storage. Market intermediaries often do not exist, and significant amounts of retail sales are made through relatively informal distribution channels like kiosks. Payments and funds-transfer systems are often inadequate. Infrastructure varies among the major emerging markets. China continues the construction and modernization of cities, highways, ports, and airports across the country.

India requires significant investment to make its market more competitive globally. Its highways, energy, telecommunications and infrastructure investments, such as the Golden Quadrilateral (GQ), a 3,633-mile expressway between the country's major population centers of Delhi, Mumbai, Chennai, and Kolkata, have made an important economic difference.

Transition Economies

Since the end of the Soviet Union, enormous change has occurred throughout central and eastern Europe as the new nations that emerged underwent a process of transition from central planning to market orientation. With the expansion of the EU eastward and the embrace of market economics by the majority of central and eastern European countries, established trading patterns shifted as many of these countries looked westward for business. During the time of the Soviet bloc (i.e., 1927 to 1991), trade took place within the political organization.

The major economies that remain in transition are Russia and Ukraine, along with smaller economies such as Armenia, Croatia, and the new countries of Central Asia. In many of these countries, privatization is ongoing, and the increasing transition of economic activity from government ownership to private ownership presents new opportunities for trade and investment.

The announcement of an intention or commitment to change does not automatically result in change itself. For example, the abolition of a centrally planned economy does not create a market economy. Laws permitting the emergence of private-sector entrepreneurs do not create entrepreneurship. The reduction of price controls may not immediately make goods available or affordable. Deeply ingrained systemic differences between the transition economies and Western firms continue. Highly prized, fully accepted fundamentals of the market economy – such as the reliance on competition, support of the profit motive, and the willingness to live with risk on a corporate and personal level – are not yet fully accepted. Major changes still need to take place. In addition, issues of corruption, gang activities, and counterfeiting continue to present Western businesses with serious challenges. Distribution channels and pricing structures are still evolving, and information about demand and channel supply can often be frustratingly limited.

Access to Financial Services in India

Programs in **microfinance** have allowed consumers, with no property as collateral, to borrow sums averaging $100 for purchases. Retail banking services are available to them. Lenders such as Grameen Bank in Bangladesh and Compartamos in Mexico have helped millions of families escape poverty.

In the product area, companies must combine advanced technology with local insights. Hindustan Lever, now part of Unilever in India learned that low-income Indians were forced to settle for low-quality products. They wanted to buy high-end detergents and personal care products but could not afford them in the quantities available. In response, the company developed extremely low-cost packaging material and small sized packaging that allowed for a product to be priced in pennies.

In Bangladesh, Grameen Phone Ltd. leases access to wireless phones to villagers. Every phone is used by an average of 100 people and generates $90 in revenue a month – up to three times the revenues generated by wealthier users who own their phones in urban areas.

The biggest challenges in developing markets are in providing essential services. Developing markets can be ideal settings for commercial and technological innovation. Global marketers often can make a realistic difference in solving some problems. Developing new technologies or products can require knowledge transfer from one market to another.

The emergence of these markets presents a great growth opportunity for companies. It also creates a chance for business, government, and civil society to join together in a common cause to help the aspiring poor to join the world economy. Lifting billions of people from poverty may help avert social decay, political chaos, terrorism, and environmental deterioration. For example, Coca-Cola has introduced "Project Mission" in Botswana to launch a drink to combat anemia, blindness, and other afflictions common in poorer parts of the world. The drink, called Vitango, contains 12 vitamins and minerals chronically lacking in personal diets.

Economic Integration and the International Manager

Economic integration simultaneously creates opportunities and challenges for the international manager. Harmonization efforts may result in standardized regulations, which can positively affect production and marketing efforts. Decisions regarding integrating markets must be assessed from four perspectives: the range and impact of changes resulting from integration, development of strategies to relate to these changes, organizational changes needed to exploit these changes, and strategies to nudge change in a more favorable direction.

Managing Change with Strategic Planning

First is to create a vision of the outcome of change. The international manager must take into consideration the change readiness within the markets themselves. That is, governments and other stakeholders, such as labor unions, may oppose the liberalization of competition, especially where national champions such as airlines, automobiles, energy, and telecommunications are concerned.

The international manager will have to develop a strategic response to the new environment to maintain a sustainable long-term competitive advantage. Those companies already present in an integrating market should fill in gaps in goods and market portfolios through acquisitions or alliances to create a regional or global company. Regional presence alone is not sufficient for success. In the future, important industrial sectors like telecom and retail will be dominated by two or three giants, leaving room only for niche players. Those with weak or no presence at all will have to create alliances for market entry.

SUMMARY

Economic integration involves agreements among countries to establish links for the movement of goods, services, and factors of production across borders. The strength of these links depends on the success of integration. Levels of integration include the free trade area, customs union, common market, and full economic union. The benefits derived from economic integration include trade creation, economies of scale, improved terms of trade, the reduction of monopoly power, and improved cross-cultural communication. However, a number of disadvantages may also exist. Most important, economic integration may work to the detriment of nonmembers by causing deteriorating terms of trade and trade diversion. No guarantee exists that all members will share the gains from integration.

Businesses are increasingly looking to emerging markets for sources of growth and developing competitive advantage because parts of the developing world have outpaced the developed countries in economic growth in the twenty-first century. With their large population base and records of economic growth, China, India, and Brazil continue to attract the attention of international businesses. Emerging markets also present the international managers with barriers to market entry in the form of restrictions on foreign investment. There are also programs that favor domestic companies, vague regulations, burdensome port and customs procedures, high-tariff barriers, and insufficient protection for intellectual property rights. Lack of infrastructure development can present international managers with significant challenges in bringing products and services to emerging markets. In transition markets like Russia, the international manager must develop strategies to succeed with deeply ingrained systemic differences between the transition economies and Western firms. Developing markets, where poverty still remains a large problem, may demand focus and goodwill, but offer important present and future opportunities for the strategic manager.

DISCUSSION QUESTIONS

1. Explain the advantages and disadvantages of economic integration in relation to challenges faced by emerging markets.
2. How can economic blocs be linked with worldwide free trade?
3. In addition to Brazil, Russia, India, and China, identify three other emerging markets that make sense for international business growth. Why do they qualify as emerging markets?

4. What are the advantages and disadvantages of serving the BOP segment in countries like India?
5. How can the WTO facilitate economic integration, considering that the biggest impediment to economic integration is the reluctance of nations to surrender a measure of their autonomy?

KEY TERMS

buffer stock	158	economic union	146
Caribbean Basin Trade Partnership Agreement (CBTPA)	149	emerging markets	158
		external economies of scale	153
cartel	157	factor mobility	150
central bank	151	free trade area	149
commodity price agreements	158	internal economies of scale	152
common agricultural policy (CAP)	156	political union	151
common market	150	trade creation	151
Cluster of Five	147	trade diversion	151
customs union	150	Treaty of Rome	154

TAKE A STAND

China: A manufacturing leader

The effects of pollution evident in the current climate of China are not only affecting its agriculture but also the everyday life of its citizens owing to high temperatures. The Massachusetts Institute of Technology (MIT) recently reported that by the end of this century, China could face deadly heat waves due to climate change. The effects of climate greenhouse gases can be noticed by a decrease in frozen areas towards Northwest China.

INTERNET EXERCISES

1. Compare and contrast two different markets for expanding trade by accessing the website of the Indian Chamber of Commerce, an industry coalition promoting world markets (www.indianchamber.org), and the China Chamber of Commerce (www.indianchamber.org).
2. Alibaba.com (www.alibaba.com) is a business-to-business e-commerce company. It operates two marketplaces: the first is an international marketplace based in English, tailored to global importers and exporters in China; the second is a Chinese marketplace that focuses on suppliers and buyers trading domestically in China. Suggest a policy for the company trying to operate in both capacities.

FURTHER RESOURCES

Bekaert, G. (1995). Market integration and investment barriers in emerging equity markets. The World Bank Economic Review,9(1), 75–107.

García-Herrero, A. and Wooldridge, P. D. (2007). Global and regional financial integration: progress in emerging markets. BIS Quarterly Review, September.

Meyer, K. E. and Su, Y. S. (2015). Integration and responsiveness in subsidiaries in emerging economies. Journal of World Business,50(1), 149–158.

Rottig, D. and de Oliveira, R. T. (2019). International expansion of Chinese emerging market multinational corporations to developed markets: a qualitative analysis of post-acquisition and integration strategies. In Chinese Acquisitions in Developed Countries. Cham, Switzerland: Springer, pp. 37–53.

Song, W., Park, S. Y., and Ryu, D. (2018). Dynamic conditional relationships between developed and emerging markets. Physica A: Statistical Mechanics and its Applications,507, 534–543.

Worldbank (2017). Available at https://datatopics.worldbank.org/world-development-indicators/stories/services-drive-economic-growth.html

7 Building Data and Knowledge

LEARNING OBJECTIVES

- Gain an understanding of the need for research
- Explore the differences between domestic and international research
- Learn where to find and how to use sources of secondary information
- Gain insight into the gathering of primary data
- Examine the need for international management information systems
- Examine the role and importance of international information systems for corporate decision processes and strategic planning

CONTENTS

VIGNETTE 7 Apple: Researching the Chinese marketplace

Apple was founded in 1976 in California. The firm's annual revenues exceed $270 million, making Apple the world's third-largest mobile phone manufacturer, after Samsung and Huawei. The iPhone represents more than 60 percent of Apple's total sales. The firm's two top markets are the USA and China, and management continuously aims to make Apple the world leader in smartphone sales.

In 2017, Apple launched the iPhone 8 in India. India's population at that time, at about 1.38 billion people, was poised to surpass China as the world's most populous country. Apple was especially anxious to launch new iPhones in India because markets in the advanced economies – in North America, Europe, and Japan – were becoming saturated, and market growth was slowing in China. Although India's per capita income of $8,000 per year was lower than that of China, the Indian economy was growing as about 7 percent annually.

Research undertaken by Apple revealed that India was already home to about 20 percent of the world's mobile phone subscribers and had become the fastest-growing market for mobiles. Apple researchers learned that India was about to experience a major surge in smartphone growth due to numerous key factors:

- *Many non-users*. The number of mobile phone users had reached 700 million, but only about 300 million Indians owned smartphones.
- *Large young population*. More than 40 percent of India's population is comprised of people under age 20. Some 20 percent of the population were 15–24 years old, a key segment for smartphone sales.
- *Internet usage patterns*. More than 500 million Indians use the Internet, and most of them rely solely on their mobile phones to go online.
- *Surging demand for apps and games*. The market for apps and games that can be played on a smartphone was growing rapidly, often more than 50 percent per year.

Apple researchers also discovered numerous emergent challenges in the Indian market. First was the problem of growing competition, and numerous Indian and Chinese smartphone brands had already entered the market. Second, India is characterized by enormous linguistic and cultural diversity. Some 30 languages are spoken by at least one million Indians, and researchers concluded that Apple would need to offer smartphones in most of these languages, as well as numerous local dialects. Some features would need to be adapted to suit cultural differences. Third, research revealed that most mobile phone users in India had already acquired a preference for Android phones. Apple would need to devise market strategies to promote iPhones, which use the iOS operating system. Finally, research revealed the Indian Government had imposed trade barriers on the smartphone market, including local content rules that required some smartphone manufacturing directly in India.

Perhaps the most pressing challenge facing Apple was deciding on appropriate pricing for iPhones. Given lower income levels, researchers discovered they would need to conduct surveys and focus groups to more precisely define the most appropriate iPhone pricing for the market. Apple also would need to gather more data to define the nature of the market opportunity in India more clearly. For example, what types of advertising and sales would be most appropriate? What types of outlets would be best suited for selling and distributing smartphones? What approaches would be needed to provide technical support? India is characterized by varying levels of infrastructure and education level. Such challenges would necessitate innovative approaches to international business research. What are your suggestions?

Sources: Mobile Ecosystem Forum, 2016 ; Dahad, 2018; United States Commercial Service, 2018; Gartenberg, 2018; CountryWatch, 2018; Central Intelligence Agency, 2019; Iyengar, 2019; Khan, 2017; Purnell and Purnell 2018.

Introduction

The most important cause of failure in international business is insufficient preparation and information. The failure of managers to comprehend cultural disparities, the failure to remember that customers differ from country to country, and the lack of investigation into whether or not a market exists prior to market entry have made international business a high-risk activity. International business research is therefore instrumental to international business success because it permits the firm to take into account different environments, attitudes, and market conditions. Fortunately, such research has become less complicated. As Vignette 7 shows, information from around the globe can be obtained quite easily.

This chapter discusses data collection and provides a comprehensive overview of how to obtain general screening information on international markets, evaluate business potential, and assess current or potential opportunities and problems. Data sources that are low cost and that take little time to accumulate – in short, secondary data – are considered first. The balance of the chapter is devoted to more sophisticated forms of international research, including primary data collection and the development of an information system.

International and Domestic Research

The tools and techniques of international research are the same as those of domestic research. The difference is in the environment to which the tools are applied. The environment determines how well the tools, techniques, and concepts work. Although the objectives of research may be the same, the execution of international research may differ substantially from that of domestic research. The four primary reasons for this difference are new parameters, new environmental factors, an increase in the number of factors involved, and a broader definition of competition.

New Environment

When going international, a firm is exposed to an unfamiliar environment. Many of the domestic assumptions on which the firm and its activities were founded may not hold true internationally. Management needs to learn the culture of the host country, understand its political systems and level of stability, and comprehend the existing differences in societal structures and language. In addition, it must understand pertinent legal issues in order to avoid violating local laws. The technological level of the society must also be incorporated in the business plan. In short, all the assumptions that were formulated over the years – often referred to as heuristics based on domestic business activities must now be reevaluated. This crucial point is often neglected because most managers are born in the environment of their domestic operations and only subconsciously learn to understand the constraints and opportunities of their business activities. The situation is analogous to learning one's native language. Being born to a language makes speaking it seem easy. Only when attempting to learn a foreign language does one begin to appreciate the structure of language and the need for grammatical rules.

Broader Definition of Competition

The international market exposes the firm to a much greater variety of competition than that found in the home market. For example, a firm may find that ketchup competes against soy sauce. Similarly, firms that offer labor-saving devices domestically may encounter competition abroad from cheap manual labor. Therefore, firms must determine the breadth of the competition, track competitive activities, and evaluate their actual and potential impact on company operations on an ongoing basis (Chandra, 2017).

Recognizing The Need for International Research

Many firms do little research before they enter a foreign market. Often, decisions concerning entry and expansion in overseas markets and selection and appointment of distributors are made after a cursory, subjective assessment of the situation. The research done is often less rigorous, less formal, and less quantitative than for domestic activities.

A major reason managers hesitate to do international research is their lack of sensitivity to differences in culture, consumer tastes, and market demands. Often managers assume that their methods are both best and acceptable to all others. Often managers are insufficiently informed about the effect of geographic boundaries and do not understand that even national boundaries need not always coincide with culturally homogenous societies. In addition, they are not prepared to accept that labor rules, distribution systems, the availability of media, or advertising regulations may be entirely different from those in the home market. Because of pressure to satisfy short-term financial goals, managers are unwilling to spend money to find out about the differences.

Managers are often unfamiliar with national and international data sources, or lack the ability to use international data once obtained. They may believe that gathering and analyzing international data is costly, in terms of time and money, and therefore not worth the investment. The Internet makes international research much easier and less expensive. It takes just one Google search, for example, to find out what typical Japanese customers eat for breakfast.

Despite managerial reservations, research is as important internationally as it is domestically. Firms must learn where the opportunities are, what customers want, why they want it, and how they satisfy their needs and wants so that the firm can serve them efficiently. Firms must obtain information about the local infrastructure, labor market, and tax rules before making a plant location decision. Doing business abroad without the benefit of research places firms, their assets, and their entire international future at risk.

Research allows management to identify and develop international strategies. The task includes the identification, evaluation, and comparison of potential foreign business opportunities and the subsequent target market selection. In addition, research is necessary for the development of a business plan that identifies all the requirements necessary for market entry, market penetration, and expansion. If obtained insights are tracked and compared, research can provide the feedback needed to fine-tune various business activities. Finally, research can provide management with the intelligence to help anticipate events, take appropriate action, and adequately prepare for global changes (Beall, 2017).

Determining Research Objectives

As a starting point for research, research objectives must be determined. They will vary depending on the views of management, the corporate mission of the firm, the firm's level of internationalization, and its competitive situation. These objectives must be embedded in a firm's internal level of readiness to participate in the global market. A review of corporate capabilities such as personnel resources and the degree of financial exposure and risk that the firm is willing and able to tolerate also needs to be conducted. Existing diagnostic tools can be used to compare a firm's current preparedness on a broad-based level. Knowing its internal readiness, the firm can then pursue its objectives with more confidence.

Going International – Exporting

A frequent objective of international research is that of foreign market opportunity analysis, which refers to broad-based research to obtain information about the general variables of a target market outside a firm's home country. When a firm launches its international activities, it will usually find the world to be uncharted territory. Fortunately, information can be accumulated to provide basic guidelines. The aim is not to conduct a painstaking and detailed analysis of the world on a market-by-market basis, but instead to utilize a broad-brush approach. Accomplished quickly and at a low cost, this approach will narrow the possibilities for international business activities.

Such an approach should begin with a cursory analysis of general variables of a country, including total and per capita GDP, mortality rates, and population figures. Although these factors in themselves will not provide any detailed information, they will enable the researcher to determine whether corporate objectives might be met in the market. For example, the offering of computer software services may be of little value to some countries if they have a low rate of computer usage. Similarly, luxury consumer products may not succeed in Tajikistan because most consumers have relatively lower incomes and less purchasing power. Such a cursory evaluation will help reduce the markets to be considered to a more manageable number – for example, from 200 to 20.

As a next step, the researcher will require information on each individual country for a preliminary evaluation. Information will highlight the fastest growing markets, the largest markets for a particular category of product or service, demand trends, and business restrictions. Although precise and detailed information on individual products may not be obtainable, information is available for general product categories or service industries. Again, this overview will be cursory but will serve to quickly evaluate and compare markets.

At this stage, the researcher must select appropriate markets for in-depth evaluation. The focus will now be on opportunities for a specific type of service, product, or brand, and will include an assessment as to whether demand already exists or can be stimulated. Even though aggregate industry data may have been obtained previously, this general information is insufficient to make company-specific decisions. For example, the demand for sports equipment should not be confused with the potential demand for a specific brand. The research now should identify demand and supply patterns and evaluate any regulations and standards. Finally, a competitive assessment needs to be made. Such an assessment is a research process that consists of matching markets to corporate strengths and providing an analysis of the best potential for specific offerings. A summary of the various stages in the determination of market potential is provided in Exhibit 7.1 (Beall, 2017; Burns et al., 2017; Central Intelligence Agency, 2019; Chandra, 2017; World Bank, 2018).

Going International – Importing

When importing, the major focus shifts from supplying to sourcing. Management must identify markets that produce supplies or materials desired or have the potential to do so. Foreign firms must be evaluated in terms of their capabilities and competitive standing.

Just as management would want to have some details on a domestic supplier, the importer needs to know, for example, about the reliability of a foreign supplier, the consistency of its product or service quality, and the length of delivery time. Information obtained through the subsidiary office of a bank or an embassy can prove very helpful. Information from business rating services and recommendations from current customers are also very useful in evaluating the potential business partner.

In addition, foreign government rules must be scrutinized as to whether exportation from the source country is possible. As examples, India may set limits on the cobra handbags it allows to be exported, and laws protecting a nation's cultural heritage may prevent the exportation of pre-Columbian artifacts from Latin American countries.

The international manager must also analyze domestic restrictions and legislation that may prohibit the importation of certain goods into the home country.

EXHIBIT 7.1 Key questions to address in researching international market potential

Stage	Key activity	Key question
(1)	Screen for the most attractive country markets	What foreign markets warrant detailed research?
(2)	Assess industry market potential	What is the aggregate demand in each market?
(3)	Assess company-level sales potential	How much demand exists for the products and services of our firm?
(4)	Determine available bases for segmentation	How much debt can the availability of big data provide?

Even though a market may exist at home for foreign umbrella handles, for example, quotas may restrict their importation to protect domestic industries. Similarly, even though domestic demand may exist for ivory, its importation may be illegal because of global legislation enacted to protect wildlife worldwide.

Market Expansion

Research objectives include obtaining more detailed information for business expansion or monitoring the political climate so that the firm can successfully maintain its international operation. Information may be needed to enable the international manager to evaluate new business partners or assess the impact of a technological breakthrough on future business operations. The better defined the research objective is, the better the researcher will be able to determine information requirements and thus conserve the time and financial resources of the firm (Beall, 2017; Burns et al., 2017; Hague et al., 2016).

Conducting Secondary Research

Finding and analyzing secondary data is a critical first step in international business research. Initially, let's examine the challenge of identifying sources of data. Then we will delve into selecting the most appropriate data from secondary sources, as well as interpreting and analyzing secondary data. We will then review contemporary phenomena – big data and data privacy.

Sources of Data

Typically, the information requirements of firms will cover both macro information about countries and trade, as well as micro information specific to the firm's activities. Exhibit 7.2 provides an overview of the types of information that are most crucial for international business executives. If each firm had to go out and collect all the information needed on-site in the country under scrutiny, the task would be unwieldy and far too expensive. On many occasions, however, firms can make use of secondary data, that is, information that already has been collected by some other organization. A wide variety of sources present secondary data. The principal ones are governments, international institutions, service organizations, trade associations, directories, and other firms. This section provides a brief review of major data sources. Details on selected monitors of international issues are presented in the Appendix at the end of this chapter (Beall, 2017; Burns et al., 2017; Hague et al., 2016; Hackett, 2018).

EXHIBIT 7.2 Key information to obtain in international market research

Macro information	Micro information
Tariffs and non-tariff trade barriers	Size of target market
Government trade policy	Income and purchasing power per capita
Nature of commercial infrastructure	Market economic growth rate
Country risk	Local laws, regulations, and standards
Volume of home country exports and imports	Nature of distribution system
Volume of target market exports and imports	Competitive activity

Governments

Most countries have a wide array of national and international trade data available. Typically, the information provided by governments addresses either macro and micro issues or offers specific data services. Macro information includes data on population trends, general trade flows among countries, and world agriculture production. Micro information includes materials on specific industries in a country, their growth prospects, and the extent and direction to which they are traded.

Unfortunately, the data are often published only in their home countries and in their native languages. Data publications mainly present numerical data and so the translation task is relatively easy. In addition, the information sources are often available at embassies and consulates, whose mission includes the enhancement of trade activities. The commercial counselor or commercial attaché can provide the information, as can government-sponsored web sites. The user should be cautioned that the printed information may be outdated and that the industry categories used abroad may not be compatible with industry categories used at home. Increasingly, government data are available on the Internet – often well before they are released in printed form. Closer collaboration between governmental statistical agencies is making data more accurate and reliable, because it is now much easier to compare data such as bilateral exports and imports to each other. Nonetheless, there are also occasional problems with government data. Exhibit 7.3 suggests that data from individual governments are not always reliable.

While many of the current data are available at no charge, governments often charge a fee for the use of data libraries. Given the depth of information such data can provide, the cost usually is a worthwhile expenditure for firms in light of the insights into trade patterns and reduction in risk they can achieve.

EXHIBIT 7.3 Politics

Government Reports May Be Unreliable

During the past few decades, China has sought to build up its economy. The nation has experienced much variability in key economic indicators, and this has varied across diverse regions in China. For example, economic growth has progressed rapidly in southeastern China, but has been much slower in western China. Many economists long had suspected that economic data published by the Chinese Government are not always reliable, and may be exaggerated to enhance China's reputation as a robust, thriving economy. The issue has become even more salient in recent years as growth of the Chinese economy has slowed to less than 7 percent annually and Chinese influence on lives elsewhere has greatly increased.

In a report issued in 2017, the governor of Liaoning province in northeastern China admitted that his government had inflated its GDP figures from 2011 to 2014. The report stated that fiscal revenues had been inflated by at least 20% during the period.

Growth in housing construction is a powerful driver of China's economy, and the picture painted by Chinese Government reports is often very bright. In reality, however, the National Bureau of Statistics in China publishes relatively limited information, which obscures real data on actual housing progress. China also has been accused of omitting key data, for example, on household consumption.

Some experts believe the methodology used by the Chinese Government to assess economic outcome is flawed. China's reputation and system for transparency in the reporting of official data may be underdeveloped.

Economists and political analysts also argue that unreliable data and sloppy statistics can hurt a country's credibility with investors. When official economic data are unreliable, potential investors will hesitate to fund new projects.

Sources: Guilford, 2015; Huang, 2017; Huang, 2018.

International Organizations

International organizations often provide useful data for the researcher. The United Nations (UN) *Statistical Yearbook* (http://unstats.un.org) is an annual publication of economic, social, and environmental statistics for more than 200 countries. However, because of the time needed for the collection of such a large amount of information, the Yearbook does not always present the most current data. More up-to-date additional information is made available by specialized substructures of the United Nations, such as the UN Conference on Trade and Development (www.unctad.org) and the International Trade Center (www.intracen.org). The World Bank (www.worldbank.org) provides a wealth of country-specific economic data, including detailed development reports, research books, and policy papers. The World Trade Organization (www.wto.org) and the Organization for Economic Cooperation and Development (www.oecd.org) also publish quarterly and annual trade data on their member-countries. The International Monetary Fund (www.imf.org) is another useful source of information. Its publications include the World Economic Outlook databases, international trade statistics, and financial data by country. Additionally, many industry-specific organizations, such as the International Air Transport Association (www.iata.org) and the Federation of International Trade Associations (www.fita.org/), provide a wealth of data to researchers.

Service Organizations

A wide variety of service organizations that provide information include banks, accounting firms, freight forwarders, airlines, international trade consultants, research firms, and publishing houses located around the world. Frequently they are able to provide information on business practices, legislative or regulatory requirements, and political stability, as well as trade and financial data.

Trade Associations

Associations such as world trade clubs and domestic and international chambers of commerce (such as the American Chamber of Commerce abroad) can provide good information on local markets. Often files are maintained on international trade flows and trends affecting international managers. Valuable information can also be obtained from industry associations. These groups, formed to represent entire industry segments, often collect a wide variety of data from their members that are then published in an aggregate form.

Directories

A large number of industry directories are available on local, national, and international levels. The directories primarily serve to identify firms and to provide very general background information, such as the name of the chief executive officer, the level of capitalization of the firm, the location, the address and telephone number, and some description of the firm's products.

Online Sources

The Internet provides abundant information and data for international market research. Exhibit 7.4 lists some of the most popular online information sources. In addition, international online computer database services can be purchased to supply information external to the firm, such as exchange rates, international news, and import restrictions. The selection of online resources depends on various factors, including the quality of data, reliability of available information, and any costs.

EXHIBIT 7.4 Information sources available via the Internet

Site	Address	Description
globalEDGE™	www.globalEDGE.msu.edu	Information, data, search engines, and diagnostic tools on various international business topics
Europa	www.europa.eu	Information, data, and resources related to the European Union
Export.gov	www.export.gov	Country-level commercial guides and other United States Government resources to support international business
UK Department for International Trade	www.gov.uk/government/organisations/department-for-international-trade	UK data and resources to support international business
Industry Canada	www.ic.gc.ca	Data and resources to support international business, especially for Canada
United Nations Conference on Trade and Development (UNCTAD)	www.unctad.org	Country fact sheets and statistics for analysis of international trade, FDI, and economic trends
World Trade Organization (WTO)	www.wto.org	Statistics on tariffs, government intervention, and economic conditions worldwide
World Bank	www.worldbank.org	National and international statistics, financial and technical information, sectoral data, trends in the world economy
World Bank Doing Business	www.doingbusiness.org	Reports on doing business in various countries
International Monetary Fund (IMF)	www.imf.org	Data and statistics on countries and economic and financial indicators

Many online databases, developed by analysts who systematically sift through a wide range of periodicals, reports, and books in different languages, provide information on given products and markets. Many of the main news agencies now have information available through online databases, providing information on events that affect certain markets. Some databases cover extensive lists of companies in given countries and the products they buy and sell. A top site for international market research is Export.gov, a major information site offered by the United States Department of Commerce International Trade Administration. The site provides a variety of databases and tools detailing international trade statistics, as well as market intelligence, guides on international business methods, and customized services. One of the most useful resources for international business research is the Country Commercial Guide published by the International Trade Administration (ITA), of the US Department of Commerce. The ITA provides comprehensive guides for more than 120 countries worldwide. A sample outline of the Guide is provided in the Appendix (Beall, 2017; Burns et al., 2017; Hague et al., 2016; Hackett, 2018; UNCTAD, 2018).

Selection of Secondary Data

A key advantage of secondary over primary data is that the former can be obtained relatively quickly and inexpensively. Secondary data should be evaluated regarding the quality of their source, their recency, and their relevance to the task at hand. Clearly, because the information was collected without the current research requirements in mind, there may well be difficulties in coverage, categorization, and comparability. For example, an "engineer" in one country may differ substantially in terms of training and responsibilities from a person in another country holding the same title. It is therefore important to be careful when getting ready to interpret and analyze data.

The ease of access to information through online searches has raised concerns about information usage. Governments and private-sector organizations are analyzing the effects of declassification programs that may place sensitive information into the hands of dangerous people.

Interpretation and Analysis of Secondary Data

Once secondary data have been obtained, the researcher must creatively convert them into information. Secondary data were originally collected to serve another purpose than the one in which the researcher is currently interested. Therefore, they can often be used only as **proxy information** in order to arrive at conclusions that address the research objectives. Proxy information is data used as a substitute for more desirable data that are unobtainable. For example, the market penetration of the smartphone may be used as a proxy variable for the potential demand for gaming apps. Similarly, in an industrial setting, information about plans for new port facilities may be useful in determining future container requirements.

The researcher must often use creative inferences, and such creativity brings risks. Therefore, once interpretation and analysis have taken place, a consistency check must be conducted. The researcher should always cross-check the results with other possible sources of information or with experts. Yet, if properly implemented, such creativity can open up one's eyes to new market potential (Beall, 2017; Burns et al., 2017; Hague et al., 2016).

Big Data

Technological advances have given rise to massive quantities of information and data, on customers, markets, and business strategies. Much of this information takes the form of big data. **Big data** refers to database systems that contain vast amounts of data that cannot be stored, managed, or analyzed with conventional software. The data arise from websites, personal electronics and apps, retail activity, and surveys, as well as sensors and other gauges in stores, factories, and on smart devices. For example, much big data is collected from smartphones. The number of smartphone users worldwide now exceeds 3 billion, about 50 percent of the world population. Smartphone ownership is common in the advanced economies – especially in Australia, Europe, and North America – where 65 percent of residents own such devices. The phones are increasingly popular in emerging markets – countries such as China, Poland, and Russia – where the ownership rate is more than 50 percent.

Very high-powered computing is required to analyze very large or highly complex data sets. Big data is so vast that it is often difficult to determine what data are relevant. Analyzing big data can be challenging, partly because of a shortage of data analysts worldwide. Most data is housed in the advanced economies, where the largest proportion of analysts are located. This complicates efforts to research emerging markets and developing economies.

The main benefit of big data is that it can answer many market research questions. The data can be used to enhance research and development, to better target products, to increase the sophistication of marketing efforts, and to reduce the time and resources needed for market adoption. Smart, a wireless service provider, uses big data to find and profitability serve micro-markets in the Philippines. In the United Kingdom, data on the origin, location, and timing of prescription drug use helped reduce delays between the release of a drug and its adoption. Big data can also help formulate strategies to improve supply chain performance, and increase the efficiency and effectiveness of logistics and distribution. The most sophisticated companies collect big data and build analysis capabilities.

Big data collection and analysis also can go far to advance the development of less-developed economies, by increasing the efficiency and effectiveness of the provision of needed products and services. The data can be used to improve health care, economic productivity, security, resource management, and other key areas. Exhibit 7.5 presents other characteristics of big data (International Telecommunications Union, 2017; McKinsey Global Institute, 2016).

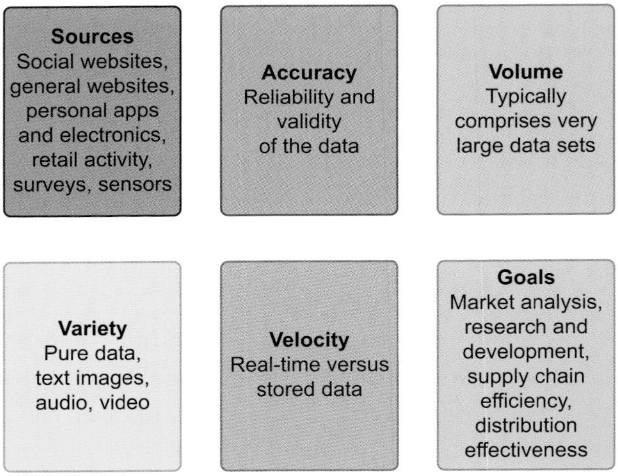

Sources
Social websites, general websites, personal apps and electronics, retail activity, surveys, sensors

Accuracy
Reliability and validity of the data

Volume
Typically comprises very large data sets

Variety
Pure data, text images, audio, video

Velocity
Real-time versus stored data

Goals
Market analysis, research and development, supply chain efficiency, distribution effectiveness

Exhibit 7.5 Characteristics of big data

Data Privacy

The attitude of society toward obtaining and using both secondary and primary data must be taken into account. Many societies are increasingly sensitive to the issue of data privacy, and the concern has grown exponentially as a result of e-business. Data privacy refers to electronic information security that restricts secondary use of data according to laws and preferences of the subjects. Readily accessible databases may contain information valuable to marketers, but they may also be considered privileged by individuals who have provided the data. Exhibit 7.6 reports on data concerns related to data privacy.

EXHIBIT 7.6 Data privacy: To share or not to share

Many believe that scientific knowledge is a public good that should be freely shared in the global research community for the betterment of humanity. Breakthroughs in the treatment and containment of infectious disease, improved water purification techniques, and the genetic modification of crops to increase yields are all examples of real-life applications of scientific innovation. Presently, however, barriers limit the free flow of scientific information around the world. Constraints on research sharing are driven mainly by policies of government and the private sector. Companies in particular are concerned about securing private data and maintaining control of proprietary information and knowledge.

Private industry finances most global research and development (R&D). The largest proportion of spending on R&D occurs in leading-edge industries, such as biotechnology, pharmaceuticals, and telecommunications. Because companies' main goal is profit maximization, it is in their interest to keep their scientific innovations proprietary. This allows for generating profits and competitive advantages from developed technologies.

One issue that has generated much controversy is the tension between intellectual property law and global health. For example, the avian flu pandemic led to public pressure for Roche to relax its patent on Oseltamivir, a drug used to treat bird influenza. Biotechnology firms worldwide have been pressured to share knowledge on treatments for HIV/AIDS, especially to benefit low-income countries in Africa where the disease is more widespread. Such situations arouse debate on whether pharmaceuticals and other firms should be forced to share their proprietary research in times of global crises, such as viral pandemics.

Governments usually avoid pressuring private companies to share their intellectual property because such efforts can stunt future innovation. By contrast, the Organisation for Economic Cooperation and Development (OECD) issued their Declaration on Access to Research Data from Public Funding because the OECD understands that innovative scientific research plays a crucial role in addressing global challenges – ranging from health care and climate change to renewable energy. Other organizations in Australia, Europe, the United States, and elsewhere have issued similar recommendations. However, there is no consensus on how best to handle such critical information. What is your view? Should governments require private companies to reveal patents and other innovations that can help solve world problems? Why or why not?

Sources: Beagrie, Beagrie, and Rowlands, 2009; Rosenberg, 2018; Wilkinson et al., 2016.

In 1995, the European Union adopted a stringent data-privacy directive that restricts access to lifestyle information. Companies are permitted to collect personal data only if the individuals consent to the collection, know how the data will be used, and have access to databases to correct or erase their information. In 2018, the European Union enacted a new law, the General Data Protection Rule (GDPR), which imposes heavy fines on companies if undeveloped data security systems result in the loss of personal information on consumers due to hacking or similar means. By contrast, restrictions on data privacy in the United States remain relatively lax. This implies that the researcher can more readily access data in the United States (Blackmer, 2016; European Commission, 2018; OECD, 2013).

Conducting Primary Research

It is typical for managers to begin research studies using secondary data, because of its easy access and low cost. In the long run, however, many relatively specific research questions cannot be answered using secondary sources, and the investigator will need to collect primary data. Thus, firms collect **primary data** directly for a specific research purpose through interviews, focus groups, surveys, observation, or experimentation. Although the research may not be conducted by the company with the need, the work must be carried out for a specific research purpose in order to qualify as primary research. Typically, primary research intends to answer such specific questions as:

- What is the sales potential for our measuring equipment in Malaysia?
- How much does the typical Greek consumer spend on fast food?
- What effect will our new type of packaging have on our green consumers in Norway?
- What service standards do industrial customers expect in Japan?

The researcher must have a clear idea of what the population under study should be and where it is located before deciding on the country or region to investigate. Conducting research in an entire country may not be necessary if, for example, only urban centers are to be penetrated. Multiple regions of a country need to be investigated; however, if a lack of homogeneity exists because of different economic, geographic, or behavioral factors. One source reports of the failure of a firm in Indonesia due to insufficient geographic dispersion of its research. The firm conducted its study only in large Indonesian cities during the height of tourism season, but projected the results to the entire population. When the company set up large production and distribution facilities to meet the expected demand, it realized only limited sales to city tourists (Beall, 2017; Burns et al., 2017; Hague et al., 2016; Hackett, 2018).

Industrial Versus Consumer Sources of Data

The researcher must decide whether research is to be conducted in the consumer or the industrial product area, which in turn determines the size of the universe and respondent accessibility. Consumers usually are a very large group, whereas the total population of industrial users may be limited. Cooperation by respondents may also vary. In the industrial setting, differentiation between users and decision-makers may be important because their personalities, their outlooks, and their evaluative criteria may differ widely. Determining the proper focus of the research is therefore of major importance to its successful completion.

Research Techniques

Once the decision has been made to collect primary data, the researcher must choose an appropriate research technique. The most common research techniques are observation, surveys, and focus groups. Firms also leverage the wealth of information available from social media to conduct research. Each provides a different depth of information and has its own strengths and weaknesses.

Observation

Observation requires the researcher to play the role of a nonparticipating observer of activity and behavior. In an international setting, observation can be extremely useful in shedding light on practices not previously encountered or understood. For example, Toyota sent researchers to California to nonchalantly observe how women get into and operate their cars. They found that women with long fingernails have trouble opening the door and operating various knobs on the dashboard. The researchers were able to comprehend the women's plight and redesign some of their automobile exteriors and interiors, producing more desirable cars.

Surveys

Survey research is useful in quantifying concepts. Surveys are usually conducted via questionnaires that are administered personally, by telephone, mail, or email. The use of the survey technique presupposes that the population under study is accessible and able to comprehend and respond to the questions posed through the chosen medium. Email surveys are suitable in countries where residents can access the Internet easily. Mail surveys depend on the quality of the local postal system. In many less-developed countries, for example, many houses are not numbered and streets may lack names. As a result, reaching respondents by mail is virtually impossible. In other countries, obtaining a correct address may be easy, but the postal system may not function well.

Since surveys deal with people who in an international setting display major differences in culture, preference, education, and attitude, just to mention a few factors, the use of the survey technique must be carefully examined. For example, in some regions of the world, recipients of letters may be illiterate. Others may be very literate, but totally unaccustomed to some of the standard research techniques common in advanced economies. Survey respondents in different countries may have different extreme response styles. Respondents may be reluctant to answer questions about sensitive issues.

In spite of all the potential difficulties, the survey technique remains a useful one because it allows the researcher to rapidly accumulate a large quantity of data amenable to statistical analysis. With constantly expanding technological capabilities, international researchers will be able to use this technique even more in the future.

Focus Groups

Focus groups are a useful research tool resulting in interactive interviews. A group of knowledgeable people is gathered for a limited period of time (two to four hours). Usually, seven to ten participants is the ideal size for a focus group. A specific topic is introduced and thoroughly discussed by all group members. Because of the interaction, hidden issues are sometimes raised that would not have one-paragraph in an individual interview. The skill of the group leader in stimulating discussion is crucial to the success of a focus group. Like in-depth interviews, focus groups do not provide statistically significant information; however, they can be helpful in providing information about perceptions, emotions, and attitudinal factors. In addition, once individuals have been gathered, focus groups are a highly efficient means of rapidly accumulating a substantial amount of information.

When planning international research using focus groups, the researcher must be aware of the importance of language and culture in the interaction process. Major differences may exist already in preparing for the focus group. In some countries, participants can simply be asked to show up at a later date at a location where they will join the focus group. In other countries, participants have to be brought into the group immediately because commitments made for a future date have little meaning. In some nations, providing a payment to participants is sufficient motivation for them to open up in discussion. In other countries, one first needs to host a luncheon or dinner for the group so that members get to know each other and are willing to interact.

Once the focus group is started, the researcher must remember that not all societies encourage frank and open exchange and disagreement among individuals. Status consciousness may result in the opinion of one participant being reflected by all others. Disagreement may be seen as impolite, or certain topics may be taboo. Unless a native focus group leader is used, it also is possible to misread the interactions among group participants completely and to miss out on nuances and constraints participants feel when commenting in the group situation. One of this book's authors, for example, used the term group discussion in a focus group with Russian executives, only to learn that the translated meaning of the term was political indoctrination session. The use of different languages in research makes it necessary to check one's translations very carefully.

Observation and focus groups are especially useful for gathering **qualitative information**, which refers to data that are not amenable to statistical analysis, but provide a better understanding, description, or prediction of given situations, behavioral patterns, or underlying dimensions. By contrast, **quantitative data** is information based on numeric and statistical relationships. In short, qualitative information is mainly words and text, while quantitative data is mainly numbers (Beall, 2017; Burns et al., 2017; Hackett, 2018). Exhibit 7.7 reports on how differences in national culture can confound knowledge development and ultimate marketing efforts.

EXHIBIT 7.7 The business Tower of Babel

All sorts of comical things can go wrong when a company translates its advertising into foreign languages. Managers at one American automaker marketed their new car – the Matador – based on an image of courage and strength. In Puerto Rico, however, the name means "killer" and proved unpopular on the nation's hazardous roads. Kellogg renamed its Bran Buds cereal in Sweden when it discovered that it roughly translated to "burned farmer." PepsiCo's innocuous-sounding "Come Alive with Pepsi" campaign led to not only one but two translation blunders. The slogan was translated in Chinese as "Pepsi brings your ancestors back from the dead," and in German as "Come Alive from the Grave."

Advertising mistakes receive much attention in the media and the international business world, but companies continue to make such blunders. The risk from such errors is especially serious when committed in the early phase of market research because findings typically are used to determine various subsequent activities, including new product development, marketing strategy, and advertising. A translation blunder that goes undiscovered at this stage sets the firm on the wrong track. Imagine spending millions of dollars on developing a new product or on entering a new market only to find that your company's surveys had asked the wrong questions!

Researchers at the Pew Research Center for the People and the Press in Washington, DC received an unwelcome surprise when they translated one of their worldwide polls into 63 languages and then back into English. The ride to the foreign languages and back again was a bit bumpier than they had imagined. In Ghana, for example, the original phrase "married or living with a partner" was first translated into one of the country's tribal languages as "married but have a girlfriend," and the category "separated" became "There's a misunderstanding between me and my spouse." The original version of a questionnaire for use in Nigeria had similar problems: "Success in life is determined by forces outside our control" initially read, "Goodness in life starts with blessings from one's personal god." In the original Nigerian Yoruba version, "fast food" was translated as "microwave food" and "the military" became "Herbalist/medicine man." Fortunately, the meanings were corrected in the final translations of the questionnaire. The lesson? Multinational researchers check your translations!

Sources: Tyekiff, 2019; Williams, 2019.

Social Media and the Internet

Data mining and other forms of research are facilitated by the wealth of information that people provide about themselves on social sites. At Facebook, for example, users provide various demographic and geographic information, as well as political affiliation, educational level, and psychographic data, such as interests, attitudes, and opinions on various topics, from favorite books and hobbies to contemporary issues. Some sites track members' shopping habits. In addition, marketers mine posts and other information published by members to better understand attitudes and preferences regarding individual brands. Such data lead to strategies for segmentation, targeting, positioning, communications, and other marketing tasks.

When consumers signal their preferences for various product features via social media, important intelligence is generated that firms use to refine current offerings and launch new ones. For example, suppose you are targeting your product to baseball fans in Japan making more than $50,000 per year. Suppose your market is single parents who consume high-culture products in each of France, Germany, and Spain. Facebook alone facilitates targeting a sizeable proportion of the world using very specific criteria at little or no cost.

Social media and the Internet provide innovative ways to present stimuli and collect data, at very low costs. For example, on a website, product details, pictures of products, brands, and the shopping environment can be portrayed with integrated graphics and sound – thus bringing the issues to be researched much closer to the respondent. In addition, the behavior of visitors to a site can be traced and interpreted regarding the interest in product, services, or information. Exhibit 7.8 shows a representation of the analytics generated from website visits.

Firms follow up data mining with online surveys, via websites or email, which provide deeper levels of primary data. Data entry can be automated so that responses are automatically fed into data-analysis software. As with other research techniques, however, differences in culture, technology level, socioec-

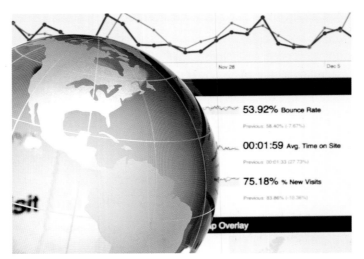

Exhibit 7.8 Google Analytics is a useful form of data that can be generated from websites
Credit: Bill Oxford/Getty Images.

onomic variables and other factors may affect the accuracy of data. In addition, electronic research may lack confidentiality and raise concerns over data privacy, which may limit the use of these tools in some nations or regions (Ahmadinejad & Asli, 2017; International Telecommunications Union, 2017; Levy, 2018).

The International Information System

Many organizations have data needs that go beyond specific international research projects. Most of the time, daily decisions must be made for which there is neither time nor money for special research. An information system can provide the decision-maker with basic data for most ongoing decisions. Defined as "the systematic and continuous gathering, analysis, and reporting of data for decision-making purposes," such a system serves as a mechanism to coordinate the flow of information to corporate managers.

To be useful to the decision-maker, the system must have certain attributes. First of all, the information must be relevant. The data gathered must have meaning for the manager's decision-making process. Only rarely can corporations afford to spend large amounts of money on information that is simply "nice to know." Any information system will have to continuously address the balance to be struck between the expense of the research design and process and the value of the information to ongoing business activities. Second, the information must be timely. Managers derive little benefit if decision information needed today does not become available until a month from now. To be of use to the international decision-maker, the system must therefore feed from a variety of international sources and be updated frequently. For multinational corporations, this means a real-time link between international subsidiaries and a broad-based ongoing data input operation. Third, information must be flexible – that is, it must be available in the form needed by management. An information system must therefore permit manipulation of the format and combination of the data. Fourth, the information contained in the system must be accurate. This is especially important in international research because information quickly becomes outdated as a result of major environmental changes. Fifth, the system's information bank must be reasonably exhaustive. Factors that may influence a particular decision must be appropriately represented in the information system because of the interrelationships among variables. This means that the information system must be based on a wide variety of factors. Sixth, the collection and processing of data must be consistent. This is to hold down project cost and turnaround time, while ensuring that data can be compared regionally. This can be achieved by centralizing the management under one manager who oversees the system's design, processing, and analysis. Finally, to be useful to managers, the system must be convenient to use. Systems that are cumbersome and time-consuming to reach and to use will not be used enough to justify corporate expenditures to build and maintain them.

The Internet enables customers to provide feedback on their experiences with a firm. Online reputation can have an important effect on a firm's prospects and can even preclude individuals from participating in business transactions. A symposium sponsored by the National Science Foundation and the Massachusetts Institute of Technology created the Reputation Research Network (http://databases .si.umich.edu/reputations/), an electronic database of studies on reputation systems and their importance for businesses seeking to preserve customer loyalty.

To build an information system, corporations use the internal data that are available from divisions such as accounting and finance and also from various subsidiaries. In addition, many organizations put mechanisms in place to enrich the basic data flow to information systems. Three such mechanisms are environmental scanning, Delphi studies, and scenario building (Enderwick, 2011; OECD, 2017).

Environmental Scanning

Any changes in the business environment, whether domestic or foreign, may have serious repercussions on the activities of the firm. Corporations therefore understand the necessity for tracking new developments. Although this can be done implicitly in the domestic environment, the remoteness of international markets requires a continuous information flow. For this purpose, some large multinational organizations have formed environmental scanning groups.

Environmental scanning activities provide continuous information on political, social, and economic affairs internationally; on changes of attitudes of public institutions and private citizens; and on possible upcoming alterations. Environmental scanning models can be used for a variety of purposes, such as the development of long-term strategies, getting managers to broaden their horizons, or structuring action plans. Obviously, the precision required for environmental scanning varies with its purpose. The more immediate and precise the application will be within the corporation, the greater the need for detailed information. On the other hand, heightened precision may reduce the usefulness of environmental scanning in strategic planning, which is long term.

Environmental scanning can be performed in various ways. One consists of obtaining factual input on a wide variety of demographic, social, and economic characteristics of foreign countries. Frequently, managers believe that factual data alone are insufficient for their information needs. Particularly when forecasting future developments, other methods are used to capture underlying dimensions of social change. One significant method is that of content analysis, which we define as a systematic evaluation of communication for the frequency of expressions.

A wide array of newspapers, magazines, and other publications are scanned worldwide in order to pinpoint over time the gradual evolution of new views or trends. Corporations also use the technique of media analysis to pinpoint upcoming changes in their line of business. This is especially important in the field of communications and information technology, where innovations create a rapidly changing business environment. For example, when Google announced the development of new software that consumers could download to their mobile phones and receive free turn-by-turn directions, investors fled traditional global positioning system (GPS) makers like TomTom and Garmin. Within hours after Google's announcement, Garmin's shares had dropped by 17 percent and TomTom's by 21 percent.

Content analysis is also useful in identifying consumer attitudes about environmental and ethical issues, such as pollution, preservation of natural resources, and animal testing, which allows firms to locate new opportunities for expanding their operations while remaining within changing moral and environmental boundaries.

Environmental scanning is conducted by a variety of groups within and outside the corporation. Quite frequently, small corporate staffs are created at headquarters to coordinate the information flow. In addition, subsidiary staff can be used to provide occasional intelligence reports. Groups of volunteers are also formed to gather and analyze information worldwide and feed their individual analyses back to corporate headquarters, where the "big picture" can then be constructed. The Internet also allows firms to find out about new developments in their fields of interest and permits them to gather information through bulletin boards and discussion groups. For example, some firms use search engines to comb through thousands of newsgroups for any mention of a particular product or application. If they find frequent references, they can investigate further to see what customers are saying.

Finally, it should be kept in mind that internationally there may be a fine line between tracking and obtaining information and the misappropriation of corporate secrets. With growing frequency, governments and firms claim that their trade secrets are being obtained and abused by foreign competitors. The perceived threat from economic espionage has led to legislation and accusations of government spying networks trying to undermine the commercial interests of companies. Information gatherers must be sensitive to these issues in order to avoid conflict.

Delphi Studies

To enrich the information obtained from factual data, corporations and governments frequently resort to the use of creative and highly qualitative data-gathering methods. One approach is through **Delphi studies**. These studies are particularly useful in the international environment because they are "a means for aggregating the judgments of a number of ... experts ... who cannot come together physically"

(Van de Ven et al., 1975). This type of research clearly aims at qualitative measures by seeking a consensus from those who know, rather than average responses from many people with only limited knowledge.

Typically, Delphi studies are carried out with groups of about 30 well-chosen participants who possess expertise in an area of concern, such as future developments of the international trade environment. The participants are asked to identify the major issues in the given area of concern. They are also requested to rank order their statements according to importance and explain the rationale behind the order. The aggregated information and comments are then sent to all participants in the Delphi group. Group members are encouraged to agree or disagree with the various rank orders and comments. This allows statements to be challenged. In another round, the participants respond to the challenges. Several rounds of challenges and responses result in a reasonably coherent consensus.

The Delphi technique is particularly valuable because it uses mail, facsimile, or electronic communication to bridge large distances and therefore makes experts quite accessible at a reasonable cost. It avoids the drawback of ordinary mail investigations, which lack interaction among participants. Several rounds may be required, however, so substantial time may elapse before the information is obtained. Also, a major effort must be expended in selecting the appropriate participants and in motivating them to participate in the exercise with enthusiasm and continuity. When carried out on a regular basis, Delphi studies can provide crucial augmentation of the factual data available for the information system.

Scenario Building

The information obtained through environmental scanning or Delphi studies can then be used to conduct a scenario analysis. A scenario analysis involves the development of a series of plausible scenarios that are constructed from trends observed in the environment, and then formally reviewing assumptions built into existing business plans and positions. Subsequently, some of these key assumptions such as economic growth rates, import penetration, population growth, and political stability are varied to examine the consequences. By projecting variations for medium-to-long-term periods, completely new environmental conditions can emerge. The conditions can then be analyzed for their potential domestic and international impact on corporate strategy.

The identification of crucial variables and the degree of variation are of major importance in scenario building. Scenario builders also need to recognize the nonlinearity of factors. To simply extrapolate from currently existing situations is insufficient, since extraneous factors often enter the picture with significant impact. The possibility of joint occurrences must be recognized as well, because changes may not come about in an isolated fashion but instead may spread over wide regions. For example, given large technological advances, the possibility of wholesale obsolescence of current technology must be considered. Quantum leaps in computer development and new generations of computers may render obsolete the entire technological investment of a corporation.

For scenarios to be useful, management must analyze and respond to them by formulating contingency plans. Such planning will broaden horizons and may prepare managers for unexpected situations. Through the anticipation of possible problems, managers hone their response capability and in turn shorten response times to actual problems.

The development of an international information system is of major importance to the multinational corporation. It aids the ongoing decision process and becomes a vital tool in performing the strategic planning task. Only by observing global trends and changes will the firm be able to maintain and improve its competitive position. Much of the data available are quantitative in nature, but researchers must also pay attention to qualitative dimensions. Quantitative analysis will continue to improve as the ability to collect, store, analyze, and retrieve data increases as a result of computer development. Nevertheless, the qualitative dimension will remain a major component of corporate research and planning activities (Beall, 2017; Burns et al., 2017; Krippendorff, 2012; Hackett, 2018; Enderwick, 2011).

SUMMARY

Constraints of time, resources, and expertise are the major inhibitors to international research. Nevertheless, firms need to carry out planned and organized research in order to explore foreign market opportunities and challenges successfully. Such research must be linked closely to the decision-making process.

International research differs from domestic research in that the environment – which determines how well tools, techniques, and concepts apply – is different abroad. In addition, the international manager must deal with duties, exchange rates, and international documentation; a greater number of interacting factors; and a much broader definition of the concept of competition.

When the firm is uninformed about international differences in consumer tastes and preferences or about foreign market environments, the need for international research is particularly great. Research objectives need to be determined based on the corporate mission, the level of international expertise, and the business plan. These objectives will enable the research to identify the information requirements.

Given the scarcity of resources, companies beginning their international effort must rely on data that have already been collected. These secondary data are available from sources such as governments, international organizations, or electronic information services. It is important to respect privacy laws and preferences when making use of secondary data.

To fulfill specific information requirements, the researcher may need to collect primary data. An appropriate research technique must be selected to collect the information. Sensitivity to different international environments and cultures will aid the researcher in deciding whether to use interviews, focus groups, observation, surveys, or web technology as data-collection techniques.

To provide ongoing information to management, an information system is useful. Such a system will provide for the continuous gathering, analysis, and reporting of data for decision-making purposes. Data gathered through environmental scanning, Delphi studies, or scenario building enable management to prepare for the future and hone its decision-making abilities.

DISCUSSION QUESTIONS

1. You are employed by National Engineering, a firm that designs subways. You are responsible for exploring international possibilities for the company. How will you go about this task?

2. What are some of the products and services the World Bank offers to firms doing business in the developing world? Refer to the bank's Projects & Operations site here: http://projects.worldbank.org/

3. Suppose you work for Apple, Nike, or another firm of your choosing, and you are tasked with conducting market research on China, India, or another emerging market, to assess prospects for product sales. What steps should you follow in conducting the research. Provide a general outline of the stages in international market research.

4. Among all the OECD countries, which derives the largest share of its GDP from the service sector? From agriculture? From industry? Refer to www.oecd.org.

5. What are the characteristics of big data? What types of international business research can you conduct using big data?

6. To which group of countries are NAFTA members most likely to export? Use the Inter-American Development Bank's export tables, located in the Research and Data section of its webpage, www.iadb.org/research/

7. Summarize the major techniques used in international business research. What research technique should you use to answer the following research questions: How do people bake cakes at home in Japan? What stores at a mall in Russia do shoppers frequent most, and what is their average expenditure per store? What are the most important job attributes to factory workers in China?

KEY TERMS

TAKE A STAND

Business research, especially the collection and manipulation of consumer data, is not without its critics. With the rapid development of information technology and the rise of e-business, consumers and analysts alike are increasingly concerned about personal privacy. Most search engines, for example, keep track of the web pages visited by users. This allows both for targeted online marketing by partners, and, in some instances, for direct marketing offline, either through mailers or that old favorite – the telemarketer call.

Questions for Debate

1. Should search engines be prohibited from storing and disseminating their users' online activity, in order to protect their privacy? Should governments introduce tighter controls for direct marketing?
2. Considering that more consumer data allows businesses to employ more targeted marketing, which saves money and boosts sales, which in turn creates jobs and stimulates the economy, should governments encourage customer research?
3. Suppose the data you have obtained from a given country to build an international database seems unreliable. What will you do?

INTERNET EXERCISES

1. China is an attractive market with rising purchasing power. Before exporting to China, most firms conduct research to understand the Chinese market better. Visit the China Business Information Center (CBIC; www.export.gov/china) and UK Department for International Trade (www.gov.uk/government/organisations/department-for-international-trade). Suppose you are hired by firms that aim to begin exporting to China three products: (a) granola bars,

(b) popular music on CDs, and (c) laptop computers. For each of these product categories, using the preceding websites, prepare a list of the information that the firm should gather prior to making a decision to export to China.

2. Show macro aggregate changes in international markets by listing the total value of three commodities exported from your country to five other countries for the last four years. For each of the countries, provide a one-paragraph statement in which you identify positive or negative trends. Give your opinion on whether or not these trends are relevant or reflect the reality of today's international business environment. What are the dangers of relying on perceived trends? You are encouraged to conduct research on products from your hometown or region.

FURTHER RESOURCES

Beall, Annel. (2019). *Strategic Market Research*. CreateSpace, www.amazon.com.

Brown, Tom, Suter, Tracy, and Churchill, Gilbert. (2018). *Marketing Research: Customer Insights And Managerial Action*. Boston: Cengage Learning.

Burns, Alvin, Veeck, Ann, and Bush, Ronald. (2017). *Marketing Research*. New York: Pearson.

Curtin, Richard (2019). *Consumer Expectations: Micro Foundations and Macro Impact*. New York: Cambridge University Press.

Leavy, Patricia. (2017). *Research Design: Quantitative, Qualitative, Mixed Methods, Arts-Based, and Community-Based Participatory Research Approaches*. New York: Guilford Press.

World Factbook 2018. (2018). Central Intelligence Agency website [online]. Available at www.cia.gov/library/publications/download/download-2018/index.html (Accessed May 1, 2020).

Appendix
A Country Commercial Guide for Indonesia

1 Doing Business in Indonesia

- Market Overview
- Market Challenges
- Market Opportunities
- Market Entry Strategy

2 Political and Economic Environment

- Indonesia – Political Environment (Links to the State Department's website for background on the country's political environment).

3 Selling US Products and Services

- Using an Agent
- Web Resources
- Establishing an Office
- Franchising
- Direct Marketing
- Joint Ventures/Licensing
- Selling to the Government
- Distribution and Sales Channels
- Selling Factors and Techniques
- E-Commerce
- Trade Promotion and Advertising
- Pricing
- Sales Service/Customer Support
- Protecting Intellectual Property
- Local Professional Services

- Indonesia – Principal Business Associations
- Due Diligence

4 Leading Sectors for US Exports and Investments

- Best Prospect Overview
- Indonesia – Agriculture
- Indonesia – Aviation
- Indonesia – Education and Training
- Indonesia – Medical Equipment
- Indonesia – Power Generation
- Indonesia – Telecommunications

5 Customs, Regulations, and Standards

- Trade Barriers
- Web Resources
- Import Tariffs
- Import Requirements and Documentation
- Labeling/Marking Requirements
- US Export Controls
- Temporary Entry
- Prohibited and Restricted Imports
- Customs Regulations
- Standards for Trade
- Trade Agreements
- Licensing Requirements for Professional Services

6 Investment Climate Statement

- Links to the US Department of Department of State's Investment Climate Statement website (www.state.gov/e/eb/rls/othr/ics/).

7 Trade and Project Financing

- Methods of Payment
- Web Resources

- Banking Systems
- Foreign Exchange Controls
- US Banks and Local Correspondent Banks
- Project Financing

8 Business Travel

- Indonesia Business Travel
- Business Customs
- Travel Advisory
- Visa Requirements
- Currency
- Telecommunications/Electronics
- Transportation
- Language
- Health
- Local Time, Business Hours, and Holidays
- Entry of Materials or Personal Belongings
- Travel Related Web Resources

Source: The International Trade Administration (ITA), US Department of Commerce, Washington DC, http://export.gov, 2019.

8

Entry and Expansion

LEARNING OBJECTIVES

- Observe how firms gradually progress through an internationalization process
- Understand the strategic effects of internationalization on the firm
- Study the various modes of entering international markets
- Understand the role and functions of international intermediaries
- Learn about the opportunities and challenges of cooperative market development
- Understand how firms can overcome market barriers by either building competitive capabilities abroad from scratch or acquiring them from local owners
- Observe a model linking managerial commitment, international expansion and corporate concerns

CONTENTS

VIGNETTE 8 **The internationalization of Harley-Davidson**

Harley-Davidson (Harley) is a US producer of motorcycles and other two-wheelers that markets more than 30 models through a network of some 1,500 dealers and other intermediaries worldwide. Founded in 1903, Harley initially focused on the US domestic market but gradually expanded sales internationally. Harley earns about half its total sales in the United States. Famous in the USA for large, powerful motorcycles, the firm also makes practical bikes for commuting and other practical needs, for sales around the world.

Global competition has been a key factor inducing Harley to internationalize. As domestic sales declined some years ago, management began to focus on international expansion. Harley undertakes exporting to offer many of its bikes to markets worldwide. Harley cooperates with local intermediaries and other partners to access the capabilities it needs to succeed in complex markets. The firm also uses foreign direct investment (FDI) to establish subsidiaries, warehousing, and assembly plants abroad.

Harley expanded proactively into Europe and enjoyed much success in the large marketplace comprising dozens of countries with diverse consumer tastes. In Germany, freeways have high speed limits that drive a need for high-performance bikes. Many European cities are crowded and feature narrow streets. Most Europeans use motorcycles for everyday commuting. Harley has had to develop a range of bikes to suit varied needs in Europe.

Harley has begun targeting emerging markets – nations such as Brazil, China, and several countries in Eastern Europe characterized by lower spending power and often complex regulation. Harley established an assembly plant in Brazil to minimize the impact of local import tariffs and other trade barriers. The firm exports parts to Brazil, which are used to construct motorcycles directly in the market.

In China, many people ride small motorcycles for commuting and other everyday needs. Average incomes in China are relatively low, and Harley has had to develop basic bikes that appeal to Chinese buyers. Harley aims to develop the leisure market in China as well. Management also set its sights on India, where millions of households enjoy substantial buying power. Harley established a subsidiary near Delhi to facilitate imports, but India imposes significant regulation and trade barriers. Harley has leveraged the services of US export promotion agencies such as the US Department of Commerce to understand complex markets better and reduce risk.

Harley management believes it must expand increasingly to markets around the world, both to reduce operating costs and to increase sales. This requires

Workers at Harley-Davidson in Shanghai get a motorcycle for sale. With the USA and China being the world's two largest economies, Harley-Davidson views China as a key market.
Credit: JOHANNES EISELE/AFP via Getty Images.

offering smaller bikes and developing intermediary networks. Harley needs to balance production and sales for domestic and international markets. The firm must strike the right balance between generating profits and managing various risks as it expands into markets around the world.

Sources: Hartley and Claycomb, 2014; Hagerty, 2015; Dun and Bradstreet, 2020; Harley-Davidson USA, 2020; Jakab, 2015.

Introduction

International business holds out the promise of large new market areas, yet firms cannot simply jump into the international marketplace and expect to be successful. They must adjust to needs and opportunities abroad, have quality products, understand their customers, and do their homework to comprehend the vagaries of international markets. The rapid globalization of markets, however, reduces the time available to adjust to new market realities.

This chapter is concerned with firms preparing to enter international markets and companies expanding their current international activities. Initial emphasis is placed on export activities with a focus on the role of management in starting up international operations and a description of the basic stimuli for international activities. Entry modes for the international arena are highlighted, and the problems and benefits of each mode are discussed. The roles of facilitators and intermediaries in international business are described. Finally, alternatives that involve a local presence by the firm are presented.

The Role of Management

Management dynamism and commitment are crucial to a firm's first steps toward international operations. Managerial commitment reflects the desire and drive on the part of management to act on an idea and to support it in the long run. Managers of firms with a strong international performance typically are active, aggressive, and display a high degree of international orientation. Such an orientation is indicated by substantial global awareness and cultural sensitivity. Conversely, firms that prove unsuccessful in international business usually exhibit minimal managerial commitment to expanding abroad.

The issue of managerial commitment is a critical one because foreign market penetration requires a vast amount of market development activity, sensitivity toward foreign environments, research, and innovation. Regardless of what the firm produces or where it does business internationally, managerial commitment is crucial for enduring stagnation and sometimes even setbacks and failure. After all, it is top management that determines the willingness to take a risk, to introduce new products, to seek new solutions to problems, and to strive to continuously succeed abroad. To achieve such a commitment, it is important to involve all levels of management early on in the international planning process and to impress on all players that the effort will only succeed with a commitment that is companywide.

Initiating international business activities takes the firm in an entirely new direction, quite different from adding a product line or hiring a few more people. Going international means that a fundamental strategic change is taking place. Companies that initiate international expansion efforts and succeed with them, typically begin to enjoy operational improvements – such as positioning strengths in competition – long before financial improvements appear.

The decision to export usually comes from the highest levels of management, typically the owner, president, chairman, or vice president of marketing. The carrying out of the decision – that is, the implementation of international business transactions – is then the primary responsibility of marketing personnel. It is important to establish an organizational structure in which someone has the specific responsibility for international activities. Without such a responsibility center, the focus necessary for success can easily be lost. Such a center need not be large. For example, just one person assigned part-time to international activities can begin exploring and entering international markets.

The first step in developing international commitment is to become aware of international business opportunities. Management must then determine the degree and timing of the firm's internationalization. For instance, a German corporation that expands its operation into Austria, Switzerland, Belgium, and the Netherlands is less international than a German corporation that launches operations in Japan and Brazil. Moreover, if a German-based corporation already has activities in the USA, setting up a business in Canada does not increase its degree of internationalization as much as if Canada had been the first "bridgehead" in North America. Management must decide the timing of when to start the internationalization process and how quickly it should progress. For example, market entry might be desirable as soon as possible because clients are waiting for the product or because competitors are expected to enter the market shortly. In addition, it may be desirable to either enter a market abroad selectively or to achieve full market coverage from the outset. Decisions on these timing issues will determine the speed with which management must mobilize and motivate the people involved in the process.

However, firmwide international orientation may take considerable time to develop. Internationalization is a matter of learning, of acquiring experiential knowledge. A firm must learn about foreign markets and institutions, but also about its own internal resources in order to know what it is capable of when exposed to new and unfamiliar conditions. The planning and execution of an export venture must be incorporated into the firm's strategic management process. A firm that sets no strategic goals for its export venture is less likely to make the venture a long-term success. As markets around the world become more linked and more competitive, the importance of developing and following a strategy becomes increasingly key to making things better.

How do firms first become interested in international business? Certain situations may lead a manager to discover and understand the value of going international and to decide to expand abroad. For example, unsolicited orders from abroad often stimulate early interest in exporting. An **unsolicited order** is an unplanned business opportunity that arises as a result of another firm's activities. Having a substantial corporate website facilitates the ability of foreign customers or distributors to find the firm and its products. Customers from abroad may place an order via the company website, leading to unplanned internationalization. When this arises, the firm may become an **accidental exporter**, and participate in international trade on account of outside demand rather than based on deliberate planning. Over time, the firm may then start planning to expand internationally.

Managers who have lived abroad and learned foreign languages or are particularly interested in foreign cultures are more likely to investigate in international business opportunities. Countries or regions with high levels of immigration may, over time, benefit from greater export success due to more ties, better information, and greater international business sensitivity by their new residents. New management or new employees can also introduce an international orientation. For example, managers entering a firm may already have had some international business experience and may use this experience to further the business activities of their new employer (Brake, 2002; Thomas & Peterson, 2018; Andersen & Andersson, 2017; Morschett et al., 2015).

Motivations to Go Abroad

Normally, management will consider international activities only when stimulated to do so. A variety of motivations can push and pull individuals and firms along the international path. An overview of the major motivations that have been found to make firms go international is provided in Exhibit 8.1. Proactive motivations represent stimuli for firm-initiated strategic change. Reactive motivations describe stimuli that result in a firm's response and adaptation to changes imposed by the outside environment. In other words, firms with proactive motivations go international because they want to; those with reactive motivations go international because they have to (Deresky, 2017; Kedia & Mukherji, 1999; Ghislanzoni et al., 2008).

Proactive Motivations
Proactive motivations are triggered by the firm as a function of corporate growth. Profits are the major proactive motivation for international business. Management may perceive international sales as a potential source of higher profits. In

EXHIBIT 8.1 Major motivations for firms to expand abroad

Proactive motivations	Reactive motivations
• Obtain profit advantages	• Stagnant or declining domestic sales
• Ability to offer unique products	• Saturated domestic markets
• Technological advantage	• Competitive pressures
• Exclusive information	• Overproduction
• Tax benefits	• Excess capacity
• Economies of scale	• Proximity to customers and ports

reality, international ventures may take some time to become profitable because of the added, sometimes unforeseen, costs of international expansion. Particularly in startup firms, initial profitability may be quite low because of the cost of preparing to go international and the losses that result from early mistakes. The gap between expectation and reality can be especially large if the firm lacks significant international experience. Even with thorough planning, unexpected influences can change the profit picture substantially. Shifts in exchange rates, for example, may drastically affect profit forecasts.

Unique products or a technological advantage can be another major motivation. A firm may produce goods or services that are not widely available from international competitors. Again, real and perceived advantages must be differentiated. Many firms believe that they offer unique products or services, even though this may not be the case internationally. If products or technologies are unique, however, they certainly can provide a competitive edge. In the past, a firm with a competitive edge could often count on being the sole supplier to foreign markets for years to come. The number of such occurrences has shrunk dramatically because of competing technologies and the frequent lack of international patent protection.

Special knowledge about foreign customers or market situations may be another proactive motivation. Such knowledge may result from particular insights by a firm, special contacts an individual may have, in-depth research, or simply from being in the right place at the right time (e.g., recognizing a good business situation during a vacation trip). Although such exclusivity can serve well as an initial motivation for international business, it will rarely provide prolonged motivation because competitors can be expected to catch up with the information advantage. Only if firms build up international information advantage as an ongoing process through, for example, broad market scanning or special analytical capabilities, can prolonged corporate strategy be based on this motivation.

Tax benefits can also play a major motivating role. Many governments use preferential tax treatment to encourage exports. As a result of such tax benefits, firms either can offer their product at a lower cost in foreign markets or can accumulate a higher profit. However, international trade rules make it increasingly difficult for governments to use tax subsidies to encourage exports.

A final major proactive motivation can involve economies of scale particularly when volume of production plays an important role. International activities may enable the firm to increase its output and therefore rise more rapidly on the learning curve. Doubling productive output can reduce production costs by a substantial amount. Additionally, studies have shown that the benefits of centralized production are substantial enough to offset any increases in transportation costs. Therefore, increased production for international markets can help reduce the cost of production and make the firm more competitive domestically (Sengupta, 2007; Knight & Liesch, 2016).

Reactive Motivations

Reactive motivations influence firms to respond to environmental changes and pressures rather than blaze new trails. Competitive pressures are one example. A company may worry about losing domestic market share to competing firms that have benefited from the economies of scale gained through international business activities. Further, it may fear losing foreign markets permanently to competitors that have decided to focus on these markets. Because market share usually is most easily retained by firms that initially obtain it, some companies may enter the international market head over heels. Quick entry, however, may result in equally quick withdrawal once the firm recognizes that its preparation has been inadequate.

Similarly, overproduction may represent a reactive motivation. During downturns in the domestic business cycle, foreign markets can provide an ideal outlet for excess inventories. International business expansion motivated by overproduction usually does not represent a full commitment by management, but rather a temporary safety valve. As soon as domestic demand returns to previous levels, international business activities are curtailed or even terminated. Firms that have used such a strategy once may encounter difficulties when trying to employ it again because many international customers are not interested in temporary or sporadic business relationships.

Declining domestic sales, whether measured in sales volume or market share, have a similar motivating effect. Goods marketed domestically may be at the declining stage of their product life cycle. Instead of attempting to push back the life cycle process domestically, or in addition to such an effort, firms may opt to prolong the product life cycle by expanding the market. Such efforts often meet with success, particularly with high-technology products that are becoming outmoded by the latest innovations. Such "just-dated" technology may enable vast progress and make such progress affordable. For example, a hospital without any imaging equipment may be much better off acquiring a "just-dated" MRI machine, rather than waiting for enough funding to purchase the latest state-of-the-art equipment.

Excess capacity can also be a powerful motivator. If equipment for production is not fully utilized, firms may see expansion abroad as an ideal way to achieve broader distribution of fixed costs. Alternatively, if all fixed costs are assigned to domestic production, the firm can penetrate foreign markets with a pricing scheme that focuses mainly on variable cost. Yet such a view is feasible only for market entry. A market-penetration strategy based on variable cost alone is unrealistic because, in the long run, fixed costs have to be recovered to replace production equipment.

The reactive motivation of a saturated domestic market has similar results to that of declining domestic sales. Again, firms in this situation can use the international market to prolong the life of their good and even of their organization.

A final major reactive motivation is that of proximity to customers and ports. Physical and psychological closeness to the international market can often play a major role in the international business activities of the firm. For example, a firm established near a border may not even perceive itself as going abroad if it does business in the neighboring country. Except for some firms close to the Canadian or Mexican borders, however, this factor is much less prevalent in the United States than in many other nations. Most European firms automatically go abroad simply because their neighbors are so close (Buckley, 2017; Deresky, 2017; Morschett et al., 2015).

In this context, the concept of psychic or **psychological distance** refers to perceptions about the proximity of an opportunity or a potential goal. Geographic closeness to foreign markets may not necessarily translate into real or perceived closeness to the foreign customer. Sometimes complex cultural variables, such as language, religion, legal, and political systems, make a geographically close foreign market seem psychologically distant. Some research has suggested that these intangibles also account for concrete differences in health, education, and consumption patterns. For example, research has shown that US firms perceive Canada to be much closer psychologically than Mexico. Even the UK, mainly because of the similarity in language, is perceived by many US firms to be much closer than Mexico or other Latin American countries, despite the geographic distances. However, in light of the reduction of trade barriers as a result of the North American Free Trade Agreement (NAFTA), and a growing proportion of the US population with Hispanic backgrounds, this long-standing perception is changing.

It is generally easier to enter foreign markets that are psychologically close. Firms new to international business benefit by entering psychologically closer markets first to gain experience before venturing into markets that are farther away. For example, US companies find it easier to expand to China or Japan, once they have developed international experience in Europe. However, psychological distance can be deceptive. For example, a British firm may see Canada as psychologically close because both countries speak English. However, the attitudes and values of managers and customers may vary substantially between the markets. Too much of a focus on the similarities may let the firm lose sight of the differences (Vaccarini et al., 2018; Evans & Mavondo, 2002).

In general, firms that are most successful in international business are usually motivated by proactive – that is, firm internal – factors. Proactive firms are also frequently more service-oriented than reactive firms. Further, proactive firms tend to be more marketing and strategy-oriented than reactive firms, which have operational issues as their major concern. Exhibit 8.2 examines the proactive efforts of an exporter. The clearest differentiation between the two types of firms can probably be made after the fact by determining as to how they initially entered international markets. Proactive firms are more likely to have solicited their first international order, whereas reactive firms frequently begin international activities after receiving an unsolicited order from abroad.

EXHIBIT 8.2 Nutcase helmets: Crash course in exporting

Nutcase makes and sells helmets for bicycles, motorcycles, and skateboarding. Headquartered in Portland, Oregon, in the United States, the firm has fewer than 50 employees, but sells its helmets in about 46 countries throughout Asia, Europe, and the Americas. The helmets emphasize creativity and innovation. Numerous colorful designs and unique styles distinguish the helmets from those of their competitors. The product is produced under a manufacturing contract in China. A manager at Nutcase noted that "In pursuing foreign markets, we needed to do market research and learn about ways of doing business in other countries … We adapt our marketing for foreign markets to suit local conditions."

For Nutcase, and countless other firms, exporting diversifies the customer base, and increases sales and profits. Compared to other entry strategies, exporting is relatively low cost, lower risk, and uncomplicated. These are big advantages for smaller firms like Nutcase that usually lack substantial human and financial resources. Nutcase managers often give advice and guidance to the firm's foreign distributors, sharing their knowledge of the product, as well as distribution and marketing in the global helmet market. When Nutcase contracts with a new distributor overseas, managers do their homework to ensure the intermediary is reliable, knowledgeable, and trustworthy. Exporters such as Nutcase locate foreign distributors using various methods. One approach is to attend trade fairs in target countries. Nutcase managers also attend bicycle races and other venues were helmet users meet.

One challenge is the unique name, Nutcase, which has a humorous connotation in English. Simultaneously it is a slang term meaning "a person with mental problems" and it also refers to a protective covering for one's "nut" (head). The firm has encountered problems in translating the name into other languages, where "nutcase" does not share the same meanings. Despite such challenges, Nutcase has persevered and enjoys a big following among helmet buyers around the world.

Sources: Cook and Raia, 2017; Nutcase Helmets (2020).

Then Federal Minister of Transport, Building, and Urban Development of Germany tries on a Nutcase helmet. Nutcase does not translate perfectly in German.
Credit: Frank Ossenbrink/ullstein bild via Getty Images.

Strategic Effects of Going International

Going international presents the firm with new environments, entirely new ways of doing business, and a host of new problems. The problems are wide ranging. They can consist of strategic considerations, such as service delivery and compliance with government regulations. In addition, the firm has to focus on startup issues, such as how to find and effectively communicate with customers and operational matters, such as information flows and the mechanics of carrying out an international business transaction. This involves various new documents, including commercial invoices, bills of lading, and shippers export declarations. The paperwork is necessary to comply with various domestic, international, or foreign regulations.

The firm needs to determine its preparedness for internationalization by assessing its internal strengths and weaknesses. This preparedness has to be evaluated in the context of the globalization of the industry within which the firm operates, since this context will affect the competitive position and strategic options available to the firm. Unusual things can happen to both risk and profit. Management's perception of risk exposure grows in light of the gradual development of expertise, the many concerns about engaging in a new activity, and uncertainty about the new environment it is about to enter. Domestically, the firm has gradually learned about the market and therefore managed to decrease its risk. In the course of international expansion, the firm now encounters new and unfamiliar factors, exposing it to increased risk and considerable expense. At the same time, because of the complexity, uncertainty, and typically higher costs associated with entering foreign markets, international ventures often fall short of initial profit expectations. In the longer term, however, as managerial expertise and familiarity with foreign markets increase, profits tend to rise. This reality, which is depicted in Exhibit 8.3, discourages many firms from undertaking international activities.

Understanding the changes in risk and profitability can help management overcome the seemingly prohibitive cost of going international. Success requires managers to be risk takers. Achieving satisfactory international performance usually takes time. It can be achieved in three ways: effectiveness, efficiency, and competitive strength. Effectiveness is characterized by the acquisition of market share abroad and by increased sales. Efficiency refers to falling costs over time that give rise to increasing profits. Competitive strength refers to the firm's position compared to other companies in the industry, and, due to the benefits of international experience, it is likely to grow. The international executive must appreciate the time and performance dimensions associated with going abroad in order to overcome short-term setbacks for the sake of long-term success (Bartlett et al., 2013; Czinkota, 2010; Yip & Hult, 2013; Morschett et al., 2015.

Technological Advances and International Market Entry

A key way that firms, large and small, reduce the costs and enhance performance in going international is by leveraging technological advances in infor-

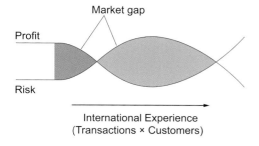

Exhibit 8.3 Profit and risk during early internationalization
Source: Czinkota, 2010.

mation, communications, manufacturing, and transportation. Such technologies have accelerated the ability of firms to enter new foreign markets and expand operations around the world. Information technology (IT) provides competitive advantages in internationalization by connecting geographically distant subsidiaries of the multinational firm. The Internet and intranets within firms' global networks facilitate instant sharing of data and critical information among company operations worldwide. Search engines enable research on markets, competitors, and business methods in individual countries. The Internet, Voice over Internet Protocol (VoIP) technologies (e.g., Skype, FaceTime), and other low-cost communications technologies facilitate efficient interaction with partners and value-chain members, greatly enhancing productivity and the pursuit of global opportunities.

Digital platforms and information flows connect the world as never before. Electronic commerce platforms and applications facilitate international buying and selling. Sharing-economy firms such as Airbnb and Uber leverage the Internet to facilitate joint creation of services between asset owners and customers.

The rise of "big data" – massive banks of information on customers and transactions – facilitates productivity and efficiencies in international marketing. Large-scale data analysis augments new customer knowledge and the development of products and experiences customized to buyer needs worldwide. Digitalization has reduced the importance of national boundaries. Online retailers such as Amazon and Alibaba leverage the Internet to enter new markets worldwide.

The Internet opens the global marketplace to smaller firms that historically lacked the resources to expand internationally. By establishing a presence on the web, even tiny enterprises can make their offerings known to a global audience.

In developing economies, the growing availability of the Internet and modern telecommunications facilitate targeting buyers with a range of products and services. Smartphones are especially transformative in developing economies. It is forecasted that by 2021 the number of smartphone users will exceed 3.8 billion, providing for countless new connections (Newzoo, 2019).

Many firms utilize social media – for example, Instagram, Snapchat, and WeChat– to connect with customers via advertising and direct sales, including potential buyers in new markets. Adidas uses Twitter and other platforms to market sportswear in emerging market countries. More than one-third of the residents of Africa now access the Internet. In Asia, about half the population is now online. Two-thirds of Latin Americans utilize Internet services. In the advanced economies, more than 70 percent of residents have become Internet mavens (Boston Consulting Group, 2015; Bughin et al., 2017).

Entry and Development Strategies

Here we will present the most typical international entry and expansion strategies. These are exporting and importing, licensing, and franchising. Another key way to expand is through a local presence, either via interfirm cooperation or foreign direct investment. These can take on many forms such as contractual agreements, equity participation, and joint ventures, or direct investment conducted by the firms alone.

Exporting and Importing

These activities can be indirect or direct. **Indirect involvement** means the firm participates in international business through an intermediary and does not deal directly with foreign customers or markets. **Direct involvement** means the firm works with foreign customers or markets with the opportunity to develop a relationship. Firms typically opt for direct involvement based on cost decisions. **Transaction cost theory** reflects the view that carrying out business interactions requires resources and causes expenses. The theory postulates that firms will evaluate and compare the costs of integrating an operation internally, as compared to the cost of using an external party to act for the firm abroad. Once it becomes easier and more efficient for a firm to conduct all the research, negotiations, shipping, and monitoring itself, rather than paying someone else to do it, the firm is likely to become a direct exporter or importer.

The end result of exporting and importing is similar to whether the activities are direct or indirect. In both cases, goods and services either go abroad or come to the domestic market from abroad, and goods may have to be adapted to suit the targeted market. However, following the indirect path to exporting, tends to limit learning and the development of expertise on how to do business abroad, information that the firm can draw on later for further international expansion. Therefore, while indirect activities represent a form of international market entry, they are usually suboptimal for gaining valuable international experience and capabilities, or for stimulating management commitment to international business.

Many firms are indirect exporters and importers, often without their knowledge. As an example, merchandise can be sold to a domestic firm that in turn sells it abroad. This is most frequently the case when smaller suppliers deliver products to large multinational corporations, which use them as input to their foreign sales. Foreign buyers may also purchase products locally and then send them immediately to their home country. While indirect exports may result from unwitting participation, some firms also choose this method of international entry as a strategic alternative that conserves effort and resources while still pursuing foreign opportunities.

Firms that opt to export or import directly typically access more opportunities, but they also face greater obstacles. Such hurdles include identifying and targeting foreign suppliers and/or customers and finding retail space, processes that can be costly and time-consuming. Many firms overcome such barriers through the use of electronic commerce. In Japan, for example, high-cost rents, crowded shelves, and an intricate distribution system have made launching new products through conventional methods challenging and expensive. Direct marketing via e-commerce eliminates the need for high-priced retail space.

As a firm and its managers gather experience with exporting, they move through different levels of commitment, ranging from awareness, interest, trial, evaluation, and finally, adaptation of an international outlook as part of corporate strategy. But not all firms progress with equal speed through all these levels. Some do so very rapidly, perhaps encouraged by success from e-commerce, and move on to other forms of international involvement such as foreign direct investment. Others may abandon exporting, owing to disappointing results or the need to allocate resources to other uses.

Increasingly, there are many new firms that either start out with an international orientation or develop one shortly after their establishment. Such *born global* firms emerge particularly in industries that require large numbers of customers, and in countries that only offer small internal markets. They tend to be small and young and often make heavy use of electronic commerce in reaching out to the world. In some countries more than one-third of new companies have been reported to export within two years. Firms, managers, and governments therefore will need to be much quicker than they have been in the past, when it comes to introducing firms to and preparing them for the international market (Cavusgil & Knight, 2015; Ghislanzoni et al., 2008).

International Intermediaries

Both direct and indirect importers and exporters frequently make use of intermediaries who can assist with troublesome yet important details such as documentation, financing, and transportation. The intermediaries also can identify foreign suppliers and customers and help the firm with long- or short-term market penetration efforts. Major types of international intermediaries are export management companies and trading companies. Together with export facilitators, intermediaries can bring the global market to the firm's doorstep and help overcome financial and time constraints. Exhibit 8.4 shows those areas in which intermediaries are typically most helpful. Management must decide how best to use intermediaries, from using their help for initial market entry to developing a long-term strategic collaboration.

EXHIBIT 8.4 Some opportunities for the support of company internationalization

- Deep knowledge about the local market, including characteristics of buyers and competitors
- Ability to navigate the local legal and regulatory environment
- Established local network and relationships with potential buyers
- Specific knowledge about potential buyers, including needs, creditworthiness, and purchasing power
- In-country services, including sales, marketing, warehousing, and technical support
- Distribution and physical delivery of product to foreign buyers

Export Management Companies

Firms that specialize in performing international business services as commission representatives or as distributors are known as export management companies (EMCs). Most EMCs are small, and many focus on specific industries or particular world regions. Their expertise enables them to offer specialized services to domestic corporations. EMCs have two primary forms of operation: they take title to goods and distribute internationally on their own account, or they perform services as agents. They often serve a variety of clients, thus their mode of operation may vary from client to client and from transaction to transaction. An EMC may act as an agent for one client and as a distributor for another. It may even act as both for the same client on different occasions.

When working as an agent, the EMC is primarily responsible for developing foreign business and sales strategies and establishing contacts abroad. Because the EMC does not share in the profits from a sale, it depends heavily on a high sales volume, on which it charges commission. The EMC thus may be tempted to take on as many products and as many clients as possible to maximize sales volume. As a result, the EMC may spread itself too thin and prove unable to represent all the clients and products it carries adequately.

EMCs that have specific expertise in selecting markets because of language capabilities, previous exposure, or specialized contacts appear to be the ones most successful and useful in aiding client firms in their international business efforts. For example, they can cooperate with firms that are already successful in international business but have been unable to penetrate a specific region. By sticking to their area of expertise and representing only a limited number of clients, such agents can provide quite valuable services.

When operating as a distributor, the EMC purchases products from the domestic firm, takes title, and assumes the trading risk. Selling in its own name, it has the opportunity to reap greater profits than when acting as an agent. The potential for greater profit is appropriate, because the EMC has drastically reduced the risk for the domestic firm while increasing its own risk. The burden of the merchandise acquired provides a major motivation to complete an international sale successfully. The domestic firm selling to the EMC is in the comfortable position of having sold its merchandise and received its money without having to deal with the complexities of the international market. On the other hand, it is less likely to gather much international business expertise (Cook & Raia, 2017; Papa & Elliott, 2016; International Trade Administration, 2016; International Trade Administration, 2018).

Compensation of EMCs

Some EMCs charge a fee to the manufacturer for market development, sometimes in the form of a retainer and often on an annual basis. The retainers vary and are dependent on the number of products represented and the difficulty of foreign market penetration. Frequently, manufacturers are also expected to pay all or part of the direct expenses associated with foreign market penetration. These expenses may involve the production and translation of promotional product brochures, the cost of attending trade shows, the provision of product samples, or trade advertising.

Alternatively, the EMC may demand a price break for international sales. In one way or another, the firm that uses an EMC must pay the EMC for the international business effort. Otherwise, despite promises, the EMC may simply add the firm and product in name only to its product offering and do nothing to achieve international success (Cook & Raia, 2017; International Trade Administration, 2016; International Trade Administration, 2018).

Trading Companies

Another major intermediary is the trading company. Such firms are especially common in Asia. In Japan, large trading companies are known as *sogoshosha*. Examples include companies such as Mitsubishi, Mitsui, and Marubeni. Such firms act as intermediaries for about one-third of the country's exports and two-fifths of its imports. They play a unique role in world commerce by importing, exporting, countertrading, investing, and manufacturing. Their vast size allows them to benefit from economies of scale and perform their operations at high rates of return, even though their profit margins are often less than 2 percent. Japanese trading companies succeed on the basis of substantial scale economies, access to capital, and enormous knowledge about opportunities both in Japan and abroad. Trading companies were long considered a Japanese phenomenon. Over time, however, the firms were established in numerous other countries. Today, in countries as diverse as Korea, Brazil, and Turkey, trading companies handle large portions of national exports (Cook & Raia, 2017; International Trade Administration, 2018).

Private-Sector Facilitators

Facilitators are entities outside the firm that assist in the process of going international. They supply knowledge and information but do not participate in the transaction. Such facilitators can come from both the private and the public sector.

Major encouragement and assistance can result from the statements and actions of other firms in the same industry. Information that would be considered proprietary if it involved domestic operations is often freely shared by competing firms when it concerns international business. The information not only has source credibility but is viewed with a certain amount of fear, because a too-successful competitor may eventually infringe on the firm's domestic business.

A second influential group of private-sector facilitators is distributors. Often a firm's distributors are engaged, through some of their business activities, in international business. To increase their international distribution volume, they encourage purely domestic firms to participate in the international market. This is true not only for exports but also for imports. For example, a major customer of a manufacturing firm may find that materials available from abroad, if used in the domestic production process, would make the product available at a lower cost. In such instances, the customer may approach the supplier and strongly encourage foreign sourcing.

Banks and other service firms, such as accounting and consulting firms, can serve as major facilitators by alerting their clients to international opportunities. While these service providers historically follow their major multinational clients abroad, increasingly they are establishing a foreign presence on their own. Frequently, they work with domestic clients on expanding market reach in the hope that their service will be used for any international transaction that results. Given the extensive information network of many service providers – banks, for example, often have a wide variety of correspondence relationships – the role of these facilitators can be major. Like a mother hen, they can take firms under their wings and be pathfinders in foreign markets (Deresky, 2017; Cook & Raia, 2017; International Trade Administration, 2016).

Public-Sector Facilitators

Government efforts can also facilitate the international efforts of firms. In the USA, for example, the Department of Commerce provides major export assistance, as do other federal organizations such as the Small Business Administration and the Export–Import Bank in the USA or Hermes in Germany. Most countries maintain similar export support organizations. Exhibit 8.5 identifies various export promotion agencies around the globe, together with their web addresses. Employees of these organizations typically visit firms and attempt to analyze their international

EXHIBIT 8.5 A sampling of export promotion agencies

Country / Organization	Agency	Website
Australia	Australian Trade Commission	www.austrade.gov.au
Canada	Export Development Corporation	www.edc.ca
France	Centre Francais du Commerce Exterieur	www.ubifrance.fr
Germany	Germany Trade and Invest	www.gtai.de/web_de/startseite
India	India Trade Promotion Organisation (ITPO)	www.indiatradepromotion.org
Japan	Japan External Trade Organization (JETRO)	www.jetro.go.jp
Singapore	International Enterprise Singapore	www.iesingapore.gov.sg/wps/portal
South Korea	Trade-Investment Promotion Agency (KOTRA)	www.kotra.or.kr/wps/portal/dk
United Kingdom	Department of Business Innovation and Skills	www.bis.gov.uk
United Nations / World Trade Organization	International Trade Centre	www.intracen.org
United States	International Trade Administration	www.ita.doc.gov

business opportunities. Through rapid access to government resources, these individuals can provide data, research reports, counseling, and financing information to firms. Government organizations can also sponsor meetings that bring interested parties together and alert them to new business opportunities abroad. Key governmental support is also provided when firms are abroad. By receiving information and assistance from their embassies, many business ventures abroad can be made easier. The ad on the next page provides an example of active government involvement in investment promotion.

Increasingly, organizations at the state and local levels also are active in encouraging firms to participate in international business. Many states and provinces have formed agencies for economic development that provide information, display products abroad, conduct trade missions, and sometimes even offer financing. Similar services can also be offered by state and local port authorities and by some of the larger cities. State and local authorities can be a major factor in facilitating international activities because of their closeness to firms.

Educational institutions such as universities and community colleges can also be major international business facilitators. They can act as trade information clearinghouses, facilitate networking opportunities, provide client counseling and technical assistance, and develop trade education programs. They can also develop course projects that are useful to firms interested in international business. For example, students may visit a firm and examine its potential in the international market as a course requirement. With the skill and supervision of faculty members to help the students develop the final report, such projects can be useful to firms with scarce resources, while they expose students to real-world problems (Bughin et al., 2015; Deresky, 2017; International Trade Administration, 2016; Mansfield & Reinhardt, 2015; UNCTAD, 2017).

Licensing

A license is a type of permission that one firm grants to another to undertake business using assets owned by the first firm. Under a licensing agreement, one firm permits another to use its intellectual property in exchange for compensation known as a royalty. The recipient firm is the licensee. The property licensed might include patents, trademarks, copyrights, technology, technical know-how, or specific business skills. For example, a firm that has developed a bag-in-the-box packaging process for milk can give the right to other firms abroad to use the same process, in exchange for royalty payments. In this way, licensing represents the export of intangibles.

Licensing has intuitive appeal to many would-be international managers. As an entry strategy, it requires neither capital investment nor detailed involvement with foreign customers. By generating royalty income, licensing provides an opportunity to exploit research and development already conducted. After initial costs, the licensor can reap benefits until the end of the license contract period. Licensing also reduces the risk of expropriation because the licensee is a local company that can provide leverage against government action.

Licensing may help circumvent host-country regulations applicable to equity ventures. It also may provide a means by which foreign markets can be tested without major involvement of capital or management time. Similarly, licensing can be used as a strategy to preempt a market before the entry of competition, especially if the licensor's resources permit full-scale involvement only in selected markets. Licensing also relieves the originating company from having to come up with culturally responsive changes in every market. As Exhibit 8.6 shows, adapting to foreign cultures can be challenging for local licensees.

A special form of licensing is trademark licensing, which involves granting another firm or an individual the right to use an established brand symbol
in exchange for payment. Trademark licensing provides substantial revenue to

---

EXHIBIT 8.6 Licensing of popular TV programs

Television shows produced in the USA are popular with audiences worldwide. In
many countries, popular programs are often based on American concepts produced by US production companies. Police dramas, situation comedies, and reality TV shows are popular television concepts, originally developed in the USA.
As local commercial stations emerged in many countries, they typically lacked
the expertise to produce hit shows cost-effectively, so they filled open hours of
airtime by purchasing programming from the USA. American companies took
advantage of high demand and generated substantial profits. During a bidding
war in the United Kingdom, for example, the price of an episode of the Simpsons
shot up to US $1.5 million.

More recently, TV networks in many countries have become adept at developing and producing their own programming. The trend was driven partly by
growing consumer demand for shows more reflective of local cultural values and
preferences.

In addition to claiming a larger share of their domestic markets, European
production companies turned the tables with licensing agreements. Now they develop winning TV shows and license concepts to other companies for production
in their own countries.

In numerous countries, new concepts are developed, tested, and exported
around the world. The British television hit Pop Idol gave rise to licensed versions
in Poland, South Africa, and the USA. In the new international television market,
winning ideas can come from any country.

Under the 1989 "Television Without Frontiers" directive, the European Union
(EU) mandated that EU television channels reserve at least 50 percent of their
output for European-made content. Over time, Europe's licensing landscape has
evolved. In 2018, the EU implemented new digital portability rules that allow
Europeans to watch online streaming services like Netflix, Amazon Video Prime,
and others wherever they travel around Europe. The EU authorized territorial licensing that allows producers to sell movies and TV shows throughout Europe.
These developments are transforming the EU into a unified digital market, where
customers in any member country can access the online programming of any of
the other 27 EU nations.

Sources: European Commission, 2008; Chalaby, 2009; Hopewell, 2018; Liao, 2018.

Pop Idol debuted in the UK in 2003. While it only aired two series in the UK, its success lead to the show launching the Idol format in dozens of countries.
Credit: Steve Finn/Getty Images.

firms – such as Nike and Louis Vuitton – that can trade on well-known names and characters. Trademark licensing permits the names or logos of designers, literary characters, sports teams, or movie stars to appear on clothing, games, foods and beverages, gifts and novelties, toys, and home furnishings. Licensors can make millions of dollars with little effort, while licensees can produce a brand or product that consumers will recognize immediately. However, trademark licensing is a realistic business venture only if the trademark is relatively well known.

Licensing entails some disadvantages. It is a relatively limited form of foreign market participation and does not in any way guarantee a basis for future expansion. Indeed, licensors run the risk of creating competitors not only in the market for which the agreement was made but for third-country markets as well (Dratler & McJohn, 2017; Licensing Journal, 2009; Lieberstein et al., 2011; Safarian & Bertin, 2014).

Franchising

Franchising is an advanced form of licensing in which a firm (the franchisor) grants the right to another, independent entity (the franchisee) to do business in a prescribed manner. The right can take the form of selling the franchisor's products, using its name, production, and marketing techniques, or using its general business approach. Usually franchising involves a combination of many of those elements. The major forms of franchising are manufacturer-retailer systems (such as car dealerships), manufacturer-wholesaler systems (such as soft drink companies), and service-firm retailer systems (such as lodging services and fast-food outlets).

The expansion or contraction of franchising results from the global economic climate. When financing is readily available and product demand is soaring, companies are eager to expand their franchise operations. Franchising allows firms to rapidly internationalize, expanding franchised outlets into numerous countries simultaneously by leveraging the resources and capabilities of entrepreneurs in each nation.

To be successful in international franchising, firms frequently offer products or selling propositions that are relatively unique. A successful franchise model is relatively standardized, fairly easy to replicate, and capable of engendering widespread customer recognition. Concurrent with this recognizability, the franchisor can and should adapt to local circumstances. Food franchisors, for example, will vary the products and product lines offered, depending on local market conditions and tastes.

Key reasons for the international expansion of franchise systems are market potential, financial gain, and saturated domestic markets. From a franchisee's perspective, the franchise is beneficial because it reduces risk by implementing a proven concept. There are also major benefits from a governmental perspective. The source country does not see a replacement of exports or an export of jobs. The recipient country sees franchising as requiring little outflow of foreign exchange, since the bulk of the profits generated remains within the country.

Franchising has been growing rapidly, but government intervention or underdeveloped legal systems, can hinder growth and performance. Many multinational corporations (MNCs) have sought to establish franchises in China, but encounter problems related to weak local intellectual property rights. Intellectual piracy remains common in the country. Franchisors are advised to register their brands in Chinese characters. Otherwise, they may be registered by someone else. In China, recovering a trademark after it has been registered by another party (including a franchisee) can be a complex undertaking. For example, Starbucks Corporation fought a legal battle against a local competitor that had registered its Chinese name – Xingbake – and was even using the coffee company's green logo. The case was resolved when the Shanghai Municipal Higher People's Court finally ruled in Starbucks' favor (Exhibit 8.7).

Selection and training of franchisees represents another problem area. In much of the world, firms struggle to identify and recruit qualified entrepreneurs. Although the local franchisee knows the market best, the franchisor still needs to understand the market for product adaptation and operational purposes. The franchisor, in order to remain viable in the long term, needs to coordinate the efforts of

Exhibit 8.7 A Starbucks store in Shenzhen, China, with its Chinese name next to the company's name
Credit: Zhang Peng/LightRocket via Getty Images.

individual franchisees – for example, to share ideas and engage in joint undertakings, such as cooperative advertising (Burton & Cross, 2001; Fladmoe-Lindquist, 2000; Icon Group International, 2018; Merrilees, 2014).

Local Presence

Many firms prefer to establish a local, stronger presence directly in important foreign markets. This is most commonly accomplished through interfirm collaboration or through full ownership of local operations via foreign direct investment (FDI). Let's explore these two entry approaches.

Interfirm Cooperation

International expansion typically is complex and potentially risky. Many firms seek to develop new products but may lack specific capabilities possessed by companies located abroad. Primarily for these reasons, many firms partner with suppliers, customers, competitors, or companies in other industries to achieve international or product development goals.

A **strategic alliance** is a type of partnership between two or more companies that aim to achieve a common, planned business objective. It is something more than a simple customer–vendor relationship but less than an outright acquisition. Alliances can take forms ranging from informal cooperation to joint ownership of worldwide operations. For example, Texas Instruments has undertaken strategic alliances with partners as diverse as Hyundai, Fujitsu, Alcatel, and Ericsson.

Firms undertake strategic alliances for various reasons. Market development is one common focus. Penetrating foreign markets is a primary objective of many companies. In Japan, Motorola shares chip designs and manufacturing facilities with Toshiba to gain greater access to the Japanese market. Some alliances aim to defend home markets. With no orders coming in for nuclear power plants, Bechtel Group has teamed up with Germany's Siemens to service existing US plants. Other options are either the sharing of risk or of resources. The costs of developing new jet engines are so vast that they force aerospace companies into collaboration. One such consortium was formed by United Technologies' Pratt & Whitney division, Britain's Rolls-Royce, Motoren-und-Turbinen Union from Germany, Fiat of Italy, and Japanese Aero Engines (made up of Ishikawajima Heavy Industries and Kawasaki Heavy Industries). Some alliances are formed to block and co-opt competitors. For example, Caterpillar formed a heavy equipment joint venture with Mitsubishi in Japan to strike back at its main global rival, Komatsu, in its home market.

The most successful alliances are those that match the complementary strengths of partners to satisfy a joint objective. Partners may have different products or functional strengths which they can build on (Mesquita & Ragozzino, 2017; Townsend, 2003).

Types of Interfirm Cooperation

Each form of alliance is distinct in terms of the amount of commitment required and the degree of control each partner has. The equity alliances – minority ownership, joint ventures, and consortia – feature the most extensive commitment and shared control. The types of strategic alliances are summarized in Exhibit 8.8, using the extent of equity involved and the number of partners in the endeavor as defining characteristics.

Informal Cooperation. In informal cooperative deals, partners work together without a binding agreement. This arrangement often takes the form of visits to exchange information about new products, processes, and technologies or may take the more formal form of the exchange of personnel for limited amounts of time. Often such partners are of no real threat in each other's markets and are of modest size in comparison to the competition, making collaboration necessary. The relationships are based on mutual trust and friendship, and may lead to more formal arrangements, such as contractual agreements or joint projects.

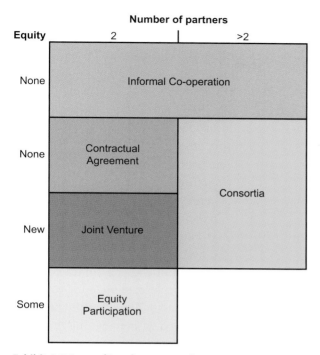

Exhibit 8.8 Types of interfirm cooperation
Source: Adapted with permission from Bernard L. Simonin, Transfer of Knowledge of International Strategic Alliances: A Structural Approach, dissertation (Ann Arbor: University of Michigan, 1991).

Contractual Agreements. Strategic alliance partners may collaborate for joint R&D, marketing, or production. Alternatively, they may use joint licensing or marketing. Nestlé and General Mills had an agreement whereby Honey Nut Cheerios and Golden Grahams were made in General Mills' US plants and shipped in bulk to Europe for packaging by Nestlé. Such an arrangement – complementary marketing (also known as piggybacking) – allows firms to reach objectives that they cannot reach efficiently by themselves. The alliance between General Mills and Nestlé evolved into a joint venture, Cereal Partners Worldwide, which markets both companies' products in Europe and Asia. In this way, cross-marketing activities represent a reciprocal arrangement whereby each partner provides the other access to its markets for a product. The New York Yankees and Manchester United sell each other's licensed products and develop joint sponsorship programs. International airlines share hubs, coordinate schedules, and simplify ticketing. Alliances such as Star (joining United and Lufthansa), Oneworld (British Airways and American Airlines), and Sky Team (Delta and Air France) provide worldwide coverage for their customers both in the travel and shipping communities.

Firms also enter contractual agreements for outsourcing. For example, General Motors buys cars and components from South Korea's Daewoo, and Siemens buys computers from Fujitsu. As corporations look for ways to simultaneously grow and maintain their competitive advantage, outsourcing has become a powerful new tool for achieving those goals. **Contract manufacturing** refers to outsourcing the production of goods so that the firm can focus on research, development, and marketing. Nike has nearly all its footwear manufactured this way, which allows the firm to concentrate on R&D and marketing. The benefits of such contracting are to improve company focus on higher value-added activities, to gain access to world-class capabilities, and to reduce operating costs.

In some parts of the world and in certain industries, governments insist on complete or majority ownership of firms. In such settings, multinational companies offer **management contracts**, an agreement whereby a firm sells its expertise in running a company while avoiding the risk or benefit of ownership. For example, using management contracts, the Marriott and Four Seasons corporations run, but do not own, numerous hotels worldwide. Many hotels, hospitals, airports, and other facilities are operated this way around the world in which a contractor supplies managerial know-how to operate an organization in exchange for compensation. In France and Japan, Disney theme parks are actually owned by separate entities, and the Walt Disney Company is mainly charged with managing the parks (Buckley et al., 2018; NCMA, 2017).

One specialized form of management contract is the **turnkey operation**, an arrangement that permits a client to acquire a complete international system, together with skills sufficient to allow unassisted maintenance and operation of the system following its completion. The client need not search for individual contractors or subcontractors or deal with scheduling conflicts or with difficulties in assigning responsibilities or blame. Instead, a package arrangement focuses responsibility on one entity, thus greatly easing the negotiation and supervision requirements and subsequent accountability. When the project is running, the system will be totally owned, controlled, and operated by the customer. Companies such as AES are part of consortia building electric power facilities around the world, operating them, and, in some cases, even owning parts of them.

Management contracts have clear benefits for the client. They provide organizational skills not available locally, expertise that is immediately available, and management assistance in the form of support services that would be difficult and costly to replicate locally. For example, hotels managed by the Sheraton Corporation have access to Sheraton's worldwide reservation system. Management contracts today typically involve training locals to take over the operation after a given time period.

Similar advantages exist for the supplier. The risk of participating in an international venture is substantially lowered, while significant amounts of control are still exercised. Existing know-how that has been built up through substantial investment can be commercialized, and frequently the impact of fluctuations in business volume can be reduced by making use of experienced personnel who otherwise would have to be laid off. Accumulated service knowledge should be used internationally. Management contracts permit firms to do so (Deresky, 2017; Cook & Raia, 2017).

Equity Participation. Many multinational corporations have acquired minority ownership in companies that have strategic importance for them to ensure supplier ability and build formal and informal working relationships. An example was the equity swap between China's Unicom and Spain's Telefonica. The partners continue operating as separate entities, but each enjoys the strengths that the other provides. For example, both telecom giants were motivated by a desire to stay competitive and gain market share in the midst of a global economic downturn. The agreement ensured cooperation in infrastructure and equipment sharing, research and development, and the provision of roaming and other services for multinational customers. The deal gave both companies access to a combined 550 million customers worldwide. Equity ownership in an innovator may also give the investing company first access to any newly developed technology. Another significant reason for equity ownership is market entry and support of global operations. For example, Telefonica has acquired varying stakes in Latin American telecommunications systems – a market that is the fastest-growing region of the world after Asia. Telefonica had evolved into one of the world's largest telecom operators (Tallman et al., 2017; Yan & Luo, 2016).

Joint Ventures. A joint venture can be defined as the participation of two or more companies in an enterprise in which each party contributes assets, has some equity, and shares risk. The venture is also considered long term. The reasons for establishing a joint venture can be divided into three groups: (1) government policy or legislation; (2) one partner's needs for other partners' skills; and (3) one partner's needs for other partners' attributes or assets. Equality of the partners or of their contribution is not necessary. In some joint ventures, each partner's contributions – typically consisting of funds, technology, plant, or labor – also vary.

The key to a joint venture is the sharing of a common business objective, which makes the arrangement more than a customer–vendor relationship but less than an outright acquisition. The partners' rationales for entering into the arrangement may vary. An example is a joint venture between Toyota and General Motors (GM). Toyota needed direct access to the US market, while GM benefited from the technology and management approaches provided by its Japanese partner. Joint ventures may be the only way in which a firm can profitably participate in a particular market since many governments restrict equity participation in local operations by foreigners. Other entry modes may be limited; for example, exports may be restricted because of tariff barriers. Joint ventures are valuable when the pooling of resources results in a better outcome for each partner than if each were to conduct its activities individually. This is particularly true when each partner has a specialized advantage in areas that benefit the venture. For example, a firm may have new technology yet lack sufficient capital to carry out foreign direct investment on its own. Through a joint venture, the technology can be used more quickly and market penetration achieved more easily. Similarly, one of the partners may have a distribution system already established or have better access to local suppliers, either of which permits a greater volume of sales in a shorter period of time.

Joint ventures also permit better relationships with local government and other organizations such as labor unions. Government-related reasons are the main rationale for joint ventures to take place in less-developed countries. If the local partner is politically influential, the new venture may be eligible for tax incentives, grants, and government support. Negotiations for certifications or licenses may be easier because authorities may not perceive themselves as dealing with a foreign firm. Relationships between the local partner and the local financial establishment may enable the joint venture to tap local capital markets. The greater experience (and therefore greater familiarity) with the local culture and environment of the local partner may enable the joint venture to benefit from greater insights into changing market conditions and needs.

Many joint ventures fall short of expectations and/or are disbanded. The reasons typically relate to conflicts of interest, problems with disclosure of sensitive information, and disagreements over how profits are to be shared. There is also often a lack of communication before, during, and after the formation of the venture. In some cases, managers have been more interested in the launching of the venture than the actual running of the enterprise. Many of the problems stem from a lack of careful consideration in advance, of how to manage the new endeavor. A partnership works on the basis of trust and commitment or not at all.

Typical disagreements cover the whole range of business decisions, including strategy, management style, accounting and control, marketing policies and strategies, research and development, and personnel. The joint venture may, for example, identify a particular market as a target only to find that one of the partners already has individual plans for it. US partners have frequently complained that their Japanese counterparts do not send their most competent personnel to the joint venture; instead, because of their lifetime employment practice, they get rid of less competent managers by sending them to the new entities.

Similarly, the issue of profit accumulation and distribution may cause discontent. If one partner supplies the joint venture with a good, the partner will prefer that any profits accumulate at headquarters and accrue 100 percent to one firm rather than at the joint venture, where profits are divided according to equity participation. Such a decision may not be greeted with enthusiasm by the other partner. Once profits are accumulated, their distribution may lead to disputes. For example, one partner may insist on a high payout of dividends because of financial needs, whereas the other may prefer the reinvestment of profits into a growing operation (Cavusgil, 1998; Yan & Luo, 2016).

Consortia. A new pharmaceutical drug can cost $1 billion to develop and bring to market. Some $7 billion goes into creating a new generation of computer chips. To combat the high costs and risks of research and development, research consortia have emerged in various countries. For example, Ericsson, Panasonic, Samsung, Siemens, Sony, Motorola, Nokia, and Psion formed a consortia called "Symbian" to develop technologies for wireless communication, and headquartered in the United Kingdom.

The European Union established several consortia to develop new technologies under the names EUREKA, ESPRIT, BRITE, RACE, and COMET. Airbus Industries, the giant aerospace company, is a consortium backed by the European Aeronautic Defence and Space Company (EADS) that emerged from the link-up of the German DaimlerChrysler Aerospace AG, the French Aerospatiale Matra, and CASA of Spain. All these units are subject to the repercussion of the UK leaving the European Union. Only time will tell us about the effect of Brexit.

Managerial Considerations. The first requirement of interfirm cooperation is to find the right partner. Partners should have an orientation and goals in common and should bring complementary and relevant benefits to the endeavor. The venture makes little sense if the expertise of both partners is in the same area; for example, if both have production expertise but neither has distribution know-how. Patience should be exercised; a deal should not be rushed into, nor should the partners expect immediate results. Learning should be paramount in the endeavor while at the same time, partners must try not to give away core secrets to each other.

Second, the more formal the arrangement, the greater the care that needs to be taken in negotiating the agreement. In joint venture negotiations, for example, extensive provisions must be made for contingencies. The points to be explored should include: (1) clear definition of the venture and its duration; (2) ownership, control, and management; (3) financial structure and policies; (4) taxation and fiscal obligation; (5) employment and training; (6) production; (7) government assistance; (8) transfer of technology; (9) marketing arrangements; (10) environmental protection; (11) record-keeping and inspection; and (12) settlement of disputes. These issues have to be addressed before the formation of the venture; otherwise, they eventually will surface as points of contention. A joint venture agreement, although comparable to a marriage agreement, should contain the elements of a divorce contract. In case the joint venture cannot be maintained to the satisfaction of partners, plans must exist for the dissolution of the agreement and for the allocation of profits and costs. Typically, however, one of the partners buys out the other partner(s) when partners decide to part ways.

A strategic alliance, by definition, also means a joining of two corporate cultures, which can often be quite different than a joint venture. To meet this challenge, partners must have frequent communication and interaction at three levels of the organization: the top management, operational leaders, and workforce levels. Trust and relinquishing control are difficult not only at the top but also at levels where the future of the venture is determined. A dominant partner may determine the corporate culture, but even then the other partners should be consulted. The development of specific alliance managers may be advised to forge the net of relationships both within and between alliance partners and, therefore, to support the formal alliance structure.

Strategic alliances operate in a dynamic business environment and must therefore adjust to changing market conditions. The agreement between partners should provide for changes in the original concept so that the venture can flourish and grow. The trick is to have a prior understanding as to which party will take care of which pains and problems so that a common goal is reached.

Government attitudes and policies have to be part of the environmental considerations of corporate decision-makers. While some alliances may be seen as a threat to the long-term economic security of a nation, in general, links with foreign operators should be encouraged. For example, the US Government urged major US airlines to form alliances with foreign carriers to gain access to emerging world markets, partly in response to the failure to achieve free access to all markets through the negotiation of so-called open-skies agreements (Cavusgil, 1998; Tjemkes et al., 2017; Yan & Luo, 2016).

Full Ownership

Some firms strive for 100 percent ownership of subsidiaries and other ventures that they develop overseas. For example, Starbucks enjoys full ownership of its subsidiary in France, which previously had been operated through a joint venture with Sigla S.A. (Grupo Vips) of Spain. The ownership switch was motivated by potential increases in profitability and operational efficiency in the growing French market. Starbucks had opened its first location at the Paris Opera House. In order to make a rational decision about the extent of ownership, management must evaluate the extent to which total control is important to the success of its international marketing activities. Full ownership may be a desirable, but unnecessary, prerequisite for international success. At other times it may be essential, particularly when strong links exist within the corporation. Interdependencies between and among local operations and headquarters may be so strong that nothing short of total coordination will result in an acceptable benefit to the firm as a whole.

Increasingly, however, the international environment is hostile to full ownership by multinational firms. Government action through outright legal restrictions or discriminatory actions is making the option less attractive. There seems to be a distinct "liability of foreignness" to which multinational firms are exposed (Wu & Salomon, 2017). Such disadvantages can result from government resentment of greater opportunities by multinational firms. But they can also be the consequence of corporate actions such as the decision to have many expatriates rotate in top management positions, which may weaken the standing of a subsidiary and its local employees.

To overcome market barriers abroad, firms can either build competitive capabilities from scratch or acquire them from local owners. The choice is often to accept a reduction in control or to lose the opportunity to operate efficiently in a country. In addition to formal action by the government, the general conditions in the market may make it advisable for the firm to join forces with local entities (Buckley et al., 2018; Tallman et al., 2017; UNCTAD, 2018).

A Comprehensive View of International Expansion

All of the developments, processes, and factors involved in the overall process of going international are linked to each other. Exhibit 8.9 presents a comprehensive view of these links. The central driver of internationalization is the level of managerial commitment. This commitment will grow gradually from an awareness of international potential to the adaptation of international business as a strategic business direction. It will be influenced by the information, experience, and perception of management, which in turn is shaped by motivations, concerns, and the activities of change agents.

Management's commitment and its view of the capabilities of the firm will then trigger various international business activities, which can range from indirect exporting and importing to more direct involvement in the global market.

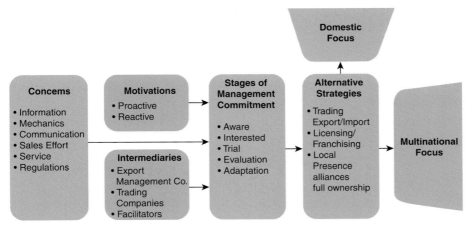

Exhibit 8.9 A comprehensive view of international expansion

Eventually, the firm may then expand further through measures such as joint ventures, strategic alliances, or foreign direct investment (Buckley et al., 2018; Dowlah, 2018).

SUMMARY

Firms do not become experienced in international business overnight, but rather progress gradually through an internationalization process. The process is triggered by different motivations to go abroad. The motivations can be proactive or reactive. Proactive motivations are initiated by aggressive management, whereas reactive motivations are the defensive response of management to environmental changes and pressures. Firms that are primarily stimulated by proactive motivations are more likely to enter international business and succeed.

In going abroad, firms encounter multiple problems and challenges, a lack of information to short fall in mechanics and documentation. In order to gain assistance in its initial international experience, the firm can make use of either intermediaries or facilitators. Intermediaries are outside companies that actively participate in an international transaction. They are export management companies or trading companies. In order for these intermediaries to perform international business functions properly, however, they must be compensated. This will result in a reduction of profits.

International facilitators do not participate in international business transactions, but they contribute knowledge and information. Increasingly, facilitating roles are played by private-sector groups, such as industry associations, banks, accountants, or consultants, and by universities and federal, state, and local government authorities.

Apart from exporting and importing, alternatives for international business entry are licensing, franchising, and local presence. The basic advantage of licensing is that it does not involve capital investment or knowledge of foreign markets. Its major disadvantage is that licensing agreements typically have time limits, are often proscribed by foreign governments, and may result in creating a competitor. The use of franchising as a means of expansion into foreign markets has increased dramatically. Franchisors must learn to strike a balance between adapting to local environments and standardizing to the degree necessary to maintain international recognizability.

Full ownership is becoming more unlikely in many markets as well as industries, and the firm has to look at alternative approaches. The main alternative is interfirm cooperation, in which the firm joins forces with other business entities, possibly even a foreign government. In some cases, when the firm may not want to make a direct investment, it will offer its management expertise for sale in the form of management contracts.

DISCUSSION QUESTIONS

1. Why is management commitment so important to export success?
2. Explain the benefits that international sales can have for domestic business activities.
3. Comment on the stance that "licensing is really not a form of international involvement because it requires no substantial additional effort on the part of the licensor."
4. How can intermediaries assist companies in their trading effort?
5. How can an export intermediary avoid circumvention by a client or customer?
6. Comment on the observation that "a joint venture may be a combination of Leonardo da Vinci's brain and Carl Lewis's legs; one wants to fly, the other insists on running."
7. Why would an internationalizing company opt for a management contract over other modes of operation? Relate your answer especially to the case of hospitality companies such as Hyatt, Marriott, and Sheraton.

KEY TERMS

accidental exporter	204	licensing agreement	219
agent	215	management contracts	226
contract manufacturing	226	managerial commitment	203
contractual agreements	225	psychological distance	208
cross-marketing activities	225	royalty	219
direct involvement	213	sogoshosha	216
distributor	215	strategic alliances	224
export management		trademark licensing	220
companies (EMCs)	215	transaction cost theory	213
franchising	221	turnkey operation	226
indirect involvement	213	unsolicited order	204
license	219		

TAKE A STAND

The European Union (EU) has implemented an agriculture policy that heavily subsidizes local producers. As a result, European farmers have increased their production capacity and are able to export large quantities of cheap foodstuffs to the international market. The EU has come under heavy scrutiny for these subsidies. Critics claim that the policy is harming agriculture in the developing world by cutting out suppliers in poor countries, where governments are unable or unwilling to dole out assistance.

Questions for Debate

1. Is there a way to make cheap food available in poor countries, without forcing people in rich countries to pay artificially high prices for it and unfairly cutting out suppliers in the developing world?
2. Does it matter that the EU is a generous international aid donor?
3. Under what circumstances are government subsidies justified?

INTERNET EXERCISES

1. What forms of export assistance are offered by the Small Business Administration (www.sba.gov) and the Export–Import Bank (www.exim.gov)?
2. Prepare a one-page memo to a foreign company introducing your product or service. Include a contact listing of ten foreign businesses looking to import your particular product. Cite the sources you used. You can find sample sources of trade leads at www.trade.gov, www.trademarch.co.uk, and www.mnileads.com/, as well as at the various sites listed in Exhibit 8.5.
3. The US Bureau of the Census tracks foreign trade statistics, at www.census.gov/foreign-trade. Using their search engine, search for the report "Profile of US Exporting Companies". Answer the following questions:
   (i)   What are the main characteristics of firms that export from the USA?
   (ii) What proportion of US exporters are small and medium-sized exporters?
   (iii) What countries are the top targets of US exporters? What factors make these countries the top markets for US firms?

FURTHER RESOURCES

Deloitte. (2017). On the Board's Agenda: What Directors Need to Know About Digital Transformation. Deloitte Center for Board Effectiveness, October 2017. Available at www.deloitte.com

Duane, S. and Domegan, C. (2019). Social marketing partnerships: Evolution, scope and substance. *Marketing Theory*, 19(2), 169–193. https://doi.org/10.1177/1470593118799810

Gao, L. and Mishra, B. (2019). The Role of Market Evolution in Channel Contracting. (Report). *Management Science*, 65(5), 2432–2441. https://doi.org/10.1287/mnsc.2018.3057

International Trade Administration, *Basic Guide to Exporting* (Washington, DC: International Trade Administration, 2018).

International Telecommunications Union, Measuring the Information Society 2017 (Geneva, Switzerland: International Telecommunications Union)

Jensen, K. R. (2017). Leading Global Innovation: Facilitating Multicultural Collaboration and International Market Success. London: Palgrave Macmillan.

Konigsberg, Alexander S. (2016). *International Franchising.* New York: Juris Publishers.

Sengupta, Jati K. (2007). *Dynamics of Entry and Market Evolution.* New York: Palgrave Macmillan.

Tjemkes, Brian, Vos, Pepijn, and Burgers, Koen. (2017). *Strategic Alliance Management.* London: Routledge.

Yan, Aimin, and Luo, Yadong. (2016). *International Joint Ventures: Theory and Practice.* New York: Routledge.

PART III

9

International Marketing

LEARNING OBJECTIVE

- How can markets for international expansion be selected?
- Coping with new challenges for the international marketing manager
- Standardized versus localized global strategies
- Facing global challenges to product, price, distribution, and communications

CONTENTS

VIGNETTE 9 Sports sponsorship

The number of big annual international sporting events has increased exponentially – from 20 in 1912 to more than 1,400 in 2018, an average of about four per day. Simultaneously, global sports sponsorship has gradually grown over the past decade to more than $65 billion per year. When companies sponsor a team or sports event, their goal is to generate brand awareness and customer loyalty for their firm and products. Marketers develop relationships with teams, organizers, and individual superstars, such as Cristiano Ronaldo and Roger Federer.

Marketers employ a wide variety of strategies, such as attaching a company's name to a stadium, sponsoring Little League baseball tournaments, and using famous sport personalities in their advertising. The Olympics and the World Soccer Cup bring marketers the largest amount of exposure to the largest number of potential customers.

For multinationals, crafting a successful global sports marketing strategy involves finding the right combination of expensive, "big-ticket" international competitions, as well as smaller-scale local and regional events. In 2019, the most popular sponsor brands in sports were all multinational firms:

- Pepsi (USA, beverages)
- Red Bull (Austria, beverages)
- Coca-Cola (USA, beverages)
- Samsung (South Korea, electronics)
- Puma (Germany, athletic apparel)
- Adidas (Germany, athletic apparel)
- Reebok (UK, athletic apparel)
- Castrol (UK, oil and gas)

Many major corporations spend large sums on sponsorship and advertising during sporting events. Marketers need to choose their partners carefully to ensure effective and engaging outcomes. One challenge of sports sponsorships is that the benefits are hard to quantify. The contribution to the sponsoring firm's bottom line is nearly impossible to measure.

Sports sponsorship might be a case of the "dog that did not bark" – more conspicuous in its absence than its presence. If Pepsi or Red Bull were to withdraw from one of the big sporting events that they currently sponsor, a competitor would quickly step in. Additionally, the company's long-standing relationships with broadcasters and organizers could be damaged. Evaluating the number of new corporate customers that sell a given sponsor's products in stores, the incremental amount of promotional/display activity, and new vending placements, can provide useful benchmarks of success. However, environmental disruptions can short change both sponsor and product as one saw during the Coronavirus attacks of 2020.

Sources: Cornwell, 2020; FINSMES, 2019; Handley, 2018; Topend Sports, 2020.

Introduction

Marketing is the activity of engaging a set of institutions and coordinating processes for creating, communicating, and delivering value from an exchange based on offerings that have value for customers, clients, partners, and society at large (American Marketing Association, 2020). The concepts of value, satisfaction, and exchange are at the core of marketing. For an exchange to take place, two or more entities should communicate physically or electronically for delivery of perceived value. During the exchange, customers should be perceived as information seekers who evaluate every offering in terms of their own needs, wants, and desires. When the offering is consistent with their needs, they tend to choose the good or service; if it is not, other alternatives are chosen.

A key task of the marketer is to recognize the ever-changing nature of needs and wants using marketing techniques, which can be applied not only to goods but to ideas and services as well. Marketers plan and execute programs that will ensure a long-term competitive advantage for the company. This task has two integral parts: (1) identifying target markets and (2) managing marketing activities. Marketing management consists of manipulating marketing mix elements to best satisfy the needs of the individual target markets. Regardless of geographic markets, the basic tasks of marketing managers do not vary; they have been called the technical universals of marketing (Kotler & Keller, 2016).

This chapter focuses on the formulation of marketing strategy and tactics for international operations. It describes what effective marketing strategy can do, how target markets are selected based on pertinent market characteristics, and how to adjust elements of the marketing program to achieve maximum effectiveness and efficiency, while attempting to exploit global and regional similarities, as in the case of sports sponsorship.

Target Market Selection

If all markets were similar in their characteristics, the firm could enter any one of them without preparation. In reality, however, markets differ along three major dimensions: physical, psychic, and economic. **Physical distance** is the geographic distance between home and target countries; its impact has decreased thanks to technological developments in transportation and communications. **Psychic distance** refers to differences in culture, language, tradition, and customs between two countries (Czinkota, 2017). **Economic distance** translates into the target's ability to pay. Generally, the greater the overall distance – or difference – between two countries, the less knowledge the marketer has about the target market. The amount of information that is available varies dramatically (Hutzschenreuter et al.,

2016). For example, although the marketer can easily learn about the economic environment from the Internet and other secondary sources, invaluable interpretive information may not be available until the firm actually enters the market. In the early stages of this assessment, international marketers can be assisted by numerous online information sources.

The process of target market selection for international business is complex. International market penetration involves identifying potential country markets and market segments within them. Rather than trying to appeal to everyone, firms can best utilize their resources by (1) identifying potential markets for entry and (2) expanding selectively over time to those deemed attractive.

Firms undertake screening research to identify the most attractive target markets. The process begins with very general criteria and ends with product-specific market analyses. Target market screening progresses in four stages: preliminary screening, estimation of market potential, estimation of sales potential, and identification of segments. Each stage should be given careful attention. The first stage, for example, should not merely reduce the number of alternatives to a manageable few for the sake of reduction, even though the expense of analyzing markets in depth is great. Unless care is taken, attractive alternatives may be eliminated (Leonidou et al., 2018). There are four stages of target market screening.

Preliminary Screening

The preliminary screening process must rely chiefly on secondary data for country-specific factors as well as product and industry-specific factors. Country-specific factors typically include those that indicate the market's overall buying power – for example, population, gross national product in total and per capita, total exports and imports, and production of cement, electricity, and steel. Product-specific factors narrow the analysis to the firm's specific areas of operation. A company such as Motorola, manufacturing for the automotive aftermarket, is interested in the number of passenger cars, trucks, and buses in use. The statistical analyses must be accompanied by qualitative assessments of the impact of cultural elements and the overall climate for foreign firms and products. A market that satisfies the levels set becomes a prospective target country.

Estimating Market Potential

Total market potential is the sales, in physical or monetary units, that might be available to all firms in an industry during a given period under a given level of industry marketing effort and given environmental conditions. The international marketer needs to assess the size of existing markets and forecast the size of future markets. A number of techniques, both quantitative and qualitative, are available for this task, such as estimation of income elasticity of demand and economic progress.

If appropriate data are available, the simplest way to establish a market-size estimate is to conduct a market audit, by adding local production and imports with exports deducted from the total. However, in many cases, data may not exist, be current, or fit the question. In such cases, market potentials may have to be estimated by methods such as analogy. This approach is based on the use of proxy variables that have been shown to correlate with the demand for the product in question. The market size for a product (such as mobile advertising) in country A is estimated by comparing a ratio for an available indicator (e.g., smartphones) for country A and country B, and using this ratio to determine advertising opportunities in country B. In some cases, a time lag in demand patterns may be seen, thus requiring a longitudinal analysis, which involves repeated observations of a phenomenon over long periods of time. For example, it is suggested that the use of wireless communication in southern Europe lags northern Europe by two years and that wireless phone use overall is tied to the state of the economy (e.g., GNP per capita). Despite the valuable insight generated through these techniques, caution should be used in over-interpreting the results.

In industrialized countries, the richest 10 percent of the population consumes 20 percent of all goods and services; in developing countries the figure may be as high as 45 percent. Therefore, even in the developing countries with low GNP figures, segments with substantial buying power may exist (Dholakia et al., 2018).

In addition to quantitative techniques that rely on secondary data, international marketers can use various survey techniques. They are especially useful when marketing new technologies. A survey of end-user interest and responses may provide a relatively clear picture of the possibilities in a new market. Surveys can also be administered through a web site or through e-mail. More research alternatives are presented in Chapter 7 of this book.

Comparing figures for market potential with actual sales will provide the international marketer with further understanding of the firm's chances in the market. If the difference between potential and reality is substantial, the reasons can be evaluated using gap analysis. Here, the market researcher seeks to identify spaces in the market between what firms are currently selling and what consumers want to purchase. The differences can be the result of usage, distribution, or product line gaps. If the firm is already in the market, part of the difference between its sales and the market potential can be explained through the competitive gap. Usage gaps indicate that not all potential users are using the product or that those using it are not using as much as they could, which suggests mainly a promotional task. Global fashion designers and retailers pay close attention to what trendy teenagers are wearing on the streets of Tokyo's Shibuya and Harajuku districts in order to spot emerging trends and develop new products for sales opportunities (Brem & Freitag, 2015).

Data from China highlights that luxury retailers are now focusing on serving the upper-middle class in Asian countries owing to the increase in disposable

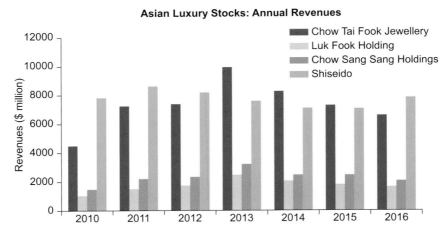

Exhibit 9.1 Asian luxury stocks: Annual revenues
Source: Khaitan, 2017.

income available with the segment (Atsmon & Dixit, 2009; Khaitan, 2017). Increasing demand of luxury products in emerging Asian countries is reflective in the revenue of four Asian luxury retailers Chow Sang Sang, Chow Tai Fook Jewellery Group, Shiseido and Luk Fook Holdings. A study by Frontera News reported that these companies returned 29%, 43%, 46%, and 62% increases in their share value during 2016. Chow Sang Sang is a jewelry brand from Hong Kong that serves consumers in China from its 150 outlets and in Macau and Hong Kong through 50 retail outlets (Exhibit 9.1).

Estimating Sales Potential

Even when the international marketer has gained an understanding of markets with the greatest overall promise, the firm's own possibilities in those markets are still not known. Sales potential is the share of the market potential that the firm can reasonably expect to get over the longer term. To arrive at an estimate, the marketer needs to collect product- and market-specific data related to:

1. Competition – strength, likely reaction to entry
2. Market – strength of barriers
3. Consumers – ability and willingness to buy
4. Product – degree of relative advantage, compatibility, complexity, trial ability, and communicability
5. Channel structure – access to retail level

In 2009, Russia was one of the fastest growing markets worldwide for new cars. It had gone from annual sales of less than 1.5 million in 2005 to nearly 3 million in 2008 and was poised to overtake Germany as the fourth-biggest car market in the world. Credit Suisse confidently predicted that sales would grow by at least 12 percent a year until 2012. By then the foreign car firms that had rushed to build factories in Russia would be producing more than 1.5 million cars a year. How wrong were they? Credit Suisse, which was used to finance the purchase of about half of all new cars, disappeared almost instantly. Thanks to the economy's reliance on exports of oil and gas, slumping energy prices immediately hit both earnings and the ruble. The tumbling domestic currency also meant that foreign car brands suddenly became much less affordable, including those made in Russia, because most of their components are still imported. In addition, foreign multinational corporations such as Renault, Ford, and General Motors amended their production plans for year 2009 in Russia and delayed their production of new models (The Economist, 2009).

Identifying Segments

Within the markets selected, individuals and organizations will vary in their wants, resources, geographical locations, buying attitudes, and buying practices (Kotler & Keller, 2016). Initially, the firm may cater to one or only a few of the segments identified. Only later will there be an expansion to other market groups if the product is innovative. Segmentation is indicated when clusters are indeed different enough to warrant individualized attention, large enough for-profit potential, and reachable through the methods that the international marketer can use. When growth potential is no longer in market development, the firm may opt for market penetration. Exhibit 9.2 presents a case in which LEGO used skillful market segmentation to expand its brand.

EXHIBIT 9.2 LEGO customer personas

LEGO group exemplifies a successful effort at international market segmentation. By leveraging a careful mix of audience targeting and social media, the firm skillfully targeted current and potential customers, differentiating them by specific market experience and response, and providing them a high-quality online experience. Management identified six distinct personas that it used to categorize LEGO customers based on purchase and usage rates. The personas ranged from current LEGO devotees to those having no experience with the brand. By actively and cleverly engaging each persona group, LEGO succeeded at encouraging them to become ardent advocates for the firm and its products. Such skillful marketing has helped LEGO become the world's fourth best-selling toy company, capturing nearly 7% of global market share for toys. LEGO has continued to sustain high growth, achieving a net profit of $688 million for the year.

Source: Peterson, 2018.

LEGO's diverse offerings and strong brand have made it one of the most profitable toy companies
Credit: Stephen M. Dowell/Orlando Sentinel/Tribune News Service via Getty Images.

Factors Affecting Expansion Strategy

Expansion strategy is determined by factors related to the market and the marketing mix. In the choice of expansion strategy, demand for the firm's products is a critical factor. When growth rates in certain markets are high and stable, the firm will most likely opt to concentrate sales in those markets. If the demand is strong worldwide, diversification may be attractive.

The uniqueness of the firm's offering with respect to competition is also a factor in expansion strategy. If lead time over competition is considerable, the decision to diversify may not seem urgent. However, complacency can be a mistake in today's competitive environment; competitors can rush new products into the market in a matter of days. Competition may present other challenges as well. For products in which fast-changing technology and service offerings can provide only temporary and sometimes questionable competitive advantage, competitive superiority claims, either explicit or implicit, will often face immediate challenge.

Depending on the product, each market will have its own challenges. Whether constraints are apparent (such as tariffs) or hidden (such as tests or standards), they will complicate all of the other factors. Nevertheless, regional integration has allowed many marketers to diversify their efforts (Verbeke & Asmussen, 2016). The opportunity to take advantage of diversification is available for all types of companies, not only the large ones. The identification of unique worldwide segments

---

EXHIBIT 9.3 Canon's Kidictionary

When optical products company Canon sought to develop new markets for its IXUS digital camera, market researchers discovered that young children were under-served. Thus, the firm decided to develop and target the segment of parents-to-be and parents with young children. The firm's research revealed that many parents prefer to buy their children digital cameras rather than smartphones.

The marketing campaign consisted of a promotion in the form of a contest called Kidictionary. The company targeted kids aged 5 to 9, and asked them to interact with an ordinary word in a creative way through photography, and then to share the results on social media. The firm also leveraged online advertising and engaged key opinion bloggers to increase participation. As a result, the campaign resulted in engagement of 40% of the market. Visits to the Kidictionary website increased by 64%, comprising new and returning visitors. The website recorded more than 5,000 visitors per month and over 180 visitors per day.

Source: Peterson, 2018.

---

for which a customized marketing mix is provided has proven to be successful for many small and medium-sized companies. Exhibit 9.3 highlights an expansion strategy used by Canon to capture an underdeveloped market.

The Product

Product adaptation decisions vary from minor ones, such as translation of a user's manual, to major ones, such as creating a more economical version of the product. Studies of product adaptation show that most products must be modified for the international marketplace one way or another. Changes typically affect packaging, measurement units, labeling, product constituents and features, usage instructions, and, to a lesser extent, logos and brand names.

Regional, Country, or Local Characteristics

The market environment and regulations mandate most product modifications. The most stringent requirements often result from government rules. Some requirements may serve no purpose other than a political one (such as protection of domestic industry or response to political pressures). Because of the sovereignty of nations, individual firms must comply, but they can influence the situation either by lobbying directly or through industry associations to have the issue raised during trade negotiations. Government regulations may be spelled out, but firms need to be ever vigilant for changes and exceptions.

Product decisions made by marketers of consumer products are especially affected by local behavior, tastes, attitudes, and traditions, all reflecting the marketer's need to gain the customer's approval. Knowledge of cultural and psychological differences may be the key to success. For example, Brazilians typically eat a light breakfast at home; therefore, Dunkin' Donuts markets doughnuts as snacks, as dessert, and for parties. To further appeal to Brazilians, doughnuts are made with local fruit fillings such as papaya and guava. While China's Kentucky Fried Chicken menu features its signature "Original Recipe" fried chicken, it also creates products that appeal to local tastes such as the Spicy Dragon Twister, Pi Dan Congee (rice porridge), Fu Young Vegetable Soup, and Egg Tart (signature dessert). Pizza Hut restaurants display upscale decor to satisfy their customers' preference for "five-star service and atmosphere at a three-star price." The casual dining atmosphere is centered on an extensive menu that covers soup, salads, appetizers, and a range of pizzas such as Seafood Catch (seafood mix, crab sticks, green pepper, pineapple), and The Hot One (chili pepper, onion, tomato, beef, spicy chicken). Even with the success of KFC and Pizza Hut in China, the company is not resting on its laurels. Yum! China is installing touchscreen kiosks in its restaurants and using face-recognition technology to process payments. Robots prepare ice cream cones and other menu options. In 2020, about half of all food orders in China at KFC, Pizza Hut, and Taco Bell restaurants were placed via mobile app or digital kiosk (Bloomberg Businessweek, 2019; Taylor & Okazaki, 2015).

Globally consumers share similar standards when it comes to evaluating and appreciating a brand name that is catchy, memorable, distinct, and says something indicative of the product (Steenkamp, 2017; Talay et al., 2015). But, because of cultural and linguistic factors, Chinese consumers expect more in terms of how the names are spelled, written, and styled, and whether they are considered lucky. Food is arguably one of the most culture-sensitive categories. Hence, PepsiCo introduced Cheetos in the Chinese market under a Chinese name, *qi duo*, roughly pronounced "chee-do," that translates as "many surprises."

Often no concrete product changes are needed, only a change in the product's positioning. Positioning is the perception by consumers of the firm's brand in relation to competitors' brands (Kotler & Keller, 2016). Nontariff barriers may affect product positioning and include product standards, testing or approval procedures, subsidies for local products, and bureaucratic red tape. The nontariff barriers affecting product adjustments usually concern elements outside the core product. Coca-Cola took a risk in marketing Diet Coke in Japan because the population is not overweight by Western standards. Further, Japanese women do not like to drink anything clearly labeled as a diet product. The company changed the name

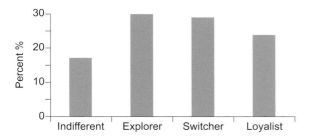

Exhibit 9.4 Distribution of four types of Chinese consumers (2013)
Source: China Internet Watch, 2013.

to Coke Light and subtly shifted the promotional theme from "weight loss" to "figure maintenance." (Betros, 2010).

A study of consumer attitudes in China classified the attitude of consumers into four categories (1) Indifferent, (2) Explorer, (3) Switcher, and (4) Loyalist (China Internet Watch, 2013). It found that 30 percent of consumers were Explorers – they consider and compare brands and conduct research before making a purchase (Exhibit 9.4).

Monitoring features of competitors' products, as well as determining how to meet and beat them, is critical to product-adaptation decisions. Competitive offerings may provide a baseline against which resources can be measured – for example, they may help to determine what it takes to reach a critical market share in a given competitive situation.

Management must take into account the stage of economic development of the overseas market. As a country's economy advances, buyers are in a better position to buy and to demand more sophisticated products and product versions. Many companies have described how they have adapted to the new global era through a process they call **reverse innovation**. For example, in India, General Electric developed a handheld electrocardiogram device that it sells for $1,000, about one-tenth of the price of the original (and much bulkier) US-developed machine. Similarly, in China, the company introduced a portable ultrasound machine priced at $15,000, again vastly cheaper than the model GE used to try to sell to the Chinese market (Immelt et al., 2009).

Packaging is an area where firms generally do make modifications. Owing to the longer time that products spend in channels of distribution, international companies, especially those marketing food products, have used more expensive packaging materials and/or more expensive transportation modes for export shipments. Food processors have solved the problem by using airtight, re-closable containers that seal out moisture and other contaminants.

The promotional aspect of packaging relates primarily to labeling. The major adjustments concern legally required bilingualism. Other governmental requirements include more informative labeling of products for consumer protection and education. Inadequate identification, failure to use the required languages, or inadequate or incorrect descriptions printed on the labels may all cause problems. Increasingly, environmental concerns are having an impact on packaging decisions. On the one hand, governments want to reduce packaging waste by encouraging marketers to adopt the four environmentally correct Rs – redesign, reduce, reuse, and recycle. The EU has strict policies on packaging waste and recycling of such materials. Depending on the packaging materials (20 percent for plastics and 60 percent for glass), producers, importers, distributors, wholesalers, and retailers are held responsible for generating the waste. In Germany, which has the toughest requirements, all packaging must be reusable or recyclable, and packaging must be kept to a minimum needed for proper protection and marketing of the product (Toto, 2018). Exporters to the EU must find distributors that can fulfill such requirements and must agree how to split the costs of such compliance.

When a product sold abroad requires repairs, parts, or service, the problems of obtaining, training, and holding a sophisticated engineering or repair staff are not easy to solve. If the product breaks down and the repair arrangements are not up to standard, the product image will suffer. In some cases, products abroad may not even be used for their intended purpose and thus may require not only modifications in product configuration but also in service frequency. For instance, snowplows exported from the USA are used to remove sand from driveways in Saudi Arabia, thus imposing product stress factors which are typically very unexpected for a snowplow.

The country of origin of a product, typically communicated by the phrase "made in (country)," has considerable influence on quality perceptions. The perception of products manufactured in certain countries is affected by built-in positive or negative assumptions about quality. For example, consumers tend hold very positive perceptions about wine from France and cars made in Japan. Such perceptions bolster exports of French wine and Japanese cars. By contrast, consumers may have negative perceptions about clothing made in Russia or computers made in Bolivia, because those countries have not established strong reputations for producing such goods. Firms may need to devise marketing approaches to overcome or neutralize such biases. The issue is especially important to developing countries that need to increase exports.

Company Considerations

Company policy will often determine the presence and degree of adaptation. Discussions of product adaptation often end with the question "Is it worth it?" The answer depends on the company's ability to control costs, to correctly estimate market potential, and, finally, to secure profitability. The decision to adapt should be preceded by a thorough analysis of the market. Formal market research with primary data collection and/or testing is warranted (Leonidou et al., 2018). From the financial standpoint, some companies have specific return-on-investment levels (e.g., 25 percent) to be satisfied before adaptation. Others let the requirement vary as a function of the market considered and also the time in the market – that is, profitability may be initially compromised for proper market entry.

India is home to 1.4 billion people with different cultures, languages, geographies, food habits, traditions, and sociocultural behaviors. No one can successfully do business in India by reading its potential from quantitative market reports. Understanding the psychological, sociological, and historical backgrounds is fundamental to hit the bull's eye. The soup concentrate manufacturer, Maggi, has leveraged research and skillful marketing to change the eating habits of Indian consumers through its promise of convenience. The brand understood the psychology of Indian mothers and positioned itself for mother–child indulgence. Nokia produced a cell phone with a dust-resistant keypad, anti-slip grip, and a built-in flashlight; truck drivers and rural consumers enjoyed these simple, yet useful, features (Chakravarthy, 2012; Varma, 2017).

Most companies aim for consistency in their market efforts. This means that all products must fit in terms of quality, price, and user perceptions. Consistency may be difficult to attain, for example, in the area of warranties. Warranties can be uniform only if use conditions do not vary drastically and if the company is able to deliver equally on its promise anywhere it has a presence. The goal of many marketers currently is to create consistency and impact, both of which are easier to manage with a single worldwide identity. Building global brands are a key way of reaching this goal. Global brands are reaching the world's mega-markets and are perceived as the same brand by consumers and internal constituents. While some of the global brands are completely standardized, some elements of the product may be adapted to local conditions (Steenkamp, 2017; Talay et al., 2015). These adjustments include brand names (e.g., Tide, Whisper, and Clairol in North America are Ariel, Allways, and Wella in Europe), positioning (e.g., Ford Fiesta as a small car in Germany but a family vehicle in Portugal), or product versions sold under the same brand name (e.g., a dozen different types of coffee sold under the Nescafé name in northern Europe alone). As revealed in Exhibit 9.5, Starbucks made numerous adjustments as it launched shops in China (Das, 2017).

Consumers worldwide associate and evaluate global brands based on three characteristics when making purchase decisions. First, global brands carry a strong *quality* signal suggested by their success across markets. Part of this is that great brands often represent great ideas and leading-edge technological solutions. Second, global brands compete on *emotion*, catering to aspirations that cut

EXHIBIT 9.5 Starbucks in China

In order to adapt to the Chinese market, Starbucks changed product texture, menu and store layout to match the local culture and food preferences. Chinese consider coffee stores to be a place for social gathering where they can socialize for hours with friends and family. Hence, Starbucks needed coffee shops with floorspace larger than those in the USA where its shops are normally about 1,200 to 1,500 square feet. For China the company started opening stores bigger than 2,000 square feet. Starbucks managers also observed that Chinese enjoy food along with their drink. In response, Starbucks began offering popular Chinese foods like curry puffs, traditional cookies, and moon cakes. Starbucks also incorporated the standard localization strategy that it deploys in every market they enter, e.g., modifying the name "Starbucks" to suit the local language. For China the name was changed to "Xing Bake" where "Xing" represents "Star" and "Bake" was pronounced as "bucks."

In addition, while tea is the traditional drink in China, the younger generation tends to prefer coffee. Hence, menus for different stores in China were adapted. For example, items on the menu for consumers in Shanghai were westernized with a standard menu and served coffee. In Beijing, stores introduced different tea-based drinks like coffee-flavored milk tea and green tea-flavored Frappuccino.

Source: Das, 2017.

Starbucks launched the mooncake in China for the mid-autumn festival
Credit: Zhang Peng/LightRocket via Getty Images.

across cultural differences. Global brands may cater to needs to feel cosmopolitan, something that local brands cannot deliver. Global brands may also convey that their user has reached a certain status both professionally and personally. This type of recognition represents both perception and reality, enabling brands to establish credibility in markets. Third, consumers choose global brands based on perceptions on how they *address social problems* linked to the nature of the product. For example, buying a BMW car addresses the desire to project an affluent social status.

Product Counterfeiting

Every year, more than one billion dollars in domestic and export sales are lost by companies worldwide because of product counterfeiting and intellectual property infringement of consumer and industrial products. The hardest hit are the software, entertainment, and pharmaceutical industries. Counterfeit goods are any goods bearing an unauthorized representation of a trademark, patented invention, or copyrighted work that is legally protected in the country where it is marketed (International Chamber of Commerce, 2017; Frontier Economics, 2017).

Four types of action can be taken against counterfeiting: legislative action, bilateral and multilateral negotiations, joint private sector action, and measures taken by individual firms. Governments have enacted special legislation and set country-specific negotiation objectives for reciprocity and retaliatory options for intellectual property protection.

Victimized firms not only lose sales but also goodwill in the longer term if customers, believing they are getting the real product, unknowingly end up with a copy of inferior quality. In addition to the normal measures of registering trademarks and copyrights, firms are taking steps in product development to prevent the copying of trademarked goods. For example, new authentication materials in labeling are virtually impossible to duplicate. Jointly, companies have formed organizations to lobby for legislation and to act as information clearinghouses.

Pricing

Pricing is a critical strategy instrument in the marketing mix and in marketing decision-making. Pricing in the international environment is more complicated than in the domestic market because of such factors as government influence, different currencies, and additional costs (Kermisch & Burns, 2018b). International pricing situations can be divided into four general categories: export pricing, foreign market pricing, price coordination, and intracompany (or transfer) pricing. As shown in Exhibit 9.6, skillful pricing strategy is essential, and top-performing global firms align pricing with sales incentives and rely on training and marketing as a tool.

Percentage of respondents who strongly agree or agree	The best	The rest
Our pricing strategy maximizes returns at customer and product levels	76%	41%
Our incentives encourage prudent pricing	80%	42%
Our salesforce has the right tools and data	77%	40%

Exhibit 9.6 Top-performing firms stand out on three pricing capabilities
Source: Kermisch and Burns, 2018b. Used with permission from Bain & Company www.bain.com/insights/is-pricing-killing-your-profits

Export Pricing

Three general price-setting strategies in international marketing are a standard worldwide price, dual pricing, and market-differentiated pricing. The first two are cost-oriented pricing methods that are relatively simple to establish, easy to understand, and cover all the necessary costs. Standard worldwide pricing is based on average unit costs of fixed, variable, and export-related costs.

In dual pricing, domestic and export prices are differentiated, and two approaches are available: the cost-plus method and the marginal cost method. The cost-plus strategy involves the actual costs, that is, a full allocation of domestic and foreign costs to the product. Although this type of pricing ensures margins, the final price may put the product beyond the reach of the customer. As a result, some exporters resort to flexible cost-plus strategy, wherein discounts are provided when necessary as a result of customer type, intensity of competition, or size of order. The marginal cost method considers the direct costs of producing and selling for export as the floor beneath which prices cannot be set. Fixed costs for plants, R&D, domestic overhead, and domestic marketing costs are disregarded. An exporter can thus lower export prices to be competitive in markets that otherwise might have been considered beyond access.

On the other hand, market-differentiated pricing is based on a demand-oriented strategy and is thus more consistent with the marketing concept. This method also allows consideration of competitive forces in setting export price. The major problem is the exporter's perennial dilemma: lack of information. Therefore, in most cases, marginal costs provide a basis for competitive comparisons, on which the export price is set (International Trade Administration, 2020).

In preparing a price quotation, the exporter should take into account unique export-related costs and, if possible, include them. They are in addition to the normal costs shared with the domestic side. They include:

1. The cost incurred in modifying the good for foreign markets.
2. Operational costs of the export operation. Examples are personnel, market research, additional shipping and insurance costs, communications costs with foreign customers, and overseas marketing communications costs.
3. Costs incurred in entering foreign markets. These include tariffs and taxes; risks associated with a buyer in a different market (mainly commercial credit risks and political risks); and dealing in other than the exporter's domestic currency i.e., foreign exchange risk (Bradsher, 2017).

The combined effect of both clear-cut and hidden costs results in export prices far in excess of domestic prices. This is called price escalation. Management must take into account the stage of economic development and buying power of the market. The analysis of a pricing study by Bain and Company, as shown in Exhibit 9.7 revealed that top performers normally integrate target pricing with incentives and capability building (Kermisch & Burns, 2018a.)

Inexpensive imports often trigger accusations of dumping – that is, selling goods overseas for less than in the exporter's home market, at a price below the cost of production, or both. Dumping ranges from predatory to unintentional. Predatory dumping is the tactic of a foreign firm that intentionally sells at a loss in another country to increase its market share at the expense of domestic producers. This amounts to an international price war. Unintentional dumping is the result of time lags between the date of sales transactions, shipment, and arrival.

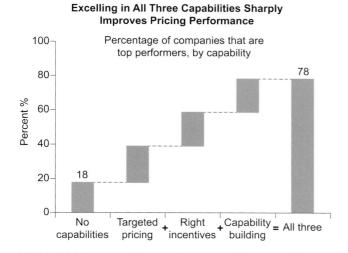

Exhibit 9.7 Targeted pricing, incentives, and building capabilities improve pricing performance
Source: Kermisch and Burns, 2018a. Used with permission from Bain & Company www.bain.com/insights/is-pricing-killing-your-profits

Prices can change in such a way that the final sales price is below the cost of production or below the price prevailing in the exporter's home market (Czinkota & Kotabe, 1997).

Price Coordination

The issue of standard worldwide pricing may be mostly a theoretical one because of the influence of environments, but if standardization is sought, it relates more to price levels and the use of pricing as a positioning tool. The single currency in European countries makes prices completely transparent for all buyers. If discrepancies are not justifiable due to market differences such as consumption preferences, competition, or government interference, cross-border purchases will occur. The simplest solution would be to have one euro-based price throughout the market. However, given significant differences up to 100 percent, that solution would lead to significant losses in sales and/or profits, as a single price would likely be closer to the lower-priced countries' level. The recommended approach is a pricing corridor that considers existing country-specific prices while optimizing the profits at a pan-European level. Such a corridor defines the maximum and minimum prices that a country organization can charge – enough to allow flexibility as a result of differences in price elasticity and competition, but not enough to attract people to engage in cross-border shopping that starts at price differences of 20 percent or higher. This approach moves pricing authority away from country managers to regional management and requires changes in management systems and incentive structures (Nagle & Muller, 2018).

Significant price gaps lead to gray markets, or parallel importation. The term refers to brand-name imports that enter a country legally but outside of authorized distribution channels. Gray markets arise when companies sell goods in one country that are priced substantially lower than prices the firm charges for the same good in other countries. In such circumstances, illicit intermediaries may enter the firm's markets by purchasing the good in the low-price country, and selling it at a higher prices in other countries, thereby subverting the firm's official distribution channels. Gray markets have flourished in mobile phones, cars, watches, and even baby powder, cameras, and chewing gum (Kyle, 2011; Zhao et al., 2016).

The phenomenon is harmful in various ways. First, the gray market will result in lower profits to the brand owner, the firm that owns the good. Second, the firm may suffer harm to its reputation because authorized distributors may refuse to honor warranties on items bought through the gray market. The proponents of gray marketing argue for their right to "free trade" by pointing to manufacturers who are both overproducing and overpricing in some markets. The main beneficiaries of gray markets are consumers, who benefit from lower prices, and discount distributors who gain access to the good. The producing firm can combat gray marketing in various ways. First, it can take steps to ensure authorized dealers do not engage in transshipments or other practices that give rise to gray markets. Second, the firm can set a similar, standardized price for its products in all it markets. Finally, the firm can undertake educational campaigns to alert buyers about the harm of gray-marketed goods, such as lack of a full warranty or after-sales service (Kyle, 2011; Zhao et al., 2016).

Transfer Pricing

Transfer, or intracompany, pricing is the pricing of sales to members of the corporate family. The overall competitive and financial position of the firm forms the basis of any pricing policy. In this, transfer pricing plays a key role. Intracorporate sales can easily change consolidated global results because they often are one of the most important ongoing decision areas in a company.

Firms utilize four main transfer-pricing approaches: (1) transfer at direct cost; (2) transfer at direct cost plus additional expenses; (3) transfer at a price derived from end-market prices; and (4) transfer at **an arm's length price**, or the price that unrelated parties would have reached on the same transaction. Doing business overseas requires coping with complexities of environmental peculiarities, the effect of which can be alleviated by manipulating transfer prices. Factors that call for adjustments include taxes, import duties, inflationary tendencies, unstable governments, and other regulations. For example, high transfer prices on goods shipped to a subsidiary and low ones on goods imported from it will result in minimizing the tax liability of a subsidiary operating in a country with a high income tax. Tax liability thus results not only from the absolute tax rate but also from differences in how income is computed. On the other hand, a higher transfer price may have an effect on the import duty, especially if it is assessed on an ad valorem basis. Exceeding a certain threshold may boost the duty substantially and thus have a negative impact on the subsidiary's posture.

Distribution

Channels of distribution provide the essential links that connect producers and customers. Developing the channel is a long-term process that cannot be readily changed. It involves relinquishing some control the firm has over the marketing of its products. The two factors make choosing the right channel structure a crucial decision. Properly structured and staffed, the distribution system will function more as one rather than as a collection of often quite different units.

Channel Design

Channel design refers to the length and width of the channel employed. Channel design is determined by factors that can be summarized as the 11 Cs: customer, culture, competition, company, character, capital, cost, coverage, control, continuity, and communication. While there are no standard answers to channel design, the international marketer can use the 11 Cs as a checklist to determine the proper approach to reach target audiences, before selecting channel members to fill key roles. The first three factors are givens in that the company must adjust its approach to the existing structures. The other eight are controllable to a certain extent by the marketer.

Customers, as represented by their demographic and psychographic characteristics, form the basis for channel-design decisions. Answers to questions such as what customers need as well as why, when, and how they buy are used to determine ways in which products should be made available to generate a competitive advantage.

Culture refers to the nature of existing channel structures in a given market.

Competitors' channels should be examined and may make up the only distribution system that is accepted both by the trade and consumers. In this case, the firm should strive to use the structure more effectively and efficiently.

Company refers to the firm's objectives for the channel. For example, the firm might have a goal of pursuing mass markets, or it might aim for niche markets. Each objective requires a different type of channel.

Character of the good being marketed will have an impact on the design of the channel. For example, perishable products may require refrigeration and other special treatment in the channel until the good reaches consumers. Other products require substantial after-sales service, which may necessitate distributors with specialized capabilities.

Capital describes the financial resources needed to set up the channel. The firm's financial strength will determine the type of channel and the basis on which channel relationships are built. The stronger the finances, the more able the firm is to establish channels it either owns or controls.

Cost refers to ongoing expenditures required to maintain a channel once it is established. Costs will vary over the life cycle of the relationship and of the product marketed. For example, advertising efforts in the channel represent on ongoing cost.

Coverage describes both the number of areas where the marketer's products are represented and the quality of that representation. The number of areas covered depends on dispersion of demand in the market and on the time elapsed since the product's introduction to the market. A company typically enters a market with one local distributor. As volume expands, the distribution base often must be adjusted.

Control refers to how much power the firm has in influencing how its goods are marketed in the foreign country. The use of intermediaries leads to some loss of control. The looser the relationship with intermediaries, the less control can be exerted. The longer the channel, the harder it is for the marketer to influence pricing, communications, and the types of outlets in which the product is sold.

Continuity refers to the efforts to develop and maintain a channel, and the channel experience for consumers, that are consistent and stable. Nurturing continuity rests heavily on the marketer because foreign distributors may have a more short-term view of the relationship.

Communication between the marketer and intermediaries determines how effectively the firm's goals are carried out, how conflicts are resolved, and ultimately how well marketing is performed in the market. Dell created a Customer Experience Council to scrutinize aspects of how the firm's channel interacts with customers.

Selection and Screening of Intermediaries

Once the basic design of the channel is determined, the international marketer must begin a search to fill the defined roles with the best available candidates. Choices must be made within the framework of the company's overall philosophy on distributors versus agents, as well as whether the company will use an indirect or direct approach to foreign markets (Jurse & Jager, 2017; Kotler & Keller, 2016).

Firms that have successful international distribution attest to the importance of finding top representatives. Various sources exist to assist the marketer in locating intermediary candidates. One of the easiest and most economical ways is to use the service of governmental agencies. Telephone directories can provide distributor lists. The firm can solicit the support of some of its facilitating agencies, such as banks, advertising agencies, shipping lines, and airlines. The marketer can take a more direct approach by placing recruitment advertising to find appropriate representatives. The advertisements typically indicate the type of support the marketer will be able to give to its distributor. Intermediaries can be screened on their performance and professionalism. An intermediary's performance can be evaluated on the basis of financial standing and sales as well as the likely fit it would provide in terms of its existing product lines and coverage. Professionalism can be assessed through reputation and overall standing or relationships in the business community. For the channel relationships to work, each party has to be open about its expectations and openly communicate changes perceived in the other's behavior that might be contrary to the agreement. The complicating factors that separate the two parties fall into three categories: ownership, geographic and cultural distance, and different rules of law. Rather than lament their existence, both parties must take strong action to remedy them. Often the first major step is for both parties to acknowledge that differences exist.

E-Commerce

E-commerce is the offering of goods and services via the Internet. Global Internet penetration is facilitated by the quality of available technology, such as the presence of 5G telephony and artificial intelligence. Technology has facilitated the growth of m(obile)-commerce, the exchange of goods and services via smartphones, a common way that developing country consumers access products and marketing information.

Many companies entering e-commerce choose to use marketplace sites, like Amazon and eBay, that bring together buyers, sellers, distributors, and transaction payment processors in one single marketplace, making convenience the key attraction. Transaction payment processors like PayPal offer services to facilitate payments around the world.

To fully serve the needs of its customers via e-commerce, the company itself must be prepared to provide 24-hour order taking and customer service; have the regulatory and customs-handling expertise to deliver internationally; and have an in-depth understanding of marketing environments, as well as customer habits and preferences, for the further development of the business relationship. The instantaneous interactivity users experience will also be translated into an expectation of expedient delivery of answers and products ordered. Many people living outside the USA, who purchase online expect US-style service. However, in many cases, these shoppers may find that shipping is not even available.

The challenges faced in terms of response and delivery capabilities can be overcome through outsourcing services or by building international distribution networks with Air express carriers, such as FedEx and UPS, who offer full-service packages that leverage their own Internet infrastructure with customs clearance and e-mail shipment notification. If a company needs help in order fulfillment and customer support, logistics centers offer warehousing and inventory management services as well as same-day delivery from in-country stocks. UPS, for example, has more than 500 supply chain facilities in 125 countries and serves more than 200 countries and territories. Some companies elect to build their own international distribution networks, especially as they open country-specific web sites. Amazon offers global services through its Fulfilled-By-Amazon model in countries like the USA, the United Kingdom, Germany, France, Japan, China, and Canada. As the company broadens its product categories, it will require additional facilities to fulfill the orders generated locally more quickly and cheaply (Li, 2018; Roberts, 2019; UPS, 2020).

Although English has historically dominated the Web, increased global Internet penetration has made localization of web content and e-commerce a requirement. In targeting international markets, it is prudent to use a company located in the specific geographic area. It has been shown that web users are three times more likely to buy when the offering is made in their own language. True to the marketing concept, smart marketers will seek to customize commercial web sites to meet customer convenience and ease-of-use needs in different countries, starting with language localization.

The marketer has to be sensitive to the governmental role in e-commerce with regard to local regulations and taxation implications. Some countries require businesses to have a "permanent establishment" or taxable entity established. Privacy issues have grown exponentially as a result of e-business as businesses collect and process personally identifiable information. Many countries, including the USA and the member-states of the European Union, have specific privacy laws requiring strict compliance by online businesses. For industries such as music and motion pictures, the Internet has proven to be both an opportunity and a threat. The Web provides a new efficient method of distribution and customization of products that has been enthusiastically embraced by music and film lovers. At the same time, it can be a channel for intellectual property violation through unauthorized distribution methods that threaten the revenue streams to artists and creative industries.

Communications

The international marketer must choose a proper combination of the various marketing communications tools like advertising, personal selling, sales promotion, and publicity – to create images among the intended target audience. The choice will depend on the target audience, company objectives, the product or service marketed, the resources available for the endeavor, and the availability of communications tools in a particular market (Percy, 2018). The focus may be on not only a product or service but the company's overall image.

Advertising

The key decision-making areas in advertising are (1) media strategy, (2) the advertising message, and (3) the organization of the advertising program. Media strategy is applied to the selection of media vehicles and the development of a media schedule. Worldwide digital ad spending, which surpassed $300 billion in 2019, varies by locale (Emarketer, 2019). Pay-per-click (PPC) is an Internet advertising model used on search engines, advertising networks, and content websites (such as blogs), where advertisers only pay when a user actually clicks on an advertisement to visit the advertisers' web sites. It has become a battlefield between global players and their local challengers. A company with "boots on the ground" will have knowledge of language, culture, and marketing jargon and will be able to localize content and not just translate it from one language to another. Currently, there are good deals to be had in other countries. For example, click costs are cheaper on the Yandex and Baidu than on Google in the USA and United

Kingdom. In markets like China and Russia, the government is an important consideration because both countries have been known to interfere in their business. Having said this, China's government seems to be encouraging and supporting Internet- and technology-related industries. An analysis of the Chinese luxury goods market by Bain and Company revealed that online sales showed a steep growth, measured as compound annual growth rate (CAGR). Managers in China proactively marketed luxury goods in the webspace (D'Arpizio et al., 2017). Luxury e-tailers held a large share of online sales, as consumption throughout China grew during 2017 (Exhibit 9.8).

Media regulations also vary. Some regulations include limits on the amount of time available for advertisements. In the EU, for example, the Audiovisual Media Services Directive (AVMSD) is a set of common rules for advertising in all audiovisual media for EU member states. Among its provisions, the directive sets an upper limit of 20 percent of total television broadcasting time that can be devoted to advertising. Internet and TV advertising for alcoholic beverages cannot be aimed specifically at minors and must not encourage immoderate consumption of such beverages (European Commission, 2020).

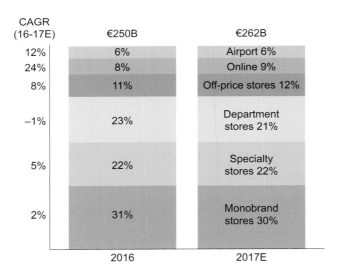

Exhibit 9.8 The off-price, online, and airport channels continue to outperform

Source: D'Arpizio, Levato, Kamel, and de Montgolfier, 2017. Used with permission from Bain & Company www.bain.com/insights/is-pricing-killing-your-profits

Note: In the exhibit, CAGR is the compound annual growth rate of each of the indicated channels.

Global media vehicles have been developed that target audiences on at least three continents and for which the media buying takes place through a centralized office. These media have traditionally been publications that, in addition to the world-wide edition, have provided advertisers the option of using regional editions. For example, the *Financial Times*, *New York Times*, *The Economist*, and *Wall Street Journal* all publish international editions in various world regions.

The Internet facilitates international marketing communications (Percy, 2018). Online editions of publications, as well as mobile editions and podcasts, can be used in tandem with print publications and broadcast media or separately. Advertisers who want to reach business travelers, for example, can buy advertising packages from CNN that may include CNN regional programming in Africa, the Middle East, Europe, the USA, Latin America (CNN en Español or Asia; CNN.com; and CNN mobile services. Advertisers in the Middle East might look to Al Jazeera as a very attractive medium. Aljazeera TV claims 40 million viewers, and Aljazeera.net is the most visited web site in the Arab world. The National Geographic Channel is available in over 150 countries, seen in more than 400 million homes and in 38 languages.

A smart approach to global marketing over the Internet might start with search engine optimization or paid placement in search marketing. With the rapid growth in the use of social media such as Facebook, LinkedIn, Twitter, YouTube, Instagram, Snapchat, and blogs, marketers are increasingly integrating public relations and viral marketing ideas into their media planning. Word-of-mouth and grassroots brand advocacy can have a powerful effect, particularly for the launch of new products and services or a new marketing push.

Developing the marketing communications message is referred to as *creative strategy*. The marketer must determine what the consumer is really buying, that is, the consumer's motivations. They will vary, depending on (1) the diffusion of the product, service, or concept into the market, (2) the criteria on which the consumer will evaluate the product, and (3) the product's positioning.

The ideal situation in developing message strategy is to have a global brand, that is, a product that is manufactured, packaged, and positioned the same around the world. However, numerous factors can force companies to abandon identical campaigns in favor of recognizable campaigns, or campaigns adapted for individual countries. Such factors include culture, of which language is the main manifestation, economic development, and lifestyles.

Many multinational corporations are staffed and equipped to perform the full range of communications activities. In most cases, however, they rely on the outside expertise of advertising agencies and other communications-related companies such as media-buying companies and specialty marketing firms. Local agencies tend to forge ties with foreign ad agencies for better coverage and customer service, and thus become part of the general globalization effort.

Personal Selling

Although advertising is often equated with the communications effort, in many cases communications efforts consist of personal selling. In the early stages of internationalization, exporters rely heavily on personal contact. The marketing of industrial goods, especially of high-priced items, requires strong personal selling efforts. In some cases, personal selling may be truly international; for example, Boeing or Northrop Grumman salespeople engage in sales efforts around the world. However, in most cases, personal selling takes place at the local level. The best interests of any company in the industrial area lie in establishing a solid base of dealerships staffed by local people. Personal selling efforts can be developed in the same fashion as advertising. For the multinational company, the primary goal again is the enhancement and standardization of personal selling efforts, especially if the product offering is standardized. When distribution is intensive, channels are long, or markets have tradition-oriented distribution, headquarters' role should be less pronounced and should concentrate mostly on offering help and guidance. The field sales manager acts as the organizational link between headquarters and the salespeople (Kotler & Keller, 2016).

Sales Promotion

Sales promotion has been used as the catchall term for promotion that is not advertising, personal selling, or publicity. Sales promotion directed at consumers involves such activities as couponing, sampling, premiums, consumer education and demonstration activities, cents-off packages, point-of-purchase materials, and direct mail. The success in Latin America of Tang, Mondelez's presweetened powder juice substitute, is for the most part traceable to successful sales promotion efforts. One promotion involved trading Tang pouches for free popsicles from the firm's Brazilian subsidiary. The company also placed coupons for free groceries in Tang pouches. In Puerto Rico, General Foods ran Tang sweepstakes. In Argentina, in-store sampling featured Tang poured from Tang pitchers by girls in orange Tang dresses. Decorative Tang pitchers were a hit throughout Latin America (Mondelez, 2020).

For sales promotion to work, the campaigns planned by manufacturers or their agencies have to gain the support of the local retailer population. As an example, retailers must redeem coupons presented by consumers and forward them to the manufacturer or to the company handling the promotion. A. C. Nielsen tried to introduce cents-off coupons in Chile and ran into trouble with the nation's supermarket union, which notified its members that it opposed the project and recommended that coupons not be accepted. The main complaint was that an intermediary, such as Nielsen, would unnecessarily raise costs and thus the prices to be charged to consumers. Also, some critics felt that coupons would limit individual negotiations, because Chileans often bargain for their purchases. Global marketers are well advised to take advantage of local regional opportunities in Brazil: gas delivery people are used to distributing product samples to households by companies such as Nestlé, Johnson & Johnson, and Unilever. The delivery people are usually assigned to the same district for years and have, therefore, earned their clientele's trust. For the marketers, distributing samples this way is not only effective, it is very economical: they are charged 5 cents for each unit distribution.

Sales promotion directed at intermediaries, also known as trade promotion, includes activities such as trade shows and exhibits, trade discounts, and cooperative advertising. For example, attendance at an appropriate trade show is one of the best ways to make contacts with government officials and decision-makers, work with present intermediaries, or attract new ones.

Public Relations

Public relations is the marketing communications function charged with executing programs to earn public understanding and acceptance, which means both internal and external communication. Internal communication is important, especially in multinational companies, to create an appropriate corporate culture. External campaigns can be achieved through the use of corporate symbols, corporate advertising, customer relations programs, the generation of publicity, as well as getting a company's view to the public via the Internet. Some material on the firm is produced for special audiences to assist in personal selling. A significant part of public relations activity focuses on portraying multinational corporations as good citizens of their host markets.

The United Nations has promoted programs to partner multinationals and NGOs to tackle issues such as healthcare, energy, and biodiversity. For example, Merck and GlaxoSmithKline have partnered with UNICEF and the World Bank to improve access to AIDS care in the hardest hit regions of the world (Gereffi et al., 2001).

Public relations activity includes anticipating and countering criticism. The criticisms range from general ones against all multinational corporations to specific complaints and certification. First-party certification is the most common variety, whereby a single firm develops its own rules and reports on compliance. This certification includes prohibitions on child labor and forced labor guarantee of nondiscrimination in the workplace. Second-party certification involves an industry or trade association fashioning a code of conduct and implementing reporting mechanisms. The chemical industry's global Responsible Care program developed environmental, health, and safety principles and codes; required participating firms to submit implementation reports; and reported aggregate industry progress. Third-party certification involves an external group, often a nongovernmental organization (NGO), imposing its rules and compliance methods onto a particular firm or industry. Fourth-party certification involves government or multilateral agencies. The United Nations' Global Compact, for instance, lists environmental, labor, and human rights principles for companies to follow; participating corporations must submit online updates of their progress for NGOs to scrutinize.

Marketing Management

Once the target market has been selected, the next step is the determination of marketing efforts at appropriate levels. A key question in international marketing concerns the extent to which the elements of the marketing mix – product, price, distribution, communications – should be standardized. The marketer also faces specific challenges of adjusting each of the mix elements in the international marketplace (Johansson & Furick, 2017). A key question is whether the firm should sell standardized products or adapt products for individual markets. For this, the international marketer must first decide what modifications in the mix policy are needed or warranted. Three basic alternatives in approaching international markets are available:

1. Make no special provisions for the international marketplace but, rather, identify potential target markets and then choose products that can easily be marketed with little or no modification.
2. Adapt to local conditions in each and every target market (the multi-domestic approach).
3. Incorporate differences into a regional or global strategy that will allow for local differences in implementation (globalization approach) (Verbeke & Asmussen, 2016).

Standardization or Adaptation

In today's environment, standardization usually means cross-national strategies rather than a policy of viewing foreign markets as secondary and therefore not important enough to have products adapted for them. Ideally, the international marketer should think globally and act locally, focusing on neither extreme: full standardization or full localization. Global thinking requires flexibility in exploiting good ideas and products on a worldwide basis regardless of their origin.

The adaptation decision will also have to be assessed as a function of time and market involvement. The more companies learn about local market characteristics in individual markets, the more they are able to establish similarities and, as a result, standardize their approach. This market insight will give them legitimacy with local constituents in developing a common understanding of the extent of standardization versus adaptation. Even when marketing programs are based on highly standardized ideas and strategies, they depend on three sets of variables: (1) the market(s) targeted, (2) the product and its characteristics, and (3) company characteristics, including factors such as resources and policy.

Factors Affecting Adaptation

Questions of adaptation have no easy answers. Marketers in many firms rely on decision-support systems to aid in program adaptation, while others consider every situation independently. All goods must, of course, conform to environmental conditions over which the marketer has no control. Further, the international marketer may use adaptation to enhance its competitiveness in the marketplace.

Exhibit 9.9 examines consumer behavior toward global brands of consumers in China. It reveals preferences of consumers towards being a first buyer, compared

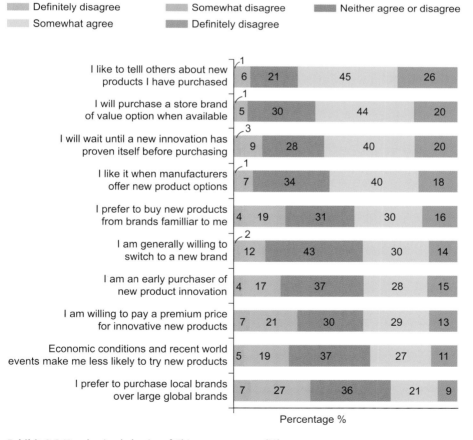

Exhibit 9.9 New buying behavior of Chinese consumers (%)

Source: Zhou, 2013. www.chinainternetwatch.com/2186/new-buying-behavior

to waiting to learn from the experiences of others. The exhibit implies how firms might benefit from orienting their global brand strategy towards adaptation versus standardization (Zhou, 2013).

Goods or services form the core of the firm's international operations. Its success depends on how well goods satisfy needs and wants and how well they are differentiated from those of the competition.

SUMMARY

The role of an international marketer is to seek new opportunities in the world marketplace and satisfy emerging needs through creative management of the firm's product, pricing, distribution, and communications policies. By its very nature, marketing is the most sensitive of business functions to environmental effects and influences. The analysis of target markets is the first of the international marketer's challenges. Potential and existing markets need to be evaluated and priorities established for each, ranging from rejection to a temporary holding position to entry. Decisions at the level of the overall marketing effort must be made with respect to the selected markets, and a plan for future expansion must be formulated. The closer that potential target markets are in terms of their geographical, cultural, and economic distance, the more attractive they typically are to the international marketer. A critical decision in international marketing concerns the degree to which the overall marketing program should be standardized or localized. The ideal is to standardize as much as possible without compromising the basic task of marketing – satisfying the needs and wants of the target market. Many multinational marketers are adopting globalization strategies that involve the standardization of good ideas, while leaving the implementation to local entities. The technical side of marketing management is universal, but environments require adaptation within all of the mix elements. The degree of adaptation will vary by market, good, or service marketed, and overall company objectives.

DISCUSSION QUESTIONS

1. Many rational reasons exist for rejecting a particular market in the early stages of screening. Describe the nature of such decisions and how managers make them. Identify irrational reasons that managers might employ in the screening process.
2. If, indeed, the three dimensions of distance as shown on page X were valid, to which countries would Chinese companies initially consider to expand internationally? Consider the interrelationships of the distance concepts.

3. Is globalization or the regional approach appropriate for the international marketer to consider standardization?
4. What can be the possible exporter reactions to extreme foreign exchange rate fluctuations?
5. Argue for and against gray marketing.
6. What if all attractive intermediaries are already under contract to competitors?

KEY TERMS

arm's length price	257	m-commerce	260
channel design	258	market audit	243
cost-plus method	254	market-differentiated pricing	254
dual pricing	254	marginal cost method	254
dumping	255	media strategy	261
e-commerce	260	positioning	248
global brands	267	price escalation	255
gray markets	256	reverse innovation	249
income elasticity of demand	242	standard worldwide pricing	254
longitudinal analysis	243		

TAKE A STAND

The past and forthcoming changes in the business environment with events like Brexit, will change the scope of international business and complicate the task of the international marketer. The UK economy was harmed in the wake of Brexit, which affected trade not only in the UK and EU, but also in other countries around the world. Unemployment in the UK increased, the economy shrank, and British firms' ability to recruit international talent took a hit. However, Brexit had a positive side for the UK. Countries like China began discussing new trade deals with the UK for mutual benefits. New agreements faced fewer regulations and fewer obligations to fulfill. Given the risks UK businesses have faced due to Brexit, the UK Government developed plans for widespread insolvencies. The Federation of Small Businesses predicted an increase in consumer prices. However, the UK is aiming to maintain some political influence over the EU, to facilitate international trade between the EU and the UK.

Questions for Debate

1. What can the UK Government do to reduce the negative impact of Brexit on imports and exports from the UK?
2. How can outsiders recapture lost market share?

INTERNET EXERCISES

1. Piracy and counterfeiting pose much harm to the software industry. Using the website of the Business Software Alliance (www.bsa.org), assess how this problem is being tackled.
2. The global advertising industry has experienced significant consolidation with a few giant communications companies owning most of the major advertising, branding, public relations, digital marketing, marketing research, and other marketing services agencies. Visit the websites of the four largest communications groups:

   www.wpp.com

   www.omnicom.com

   www.interpublic.com

   www.publicis.com

   From the information they provide about their companies, create a shortlist of five global advertising agencies that a global marketer might consider working with to create a global advertising campaign and provide advertising services in most major countries.

FURTHER RESOURCES

Brown, T., Suter, Tracy, and Churchill, Gilbert. (2018). *Marketing Research: Customer Insights And Managerial Action*. Boston: Cengage Learning.

Henshall, J. (2016). Global Transfer Pricing: Principles and Practice. London: Bloomsbury Professional.

Khanna, Tarun and Palepu, Kishna. (2010). *Winning in Emerging Markets: A Road Map for Strategy and Execution*. Boston: Harvard Business Review Press.

Kim, W. Chan and Mauborgne, Renee. (2018). *Blue Ocean Marketing*. Boston: Harvard Business Review Press.

Leach, Will. (2018). *Marketing to Mindstates: The Practical Guide to Applying Behavior Design to Research and Marketing*. Austin, TX: Lioncrest Publishing.

10 Services

CONTENTS

VIGNETTE 10 Labor mobility and the global services sector

Globalization has had major implications for international business – from the worldwide spread of digital technologies and resulting productivity gains to the increased pace of internationalization and the appearance of "born global" firms. Analysts point to labor mobility as the last remaining bastion of pre-globalization economics. Workers have moved around at a far slower pace than all the other factors of production. Two reasons are commonly cited for this: (1) people are culturally embedded and closely connected to their communities and familial networks and (2) would-be migrants face various regulations and restrictions that block their free movement across national borders.

However, growing ease of international travel, the "homogenization" of lifestyles worldwide, and gradual liberalization of international markets are facilitating greater cross-national labor mobility. The Internet facilitates the ability to find overseas jobs. The most powerful motivator for worker migration is financial – people are more willing to move abroad if they can make more money.

Increased labor mobility has numerous potential benefits. Companies benefit through savings on labor costs, which are then passed on to consumers in the form of lower prices on goods and services. Immigrants enjoy better wages and a higher standard of living, while their home countries receive remittances. Concerns over depressed wages and large-scale job losses by natives of countries that are net recipients of migrants have been countered by statistics that suggest that immigration has no effects on average wages or on the return to capital in the receiving country. It simply leads to an increase in total employment, even during bad economic times. However, domestic political pressure from interested constituent groups has pushed many governments in the developed world to adopt strict entry laws.

Despite such measures, the new global job shift is certain to continue. Research points to a growing shortage of workers in the services sector worldwide. By 2030, shortages of talent in key service industries could reach 85 million people, costing companies trillions of dollars in lost economic opportunity. Services industries most likely to experience employee shortages include knowledge-intensive fields, especially financial and business services, as well as professions related to technology, media, and telecommunications. Managers who seek to work abroad will need to be increasingly footloose. The workplace of tomorrow is likely to be truly global.

Sources: Kerr and Kerr, 2016; Nath and Liu, 2017; McLaren, 2018; UNCTAD, 2020; World Trade Organization, 2020.

Introduction

Services are a major component of world trade. Traditionally, international business emphasized companies that make and sell products – tangible merchandise such as cars, computers, and clothing. In the modern era, however, firms that produce services are key global players as well. Services are deeds, efforts, or performances delivered directly by individuals working in banks, hotels, retailers, and other firms in the services sector.

Google is a popular services firm that has internationalized rapidly. The Standard Bank of South Africa is a leading financial services firm that provides loans to customers throughout Africa. The French firm Sodexho manages the food and beverage operations of government agencies, universities, and hospitals around Europe. Services face various challenges in international business that distinguish them from products. For example, services are intangible, which complicates exporting and mass production.

This chapter will highlight international business dimensions that are specific to services as role of services in the world economy, opportunities and new problems that have arisen because of increasing service trade. We will focus on worldwide transformations of industries due to profound changes in globalization and technologies, and outline the steps that firms need to undertake to offer products or services internationally.

Differences Between Services and Goods

Services often accompany goods, but they are also, by themselves, an increasingly important part of the economy. One author has contrasted services and products by stating that "a good is an object, a device, a thing; a service is a deed, a performance, an effort." That definition, although quite general, captures the essence of the difference between goods and services. Services tend to be more intangible, personalized, and custom-made than goods. Services also are typically using a different approach to customer satisfaction. Service firms do not have products in the form of pre-produced solutions to customer's problems; they have processes as solutions to such problems (Gronroos, 2006).

Services are the fastest growing sector in world trade, and employment in the services sector is becoming increasingly global. These major differences add dimensions to services that are not present in goods. Services may complement goods; at other times, goods may complement services. The offering of goods that are in need of substantial technological support and maintenance may be useless if no proper assurance for service can be provided (Mattoo et al., 2007). For this reason, the initial contract of sale often includes important service dimensions.

This practice is frequent in aircraft sales. When an aircraft is purchased, the buyer contracts not only for the physical good – namely, the plane – but often for the training of personnel, maintenance service, and the promise of continuous technological updates. Similarly, the sale of computer hardware depends on the availability of proper servicing and software.

In an international setting, proper service support can often be crucial. Particularly for newly opening markets or for goods new to market, providing the good alone may be insufficient. The buyer wants to be convinced that proper service backup will be offered for the good before making a commitment. On a smaller scale, individual consumers' selection of a household appliance from a particular vendor is often motivated by the quality of after-purchase service, ease of delivery, technical support in case of malfunction, and so forth. Retailers need to recognize that the quality of a product is just as important as the quality of the service system in which it is embedded. This is especially true in the case of e-commerce (Exhibit 10.1). As the number of online vendors has exploded in recent years, offering a superior product no longer guarantees a competitive edge. Customer satisfaction and e-loyalty can be a function of many tangible and intangible elements, such as physical elements of the vendor site's perceived security (e.g., secure checkout) (Li, 2018). With rising concerns about identity theft, this last element is likely to only increase in importance.

EXHIBIT 10.1 Amazon

Amazon, the global e-commerce giant, has long sought to dominate global retail markets using low prices, easy availability of goods and services, and superior customer service. Amazon's site offers search functionality and smart categorization. Amazon is "customer obsessed," and demonstrates the critical importance of a high-quality customer experience in global e-commerce. Founded in 1994 in the USA, Amazon expanded into Europe in 1998 by acquiring online booksellers in Germany and the UK. Today Amazon is active in 13 countries. Possession of leading technologies and large size has helped the firm dominate e-commerce in key markets worldwide. In several countries, for example, Amazon has avoided the problem of expensive local labor by leveraging robotics. The firm acquired KIVA Robotics in 2016 and became the first e-commerce company to massively deploy robot warehouse management technologies (Holley, 2019; Li, 2018).

One international market where Amazon has struggled is China. Amazon initially entered China in 2004 by acquiring Joyo, a local e-commerce firm in retailing. In China, Amazon put much weight on its technological strengths, while largely ignoring the imperative of skillful marketing strategy. The firm emphasized a standardization strategy, and neglected to sufficiently adapt to local culture and business customs in China. In this way, Amazon failed to achieve a high level of responsiveness to the needs and characteristics of Chinese consumers. The firm paid limited attention to online shopping habits in China, and proved somewhat inflexible in dealing with suppliers and third-party suppliers.

Over time, Amazon's China market share shrank, just as local competitors – Alibaba, JD.com, and Pinduoduo – gained strength. The Chinese Government also implemented various regulations that hindered Amazon's progress. In 2019, Amazon announced it would close its domestic e-commerce business in China. Amazon's failure in China demonstrates the importance of understanding local conditions and adopting an appropriate business model accordingly.

Source: Casna, n.d.; Li, 2018.

The link between goods and services often brings a new dimension to international business efforts. The knowledge that services and goods interact, however, is not enough. Successful managers must recognize that different customer groups will frequently view the service–good combination differently. The type of use and the usage conditions will affect evaluations of the market offering. For example, the intangible dimension of "on-time arrival" by airlines may be valued differently by college students than by business executives. Similarly, a passenger arriving at his or her final destination will judge a 20-minute delay differently than by one who has just missed an overseas connection. As a result, adjustment possibilities in both the service and the goods areas emerge that can be used as a strategic tool to stimulate demand and increase profitability. Service and goods elements may vary substantially in any market offering. The manager must identify the role of each and adjust them all to meet the desires of the target customer group. By rating the offerings on their dominant (in)tangibility, the manager can compare offerings and also generate information for subsequent market positioning strategies.

Stand-Alone Services

Services do not have to come in unison with goods. They can compete against goods and become an alternative offering. For example, rather than buy an in-house computer, the business executive can contract computing work to a local or Foreign Service firm. Similarly, the purchase of a car (a good) can be converted into the purchase of a service by leasing the car from an agency. Services therefore can transform the ownership of a good into its possession or use. This transformation can greatly affect business issues such as distribution, payment structure and flows, and even recycling. Services by themselves can satisfy the needs and wants of customers. Entertainment services such as movies or music offer leisure time enjoyment. Insurance services can protect people from financial ruin in case of a calamity. Services may also compete against one another. As an example, a store may have the option of offering full service to customers or of converting to the self-service format. With automated checkout services, customers may have to be self-sufficient with other activities such as selection, transportation, packaging, and pricing.

Popular services in international trade include retailing; architectural, construction, and engineering services; banking, finance, and insurance; education and training; publishing; entertainment; e-commerce and information services; professional business services; transportation; travel and tourism (OECD, 2020).

Services differ from goods most strongly in their **intangibility**: they are frequently consumed rather than possessed. Though the intangibility of services is a primary differentiating criterion, it is not always present. For example, publishing services ultimately result in a tangible good – namely, a book. Similarly, construction services eventually result in a building, a subway, or a bridge. Even in those instances, however, the intangible component that leads to the final good is of major concern to both the producer of the service and the recipient of the ultimate output, because it brings with it major considerations that are nontraditional to goods.

Another major difference concerns the storing of services. Due to their nature, services are difficult to inventory. If they are not used, the "brown around the edges" syndrome tends to result in high **perishability**. Unused capacity in the form of an empty seat on an airplane, for example, becomes nonsalable quickly. Once the plane has taken off, selling an empty seat is virtually impossible except for an in-flight upgrade from coach to first-class and the capacity cannot be stored for future use. The difficulty of keeping services in inventory makes it troublesome to provide service back-up for peak demand. To maintain **service capacity** constantly at levels necessary to satisfy peak demand would be very expensive. The business manager must therefore attempt to smooth out demand levels through pricing or promotional tools in order to optimize overall use of capacity.

For the services offering, the time of production is usually very close to or even simultaneous with the time of consumption. This often means close **customer involvement** in the production of services. Customers frequently either service themselves or cooperate in the delivery of services. As a result, the service provider may need to be physically present when the service is delivered. This physical presence creates both problems and opportunities, and introduces a new constraint that is seldom present in the marketing of goods. For example, close interaction with the customer requires a much greater understanding of and emphasis on the cultural dimension of each market. A good service delivered in a culturally

Exhibit 10.2 UK Customer Satisfaction Index (UKCSI) 2019
Source: The Institute of Customer Service (2020). UK Customer Satisfaction Index. Available at:
www.instituteofcustomerservice.com/ukcsi

unacceptable fashion is doomed to failure. Even in a domestic setting, international exposure can make a service culturally controversial. A common pattern of internationalization for service businesses is therefore to develop stand-alone business systems in each country (Czinkota et al., 2009). In the United Kingdom, the National Customer Satisfaction Index (UKCSI) reflects the level of buyer contentment in various services industries (Exhibit 10.2).

The close interaction with customers points to the fact that services often are custom-made. This contradicts the desire of the firm to standardize its offering; yet at the same time, it offers the service provider an opportunity to differentiate the service. The concomitant problem is that, in order to fulfill customer expectations, service consistency is required. For anything offered online, however, consistency is difficult to maintain over the long run. Therefore, the human element in the service offering takes on a much greater role than in the offering of goods. Errors may enter the system, and unpredictable individual influences may affect the outcome of the service delivery. The issue of quality control affects the provider as well as the recipient of services. Efforts to increase control through service uniformity may sometimes be perceived by customers as the limiting of options. Since research has shown that the relative importance of the serviced quality dimensions varies from one culture to another, one single approach to service quality may therefore have a negative market effect (Cunningham et al., 2006).

Buyers have more difficulty observing and evaluating services than goods. This is particularly true when the shopper tries to choose intelligently among service providers. Even when sellers of services are willing and able to provide more market transparency, the buyer's problem is complicated: customers receiving the same service may use it differently. Because production lines cannot be established to deliver an identical service each time, and the quality of a service cannot be tightly controlled, the problem of service heterogeneity emerges, meaning that services may never be the same from one delivery to another (Schweidel et al., 2008). For example, the counseling by a teacher, even if the same person provides it on the same day, may vary substantially depending on the student. But over time, even for the same student, the counseling may change. As a result, service offerings are not directly comparable, which makes quality measurements quite challenging. Therefore, service quality may vary for each delivery. Nonetheless, maintaining service quality is vitally important, since the reputation of the service provider plays an overwhelming role in the customer's choice process.

Services often require entirely new forms of distribution. Traditional channels frequently are multi-tiered and long, and therefore slow. They often cannot be used at all because of the perishability of services. A weather news service, for example, either reaches its audience quickly or rapidly loses value. As a result, direct delivery and short distribution channels are required for international services. When they do not exist, service providers need to be distribution innovators to reach their market. Increasingly, many services are "footloose," in that they are not tied to any specific location. Advances in technology make it possible for firms to separate production and consumption of services. As a result, labor-intensive service performance can be moved anywhere around the world where qualified, low-cost labor is plentiful. As communication technology further improves, services such as teaching, medical diagnosis, or bank account management can originate from any point in the world and reach customers around the globe (Loungani et al., 2017).

The unique dimensions of services exist in both international and domestic settings, but their impact has greater importance for the international manager. For example, the perishability of a service, which may be a mere obstacle in domestic business, may become a major barrier internationally because of the longer distances involved. Similarly, quality control for international services may be much more difficult because of different service uses, changing expectations, and varying national regulations. Services are delivered directly to the user and are therefore frequently much more sensitive to cultural factors than are products. Their influence on the individual abroad may be welcomed or greeted with hostility. For example, countries that place a strong emphasis on cultural identity have set barriers inhibiting market penetration by foreign films. France leads a major effort within the European Union, for instance, to cap the volume of US produced films in order to obtain more playing time and visibility for French movies.

Role of Services in the World Economy

The rise of the services sector is a global phenomenon. In North America, Europe, Japan, and other developed areas, services account for 70 percent or more of Gross National Product (GNP). In China, India, and other emerging countries, services typically represent between 50 and 60 percent of GNP (Central Intelligence Agency, 2020). With growth rates higher than other sectors, such as agriculture and manufacturing, services are instrumental in job creation in these countries. In addition, services exports are very important to emerging markets and developing economies. On average, 25 percent of developing and emerging economy exports are service exports (United Nations Conference on Trade and Development, 2020; World Trade Organization, 2020).

In the early stages of economic development, countries typically concentrate on making and selling commodities and basic products. As they develop, countries manufacture increasingly sophisticated products. However, growing economic development means that worker wages rise over time. Consequently, in the long run products manufacturing becomes concentrated in countries characterized by low-cost labor, such as China, Mexico, and Poland. In the latter stages of development, as local labor wages have become relatively high (e.g., in Canada, Japan, the USA, and the nations of Europe), the relative importance of the services sectors increases. Numerous late-stage economies – such as Singapore, Hong Kong, and the United Arab Emirates – have developed very strong service sectors. Worldwide, artificial intelligence, robotics, and digital technologies continue to increase the efficiency of manufacturing (Forbes, 2020). In such an environment, the services sector continues to grow. As more countries expand their services activities, the global services business will become more competitive.

The service sector accounts for all of the growth in total non-farm employment. Most of the large management consulting firms derive more than half of their revenue from international sources. The largest law firms serve customers around the globe, some of them in over a hundred countries. Competition in global services is rising rapidly at all levels. Hong Kong, Singapore, and western Europe are increasingly active in service industries such as banking, insurance, and advertising. Years ago, US construction firms could count on a virtual monopoly on large-scale construction projects. Today, firms from China, France, Sweden, and other countries are taking a major share of the international construction business. These facts demonstrate that many service firms and industries have become truly international and formidable in size. One such industry is healthcare. In this context, Exhibit 10.3 explains the growth of international medical tourism (Lunt et al., 2016).

EXHIBIT 10.3 Medical tourism as an alternative to domestic healthcare

Medical tourism is a type of service that many consumers from advanced economies pursue by traveling to another country for healthcare. Many thousands of residents from North America, Europe, and other advanced areas travel abroad annually for care. The main rationale is that medical procedures are cheaper in many foreign countries. A medical procedure in India can cost 70 percent less than in the West. Moreover, patients from Canada, the United Kingdom, and other countries with public healthcare systems may seek treatment abroad to avoid long wait periods for desired procedures.

Top destinations for seeking healthcare abroad include Thailand, India, Brazil, and Turkey. Many Americans venture to Mexico to obtain low-cost dental surgery. Patients Without Borders, an organization that facilitates medical tourism, estimates that the market for this practice is approaching US$100 billion per year. Approximately 25 million patients worldwide travel abroad for medical procedures each year, spending an average of US$3,500 per visit.

Commonly sought procedures include cosmetic surgery, dentistry, and heart surgery, as well as procedures related to ophthalmology and orthopedics. However, medical tourism can be risky. For one, communication may be a challenge if the patient does not speak the local language. In some cases, medication is counterfeit and medical skills may be inferior. However, the global spread of superior technologies and international accreditation standards is giving patients greater confidence in the quality of care received abroad.

Medical tourism is a boon for healthcare providers in the developing world. Internationally accredited medical centers in emerging markets are eager to accommodate an ever-growing stream of Western patients. In some countries, governments develop support infrastructure to promote their healthcare services internationally. Companies have sprung up to assist patients with procedures, trip planning, and in-country support, such as airport transfers, after-care arrangements, hospital liaisons, and dispute mediation.

As medical costs in mature markets continue to surge and demand for elective procedures such as cosmetic and dental surgery rises, medical tourism is rapidly evolving into a viable healthcare alternative.

Sources: Lunt, Horsfall, and Hanefeld, 2016; Patients Beyond Borders, 2020.

The United Nations Conference on Trade and Development (UNCTAD) reported that in various economies, the share of services as a percentage of gross domestic product (GDP) has increased significantly in recent decades (Exhibit 10.4)

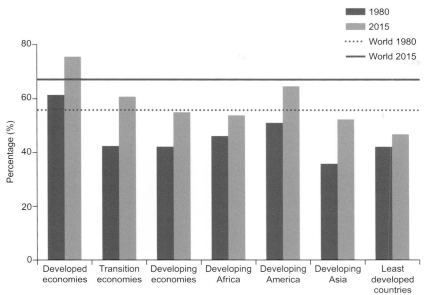

Exhibit 10.4 Share of services in gross domestic product by income level and region, 1980 and 2015 **Source**: *The role of the services economy and trade in structural transformation and inclusive development. Multi-year Expert Meeting on Trade, Services and Development Fifth session* by Trade and Development Board © 2017 United Nations. Reprinted with the permission of the United Nations.

(UNCTAD, 2017). The services sector is bringing much structural transformation to both developed and developing economies. For example, information and communications technology (ICT) services have had a huge impact on industries in energy, finance, and healthcare, greatly increasing their effectiveness and efficiency.

Global Transformations in the Services Sector

Technological advances, globalization, and integration of national economies have had an enormous impact on internationalization of the services sector. Beginning in the 1980s, nations worldwide began to substantially reduce government regulation and interference in global services trade. For example, deregulatory efforts in the transportation sector led to numerous new air carriers and rising competition in the international airline industry. In turn, rising competition resulted in lower prices, which stimulated demand and led to further, dramatic increases in international air travel (Morrison & Winston, 1995). A similar trend followed in the banking and finance industries. Deregulation increased the ability of banks and financial institutions to establish operations in more countries, and also allowed them to create new financial instruments and practices. However, liberalization also led banks to undertaking riskier ventures, which paved the way for the global financial crisis that began in 2007 (Tooze, 2018).

The 1990s saw the liberalization of economies in socialist or communist countries, bringing formerly protectionist states into global trade. Numerous countries – for example, China, India, Indonesia, and Russia – adopted free market norms. The transition opened much of the world to freer international trade and investment. India as well as numerous other countries in Asia and Eastern Europe have become some of the most cost-effective locations for producing various services offered online or by telephone. Today, China is home to four of the world's eight largest banks, which provide financial services around the world (Hu & Wooldridge, 2016).

In another major trend, technological advances since the 1990s have fostered a revolution in global services trade (McKinsey Global Institute, 2016). Technology offers new ways of doing business and permits businesses to expand their horizons internationally. The rise of information communications technology (ICTs), the Internet, and digital technologies in the 2000s greatly increased the efficiency of international trade in services. The Internet made possible service exchanges that previously were prohibitively expensive. For example, Sweden's Skanska, one of the world's largest construction companies, is leveraging the Internet of Things (IoT), artificial intelligence, and other digital technologies to coordinate countless local construction projects at sites around the world. Using digital technologies allows the firm to better connect coworkers, partners, subcontractors, and customers through updated technologies and coordinate the large amounts of data used in building projects (Snow, 2019). Technology innovations have also spilled over into the small businesses arena, allowing for online access to the same kind of planning, management, and accounting tools that big companies use. Technology has also sharply reduced the **cost of communication**. Fiber optic cables have made the cost of international links trivial. An international phone call in the 1980s typically cost $2.00 per minute, but today calling is essentially free.

The Internet and web technology have improved the transaction economics of services and succeeded in making many formerly location-bound services tradable (International Telecommunications Union, 2019). Simultaneously, the increased use of outsourcing by firms has led to a greater need for global service performance (Chesterman & Fisher, 2010). For example, more use of just-in-time inventory systems has created the need to coordinate the supply chain function better and has resulted in the creation of more service intermediaries (Wisner et al., 2016). Retailing is a key industry in the services sector. Consumers around the world patronize foreign retailers, shopping online for cosmetics, personal care, baby food, and other offerings (Exhibit 10.5).

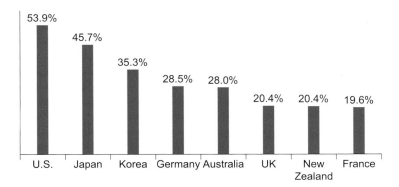

Exhibit 10.5 Top eight countries from which China's cross-border online shoppers are willing to buy commodities
Source: iResearch, 2016.

Service industry expansion is not confined to labor-intensive services and is therefore better performed in areas of the world where labor possesses a comparative advantage. Technology-intensive services are becoming the sunrise industries of this century. Increasingly, firms in various industries can use technology to offer a presence without having to be there physically. Banks, for example, can offer their services through automatic teller machines, telephone, or Internet banking. Consultants can advise via videoconferences, and teachers can teach the world through multimedia classrooms. Physicians can advise and even perform operations in a distant country if proper links can drive robotized medical equipment.

Due to the growth of corporate websites, some firms, particularly in the service sector, can quickly become unplanned participants in the international market. For example, potential customers from abroad can visit a website and request the firm to deliver internationally as well. Of course, the firm can choose to ignore foreign interests and lose out on new markets. Alternatively, it can find itself unexpectedly an international service provider. Industries such as retailers and consultancies are examples of services that have become international in this way.

Many service providers have the opportunity to become truly global players. Knowledge, the core of many service activities, can attain global reach, often without requiring a local presence, especially if the service can be delivered via the Internet. Service providers therefore may have only a minor need for local establishment, because they can operate without premises. Exhibit 10.6 looks at haitao, a cross-border service in China that makes shopping internationally easier for users.

EXHIBIT 10.6 The haitao sensation in China

As the middle class expands in China, more and more Chinese consumers enjoy internet shopping. Many have become enthusiastic buyers of imported products using foreign online retailers. The phenomenon, called "haitao," refers to cross-border internet shopping. An important market-creating service innovation, the haitao market represents more than US$120 billion in annual transactions, benefiting many popular brands in the USA and other Western countries. To accommodate the trend, numerous online sites offering haitao service have emerged in China. Coach, Gucci, Burberry, and other popular companies have embraced the opportunity – China's population now exceeds 1.4 billion people and the Chinese retailing market has expanded rapidly in recent years. E-commerce companies like www.tmall.hk, Amazon.cn, and Gmarket.co.kr specialize in serving the online Chinese market. The diagram highlights the top categories of goods that Chinese buy online. Haitao is a service innovation that has created new market spaces and shopping opportunities. The phenomenon emerged in part because many Chinese are passionate about Western brands, but often cannot buy them in China. Many Chinese prefer trusted Western brands because many such products sold in China are counterfeit.

Top 10 categories of commodities China's cross-border online shoppers have ever bought (Kenichi Ohmae 3 Cs are corporation, customer, and competitor)

Sources: Liu and Hong, 2016; iResearch, 2016; The Milan City Journal, 2020.

Challenges in Services Trade

Despite the sector's importance, services are characterized by significant challenges. These are of sufficient importance to merit a brief review.

Data Collection

The data collected on services trade are unreliable. Service transactions are often invisible statistically as well as physically. For example, the trip abroad of a consultant for business purposes may be hard to track and measure. The interaction of variables such as citizenship, residency, location of the transaction, and who or what (if anything) crosses national boundaries further contributes to the complexity of services transactions. Imagine that an Irish citizen working for a Canadian financial consulting firm headquartered in Sweden advises an Israeli citizen living in India on the management of funds deposited in a Swiss bank. Determining the export and import dimensions of such a service transaction is challenging. The fact that governments have precise data on the number of trucks exported down to the last bolt but little information on reinsurance flows, reflects past governmental inattention to services. Consequently, estimates of services trade vary. Total actual volume of services trade is likely to be larger than the amount shown by official statistics. Consider the problem of services data collection in industrialized countries, with their sophisticated data gathering and information systems. Now imagine how many more problems are encountered in countries lacking such elaborate systems and unwilling to allocate funds for them. Insufficient knowledge and information have led to a lack of transparency, which makes it difficult for nations either to gauge or to influence services trade. As a result, regulations are often put into place without precise information as to their repercussions on actual trade performance.

Global Regulation of Services

Global obstacles to service trade can be categorized into two major types: barriers to entry and problems in performing services abroad. Barriers to entry are often explained by reference to "national security" and "economic security." For example, the impact of banking on domestic economic activity is given as a reason why banking should be carried out only by nationals or indeed should be operated entirely under government control. Sometimes the protection of service users is cited, particularly of bank depositors and insurance policyholders. Another justification used for barriers is the infant-industry argument: "with sufficient time to develop on our own, we can compete in world markets." Often, however, this argument is used simply to prolong the ample licensing profits generated by restricted entry. Yet defining a barrier to services is not always easy. For example, Taiwan gives an extensive written examination to prospective accountants (as do most countries) to ensure that licensed accountants are qualified to practice. The examination is given in Chinese. The fact that few German accountants, for example, read and write Chinese and hence are unable to pass the examination, does not necessarily constitute a barrier to trade in accountancy services.

Service companies also encounter difficulties once they have achieved access to the local market. One reason is that rules and regulations based on tradition may inhibit innovation. A more important reason is that governments pursue social objectives through national regulations. The distinction between **discriminatory** and **nondiscriminatory regulations** is of primary importance here. Regulations that impose larger operating costs on Foreign Service providers than on the local competitors, that provide subsidies to local firms only, or that deny competitive opportunities to foreign suppliers are a proper cause for international concern. The problem of discrimination becomes even more acute when foreign firms face competition from government-owned or government-controlled enterprises. On the other hand, **nondiscriminatory regulations** may be inconvenient and hamper business operations, but they offer less cause for international criticism. Yet such national regulations can be key inhibitors for service innovations. For example, in Japan pharmaceuticals cannot be sold outside of a licensed pharmacy. Similarly, travel arrangements can only be made within a registered travel office and banking can only be done during banking hours. As a result, innovations offered by today's communications technology cannot be brought to bear in these industries. All of these regulations make it difficult for international services to penetrate world markets. At the governmental level, services frequently are not recognized as a major facet of world trade or are viewed with suspicion because of a lack of understanding, and barriers to entry often result. To make progress in tearing them down, much educational work needs to be done (Ghemawat, 2017).

In a major breakthrough in the Uruguay Round, the major GATT participants agreed to conduct services trade negotiations parallel with goods negotiations. The negotiations resulted, in 1995, in the forging of a **General Agreement on Trade in Services (GATS)** as part of the World Trade Organization, the first multilateral, legally enforceable agreement covering trade and investment in the services sector. Similar to earlier agreements in the goods sector, GATS provides for most-favored-nation treatment, national treatment, transparency in rule-making, and the free flow of payments and transfers. Market-access provisions restrict the ability of governments to limit competition and new-market entry. In addition, sectoral agreements were made for the movement of personnel, telecommunications, and aviation. However, in several sectors, such as entertainment, no agreement was obtained. In addition, many provisions, due to their newness, are very narrow. Future negotiations will be required to further improve the international flow of services (UNCTAD, 2020).

Corporations and Services Trade

Historically, international business was the domain of firms that make and sell tangible products. Today, companies that specialize in services have become key international players as well. However, services are distinct from products and reflect various unique characteristics. Firms that offer services internationally face diverse challenges and opportunities.

E-commerce

Electronic commerce has opened up new horizons for global services reach, and has drastically reduced the meaning of distance. For example, when geographic obstacles make the establishment of retail outlets cumbersome and expensive, firms can approach their customers via the Internet. Government regulations that might be prohibitive to a transfer of goods may not have any effect on the international marketing of services. Also, regardless of size, companies are finding it increasingly easy to appeal to a global marketplace. The Internet can help service firms in developing and transitional economies overcome two of the biggest barriers they face: gaining credibility in international markets and saving on travel costs. Little-known firms can become instantly "visible" on the Internet. Even a small firm can develop a polished and sophisticated Internet presence and promotion strategy. Customers are less concerned about geographic location if they feel the firm is electronically accessible. An increasing number of service providers have never met their foreign customers except "virtually" online. A quantitative assessment conducted by the WTO's Electronic Commerce Council indicated that the share of value-added that potentially lends itself to electronic commerce exceeds 30 percent of GDP, most importantly distribution, finance, travel, and business services (Chaffey et al., 2019; Dinlersoz & Pereira, 2007; WTO Electronic Commerce, 2020).

Nonetheless, several notes of caution must be kept in mind. First, introduction of the Internet occurred at different rates in different countries. In developing countries, millions of businesses and consumers do not have access to electronic business media. At the same time, firms need to prepare their internet presence for global visitors. Language is critical to accessing retailers and other online sites. In 2020, the most common language used for websites was English, accounting for 25 percent of internet sites. This was followed by Chinese, with approximately 20 percent, and Spanish with 8 percent, of total sites. Japanese, Russian, and French each accounted for only 3 percent of websites worldwide. Historically, English dominated the Internet. But as countries began using the Internet in the 1990s, their firms and other organizations launched sites in their own languages. Multinational firms create websites in multiple languages to accommodate retailing and other services offered online. Chinese has assumed growing importance online, and may soon surpass English. This arises because China is home to 1.4 billion people, more than four times the population of the USA. China's middle class is growing rapidly, and expected to surpass 500 million in 2022; many more Chinese are acquiring the affluence needed to become online shoppers (Cheng, 2019; Sitsanis, 2019).

International Sectors

Although many services firms operate globally, most do not perceive the benefits of internationalization. Services that are efficiently performed in the home market may have great potential for internationalization (Patterson & Cicic, 1995; WTO Electronic Commerce, 2020).

Financial institutions can offer some functions very competitively internationally in the field of banking services. US banks possess advantages in fields such as mergers and acquisitions, securities sales, credit cards, and asset management. Banks in Europe and Japan are boosting their leadership through large assets and capital bases.

Construction, design, and engineering services also have great international potential. Providers of these services can achieve economies of scale not only for machinery and material but also in areas such as personnel management and the overall management of projects. Particularly for international projects that are large scale and long term, the experience advantage weighs heavily in favor of international firms. Firms knowledgeable about underwriting, risk evaluation, and operations can sell insurance services internationally. Firms offering legal and accounting services can aid their clients abroad through support activities; they can also help firms and countries improve business and governmental operations. Many small and medium-sized firms insufficiently exploit knowledge of computer operations, data manipulations, data transmission, and data analysis internationally.

Similarly, communication services have substantial future international opportunities. For example, firms experienced in the areas of videotext, home banking, and home shopping can find international success, particularly where geographic obstacles make the establishment of retail outlets cumbersome and expensive. In addition, global communication services can lead to collaboration, which greatly expands the capability of corporations.

Many institutions in the educational and corporate sectors have developed expertise in teaching services. There are large markets in training, motivation, and in the teaching of operational, managerial, and theoretical issues. It is time to take education global! Too much good and important knowledge is not made available to broad audiences. More knowledge must be communicated, be it through distance learning, study and teaching abroad, or attracting foreign students into the domestic market. The latter option can spur a service industry in itself. Many question, however, whether international education creates a stronger foreign competition. We believe that any competition, which is able to easily destroy its creators, was not built on strong pillars; new interests and capabilities will make education the jungle gym of the future with a slide toward the pool of knowledge.

Management consulting services are provided by firms and individuals to many countries and corporations. Of particular value is management expertise in areas where many developing economies need the most help, such as transportation and logistics. Major opportunities also exist for industries that deal with societal problems. For example, firms that develop environmentally safe products or produce pollution-control equipment can find new markets, as nations around the world increase their awareness of and concern about the environment and tighten their laws. Similarly, advances in healthcare or new knowledge in combating AIDS offer major opportunities for global service success.

Tourism represents a major service export whose positive impact has been sharply curtailed by Coronavirus. Whenever people visit a foreign country and spend money, it registers a positive effect on the nation's current account, with the same effect as an export. International tourism has grown in recent years, partly due to the global rise of e-commerce. For example, the explosion of internet usage in China helped grow the online travel booking market in that country. However, tourism is vulnerable to conditions in the economy and the world at large. As Exhibit 10.7 shows, the widespread outbreak of illnesses can have major consequences (Business Insider, 2020).

EXHIBIT 10.7 Coronavirus and the global tourism industry

The spread of the coronavirus, COVID-19, around the world had a palpable impact on the tourism industry. The virus affected both supply and demand, as industry workers and tourists largely stayed home during the pandemic. Countries depend heavily on the arrival of tourists from abroad. As the virus emerged in 2020, however, international tourist arrivals decreased by 20–30 percent, a loss of some US$50 billion. Many countries imposed quarantines, entry bans, or other restrictions on citizens of or recent travelers to areas most affected by COVID-19. Worldwide, for months, tourist attractions closed – museums, amusement parks, and sports venues, as well as countless restaurants, bars, and coffee shops.

Companies most affected by the pandemic are typical of the global services sector, including airlines, hotels, restaurants, casinos, and the cruise industry. Airports in Congo, El Salvador, Portugal, and several other countries were closed. Atlanta International Airport closed one of its runways to allow airlines to park unused aircraft there. The worst hit areas were Europe and the Asia-Pacific region, which expected to sustain tens of billions of dollars in losses. Experts said the coronavirus was the biggest threat to the tourism industry since World War II.

The virus outbreak, in essence, created a "perfect storm" for the tourism industry. The ensuing global economic downturn further damaged the industry. However, analysts were optimistic for a rebound in the economy and global tourism in the wake of developing effective treatments and a vaccine.

Sources: Business Insider, 2020; United Nations World Tourism Organization, 2020.

An attractive international service mix can also be achieved by pairing the strengths of different partners. For example, information technology from one country can be combined with the financial resources of other countries. The strengths of the partners can then be used to offer maximum benefits to the international community. Combining international advantages in services may ultimately result in the development of an even more drastic comparative lead. For example, if a firm has an international head start in such areas as high technology, information gathering, information processing, information analysis, and teaching, the major thrust of its international services might not be to provide these service components individually but rather to enable clients, based on a combination of competitive resources, to make better decisions.

For many firms, participation in the Internet will offer the most attractive starting point in marketing their services internationally. The setup of a website will allow visitors from any place in the globe to come see the offering. Of course, the most important problem will be how to communicate the existence of one's site and how to entice visitors to come. For that, often very traditional advertising and communication approaches need to be used. In some countries, for example, one can find rolling billboards announcing websites and their benefits. Overall, however, one needs to keep in mind that not everywhere do firms and individuals have access to or make use of the new e-commerce opportunities.

Exhibit 10.8 highlights the world's largest internet companies. They generate revenue through online sales, financial transactions, paid advertising, cloud computing, and other services. Internet companies are dominated by firms based in China and the USA. In a dynamic industry, however, innovation and technological change are constant – new entrants can grow quickly and displace current leaders.

Services Offered Internationally

For services that are delivered mainly in support of or in conjunction with goods, the most sensible approach for the international novice is to follow the path of the good. For years, many large accounting and banking firms have done this by determining where their major multinational clients have set up new operations

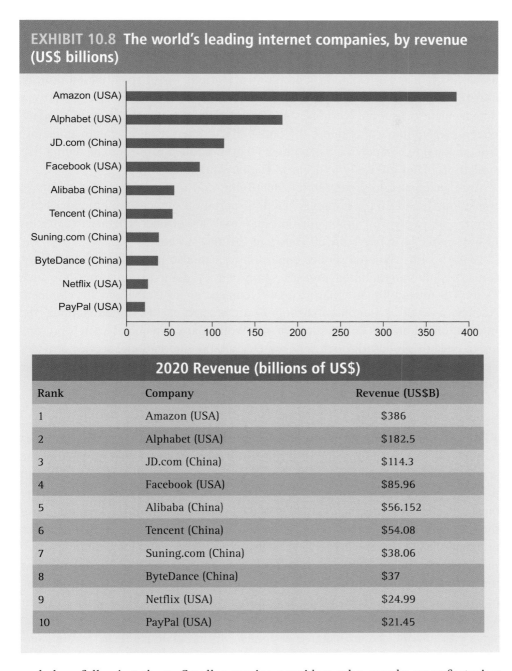

EXHIBIT 10.8 The world's leading internet companies, by revenue (US$ billions)

Rank	Company	Revenue (US$B)
1	Amazon (USA)	$386
2	Alphabet (USA)	$182.5
3	JD.com (China)	$114.3
4	Facebook (USA)	$85.96
5	Alibaba (China)	$56.152
6	Tencent (China)	$54.08
7	Suning.com (China)	$38.06
8	ByteDance (China)	$37
9	Netflix (USA)	$24.99
10	PayPal (USA)	$21.45

and then following them. Smaller service providers who supply manufacturing firms can determine where the manufacturing firms are operating internationally. Ideally, of course, it would be possible to follow clusters of manufacturers abroad to obtain economies of scale internationally while simultaneously looking for entirely new client groups.

Service providers whose activities are independent from goods need a different strategy. These individuals and firms must search for market situations abroad that are similar to the domestic market. Such a search should be concentrated in their area of expertise. For example, a design firm learning about construction projects abroad can investigate the possibility of rendering its design services. Similarly, a management consultant learning about the plans of a country or firm to computerize its operations can explore the possibility of overseeing a smooth transition from manual to computerized activities. What is required is the understanding that similar problems are likely to occur in similar situations.

Another opportunity consists of identifying and understanding the points of transition abroad. If, for example, new transportation services are introduced in a country, an expert in containerization may wish to consider whether to offer his or her service to improve the efficiency of the new system.

Leads for international service opportunities can also be gained by staying informed about international projects sponsored by domestic organizations such as the US Agency for International Development or the Trade and Development Agency, as well as international organizations such as the United Nations, the International Finance Corporation, or the World Bank. Frequently, such projects are in need of support through services. Overall, the international service provider needs to search for similar situations, similar problems, or scenarios requiring similar solutions to formulate an effective international expansion strategy.

Strategic Indicators

To be successful in the international service offering, the manager must first determine the nature and the aim of the services-offering core – that is, whether the service will be aimed at people or at things and whether the service act in itself will result in tangible or intangible actions. During this determination, the manager must consider other tactical variables that have an impact on the preparation of the service offering. For example, in conducting research for services, the measurement of capacity and delivery efficiency often remains highly qualitative rather than quantitative. In communication and promotional efforts, the intangibility of the service reduces the manager's ability to provide samples. This makes communicating the service offered much more difficult than communicating an offer for a good. Brochures or catalogs explaining services often must show a proxy for the service to provide the prospective customer with tangible clues. A cleaning service, for instance, can show a picture of an individual removing trash or cleaning a window. However, the pictures will not fully communicate the performance of the service.

Service exporters have three ways to gain credibility abroad: (1) providing objective verification of their capabilities perhaps through focusing on the company's professional license or certification by international organizations, (2) providing personal guarantees of performance, including referrals and testimonials by satisfied customers, and (3) cultivating a professional image through public appearances at international trade events or conferences and promotional materials such as a website. Due to the different needs and requirements of individual consumers, the manager must also pay attention to the two-way flow of communication. In the service area, mass communication often must be supported by intimate one-on-one follow-up.

The role of personnel deserves special consideration in international service delivery. The customer interface is intense; therefore, proper provisions need to be made for training of personnel both domestically and internationally. Major emphasis must be placed on appearance. Most of the time the person delivering the service – rather than the service itself – will communicate the spirit, value, and attitudes of the service corporation. Since the service person is both the producer as well as the marketer of the service, recruitment and training techniques must focus on dimensions such as customer relationship management and image projection as well as competence in the design and delivery of the service (Chaffey et al., 2019).

This close interaction with the consumer will also have organizational implications. While tight control over personnel may be desired, the individual interaction that is required points toward the need for an international decentralization of service delivery. This, in turn, requires delegation of large amounts of responsibility to individuals and service "subsidiaries" and requires a great deal of trust in all organizational units. This trust, of course, can be greatly enhanced through proper methods of training and supervision. Sole ownership also helps strengthen this trust. Research has shown that service firms, in their international expansion, tend to greatly prefer the establishment of full-control ventures. Only when costs escalate and the company-specific advantage diminishes will service firms seek out shared-control ventures (Czinkota et al., 2009).

The areas of pricing and financing require special attention. Because services cannot be stored, much greater responsiveness to demand fluctuation must exist, and therefore greater pricing flexibility must be maintained. At the same time, flexibility is countered by the desire to provide transparency for both the seller and the buyer of services in order to foster an ongoing relationship. The intangibility of services also makes financing more difficult. Frequently, even financial institutions with large amounts of international experience are less willing to provide financial support for international services than for products. The reasons are that the value of services is more difficult to assess, service performance is more difficult to monitor, and services are difficult to repossess. Therefore, customer complaints and difficulties in receiving payments are much more troublesome for a lender to evaluate in the area of services than for goods.

Finally, the distribution implications of international services must be considered. Usually, short and direct channels are required. Within these channels, closeness to the customer is of overriding importance to understand what the customer really wants, to trace the use of the service, and to aid the customer in obtaining a truly tailor-made service. Trade brings about various challenges and opportunities in the ethical and social responsibility domain of international business.

SUMMARY

Services are increasingly important in international trade. They need to be considered separately from trade in merchandise because they no longer simply complement goods. Often, goods complement services or compete with them. Service attributes such as intangibility, perishability, custom design, and cultural sensitivity frequently make international trade in services more complex than trade in goods. International growth and competition in this sector are intensifying. Firms leverage services to increase competitive advantage in international competition, particularly in light of new facilitating technologies, which encourage electronic commerce. Most services firms operate only domestically, but would benefit by going global. Historical patterns of service providers following manufacturers abroad have become partially obsolete as stand-alone services become more important to world trade. Management must therefore assess its vulnerability to service competition from abroad and explore opportunities to provide services internationally.

DISCUSSION QUESTIONS

1. How does the Internet facilitate offering services internationally?
2. Discuss the future of services internationalization. Which services do you expect to migrate abroad and why?
3. Why does the international sale of services differ from the sale of goods?
4. Discuss the benefits and drawbacks of services internationalization for companies in both the developed and the developing worlds.

KEY TERMS

communication services	288	General Agreement on Trade	
consulting services	289	in Services (GATS)	286
cost of communication	282	infant-industry	285
customer involvement	276	insurance services	288
discriminatory regulations	286	intangibility	276
economic security	285	market transparency	278
engineering services	288	national security	285

TAKE A STAND

As the volume of global products trade rose from the middle of the twentieth century, countless manufacturing jobs were lost in developed economies. Jobs were essentially shipped abroad to low labor-cost countries such as China and Mexico. As products manufacturing declined, services became the most prominent component of GNP in the developed countries. Then, with the rise of the Internet and digital technologies in the 1990s and 2000s, firms in the services sector began relocating jobs to lower wage countries like India, Poland, and the Philippines. Unions and activists began pressuring governments in the developed world to limit such outsourcing of services jobs. Many governments responded, and some have implemented tax or monetary penalties on companies that engage in offshoring. However, cheaper labor leads to lower costs for both goods and services, which benefits many consumers at home. At the same time, there are domestic losers of outsourcing, such as those who lose their jobs or are unable to find new ones when industries move offshore.

Questions for Debate

1. Do lower costs for businesses and consumers make up for lost jobs in those countries using such outsourcing?
2. What should governments do to keep services from moving overseas?

INTERNET EXERCISES

1. Find the most current data on the five leading export and import countries for commercial services. The information is available on the World Trade Organization site www.wto.org – click the statistics button.
   What are the key services, exports, and imports of your country? What is the current services trade balance?
2. Globalization facilitates company internationalization, but it can also expose firms to new challenges. Among the most pressing are variable economic conditions abroad; corruption, inefficiency, and the political agendas of national governments; and the growing presence of powerful, new competitors. How do globalization challenges affect the international performance of firms in the services sector? Consider using www.globalEDGE.msu.edu.

FURTHER RESOURCES

Chesterman S., and Angelina Fisher. (2010). *Private Security, Public Order: The Outsourcing of Public Services and Its Limits.* Oxford, MA: Oxford University Press.

Czinkota, M. (2019). WTO as a Reflection of Emerging "New" World Order. EastWest Institute. www.eastwest.ngo/idea/wto-reflection-emerging-"new"-world-order

International Telecommunications Union. (2019) Measuring the Information Society 2018. Geneva, Switzerland: International Telecommunications Union.

Mattoo, A., Stem, Robert M., and Zanini, Gianni (eds.). (2007). *A Handbook of International Trade in Services.* Oxford, U.K: Oxford University Press.

United Nations Conference on Trade and Development. (2017). The role of the services economy and trade in structural transformation and inclusive development. [online]. Available at https://unctad.org/meetings/en/SessionalDocuments/c1mem4d14_en.pdf.

11 International Supply Chain Management

CONTENTS

> ## VIGNETTE 11 The impact of COVID-19 on the world's supply chains
>
> COVID-19, a pandemic of 2020, has disrupted the predictions made by the World Trade Organization (WTO). A statistical review published by WTO in 2018 reported that world merchandise trade went through its strongest growth period in 2017 and was expected to continue to increase its growth in the future (WTO, 2018). The upsurge forecasted in international trade by the WTO anticipated an increase in not only the volume but also the complexity in international supply chain practices. Anecdotes indicated that during the pandemic, only 20% of supply of essentials was available although demand was very high. As a result, some retailers were increasing their selling price on a daily basis. Hence, the focus of industry and government shifted from long-term growth to short-term fulfillment. Governments encouraged companies like Amazon and eBay to deliver rapidly during the period of uncertainty. These companies mobilized their plans and resources to deal with the crisis. But their employees were worried about their own safety. Hence, the main challenge for companies during this period was to demonstrate their level of resilience by ensuring secure logistics handling capacity. Frustration of employees combined with the needs of companies like Amazon to ensure safety precaution measures.
>
> **Source:** World Trade Organization, 2018.

Introduction

An increase in the display of international products on the shelves of the retail sector, new trade agreements between Europe and Asian countries, the impact of Brexit on the United Kingdom, and the increasing dominance of China in international trade are making international logistics and supply chains highly complex. While digital technologies help simplify processes, an increase in regulatory and compliance-related requirements at the local level have led to growing adjustment needs. Many firms excel in developing supply chains and Exhibit 11.1 presents the overall top 25.

This chapter will focus on international logistics and supply chain management. Primary areas of concentration will be the links between the firm, its suppliers, and its customers, as well as transportation, inventory, packaging, and storage issues. The logistics management problems and opportunities that are peculiar to international business will also be highlighted. We will see how advances in logistics have led to more efficient production and consumption patterns. Changes in

EXHIBIT 11.1 Gartner's top 25 supply chains for 2018

2018 Rank	Company	2017 Rank	2016 Rank	2015 Rank
1	Unilever	1	1	3
2	Inditex (Zara)	3	6	5
3	Cisco Systems	4	7	6
4	Colgate-Palmolive	9	13	9
5	Intel	6	4	3
6	Nike	8	11	10
7	Nestle	7	10	17
8	PepsiCo	11	15	15
9	H&M	5	5	7
10	Starbucks	10	12	12
11	3 M	12	14	14
12	Schneider Electric	17	18	NA
13	Novo Nordisk	NA		
14	HP Inc.	19	17	NA
15	L'Oreal	20	19	22
16	Diageo	23	NA	NA
17	Samsung Electronics	25	8	8
18	Johnson & Johnson	13	21	21
19	BASF	16	20	NA
20	Walmart	18	16	13
21	Kimberly-Clark	21	24	20
22	The Coca-Cola Co.	14	9	11
23	Home Depot	NA	NA	NA
24	Adidas	NA	NA	NA
25	BMW	22	22	NA

Sources: Gilmore, 2018; Gartner Inc., 2018.

logistics-related capabilities of countries worldwide has changed the quality and standards of life of people, by bridging the geographical gap between the location of markets and of production.

Supply Chain Management

Logistics itself has been practiced for millennia and has regularly given the opportunity for efficiency and advancement to entire industries. For example, one of us authors still has the historical description of how the Eißfeld family used the acquisition of two ships, the Seestern and the Polyp, to install a steam engine in addition to the sails. Henceforth, these two ships managed to get out to the shoals earlier, harvest more fish, and return them to waiting customers more quickly. They may not have called it logistics, but their actions led to great content. On the academic side, the definition of logistics originated in academic texts in 1961 from the context of the military as a practice that dealt with procurement, maintenance, and transportation of personnel, material, and facilities (Corominas, 2017). The field later expanded and became an important part of the field of supply chain. Prof Bernard Lalonde, the father of the modern supply chain management, linked concepts like customer service, profitability, return on investment, merger and acquisitions, working capital, operation cost, optimization and shareholder value with brand reputation, inventory availability, early payment discount, and customer complaints.

A supply chain consists of manufacturers of raw material, intermediate product manufacturing companies, manufacturers of products for consumption by end customers, wholesalers, distributors, and retailers. Once connected, all these players can and should exchange information, which allows managers to plan the integration of various activities. One goal is to ensure a smooth flow of recycling and returns-related activities from an end user to the manufacturer. Another is efficient warehousing that allows tracking of inventory. One area where product tracking could be especially beneficial is the incorporation of data into production processes. On the consumer level, drug packaging can help to protect patients from dangerous counterfeits. Countries have begun to implement laws that require pharmaceutical companies to use tracking technologies.

Development of Supply Chain Management as a Discipline

During the 1950s and 1960s, the supply chain philosophy promoted traditional concepts such as mass manufacturing with cost reduction and improved productivity, which gradually moved during the 1970s towards the adoption of technology for production planning and scheduling combined with strong control over inventory using material requirements planning (MRP) programs. Furthermore, the growth of international business in the next decades encouraged manufacturers to adopt practices based on concepts such as just-in-time (JIT), total quality management (TQM), and business process re-engineering (BPR). While MRP and ERP (enterprise resource planning) enable companies to link both buyers and suppliers, JIT ensures that inventory is pushed into the market for sale to reduce the cost of warehousing and investments into production, and TQM reduces the losses by diminishing the returns from dissatisfied consumers.

International Supply Chain Management

An international supply chain benefits the manufacturer through the procurement of comparatively higher-quality products at lower costs. The international expansion of the supply chain of a firm involves expanding both in breadth and depth to enable penetration and create superior relationships. A main issue in the current state of international business is that consumers are becoming highly conscious about the green behavior of manufacturers and notice the efforts made by the manufacturer to reduce environmental degradation and consumption of natural resources. Simultaneously, manufacturers today create benchmarks for other players in the industry through trial and error and by using an ongoing process to learn how to reduce waste, lower inventory requirements, and improve purchasing costs.

Businesses engaged in international markets moved from manufacturing during the early 1970s, to quality consciousness a decade later. The dynamics of international business changed again in the twenty-first century with the advent of e-commerce and the emergence of supply chains required for e-business. Managers of international firms realized that they needed to adopt a combination of push and pull strategy. An international firm should achieve collaboration between the downstream and upstream suppliers and optimize its level of efficiency. McKinsey & Company conducted surveys of executives about future challenges to the supply chain and how prepared companies are to meet them (Exhibits 11.2 and 11.3).

Some of the critical issues in managing the efficiency of a supply chain are fulfilling the orders starting from the customer touchpoints where orders are recorded, coordinating these within the company for delivering the right order at the right time, and managing customers for future orders (In et al., 2019). Two main aspects of an efficient supply chain are (1) back-office support that follows good accounting and finance practices with appropriate packaging and supply chain arrangements, and (2) a smooth flow of goods and information and a payment realization process based on cooperation and trust between parties (Narayanaswami et al., 2019). When working well, these two elements efficiently enhance the engagement of partner organizations, their people, and procedures.

Different business functions such as order management, demand forecasting, warehousing infrastructure, and distribution structure, all influence a supply chain. Uncertainty in a supply chain can be reduced by controlling the inventories, eliminating risk, minimizing delays, and enhancing the spirit of customer service. Information technology has also helped improve supply chain management capabilities because of stronger communications and collaborations.

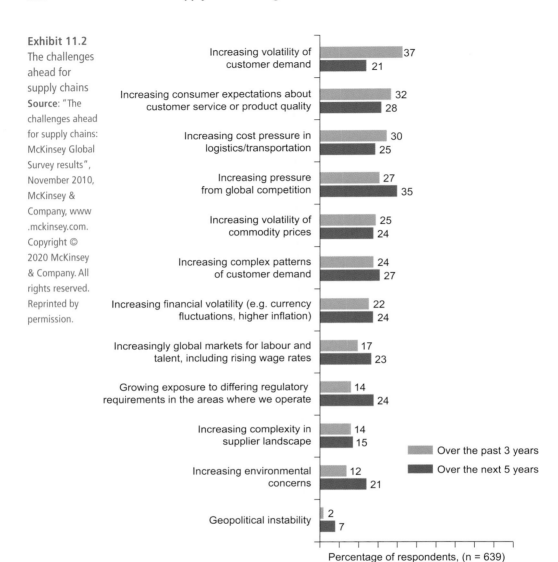

Increasing volatility of customer demand — 37 / 21

Increasing consumer expectations about customer service or product quality — 32 / 28

Increasing cost pressure in logistics/transportation — 30 / 25

Increasing pressure from global competition — 27 / 35

Increasing volatility of commodity prices — 25 / 24

Increasing complex patterns of customer demand — 24 / 27

Increasing financial volatility (e.g. currency fluctuations, higher inflation) — 22 / 24

Increasingly global markets for labour and talent, including rising wage rates — 17 / 23

Growing exposure to differing regulatory requirements in the areas where we operate — 14 / 24

Increasing complexity in supplier landscape — 14 / 15

Increasing environmental concerns — 12 / 21

Geopolitical instability — 2 / 7

Over the past 3 years
Over the next 5 years

Percentage of respondents, (n = 639)

Materials Management

Export supply chain management skills facilitate the identification of attractive sources of supply and help firms develop a low-cost competitive supply position in export markets. The automobile industry was the first to adopt a comprehensive view of supply chain management with an emphasis on supplier relations. Ford cars are one of the best examples of a supply chain strategy that integrates all activities. While previously Ford had been the most vertically integrated American automotive company, it stopped making its own glass and purchased a share in a

by percentage of top response to the most significant challenges in the future

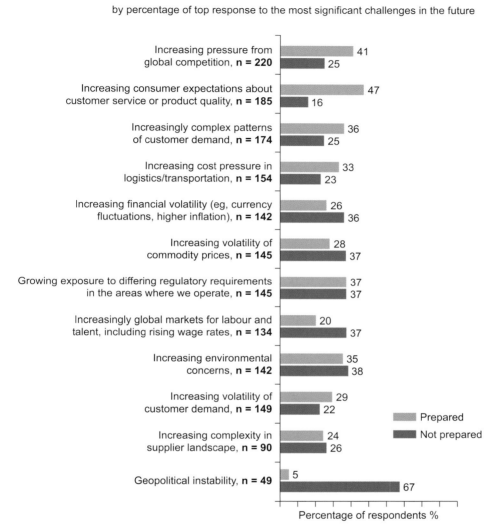

Exhibit 11.3
Companies'
level of
preparedness
to meet
supply chain
challenges
Source: "The
challenges
ahead for
supply chains:
McKinsey Global
Survey results",
November 2010,
McKinsey &
Company, www
.mckinsey.com.

glass producer. This allowed Ford to use the glass producer's design and technology expertise, while still dictating specifications. This is an example of an **extended enterprise**, where the entire supply chain is integrated into a single organization.

Technological Advancements

Effective communications also facilitate more accurate demand forecasting and efficient production planning, rather than just reviewing the past to predict the future. The use of technology to manage the supply chain allows brand managers to share issues or feedback and related market information in a timely manner. Advances in information technology (IT) have been crucial to progress in supply chain management and supplier coordination. ERP software integrates different departmental functions and commercial sales activities using business-to-business commercial software.

As a result of successfully implementing these systems considerations, the firm can develop just-in-time (JIT) delivery for lower inventory cost, electronic data interchange (EDI) for more efficient order processing, and early supplier involvement (ESI) for better planning of goods development and movement. In addition, the use of such a systems approach allows a firm to concentrate on its core competencies and to form outsourcing alliances with other companies (Mangan & Lalwani, 2016). For example, a firm can choose to focus on manufacturing and leave all aspects of order filling and delivery to an outside provider. By working closely with customers such as retailers, firms can also develop efficient customer response (ECR) systems, which can track sales activity on the retail level. As a result, manufacturers can precisely coordinate production in response to actual shelf replenishment needs, rather than based on forecasts. An enterprise resource planning (ERP) system that integrates business processes with business activities in real time allows companies to remotely handle the complex elements of supply chain management in different locations.

The use of partner engagements for transporting international supplies and technology for tracking and managing international supplies has become even more efficient with the use of smart technology, which automates complex tasks at higher speeds and with precision, thereby reducing the chances of human error. Integration and alignment of supply chain functions today is being empowered by the Internet of Things (IoT), using radio frequency identification (RFID) with cloud computing and analytics. The Internet of Things facilitates interaction between objects using electronic equipment programmed for their specific function, such as tracking the location of raw material, finished products, and supplies through RFID tagging, thereby converting events and information into cryptocurrency. The timely arrival of a shipment acknowledge by RFID and the issuance of a goods receipt note (GRN) resolves many supply chain-related issues faced by both transporter and receiver, by notifying them about the real-life situation, thereby strengthening business associations by increasing transparency and confidence. The Internet of Things also monitors the environment in which goods are being transported and provides notification of variances in terms of moisture, temperature, or humidity required for the storage of products that are either perishable or environmentally sensitive in accordance with the required standards. Application of IoT also assists companies in recording every transaction and event, which makes information about material in transit available to everyone across the supply chain.

Companies like CISCO are developing different modules to apply IoT for supporting accidents or incidents beyond control, such as for an air ambulance operation by collaborating with the California Shock Trauma Air Rescue service. The service is designed to provide instant support at the location of an incident using "geo-matching" programs and to monitor the progress remotely. Exhibit 11.4 highlights Amazon's use of technology to manage multiple components of its supply chain.

EXHIBIT 11.4 Amazon

The e-commerce giant Amazon has transformed not only the retail sector but also the shopping experience of customers. Using latest technologies available, the company created a selling services portal for manufacturers and helped them managed their supply chain efficiently. Since then, the company has been working with suppliers to innovate its online retail combined with supply chain and inventory management services. Using technological advancements such as deliveries made using drones and management of its warehouse inventory using robots, Amazon has excelled in its business, gained a competitive edge, and given a tough time to real-time retailers while generating wealth for its shareholders by not only innovating its supply chain for a superior customer experience, but also increasing the scope of its business through fulfillment services including warehousing and distribution. An analysis of retail sectors conducted by the Australian Investment Bank Macquarie in 2015 indicated that Amazon's policies to use digital technologies for managing customer expectations and their supply chain has helped them earn 26 cents per dollar of sale.

Source: Caudell, 2019.

Floor workers in Amazon's warehouse use technology to track inventory and improve shipping
Credit: Emanuele Cremaschi/Getty Images.

Dimensions of an International Supply Chain

An international supply chain is the design and management of a system that controls the forward and reverse flow of materials, services, and information into, through, and out of the international corporation. It encompasses the total movement concept by covering the entire range of operations concerned with movement, including both exports and imports. By taking a systems approach, the firm explicitly recognizes the links among the traditionally separate supply chain components within and outside a corporation. Incorporating the interaction with outside organizations and individuals such as suppliers and customers, managers are able to figure out the market demand more precisely and more quickly (Cho et al., 2019).

Two major phases in the movement of materials are of logistical importance. First is **materials management**, or the timely movement of raw materials, parts, and supplies into and through the firm. The second phase is **physical distribution**, which involves the movement of the firm's finished product to its customers. In both phases, movement is seen within the context of the entire process. Stationary periods (storage and inventory) are therefore included. The basic goal of supply chain management is the effective coordination of both phases and their various components to result in maximum cost-effectiveness while maintaining service goals and requirements.

Key to efficient supply chain management for any business are three major concepts: (1) the systems concept, (2) the total cost concept, and (3) the trade-off concept. The **systems concept** is based on the notion that materials-flow activities within and outside of the firm are so extensive and complex that they can be considered only in the context of their interaction. Instead of each corporate function, supplier, and customer operating with the goal of individual optimization, the systems concept stipulates that some components may have to work sub-optimally to maximize the benefits of the system as a whole. The systems concept intends to provide the firm, its suppliers, and its customers, both domestic and foreign, with the benefits of synergism expected from the coordinated application of size.

In order for the systems concept to work, information flows and partnership trust are instrumental. Supply chain management capability is highly information dependent, because information availability is key to planning and process implementation. Long-term partnership and trust are required in order to forge closer links between firms and managers. A logical outgrowth of the systems concept is the development of the **total cost concept**. To evaluate and optimize logistical activities, cost is used as a basis for measurement. The purpose of the total cost concept is to minimize the firm's overall supply chain management cost, by implementing the systems concept appropriately. Implementation of the total cost concept requires that the members of the system understand the sources of costs.

The **trade-off concept** recognizes the links within supply chain systems that result from the interaction of their components. For example, locating a warehouse near the customer may reduce the cost of shipment. However, additional costs are associated with new warehouses. Similarly, a reduction of inventories will save money but may increase the need for costly emergency shipments. Managers can maximize the performance of supply chain systems, only by formulating decisions based on the recognition and analysis of such trade-offs. A trade-off of costs may go against one's immediate interests (Beske-Janssen et al., 2019). Consider a manufacturer producing several different goods. The goods all use one or both of two parts, A and B, which the manufacturer buys in roughly equal amounts. Most of the goods produced use both parts. The unit cost of part A is $7, of part B, $10. Part B has more capabilities than part A; in fact, B can replace A. If the manufacturer doubles its purchases of part B, it qualifies for a discounted $8 unit price. For products that incorporate both parts, substituting B for A makes sense to qualify for the discount, since the total parts cost is $17 using A and B, but only $16 using B only. Part B should therefore become a standard part for the manufacturer. But departments assembling products that only use part A may be reluctant to accept the substitute part B because, even discounted, the cost of B exceeds that of A. Use of the trade-off concept will solve the problem.

Integration of the three concepts – system, total cost, and trade off – has resulted in the new paradigm of supply chain management with a series of value-adding activities, which connect a company's supply side with its demand side. The Ohio State University Global SMC forum has defined such integration as "the integration of business processes from end user through original suppliers, that provide products, services, and information that add value for customers." This approach views the supply chain of the entire extended enterprise, beginning with the supplier's suppliers and ending with consumers or end users. The perspective encompasses the entire flow of funds, products, and information that form one cohesive link to acquire, purchase, convert/manufacture, assemble, and distribute goods and services to the ultimate consumers. The implementation effects of such supply chain management systems can be major, especially when the company is in the phase of international expansion.

A significant characteristic of the centralized approach to the international supply chain is the existence of headquarters staff who retain decision-making power over supply chain activities affecting international subsidiaries. If headquarters exerts control, it must also take the primary responsibility for its decisions (Lee et al., 2019). Clearly, ill may arise if local managers are appraised and rewarded on the basis of performance they do not control. This may be particularly problematic if headquarters staff lack information or expertise. To avoid internal problems, both headquarters staff and local management should report to one person. The internationally centralized decision-making process leads to an overall supply chain management perspective that can dramatically improve profitability.

When a firm serves many international markets that are diverse in nature, total centralization might leave the firm unresponsive to local adaptation needs (Tatoglu et al., 2016). If each subsidiary is made a profit center in itself, each one carries the full responsibility for its performance, which can lead to greater local management satisfaction and better adaptation to local market conditions. Yet often such decentralization deprives the supply chain function of the benefits of coordination. The same argument also applies to the sourcing situation, where the coordination of shipments by the purchasing firm may be much more cost-effective than individual shipments from many small suppliers around the world. Once products are within a specific market, however, increased input from local supply chain operations should be expected and encouraged. At the very least, local managers should be able to provide input into the supply chain decisions generated by headquarters. Headquarters can then either adjust its international supply chain strategy accordingly or explain to the manager why system optimization requires actions different from the ones recommended.

A third option, used by some corporations, is the systematic outsourcing of supply chain capabilities. By collaborating with shipment firms, private warehouses, or other specialists, corporate resources can be concentrated on the firm's core product. Many firms whose core competency does not include supply chain find it more efficient to use the services of companies specializing in international shipping. This is usually true for smaller shipping volumes – for example, in cases when smaller import–export firms or smaller shipments are involved. Such firms prefer to outsource at least some of the international supply chain functions, rather than detract from staff resources and time. The resulting lower costs and better service make such third parties the preferred choice for many firms.

Going even further, **one-stop supply chain** allows shippers to buy all the transportation modes and functional services from a single carrier, instead of going through the pain of choosing different third parties for each service. One-stop supply chain ensures a more efficient global movement of goods via different shipment modes. Specialized companies provide EDI tracking services and take care of cumbersome customs procedures; they also offer distribution services, such as warehousing and inventory management.

Finally, third parties may even provide some of the international shipper's logistical functions. This rapidly growing trend offers benefits to both carriers and shippers. While the cost savings and specialization benefits of such a strategy seem clear, one must also consider the loss of control for the firm, its suppliers, and its customers that may result from such outsourcing. Yet contract supply chain does not and should not require the handing over of control. Rather, it offers concentration on one's specialization – a division of labor. The control and responsibility toward the supply chain remain with the firm, even though operations may move to a highly trained outside organization.

Alignment

An agile supply chain that operates in an international domain links up different organizations with one or more of the upstream and downstream flows of goods. Products, services, finances, and information flow from a source to a customer, co-ordinated with the help of talent and technology for intense collaborative culture within the supply chain partners. Managing a supply chain develops a network of interconnected businesses and teams involved in the fulfillment of customer needs. They coordinate the movement and storage of inventory of raw material at the point of origin to the point of consumption, which is unlike the decisions made for domestic operations by managers based on experience and knowledge of trends and heuristics.

Infrastructure

An established shipment network works as the infrastructure required for the international supply chain (Srai & Gregory, 2008). Around the globe, however, major infrastructural variations will be encountered. Some countries may have excellent inbound and outbound shipment systems but weak internal shipment links. This is particularly true in former colonies, where the original shipment systems were designed to maximize the extractive potential of the countries. In such instances, shipping to the market may be easy, but distribution within the market may represent a very difficult and time-consuming task. Infrastructure problems can also be found in countries where most shipment networks were established between major ports and cities in past centuries. The areas lying outside the major shipment networks will encounter problems in bringing their goods to market. The firm's supply chain platform, which is determined by a location's ease and convenience of market reach under favorable cost circumstances, is a key component of a firm's competitive position. Because different countries and regions may offer alternative supply chain platforms, the firm must recognize that such alternatives can be the difference between success and failure. Policy makers in turn must recognize the impact they have on the quality of infrastructure. Government planning enables supply chain capabilities and substantially affects supply chain performance on the corporate level. In an era of foreign direct investment flexibility, the public sector's investment priorities, safety regulations, tax incentives, and transport policies can have major effects on the supply chain decisions of firms.

Modes Available

International shipment frequently requires ocean or airfreight modes, which many corporations rarely use domestically. In addition, combinations such as land bridges or sea bridges may permit the transfer of freight among various modes of shipment, resulting in intermodal movements. The international supply chain manager must understand the specific properties of the different modes to be able to use them intelligently.

Water shipment is a key mode for international freight movement. Three types of vessels operating in ocean shipping can be distinguished by their service: liner service, bulk service, and tramp or charter service. Liner service offers regularly scheduled passage on established routes. Bulk service mainly provides contractual services for individual voyages or for prolonged periods of time. Tramp service is available for irregular routes and scheduled only on demand.

In addition to the services offered by ocean carriers, the type of cargo a vessel can carry is also important. The most common are conventional (break bulk) cargo vessels, container ships, and roll-on-roll-off vessels. Conventional cargo vessels are useful for oversized and unusual cargoes but may be less efficient in their port operations. Container ships carry standardized containers that greatly facilitate the loading and unloading of cargo and intermodal transfers (Exhibit 11.5). As a result, the time the ship has to spend in port is reduced, as are the port charges. Roll-on-roll-off (RORO) vessels are essentially oceangoing ferries. Trucks can drive on to built-in ramps and roll off at the destination. Another vessel similar to the RORO vessel is the LASH (lighter aboard ship) vessel. LASH vessels consist of barges stored on the ship and lowered at the point of destination. The individual barge can then operate on inland waterways, a feature that is particularly useful in shallow water.

The total volume of airfreight in relation to total shipping volume in international business remains quite small – approximately 20 percent of the world's

Exhibit 11.5 A great deal of international shipping is facilitated through container ships
Credit: David McNew/Getty Images.

manufactured exports by weight, travel by air. The figure is higher for advanced economies, which export more high-value items. Those are likelier to be shipped by air, particularly if they have a high density, that is, a high weight-to-volume ratio. Airlines continue to make major efforts to increase the volume of airfreight. In addition, some airfreight companies and ports have specialized and become partners in the international supply chain effort. The international supply chain manager must make the appropriate selection from the available modes of shipment. The decision will be heavily influenced by the needs of the firm and its customers. The manager must consider the performance of each mode on four dimensions: transit time, predictability, cost, and noneconomic factors.

Transit Time

The period between departure and arrival of the carrier varies significantly between ocean freight and airfreight. For example, the 45-day transit time of an ocean shipment can be reduced to 24 hours, if the firm chooses airfreight. The length of transit time can have a major impact on the overall operations of the firm. As an example, a short transit time may reduce or even eliminate the need for an overseas depot. Also, inventories can be significantly reduced if they are replenished frequently. As a result, capital can be freed up and used to finance other corporate opportunities. Transit time can also play a major role in emergency situations. For example, if the shipper is about to miss an important delivery date because of production delays, a shipment normally made by ocean freight can be made by air.

   Overall, it has been estimated that each day that goods are in transit adds about 0.8 percent to the cost of the goods. Perishable products require shorter transit times. Transporting them rapidly prolongs the shelf life in the foreign market. Air delivery may be the only way to enter foreign markets successfully with products that have a short life span. International sales of cut flowers have reached their current volume only as a result of airfreight. The interactions between different components of the supply chain process and their effect on transit times must be considered because, unless a smooth flow throughout the supply chain can be assured, bottlenecks will deny any timing benefits from specific improvements.

Predictability

Providers of both ocean freight and airfreight services wrestle with the issue of reliability. Both modes are subject to the vagaries of nature, which may impose delays. Yet, because reliability is a relative measure, the delay of one day for airfreight tends to be seen as much more severe and "unreliable" than the same length of delay for ocean freight. However, delays tend to be shorter in absolute time for air shipments. As a result, arrival time via air is more predictable. This attribute has a major influence on corporate strategy. For example, because of the higher predictability of airfreight, inventory safety stock can be kept at lower levels. Greater predictability can also serve as a useful sales tool because it permits more precise delivery promises to customers. If inadequate port facilities exist, airfreight may, again, be the better alternative. Unloading operations for oceangoing vessels are more cumbersome and time-consuming than for planes. Merchandise shipped via air is likely to suffer less loss and damage from exposure of the cargo to movement. Therefore, once the merchandise arrives, it is more likely to be ready for immediate delivery – a fact that also enhances predictability.

Another important aspect of predictability is the capability of a shipper to track goods at any point during the shipment. Tracking becomes particularly important as corporations increasingly obtain products from and send them to multiple locations around the world. Being able to coordinate the smooth flow of a multitude of interdependent shipments can make a vast difference to a corporation's performance. Tracking allows the shipper to check on the functioning of the supply chain and to take remedial action if problems occur.

Cargo can also be redirected if demand suddenly changes. However, such enhanced corporate response to the predictability issue is only possible if an appropriate information system is developed by the shipper and the carrier, and is easily accessible to the user. Due to rapid advances in information technology, the ability to know where a shipment is, has increased dramatically, while the cost of this critical knowledge has declined. Focus on e-business explains this further.

Cost of Shipment

Studies of customs data have demonstrated that shipment costs (both explicit and in terms of transit time) pose a barrier to trade at least as large as, and frequently larger than, tariffs. Global trade negotiations have steadily reduced tariff rates. As tariffs become a less important barrier to trade, the impact of shipment expenses on total trade costs is on the rise. The physical density and the value of the cargo will affect the decision. Bulky products may be too expensive to ship by air, whereas very compact products may be more appropriate for airfreight shipment. High-priced items can absorb shipment costs more easily than low-priced goods because the cost of shipment as a percentage of total product cost will be lower. As a result, sending diamonds by airfreight is easier to justify than sending coal. Alternatively, a shipper can decide to mix modes of shipment in order to reduce overall cost and time delays. For example, part of the shipment route can be covered by air, while another portion can be covered by truck or ship. Most important, however, are the supply chain considerations of the firm. The manager must determine how important it is for merchandise to arrive on time, which, for example, will be different for standard garments versus high-fashion dresses. The effect of shipment cost on price and the need for product availability abroad must also be considered. Simply comparing shipment modes on the basis of price alone is insufficient.

Non-Economic Factors

The shipment sector, nationally and internationally, both benefits and suffers from government involvement. Even though shipment carriers are one prime target in the sweep of privatization around the globe, many carriers are still owned or heavily subsidized by governments. As a result, governmental pressure is exerted on shippers to use national carriers, even if more economical alternatives exist. Such **preferential policies** are most often enforced when government cargo is being transported. Restrictions are not limited to developing countries. The manager must factor in all corporate, supplier, and customer activities that are affected by the modal choice and explore the full implications of each alternative.

Export Documentation

A firm must deal with numerous forms and documents when exporting to ensure that all goods meet local and foreign laws and regulations. In the simplest form of exporting, the only documents needed are a bill of lading and an **export declaration**. In most countries, these documents are available either from the government or from shipment firms. The shipper's export declaration provides proper authorization for export and serves as a means for governmental data collection efforts. A **bill of lading** is a contract between the exporter and the carrier indicating that the carrier has accepted responsibility for the goods and will provide shipment in return for payment. The bill of lading can also be used as a receipt and to prove ownership of the merchandise. There are two types of bills of lading, negotiable and nonnegotiable. **Straight bills of lading** are nonnegotiable and are typically used in prepaid transactions. The goods are delivered to a specific individual or company. **Shipper's order bills** of lading are negotiable; they can be bought, sold, or traded while the goods are still in transit and are used for letter of credit transactions.

The customer usually needs the original or a copy of the bill of lading as proof of ownership to take possession of the goods. The buyer needs the invoice to prove ownership and to arrange payment. Some governments use the **commercial invoice** to assess customs duties.

Other export documents that may be required include export licenses, consular invoices (used to control and identify goods, they are obtained from the country to which the goods are being shipped), certificates of origin, inspection certification, dock and/or warehouse receipts, destination control statements (serve to notify the carrier and all foreign parties that the item may only be exported to certain destinations), insurance certificates, shipper's export declarations (used to control exports and compile trade statistics), and export packaging lists.

The documentation required depends on the merchandise in the shipment and its destination. The number of documents required can be quite cumbersome and costly, creating a deterrent to trade. To ensure that all documentation required is accurately completed and to minimize potential problems, firms just entering the international market should consider using **freight forwarders**, who specialize in handling export documentation. Freight forwarders increasingly choose to differentiate themselves through the development of sophisticated information management systems, particularly with electronic data interchange (EDI).

Terms of Shipment and Sale

The responsibilities of the buyer and the seller should be spelled out as they relate to what is and what is not included in the price quotation and when ownership of goods passes from seller to buyer. **Incoterms** have been the internationally accepted standard definitions for terms of sale set by the International Chamber of Commerce (ICC) since 1936. The new Incoterms also clarify the loading and unloading requirements of both buyers and sellers. Although the same terms may be used in domestic transactions, they gain new meaning in the international arena.

There are four categories of terms: "E"-terms are where the seller makes the goods available to the buyer only at the seller's own premises; "F"-terms are where the seller is called upon to deliver the goods to a carrier appointed by the buyer; "C"-terms are where the seller has to contract for carriage but without assuming the risk of loss or damage to the goods or additional costs after the dispatch; and finally "D"-terms are where the seller has to bear all costs and risks to bring the goods to the destination determined by the buyer.

Prices quoted **ex-works (EXW)** apply only at the point of origin, and the seller agrees to place the goods at the disposal of the buyer at the specified place on the date or within the fixed period. All other charges are for the account of the buyer. One of the new Incoterms is **free carrier (FCA)**, which replaced a variety of FOB terms for all modes of shipment except vessel. FCA (named inland point or place of delivery) applies only at a designated inland shipping point. The seller is responsible for loading goods into the means of shipment; the buyer is responsible for all subsequent expenses. If a port of exportation is named, the costs of transporting the goods to the named port are included in the price.

Free alongside ship (FAS) at a named US port of export means that the exporter quotes a price for the goods, including charges for delivery of the goods alongside a vessel at the port. The seller handles the cost of unloading and wharfage; loading, ocean shipment, and insurance are left to the buyer. **Free on board (FOB)** applies only to vessel shipments. The seller quotes a price covering all expenses up to, and including, delivery of goods on an overseas vessel provided by or for the buyer. Under **cost and freight (CFR)** to a named overseas port of import, the seller quotes a price for the goods, including the cost of shipment to the named port of debarkation.

The cost of insurance and the choice of insurer are left to the buyer. With **cost, insurance, and freight (CIF)** to a named overseas port of import, the seller quotes a price including insurance, all shipment, and miscellaneous charges to the point of debarkation from the vessel. If anything other than waterway transport is used, the terms are CPT (carriage paid to) or CIP (carriage and insurance paid to). With delivered duty paid (DDP), the seller delivers the goods, with import duties paid, including inland shipment from import point to the buyer's premises and delivered duty unpaid (DDU) only the destination customs duty and taxes are paid by the consignee.

Ex-works signifies the maximum obligation for the buyer; delivered duty paid puts the maximum burden on the seller. The exporter should therefore learn what importers usually prefer in the particular market and what the specific transaction may require. Increasingly, exporters are quoting more inclusive terms. The benefits of taking charge of the shipment on either a CIF or DDP basis include the following: (1) exporters can offer foreign buyers an easy-to-understand "delivered cost" for the deal, (2) by getting discounts on volume purchases for shipment services, exporters cut shipping costs and can offer lower overall prices to prospective buyers, (3) control of product quality and service is extended to transport, enabling the exporter to ensure that goods arrive to the buyer in good condition, and (4) administrative procedures are cut for both the exporter and the buyer. When taking control of shipment costs, however, the exporter must know well in advance what impact the additional costs will have on the bottom line.

Starbucks is one of the top buyers of coffee in the world. As shown in Exhibit 11.6, the company's focus on quality requires a commitment to both suppliers and a complex international transportation plan.

EXHIBIT 11.6 Starbucks

Starbucks offers coffee to consumers through 22,000 stores scattered across six different continents. Raw material for the coffee bought by all the consumers across these different stores is sourced by the company from either Latin America or Africa, and its product development departments works on the material received to create blends suited to the tastes of local consumers in local markets. Boyer studied the supply chain of Starbucks and reported that Starbucks makes 70,000 deliveries to its 22,000 retail outlets located in 65 different countries. Managing delivery at such a scale requires the company to control both backward and forward integration of its supply chain with its organizational processes so that, although the coffee is localized, customer experience across all 22,000 stores is similar. For this, Starbucks sources coffee beans from approved suppliers from coffee plantations across eight different locations, namely Brazil, Columbia, Kenya, Saudi Arabia, Guatemala, Mexico, Hawaii, and Tanzania. Starbucks works with these suppliers to ensure they provide high-quality beans. For this, Starbucks developed and introduced sustainability standards, called Coffee and

Farmer Equity, with training modules for managing these standards. Also, the company bought a coffee plantation in Costa Rica to develop an internal capability to fulfill demand in case of shortages. To ensure efficiency in manufacturing and the supply chain, Starbucks opened processing and distribution centers to roast, pack, and dispatch the beans to regional warehouses for a smooth supply to retail stores.

Source: Romanoff, 2016.

Starbucks has a number of central roasteries, such as this one in New York that opened in 2018
Credit: Gary Hershorn/Getty Images.

The Cost of International Inventory

Inventories tie up a major portion of corporate funds. Capital used for inventory is not available for other corporate opportunities. Annual **inventory carrying costs** (the expense of maintaining inventories) are heavily influenced by the cost of capital and industry-specific conditions (Wu et al., 2019). A company with a 36 percent inventory carrying cost will pay for its inventory twice in two years: once to purchase it and a second time to carry it for about 25 months. Therefore, inventory management is critical for make/buy, make-to-order/make-to-stock, and other top-level decisions. In addition, **just-in-time inventory** policies, which minimize the volume of inventory by making it available only when it is needed, are increasingly required by multinational manufacturers and distributors engaging in supply chain management. They choose suppliers on the basis of their delivery and inventory performance and their ability to integrate themselves into the supply chain. Proper inventory management may therefore become a determining variable in obtaining a sale.

The purpose of establishing inventory systems – to maintain product movement in the delivery pipeline and to have a cushion to absorb demand fluctuations – is the same for domestic and international operations. The international environment, however, includes unique factors such as currency exchange rates, greater distances, and duties. At the same time, international operations provide the corporation with an opportunity to explore alternatives not available in a domestic setting, such as new sourcing or location alternatives. In international operations, the firm can make use of currency fluctuation by placing varying degrees of emphasis on inventory operations depending on the stability of the currency of a specific country. Entire operations can be shifted to different nations to take advantage of new opportunities. International inventory management can therefore be much more flexible in its response to environmental changes. In deciding the level of inventory to be maintained, the international manager must consider three factors: the order cycle time, desired customer service levels, and use of inventories as a strategic tool.

The total time that passes between the placement of an order and the receipt of the merchandise is referred to as order cycle time. Two dimensions are of major importance to inventory management: the length of the total order cycle and its consistency. In international business, the order cycle is frequently longer than in domestic business. It comprises the time involved in order transmission, order filling, packing and preparation for shipment, and shipment. Order transmission time varies greatly internationally depending on the method of communication. The order-filling time may also increase because lack of familiarity with a foreign market makes the anticipation of new orders more difficult. Packing and shipment preparation requires more detailed attention. Finally, of course, shipment time increases with the distances involved. Larger inventories may have to be maintained both domestically and internationally to bridge the time gaps. Consistency, the second dimension of order cycle time is also more difficult to maintain in international business. Depending on the choice of shipment mode, delivery times may vary considerably from shipment to shipment. The variation may require the maintenance of larger safety stocks to be able to fill demand in periods when delays occur.

International Packaging

Packaging is instrumental in getting the merchandise to the ultimate destination in a safe, maintainable, and presentable condition. Packaging that is adequate for domestic shipping may be inadequate for international shipment because the shipment will be subject to the motions of the vessel on which it is carried. Added stress in international shipping also arises from the transfer of goods between different modes of transportation. The responsibility for appropriate packaging rests with the shipper of goods. Packaging decisions must also take into account differences in environmental conditions – for example, climate. When the ultimate destination is very humid or particularly cold, special provisions must be made to prevent damage to the product. The task becomes even more challenging when one considers that, in the course of long-distance shipment, dramatic changes in climate can take place. Still famous is the case of a firm in Taiwan that shipped drinking glasses to the Middle East. The company used wooden crates and padded the glasses with hay. Most of the glasses, however, were broken by the time they reached their destination. As the crates traveled into the dry Middle East, the moisture content of the hay dropped. By the time the crates were delivered, the thin straw offered almost no protection.

The weight of packaging must also be considered, particularly when airfreight is used, as the cost of shipping is often based on weight. At the same time, packaging material must be sufficiently strong to permit stacking in international transportation. Another consideration is that, in some countries, duties are assessed according to the gross weight of shipments, which includes the weight of packaging. Obviously, the heavier the packaging, the higher the duty will be. The shipper must pay sufficient attention to instructions provided by the customer for packaging. For example, requests by the customer that the weight of any one package should not exceed a certain limit or that specific package dimensions should be adhered to, usually are made for a reason. Often, they reflect limitations in shipment or handling facilities at the point of destination.

Although the packaging of a product is often used as a form of display abroad, international packaging can rarely serve the dual purpose of protection and display. Therefore, double packaging may be necessary. The display package is for future use at the point of destination; another packaging surrounds it for protective purposes (Richards, 2017). One solution to the packaging problem in the international supply chain has been the development of intermodal containers – large metal boxes that fit on trucks, ships, railroad cars, and airplanes and ease the frequent transfer of goods in international shipments. Developed in different forms for both sea and air shipment, containers also offer better utilization of carrier space because of standardization of size. The shipper therefore may benefit from lower shipment rates. In addition, containers can offer greater safety from pilferage and damage. Of course, at the same time, the use of containers allows thieves to abscond with an entire shipment, rather than just parts of it. The rise in cargo theft and pilferage has given birth to a whole new industry of "risk consultancies," which are contracted by exasperated ship owners to safeguard their vessels. In addition to providing armed guards on ships and offering their own crafts as escorts, "consultancies" are responsible for parleying with pirates, paying ransoms, and outfitting ships with barbed or electric wires and water cannons to make it hard for pirates to clamber aboard.

Container traffic is heavily dependent on the existence of appropriate handling facilities, both domestically and internationally. In addition, the quality of inland shipment must be considered. If shipment for containers is not available and the merchandise must be unpacked and reloaded the expected cost reductions may not materialize (Kabir et al., 2019). In some countries, rules for the handling of containers may be designed to maintain employment. Overall, cost attention must be paid to international packaging. The customer who ordered and paid for the merchandise expects it to arrive on time and in good condition. Even with re-placements and insurance, the customer will not be satisfied if there are delays. Dissatisfaction will usually translate directly into lost sales.

Exhibit 11.7 highlights the case of Shipwire's storage, packaging, and fulfillment solutions that can provide streamlined operations for many components of the international supply chain.

EXHIBIT 11.7 Shipwire

Shipwire offers safe and secure warehouse storage facilities to its clients through its warehouses located in countries such as the USA, China, Europe, Australia, and Asia. An enterprise-grade warehouse management system (WMS) enables Shipwire not only to offer secured storage for their items, but also to under-take smooth but complicated shipping and special handling procedures. Shipwire has also introduced a smart shipping platform that offers best shipping couriers, packaging options, and routes for customers' products, which helps to reduce shipping and fulfillment costs. The company uses a cloud-based platform that supports their logistics requirements and enables them to manage a global logis-tics network consisting of warehouses that ship material to both international and national locations and to the end users at the retail stores.

Source: Gilbert, 2020.

Managing International Inventories

Although the international supply chain is discussed as a movement or flow of goods, a stationary period is involved when merchandise becomes inventory stored in warehouses (Companik et al., 2018). Heated arguments can arise within a firm over the need for and utility of warehousing internationally. On the one hand, cus-tomers expect quick responses to orders and rapid delivery. Accommodating the customer's expectations would require locating many distribution centers around the world. On the other hand, warehouse space is expensive. In addition, the larger volume of inventory increases the inventory carrying cost. Fewer warehouses allow for consolidation of shipments and therefore lower shipping rates to the warehouse. However, if the warehouses are located far from customers, the cost of outgoing transportation increases. The international logistician must consider the tradeoffs between service and maintenance of the supply chain in order to determine the appropriate levels of warehousing and distribution.

The location decision addresses as to how many distribution centers to have and where to locate them. The availability of facilities abroad will differ from the domestic situation. Also, the standards and quality of facilities can vary widely. As a result, the storage decision of the firm is often accompanied by the need for large-scale, long-term investments. Despite the high cost, international storage facilities should be established if they support the overall supply chain effort. Once the decision is made to use storage facilities abroad, the warehouse conditions must be carefully analyzed. As an example, in some countries warehouses have low ceilings. Packaging developed for the high stacking of products is therefore unnecessary or even counterproductive. In other countries, automated warehousing is available, thus proper barcoding of products and the use of package dimensions acceptable to the warehousing system are basic requirements. In contrast, in warehouses still stocked manually, weight limitations will be of major concern. And, if no forklift trucks are available, palletized delivery is of little use.

To optimize the supply chain system, the logistician should analyze international product sales and then rank order products according to warehousing needs. Products that are most sensitive to delivery time might be classified as "A" products. "A" products would be stocked in all distribution centers, and safety stock levels would be kept high. Alternatively, the storage of products can be more selective, if quick delivery by air can be guaranteed. Products for which immediate delivery is not urgent could be classified as "B" products. They would be stored only at selected distribution centers around the world. Finally, products for which there is little demand would be stocked only at headquarters. Classifying products enables the international logistician to substantially reduce total international warehousing requirements and still maintain acceptable performance levels.

Foreign Trade Zones

Areas where foreign goods may be held or processed and then re-exported without incurring duties are called foreign trade zones. Such special zones can be found at major ports of entry and also at inland locations near major production facilities. The existence of trade zones can be quite useful to the international firm. For example, in some countries the benefits derived from lower labor costs may be offset by high duties and tariffs. As a result, the location of manufacturing and storage facilities in these countries may prove uneconomical. Foreign trade zones are designed to exclude the impact of duties from the location decision (and hopefully attract more local labor). Trade zones can also be useful as transshipment points to reduce supply chain costs and redesign marketing approaches based on physical proximity. All parties to the arrangement can benefit from foreign trade zones. The government maintaining the zone achieves increased employment and investment. The firm using the trade zone obtains a spearhead in the foreign market without incurring all of the costs customarily associated with such an activity. As a result, goods can be reassembled, and large shipments can be broken down into smaller units. Also, goods can be repackaged when packaging weight becomes part of the duty assessment. Finally, goods can be given domestic "made-in" status if assembled in the foreign trade zone. Thus, duties may be payable only on the imported materials and component parts rather than on the labor that is used to finish the product (Exhibit 11.8).

Governments also have established export processing zones and special economic areas. The common dimensions for all such zones are introduced by the governments' desire to stimulate the economy, particularly the export side of international trade. Export processing zones usually provide tax- and duty-free treatment for production facilities whose output is destined abroad. The maquiladoras of Mexico are one example of a program that permits firms to take advantage of

Exhibit 11.8 McDonald's maintains storage and supply units that coordinate with local and regional intermediaries and distributors to minimize inventory costs while supporting restaurant operations
Credit: Oli Scarff/Getty Images.

sharp differentials in labor costs. Firms can carry out the labor-intensive part of their operations in Mexico while sourcing raw materials or component parts from other nations.

One country that has used trade zones very successfully for its own economic development is China. Through the creation of **special economic zones**, in which there are substantial tax incentives, low prices for land and labor, and no tariffs, the government has attracted many foreign investors bringing in billions of dollars. The investors have brought new equipment, technology, and managerial know-how and have increased local economic prosperity substantially. The job generation effect has been so strong that the central Chinese Government has expressed concern about the overheating of the economy and the inequities between regions with and without trade zones. For the logistician, the decision whether to use such zones is mainly framed by the overall benefit for the supply chain system. Clearly, additional transport and re-transport are required, warehousing facilities need to be constructed, and material handling frequency will increase. However, the costs may well be balanced by the preferential government treatment or by lower labor costs.

The Supply Chain and E-Business

The term e-business refers to online business, while supply chain links operational activities of an organization like procurement and processing of raw material to be converted into a finished product ready for sale and consumption with the flow of information, materials, and services (Barrad & Valvarde, 2020). The Internet has been instrumental in transforming supply chain management; supply chains have become more cost-effective as the exchange of information has become more efficient, communications between customers and suppliers have become quicker and easier, and associated costs have reduced (Hastig & Sodhi, 2020).The Firms use internet-based intranets for communications and extranets for inventory management. Managers now use the Internet not only to conduct many more global comparisons among suppliers and select from a wide variety of choices, but also to manage different components of the supply chain such as procurement, inventory management, supply chain management, and customer service (Georgise et al., 2020). Today, with the help of the Internet, firms are much more informed in the structure of their supplier network. As a consequence, the supply base of many firms has become much broader with fewer participants.

Many firms use their websites as a marketing and advertising tool and are expanding them to include order-taking capabilities. The development of new technologies and digital processes has led to dramatic growth in net e-commerce revenue. Companies wishing to enter e-commerce will not have to do so on their own (Hinson et al., 2018). Hub sites (also known as virtual malls or digital intermediaries) bring together buyers, sellers, distributors, and transaction payment processors in a single marketplace, making convenience the key attraction. The future is also growing brighter for hubs in the consumer-to-consumer market, where companies like eBay are setting high standards of profitability.

Firms must remember that websites should encourage business, not preclude it. If prospective customers cannot easily and rapidly find what they are looking for on a website, they are likely to move on and find another site that makes its information and interactivity more apparent (King et al., 2017). For industries such as music and motion pictures, the Internet is both an opportunity and a threat. The Web provides a new, efficient method of distribution and customization of products. At the same time, it can be a channel for intellectual property violations through unauthorized posting on other websites where these products can be downloaded.

The heart of Dell's success is its integrated supply chain, which has enabled rapid product design, fabrication, and assembly, as well as direct shipment to customers. Inventories have been dramatically reduced through extensive sharing of information, a prudent choice given the risk of technological obsolescence and reductions in the cost of materials that can exceed 50 percent a month. Even with reduced inventories, Dell's strategic use of information has made possible a dramatic reduction in the elapsed time from order to delivery, giving Dell a significant competitive advantage (Exhibit 11.9).

Exhibit 11.9 Dell's integrated supply chain helps the company innovate products, like this foldable tablet
Credit: Jerod Harris/Getty Images for Dell.

A high premium has been placed on speed and process efficiency, blurring the traditional boundaries between supplier, manufacturer, and customer. Therefore, in Dell's new virtual corporation, inventories are reduced by use of timely information; emphasis on physical assets is being replaced by emphasis on intellectual capabilities; and proprietary business knowledge is being increasingly shared in open, collaborative relationships. This extensive integration of the supply chain can be viewed as a shift from vertical corporate integration to a virtually integrated corporation. For instance, peripherals, such as monitors, keyboards, speakers, and mice, need not be gathered in one location prior to shipment to the customer. Manufactured by separate suppliers and labeled with the Dell logo, shippers gather them from all over North America, match them overnight, and deliver them as complete hardware sets to customers as if they had all come from the same location. (National Research Council, 2000)

Supply Chain and Security

The entire field of supply chain management and supply chains has been thoroughly affected by newly emerging security concerns. After the terrorist attacks of 2001, companies have had to learn that the pace of international transactions has slowed down and that formerly routine steps now take longer. In decades past, many governmental efforts and negotiations were devoted to speeding up transactions across borders. Now, national security reasons are forcing governments to erect new barriers and conduct new inspections in order to safeguard businesses and consumers. The supply chain is one of the business activities most affected. Modern shipment systems have proved to be critical to terrorist activities. They provide the means for the perpetrators to quickly arrive at, and depart from, the sites of attacks. Terrorists have even used shipment systems themselves to carry out their crimes.

Supply chain systems are often the targets of attacks. These systems are the true soft spots of vulnerability for both nations and firms. Consider the vulnerability of pipelines used for carrying oil, natural gas, and other energy sources. The need to institute new safeguards for international shipments will affect the efficiency with which firms can manage their international shipments. There is now more uncertainty and less control over the timing of arrivals and departures. There is also a much greater need for internal control and supervision of shipments. Cargo security will increasingly need to ensure not only that nothing goes missing, but also that nothing has been added to a shipment. Firms with a just-in-time regimen are exploring alternative management strategies. Planning may also include a shift of international shipments from air carriage to sea.

During the 2009 summit of the North American Free Trade Agreement (NAFTA) members, participants identified border security regulations as one of the most pressing areas of concern (Lester & Manak, 2018). Some supported customs preclearance throughout all the NAFTA countries, pointing out that if only one entry/exit point is secured while others are note, this will create a competitive disadvantage for all members. 9/11 ushered in a more stringent security regime, with some unintended consequences for trade. For example, a cargo shipment may be cleared, but the truck driver may not; critical or perishable cargo can linger in custom's limbo for weeks awaiting clearance; also consider that impounded goods are subject to ongoing storage fees which can become quite substantial. There are claims that some suppliers have begun sending two trucks with the same critical cargo across the border to make sure that at least one gets through in the required time period.

Supply Chain and Environmental Sustainability

The logistician plays an increasingly important role in allowing the firm to operate in an environmentally conscious way. Environmental laws, expectations, and self-imposed goals set by firms are difficult to adhere to without a supply chain orientation that systematically takes such concerns into account. Because laws and regulations differ across the world, the firm's efforts need to be responsive to a wide variety of requirements. One supply chain orientation that has grown in importance due to environmental concerns is the development of reverse distribution systems. Such systems are instrumental in ensuring that the firm not only delivers the product to the market, but also can retrieve it from the market for subsequent use, recycling, or disposal. To a growing degree the ability to develop such a reverse supply chain is a key determinant for market acceptance and profitability.

Society also recognizes that retrieval should not be restricted to short-term consumer goods, such as bottles. Rather, it may be even more important to devise systems that enable the retrieval and disposal of long-term capital goods, such as cars, refrigerators, air conditioners, and industrial goods, all with the least possible burden on the environment. Managers are often faced with the trade-offs between environmental concerns and logistical efficiency. Companies increasingly need to learn how to achieve environmental and economic goals simultaneously. From the perspective of materials management and physical distribution, environmental practices are those that bring about fewer shipments, less handling, and more direct movement. Such practices need to be weighed against optimal efficiency routines, including just-in-time inventory and quantity discount purchasing.

On the shipment side, supply chain managers will need to expand their involvement in carrier and routing selection. For example, shippers of oil or other potentially hazardous materials will increasingly need to ensure that the carriers used have excellent safety records and use only double-hulled ships. Society may even expect corporate involvement in choosing the route that the shipment will travel, preferring routes that are far from ecologically important and sensitive zones. Firms will need to assert leadership in such consideration of the environment to provide society with a better quality of life.

Supply Chain and Waste Management

Waste created through various activities like overproduction, inappropriate processing, expired inventory, defective inventories, etc. in a supply chain impacts the environment negatively with contamination of water, air, or land. Hence, local governments try to control waste through legislation that involves the protection of the environment and preservation of resources. These initiatives require planning, authorization, operational control, and efficient disposal of waste to be managed voluntarily by organizations, with transparency not only to manage public perception, but also to ensure that the soul of their business is responsible and ethical in philosophy.

On the consumer level, in Europe, every citizen generates 1.69 kg of waste every day and 60% of waste generated comes from packaging of products purchased by consumers. Management of waste involves treatment of waste collected for the purpose of either recycling or disposal. Recycling of a product requires a reverse supply chain, which concerns the handling and disposition of returned products and the use of related materials and information. With the gradual rise in price of oil and other commodities, companies are beginning to see used products less as trash and more as the sum of their raw materials, energy, and labor. This new attitude has intensified the search for innovative ways to extract maximum value from product returns. More and more companies are entering the reverse supply chain business. Some companies choose to keep the reverse supply chain effort in-house.

Given the finite supply of valuable resources, such as steel, copper, aluminum, and petroleum, that are extensively used in many manufacturing sectors, recycling makes not only environmental but also economic sense. Commercial recycling is already an established industry in many developing countries and could be a future source of economic growth for them. Governments have tried to promote control of waste-related practices at the company level with the introduction of Extended Producers' Responsibility (EPR). EPR is a policy that holds producers or manufacturers responsible for the waste their supply chain produces along the entire life cycle of their product to minimize the effect of waste on the environment. EPR is a product stewardship model that, if integrated into the supply chain, initiates a reverse supply chain with efficient product design, production, and consumption to discourage waste and link supply chain with principles of a circular economy. The circular economy-based model of production promotes the reduction, reuse, and recycling of waste with the use of biodegradable material for production so that after consumption waste does not cause environmental hazards.

SUMMARY

Supply chain management in an international context goes beyond the flow of material into, through, and out of international corporations (Kache & Seuring, 2017). Today, it is about competitiveness that is becoming increasingly dependent on efficient management of its traditional practices such as materials management and physical distribution, with environmental consciousness and concepts such as waste management (Foo et al., 2018). Recognition of the needs of the firm combined with demands of its suppliers and customers, to develop trade-offs between various supply chain components, are important for a business to ensure that its business nurtures a responsibility toward both environmental and overall sustainability issues. Having an understanding of shipment infrastructures in other countries and modes of shipment, such as ocean shipping and airfreight, helps the international manager to make informed choices based on a knowledge of customer demands, transit times, predictability, and cost requirements. In addition, noneconomic factors such as government regulations weigh heavily in this decision. Inventory management is an important consideration for an efficient supply chain. Inventories abroad are expensive to maintain yet often crucial for international success. Customers often just don't want to wait! The logistician must evaluate requirements for order cycle times and customer service levels to develop an international inventory policy that can also serve as a strategic management tool. International packaging is important because it ensures the arrival of the merchandise at the ultimate destination in a safe environment and undamaged. In developing packaging, climate, handling conditions, and merchandise presentation requirements must be considered. The supply chain manager must also deal with international storage issues and determine where to locate inventories. International warehouse space will have to be leased, often for a rather long period, or purchased. Decisions will have to be made about utilizing foreign trade zones. International supply chain management is increasing in importance. Managing a supply chain function so that it can respond quickly and efficiently to environmental demands and exposure will increasingly be a requirement to ensure the success of global supply chains.

DISCUSSION QUESTIONS

1. Explain the key aspects of international supply chain management.
2. How can sourcing strategies and working capital disrupt the international supply chain?
3. Explain how a company can use EPR to derive economic value and competence in the international supply chain.
4. How can an international firm reduce its order cycle time?
5. What role can technology play in improving the distribution function of an international supply chain?

KEY TERMS

TAKE A STAND

Founded in 1874, the UPU is an international postal organization based in Switzerland. In 1969, the UPU's developed country members implemented discounts for poor nations when shipping small parcels. China then was isolated with few outward shipments. As a result, Chinese shipping cost were very low due to a subsidy. Face cream was more affordable to ship to American consumers from China than it was from Los Angeles. Today, however, China delivers more than 1 billion small packages a year to the USA, but the special discount treatment continues.

The USA announced that as of October 17, 2018 it was withdrawing from the agreement. The goal was to arrive at competitive and fair global shipping rates.

Questions for Debate

1. Will the price advantage of many Chinese e-commerce vendors decline?
2. Is the rapid abandonment of international agreements acceptable?
3. How long should preferential agreements remain in effect?

INTERNET EXERCISES

Based on the use of the artificial intelligence, the program Watson, by IBM, is used to support the supply chain module via predictive analysis to smooth the delivery process.

1. How, in the age of disruption, can companies meet expectations of customers when one in every three organizations reports losses year on year because of supply chain disruptions?
2. Can an agile supply chain help businesses survive and succeed internationally?
3. Go to the website of IBM using the following link to understand how companies can adapt to current business needs:
    https://mediacenter.ibm.com/media/How+AI+can+revolutionize+your+supply+chain+now/0_0bdxyurc

FURTHER RESOURCES

Mangan, J. and Lalwani, C. (2016). *Global logistics and supply chain management*. John Wiley & Sons.

Richards, G. (2017). *Warehouse management: a complete guide to improving efficiency and minimizing costs in the modern warehouse*. Kogan Page Publishers.

Tatoglu, E., Glaister, A. J., and Demirbag, M. (2016). Talent management motives and practices in an emerging market: A comparison between MNEs and local firms. *Journal of World Business*, *51*(2), 278–293.

Wu, Q., Muthuraman, K., and Seshadri, S. (2019). Effect of financing costs and constraints on real investments: The case of inventories. *Production and Operations Management*, *28*(10), 2573–2593

12 Managing Globally

CONTENTS

VIGNETTE 12 Global talent crunch

A shortage of skilled employees will have a significant impact on the world's economic growth by 2030. Korn Ferry, a global consulting firm synchronizing talent and strategy, estimated a talent crunch between supply and demand as early as 2020.

London's financial market dominance is under threat with a shortage of more than half a million workers in the financial and business sectors in the UK alone. They also project that technology advancements will be hindered with the labor shortage of more than 700,000 workers with a potential annual revenue loss of $103.25 billion by 2030. Singapore will be one of the hardest hit by the shortage in the financial sector.

Globally, the study projected a potential crisis:

- The USA, Japan, France, Germany, and Australia are faced with the largest threat in the near term with a combined loss of $1.876 trillion by 2020.
- India is the only economy in the study addressing this crisis with a potential talent surplus in 2025 and 2030.
- Global financial and business services are projected to have the largest shortages of 10.7 million workers by 2030.
- Manufacturing, which currently has a surplus of skilled workers, could face a deficit crisis of 7.9 million workers by 2030.

Left unaddressed, this talent crisis will impede global growth and could have a significant impact on the world's economy. This shortage will create 85.2 million unfilled jobs and nearly $0.5 trillion in unrealized revenue. Companies must mitigate their potential talent crisis now to protect their future. Small economies, such as Hong Kong and Singapore, need to start upskilling their existing workforce.

Having the right talent is an organization's greatest competitive advantage. A successful future will be an effective partnership between people and technology and organizations need to address the talent shortages before they are critical.

Sources: Korn Ferry (2020a); PricewaterhouseCoopers (2020); Talent Mobility, 2020; Lindblad, C. (2018).

Introduction

The importance of the quality of the workforce – from the executive level down to the factory floor – cannot be overemphasized, regardless of the stage of globalization. While in the early stages, the focus is typically on understanding cultural differences, as firms become more global, they move toward integrating country-to-country differences within the overall corporate culture.

The competency that companies indicated as most contributing to global success was having a global mindset (67%), signaling an understanding that the ability to work globally is different from working domestically in one's own country. The next top critical competencies for global success were cultural intelligence (64%), strategic thinking (64%), and being adaptable to change (47%) (Dubberke, 2017; Beaman, 2012).

When companies are successful in the development of new and effective HR management strategies, both of these challenges – having a quality workforce and a global mindset – could prove to be a blessing in disguise. The first potential problem stems from shifting demographic trends. Developed economies are typically characterized by aging populations and low birth rates. As experienced employees retire, the pool of available replacements gets progressively smaller. Therefore, companies have to develop strategies for coping with talent shortages. Among these strategies should be the development of corporate cultures that are more accepting of ethnic and gender diversity, given the prevalent global demographic trends. Their primary motivation is to attract managerial talent from developing countries with rapidly expanding markets, such as India and China, because of their specific local knowledge and understanding of consumers (Doh & Stumpf, 2013; PricewaterhouseCoopers, 2020).

Managing Managers

The importance of the quality of the workforce in international business cannot be overemphasized, regardless of the stage of internationalization of the firm. Those in early stages of internationalization focus on understanding cultural differences, while those more advanced are determined to manage and balance cultural diversity with a goal to integrate differences within the overall corporate culture. International business systems are complex and dynamic, and they require competent people to develop and direct them. Firms need to create a pipeline of future leaders with global management experience. Many managers may see an international assignment as a career enhancement. Firms will need to develop programs designed to give individuals that critical international experience. The majority of employees indicate that communicating with them before, during, and after their international experience is the most important aspect of optimizing their international assignment (BGRS, 2016).

Early Stages of Globalization

In the early stages, the marketing or sales manager of the firm is usually responsible for initiating export activities. As sales increase, an export manager will be appointed and given the responsibility for handling export documentation, developing and maintaining customers, interacting with the firm's intermediaries, and planning for overall market expansion.

Typically, firms will hire an experienced export manager from outside the firm, rather than promote an inexperienced candidate from within. The reason for this is that knowledge of the product or industry is less important than international experience. In the early stages, a highly entrepreneurial spirit with a heavy dose of trader mentality is required. As the firm progresses from exporting to an international division to foreign direct involvement, human resources planning activities will initially focus on needs vis-à-vis various markets and functions. Existing personnel can be assessed and plans made to recruit, select, and train employees for positions that cannot be filled internally. The four major categories of overseas assignments are:

1. a CEO, to oversee and direct the entire operation
2. functional heads, to establish and maintain departments and ensure their proper performance
3. trouble-shooters, who are utilized for their special expertise in analyzing, and thereby preventing or solving particular problems
4. white- or blue-collar workers.

Many technology companies have had to respond to shortages in skilled employees by globalized recruitment using websites or by hiring headhunters in places such as China and India. Colgate-Palmolive (with 80 percent of its sales outside the USA) has eight non-native Americans in its brain trust of nine top operating executives – including people from India and Colombia. More than half of the 200 people in its senior management ranks, including those in staff and support roles, are not originally from the USA (Colgate-Palmolive, 2017).

One of the major sources of competitive advantage for global corporations is their ability to attract talent from around the world. Corporations need systematic management development programs, with the objective of creating and carefully allocating management personnel. Increasingly, corporations call for international experience as a prerequisite for advancement. The biggest talent management challenges are attracting talent with relevant global skills, the readiness of our workforce, and retention of that key talent. Managers in global assignments are concerned about their future – 64% of them according to a Cartus survey (Global Relocation Trends, 2018).

In global corporations, there is no such thing as a universal global manager, but rather a network of global specialists, in four general groups of managers that have to work together. Global business (product) managers have the task to further the company's global efficiency and competitiveness. Country managers have to be sensitive and responsive to local market needs and demands and, at the same time, be aware of global implications. Functional managers have to make sure that the corporation's capabilities in technical, manufacturing, marketing, human resources, and financial expertise are linked and can benefit from one another. Corporate executives at headquarters have to manage interactions among the three groups of managers, as well as identify and develop the talent to fill the positions.

Global companies should show clear career paths for managers assigned overseas and develop the systems and the organization for promotion (Exhibit 12.1). This approach serves to eliminate many of the perceived problems and thus motivates managers to seek out foreign assignments. Furthermore, when jobs open up, the company can quickly determine who is able and willing to take them. Foreign assignments can occur at various stages of the manager's tenure. In the early stages, assignments may be short term, such as a membership in an international task force or 6 to 12 months at headquarters in a staff function. Later, an individual may serve as a business-unit manager overseas. Many companies use cross-postings to other countries or across product lines to further an individual's acculturation to the corporation. A period in a head office department or a subsidiary will not only provide an understanding of different national cultures and attitudes but also improve an individual's "know-who" and therefore establish unity and a common sense of purpose, necessary for the proper implementation of global programs.

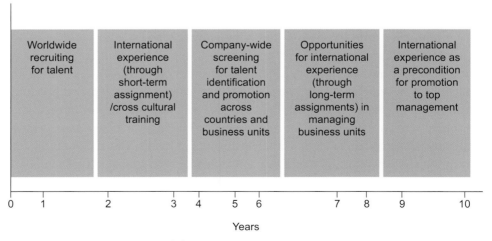

Exhibit 12.1 A corporate career path for a manager assigned overseas

Sources for Management Recruitment

The location and the nationality of candidates for a particular job are the key issues in recruitment. A decision will have to be made on whether to recruit from within the company or, in the case of larger corporations, from within other product or regional groups, or to rely on external talent. Similarly, decisions will have to be made about whether to hire or promote locally or use expatriates; that is, home-country nationals or third-country nationals (citizens of countries other than the home or host country). Typically, 43% of expatriates are posted in subsidiaries, while the remaining 57% are given assignments to the country where their company is headquartered (i.e., they are inpatriates). Hampered in their global aspirations by a lack of managerial talent, Chinese companies and multinationals operating in China alike have intensified their competition for capable global managers. In general, the choice process between expatriates and locals is driven by (1) the availability and quality of the talent pool, (2) corporate policies and their cost, and (3) environmental constraints on the legal, cultural, or economic front. Many countries still resist letting jobs go abroad, but there is increasing pressure to source employment globally. In the new economy in which the physical location of work may not matter, the choice of becoming an expatriate may be the employee's. Today's high-tech globalized workplace spawns a new trend in cross-border HR international telecommuting, whereby an employer in one country arranges for one of its own employees to work from a home overseas. Now even a top performer might successfully telecommute "from the other side of the globe" with a computer, smartphone, printer, express courier delivery, and videoconferencing (Radu, 2018; Dowling, 2013; Brunelli, 2012). The biggest issues are managing between multiple time zones – from Spain, to the United States, to Japan – and making sure that all employees understand each other and are on the same page.

Employees rate the excitement of moving abroad and the desire to work overseas as first in their decision-making. This is closely followed by how an international assignment will enhance their résumé (Cigna Health and Life Insurance Company, 2015). Expats say they need more communication and support when taking an overseas appointment. These include assistance with local culture, employer-sponsored resources, and repatriation assistance. Expats are aware that their employers must balance the considerable costs of mobility programs with the employer's demand for global talent. Some expats have made a career of taking different global assignments.

Selection Criteria for Overseas Assignments

The traits that have been suggested as necessary for the international manager range from the ideal to the real (Exhibit 12.2). One characterization describes "a flexible personality, with broad intellectual horizons, attitudinal values of

EXHIBIT 12.2 Necessary traits for the international manager

Competence	Adaptability	Personal characteristics
Technical knowledge	Interest in overseas work	Age
Leadership ability	Relational abilities	Education
Experience, past performance	Cultural empathy	Sex
Area expertise Language	Appreciation of new management styles	Health Marital status
	Appreciation of environmental constraints	Social acceptability
	Adaptability of family	

cultural empathy, general friendliness, patience and prudence, impeccable educational and professional (or technical) credentials – all topped off with immaculate health, creative resourcefulness, and respect of peers. If the family is equally well endowed, all the better" (Emerald Insight, 2007). In addition to being flexible and adaptable, they have to be able to take action where there is no precedent. Their relative importance may vary dramatically, of course, depending on the firm's situation, as well as where the choice is being made. Americans are particularly good at business literacy, while Latin Americans have developed the ability to cope with complex social relations.

An expatriate manager usually has far more responsibility than a manager in a comparable domestic position and must be far more self-sufficient in making decisions, conducting daily business, and leading others. However, regardless of management skills, being in a new environment still requires the ability to adapt to local conditions. For this reason, cultural knowledge and language ability should be key selection criteria. Yet 80% of companies do not assess the adaptability of international assignment candidates. Worrisome still is that less than one-third of firms use any type of self-assessment tool, or tools that can equip potential international assignees (BGRS, 2016). Corporations may prefer to hire managers with area expertise, which may include the knowledge of the way of "doing business" in that region or area of the world, such as how holidays are observed or which ministers to contact to do business.

The manager's own motivation determines the viability of an overseas assignment and consequently its success. Adaptability means a positive and flexible attitude toward change. The manager assigned overseas must progress from factual knowledge of a culture to interpretive cultural knowledge, trying as much as possible to become part of the new scene, which may be quite different from the one at home. Since an assignment often puts a strain on the manager's family, the adaptability criterion extends to the family, too. Historically, family adjustment, children's education, partner resistance, difficult location, and partner's career have been the top five choices (Brookfield Global Relocation Services, 2012a; Fryer, 2009).

Despite all of the efforts made by global companies to recruit the best people available, demographics still play a role in the selection process. Because of the level of experience typically needed, many foreign assignments go to managers in their mid-30s or older. Normally, companies do not recruit candidates from graduating classes for immediate assignment overseas. They want their international employees to become experienced with the corporate culture mindset, and this can best be done at the headquarters location.

Employees are posted to ever more countries, yet threats like natural disasters, terrorism, and medical endemics loom large. More than half of organizations (50.7%) have experienced an incident at some point where the health and safety of someone on a global assignment, or their accompanying dependents, was affected (Wells, 2016). Firms must analyze candidates' background, religion, race, and sex and how a candidate may be rejected by the host environment. Of the 82 leaders surveyed, 32% said they had turned down an international assignment because they did not want to move their families, and 28% said they had done so to protect their marriages. Virtually none of the men had turned down an international assignment because of cultural concerns, but 13% of the women had (Groysberg & Abrahams, 2014). Exhibit 12.3 looks deeper into gender diversity in the international workplace.

EXHIBIT 12.3 Gender diversity

In 2017, women held 14.5% of the total board seats among companies providing disclosure. For women in the boardroom, it's one step forward, but women have a long way to go when it comes to assuming leadership on boards.

The USA, once the leader in female directors, is lagging Europe where mandates have forced corporations to boost the ratio of women holding board seats. In Italy, Germany, and several other European nations, the number of women on big company boards has tripled and, in some cases, quadrupled in recent years, according to a new report by the Corporate Women Directors International, a research and advocacy group. France passed a law in 2011 requiring that blue-chip firms fill at least 40% of board seats with women and gave them six years to meet the requirement. In that time, the share of directors at the country's biggest companies more than doubled to 43% of board representation. In Norway, the first European country to set a 40% quota for women on corporate boards more than a decade ago, only 15 of the country's 200 biggest companies have a female CEO, according to Norwegian Government data – roughly the same number as in the USA. Other countries have had just a few years' experience with the boardroom quotas. In the UK, a government-backed, business-led commission is urging major British firms to fill at least a third of all board seats with women by 2020. Today women make up 26% of major company board seats there.

Many organizations are working to eliminate any institutional reasons women are denied advancement by using more quantifiable metrics in evaluating performance and leadership potential. According to the survey, 42% of women say that the pay gap is the most important issue. Indeed, there is a significant pay gap between men and women, on average. Getting women into more senior positions should help reduce much of the pay discrepancy, eradicating out-of-date philosophies. The pay gap shrinks considerably when men and women have the same title and the same role at the same company.

Forty percent of women professionals say they have missed a promotion or an opportunity simply because they are female, according to a new Korn Ferry study. Indeed, 44% of the respondents said their most important advice to other women is to develop a strong network, while 32% said it was to have confidence. Experts say the statistic is a reminder that organizations need to develop a strong pipeline of female leaders.

Sources: Globewomen.org., 2020; Korn Ferry, 2020b; MacDougall, A., Valley, J., Bettel, C., Param, A., Schmidt, J., Sigurdson, A., Strachan, T., and Suppa, 2017; Fuhrmans, 2020.

Oracle CEO Safra Catz is one of only 33 women who are CEOs of Fortune 500 companies
Credit: Justin Sullivan/Getty Images.

Because of the cost of transferring a manager overseas, many firms go beyond standard selection procedures and use adaptability screening as an integral part of the process. During the screening phase, the method most often used involves interviewing the candidate and the family. The interviews are conducted by senior executives, human relations specialists within the firm, or outside firms. Interviewers ask the candidate and the family to consider the personal issues involved in the transfer – for example, what each will miss the most. In some cases, candidates themselves will refuse an assignment. In others, the firm will withhold the assignment on the basis of interviews that clearly show a degree of risk. The candidate selected will participate in an orientation program on internal and external aspects of the assignment. Internal aspects include issues such as compensation and reporting. External aspects are concerned with what to expect at the destination in terms of customs and culture. The extent and level of the programs will vary; currently, 56% offer family training for their executives, 32% offer employee and spouse only training, and 5% offer only limited training. Companies that have the lowest failure rates typically employ a four-tiered approach to expatriate use (1) clearly stated criteria, (2) rigorous procedures to determine the suitability of an individual across the criteria, (3) appropriate orientation, and (4) constant evaluation of the effectiveness of the procedures.

Culture Shock

The effectiveness of orientation procedures can be measured only after managers are overseas and exposed to security and socio-political tensions, health, housing, education, social network and leisure activities, language, availability of products and services, and climate. **Culture shock** is the term used for the pronounced reactions to the psychological disorientation that is experienced in varying degrees when spending an extended period of time in a new environment.

One 2018 survey identifies those cities with the highest personal safety ranking based on internal stability, crime, effectiveness of law enforcement, and relationships with other countries. Western European cities continue to enjoy some of the highest quality of living worldwide. Vienna occupies the first place for overall quality of living, followed by Zurich (2), Munich (tied 3), Dusseldorf (6), Frankfurt (7), Geneva (8), Copenhagen (9), and Basel (10). New Zealand and Australia continue to rank highly in quality of living: Auckland (tied 3), Sydney (10), Wellington (15), and Melbourne (16) all remain in the top 20. Singapore (25) remains the highest-ranking city in the Asia-Pacific region. In North America, Canadian cities take the top positions in the ranking. Vancouver (5) is again the region's highest-ranking city, and Toronto and Ottawa follow in 16th and 18th place. San Francisco (30) is the highest-ranking US city, followed by Boston (35) and Honolulu (36). In South America, Montevideo (77) ranks highest for quality of living. Sana'a (229) in Yemen, Bangui (230) in the Central African Republic, and Baghdad (231) in Iraq are the region's three lowest-ranked cities for quality of living (Mercer, 2019).

The culture shock cycle for an overseas assignment may last about 14 months. Often, goals set for a subsidiary or a project may be unrealistic or the means by which they are to be reached may be totally inadequate. All of these lead to external manifestations of culture shock, such as bitterness and even physical illness. In extreme cases, they can lead to hostility toward anything in the host environment (Mitchell & Myles, 2010).

Four distinct stages of adjustment exist during a foreign assignment. The length of the stages is highly individual. The four stages are:

1. Initial euphoria when the expat enjoys the novelty and views the experience as a spectator.
2. Irritation and hostility begins to develop when the expat starts to experience cultural differences, such as the concept of time, weather.
3. The expat has to make adjustments to begin adapting to the situation, which in some cases leads to biculturalism or "going native."
4. The re-entry when an expat returns home to face a possibly changed corporate environment, management, and goals.

The manager may fare better at the second stage than other members of the family, especially if their opportunities for work and other activities are severely restricted. The fourth stage may actually cause a reverse culture shock when the adjustment phase has been highly successful, and the return home is not desired. The home environment that has been idealized during the tour abroad may not be perfect after all, and the loss of status and benefits enjoyed abroad may generate feelings of frustration. Firms themselves must take responsibility for easing one of the causes of culture shock: isolation. By maintaining contact with the manager beyond business-related communication, some of the shock may be alleviated.

Compensating Global Managers

A firm's expatriate compensation program has to be effective in:

1. providing an incentive to leave the home country on a foreign assignment
2. maintaining a given standard of living
3. taking into consideration career and family needs
4. facilitating re-entry into the home country.

To achieve these objectives, firms pay a high premium, beyond base salaries, to induce managers to accept overseas assignments. The costs to the firm are 2 to 2.5 times the cost of maintaining a manager in a comparable position at home. Corporate cost-cutting has been eroding some of the benefits packages of the past years.

Compensation can be divided into two general categories: (1) base salary and salary-related allowances and (2) non-salary-related allowances. Although incentives to leave home are justifiable in both categories, they create administrative complications for the personnel department in tying them to packages at home and elsewhere. As the number of transfers increases, firms develop general policies for compensating the manager rather than negotiate individually on every aspect of the arrangement.

Base salary, as with domestic positions, depends on qualifications and responsibilities. To ensure the manager maintains the same standard of living experienced at home, most compensation packages include cost-of-living allowances (COLA). The costs of living abroad vary and are tracked regularly, as shown in Exhibit 12.4.

Some firms offer a foreign-service premium, which is, in effect, a bribe to encourage a manager to leave familiar conditions and adapt to new surroundings. Usually, it is calculated as a percentage range of 10 to 25 percent of base salary. One variation of the straightforward percentage is a sliding scale by amount – 15 percent of the first $20,000, then 10 percent, and sometimes a ceiling beyond which a premium is not paid. Another variation is by duration, with the

EXHIBIT 12.4 International cost comparisons

The US Department of State publishes quarterly report indexes of living costs abroad, quarters allowances, hardship differentials, and danger pay allowances. For each post, two measures are computed: (1) a government index to establish post allowances for US Government employees and (2) a local index for use by private organizations. The government index takes into consideration prices of goods imported to posts and price advantages available only to US Government employees.

The local index is used by many business firms and private organizations to determine the cost of living allowance for their American employees assigned abroad. Local index measures of 18 key countries around the world are shown here in the table. Maximum housing allowances, calculated separately, are also given. Also included are cost-of-living hardship and a differential rate percentage. (Danger pay can also be found: Kabul, Afghanistan; Algiers; Algeria; and Port-a-Prince, Haiti.)

The reports are issued four times per year under the title US Department of State Indexes of Living Cost, Abroad, Quarters Allowances and Hardship Differentials.

Local cost of living index measures of 18 key countries

Cost of living index (Washington, DC = 100)			Maximum annual housing allowance		
Location	Cost of living survey date	Index	Family of 2	Cost of living hardship	Cost of living allowance % of spendable income
Buenos Aires	Oct. 2017	130	$56,500	10	30
Canberra	Jan. 2017	139	$23,200	0	25
Brussels	Jan. 2017	125	$43,900	0	30
Brasilia	Oct. 2018	147	$29,600	10	10
Shanghai	Jan. 2017	142	$17,900	10	35
Cairo	Jan. 2017	83	$17,900	20	0
Paris	Jan. 2017	150	$75,900	0	50
Frankfurt	Jan. 2017	128	$38,600	0	10
Hong Kong	Jan. 2017	134	$114,300	0	30
New Delhi	Jan. 2017	99	$17,900	25	0
Tokyo	Jan. 2017	148	$89,800	0	42
Mexico City	Apr. 2017	95	$47,900	15	0
The Hague	Jan. 2017	142	$59,900	0	25
Moscow	Jul. 2017	133	$90,900	20	25
Cape Town	Jan. 2017	85	$17,900	10	0
Geneva	Oct. 2017	152	$94,300	0	60
London	Jan. 2017	180	$73,700	0	50
Hanoi	Oct. 2017	91	$46,800	20	0

Sources: US Department of State, 2017b; US Department of State, 2017a.

percentages decreasing with every year the manager spends abroad. Despite the controversial nature of premiums paid at some locations, they are a generally accepted competitive practice.

In addition, hardship allowances compensate managers for relocating to difficult environments, such as countries that are politically or economically unstable or where the living conditions are unhealthy and isolation. For example, hardship premiums vary from 20 percent (Moscow) to 30 percent (Vladivostok).

Since housing costs and related expenses are typically the largest expenditure in the expatriate manager's budget, firms usually provide a housing allowance commensurate with the manager's salary level and position.

One of the major determinants of the manager's lifestyle abroad is taxes. A US manager earning $100,000 in Canada would pay nearly $40,000 in taxes – in excess of $10,000 more than in the USA. For this reason, 90% of US multinational corporations have tax-equalization plans. When a manager's overseas taxes are higher than at home, the firm will make up the difference. However, in countries with a lower rate of taxation, the company simply keeps the difference. The firm's rationalization is that it does not make any sense for the manager in Hong Kong to make more money than the person who happened to land in Singapore. Tax equalization is usually handled by accounting firms that make the needed calculations and prepare the proper forms. Managers can exclude a portion of their expatriate salary from US tax; in 2021, the amount was $108,700 – the annual amount is indexed for inflation (Courtesy of Thomas B. Cooke, Esq.). The amount expatriates can exclude or deduct for housing costs has been limited in the last few years.

Non-Salary-Related Allowances

Other types of allowances are made available to ease the transition into the period of service abroad. Typical allowances during the transition stage include:

1. a relocation allowance to compensate for moving expenses
2. a mobility allowance as an incentive for managers to go overseas, usually paid in a lump sum and as a substitute for the foreign service premium
3. allowances related to housing, such as home sale or rental protection, shipment and storage of household goods, or provision of household furnishings in overseas locations
4. automobile protection that covers possible losses on the sale of a car (or cars) at transfer and having to buy a car overseas, usually at a higher cost
5. travel expenses, using economy class transportation, except for long flights (for example, from Washington to Taipei)
6. temporary living expenses, which may become substantial if housing is not immediately available.

Also, companies are increasingly providing support to make up for income lost by the accompanying spouse.

Education for children is one of the major concerns of expatriate families. In many cases, children may attend private schools, perhaps even in a different country. Firms will typically reimburse for such expenses in the form of an education allowance. In the case of college education, firms reimburse for one round-trip airfare every year, leaving tuition expenses to the family.

Finally, firms provide support for medical expenses, especially for medical services at a level comparable to the expatriate's home country. Other health-related allowances are in place to allow the expatriate to periodically leave the challenging location for rest and relaxation.

Some expatriates in Mexico City get $300 to $500 per family member each month to cover a getaway from the pollution of the city (Wood, 2018).

Exhibit 12.5 provides a visual comparison between practices appropriate to developed (USA, UK, and Singapore) and developing locations. China was cited as the most challenging destination for program managers by 14% of respondents, followed by Brazil (10%), India (9%), and Russia (8%).

The method of payment compensation, especially in terms of currency, is determined by a number of factors. The most common method is to pay part of the salary in the local currency and part in the currency of the manager's home country. Host-country regulations, ranging from taxation to the availability of foreign currency, will influence the decision. Firms themselves look at the situation from the accounting and administrative point of view and, in most cases, prefer to pay in local currencies to avoid burdening the subsidiary. The expatriate naturally will

EXHIBIT 12.5 Compensation comparison between developed and developing locations

Element	Developed location	Developing location
Foreign service premium	Not offered	Required
Hardship premium	May not be included if company does not expect assignments to qualifying locations	Required
Rest & relaxation leave	May not be included even if company includes a hardship allowance in policy	Standard
Goods and services allowance	Cost-of-living allowances (COLA)	May be provided at expatriate level even in locations with a negative index, even if some elements(e.g., meals, "shopping leave") are provided directly
Home leave	Once per year to home location	May be provided more frequently and other destinations may be covered
Host transportation	Allowance may be provided; if car/drive, typically only for employee	Car and driver may be provided for spouse as well

Source: Atlas Van Lines, Inc., 2018; Brookfield Global Relocation Services, 2012b.

want to have some of the compensation in his or her own currency for various reasons; for example, if exchange controls are in effect, getting savings out of the country upon repatriation may be very difficult.

Global Workforce

In 2017 the combined reshoring and related foreign direct investment announcements surged, adding over 171,000 jobs in 2017, with an additional 67,000 in revisions to the years 2010 through 2016. This brings the total number of manufacturing jobs brought to the USA from offshore to over 576,000 since the manufacturing employment low of 2010. The 171,000 reshoring and FDI job announcements equal 90% of the 189,000 total manufacturing jobs added in 2017 (Reshoring Initiative, 2018). The same market forces that have pushed American jobs overseas are now bringing some of those jobs back. Recently, labor costs in places such as China have been rising, and when paired with high international shipping costs, offshore production presents less of a discount than it once did. Recently, General Electric shifted production of a water heater from China to a plant in Louisville, Kentucky. The move brought hundreds of manufacturing and engineering jobs back to the USA (Sauter & Stebbins, 2016).

None of the firm's objectives can be realized without a labor force, which can become one of the firm's major assets or one of its major problems, depending on the relationship that is established. Because of local patterns and legislation, headquarters' role in shaping the relations is mainly advisory, limited to setting the overall tone for the interaction. However, many of the practices adopted in one market or region may easily come under discussion in another, making it necessary for multinational corporations to set general policies concerning labor relations. Often multinational corporations have been instrumental in bringing about changes in the overall work environment in a country.

Labor strategy can be viewed from three perspectives:

1. The participation of labor in the affairs of the firm, especially as it affects performance and well-being.
2. The role and impact of unions in the relationship.
3. Specific human resource policies, in terms of recruitment, training, and compensation.

Labor Participation in Management

Over the past quarter-century, many changes have occurred in the traditional labor management relationship as a result of dramatic changes in the economic environment and the actions of both firms and the labor force. The role of the worker is changing both at the level of the job performed and in terms of participation in the decision-making process. To enhance workers' role in decision-making, various techniques have emerged: self-management, codetermination, minority board membership, and works councils. In striving for improvements in the quality of work life, programs that have been initiated include flextime, quality circles, and work-flow reorganization. Furthermore, employee ownership has moved into the mainstream.

The degree to which workers around the world can participate in corporate decision-making varies considerably. Rights of information, consultation, and co-determination develop on three levels:

1. The shop-floor level, or direct involvement – for example, the right to be consulted in advance concerning transfers.
2. The management level, or through representative bodies – for example, works-council participation in setting new policies or changing existing ones.
3. The board level – for example, labor membership on the board of directors.

In some countries, employees are represented on the supervisory boards to facilitate communication between management and labor, thereby giving labor a clearer picture of the financial limits of management and providing management with a new awareness of labor's point of view. The process is called **codetermination**. In Germany, companies have a two-tiered management system with a supervisory board and the board of managers, which actually runs the firm. The supervisory board is legally responsible for the managing board. In some countries, labor has **minority participation**. In the Netherlands, for example, works councils can nominate (not appoint) board members and can veto the appointment of new members appointed by others. In other countries, such as the USA, codetermination has been opposed by unions as an undesirable means of cooperation, especially when management–labor relations are confrontational.

A tradition in labor relations, especially in Britain, is **works councils**. They provide labor with a voice in corporate decision-making through a representative body, which may consist entirely of workers or of a combination of managers and workers. The councils participate in decisions on overall working conditions, training, transfers, work allocation, and compensation. Around 10 million workers across the EU have the right to information and consultation on company decisions at the European level through their EWCs (European Works Council). The Works Council Directive applies to companies with 1,000 or more employees, including at least 150 in two or more member states (Mueller, 2012).

The countries described are unique in the world. In many countries and regions workers have few, if any, of these rights. The result is long-term potential for labor strife in those countries and possible negative publicity elsewhere. Over a ten-year period Canada (186), Spain (170), Denmark (164), Italy (88), and Finland (75) are the countries that are leading in days lost in all industries and services (Hale, 2008).

In addition to labor groups and the media, investors and shareholders scrutinize multinationals' track records on labor practices. As a result, a company investing in foreign countries should hold to international standards of safety and health, not simply local standards. This can be achieved, for example, through the use of modern equipment and training. Local labor also should be paid adequately. This increases the price of labor, yet ensures the best available talent and helps avoid charges of exploitation.

Companies subcontracting work to local or joint-venture factories need to evaluate industrial relations throughout the system not only to avoid lost production owing to disruptions such as strikes, but to ensure that no exploitation exists at the facilities. Several large firms, such as Adidas and Nike, require subcontractors to sign agreements saying they will abide by minimum wage standards. The area of labor compliance is captured by reference to seven core standards (dealing with forced labor, child labor, discrimination, wages and benefits, working hours, freedom of association, and disciplinary practices). While companies have long been opposed to linking free trade to labor standards, the business community is rethinking its strategy mainly to get trade negotiations moving.

The Role of Labor Unions

The role of labor unions varies from country to country, often because of local traditions in management–labor relations. The variations include the extent of union power in negotiations and the activities of unions in general. In Europe, especially in the northern European countries, collective bargaining takes place between an employer's association and an umbrella organization of unions, on either a national or a regional basis, thereby establishing the conditions for an entire industry. At the other end of the spectrum, negotiations in Japan are on the company level, and the role of larger-scale unions is usually consultative. Another striking difference emerges in terms of the objectives of unions and the means by which they attempt to attain them. In the United Kingdom, for example, union activity tends to be politically motivated and identified with political ideology. In the USA, the emphasis has always been on improving workers' overall quality of life. Ikea's plans for penetrating the all-important retail market of India has hit some serious obstacles. Problems are due to a stipulation by the government that at least 30% of Ikea's inventory must be made in India. This has led the company into a head-on fight with poor manufacturing quality, low local labor standards, and miles of red tape (Chew, 2016).

Investment decisions can also be guided by union considerations. For example, of the more than 30 automobile plants in the USA owned by foreign companies, none has been organized by the United Auto Workers (UAW). Foreign car makers have located plants in southern states where the UAW has little presence and where right-to-work laws prevent unions from forcing employees to join and pay dues. In northern states, they have mostly chosen locations in rural areas away from UAW strongholds. The number of US workers in unions declined sharply in the previous year, the Bureau of Labor Statistics reported in 2018, with the percentage slipping to 10.5 percent, the lowest rate in more than 70 years (US Bureau of Labor Statistics, 2019). Levels of union density vary widely across the EU states, from over 70% in Finland and Sweden to 8% in France.

To maintain participation in corporate decision-making, unions are taking action individually and across national boundaries. Individual unions refer to contracts signed elsewhere when setting the agenda for their own negotiations. Supranational organizations such as the as the AFL–CIO – which is affiliated with the International Trade Union Confederation (ITUC), the worldwide union network (based in Brussels the ITUC represents 175 million workers through its 311 affiliated organizations within 155 countries) – and industry-specific organizations such as the International Metal Workers' Federation exchange information and discuss bargaining tactics. The goal is also to coordinate bargaining with multinational corporations across national boundaries. The International Labour Organization, a specialized agency of the United Nations, has an information bank on multinational corporations' policies concerning wage structures, benefits packages, and overall working conditions (Exhibit 12.6).

Exhibit 12.6 The International Labour Organization was created by the UN in 1919 as part of the Paris Peace Conference. During its centennial, German Federal President Frank-Walter Steinmeier addressed the ILO about taxation of digital corporations.
Credit: picture alliance/Getty Images.

In some cases, globalization can worsen labor standards, and international investment agreements can sometimes shift bargaining power toward multinational firms and away from developing countries' governments. Multinational firms often care not only about costs, but also about the quality of their finished goods and labor force, about reputation and about good governance in host economies (Mosley, 2016).

Human Resource Policies

The term **quality of work** has come to encompass various efforts in the areas of personal and professional development. Its two clear objectives are to increase productivity and to increase the satisfaction of employees. Of course, programs leading to increased participation in corporate decision-making are part of the programs; however, this section concentrates on individual job-related programs – work redesign, team building, and work scheduling (Collins, 2017; Shimizu et al., 2014).

By adding both horizontal and vertical dimensions to the work, **work redesign programs** attack undesirable features of jobs. Horizontally, task complexity is added by incorporating work stages normally done before and after the stage being redesigned. Vertically, each employee is given more responsibility for making the decisions that affect how the work is done.

Closely related to work redesign are efforts aimed at **team building**. For example, in car plants, work is organized so that groups are responsible for a particular, identifiable portion of the car, such as interiors. Each group has its own areas in which to pace itself and to organize the work. The group must take responsibility for the work, including inspections, whether it is performed individually or in groups. The group is informed about its performance through a computer system. The team-building effort includes job rotation to enable workers to understand all facets of their jobs. Another approach to team building makes use of **quality circles**, in which groups of workers regularly meet to discuss issues relating to their productivity. Team building efforts have to be adapted to cultural differences, and in cultures that are more individualistic, incentive structures may have to be kept at the individual level and discussions on quality issues should be broad-based rather than precise.

Flexibility in **work scheduling** has led to changes in when and how long workers are at the workplace. Flextime allows workers to determine their starting and ending hours in a given workday – for example, they might arrive between 7:00 and 9:30 a.m. and leave between 3:00 and 5:30 p.m. . The idea spread from Germany to the European Union and to other countries such as Switzerland, Japan, New Zealand, and the USA. Some 40% of the Dutch working population holds flex- or part-time positions. Accounting giant KPMG unveiled its new Flexible Future program. The options include a four-day workweek and a 20% reduction

EXHIBIT 12.7 Powerful profit driver or wasteful indulgence?

Thomson Reuters' ASSET4 database collected and analyzed data from over 3,500 organizations, from 43 countries, on employee relations, work culture, and company performance between 2002 to 2014. Most important aspect was the employment quality, which includes the quality of the firm's benefits package and job conditions. The second aspect gauges the health and safety of the workplace. Training encompasses professional development and educational opportunities for its workers. The final aspect is workplace diversity, which includes equal opportunities for career advancement, human rights, and labor laws.

Overall, the findings are consistent with the concept that treating employees well leads them to work harder and be more efficient. The impact of employee-friendly (EF) culture on a firm's value is stronger in nations with more stringent protection for investors and at companies that have better board governance, more independent directors, and incentive packages for managers that are tied to performance. The results suggest that creating EF culture is worth the value when managers make choices that are in line with the shareholders interest.

Companies in the tech sector such as Google, Yahoo, and Microsoft have historically led the way in showering employees with perks, such as free meals and on-site perks as well as generous benefit packages, but now other companies are following. The Virgin Group implemented a paternity policy that gives fathers up to 12 months paid leave, while other firms have been experimenting with four-day workweeks and **flextime**. The length of time of the study allowed them to analyze the effects after the enactment of laws requiring more lenient parental leave in several European countries, which improved the EF on the workplace. They found that the implementation of more generous leave guidelines had a positive effect on the value of firm with its employees.

Source: Fauver, McDonald, and Taboada, 2018; Great Place to Work® Institute, 2018; Palmquist, 2018.

in base pay, a 4- to 12-week sabbatical at 30% base pay, a combination of the two options, or sticking with the status quo (KPMG, 2019; Hewlett, 2009). Exhibit 12.7 considers whether these types of quality of work benefits drive profit or are wasteful indulgences.

Firms around the world also have other programs for personal and professional development, such as career counseling and health counseling. All of these are dependent on various factors external and internal to the firm. Of the external factors, the most important are the overall characteristics of the economy and the labor force. Internally, either the programs must fit into existing organizational structures or management must be inclined toward change. In many cases, labor unions have been one of the major resisting forces. Their view is that firms are trying to prevent workers from organizing by allowing them to participate in decision-making and management.

Global Networks

Headquarters considers each unit as a source of ideas, skills, capabilities, and knowledge that can be utilized for the benefit of the entire organization. The network avoids the problems of duplication of effort, inefficiency, and resistance to ideas developed elsewhere by giving subsidiaries the latitude, encouragement, and tools to pursue local business development within the framework of the global strategy.

Managers at both headquarters and the country organizations must bridge the physical and cultural distances separating them. If country organizations have competent managers who rarely need to consult headquarters about their challenges, they may be granted high degrees of autonomy. In the case of global organizations, local management must understand overall corporate goals, in that decisions that meet the long-term objectives may not be optimal for the individual local market.

Many of the most successful global companies have adopted approach that provides clear global strategic direction along with the flexibility to adapt to local opportunities and requirements. The term glocal has been coined to describe this approach. Mondelēz International describes the company's strategy as "A world full of differences. Different lives. Different views. Different tastes. But really, we're all the same." Being big *and* small benefits the company by having the scale and resources of a global powerhouse, but also the speed, creativity, and agility of a fresh new start-up.

Companies that have adopted this approach have incorporated the following four dimensions into their organizations (Czinkota & Ronkainen, 2014):

1. the development and communication of a clear corporate vision
2. the effective management of human resource tools to broaden individual perspectives and develop identification with corporate goals
3. to work effectively across boundaries, management need to have representatives from different countries, regions, and cultures
4 the internal cooperation.

The first dimension relates to a clear and consistent long-term corporate mission that guides individuals wherever they work in the organization. Examples of this are Johnson & Johnson's corporate credo of customer focus, Coca Cola's mission of leveraging global beverage brand leadership "to refresh the world, inspire moments of optimism and happiness, and create value and make a difference," Nestlé's vision to make the company the "reference for nutrition, health, and wellness," and Samsung's "create superior products and services, thereby contributing to a better global society." IBM has established three values for the 21st century: dedication to every client's success, innovation that matters (for the company and the world), and trust and personal responsibility in all relationships. But formulating and communicating a vision cannot succeed unless individual employees understand and accept the company's stated goals and objective.

The second dimension relates to the development of a cooperative mind-set among region/country organizations to ensure effective implementation of global strategies. Managers may believe that global strategies are intrusions on their operations if they do not have an understanding of the corporate vision, if they have not contributed to the global corporate agenda, or if they are not given direct responsibility for its implementation. Defensive, territorial attitudes, can lead to the emergence of the "not-invented-here" syndrome, that is, country organizations objecting to or rejecting an otherwise sound strategy.

For example, in an area structure, units (such a China) may operate quite independently. To tackle this problem, monthly management meeting can be set up to supervise regional operations, with each committee including representatives of the major functions (e.g., manufacturing, marketing, and finance). For example, Yum! Brands has a structure that emphasizes its individual brands, including KFC, Pizza Hut, Taco Bell, and Long John Silver's, but also has three operational units: one for the US market, an international division, and a separate China Division (covering mainland China, Thailand, and KFC Taiwan) because of the size and strategic importance of China (Exhibit 12.8).

The network avoids the problems of duplication of effort, inefficiency, and resistance to ideas developed elsewhere by giving subsidiaries the latitude, encouragement, and tools to pursue local business development within the framework of the global strategy. Headquarters considers each unit as a source of ideas, skills, capabilities, and knowledge that can be utilized for the benefit of the entire organization. This means that the subsidiaries must be upgraded from the role of implementation and adaptation to that of contribution and partnership in the development and execution of worldwide strategies. Efficient plants may be converted into international production centers, innovative R&D units may become centers of excellence (and thus role models), and leading subsidiary groups may be given a leadership role in developing new strategy for the entire corporation.

Allowing maximum flexibility at the country-market level takes advantage of the fact that subsidiary management knows its market and can react to changes quickly. Problems of motivation and acceptance are avoided when decision-makers are also the implementors of the strategy. On the other hand, many marketers

Exhibit 12.8 Yum! Brands has a separate division for China, which avoids redundancies and provides a local focus to the business
Credit: Zhang Peng/LightRocket via Getty Images.

faced with global competitive threats and opportunities have adopted global strategy formulation, which by definition requires some degree of centralization. What has emerged as a result can be called coordinated decentralization. This means that overall corporate strategy is provided from global or regional headquarters, but subsidiaries are free to implement it within a range of options established in consultation between headquarters and the subsidiaries.

However, moving into this new mode may raise significant challenges. Among these systemic difficulties are a lack of widespread commitment to dismantling traditional national structures, driven by an inadequate understanding of the larger, global forces at work. Power barriers – especially if the personal roles of national managers are under threat of being consolidated into regional organizations – can lead to proposals being challenged without valid reason. Finally, some organizational initiatives (such as multicultural teams or corporate chat rooms) may be jeopardized by the fact that people do not have the necessary skills (e.g., language ability, knowledge of Six Sigma) or that an infrastructure (e.g., intranet) may not exist in an appropriate format.

One particular case is of special interest. Organizationally, the forces of globalization are changing the country manager's role significantly. With profit-and-loss responsibility, oversight of multiple functions, and the benefit of distance from headquarters, country managers have enjoyed considerable decision-making autonomy as well as entrepreneurial initiative. Today, however, many companies have to emphasize the product dimension of the product–geography matrix, which means that the power has to shift, at least to some extent, from country managers to worldwide strategic business unit and product line managers. Many of the previously local decisions are now subordinated to global strategic moves. However, regional and local brands still require an effective local management component. Therefore, the future country manager will have to have diverse skills (such as government relations and managing entrepreneurial teamwork) and wear many hats in balancing the needs of the operation for which the manager is directly responsible with those of the entire region or strategic business unit. To emphasize the importance of the global/regional dimension in the country manager's portfolio, many companies have tied the country manager's compensation to the way the company performs globally or regionally, not just in the market for which the manager is responsible.

The human factor in any organization is critical. Managers both at headquarters and in the subsidiaries must bridge the physical and mental distances separating them. If subsidiaries have competent managers who rarely need to consult headquarters about their problems, they may be granted high degrees of autonomy. In the case of global organizations, subsidiary management must understand the corporate culture because subsidiaries must sometimes make decisions that meet the long-term objectives of the firm as a whole but that are not optimal for the local market.

In today's environment, the global business entity can be successful only if it is able to move intellectual capital within the organization – that is, transmit ideas and information in real time. If there are impediments to the free flow of information across organizational boundaries, important updates about changes in the competitive environment might not be communicated in a timely fashion to those tasked with incorporating them into strategy. For example, Procter and Gamble makes recruitment and teaching future leaders a priority for its top executives. All of the top officers at the company teach in the company's executive education programs and act as mentors and coaches for younger managers. P&G takes global executive development seriously and grooms its top management prospects through a series of career building assignments across business units and geographies. Eighty-five percent of the company's top management has had one or more international assignments. WPP, the global marketing services group, has developed a graduate marketing fellowship program, for promising global managers, comprising three one-year rotations with individual companies within the group's global network and requiring an international assignment.

Another method to promote internal cooperation for global strategy implementation is the use of international teams or councils. In the case of a new product or program, an international team of managers may be assembled to develop strategy. While final direction may come from headquarters, it has been informed of local conditions, and implementation of the strategy is enhanced because local-country managers were involved in its development. The approach has worked even in cases involving seemingly impossible market differences. In some cases, it is important to bring in members of other constituencies (e.g., suppliers, intermediaries, service providers) to such meetings to share their views and experiences and make available their own best practice for benchmarking. In some major production undertakings, technology allows ongoing participation by numerous internal and external team members.

SUMMARY

A business organization is the sum of its human resources. Firms attract international managers from a number of sources, both internal and external. In the earlier stages of internationalization, recruitment must be external. Later, an internal pool often provides candidates for transfer. The decision then becomes whether to use home-country, host country, or third-country nationals. If expatriate managers are used, selection policies should focus on competence, adaptability, and personal traits. Policies should also be set for the compensation and career progression of candidates selected for out-of-country assignments. At the same time, the firm must be attentive to the needs of local managers for training and development.

Labor can no longer be considered as simply services to be bought. Increasingly, workers are taking an active role in the decision-making of the firm and in issues related to their own welfare. Various programs are causing dramatic organizational change, not only by enhancing the position of workers but also by increasing the productivity of the work force. Workers employed by the firm are usually local, as are the unions that represent them. Their primary concerns in working for a multinational firm are job security and benefits. Unions therefore are cooperating across national boundaries to equalize benefits for workers employed by the same firm in different countries.

In today's environment, the global business entity can be successful only if it is able to move intellectual capital within the organization – that is, transmit ideas and information in real time. If there are impediments to the free flow of information across organizational boundaries, important updates about changes in the competitive environment might not be communicated in a timely fashion to those tasked with incorporating them into strategy.

DISCUSSION QUESTIONS

1. Industry analysts have determined that the company has institutionalized a "process that encourages, rewards, moves around, provides incentives, and closely manages the careers of the best performers worldwide, no matter their national origin." Colgate is a good example of how to implement a successful human global teamwork strategy. www.colgatepalmolive.com/en-us/core-values. Is this the best way to promote and why?
2. What are the most important criteria for selecting an expatriate manager during the selection process? How do you weight them on importance?
3. Your new manager moves from Houston, Texas, to Mumbai, India. What compensation package (salary and non-salary) would keep the manager happy and production high?
4. How transferable are quality-of-work programs from one market to another?
5. What are the general policies that the multinational corporation should follow in dealing (or choosing not to deal) with a local labor union?
6. Is there more to the "not-invented-here" syndrome than simply hurt feelings on the part of those who believe they are being dictated to by headquarters?

KEY TERMS

area expertise	336	housing allowance	343
base salary	341	interpretive cultural knowledge	336
codetermination	346	minority participation	346
coordinated decentralization	353	not-invented-here syndrome	352
cost-of-living allowance	341	quality circles	349
culture shock	339	quality of work	349
education allowance	343	tax-equalization plans	343
expatriates	335	team building	349
flextime	350	work redesign programs	349
foreign-service premium	341	work scheduling	349
glocal	351	works councils	346
hardship allowances	342		

TAKE A STAND

Spurred by competitive pressures, global knowledge networks enable multinationals to share information and best practices across geographically dispersed units and time zones. Corporations save millions of dollars and achieve global objectives each year through knowledge transfer and feedback. Whether the goal is customer loyalty, increased production efficiency, or retention of skilled employees, a knowledge-sharing network focused on improvement of operational practices worldwide, helps multinationals meet the challenge of building a cohesive global corporate culture.

Questions for Debate

Should there be a worldwide knowledge-sharing network for multinationals even when their goals and missions are significantly different?

INTERNET EXERCISES

A survey of 19 countries reveals the top challenges for women across the globe. What are the cultural reasons that challenges may be very different?
   www.womenatworkpoll.com/ and www.theatlantic.com/sponsored/thomson-reuters-davos/the-top-five-issues-for-working-women-around-the-world/762/

FURTHER RESOURCES

Brewster, C., Smale, A., and Mayrhofer, W. (2017). Globalisation and human resource management. *A Research Agenda for Human Resource Management*, 201.

Crovini, C., Ossola, G., and Marchini, P. L. (2018). Cyber Risk. The New Enemy for Risk Management in the Age of Globalisation. *Management Control*.

Echevarría, S. G., and Núñez, T. V. (2016). Economic-Social Order in Globalisation: The Orientation of International Management. In *Internationales Management und die Grundlagen des globalisierten Kapitalismus* (pp. 501–522). Springer Gabler, Wiesbaden.

Hanson, D., Hitt, M. A., Ireland, R. D., and Hoskisson, R. E. (2016). *Strategic management: Competitiveness and globalisation*. Cengage AU.

Krugman, P. (2017). Crises: The price of globalisation? In *Economics of Globalisation* (pp. 31–50). Routledge.

Potrafke, N. (2015). The evidence on globalisation. *The World Economy*, *38*(3), 509–552.

Velis, C. and International Solid Waste Association. (2017). Global recycling markets: plastic waste: A story for one player–China. A report from the ISWA Task Force on Globalisation and Waste Management.

PART IV

13 Ownership, Governance, and Sustainability

LEARNING OBJECTIVES

- Explore how differing ownership structures affect how organizations respond to stakeholder interests
- Explain how stakeholders' preferences may vary across borders
- Examine how companies conduct their activities to pursue both operational and financial goals and objectives
- Review goals, structures, and participants in corporate governance
- Discuss how the quality of corporate governance affects an organization's reputation
- Differentiate between governance, responsibility, and sustainability
- Identify the attributes that society increasingly expects from responsible organizations

CONTENTS

VIGNETTE 13 Unilever's governance and sustainable operations

Unilever is a British–Dutch consumer goods company joint-headquartered in Rotterdam, Netherlands, and London, United Kingdom. The firm's products, offered in 190 countries, comprise four main categories: personal care (36% of sales), food (25%), beverages (19%), and cleaning agents (18%). Unilever's 400 brands include Ben & Jerry's, Best Foods, Dove, Flora, Knorr, Lipton, Lux, Magnum, Noxzema, Pepsodent, Vaseline, and many others. Unilever has 170,000 employees worldwide and revenue of more than 50 billion euros (about $60 billion in April 2020). The largest proportion of Unilever's sourcing and marketing activities are concentrated in emerging markets – especially Brazil, China, India, Mexico, and Russia. Such markets are promising because of their large populations and rapid expansion of the middle class.

Unilever is dual listed – it is a registered corporation in both the Netherlands and the UK, but the two companies operate as a single business, with a common board of directors. Its governance is based on the public limited company (PLC) model in the UK and the *naamloze vennootschap* (NV) model in the Netherlands. Accordingly, Unilever is owned by shareholders, and its shares are traded on public stock markets around the world. The firm is responsible to shareholders to maximize profits, to consumers to maximize value, and to society to ensure sustainable operations.

But such goals often conflict with each other. Just as many Unilever customers are "going green," many also increasingly shop online. Competition is rising from Amazon, Alibaba, and other online providers. Other top competitors include Nestlé and Procter & Gamble. Natural resource shortages are affecting the costs of chemicals, food ingredients, and other key inputs. Unilever's value chain activities are closely tied to environments characterized by rapid economic and social development, as well as under-protected natural environments. For example, Unilever's palm oil plantations have contributed to deforestation in Indonesia. The firm's product packaging activities were once a significant environmental threat, affecting natural habitats in various countries.

Management is committed to addressing big social and environmental problems such as poverty, pollution, and healthcare. Specifically, in recent years, Unilever has undertaken the following initiatives:

- Improve health and well-being for people worldwide by addressing global hunger, improving nutritional standards, and increasing access to health and hygiene. For example, Unilever's global hand-washing campaign aims to reduce contagious disease in Africa and Asia.

- Reduce environmental impact by decreasing greenhouse gas emissions, factory waste, and water usage, and by increasing sustainable sourcing. For instance, the firm is developing laundry detergents that clean clothes in a few minutes with minimal energy and water usage.
- Enhancing the livelihoods of millions of workers by improving opportunities for women, ensuring fairness in the workplace, and emphasizing sourcing from small-scale farmers. For example, the firm sources cashews from small farmers in Ghana.

By 2030, Unilever aims to halve its environmental footprint in the production and use of its products, while simultaneously growing the firm's businesses. These are challenging goals that will necessitate skillful governance of the firm's operations worldwide.

Sources: Gunther, 2013; Walt, 2017; Unilever, 2019.

Introduction

A Corporation, then, or a body politic, or body incorporate, is a collection of many individuals united into one body, under a special denomination, having perpetual succession under an artificial form, and vested, by policy of the law, with the capacity of acting, in several respects, as an individual, particularly of taking and granting property, of contracting obligations, and of suing and being sued, of enjoying privileges and immunities in common, and of exercising a variety of political rights, more or less extensive, according to the design of its institution, or the powers conferred upon it, either at the time of its creation, or at any subsequent period of its existence.

– Stewart Kyd, *A Treatise on the Law of Corporations*, 1793, p. 13

Global business is conducted by many different types of organizations for many different purposes. Although it may appear at times that global business is dominated by the publicly traded corporation, and for the sole purpose of profit, these are only large parts of a much more complex global business environment. Fundamentally a corporation is a company that conducts business as a legal entity separate and distinct from its owners, but still enjoying the same rights and responsibilities as individual people. Alongside corporations, this chapter will explore the different forms of business organizations used today around the world, their governance and goals, and, ultimately, their ability to pursue sustainability. We begin our discussion by deepening our understanding of ownership, the legal construct so often associated with global business – the corporation, and then ultimately the roles and responsibilities of corporations by and for their major stakeholders (Kyd, 1793; Wright et al., 2013).

Ownership

A business may be owned by a single individual (sole proprietorship, corporation sole), a few private individuals (partnership), a multitude of private owners who may exchange their ownership portions (publicly traded company or corporation), or even partially or wholly by government. A quick survey of the businesses operating up and down the street of any major city in most countries will likely yield a mixture of these ownership forms. Businesses in all parts of the globe cover the extremes of the ownership spectrum, from the owner-operator of a fruit cart on the corner, to a publicly traded Anglo-Dutch mining concern, to a publicly traded Russian oil company largely controlled by the Russian Government.

Most companies begin as the creations of entrepreneurs, individuals or a small number of individual partners, with an idea. Whether those individuals or their families can retain control over time is a different story for every company. Just consider the following businesses configurations found around the globe:

- Porsche (Germany). Founded in the 1930s, the company in recent years has been both publicly traded and yet controlled by only two families, the Porsche and Piëch families. The inter-related and often feuding families maintained their control by holding all of the voting shares in the company, while the publicly traded shares carried no voting power and therefore little influence on the company. In 2008, Porsche attempted to take control of Volkswagen (VW), another European automaker controlled by Ferdinand Piëch of the same Piëch family; then VW attempted to take control of Porsche! After two years of inter-family feuding, the two companies merged.
- Rosneft (Russia). Rosneft is part-owned by the Russian Government and large oil companies from China and the United Kingdom. Created from a number of different government-controlled businesses, Rosneft sold a portion of its ownership to the public market to raise capital to repay debt obligations. After acquiring another oil company in 2013, Rosneft became the world's largest publicly traded petroleum company, but is still operated and controlled by the Russian Government.
- Microsoft (USA). One of the largest and sometimes most profitable companies in the world in recent years, Microsoft began as a partnership of two private individuals, Bill Gates and Paul Allen. The partners eventually sold the majority of the company's ownership to the public marketplace, although

both retained small shares. The company today is led by professional management, which holds a relatively small stake in the company.

- Cargill, Incorporated (USA). Thought by many to be the largest privately held company in the world, Cargill is a diversified multinational company with more than $120 billion in sales. Although operating in nearly 70 countries and employing more than 150,000 people worldwide, the company is still owned by descendants of the founders (90 percent), with the remaining shares (10 percent) held by employees. Like Microsoft, Cargill is led by non-family management.

These four companies show how ownership and control can diverge. Do the owners of the company run the company? Can a government-owned and -controlled company gain access to capital in the public marketplace? Can a family-owned and -run company be globally competitive? Can professional management successfully create value for a privately held business? These are just a few of the questions that a deep understanding of the modern corporation can address (Wright et al., 2013; Pinto & Branson, 2018).

The Corporation

The people who own a business and the people who operate a business may, however, be very different groups. The creation of the corporation, as described by Stewart Kyd in 1793 in the opening quote, solved a number of fundamental dilemmas faced by small businesses created by individuals.

- A corporation is legally separated from its owner(s). If it loses money, acquires debts, or incurs legal liabilities, the individual owners can lose no more than what they have invested in the company. The owners are not legally liable for debts or obligations to creditors beyond their ownership investment. This is what is meant by the oft-used phrase "limited liability."
- A corporation can be perpetual. As opposed to individuals or families, who may die, a corporation cannot die in the normal human sense of the word. A corporation may go bankrupt, it may be acquired, or it may be intentionally closed. But in terms of potential, it can continue to operate in perpetuity, beyond the lives of its creators, owners, friends, and adversaries.
- A corporation is a legal creation but is deemed to have rights and responsibilities like a person. As such, a corporation can buy or sell, sue or be sued, borrow and lend, conduct business – all as a member of society. With these legal rights, it has the responsibility to follow all laws of the state and can be held accountable for failing to act in a legal manner. Unlike human beings, however, it may have no moral conscience (Czinkota, 2019).

The creation of corporations had an enormously powerful influence on the growth of global commerce (Czinkota, 2019). The creation of a legally separate but legally responsible entity allowed the organization to raise capital independent of the financial health of any of the individual owners, to contract for purchasing and sale, and to survive the working life spans of its human creators. It may also have freed the business entity to act as if a machine, allowing it to develop a multitude of social, cultural, and moral concerns just like the human individual (Kyd, 1793; Gordon & Ringe, 2018).

Stakeholders

A **stakeholder** is an individual with some type of interest in a business. In theory, a stake is an interest or a share in some organization or undertaking. Stakes themselves may be differentiated as to whether they are interests, rights, or ownership stakes. Exhibit 13.1 summarizes the major, potential **stakeholders** in the firm. An *interest* is when a person or group is potentially affected by the actions of an organization or firm. The community in which a company operates, employing many of the people in the community, frequently opposes the closing of the firm citing its interest. A *right* is when a person or group has a legal claim, a contract, or some other existing arrangement to be treated in a certain way or have a particular right protected. This may be expressed in a variety of ways, including a right to be treated fairly, or an expectation that a firm will stand behind the quality of a product purchased from it. Ownership, the strongest form of stake, is when a person or group holds legal title to an asset such as a firm. Of course, this then raises the question of whether the owner of a firm has dictatorial power or must also consider the interests of nonowners.

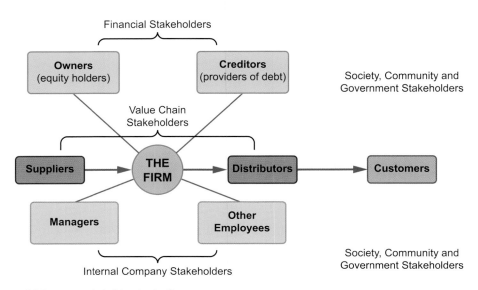

Exhibit 13.1 Stakeholders in the firm

Any analysis of corporate stakeholders must include all three levels of stakeholder interest. Depending on the country and culture of the firm itself, however, they may have very different voices in the vision, strategy, and operation of the firm. As described in the following sections, the power and influence of those having an interest versus a right versus legal title (ownership) often serves to differentiate the business environments of countries.

Financial Stakeholders

The two primary financial stakeholders of the firm, namely the providers of capital for both investment and operation, are shareholders and creditors. Shareholders are the actual owners of the firm, holding title to the firm's assets and operations as a result of their capital investment. Creditors, typically bank loans (Europe and Asia) or debt markets (Anglo-American markets), lend capital to the firm in exchange for promised repayment of both the principal amount and a return (interest). In the event that the firm cannot repay its debt obligations in a timely manner, the creditors hold a legal right over specific assets of the firm.

Business Stakeholders

The business stakeholders in the firm, its suppliers and customers, are the core of what business strategists term the value chain. The company purchases products and services from its suppliers, then combines, alters, and creates its own products and services from those and, in turn, sells its finished products and services to its customers. Most of these transactions are conducted under contract. How the company conducts its business affects the operations and livelihood of its business stakeholders. Many scholars and experts tend to believe that customers should be the focus of management action, in order to optimize the performance of the firm. Many also believe that society in general is a key stakeholder of the firm. Accordingly, businesses should operate in a manner that is socially responsible and ensures ongoing sustainability to appreciate and protect the environment external to the firm.

Internal Stakeholders

The internal stakeholders of the firm are all those employed by the firm, including management, leadership, and all the international internal locations of company operations. Workers and managers are hired to conduct the product and service procurement, purchasing, processing, production, and distribution of the company's products and services. Leadership and management may also provide most of the strategic vision and direction of the operations of the firm. Leadership may hold no ownership, partial ownership, or even complete ownership in the firm. Internal stakeholders hold both rights and interest stakes.

Community and Society Stakeholders

The corporation may be a legal construct, but it also has a great influence and impact on the local community and society as a whole. Community and society are the social stakeholders. Although more distant from the actual operations and transactions of the firm and its business, social stakeholders may be severely affected by the success or failure of the corporation both locally and globally, its investments and divestments, its employment and involvement, and its longevity and environmental stewardship. Social stakeholders hold interest stakes. As discussed in the following section, depending on the cultural and business culture in which the corporation operates, the voices of different stakeholder groups are more and less pronounced.

Government Stakeholders

Governments typically benefit enormously from the economic activity of firms and the private sector generally. Governments have an interest in economic development and the creation of jobs, which corporations provide. Governments rely on the revenues provided by taxes, which arise directly and indirectly from the private sector. Corporations also provide various goods and services that governments need in order to achieve their goals. In some countries, the government may own individual firms, termed *state-owned enterprises (SOEs)*, that provide huge revenues and value to the government and to society generally (Pinto & Branson, 2018; Gordon & Ringe, 2018; Henisz, 2017).

The Corporate Objective

So what is the goal – the objective – of the corporation? If the answer is "to earn a profit," then it has to be made very clear: For whom? In Europe and North America, the traditional view held that the objective of the corporation, and therefore the goal of management, is to maximize the value of shareholders. Maximization of shareholder value refers to the pursuit of the interests of corporate shareholders, primarily the profitability of the organization, over and above the interests of other stakeholders. This would then imply that the stockholder is the primary stakeholder and all other stakeholders are of lesser priority. This is not, however, the universally accepted view. In many cultures, the objective of the corporation is seen as including the interests of various stakeholders, simultaneously. Before moving on to discuss the different possible objectives of the corporation, we first need to explore how profit may be derived from the corporation – the operational goals of the corporation (Gordon & Ringe, 2018; Carroll et al., 2018; Henisz, 2017).

Operational Goals

It is one thing to say "maximize value," but it is quite another to do it. The management objective of maximizing profit is not as simple as it sounds, because the measure of profit used by ownership/management differs between the privately held firm and the publicly traded firm. In other words, is management attempting to maximize current income, capital appreciation, market share, or some other variable? In general, management makes strategic and operational decisions that grow sales and generate profits, and then distributes those profits to ownership in the form of dividends. Capital gains refer to the change in the share price as traded in the equity markets. Capital gains may arise from various factors, reflecting forces that are not in the direct control of management. In some countries in Asia, managers tend to focus on maximizing the firm's sales in its key markets, that is, market share.

Publicly Traded or Privately Held

Most of the world's businesses are privately held, either by an individual, a family, or by partnership. While the USA and the UK have a large number of publicly traded companies, the market in most other countries are dominated by private firms, many of which are family owned (World Bank, 2019a). For example, in a study of 5,232 corporations in 13 western European countries, family-controlled firms represented 44 percent of the sample compared to 37 percent that were widely held (Mueller & Philippon, 2011).

A privately held firm has a relatively simple objective: maximize current and sustainable income. The privately held firm does not have a share price (it does have a value, but this is not a publicly visible, market-determined value in the way in which we see share price markets work every day). Therefore, it simply focuses on generating current income, primarily dividend income, to generate the returns to its ownership. If ownership is a family, the family may also place great emphasis on the ability to sustain those earnings over time while maintaining a slower rate of growth that can be managed by the family and for the family. It is, therefore, critical that we understand the nature of ownership's financial interests from the start if we are to understand the strategic and financial goals of management.

Over time, however, some firms may choose to go public via an initial public offering (IPO) – the first sale or issuance of shares of ownership (stock) in a company to the market. A private firm that issues its shares to the public market would henceforth be classified as publicly traded. Following an IPO, the firm becomes subject to many of the increased legal, regulatory, and reporting requirements in most countries surrounding the sale and trading of securities. In many countries, going public means that the firm will now have to disclose a sizable degree of financial and operational detail, publish this information regularly, comply with sophisticated government rules and regulations, and comply with all the specific operating and reporting requirements of the specific exchange on which it is

> ## EXHIBIT 13.2 The benefits of family
>
> Research indicates that, as opposed to popular belief, family-owned firms in some highly developed economies typically outperform publicly owned firms. This is true not only in western Europe, but also in the USA. A recent study of firms included in the S&P500 found that families are present in fully one-third of the S&P500 and account for 18 percent of its outstanding equity. An added insight is that firms possessing a CEO from the family also perform better than those with outside CEOs. Interestingly, it seems that minority shareholders are actually better off, according to this study, when part of a family-influenced firm. In such firms, internationalization and innovation are associated with superior organizational performance.
>
> **Source:** Anderson and Reeb, 2003; Braga, Correia, Braga, and Lemos, 2017.

traded. As discussed in Exhibit 13.2, family-controlled firms all over the world may outperform publicly traded firms in terms of financial performance.

Shareholder Wealth Maximization

The Anglo-American markets (primarily the United Kingdom and the USA) long held the philosophy that a firm's objective should follow the shareholder wealth maximization model. More specifically, the management of the firm should strive to maximize the return to shareholders while enduring acceptable levels of risk. According to this model, the firm exists for the benefit of its stockholders (owners of equity), and the pursuit of profit on their part is the primary motivation for all of management's activities. The interests of all other stakeholders are secondary to the primary purpose of creating shareholder value. In fact, in numerous countries, by law, the company's managers must fulfill their fiduciary responsibility, which refers to a relationship between two parties whereby one party has the trust and legal and ethical duty to act in the best interests of the other. Managers obligated to exercise fiduciary responsibility must be concerned with the interests of stockholders over and above all other interests in the conduct of the business (Pinto & Branson, 2018; Gordon & Ringe, 2018; Kershaw, 2018)

The strength of the shareholder wealth maximization model is its clear focus on the returns to a specific stakeholder, the stockholder. The stockholder is the provider of the equity capital for the creation and sustenance of the corporation, and the "returns" to the stockholder are traditionally refined even further to focus on the financial returns to shareholders, as measured by the sum of capital gains (the change in share price) and dividends (distributions of income to shareholders) (Binder, 2019; Bosse & Phillips, 2016).

Ownership versus Management

One of the biggest weaknesses of the shareholder wealth maximization model has long been considered the failure of management to always act in the best interest of shareholders. More recently, attention has focused on whether firms behave in the interests of society in general. **Agency theory** is the study of how shareholder and management's interests may diverge (the agency problem) and how a firm can motivate management to act like owners when managing the corporation (agency interests). Because management's total income arises from the company's operations, it may be reluctant to undertake any risky activity that may endanger its own income.

A second issue arising from the separation of ownership and management is share concentration. The USA and UK stock markets have been characterized by widespread ownership of shares, many investors holding shares, but no real strength of concentrated ownership. Management owns only a small proportion of stock in its own firms. In contrast, in the rest of the world, ownership is usually characterized by controlling shareholders. Typical controlling shareholders are:

1. Government (e.g., privatized utilities)
2. Institutions (such as banks in Germany)
3. Family (such as in France and Italy in Europe and increasingly in Asia)
4. Consortia (such as *keiretsus* in Japan and *chaebols* in South Korea)

Control is enhanced by ownership of shares with dual voting rights, interlocking directorates, staggered election of the board of directors, takeover safeguards, and other techniques not used in the Anglo-American markets (Clarke, 2017; Kershaw, 2018; Wright et al., 2013).

Stakeholders and Capitalism

> Corporations have neither bodies to be punished, nor souls to be condemned; they therefore do as they like.
> – Edward Thurlow (1st Baron Thurlow), 1731–1806,
> as quoted by John Poynder in Literary Extracts, 1844, vol. 1, p. 2.

In countries like Germany and Japan, the management of the corporation strives to operate the firm in the interest of multiple stakeholders, not just the shareholders. Thus, **stakeholder capitalism** refers to operating a firm or organization in a manner that attempts to balance the interests of all stakeholders of the organization (stockholders, employees, creditors, suppliers, customers, and community). It does indeed try to earn returns for its stockholders – so it is a capitalist structure, but it also

EXHIBIT 13.3 German stakeholder practices

German companies frequently are used to exemplify stakeholder capitalism whereby workers and the community exert influence nearly equal to those of owners. Thus, German stakeholder practices are thought to strengthen the German business sector, taking a longer-term focus on competitiveness and employment consistent with the interests of the multitude of stakeholders.

First and foremost, German companies are required by law to consider and act in the interest of all stakeholders. Second, German companies structurally have two boards: (1) a supervisory board, in which worker representatives hold half the seats and the board itself monitors all general interest issues and activities, and (2) a managerial board, which is charged with the oversight of the ongoing operations of the company, in which the voting equity ownership holds power. As with all systems of corporate governance, there will be occasions where the interests of different stakeholder groups diverge – traditionally characterized as profits versus jobs.

Many of the inherent behaviors of the German corporate governance system were evident during the 2008–2009 recession. As corporate sales and profitability fell, management was under increasing pressure to cut costs and employment to protect shareholder interests. As opposed to the shareholder wealth-maximizing firms of the Anglo-American markets, many German firms cut their dividends, not their employment.

Source: Bobillo, Rodríguez-Sanz, and Tejerina-Gaite, 2017; Corning, 2018.

takes into consideration the interests of many of the other stakeholders when making strategic and operating decisions about the company. Depending on the country, the two stakeholder groups that generally gain a larger voice are employees and creditors, while government is seen to intervene more often in the workings of the firm. Many have argued that by pursuing the interests of multiple stakeholders, the corporation is exhibiting a type of moral character not found in purely shareholder wealth–focused enterprises. Exhibit 13.3, German Stakeholder Practices, illustrates how that system reacted differently to the recent global recession.

Although stakeholder capitalism may avoid the flaw of shareholder wealth maximization's singular focus on short-term profitability, it has its own set of challenges. First and foremost, finding common ground between multiple stakeholder interests often proves daunting, slowing decision making and often the ability to move quickly enough to remain competitive.

Both models have their strengths and weaknesses, and two trends in recent years have led to a growing focus on the shareholder wealth form. First, as more of the non–Anglo-American markets privatized industry, a shareholder wealth focus was believed to attract capital from outside investors, many of whom are in other countries. Second, and still quite controversial, many analysts believe that shareholder-based multinationals are increasingly dominating their global industry segments. Success wins followers (Kluyver, 2013; Gordon & Ringe, 2018; Carroll et al., 2018).

Corporate Governance

Corporate governance is the relationship among stakeholders that is used to determine and control the strategic direction and performance of the corporation. Although the governance structure of any company – domestic, international, or multinational – is fundamental to its very existence, this very subject has become the lightning rod of political and business debate in the past few years as failures in governance in a variety of forms have led to corporate fraud and failure. Abuses and failures in corporate governance have dominated global business news in recent years. Beginning with the accounting fraud and questionable ethics of business conduct at Enron (culminating in its bankruptcy), failures in corporate governance have raised issues about the very ethics and culture of the conduct of business (Gordon & Ringe, 2018; Carroll et al., 2018; Clarke, 2017). Exhibit 13.4 provides a framework on the structure of corporate governance.

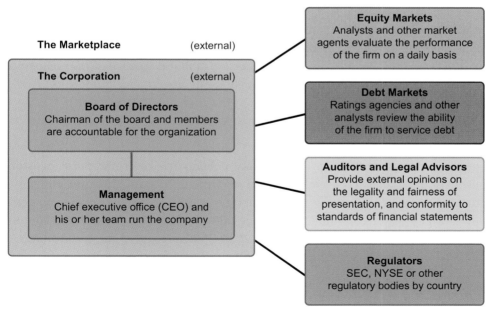

Exhibit 13.4 The structure of corporate governance

The Goal of Corporate Governance

The single overriding objective of corporate governance in the Anglo-American markets is the optimization over time of the returns to shareholders (Borlea & Monica Violeta, 2013). To achieve this, good governance practices should focus the attention of the board of directors of the corporation on this objective by developing and implementing a strategy for the corporation that ensures corporate growth and improvement in the value of the corporation's equity. At the same time, it should ensure an effective relationship with stakeholders.

One of the most widely accepted statements of good corporate governance practices is that established by the Organization for Economic Cooperation and Development (OECD) (OECD, 2015):

- The rights of shareholders. The corporate governance framework should protect shareholders' rights.
- The equitable treatment of shareholders. The corporate governance framework should ensure the equitable treatment of all shareholders, including minority and foreign shareholders. All shareholders should have the opportunity to obtain effective redress for violation of their rights.
- The role of stakeholders in corporate governance. The corporate governance framework should recognize the rights of stakeholders as established by law and encourage active cooperation between corporations and stakeholders in creating wealth, jobs, and the sustainability of financially sound enterprises.
- Disclosure and transparency. Business dealings succeed best when full information is available to facilitate collaboration, cooperation, and collective decision-making. Transparency implies that timely and accurate disclosure is made on all material matters regarding the corporation, including the financial situation, performance, ownership, and governance of the company.
- The responsibilities of the board. The corporate governance framework should ensure the strategic guidance of the company, the effective monitoring of management by the board, and the board's accountability to the company and the shareholders.

Corporate governance of any organization, publicly traded or not, must focus on four basic principles: (1) accounting and reporting, (2) board structure, composition, and reward, (3) executive ethics, and (4) executive and management compensation. Many major corporate governance failures, including those at the core of the global financial crisis that began in 2007–2008 at some of the world's largest financial institutions, involved failures in one or more of these elements.

The Structure of Corporate Governance

Our first challenge is to capture the meaning of "corporate governance." A modern corporation's actions and behaviors are directed and controlled by both internal and external forces.

The internal forces, the officers of the corporation (such as the chief executive officer) and the board of directors of the corporation (including the chairman of the board), are those directly responsible for determining both the strategic direction and the execution of the company's future. But they are not acting within a vacuum; they are subject to the constant prying eyes of the external forces in the marketplace who question the validity and soundness of their decisions and performance. These include the equity markets in which the shares are traded, the analysts who critique their investment prospects, the creditors and credit agencies who lend them money, the auditors and legal advisors who testify to the fairness and legality of their reporting, and the multitude of regulators who oversee their actions in order to protect the investment public.

The Board of Directors

The legal body that is accountable for the governance of the corporation is its board of directors. The board is composed of both employees of the organization (inside members) and senior and influential nonemployees (outside members). Areas of debate surrounding boards include the following: (1) the proper balance between inside and outside members, (2) the means by which board members are compensated for their service, and (3) the actual ability of a board to adequately monitor and manage a corporation when board members are spending sometimes fewer than five days a year in board activities. Outside members, very often the current or retired chief executives of other major companies, may bring with them a healthy sense of distance and impartiality, but also may lack substantial understanding of the true issues and events within the company. In German companies, the distinction between the governing board and the management board provides a different set of dilemmas on these same internal versus external trade-offs.

Officers and Management

The senior officers of the corporation – the chief executive officer (CEO), the chief financial officer (CFO), and the chief operating officer (COO) – are not only the most knowledgeable of the business, but the creators and directors of its strategic and operational direction. The management of the firm is, according to theory, acting as a contractor – as an agent – of shareholders to pursue value creation. They are motivated by salary, bonuses, and stock options (positively) or the risk of losing their jobs (negatively). They may, however, have biases of self-enrichment or personal agendas that the board and other corporate stakeholders are responsible for overseeing and policing. In the majority of large US companies, the CEO is also the chairman of the board. This is, in the opinion of many, a conflict of interest and not in the best interests of the company and its shareholders. British-based corporations are more aggressive and consistent in separating these roles.

Equity Markets

The publicly traded company, regardless of country of residence, is highly susceptible to the changing opinion of the marketplace. The equity markets themselves, whether they be the New York Stock Exchange (NYSE), London Stock Exchange, or Mexico City Bolsa, should reflect the market's constant evaluation of the promise and performance of the individual company. The analysts are those self-described experts employed by the many investment banking firms who also trade in the client company shares. They evaluate the strategies, plans for execution of the strategies, and financial performance of the firms on a real-time basis, and depend on the financial statements and other public disclosures of the firm for their information.

Debt Markets

Although the debt markets (banks and other financial institutions providing loans and various forms of securitized debt, like corporate bonds) are not specifically interested in building shareholder value, they are indeed interested in the financial health of the company. Their interest, specifically, is in the company's ability to repay its debt in a timely and efficient manner. These markets, like the equity markets, must rely on the financial statements and other disclosures (public and private in this case) of the companies with which they work.

Auditors and Legal Advisors

Auditors and legal advisors are responsible for providing an external professional opinion as to the fairness, legality, and accuracy of corporate financial statements. In this process, they attempt to determine whether the firm's financial records and practices follow what in the USA is termed *generally accepted accounting principles (GAAP)* with regard to accounting procedures. Auditors and legal advisors are hired by the firms they are auditing, leading to a rather unique practice of policing their employers.

Regulators

Publicly traded firms are subject to the regulatory oversight of both governmental organizations and nongovernmental organizations. In the USA, the Securities and Exchange Commission (SEC) is a careful watchdog of the publicly traded equity markets, both in the behavior of the companies themselves in those markets and of the various investors participating in those markets. The SEC and other such authorities around the world require a regular and orderly disclosure process of corporate performance in order that all investors may evaluate the company's investment value with adequate, accurate, and fairly distributed information. This regulatory oversight is often focused on when and what information is released by the company, and to whom (Clarke, 2017; Wright et al., 2013; Gordon & Ringe, 2018).

Publicly traded firms are typically also subject to the rules and regulations of the exchange where their shares are traded. The largest stock exchanges in the world, in order of total market capitalization, include:

- New York Stock Exchange (USA)
- NASDAQ (USA)
- TMX Group (Canada)
- London Stock Exchange Group (UK)
- Japan Exchange Group (Japan)
- Shanghai Stock Exchange (China)
- Euronext (Europe)
- Hong Kong Stock Exchange
- Shenzhen Stock Exchange (China)
- TMX Group (Canada)

These organizations, categorized as "self-regulatory" in nature, typically construct and enforce standards of conduct for both their member companies and themselves in the conduct of share trading (Christiansen & Koldertsova, 2008; World Federation of Exchanges, 2018).

Comparative Corporate Governance

The origins of the need for a corporate governance process arise from the separation between ownership and management, and from varying views of culture. As described in Exhibit 13.5, the various corporate governance systems may be

EXHIBIT 13.5 Comparing corporate governance regimes

Regime basis	Characteristics	Examples
Market based	Efficient equity markets; dispersed ownership	Australia, Canada, United Kingdom, USA
Family based	Management and ownership is combined; family/majority and minority shareholders	France, Hong Kong, Indonesia, Malaysia, Singapore, Taiwan
Bank based	Government influence in bank lending; lack of transparency; family control	Germany, South Korea
Government affiliated	State ownership of enterprise; limited transparency; no minority influence	China, Russia

Source: Based on J. Tsui and R. Shieh, "Corporate Governance in Emerging Markets: An Asian Perspective," in F. Choi, ed. *International Finance and Accounting Handbook, 3rd ed.* (New York: Wiley, 2004).

classified by regime. The regimes in turn reflect the evolution of business owner-ship and direction within the countries over time.

Market-based regimes, such as those of the USA, Canada, and the United King-dom, are characterized by relatively efficient capital markets in which the own-ership of publicly traded companies is widely dispersed. Family-based systems, such as those characterized in many of the emerging markets, Asian markets, and Latin American markets, not only started with strong concentrations of family ownership (as opposed to partnerships or small investment groups, which are not family based), but have continued to be largely controlled by families even after going public. Bank-based and government-based regimes are those reflecting markets in which government ownership of property and industry has been the constant force over time, resulting in only marginal "public ownership" of enter-prise, and, even then, subject to significant restrictions on business practices.

These regimes are, therefore, a function of at least four major factors in the evolution of corporate governance principles and practices globally: (1) finan-cial market development, (2) the degree of separation between management and ownership, (3) the concept of disclosure and transparency, and (4) the historical development of the legal system.

Financial Market Development

The depth and breadth of capital markets is critical to the evolution of corporate governance practices. Country markets that have had relatively slow growth (as in the emerging markets) or have industrialized rapidly utilizing neighboring capital markets (as is the case of western Europe) may not form large public equity market systems. Without significant public trading of ownership shares, high concentrations of ownership are preserved and few disciplined processes of governance develop.

Degree of Separation of Management and Ownership

In countries and cultures in which the ownership of the firm has continued to be an integral part of management, agency failures have been less of a problem. In countries like the USA, in which ownership has become largely separated from management (and widely dispersed), aligning the goals of management and own-ership is much more difficult.

Disclosure and Transparency

The extent of disclosure regarding the operations and financial results of a com-pany vary dramatically across countries. Disclosure practices reflect a wide range of cultural and social forces, including the degree of ownership that is public, the degree to which government feels it needs to protect investors' rights, and the extent to which family-based and government-based business remains central to the culture. Transparency, a parallel concept to disclosure, reflects the visibility of decision-making processes within the business organization.

Good Governance and Corporate Reputation

Does good corporate governance matter? This is actually a difficult question, and, historically, the realistic answer has been largely dependent on outcomes. For example, as long as Enron's share price continued to rise dramatically for a decade, questions over transparency, accounting propriety, and even financial facts were largely overlooked by many of the stakeholders of the corporation. Yet, eventually, the fraud, deceit, and failure of the multitude of corporate governance practices resulted in the bankruptcy of the firm. It not only destroyed the wealth of investors, but the careers, incomes, and savings of so many of its basic stakeholders – its own employees. Ultimately, yes, good governance does matter. A lot.

Good corporate governance is dependent on a variety of factors, one of which is the general governance reputation of the country of incorporation and registration. Exhibit 13.6 presents selected recent rankings of countries based on the quality of their governance. Governance in this case is measured using six variables: public accountability, political stability and absence of violence, government effectiveness, regulatory quality, rule of law, and control of corruption. As the quality of national governance rises, so does economic prosperity, leading to higher living standards for citizens. Nations that score high on governance – for example, Canada and Australia – tend to have higher living standards. By contrast, countries with the lowest governance scores – for example, Nigeria and Venezuela – tend to have lower living standards. In addition, good governance (at

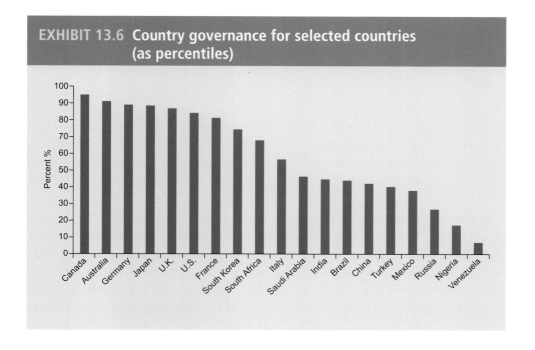

EXHIBIT 13.6 Country governance for selected countries (as percentiles)

Country	Score
Canada	95
Australia	92
Germany	90
Japan	89
UK	87
USA	85
France	82
South Korea	75
Italy	68
South Africa	57
India	46
Saudi Arabia	45
Brazil	44
China	42
Turkey	40
Mexico	38
Russia	27
Nigeria	18
Venezuela	7

Sources: Kaufmann, Kraay, and Mastruzzi, 2010; World Bank, 2019b.

both the country and corporate levels) is closely associated with the cost of capital, returns to shareholders, and corporate profitability. Finally, countries characterized by superior governance are viewed as less risky and thus are able to attract substantial inward investment, both as portfolio investment and foreign direct investment.

A second way of valuing good governance is by measuring the attitudes and tendencies of the large global institutional investors, who ultimately decide where capital may go. A study by McKinsey surveyed more than 200 institutional investors as to the value they placed on good governance. The survey results indicated that institutional investors would be willing to pay a premium for companies with good governance within specific country markets. Although this is not exactly equivalent to saying who has "good" or "bad" corporate governance globally, it does provide some insight as to the countries, in the opinion of institutional investors, where good governance is scarce. It is again important to note that most of the emerging market nations have relatively few publicly traded companies even today (Crane & Matten, 2016; de los Reyes et al., 2017; Kaufmann et al., 2010).

Corporate Governance Reform

Within the USA and the UK, the main corporate governance problem is the one treated by agency theory: With widespread share ownership, how can a firm align management's interest with that of the shareholders? Because individual shareholders do not have the resources or the power to monitor management, the US and UK markets rely on regulators to assist in the agency theory monitoring task. Outside the USA and the UK, large controlling shareholders are in the majority (including Canada). They are able to monitor management in some ways better than regulators. However, controlling shareholders pose a different agency problem. How can minority shareholders be protected against the controlling shareholders?

In recent years, reform in the USA and Canada has been largely regulatory. Reform elsewhere has been largely in the adoption of principles rather than stricter legal regulations. The principles approach is softer, less costly, and less likely to conflict with other existing regulations.

Transparency, Accounting, and Auditing

The concept of transparency is also one that has been raised in a variety of different markets and contexts. Transparency is a rather common term used to describe the degree to which an investor – either existing or potential – can discern the true activities and value drivers of a company from the disclosures and financial results reported. For example, Enron was often considered a "black box" when it came to what the actual operational and financial results and risks were for its multitude of business lines. The consensus of corporate governance experts is that all firms, globally, should work toward increasing the transparency of the firm's risk–return profile.

The accounting process itself has now come under debate. The US system is characterized as strictly rule based, rather than conceptually based as is common in western Europe. Many critics of US corporate governance practices point to this as a fundamental flaw, in which constantly more clever accountants find ways to follow the rules, yet not meet the underlying purpose for which the rules were intended. An extension of the accounting process debate is that of the role and remuneration associated with auditing. This is the process of using third parties, paid by the firm, to vet their reporting practices as being consistent with generally accepted accounting principles.

Minority Shareholder Rights

Finally, the issue of minority shareholder rights continues to be debated in many of the world's largest markets. Emerging markets are still largely characterized by

EXHIBIT 13.7 Corporate governance reform in China

The Chinese Government has made improvements to China's corporate governance structure by revising its securities and company laws. Notable changes include greater financial disclosure requirements, improved protection of minority shareholders' rights, and clearer guidelines on the role of supervising boards.

Significant progress has also been made in improving corporate governance in both the banking and equity markets. The government has also introduced a share reform program, mandating that non-tradable shares in state-owned enterprises (SOEs) can be converted into tradable shares. Regulators also have sought to decrease financial risk in China's banking system.

China has a two-tier board governance structure for companies that is similar to the German system, with a board of directors and a supervisory board. However, supervisory boards in China typically rubber-stamp decisions made by the board of directors. In Chinese public-held companies, at least one-third of the boards should constitute independent directors. In practice, however, these directors have very limited ability to influence how their companies are run. Financial disclosure requirements of Chinese listed companies are relatively weak.

In SOEs, managers have very little stake because they are usually government officials appointed by the state. By their nature, government exerts a strong managerial influence on state enterprises and many senior managers see their role as that of keeping the government happy at all costs.

Reform of SOEs' share structures is underway, but much uncertainty remains. A lack of transparency reduces prospects for China's equity markets to grow and function properly. The central government in Beijing has encouraged companies to make substantive improvements in corporate governance. Local firms are encouraged to list their shares on the Hong Kong stock exchange, which has a more internationally accepted corporate governance system for listed companies. China's corporate governance system is improving albeit slowly and with significant uncertainty.

Sources: Cheung, 2017; Jia, Huang, and Man Zhang, 2019; Molnar, 2017.

the family-based corporate governance regime, where the family remains in control even after the firm has gone public. But what of the interests and voices of the other shareholders? Exhibit 13.7 addresses minority shareholder rights.

Poor performance of management usually precipitates changes to management, ownership, or both. Such change can be affected through a variety of paths. In times gone by, and depending on the culture and accepted practices of the country and corporate culture, shareholders who believed management was consistently under-performing might have either simply remained quietly disgruntled or, at the opposite extreme, sold their shares. Over the past decade in many of the world's larger markets, however, shareholder activism has resulted in a number of more direct and aggressive actions. Now, disgruntled shareholders may actively seek the board's and other shareholders' support in removing and replacing management.

Executive Pay

Seemingly excessive compensation by many corporations, particularly in the USA, is often hotly debated. Issues spanned the full spectrum of the role compensation plays in business, from the financial incentives for individuals and organizations to the bonuses paid executives. Executive pay differs dramatically across countries. Many analysts believe that excessive pay led to the global financial crisis. It is estimated that the average senior executive in the USA today receives 400 times the pay of the company's lowest paid worker (Simmering, 2020). This is a significant difference from the ten times estimate for workers in Japan and western European firms.

Corporate Responsibility and Sustainability

As a result of globalization, this growing responsibility and role of the corporation in society has added an additional level of complexity. We shall simplify the diversity in the number of different principles under considerations. Sustainability is often described as a goal, while responsibility is an obligation of the corporation. **Sustainability** refers to activities that meet the needs of the present without harming the ability of future generations to meet their own needs. **Corporate social responsibility (CSR)** refers to operating a company in a manner that will assure both a profitable and sustainable future for the organization's primary stakeholders while having positive impacts on both society and the environment. In light of frequently different expectations and abilities, it is little wonder that there can be a wide variety of plans and outcomes.

The term "sustainable" has evolved greatly within the context of global business in the past decade. The primary objective of a family-owned business was the "sustainability of the organization" by assuring the long-term ability of the company to remain commercially viable and provide security and income for future generations of the family. Nowadays, sustainability includes the use and replenishment of resources around the globe. As reflected in Exhibit 13.8, consumer attitudes on sustainability and protecting the natural environment vary significantly between Europe and the USA (Crane & Matten, 2016; Chandler, 2017).

> ### EXHIBIT 13.8 Consumer attitudes on sustainability and the environment
>
> Consumer attitudes toward sustainability and environmental protection vary between Europe and the USA. In Europe, surveys find that consumers are preoccupied with environmental considerations in their purchasing habits. However, such concerns vary from country to country. Italian shoppers are the most likely to want to buy products with environmentally friendly packaging (81%), followed by consumers in Spain (75%), and then Greece and France (74%). German consumers are least likely to buy products with recyclable packaging (62%). Consumers in Greece are most likely to prefer to buy products that respect the environment (83% of all Greek consumers). This is followed by Italy (82% of consumers), Spain (78%), and France (71%). Consumers in Germany and the Netherlands (62% each) score lower on preference for buying products that respect the environment.
>
> In the USA, only about 48% of consumers say that they would definitely or probably change their consumption habits to reduce their impact on the environment. However, the market for sustainable fast-moving consumer goods (FMCG) is growing rapidly and reached $128 billion in the USA in 2018. The market is expected to reach $150 billion by 2021. Sustainable purchase intent is driven largely by Millennials, who are twice as likely as Baby Boomers (75% vs. 34%) to say that they are definitely or probably changing their habits to reduce their impact on the environment. American Millennials are also more inclined to pay more for products that contain environmentally friendly or sustainable ingredients (90% vs. 61%), organic/natural ingredients (86% vs. 59%), or products that have social responsibility claims (80% vs. 48%).
>
> **Sources:** Packaging Europe, 2018; Nielsen, 2018.

The Triple Bottom Line

Many corporations publicly link their corporate objective to the pursuit of the triple bottom line – profitability, social responsibility, and environmental sustainability. They refer to a desire to ensure that future generations are not harmed by actions taken today. Is this a softer and gentler form of market capitalism going beyond financial profit alone?

There are a variety of theoretical rationalizations for this more expanded view of corporate responsibilities, one of which divides the arguments along two channels, the economic channel and the moral channel:

- The economic channel argues that by pursuing corporate sustainability objectives, the corporation pursues profitability combined with a longer-term perspective using enlightened self-interest.

- The moral channel argues that because the corporation has all the rights and responsibilities of a citizen, it also has the moral responsibility to act in the best interests of society and society's future, regardless of the impact on profitability. Taking actions leads to costs. Corporations have to appreciate and decide which channel to pursue.

Consider the case of a manufacturing plant that produces effluents and can disperse those through the environment without legal liabilities or requirements. However, removal of effluents in-house reduces environmental costs on society. If society increasingly expects the corporation to act in this way, corporate obligations will add up but so will the corporate reputation.

Would a large multinational integrated oil and gas company really be expected to pursue wind or biofuels research and development when it has no experience or competence in these scientific or technology areas? Should that same company, when developing oil fields in sub-Saharan Africa, also be expected to build schools and hospitals and provide ongoing educational or medical services (Carroll et al., 2018; Rasche et al., 2017; Chandler, 2017)?

Perceptions on Responsibility

Differing perceptions of corporate responsibility are presented in Exhibit 13.9. The listing reports key issues related to sustainable business practices and activities in the workplace. It indicates that companies in different countries differ on corporate responsibility issues.

EXHIBIT 13.9 Ranking corporate responsibility issues

Global rank	Issue	Global	Brazil	Germany	Mexico	Russia	South Africa	United Kingdom	United States
1	Reduce greenhouse gas emissions	3.6	3.3	4.5	2.8	2.8	2.6	4	4
2	Promote efficient use of energy	3.3	2	4.2	3	3.5	2.3	3	3
3	Promote conservation of clean water	3.2	3.8	3.8	3.1	3.3	1.6	2.8	2.8
4	Ensure worker health and well-being	2.7	1.3	3.1	2.8	3.3	1.8	1.6	1.6
5	Provide learning opportunities for workers	2.7	2.4	2.9	3.6	3	2.3	2.2	2.2

EXHIBIT 13.9 (cont.)

Global rank	Issue	Global	Brazil	Germany	Mexico	Russia	South Africa	United Kingdom	United States
6	Ensure equal opportunities for employment	2.4	0.7	3	2.4	1.8	2.4	2.1	2.1
7	Reduce hunger, including reducing food waste	2.2	2	1.8	2.4	0.5	1.4	2.1	2.1
8	Reduce pollution of terrestrial ecosystems	2.1	1.7	2	2	2.7	0.75	1.7	1.7
9	Ensure fair labor practices in the value chain	1.9	2.2	2.6	2.7	2.2	1	1.5	1.5
10	Ensure equal pay for equal work, men and women	1.8	3	1.9	1.7	1	2.2	2.4	2.4

Sources: PricewaterhouseCoopers, 2018; Gitman, 2018.

A Question of Trust

Many issues depend on the degree of trust that individuals have in business. A trusted business is likely to receive society's support. Unreliable firms, however, may receive more regulatory oversight.

An interesting example is provided by surveys of attitudes and trust. Exhibit 13.10 presents the results of Edelman's Trust Barometer, over two decades. The results suggest that trust in business tends to be highest in emerging market countries, as reflected by Brazil and China in the exhibit. Perhaps this arises because people in such economies tend to experience significant gains in personal wealth and general economic conditions. By contrast, trust in business in advanced economies – Germany, Japan, United Kingdom, and the USA – is substantially lower. In 2019, trust in business is lowest in Russia, with only 34% of respondents stating that they trust business to do what is right. This is followed by Japan, which registers just 44% trust in business. It should be noted that Russia and Japan have experienced stagnant economies for the past several years (Carroll et al., 2018; Crane & Matten, 2016; Rasche et al., 2017; Chandler, 2017).

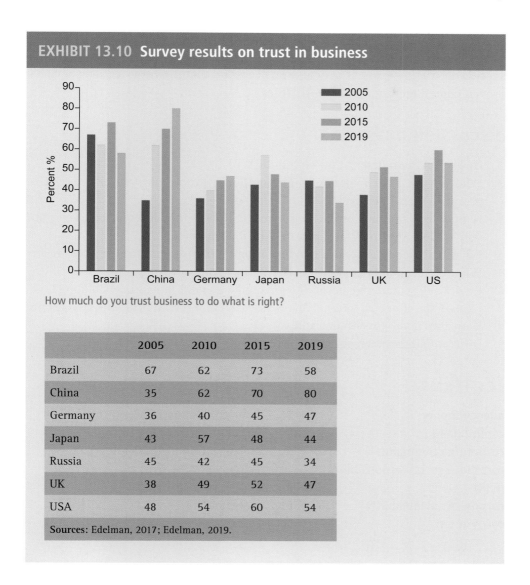

EXHIBIT 13.10 **Survey results on trust in business**

How much do you trust business to do what is right?

	2005	2010	2015	2019
Brazil	67	62	73	58
China	35	62	70	80
Germany	36	40	45	47
Japan	43	57	48	44
Russia	45	42	45	34
UK	38	49	52	47
USA	48	54	60	54

Sources: Edelman, 2017; Edelman, 2019.

SUMMARY

The nature of corporate ownership structures vary around the world. They affect how organizations respond to stakeholder interests. Goals, structures, and participants in corporate governance, as well as the quality of corporate governance, affect the reputation and social responsibility of companies.

National governments and societies worldwide increasingly demand good corporate governance. Good business capability may not be sufficient for long-term success. In coming years, it may also be necessary that the corporation establish a proven commitment to its responsibilities.

DISCUSSION QUESTIONS

1. How would you describe a corporation?
2. Who are the stakeholders of a corporation? How would you either rank or prioritize their interests?
3. How do corporations profit their owners? How is this different between publicly traded companies and privately held companies?
4. What is shareholder wealth maximization? What is your attitude towards it?
5. What is stakeholder capitalism? Does it have a future?
6. How would you define corporate governance to aid in its understanding?
7. Explain the effects of internal forces vs. external forces in corporate governance
8. How does good governance add value?
9. Differentiate between corporate responsibility and corporate sustainability

KEY TERMS

agency theory	371	fiduciary responsibility	370
capital gains	369	initial public offering (IPO)	369
corporate governance	373	maximization of shareholder	
corporate social responsibility		value	368
(CSR)	383	stakeholder capitalism	371
corporate sustainability	384	stakeholders	366
corporation	363	transparency	374

TAKE A STAND

A corporation has a multitude of stakeholders, including employees and owners. During major downturns in business, companies suffer losses in sales and, ultimately, profits. One regular response by businesses during bad economic times is to reduce costs, which may include laying off workers to reduce wage and other labor-related expenses.

Questions for Debate

1. In times of recession, how can companies stay competitive and profitable?
2. Should companies try to preserve and even increase employment? Why and how?

INTERNET EXERCISES

1. The quality of governance determines the success of corporations and countries alike. At its Worldwide Governance Indicators site, (http://info.worldbank.org/governance/wgi), the World Bank provides measures of governance for countries worldwide. Researchers use information at the site to analyze the quality of governance in individual countries, and to assess their attractiveness for business and investment. Visit the site and answer the following questions: What indicators does the World Bank use to measure governance? Choose two countries from the site's database. How well does each country rank in terms of key governance indicators? Based on your review, which country appears most attractive for doing business?

2. Corporate governance is defined variously at different sites online. Enter the phrase "corporate governance" in your browser and find three different explanations of the term. Based on examining these explanations, identify the major characteristics and issues related to corporate governance. What minimum facts about corporate governance should an international manager know?

3. The websites for Cargill (USA, www.cargill.com), WPP (United Kingdom, www.wpp.com), and Kao (Japan, www.kao.com) contain substantial information about these firms' sustainability goals. Visit each site, or simply enter the firm name and "sustainability" in your browser, and answer the following questions. Which firm appears most effective in terms of its sustainability goals? Justify your answer.

   How do the sustainability goals of a food company (Cargill) differ from those of an advertising agency (WPP) and from a cosmetics company (Kao)? Based on your reading of these sites, compile a list of the general sustainability goals that you think firms should adopt for success in international business.

FURTHER RESOURCES

Bosse, Douglas and Phillips, Robert. (2016). Agency Theory and Bounded Self-Interest., *Academy of Management Review*, 41(2), 276–297.

Chandler, David. (2017).*Strategic Corporate Social Responsibility: Sustainable Value Creation*, 4th ed. Thousand Oaks, CA: Sage.

Clarke, Thomas. (2017). *International Corporate Governance: A Comparative Approach*. New York: Routledge, 2017.

Crane, Andrew and Matten, Dirk. (2016). *Business Ethics: Managing Corporate Citizenship and Sustainability in the Age of Globalization*. Oxford: Oxford University Press.

Henisz, Witold . (2017). *Corporate Diplomacy: Building Reputations and Relationships with External Stakeholders*. New York: Routledge.

Pinto, Arthur and Branson, Douglas. (2018). *Understanding Corporate Law*. Durham, NC: Carolina Academic Press.

Rasche, Andreas, Morsing, Mette, and Moon, Jeremy. (2017). *Corporate Social Responsibility: Strategy, Communication, Governance*. New York: Cambridge University Press.

14 Digital Contributions for International Business

LEARNING OBJECTIVES

- Discuss technology as tools for local needs
- Explore problems of international electronic crime
- Explore regulation of international online commerce
- Adapt online communication across cultures
- Identify security issues in international e-commerce
- Identify strategic issues in international digital business
- Explore challenges in social media across countries
- Identify the impact of technology infrastructure on business choices

CHAPTER CONTENTS

VIGNETTE 14 WeChat: Jumpstarting an electronic payment system

WeChat is known as a "super app" since it spans a number of different social media functions, including text messaging, postings, and making payments. Founded by the Chinese e-commerce firm Tencent in 2011, WeChat had reached 902 million active daily users by 2018.

In a move little noticed outside China at the time, WeChat launched its payment service on Chinese New Year's Eve in 2014, a carefully timed event. Historically in China, so-called "red envelopes" with cash have been given by parents to children and by employers and managers to employees on New Year's Eve as an annual present. The "virtual" red envelopes that could now be sent caused quite a bit of excitement especially to the recipient since the sender can now dispatch money to a group of individuals. Money received can be stored in an electronic "wallet" and can be sent to friends, used to make purchases, or – if the user linked his or her bank account with WeChat – be transferred to the user's bank account (Lee, 2018).

The "red envelope" stunt resulted in eleven million transfers and five million bank accounts being linked to WeChat accounts. This dramatic beginning helped "jump start" a payment system that otherwise would have faced a serious chicken-and-egg problem: Potential payers fail to join the system before a sufficient number of potential recipients have joined. In return, potential recipients have little incentive to join until payers are signed up to transfer this way, resulting in a stand-off. The dramatic start allowed WeChat to immediately rise to a serious competitor to Alipay, founded a decade earlier as part of the Alibaba Group (Lee, 2018; Erisman, 2017; Clark, 2016).

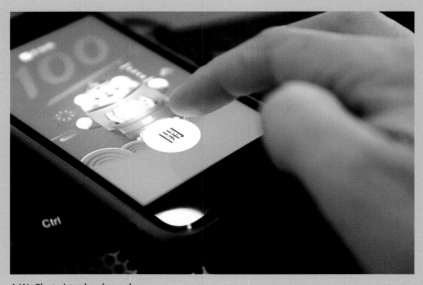

A WeChat virtual red envelope

Introduction

The world – and the way that business is transacted – has changed a great deal over the past decades. The exponentially growing Internet and opportunities for wireless, mobile connections have led to a large number of platforms. The distinction between personal interaction and business communication has blurred considerably, and many opportunities for e-commerce have emerged. It is now possible for people to have online "friends" in different parts of the world that they would never have had an opportunity to "meet" before this technology. On the other hand, electronic communications, connections, and commerce provide a very different experience in different countries depending on context, culture, government regulation, and infrastructure. In much of the developing world, Internet connections take place mostly through phones and other small devices, requiring significant adaptations to platforms. Ambivalent government attitudes toward the Internet, which can be seen both as a formidable engine for economic growth and a serious threat to long held values of privacy and endangerment of political survival of existing regimes, have resulted in heavy regulation and if not outright censorship in some countries.

Digital Business

Moore's Law postulates that every two years the capacity of computers doubles (Moore, 2006). Over the last decade, a number of technologies have converged into a cluster of "digital" tools. Although computers and telecommunications technology have existed for decades, the power of these tools has continued to increase dramatically to the point that business decisions and operations can be based on a staggering amount of data and processing. In addition, advances in communications technology have contributed to a world where a growing majority of consumers are connected to the Internet and are able to receive, analyze, and transmit large amounts of data.

In addition to websites, e-mail capabilities, and apps, an increasing number of electronic payment systems make a growing number of prepaid and credit transactions increasingly convenient. The line between online and traditional purchases has become blurred as technologies have evolved. For example, ApplePay makes it possible to make a payment in a retail store originally set up to take conventional credit and debit card payments. In some countries, it is a common practice to pay for vending machine purchases through a mobile phone. Smartphone apps make it possible for individuals to make electronic payments to each other – for example, to pay for babysitting services or to settle a restaurant check shared among several individuals. In rural Eastern Africa, where most residents had historically been denied access to banking services, mobile phone banking is spreading rapidly, in part because of an average of 80% mobile phone penetration rate across Africa (Chironga et al., 2017). Trust is an important issue given reports of network breaches. It is important for the customer to be assured both that the electronic service provider itself is legitimate and that it has the resources to keep its data and communications flow secure.

Consumers today can view and download high-quality video recordings that could not have been accommodated by existing bandwidth and processing power available two decades ago. To put things in perspective, the iPhone X has over one million times the memory and some 100,000 times the processing power of the total computing power available to NASA in getting the Apollo astronauts to the moon (Kendall, 2019). Laptop and desktop computers, in turn, feature several times the power of the iPhone.

Before the Internet, the cost of making extended voice phone calls between countries was usually quite high, making calls to friends and family in other parts of the world an unaffordable luxury to many. Some countries today still impose high charges on incoming and outgoing calls, but a number of Voice Over Internet Protocol (VOIP) services such as Skype typically provide free or low-cost voice and video connections, which is subsidized by its upgradable higher-quality features.

The Internet

Computers and other devices across the world are connected through the Internet. Because of the complexity of the technology involved, it is difficult to pinpoint exactly what constitutes the Internet as such. However, although traffic may originate through cellular phone networks or local connections to homes and commercial buildings, the data are generally directed toward several high capacity "backbone" lines across the world. By allowing for data to travel through any number of different paths between computers and server systems, the original intent was to make the Internet sufficiently resilient that it could withstand the loss of large numbers of connection points, whether through natural disasters, war, or terrorism. Today, it has become evident that despite the flexible design, the Internet is, in fact, quite vulnerable to weak points and bottlenecks, especially given the large bandwidth needed to carry dense content used today (International Organization for Standardization, 2018).

Different countries are, in principle, assigned different domain name suffixes: .jp for Japan, .cn for China, and .de for Germany. For example, Walmart's Brazil website is at the domain www.walmart.com.br and Costco's Japan site is at www.costco.co.jp. In practice, however, websites based in different countries may use another domain suffix, obscuring the site's origin. The domain suffix assigned for the USA – .us – is rarely ever used, and sites around the world use suffixes such as .com, .net, and .org. For example, Procter & Gamble's German site is at de.pg.com and Ikea's Slovakian site is at www.ikea.com/sk/sk. In addition, firms may use their home country suffixes for their foreign subsidiaries. Where you are located in the world will often determine the site to which you are sent. In Japan, for example, www.google.com will take you to a Japanese language site that you can access in most of the rest of the world at the address www.google.co.jp.

A browser transmits a lot more information than a user enters, to the server hosting a website. Among other things, this helps the server ensure that regionally appropriate content is "rendered" (i.e., formatted) in a manner suitable for display on the type of screen in use. Some of this information can also be used for market research purposes and to evaluate the performance of a site. By default, the name and version of the browser, the device operating system, and the visitor's IP address will be provided. The browser and device information can be used to optimize the rendering of a particular page, and the IP information can identify the location of the user. Depending on the level of specificity on interest, an IP address can identify:

- The specific computer used if a static ("always on") connection is temporarily assigned
- The firm or service provider from which a connection is made
- City or geographic region from which the access is made
- The country of access: Rendering decisions may be based both on the specific language to be used – for example, French for France, Brazilian Portuguese for Brazil, British English for the UK, and American English for the USA – and the selection of locally relevant content such as authorized sellers and service providers

Information on the user's location and the type of device can render pages so that the format is optimized for varying screen sizes. It is even possible to optimize the appearance of a page for the user's choice of browsers (e.g., Chrome, Firefox, Safari, or Internet Explorer). Today, several browsers allow for a "private" browsing mode where some or all of this information is altered or withheld, and various Virtual Private Network (VNP) providers may be used to disguise one's identity and location. This capability is desired by many both to preserve privacy and to be able to access content made available only to select geographic areas.

Digital Infrastructure and Internet Penetration across the World

Available infrastructure varies considerably among regions. Although internet access speeds are generally faster and more reliable in developed countries, costs have come down dramatically over time. South Korea offers higher speed access than what is seen in most European and North American countries, in part because the country's high population density has made it cost effective to roll out the newest wiring nationwide. In contrast, in countries such as the USA, there is often a heavy dependence on legacy infrastructure – including forty-year-old phone lines not originally designed with internet traffic in mind. Ironically, countries with the most limited existing infrastructure may end up ahead. In a process known as "leap frogging," countries implementing technology for the first time will often skip earlier stages of the older generations of technology still in use throughout developed countries, going directly to the newer technology (Diop, 2017).

Running new wires and performing the needed retrofitting can be a costly and labor-intensive practice, and in developed countries, private property rights often make it cumbersome to secure the needed real estate permissions. In addition, much of the cost of cellular phone networks comes from the cost of acquiring the right to use scarce and highly coveted frequency spectra. Where there is less demand for these rights, wireless connections can often be more cost effective and easier to install.

Although internet access is limited, there are currently more than one billion mobile subscribers in India since cheap phones and low priced service plans are readily available (Rai, 2016). In a country with high rates of illiteracy, there have even been attempts to create a "speaking" Internet where users choose links based on spoken prompts (Singh, 2017). This technology makes it possible for firms to reach customers at the "Bottom of the Pyramid."

Internet penetration rates – the percentage of the population using the Internet in some form at least once a month – are now growing across the world. Although not everyone will have individual access at home or through a mobile device, an increasing proportion of people can connect at work, in cyber cafes, at libraries, or through borrowed devices. Even in Brazilian *favelas* – illegally constructed slums – access to the Internet through a wired computer can often be bought by the hour at a modest cost.

In many countries, the primary means of accessing the Internet is through smartphones. For this reason, it is increasingly critical to develop parallel formatting of content for display on a smaller screen. In fact, search engines heavily favor sites with a small screen display capability. An interesting contrast is Brazil, where consumers appear to have difficulty transitioning to the smaller mobile screens and thus prefer to make their purchases through full sized desktop or laptop computers (Euromonitor International, 2018a).

In China, it is estimated that some 72.5% of households had an internet broadband connection in early 2018, typically in the form of a 3G or 4G mobile system. This figure is up from just 61.4% a year earlier. Ironically, it is widely believed that China will beat the USA in the spread of 5G connectivity across large parts of the country since this technology is highly favored by the government. Based on the MOSAIC Global system – a system that classifies consumers based on their resources and lifestyle orientations – 54% of metro Chinese consumers fall into the Progressive Pioneer category, the fastest adopters of new technology. Although Americans are generally known to view new innovations favorably, the corresponding figure for urban US residents is only 24%. This suggests that some digital innovations are likely to spread considerably faster in China. It is also expected that China, with its closer cultural ties to other Southeast Asian countries, will have an edge in penetrating these markets (Wang, 2018).

Internet access is uneven in India, which Euromonitor International ranked as 49th out of the 50 countries they examined in 2017 for their Digital Consumer Index. Although only 16% of households were found to have desktops and 10% to have laptops, mobile access – which is considerably less expensive than setting up wired home connections – is increasing. Many of the poorest households tend to live on a subsistence, day-to-day basis, but low-cost mobile sets and plans are becoming increasingly available. (Euromonitor International, 2018c). Longer commutes in increasingly congested urban areas are also contributing to increasing mobile usage (WARC, 2018).

Worldwide, the overall penetration rate is estimated at 63.9%. Although rates tend to be higher in developed countries, these are rising fast in Latin America and in China.

Internet Security

The proliferation of digital shopping, payment, banking, and communications platforms have contributed to concerns about hacking and security. As the world becomes connected through the Internet, systems become vulnerable. A bank is subject not just to attacks by local hackers – each of which may individually have very low rates of success – but also to incursions from criminals across the world. Thus, businesses are vulnerable to attempted intrusions from countries that may lack the resources and/or interests in cracking down on such criminal activity. Today, firms are in a difficult position in that they need to rely on technology that readily connects networks across the world, but also faces increasing security risks. Policy makers are worried about the potential for "cyberwarfare" – attacks on electrical power grids, financial networks, voting systems, and communication networks that can potentially affect many competitors around the globe. It may be difficult for networks to reliably identify, let alone conclusively prove, the origin of attacks. This is especially the case when the distinction between governments, cyber criminals, and terrorist groups becomes blurred.

With the large number of dedicated hackers worldwide, cyber criminals are often able to identify and exploit vulnerabilities not originally anticipated. When these vulnerabilities are discovered, creating the required patches and security updates may take time because of the complexity of the issues involved. In 2011, a flaw in common microprocessors that left data vulnerable to hacking was identified.

Although this vulnerability could have been circumvented with software coding, this would have taken a heavy toll on computer and device speed. Even after the problem was addressed in new chips, it took years before most of the devices affected by the flaw were made secure. It now appears that a newly discovered flaw may cause similar problems (Whittaker, 2019).

Hackers in North Korea are estimated to have stolen insights worth at least $700 million, and to have attempted to steal as much as $2 billion between 2017 and 2019, potentially both as a source of funding for the country's military programs and to actively build up the capability to inflict serious injury on the economies of targeted countries. The *Wall Street Journal* suggests that it is possible that North Korea's willingness to negotiate about possible curtailment of its nuclear weapons program may be based on the expectation that its cyber-terrorism capabilities leave it with a highly powerful weapon (Tally and Volz, 2019). As shown in Exhibit 14.1, a hidden portion of the Web provides vast opportunities for shady activities.

EXHIBIT 14.1 The "Dark Net"

A great deal of internet content is only available through the "Dark Net," a portion of the Internet that must usually be accessed with a special browser. In addition, certain sites require a special invitation before they can be "seen" by a user. Although some individuals use the Dark Net primarily as a means of protecting their privacy, a great deal of "shadowy" and illegal business is often done here. A 2016 article in *Vanity Fair* described the Dark Net as "a wilderness where wars are fought and hackers roam." Some of the more popular items available here include pornography, drugs, and stolen data. Yet, even in this lawless land, the power of readily available information is evident. *Vanity Fair* observes that "illegal narcotics sold over the Dark Net tend to be purer, and therefore safer, than those sold on the street – this because of the importance to the sellers of online customer ratings" (Bartlett, 2016). Ironically, much of the technology used in the Dark Web and the foundation for TOR, the most popular browser used here, was originally developed by various US Government agencies (McMillan, 2017).

In order to prevent governments across the world from tracking financial transactions, these are usually executed using *cryptocurrencies* such as Bitcoin. The details of how these work are complex, but the general idea is that transaction records are combined in chains of records ("blockchains") that are encrypted and verified by a number of individuals in a chain. The chains are maintained in a decentralized fashion by a number of individuals known as "miners." This group helps avoid dependence on a centralized institution. A limited supply of coins

is released over time, and "miners" can capture these through high-comput-
ing-power-intensive hardware and software, and then resell the limited amount
of virtual currency that exists. In addition, the "miners" use various digital means
to decipher and validate transactions and receive commissions for this. In order
to ensure that a miner has a sufficient interest in a transaction to vet it accurately,
the miner must generally present "proof of work done" by performing these
elaborate computations. Through a variety of high-computing-processing-power
and bandwidth-intensive verifications, cryptocurrencies can then be transferred.
Recipients can convert the cryptocurrency into conventional currencies of different countries or exchanges, based on the same type of supply and demand relations that exist with conventional currencies. Alternatively, they can use the
currency for future transactions.

   As recent news stories indicate, cryptocurrencies can potentially decline in
value with little warning, and are, at least indirectly, vulnerable to hacking. Although some users are attracted to this type of secret, non-government-issued
currency out of distrust of governments at a more ideological level, cryptocurrencies are used heavily by organized crime groups. For example, a number of
hackers across the world are known to send out "ransomware" code in email
attachments opened by unsuspecting recipients, often through corporate email
accounts. The ransomware will then proceed to encrypt the data on an infiltrated
computer, after which the owner is notified that the data can be decrypted for
a given fee. Since important business data and content of great personal senti-
mental value are often involved, many victims choose to pay the ransom. To avoid
detection, the intruders often demand payment in cryptocurrency. Ironically, with
the complexities involved, perpetrators of ransomware attacks have often found
themselves tasked with providing a great deal of "customer service," in walking
customers through the process of buying cryptocurrency and transferring this to
the intruder (McMillan, 2017). Cryptocurrencies are also frequently used to make
payments among drug dealers and their customers and distributors.

   In principle, more-developed countries would seem to be better able to protect themselves against hackers than less-developed ones. However, many hacks
are accomplished through sophisticated technology. The technique of phishing
involves hacking into computer networks and accounts with the use of passwords,
login information, and personal user details obtained from unsuspecting computer users responding to fraudulent inquiries ostensibly from network and other
administrators within their organization. This process exploits the reality that
many consumers and business computer users in developed countries are com-
placent enough to open innocuous-looking attachments to emails, permitting the

installation of keylogging software transmitting passwords and other information to hackers. Some will even follow instructions ostensibly sent by the local "network administrator" or "human resources division" to go to a designated site and enter, among other things, their login and password information.

Although training and interception techniques may help reduce the frequency with which a firm's employees fall for intrusion attempts into their systems, the direct and indirect costs of dealing with and preventing such breaches are considerable. Increasingly, larger firms have high-ranking security officers with large staffs charged with monitoring systems and setting up preventive measures. In addition, it may be necessary to restrict the activities of users, which can result in lost productivity and obstacles to completing the required work.

Electronic Commerce

Electronic commerce involves a number of practices such as:

- The sale of tangible and electronic products online
- Performing marketing research through electronic interfaces
- Providing customer service and maintaining contact with customers
- Advertising and promoting brands in electronic settings.

An increasing amount of business done across the world is done on the Internet. The extent to which consumer purchases are favored in a particular country varies greatly based on factors such as trust in online systems, availability of secure, reliable, and reasonably priced shipping options, and the legal and regulatory burdens that online sellers face. In addition, for online transactions to be efficient, customers must have access to online payment systems. In developed countries, early purchases were generally made using credit or debit cards, but these were less readily available in developing countries. Various systems have evolved. For example, many online purchases in Indonesia are completed using ATM machines.

The amount of business-to-business (B2B) trade online is estimated to be even greater than purchases made by consumers (Laudon & Traver, 2017). With greater incentives, business customers have been more receptive to online commerce. In China, a fragmented group of manufacturers were historically connected with a splintered retail system through inefficient and costly state enterprises. Although finding reliable shippers to deliver from buyers to sellers was difficult in the early days, there were strong incentives to bypass the expensive intermediaries that drove up costs and ate into already very low margins (Clark, 2016). Today, digital payment systems have spread in China to the extent that such payments are now accepted even by many street merchants who ask customers to scan QR codes to direct payments (Euromonitor International, 2018b). In India, recent government policies that have greatly reduced the supply of currency notes have contributed to a significant growth in digital payments (Anto & Nag, 2018).

Economics of Consumer e-Commerce

It is a commonly believed myth in developed countries that online merchants have lower costs than traditional brick-and-mortar stores (Reagan, 2017). This is the case for a limited number of items that have sufficiently high value-to-bulk ratios and absolute (dollar) margins. Amazon makes more than half of its profits on Amazon Web Services, its cloud computing unit. Its "legacy" business of selling tangible merchandise accounts for a very small part of total earnings – and actually sustains losses at the global level (Owens, 2018). Although some high value-to-bulk ratio items such as smartphones and other electronic products can be handled efficiently, much of the bulkier traditional merchandise, such as print books, household goods, and other low cost merchandise, is likely to be sold at a loss because of the high handling costs relative to the limited dollar margins involved.

It is certainly true that brick-and-mortar merchants often face high costs of real estate – especially in premium markets such as London, Shanghai, Dubai, New York, and Singapore. By consolidating inventory to a limited number of distribution centers, costs of over- and under-stocks can be reduced. High-service retail stores can run up high labor costs. This argument, however, overlooks the considerable amount of work that the customer does in modern self-service stores:

1. The customer walks around the store, collecting the items that he or she wants to buy.
2. The customer then brings these items to the cashier, or possibly even uses a self-checkout system.
3. The cashier rings up the purchase and may or may not bag it for the customer. Increasingly, in high-labor-cost markets, customers are expected to bag their own purchases.
4. The customer hauls away the purchase, whether by car, foot, or public transportation.

In an online setting, *the seller has to do all the work performed by the customer in the traditional retail setting or hire someone else to do this.* Thus, the online merchant has to hire someone to walk around and collect all the items for a purchase. Amazon distribution centers have employees who are estimated to walk ten miles or more per day to assemble items for packaging (Exhibit 14.2). For items selling at high volumes, some automation can be implemented to reduce the human labor needed, but not even Amazon – likely the most sophisticated online merchant around – has managed to do this for lower volume products. In addition, unless the online seller has sufficient economies of scale to be able to set up its own distribution systems across vast areas, it must pay someone else to deliver.

Exhibit 14.2 A worker at an Amazon fulfillment center may walk ten miles per day because they become a stand-in for each customer finding the product on a shelf and bringing it to a central "check out" location
Credit: CHRIS J RATCLIFFE/AFP via Getty Images.

These costs can be especially high in European Union (EU) countries where labor costs are relatively high, even for semi-skilled labor.

In contrast, labor costs are generally considerably less in developing countries. With the scarcity of land in China in particular, real estate costs can be high. With labor as a smaller part of the costs of distribution and the total cost of a product, online sales of consumer goods can be made more cost effective. In the USA, online ordering of groceries for delivery has proven highly problematic since items, which are often perishable, must be collected from different parts of a warehouse to fulfill an order. This order must then be dispatched to the customer, and at least some of the contents must be kept refrigerated until they reach the customer. To increase efficiency, attempts are made to make deliveries to multiple customers on the same trip, causing delays and perishability problems. Where costs of labor are low relative to the value of the goods, compiling orders and delivering these to customers with a short delay is more cost effective.

For the customer, comparing prices from different sellers is relatively easy, and with hard-earned money from low paying jobs, there are strong incentives to comparison shop extensively both online and among different retail locations. Chinese consumers – who have an extensive history of aggressive haggling with merchants – tend to be particularly price sensitive. Today, many young adults live with their families and, as a result, have limited expenses. This means that, although their incomes are fairly modest by the standards of developed countries, a great deal of this income is available for discretionary purchases such as electronics and clothing. The US based electronics retail chain Best Buy attempted to set up its traditional retail format stores in China, betting that a sufficient number of increasingly affluent Chinese consumers would be willing to pay for high levels of service. Although many consumers enjoyed coming to Best Buy stores as a showroom, sales were limited as consumers tried to find better deals elsewhere. For high ticket items such as electronics, many would search extensively, both online and with other brick-and-mortar retailers, for a lower price. With low costs of low skilled labor, the cost of packaging and shipping were much less of an issue (Owens, 2018).

Low labor costs and foreign postal rates have allowed Chinese merchants to sell low priced specialty products to foreign countries using venues such as eBay and Amazon. Such shipments often take weeks, and domestic sellers often highlight their local presence to imply more timely deliveries. Foreign online merchant delay can be mitigated somewhat by going with a seller that has favorable ratings and reviews from past customers. However, this dependence on a demonstrated history of customer satisfaction means that it can be very difficult for merchants to present a high-performance track record.

Competition between Online Merchants

In China, competition between merchants – both online and in the brick-and-mortar setting – has tended to focus heavily on price. eBay and other foreign firms have found it difficult to compete within China, in part because of an inadequate understanding of the local markets. By contrast, Amazon has been quite successful in India, where it is generally considered the preferred online merchant. However, with Walmart's purchase of a 77% stake in the troubled Indian online merchant Flipkart, this competitor will be able to develop sophisticated infrastructure and programs to compete aggressively (Rein, 2011).

Customs Issues

Depending on the laws and regulations of the recipient country, getting merchandise shipped from abroad through customs can be a difficult and lengthy process. Inspectors may be not only looking for duties to be imposed, but also deciding whether the foreign product meets safety standards and regulations. In addition, time-consuming paperwork is often involved. There is also the risk that innocuous-looking shipments may hide contraband. Furthermore, in today's international environment, there are hundreds of thousands of packages that are shipped daily, and these are difficult to inspect except by sampling. Customs officials have adopted increasingly sophisticated technology available to "scan" containers to search for suspect merchandise arriving in them. For example, programs can compare how much declared merchandise should weigh and how much the shipment actually weighs. Discrepancy can help identify wrongful content.

Merging Online Media and Retail

A number of online merchants have attempted, in various ways, to enter retail markets. Retailer loyalty programs have become increasingly popular across the world, and large amounts of data are now available on customers' purchase histories. Some loyalty programs integrate online and retail purchases, allowing one to know different facets of the same consumer (Sponder & Khan, 2018a).

As the availability of data about individuals and businesses grows, increasing opportunities for "data enhancement" exist. Customers can now be matched across databases and be integrated into one central system. Privacy regulations limit this practice, especially in the EU. Credit rating systems can segment borrowers into those who are more likely to make required payments quickly and those who need help in meeting their obligations. This can result in different offers to different customers for the same good or service (Turban et al., 2018).

Information technology can also be used to profile the shopping and spending patterns of citizens of different countries. Duty free shops at the Frankfurt International Airport scan customers' passports when purchases are made in order to develop information about the purchase behaviors of travelers from different parts of the world. The data reveals that, on the average, Brazilian visitors spend about twice as much as the average visitor, Koreans three times as much, and Chinese visitors – a highly select group of the country's population who can afford such overseas travel – spend *five* times as much (X-Ray Mega Airport, 2015).

Legal Issues

Questions of which laws govern purchases across countries have always been complex, increasingly so with the number of purchases made directly by an end customer from a foreign seller. Even if domestic courts are willing to assume jurisdiction in a dispute with a foreign seller, the potential to enforce a judgment may be limited, and for modest amounts of money involved, judicial solutions may be uneconomical. Sellers often attempt to stipulate in warranty statements or other documentation the jurisdiction whose laws and courts will govern.

Culture and Customization

Website content must be customized and adapted to the cultural context of customers much the same way that tangible products are adapted. Spellings, word meanings, and colloquial expressions differ significantly between US and British

English, for example. Other languages differ in the way they are spoken and written between countries. There are differences in word usage and meanings across different dialects of Spanish and between the Swiss, Austrian, and German versions of the German language. Similarly, some cultures favor more direct expressions than others where the need to "read between the lines" is favored.

Country Culture, Product Positioning, and Internet Practices

With internet content readily available between countries, preventing the flow of "inappropriate" content between countries can be a problem. In the USA, it is generally considered unseemly for actors and actresses at the top of their careers to appear in television advertisements. Although celebrity endorsements can be lucrative, appearing in ads is likely to come across as a move to cash in on a past career that is now headed downward. By contrast, in Japan and many other Asian countries, a successful actress or actor is expected to appear in numerous advertisements as a means of *proving* her or his star power. In addition, when US celebrities do endorse products, they are generally expected to limit these endorsements to a small number of brands or products. There was some controversy when golf champion Tiger Woods endorsed a handful of products in different categories. In Asia, on the other hand, no advertiser can expect to be able to maintain the exclusivity of a major celebrity to its brand.

A firm can block advertisements by content and geography. Often, however, sophisticated web surfers can circumvent these measures. More importantly, it is considerably more difficult to keep these ads from showing up on social media sites. If the site on which the ad has first been posted complies with a takedown request, it can be reposted on other sites, possibly in jurisdictions that are less likely to cooperate.

Certain brands attempt to maintain clearly distinct images in different countries. In the USA, for example, Pizza Hut is considered a basic fast food chain and has limited distinction. In certain countries, however, it is positioned as a much fancier establishment, featuring servers and sit-down service (Doland, 2016). In the USA and most of the world, Coca Cola is very particular about associating itself with consistent colors to identify the specific product, such as regular or diet Coke. With opportunities to associate its product with hugely popular soccer events in Brazil, a larger assortment of colors has been permitted (Exhibit 14.3). However, with social media users having friends across countries, users can introduce their own product positioning. Exhibit 14.3 provides an example of changing the brand uses of color.

Website Cultural Customization

Tastes and values differ between countries. As a result, **website cultural customization**, or the adaptation of website language and other content to the expectations

Exhibit 14.3 Coca Cola celebrating Brazilian colors
Source: AMA/Corbis via Getty Images.

of local culture, is often critical in connecting with consumers. Laws and local mores may limit what can be depicted in some countries. Western advertisements often have to be greatly toned down in order to be permissible in Arab countries and more conservative states elsewhere. Showing even the unveiled face of a woman may be deemed impermissible in conservative countries such as Iran and Saudi Arabia. In addition, permitted advertising practices vary. South American advertisements – and even European ones – can be much more explicit than what US networks would tolerate. Comparative advertising suggesting that one's product is superior to that of a competitor – even if the claims are entirely true and can be readily substantiated – is illegal in much of the world. Even if not explicitly illegal, in most Asian countries, such advertising could come across as unseemly immodest and could backfire (Nye et al., 2008).

eBay, when it attempted to enter China, relied on the "clean" minimalistic design that customers had come to expect in the West. However, Chinese customers, who had been used to a "busier" interface with extensive pop-ups and information content tended to find this design boring and lacking in information to find the best bargains available (Clark, 2016).

Cultural values greatly influence choices, and advertising compatible with such values will likely be more successful. Singh and Pereira (2005) make suggestions based on Hofstede's cultural dimensions (Hofstede et al., 2002). They suggest, for example, including the "CEO's Vision Statement" in a site intended for a high power distance culture where, with a major emphasis on status and hierarchy, the thoughts of the CEO would be important in evaluating the credibility of the firm. Similarly, in a more "collectivistic" culture that focuses on group cohesiveness and rewards, greater emphasis can be put on photos and descriptions of group, as opposed to individual, activities, to better match the lifestyle of the culture. For countries high in uncertainty avoidance, emphasis can be placed on wide use of the product and satisfaction guarantees offered.

Search Engines

Search engines allow internet users to quickly access a great deal of information based on search terms specified. In much of the world, "google" has become a verb to describe an online search for information. As an increasing number of internet users across the world employ various methods to protect privacy, statistics of search activity and the impact of the different search engines become less reliable. However, although access to Google is mostly blocked in China, it is estimated to have an 87.1% share of the overall global search market, with a greater share in mobile device searches (Net Market Share, 2018; StatCounter GlobalStats, 2017). The Chinese search engine Baidu dominates the Chinese market with an estimated overall share of 81% (Armstrong 2016); however, its total share in the rest of the world is estimated to be less than one percent (StatCounter GlobalStats, 2017).

Modern search engines use **algorithms**, or complex collections of rules that come together to predict the results likely to be of greatest interest to the searcher. Each major search engine maintains its own proprietary algorithms. However, the links pointing to a site are generally by far the most important factor. As search engines came about in the late 1990s, their results were driven in large part by the presence of relevant keywords in the text of a web page. This arrangement, however, tended to result in a large number of false positives – pages that turned out not to be relevant – and false negatives – relevant pages that were missed because the keywords in question were not used as heavily as they were in other, less relevant sites. In addition, website operators could blatantly manipulate search engines by "spamming" or overloading their pages with popular keywords.

Although we refer broadly to languages such as English, Spanish, Portuguese, and Chinese, there are major differences in the ways in which these languages are spoken in different regions. In the Spanish language, for example, words that are perfectly innocuous in one region may take on off-color meanings in other areas. The HTML system allows website creators to include certain "tags" not visible to the reader in order to communicate information to search engines. For example, tags can be used to specify relevant key words and the title of a given page. Google allows website designers offering multiple languages to identify content appropriate for different regions using the "hreflang" attribute tag. Here, website designers can specify both an applicable language and a region of the world for which the content is intended. Based on the specifications in the "hreflang" tag, different pages may be rendered to viewers in the USA than those shown to the site in the UK and other countries where British spelling and language use are more common. In practice, however, the proper use of this tool appears to be poorly understood among website designers (Hunt, 2018). A 2017 study found that the majority of websites surveyed used this feature incorrectly. In addition to bringing searchers to the wrong website sections, such errors may also result in a reduced ranking of the site (Lebedeva, 2017).

Search engines guard their algorithms closely and release limited information about the specifics of rules involved. This is done both to protect their intellectual property from competing search engines and to prevent website designers from using insights to "game" the system, designing their sites for maximum ranking rather than for appropriate content. Because of this secrecy, information on the exact ways in which content across different languages on a site are integrated is lacking.

Some algorithms are language dependent; that is, they are likely to work better within some languages than within others. There is considerable variation in the way that languages are spoken in practice. In areas of the world where there is a strong premium on consensus building and face saving – such as China – languages are likely to be "high context" such that a great deal of background must be "read between the lines" of the literal message based on a social understanding that develops. As such, words may take on different meanings – and different degrees of specificity – depending on the context in which they are expressed. By contrast, in lower context languages, meanings of words tend to be less sensitive to the context (Southern, 2018).

Social Media

Social media come in a number of different forms. They have been developed only since the early 2000s. Generally, the idea is that users create and share their own content and possibly comment upon content created by others. In some fora, content from the outside may be shared through hyperlinks, while in other fora the types of content are more limited. For example, photo and video sharing sites mostly involve posting content that one has created and commenting on that posted by others.

Social media have tremendous potential to connect individuals across the world in fora such as reddit.com, particularly those who share specialized interests. For example, parents of children on the autism spectrum and others interested in this condition are often drawn to fora in which others can contribute. Content can readily be shared and re-shared, creating abundant opportunities for information to spread widely and rapidly. With the option to link to blogs, conventional media, and commercial sites, a great deal of content can be introduced. In turn, advertisers can target prospective customers within geographic areas of interest based on any combination of demographic information that readers have provided. Many bloggers and "YouTubers" create their content primarily for themselves and the ability to share with others. Many derive significant advertising revenue for their work. Advertising is increasingly based on the location of the viewer rather than that of the creator. Thus, a resident of the Netherlands may watch a Chinese language video on a Chinese site but be exposed to a Dutch language advertisement from a local advertiser. International brokers, such as Google, match advertisers who want to reach viewers in specific geographic regions, possibly integrating information about viewers' previous activity to enhance the fit (Exhibit 14.4). For example, for Procter & Gamble, which uses many different brand names across the world, it is important both that the customer targeted has demonstrated an interest in the product category *and* that he or she lives in a region where the brand name advertised is available.

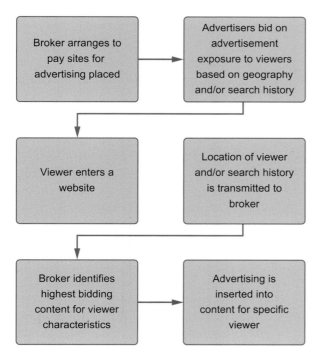

Exhibit 14.4 Brokering of advertising in online content

In recent years, a number of mainstream firms have faced the embarrassment of having their advertisements showing up on so-called "fake news" sites or sites featuring hate speech or other objectionable content. Coca-Cola Co., Procter & Gamble, Amazon.com Inc., and Microsoft Corp, all experienced problems with their ads, brokered through Google, showing up on sites promoting racial hatred (Bond et al., 2017). As a result, many have taken steps to control where their ads are placed.

Diffusion of Social Networks within and between Countries

A social networking platform may spread between certain countries but may fail to get much of a following in other countries. Because of censorship, for example, only members of certain elite groups in China are permitted access to Facebook. In Russia and surrounding countries, there appears to be a preference for local adaptations of Western social network platforms (Turban et al., 2018). One reason, discussed below, is the practice of some countries of actively blocking access to "objectionable" sites. Another problem is that as one platform gets a following in a country, others may have difficulty gaining the needed critical mass to take off.

Social media sites often encounter major "chicken-and-egg" problems. That is, for a platform to be a success, two outcomes must be achieved, each of which requires the other one to happen first. For example, you would likely find it unattractive to join a new social media site if your friends are not on it, but they will wait to join until you do. Occasionally, one platform may "unseat" another. MySpace.com had a wide following and was regarded as a powerful force during 2005 and 2009. However, its following started to drop significantly as Facebook gained traction.

The principle of *network economies* indicates that some innovations will be increasingly valuable as more people adopt it. If a social networking system with a critical mass has established itself in an area, new platforms seem unattractive. If only the founders of some of these platforms could arrange to merge their systems, they might, together, have a better shot at gaining traction.

We will now consider different types of social media and the opportunities associated with each. Exhibit 14.5 lists examples, characteristics, and international considerations for each type.

Blogs

In 1993, the European Organization for Nuclear Research (CERN), based in Geneva, Switzerland, released the HyperText Transfer Protocol (HTTP) for royalty-free use across the world as a means of generating online content (Isaacson, 2014). This represented a relatively easy and efficient opportunity to generate formatted

EXHIBIT 14.5 Popular social networking sites across the world

Type	Description	Example platforms	International considerations
Blogs	Fora in which one or more individuals add written and other content over type	blogspot.com (USA), blogspot.in (India), WordPress.com (USA, baidu.com (China), blog.sina.com.cn (China), blog.163.com (China),	For areas where internet access is mostly by phone, content should be small screen friendly
Video	Fora in which individuals can upload and comment on video material created with a cell phone or other cameras	youtube.com (USA, youko.com (China), qq.com (China), daum.net (Korea), zing.vn (Vietnam)	Limited bandwidth in some areas make sharing of high resolution video difficult; delays and interruptions may be considerable
Microblogs	Fora, usually with networks of friends or other connections, in which brief updates are shared, possible links to other content	facebook.com (USA), twitter.com (USA), weibo.com (China), wechat.com (China),	Access to Facebook, Twitter, and many other sites are blocked by certain countries
Photo sharing	Sites for sharing photos and/or other graphics	instagram.com (USA), t.qq.com (China)	Instagram is widely used across countries; users often hashtag in multiple languages
Review sites	Customer reviews of dining and other establishments	Yelp.com (USA), dianping.com (China)	Dependent on geographic databases for each location

pages that could be read by users accessing the Internet with a browser. By the late 1990s, this, in turn, led to the growth of blogs, or fora in which an individual could readily add content frequently.

A basic blog is much like the traditional diary, although it is intended to be read by others rather than being a secret venue for recording one's innermost feelings and thoughts. Blogs can be hosted either among various blogging services around the world or on one's own website, using a platform such as WordPress. Google's

Blogspot.com and WordPress.com host blogs from writers in much of the Western world. In China, platforms such as Sina Blog, Hui Xiu, and Zhizu.com are popular. The language of a blog and the location of its author are separate issues. A number of Chinese language websites are hosted on Blogspot, for example.

Motivations of influencers who create internet content differ significantly. As discussed earlier, some bloggers derive considerable income from advertising revenue. Fashion and beauty bloggers are seen creating content "in paid partnership" with brands featured. The US Federal Trade Commission has issued regulations that bloggers must disclose when they are being compensated by brands or other "partners." Since the content is being circulated worldwide, viewers in other countries will usually see these disclosures as well. As other countries and treaty organizations such as the European Union (EU) develop their own regulations, simultaneous compliance with disparate rules may complicate the dissemination of such sponsored social media content. Others may blog more for purposes of self-expression or based on a genuine desire to help others or to achieve true control and direction of their materials. Some like to share their obsessions. Ruth Crilly, described by Marie Claire (2017) as "fashion-model-turned-blogger," created the site "A Model Recommends" (www.amodelrecommends.com/) "to share an insight into the life of a model and give everyone access to the same tips and pro techniques that she enjoys on set."

Many blogs written by people across the world are written in English even if that is not the author's primary language. This is especially the case for fashion blogs. Some contain both writing in the writer's native language along with a complete or partial English language translation. Others are written entirely in an international language, although the name of the blog, by tradition, is often in English.

Writing in different languages may entail various amounts of effort. Today, touch typing is generally part of the primary or secondary school curriculum in countries whose language is based on the Latin alphabet. Things are often more complicated for speakers of languages such as Chinese and Japanese, whose writing is done with pictograms, or images that represent phrases or concepts. For each individual word, the writer will typically type in a phonetic spelling and will then select the appropriate character from a menu of options. This can make the process of writing lengthy passages quite tedious.

Despite the difficulties in writing content in some languages, a great amount is, nevertheless, created. In Japan, entire novels known as *kaitai* are written on mobile phones using the phonetic pulldown approach. With such abundant content available to readers in their preferred language, firms need to monitor, learn from, and possibly respond to content in multiple languages. This is particularly the case when customers from around the world send in comments or questions.

Top bloggers frequently develop a considerable following – often across countries – and can have a considerable impact as opinion leaders. It is helpful for firms to set up Google Search alerts to receive a notification when one's brand is mentioned in the blogosphere. Bloggers who have given favorable reviews can be sent samples of new products and can be given early alerts to forthcoming offerings. Some bloggers tend to focus primarily on their own language, while others either blog entirely in English, provide an English language translation for the material they provide, or make use of existing translation software. Fashion bloggers, in particular, often try to get a global following by blogging in English – some with better results than others.

Microblogs, Video, and Other Media Sharing Sites

Twitter was originally intended as a forum for expressing concise messages on a "no frills" page emphasizing text. Today, however, the distinction between **microblogs** and photo sharing sites has blurred considerably. Facebook supports links to external content and the inclusion of photos and other illustrations. In addition, **photo sharing sites** such as Instagram provide the option for both extended descriptions and the use of hashtags (e.g., #selfie, #fashionista, #uggs, or #globetrotter). Those writing in foreign languages will often employ a combination of native language and English language tags, some overlapping and others emphasizing different ideas. The extensive use of hashtags allows a user to be discovered and "followed" by others across the world. The US President Donald Trump became a heavy user of Twitter communication, which allowed him to be in touch directly with the global population. This connectivity in turn has given a significant boost to the use of media sharing sites.

Some platforms – such as Instagram and the Chinese sites *Huaban* (huaban.com) and Duitang (www.duitang.com) – are intended primarily to share links to content external content from other sites. Platforms such as Instagram and the Chinese site *Youmeitu* (www.youmeitu.com) emphasize user generated photos, graphics, and videos. *Zhipin* (www.zhipin.com) features user generated photos with a section dedicated to the promotion of the online stores of Chinese designers and independent fashion labels.

Users of photo sharing sites can gain large followings, especially if they use hashtags extensively so that their material will appear in search results. When the user allows for this, his or her popular photos may be "reposted" by others, causing some to "go viral." Some will use a combination of photo sharing and video sharing, where they use the latter for more elaborate updates and product reviews.

YouTube is the dominant forum for user generated video in the Western world. Firms can post user guides, product information, and promotional materials to reach customers and interested parties. Individuals who develop a sufficient

Exhibit 14.6 YouTube, Twitch, and eSports personality Richard Tyler Blevins, better known as Ninja, has gained an important following and reportedly earned over $20 million through subscriptions and advertising

Credit: Amy Lemus/NurPhoto via Getty Images.

following can share in advertising revenues, sometimes deriving considerable income from this source (Exhibit 14.6).

The American Logan Paul was one of several social media influencers featured on a 2016 episode of the American CBS magazine show *60 Minutes.* He creates a number of brief and largely unrehearsed "slapstick" video segments in which firms pay heavily to be featured. As he was followed by the TV crew on Hollywood Boulevard in California, he was approached by fans from France, Kuwait, Israel, Sweden, and Mongolia.

In China, the video sharing market is somewhat fragmented, with about ten major players (Euromonitor International, 2018b). Some of these sites feature blatantly pirated content from abroad while others are dedicated to individual video sharing or locally generated content. Opinion leaders on sites such as *Soku* (www .soku.com) can gain sizable followings and are often wooed by brands eager for exposure.

TikTok focuses on very brief video clips and has gained a considerable following, both among viewers and posters. In an attempt to attract users from across the world, TikTok maintains active offices in cities across the world, including Los Angeles, New York, London, Paris, Berlin, Dubai, Mumbai, Singapore, Jakarta,

Seoul, and Tokyo. Getting an idea or message across within a few seconds presents major creative challenges. In some cases, such briefly expressed ideas may be better understood across cultures. In other cases, the symbols expressed may be culture specific and lack additional context that could aid understanding in different settings. For example, a brief scene can play on the American stereotype that police officers eat doughnuts and not be understood in settings where there is not at least a close analogue.

A number of specialty social media platforms exist. In China, it is estimated that matchmaking networks – intended to lead to eventual marriage – account for some 30% of total social media revenue as family pressures mount on both single women and men to find a spouse (IBISWorld, 2018). WeChat – owned by the Chinese firm Tencent – specializes in chatting and informal money transfers between friends. Other platforms emphasize professional networking.

Censorship

Internet **censorship** comes in two forms. China, Russian, Egypt, Iran, and Cuba, are among countries that use "firewalls" to automatically block selected foreign and domestic sites so that these cannot generally be accessed within the country. In other cases, countries impose laws on the types of material that may (not) be posted online. Although it can be difficult for a government to prevent a resident of another country from posting such material, its own citizens can be prosecuted for participating in – or merely accessing – sites deemed objectionable (Dou, 2017; Jacobson, 2017; Malsin, 2018).

When we think of censorship, the image that comes to mind is usually that of a government that wants to suppress political dissent or embarrassing information about its leaders' opulent lifestyles. In reality, censorship goes much beyond this. Chinese censors, for example, have been known to block access to the US magazine *Parenting*, a publication about a topic not normally considered political per se. On closer inspection, however, it is readily apparent that such a periodical is likely to contain many "subversive" ideas about raising children to be independent and critical thinkers who question existing rules, institutions, values, and authority in general. Some content may be disfavored simply as being too "frivolous" or for offending officials' sensibilities. For example, Chinese movie censors have only recently begun to allow "monster" movies.

The Internet has been credited with facilitating reform in many authoritarian countries. In 2010, for example, established regimes were greatly weakened in Tunisia and throughout North Africa during the so-called Arab Spring. However, although technological advances facilitate certain types of communications among citizens, advances in technology also provide opportunities for increasingly effective and onerous censorship. In 2005, Chinese sensors blocked dissident Isaac

Mao's blog on isaacmao.com. However, he was able to evade censors by simply relaunching at notisaacmao.com. Today, technology allows censors to spot and block such moves with little delay.

There are various ways to access "banned" content. One is to use a **Virtual Private Network (VPN)**. These were created to enhance the security of internet communication. They use a remote server to encrypt information transmitted through the Internet. With the high value placed on free speech in the USA, controversy has arisen as technology developed by US companies appears to be used in firewalls (Malsin, 2018).

Countries divide approaches and motivations for censorship into three categories: imposition of traditional values, maintenance of political stability, and national security. Some countries are motivated by all three while some are motivated by different combinations of two.

In addition to direct censorship, authoritarian states have other high-tech tools available to subvert open communication online. It is possible to "throttle" – or slow down – traffic to and from objectionable websites to reduce their appeal. "Bots," automated social media accounts run by algorithms, and "trolls," real users who initiate online conflicts, can automatically generate massive amounts of content to counter and/or obscure dialogue between actual people (Premium Official News, 2018).

All countries limit expression to some extent. Bans on the deliberate misrepresentation of facts in order to perpetrate fraud are generally seen as an unavoidable measure to maintain a functional economy. Beyond that, views of what constitutes censorship vary between cultures, often on the basis of deeply held values. Historically, in the USA, the philosophy has generally been, as the late Supreme Court Justice Louis Brandeis put it, that "The remedy [for bad speech] ... is more speech" that can set the record straight. As a result, it would seem highly improper to limit expressions of opinions, and generally, with the exceptions of slander, libel, or fraud, prior restraint is considered unacceptable. Some countries make it illegal to deny that the Nazi Holocaust occurred – fearing the distress that such claims can cause to survivors and their descendants and the potential that such information could spur the growth of dangerous groups threatening democracy. The American view has tended to be that such ideas are best dispelled by other communication demonstrating inaccurate and deceptive nature.

Policy makers in the European Union (EU) have tended to see a "right to be forgotten" as a fundamental human right more important than the unrestrained dissemination of true information. That is, there is a feeling that negative things that an individual may have done or said in the past should not be readily available for others to find, especially not years after the fact. As a result, search engines are required, upon request, to evaluate if certain URLs deemed to be in violation of an individual's "right to privacy" should be suppressed from search results. Historically, the suppression requirement has only been applied to the search engine versions available in the EU. Pressure is now being placed on search engines to impose such suppression worldwide.

Sentiment Analysis

Sentiment involves computer analysis of social media content (Liu, 2015). This term refers to the idea that a person's overall feelings, or sentiment toward some brand or other object of interest, can be distilled from his or her online writings. That is, using artificial intelligence, computer algorithms can be used to "read" and understand human language, in turn allowing for classification of social media content. Although firms around the world are working on this technology, most of the known work appears to have been done on English language content. Because of the rapid development of this field and extensive technology involved, work on sentiment analysis tends to be heavily proprietary, and industry work generally runs ahead of academia. Although firms must strike a balance between the need to impress customers with the capability of their technology and the desire to keep competitors from knowing what they are currently developing.

The analysis can be based on a variety of content. Currently, words, phrases, and hashtags can be assessed. Some of the technology involves algorithms that interpret content. In its most basic form, such analysis focuses on whether the sentiment expressed is likely to be positive or negative, or the statistical extent to which a concept (such as a brand) is associated with other concepts. Content containing a brand with a large number of hashtags can be particularly useful in identifying common associations. In more advanced work, artificial intelligence is used to gain a deeper understanding of the thoughts expressed and the reasoning behind such outlook and opinions. This can be especially useful to gauge the impact of current events and can serve as an "early warning" when tastes, opinions, and values are undergoing change. Future advances may allow for the interpretation and analysis of photos and other media.

The need for sentiment analysis is especially critical in emerging markets, where less is known – at least by foreign firms – and more is at stake as large numbers of consumers are forming their brand preferences. Adapting English language-based research for such work can be tricky for a number of reasons. Languages differ in their structure. New slang terms and words come about over time. Some languages heavily emphasize euphemisms, and figures of speech tend to be language specific. In addition, problems of identifying irony and sarcasm, which are often expressed through subtleties and indirection, can be significant (Liu 2015).

SUMMARY

The Internet and other digital tools allow organizations to reach customers and other individuals with increasing speed and more complex content. Since the takeoff of the "information superhighway" in the mid-1990s, an increasing number of people across the world have access to the Internet, with a growing number of consumers now shopping and communicating online. Although the growth of electronic commerce has been greatly influenced by technological advances, cultural, legal, economic, and infrastructure differences have brought about differing experiences across world regions, and communications approaches must be adjusted based on the region of interest. Because of the wide availability of information released in different parts of the world, greater efforts in coordination are required to assess the impact of content that may be accessed in areas other than those for which it was intended.

DISCUSSION QUESTIONS

1. What are some developments in internet use, e-commerce, and social media currently in the news?
2. Favorable social media coverage is considered much more credible by consumers than advertising. However, social media is also a way for unfavorable views of a company and its practices to spread, potentially across borders. What can firms do to address such risks?
3. If Apple were to pursue lower priced phones for developing countries, what might be possible repercussions from individuals and social media?

KEY TERMS

algorithms	407	microblogs	413
blogs	411	phishing	399
censorship	415	photo sharing sites	413
cyberwarfare	397	sentiment	417
domain name suffixes	394	social media	408
electronic commerce	400	virtual private network (VPNs)	416
firewalls	415	website cultural customization	405
leap frogging	396		

TAKE A STAND

In the USA, the right to free speech has historically been deeply valued, and with very limited exceptions, other considerations – such as the negative social impact that some speech may have – have generally had to yield. Within European Union countries, however, the "right to be forgotten" is viewed as an inherent civil right. As a result, EU governments have forced Google to set up a process where individuals can ask to have links to certain types of negative information about them deleted from search results shown in Europe.

Questions for Debate

1. Which values are, ultimately, most important?
2. Should search engine firms whose values emphasize free speech challenge laws requiring them to suppress information?

INTERNET EXERCISES

1. Using Google Translate to search on Instagram, Baidu, or Google Images, what are some of the differences that you see in the way that different products are being depicted and discussed? In what context is the product used – for example, individually or as part of a group? Does it reflect cultural values, status, and/or relationships between people?
2. IKEA's main website, www.ikea.com/, provides a gateway to sites designed for a number of different countries. Selecting a few country sites, what are some differences you see? What may be some possible explanations for these differences?

FURTHER RESOURCES

Bartlett, J. (2016). *Cypherpunks write code. (BOOK EXCEPT)(Dark Net: Inside the Digital Underworld)(Excerpt).* 104(2), 120–123. https://doi.org/10.1511/2016.119.120

Brock, D. and Moore, G. (2006). Understanding Moore's law: four decades of innovation. Philadelphia, Pa: Chemical Heritage Foundation.

Clark, D. (2016). Alibaba: the house that Jack Ma built. New York: Ecco, an imprint of HarperCollins Publishers.

Erisman, P. (2017). *Six billion shoppers: the companies winning the global e-commerce boom* (First US edition.). New York, NY: St. Martin's Press.

15 International Business: the Soul and the Future

LEARNING OBJECTIVES

- To outline the risk and exposure of firms operating in the global marketplace
- To consider responsibilities for the soul of the international firm
- To learn about the obligations that support a firm in its planning for curative marketing
- To help analyze current and future prospects for international business employment

CONTENTS

VIGNETTE 15 Global firms need a soul

In a time when so many people and so much of society are exclusively engaged in so-called practical pursuits of advancing in the world, knowing the latest fads and trends, and pursuing the gods of wealth and technology, we need to take a step back. Let us ask, as Blessed Pope Paul VI and Pope Emeritus Benedict XVI did in their encyclical letters *Populorum Progressio* (1967) and *Caritas in Veritate* (2009), what makes for real development and progress? Is it simply having more wealth and technology? Or should we not adhere to what Pope Paul VI called a "full-bodied humanism" that "will enable our contemporaries to enjoy the higher values of love and friendship, of prayer and contemplation, and thus find themselves." Should business and politics not have a higher calling than merely gaining more wealth or satisfying more desires? Can we not, as Pope Emeritus Benedict advised, make such things as love, friendship, beauty, and the call to immortality, the overriding "principle not only of micro-relationships (with friends, with family members, or within small groups) but also of macro-relationships (social, economic, and political ones)." Can business and politics not have a soul?

This is the pressing question. How can the focus on personal success prevalent in capitalism be synthesized with care for the greater society? We can learn from the performance of body and soul, not only by understanding what was done before us but also by appreciating the changes that do and will occur. International business reaches every corner of our world today and affects the souls of individuals, firms, and societies. In our global community, in many ways, we often miss out on commonality. Independent thought should reflect the presence and absence of a good. This reminds of the Bavarian beer and Brez'n experience where visitors fearlessly occupy any free seat around the table and accept the existence of joint intentions. The value of international business comes from the desire of people to experience and appreciate the differences between cultures. The need for and acceptance of the soul gives us a common path and provides a joint perspective underpinned by a broadly supported objective.

Source: Czinkota and Horkan, 2019.

Introduction

When the long-standing rivalry between socialism and market orientation was resolved, market forces and the recognition of demand and supply directly affected human rights and the extent of **freedom**. With all humility and gratefulness, we can conclude: Markets were right! In country after country, market forces have demonstrated typically greater efficiency and effectiveness in their ability to satisfy the needs of people. International business has been instrumental in stimulating these newly emerging market forces. In spite of complaints about the slowness of change, biases in wealth distribution, and the inequities inherent in societal upheavals, a large majority of participants in market-oriented conditions are now better off than they were before. Without the transition provided by international business, these changes would not have come about that swiftly and efficiently. Moreover, international business provides the opportunity to acquire resources without the deployment of force. Why fight if you can trade? Countries that have been historic enemies such as France, England, and Germany are now all united in collaboration through international business. The field is, therefore, at the very least contributing to freedom from war while providing additional choices and freedom for consumption. The focus and aim of international business is on crossing borders. International business does so in all corners of the globe, in the glamorous ones as well as in the small and remote ones where others do not see the efforts. By operating both in the limelight and well outside of it, international business offers the freedom to exercise virtue to both the seller and the buyer – be it in decisions of supplying or purchasing, pricing or selecting.

Globalization

The term "Soul of Globalization" became alive at the Fez Festival of Music in 2001 with inspiration from an anthropologist and a Sufism scholar Faouzi Skali with a diverse group of participants with vastly different voices and multi-cultural characteristics. One of the remarkable feature of the event were points raised by French journalist Pierre Barrat about the need for bridges that link civil society with international institutions such as the World Bank. Highlights were also considerations of global inequality, risk, and the need for a homogeneous culture that is tolerant and promotes education.

A report by Boston Consulting Group claimed that globalization is evolving based on a combination of economic nationalism that uses digital integration and more broad based consumer behavior (Battacharya et al., 2018). In previous models, each national entity marketed a range of different products and services. These targeted different customer segments, utilizing different strategies with little or no coordination of operations between countries. As national markets become increasingly similar and implementation of scale for economies grew in importance, there was also a rise in inefficiencies due to non-standardization of product and program development. Simultaneously, the lack of control by executives over the number of customers and competitors operating globally throughout the major markets called for stronger coordination and integration of strategies. This chapter will discuss the soul of business, combined with key considerations about the business and the encouragement of curative marketing implementation. Suggestions will also be offered about employment alternatives and opportunities, and the ways to prepare for them.

The Soul of Business

Globalization has resulted in economic prosperity for many countries and modern lifestyle for people across the world. Switzerland was nominated by Bertelsmann Stiftung (Weiß, 2018) in the Globalization Index as the champion country that gained maximum benefits in terms of per capita income, followed by Japan and Finland. Today, globalization refers to a business orientation based on the belief that the world is becoming more homogeneous and that distinctions between national markets may eventually even disappear. Companies need to formulate their international strategies across markets rather than within. Ongoing exchange of knowledge is likely to increase the efficiency and effectiveness of trade and investment across national borders.

Nowadays, one discusses and often reevaluates the meaning and adjustment of key traditional business pillars such as risk, competition, profit, and ownership. These business pillars are insufficient for the modern age. Many of today's business executives gradually discover that their activities are but one component of society. Emotional subcomponents such as politics, security, and religion are only some of the other dimensions that, historically, society at large holds in higher esteem than economics and business. Those who act and argue based on business principles alone may increasingly find themselves ignored because the soul and innovation often inspire new business perspectives.

Furthermore, the old pillars need refurbishing, placing a seat on top to give the customer his rightful priority. The concept of the soul of business recognizes the load-bearing columns of truthfulness, simplicity, participation, and responsibility, which managers need to incorporate into their business practices for a shining performance. Crucial is competitiveness based on quality, value, and ethics with a strong financial bottom-line. There is newly emerging attention to the issue of whether market activities alone are sufficient to ensure individual happiness. Companies cannot just reuse old approaches but must respond to changing societal requirements. Innovative and comprehensive responses to requirements in products, packaging, pricing, distribution, and promotion are necessary.

But how to instill these new columns into business operations? One solution is to promote mindfulness in corporate life. It is easy to lose sight of what is important, when spending each day laboring in an office far from the impacts of one's work. The same mindfulness also needs to be considered under conditions of work-from-home offices. One can also specifically focus on how to bring the soul back into the business curriculum. For this, we can look to the tenets of the

Jesuits, whose vigorous promotion of honor and service deserves our praise and emulation. If businesses are to thrive in this era, they must rediscover their soul. We need companies like the old GM – a car company of car people. Passion and commitment to excellence is the soul of business, and just as the body dies without its soul, so does business.

However, it is important to note that recessions are not seen as a signal of decline on the world stage but rather as an opportunity to move forward in new directions with new determination, and in pursuit of different rules. For example, if one demands that government provides great protection from competition, then we have to be willing to give up a certain amount of privacy and price flexibility. The acknowledgment of the soul helps to delineate interactions and limitations.

The new and crucial joint responsibility of humanity, business, and faith can and should be used to humanize behavior, expectations, and cultivation. Religious connectivity with commerce has had an important role for ages. There is, for example, the ejection of the money changers from the synagogue by Jesus and the creation of the honorable merchant, developed by the German Hanse Trading Group in the 13th century (Czinkota, 2019a). However, society often describes business as soulless, and the growing application of technology and artificial intelligence might even further distance business from the soul.

Thus, the integration of the soul with international business is increasingly pressing. (Szabó, 2019). Companies focus too much on hedging risks, ousting their competitors, maximizing profits, and expanding assets, and they forget the cardinal rule of human decency and reverence for others. Business without soul takes on a sinister character, which charges exorbitant rates for on-flight pillows or hotel minibar snacks. Business is meant to create value, for itself and the customer, not leach off resources unreasonably.

Trade can also be a tool to deal with crises. From refugee flows and spy wars, to the macro conflict of global terrorism, all affect and should be affected by the soul. Corporations are increasingly expected to play a stronger role as a collaborator with government and society in finding solutions to often-unforeseen future challenges. Winner-takes-all competition begins to give way to a strategy based on global collaboration. Money is no longer the only or ultimate outcome of business efforts. Self-sufficient, societally supportive, and leading is how many business executives like to see themselves. Yet their activities are only one slice of a floating sphere formed by a score of other components integral to society. But wealth seems to have won out. Concurrently, technology and artificial intelligence may contribute to further alienate business from the soul. Two fatal crashes involving Boeing 737 Max 8 planes have faltered public confidence in the aviation giant. Volkswagen's Teutonic attraction to honesty was deflected by its cheating on the emissions of diesel engines. Church child abuse scandals reveal a faith's failure to organize and govern human behavior. All these cases weaken the public and private perception of business and society, without leadership or respect.

Since the 1990s, government again has begun to play a growing role in business. New global regulations and restrictions have emerged because markets are not always successful with self-regulation. Today, the traditional role and effectiveness of the World Trade Organization are challenged. Multilateral agreements appear to be at a standstill or even in retrenchment. At the same time, the Trump administration's deregulation brought confidence to the US domestic economy. A 2018 survey by the National Association of Manufacturers showed that more than 92 percent of respondents maintained a positive outlook for their firms. Nearly a half-million new manufacturing jobs were created within two years. However, the reach of the Coronavirus annulled many such gains and confronted all players in the economy with new thinking and requirements to learn (Exhibit 15.1).

EXHIBIT 15.1 Risk of COVID-19 indicates important learning opportunities

The coronavirus has been the firing pin for major innovations. In many educational institutions, less than half of the customary study time is invested in the 2020 academic spring semester. There is some distance learning, but in many instances, the faculty is very much dependent on technology that they learn from students rather than the traditional reverse flow. Just consider that traditionally, the entire sector has not distinguished itself with high-speed change. In the university sector, if one could implement time travel for professors and their students, they could be safely delivered to a university town and be rapidly functional in their work. There still remains the amphitheater seating of chairs. There is the black or white board to communicate information. There is the professor upfront moving from one side of the room to the other, while students take notes or raise their hand indicating readiness for comment.

Any changes to this model require approval by at least four faculty committees, each one of which needs substantial time to investigate the potential repercussions of alterations. Then there are reviews by board members, insights from administrators, and the "Fingerspitzengefuehl" of financial liaison. Woe the planner of change who is likely to encounter a lead time of what seems like forever. The bottom line: change for education is very difficult and hard to achieve.

How has the education system performed under virus conditions? We can attribute to it, very high degrees of rapidity, focus, transparency, and adaptation which have led to significant changes. Students, by the tens of thousands, are have shifted their main residence within a week. Faculty members have at the same time solidified new course materials and given major thought to content delivery under entirely new conditions. Administrators have had to rapidly find ways to work with the complaining, and even incensed, students and parents.

Long-term contemplations must now be considered and decided on with a new kind of time framework – we suggest 10 days for adaption of innovation. A textbook which was developed over 40 years now needs a revision time measured in weeks. The virus has given us a way to cope with complexity using extraordinary speed. There are now innovations which are finally accepted and which pump new energy and strength into the body politic. The best infusion is yet to come. The post-viral times will not necessarily be convenient or tranquil, but there may be many more opportunities for innovation and creativity. Sometimes it takes a large hurdle to overcome obstacles, but focus and collaboration achieve much progress. This may be a time for a new jointness of purpose.

Source: Czinkota, 2020.

Mutual (Inter)dependence

When a business transaction takes place, there is often joy associated with receiving the goods or services requested. Therefore, we are better off after the transaction than before, which is of course why we engage in the relationship at all. The same tends to apply to the other party, where typically money is received. We can conclude that both seller and buyer feel better off than before.

By obtaining goods from others, we have also learned about the dependence which a transaction can precipitate. For example, during the COVID-19 epidemic, countries had to find out that they did not have sufficient capability or capacity to produce highly necessary products. Orders had to be placed abroad, and customers sometimes found that, in the priority of things, their distance from the market led to slower servicing. Without knowledge, such conditions highlighted that without tracking or focus it can be easy to expose oneself to dependent conditions. A few pennies saved may result in growing exposure to dependence.

Kenichi Ohmae, an economic theorist from Japan, identified a segment of consumers emerging in the triad of North America, Europe, and the Far East. These consumers had similar educational backgrounds, income levels, lifestyles, use of leisure time, and aspirations. One reason given for the similarities was a high level of purchasing power and higher diffusion rates for certain products. They also share a developed infrastructure, such as diffusion of telecommunication and common platforms such as Microsoft Windows and the Internet. The similarity of these consumer segments across the globe sets a strong example for the potential satisfaction that interdependence between nations can give.

As transactions continue, one experiences limitations to one's course of action. For example, in the short term it might be desirable to cut off a trading partner from one's goods, in order to minimize dependence. However, frequently one discovers that such dependence is not a one-way street. Rather it is likely to be a condition of interdependence. While one can take business away from a partner, the same party in reciprocity can take business away as well. What may have been a long-term positive business relationship can quickly become a disappointing non-relationship. A true experience of interdependence.

Freedom

Interdependence represents a crucial link for increased market freedom. What does freedom have to do with international business? Freedom is about options. If there is no alternative, there is no freedom. A true alternative provides the opportunity to make a decision, to exercise virtue. In the blaze of the Klieg lights, it is easy to make the "right" decision. That is not an exercise in virtue, because real alternatives are effectively removed. The true selection among alternatives takes place in the darkness of night when nobody is looking. In reciprocal causality, freedom both causes and facilitates international business, while international business itself is a key support of freedom's cause. The focus and aim of international business is on crossing borders, with the goal of providing more choice for consumers and letting them be the ones to maximize their satisfaction. International business does so in all corners of the globe, in the glamorous ones as well as in the small and remote ones. When the long-standing rivalry between socialism and market economy came to an end, market forces directly improved human rights and the extent of freedom. Exchanges through markets have clearly demonstrated a greater ability to satisfy the needs of people. Now they must demonstrate their ability to persist through continuity and balance (Czinkota & Ronkainen, 2003).

One key dimension of freedom is to allow people outside of the box. National borders are where business, government, and people usually find their frontier. The idea of freedom wants to know no international boundaries. It thrives on how to successfully cross national borders, on coping with local differences once the crossing is done, and on profitably reconciling any conflicts. Domestic borders limit economic expansion, while international approaches contain the freedom of wide opportunities.

Trust

Trust is a valuable corporate asset since it typically translates into fulfilled expectations, which allow for better forecasts, less uncertainty in the future, and more realism. **Trust bridges**, developed by shared expectations and experiences, allow people to get to know each other quicker, and help establish fair business practices on global terms. Connections that bring people together and lead to greater trust can be built upon a shared alma mater, military service, same work experience, sports fans for the same team, and even practicing the same religion. People are more likely to bond over these personal preferences and organizations because they already share a similar interest; therefore, they expect to share similar values.

If two companies operate in similar environments and share values, they are more likely to connect and establish warm and trusting relationships. This ultimately establishes credibility and allows business to select patterns based on trust rather than strictly on proximity or financial measures. Trust is developed through interaction, although there are other spillover effects that come into play. An example would be where two organizations that are led by former sports champions might be more likely to trust each other, particularly when it comes to sports. This may also connote, but does not necessarily require, trust in financial matters. It is important to note that trust is an extension of confidence, so high expectations often accompany trust. One such trust-enhancing activity is especially present in the German model for developing trust, which, due to its reliance on standardized training and internships, focuses on keeping processes flowing on account of having confidence in and reliance on others' work. In contrast, less training in the USA often leads to a lack of trust and little confidence in work. Therefore, trust bridges may not be as visible in the American corporate world.

Curative Marketing

Curative international marketing, in the sense of restoring and developing international economic health, may be the next business direction. "Restoring" indicates something lost which once was there. "Developing" refers to new issues to be addressed with new tools and frames of reference. "Health" in turn positions the issue as important to overall welfare, which marketing needs to address, resolve, and improve. Managers must deliver joy, pleasure, fulfillment, safety, personal growth, and achieve advancement towards a better society, and do so across borders.

Curative marketing's two perspectives consist of looking back for what marketing has wrought and making up for errors with future action. Global problems benefit from a global approach. Curative international marketing needs to draw on jurisprudence, cultural anthropology, philosophy, and history to assemble the power for change. One wonders about the validity of international business being too important to be left to managers, consonant with Keynes questioning "how and whether economics should rule the world" (Czinkota, 2016).

At the business level growth is not just important, but the key issue for survival. Executives planning to merely maintain market share, or to minimize growth, would last a very short time in their job. More is expected. "Citius, altius, fortius" (faster, higher, stronger) may be a great motto for the Olympics, but leads to unexpected repercussions for managers and their customers.

International managers need to focus on past errors and mistakes inflicted by their discipline and sweep these out from under the carpet in the spirit of "Wiedergutmachung" or restitution for imposed wrongful actions. Management's disregard of local idiosyncrasies has sometimes been like bringing snakes to Guam, which almost exterminated all local birds. Examples of heavy held burdens inflicted by outsiders were the smallpox, flu, and typhus viruses introduced by the conquistadores to the Incas of Peru.

Negative effects may result from the misleading of consumers, or simply from unawareness or neglect. This is one key reason for the emergence of the concept of curative marketing, which accepts responsibility for particularly international problems that business has caused. It then uses marketing's capabilities to set things right even for the long term and works to increase the well-being of the individual and society on a global level. Curative marketing provides the concept and context for making conditions better than they are. For new ventures, it is the obligation of international managers to understand local conditions and to anticipate and limit possible ill effects. Managers must avoid causing short or long term harm and make restitution for any past damages. Not everything that can be done should be done. Marketing ought to have its own Hippocratic Oath: "First do no harm" should guide to help make people be better off and actually feel better. See Exhibit 15.2 for an example of curative marketing.

EXHIBIT 15.2 Georgetown University exercises curative marketing

© Michael R. Czinkota

An example is the efforts by Georgetown University to seek forgiveness and make good for its selling of slaves more than 200 years ago – even though doing so had a major survival effect on the continuing viability of the institution. The descendants of the victims, as far as identified, have now been provided with enhanced access to higher education and help with their social progress. In 2019, Georgetown undergraduates, in a historic vote, approved to pay $27.20 each semester to create a fund for the descendants of the 272 slaves that were sold in 1838 (Jonnalagadda, 2019). The vote passed at 66.1%, a much higher voter turnout than in previous years for a student referendum. Lee Baker, a descendant of the 272 slaves, stated that "Regardless of what happens, we will know that Georgetown University students practiced solidarity and decided to ensure that such a historic injustice has a permanent lens for awareness, analysis and action" (Jonnalagadda, 2019). Georgetown will continue to grapple with its difficult legacy of slavery, according to Richard Cellini (COL '84, LAW '87), who is the founder of the Georgetown Memory Project, an independent nonprofit that has located 8,298 direct descendants of the GU272 since 2015 (Jonnalagadda, 2019). Georgetown is the first in the country to establish a reconciliation fund, even though many other prestigious universities also have slavery in their past.

Source: Czinkota, 2019b; Jonnalagadda, 2019.

Curative marketing can help understanding, propel interaction, and overcome past shortcomings. China, for example, tries to heal past wounds in areas such as food safety, environmental protection, and medical security. It may well be that, with growing attribution of self-responsibility, companies can use curative marketing as their set-aside for competitiveness in international business. It is not just the big things which make a difference!

Future Dimensions

By studying this book, you have learned about the intricacies, complexities, and thrills of international business. Of course, a career in international business is more than jet-set travel between New Delhi, Tokyo, Frankfurt, and New York. It is hard work and requires knowledge and expertise. Yet, in spite of the difficulties, international business expertise may well become a key ingredient for corporate advancement. Preparing for such expertise is, however, not easy.

Today, for their students studying overseas, universities are developing contingency plans with planned responses for crises ranging from the outbreak of war to students being taken hostage. Many emergency response strategies include a complete extraction plan should all students studying abroad need to be brought back to the home campus. Also common are pre-departure orientation programs where students are informed about risky conditions abroad and how those risks vary from site to site. The total disruption of transportation and logistics during the Coronavirus outbreak of 2020 demonstrated how important it is to prepare for significant alterations in customary activities.

Businesses will shift from western-dominated management approaches to more inclusive and integrated ones that include Asian cultural elements. Perhaps rule-based firms can add more "family feeling" and relation-based dimension to their organizational culture in order to provide more unity in far-flung global organizations. There will be an increased value placed on charismatic leadership to unify global companies behind a strategic vision. Firms with a charismatic leader – someone who has the ability to earn trust, who has good interpersonal skills, who is good at cultivating relationships, and who is generous in his or her treatment of loyal friends and employees – may have a competitive advantage. On the micro level, however, ongoing culture clashes will continue, often giving a boost to fundamentalism. In many regions of the world, different cultural groups will grow their contacts as immigration increases. For example, it will be a new experience for many white English-speaking Americans to be exposed to large groups of Latinos. Similarly, "western" Europeans will become exposed to the influx and major competition from what used to be communist neighbors. A 2008 survey in South Korea found that 42 percent of the population had never spoken to a foreigner (Sang-Hun, 2009).

All these moves will change cultures. Culture is the result of learned behavior and adjustment to new conditions. Opening up to others on a such a gigantic scale, as the world has done within a relatively short time, will bring some individual xenophobia, but also the reward of growing flexibility, better understanding, and rising tolerance levels. Mobility may well create a new generation of innovators and risk takers. Already, innovators like Elon Musk or Google's engineers are changing the methods of mobility. Electric vehicles and self-driving cars are becoming more and more prevalent, so it is important to consider both mobility patterns and the means of mobility.

Given the importance of families in making expatriate decisions, some employers are offering new types of foreign postings. More people are being sent on short-term "commuter" assignments, where they do not need to uproot their families. The commuting trend is particularly common in Europe: a banker from Vienna, Austria, for instance, may spend Monday to Friday working in Dresden, Germany, and then fly home for the weekend. In some cases, where the locations are not too far from each other, a daily commute may be feasible. Technology has allowed companies to take unique advantage of strengths that are present in different parts of the world.

Businesses in search of economic vitality look to Asia and other developing regions for growth. Market economies like China and India will continue to increase their influence on the world. Economic power will shift globally to Asia, in terms of investment, output, and the integration of Eastern business practices. Asian players will have a major role, but they will pursue differentiated paths. China will continue to be the player to watch. Success in China will be the crucial indicator of global competitiveness. "If you can make it there, you can make it anywhere" will be the guiding anthem for businesses seeking global competitive advantage. Chinese firms themselves will become more aggressive in pursuit of global ambitions. The challenge for Chinese firms will be in adapting business strategies to become more consumer-driven with greater branding power.

India will continue to be the other major player. In its efforts to rival China for rapid growth, India will look for competitive advantage in services and technology.

As India reduces its barriers to trade and investment, companies are likely to see it both as a primary place for process outsourcing and as an important market for goods. The country's linkages in the communications and information sectors are likely to soar. With an enduring democratic tradition, close alignment with the rule of law, and widespread facility with the English language, India will be a must for marketers. Understanding how to bridge the divide between the growing class of affluent urban Indians and the lagging bulk of the population in rural markets will be a challenge to new market entrants.

The global services economy will be a knowledge-based economy and its most precious resource will be information and ideas. Unlike the classical factors of production – land, labor, and capital – information and knowledge are not bound to any region or country but are almost infinitely mobile and infinitely capable of expansion. International business has made important contributions to this transition process. Trade and investment have offered the populace in these nations a new perspective, new choices, new jobs, and new alternatives for marketing their products and services. At the same time, the bringing together of two separate economic and business systems has resulted in new, and sometimes devastating competition, a loss of government-ordained trade relationships, and substantial dislocations owing to the adjustment process.

Employment with a Large Firm

One career option in international business is to work for a large multinational corporation. These firms constantly search for personnel to help them in their international operations. Many multinational firms, while seeking specialized knowledge such as languages, expect employees to be firmly grounded in the practice and management of business. Rarely, if ever, will a firm hire a new employee at the starting level and immediately place him or her in a position of international responsibility. Usually, a new employee is expected to become thoroughly familiar with the company's internal operations before being sent abroad. Companies send managers abroad to reflect the corporate spirit, to be tightly wed to the corporate culture, and to be able to communicate well with both local and corporate management personnel. In this liaison position, the manager needs to be exceptionally sensitive to both headquarters and local operations. As an intermediary, the expatriate must be empathetic, understanding, and yet fully prepared to implement the goals set by headquarters.

It is very expensive for companies to send an employee overseas. The annual cost of maintaining a manager overseas is a multiple of the cost of hiring a local manager. Companies want to be sure that the expenditure is worth the benefit. Failure not only affects individual careers, but also sets back the business operations of the firm. Therefore, firms increasingly use training programs for employees destined to go abroad.

Even if a position opens up in international operations, there is some truth in the saying that the best place to be in international business is on the same floor as the chief executive at headquarters. Employees of firms that have taken the international route often come back to headquarters to find only a few positions available for them. After spending time in foreign operations, where independence is often high and authority significant, a return to a regular job at home, which sometimes may not even call on the many skills acquired abroad, may turn out to be a difficult and deflating experience. Such encounters lead to some disenchantment with international activities as well as to financial pressures and family problems, all of which may add up to significant executive stress during re-entry.

Employment with Small or Medium-Sized Firms

A second option is to begin work in a small or medium-sized firm. Very often, such firms have only recently developed an international outlook, and the new employee will arrive on the "ground floor." Initial involvement will normally be in the export field – evaluating potential foreign customers, preparing quotes, and dealing with activities such as shipping and transportation. With a very limited budget, the export manager will only occasionally visit international markets to discuss business strategies with distributors abroad. Most of the work will be done by email, by videoconference, or by telephone. The hours are often long because of the need, for example, to reach a contact during business hours in Hong Kong or Vietnam. Yet the possibilities for implementing creative business transactions are virtually limitless. It is also gratifying and often rewarding that one's successful contribution will be visible directly through the firm's growing export volume.

Alternatively, international work in a small firm may involve importing. Decisions often must be based on limited information, and the manager is faced with many uncertainties. Often things do not work out as planned. Shipments are delayed, letters of credit are canceled, and products almost never arrive in exactly the form and shape anticipated. Yet the problems are always new and offer an ongoing challenge.

As a training ground for international activities, there probably is no better starting place than a small or medium-sized firm. Later on, the person with some experience may find work with a trading or export management company resolving other people's problems and concentrating almost exclusively on the international arena.

Self-Employment

A third alternative is to hang up a consultant's shingle or to establish a trading firm. Many companies are in need of help for their international business efforts and are prepared to part with a portion of their profits in order to receive it. Yet it requires in-depth knowledge and broad experience to make a major contribution from the outside or to run a trading firm successfully.

Specialized services that might be offered by a consultant include international market research, international strategic planning, or, particularly desirable, beginning-to-end assistance for international entry or international negotiations. The advantage of this career option is the opportunity to become a true international entrepreneur. Consultants and those who conduct their own export–import or foreign direct investment activities work at a higher degree of risk than those who are not self-employed, but they have an opportunity for higher rewards.

Opportunities for Women in Global Management

As firms become more involved in global business activities, the need for skilled global managers is growing. Concurrent with this increase in business activity is the ever-growing presence and managerial role of women in international business. Even in regions where, because of cultured conditions, women might struggle to succeed as managers, expatriates are not seen as local women, but rather as foreigners who happen to be women.

There appear to be some distinct advantages for a woman in a management position overseas. Among them are the advantages of added visibility and increased access to clients. Foreign clients tend to assume that "expatriate women must be excellent, or else their companies would not have sent them." It also appears that companies that are larger in terms of sales, assets, income, and employees send more women overseas than smaller organizations. Further, the number of women expatriates is not evenly distributed among industries. Industry groups that utilize growing numbers or percentages of women expatriates include banking, electronics, petroleum, publishing, diversified corporations, pharmaceuticals, and retailing and apparel.

It is here where international business academics are, or should be, the guardians who separate fact from fiction in international trade policy discussions. Qualified not by weight of office but by expertise, international business academics are the indirect guarantors of and guides toward reasonableness and fairness. Without their input and impact, public apathy and ignorance may well lead trade astray.

SUMMARY

This final chapter has provided an overview of the changes facing international managers and alternative managerial responses to these changes. International business is undergoing continuous and complex alterations. "May you live in interesting times" is an ancient Chinese curse. For the international manager, this curse is a call to action. In particular, the issue of the corporate and individual soul and its effect on management's mission and outlook will increasingly lend specificity to the rectitude and character of firms. In addition, there is a growing concern dealing with the curative aspects of business, where particularly marketers are encouraged to make up for past wrongdoings and prepare themselves and their environment for mindful and responsible business leadership. Observing changes and analyzing how best to incorporate them into the international business mission is the bread and butter of the manager. The frequent changes make international business so fascinating to those active in the field. International business managers could well have been the subjects of the old Native American proverb: "when storms come about, little birds seek to shelter while eagles soar." May you be an eagle!

DISCUSSION QUESTIONS

1. How can global firms benefit from curative marketing?
2. What is the role of the "soul of business" in the integration of business processes for globalization?
3. Suggest ways in which governments can shape the competition between local and multinational firms.
4. How would our lives and our society change if imports were banned?

KEY TERMS

columns	423	soul of business	423
curative marketing	422	traditional business pillars	423
freedom	421	trust bridge	427
interdependence	426	Wiedergutmachung	429

TAKE A STAND

Advanced strategic planning requires resources and capabilities that will help managers cope with competition and adverse conditions such as terrorism. Terrorism today comes in various asymmetrical forms, such as food terrorism, which has become an ongoing challenge for food companies operating in global markets. Actors involved in food terrorism use their destructive power to sow panic and initiate triggers with new frictions for global commerce. Thus, operational, process, and strategic innovations that shield the firm are increasingly prudent investments for every firm that aims to go global. In such cases, environmental scanning is a key step in the planning process.

Questions for Debate

1. Does the symmetry of terrorism lower its risk?
2. Should consumers worry about terrorism?

INTERNET EXERCISES

1. Using World Bank data for gross domestic product (www.worldbank.org) and annual revenue information available on the websites of individual corporations, calculate how the largest corporations might rank among countries if their annual corporate revenue were ranked as GDP.
2. Using World Trade Organization data shown on the International Trade page of its website (www.wto.org), determine the following information: (a) the fastest growing traders, (b) the top ten exporters and importers in world merchandise trade, and (c) the top ten exporters or importers of commercial services.

FURTHER RESOURCES

Czinkota M. and Ronkainen, Ilkka A. (2009). Trends and Indications in International Business – Topics for Future Research. Management International Review.

Czinkota, M. and Charles J. Skuba. (2020). Business Not as Usual. Marketing Management, Summer 2010.

CASE STUDIES

CASE STUDY 1
Alibaba and Its Influence on International Markets

This case addresses the vast effect that e-commerce has not only on B2B interactions, but also on the consumer side benefits. By the end of the case, you will be able to identify how popular goods can be tweaked to better fit a new culture and see how strategic flexibility can lead to success at the global level.

Alibaba, the Chinese e-commerce giant, is extending its many tentacles into international markets as part of its aspiration to become a global business. During 2019, AliExpress, an e-commerce arm of Alibaba that sells products from Chinese retailers to customers in 150 countries, was setting up operations in Italy, Russia, Spain, and Turkey to allow retailers from those countries to sell their goods to domestic and international customers.

Alibaba's approach to building an international business is twofold: In developed e-commerce markets, the company is working to get international brands to sell to customers in China through Tmall, acting as a "gateway to China," according to the company; and in developing markets, the approach is to build or buy e-commerce marketplaces and acquire customers in those markets.

The first piece of Alibaba's strategy – the "gateway to China" – is to get established international brands in developed markets to work with the marketplace by making it easier for those brands to appeal to and target Chinese customers. This has played out in a series of initiatives. The Tmall Luxury Pavilion, launched in 2017, offers a more high-level customer experience, only open to people Alibaba knows would be shopping for luxury brands. Since 2017, 80 brands, including Burberry, Valentino, Versace, and Stella McCartney, have joined. Outside luxury category, Alibaba has positioned itself as a partner for mass brands to create new products better targeted to Chinese customers. The Tmall Innovation Center works with international brands like Unilever and Mars to offer research development and data resources to drive China-specific product development.

For less-established brands in developed markets, there is Taobao Global. Taobao Global works with small and medium-sized brands without the resources to set up their own teams and operations in China, to help them get access to Alibaba customers by setting them up with merchants who will sell their products on Taobao, Alibaba's other consumer marketplace.

To target developing e-commerce markets, Alibaba is adopting a "local-to-local" strategy. It's either acquiring or investing in companies that have existing links to local customers to introduce them to Chinese customers, or setting up bridges in-house that make it easier for customers in other countries to shop through Alibaba, and businesses in other countries to sell there.

AliExpress is a growing part of this strategy. It is a small to medium-sized business platform that sells products from retailers in China to customers internationally, and is now being expanded to invite similar sized sellers from other countries to expand from their own markets into those of other countries – except China, where they would sell through Tmall or Taobao. Alibaba.com, meanwhile, is the company's international B2B business, linking businesses to a network of suppliers while enabling otherwise expensive logistics like cross-border shipping. Most recently, Alibaba.com partnered with Office Depot in March 2019 to join forces on inventory and domestic shipping. Exhibit 1.5 shows Alibaba's sales share in China.

Top 10 e-commerce retailers in China as of June 2018, by sales share

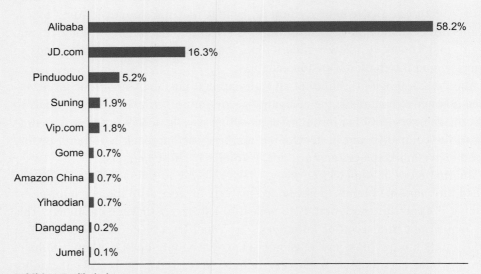

Exhibit 1.5 Alibaba's success
Source: Blazyte, 2018.

Alibaba's success in e-commerce sets a precedent for the opportunity that e-commerce creates for multinational corporations all over the world, and connects cultures more than ever before through increased product availability and adaptability to different cultures.

DISCUSSION QUESTIONS

1. How does Alibaba's success contribute to the rising opportunity presented by e-commerce?
2. Provide two examples of how Alibaba's services have brought countries closer together than ever before.
3. How do you see the relationship between Alibaba and its Western counterpart, Amazon?

Contributed by: Avdyushka Gupta

This case addresses the dichotomy presented between international trade and the Indian concept of Gram Swaraj, or self-sustenance. After working through the case, you will be familiarized with an international perspective on trade that contradicts the current norms and the questions that arise for global players, notably developing countries.

Mahatma Gandhi is said to have been one of the most iconic thinkers of his time. He did not accept many of the assumptions of classical economics; in fact, he critiqued them deeply. For example, Gandhi disagreed with the basic capitalist assumption that consuming products and satisfying one's wants leads to happiness. Gandhi believed these ever-multiplying wants make the person a slave of their desires and hence keeps them at a distance from true freedom. He notably perceived the dangers of extensive centralization and wanted to move India in the direction of a more decentralized kind of economy. He believed that every village should attain Gram Swaraj.

The essence of Gram Swaraj lay in self-sustenance, a freedom so deep that there is no need of reliance on anyone else. Gandhi believed in creating independent units of villages that did not need to rely on others. They would ensure that they themselves took care of their own basic needs. Some claim that this concept was remindful of the structure of Israeli kibbutz, as given in the Encyclopedia Britannica. This was also deeply rooted in the idea of Swadeshi, the movement for India's independence through the boycott of foreign goods. Gandhi believed it to be extremely sinful to purchase products made abroad when weavers and artisans nearby were suffering because of lack of work. He strongly opposed industrialization because he saw it as something that was taking away jobs and producing products at speeds that were much higher than the speeds of consumption.

Jobless growth may be rooted in extensive mechanization and industrialization. Are workers getting replaced by machines? Are they pushed aside by too many products? Growth may be seen, but the people remain unemployed. Companies invest in the manufacturing of demand, which leads to wasteful levels of consumption and has a major environmental impact. The high level of energy that a centralized economy consumes was another worrisome impact according to Gandhi. His solutions were a control of wants, feeling of solidarity, and promotion of your neighbor. Gandhi's idea of Gram Swaraj holds the key.

The concept of Gram Swaraj fundamentally contradicts international trade, upon which our world today is highly dependent. The advent of e-commerce and ease of transportation have made it much easier to sit in one corner of the globe and purchase merchandise from another. The whole world seems to have become one big market. There are many repercussions. World trade and globalization may lead to a merging of cultures and less diversity. Gram Swaraj, on the other hand, proposes unity in diversity. If the concept of Gram Swaraj is ever put into action by any country, it would be perceived as the taking on of extreme protectionist policies. A solution may be a middle path.

Multinational corporations can lead the change towards a more sustainable and caring world. Leaders of this movement can be the multinational giants that have helped us arrive at this point in history.

There can be multiple creative solutions to incorporate aspects of Gram Swaraj into the current workings of global trade. One such example is the relocation of large manufacturing units into smaller plants in numerous areas. In this manner, a centralized power can be held by the MNCs, and the decentralization of the production units will lead to not only less energy consumption but also the development of these numerous areas. This is essentially important in the case of fast-moving consumer goods (FMCGs).

Though International Trade and Gram Swaraj seem to be on opposite ends of the spectrum, it is possible to incorporate the positives of both systems to create a new and more enhanced system. The scales should not be tipped in favor of either extreme, but instead an acceptable balance should be struck.

The differences between Gram Swaraj and international trade as we know it are not insurmountable, and the case gives an opportunity to provoke thought on the best method of international trade for everyone, especially developing countries.

DISCUSSION QUESTIONS

1. Which method is fundamentally more effective, and why?
2. What concessions could be reasonably made from the current international trade focus on demand to become a more sustainable and responsible global economy?
3. Can you find companies that have implemented aspects of Gram Swaraj successfully? How did they implement the changes, and are they ahead of their industry? Is sustainability an increasing trend?

Acculturation of people from different religions toward activities of joy in the local area and influence of diversity in the culture of a local area, reflects on the power of intercultural initiatives on both businesses and consumers. This aspect of internationalization can be noticed in varied conceptualization of Diwali by firms in China when their artisans crafted a flamboyant Lakshmi with oriental features wearing fashion jewelry and Ganesha playing cricket or a musical instrument, or McGanesha created by American artists for Indian Americans.

INTRODUCTION

Deepavali or Diwali is a Hindu festival of lights and represents the victory of right over wrong, light over darkness, good over evil, and knowledge over ignorance during the first month of the Hindu Lunar Calendar. The festival marks the beginnings of a new calendar for businesses and, on a domestic front, people leave their doors and windows open for the goddess of wealth to walk into their life. For Hindus the five days of Diwali are very busy days filled with social engagement and activities such as cleaning the house, for welcoming the Goddess of wealth, Lakshmi, for her blessings of good fortune, along with her son Ganesha, a symbol of good luck. However, Diwali means different things for different types of Hindus. People in the northern part of India link Diwali with celebrations based on the return of Prince Ram of Ayodhya with his wife Sita and brother Lakshman after 14 years. However, people in the western part of India relate Diwali with the departure of King Bali by Lord Vishnu to rule the netherworld. At the same time, in the southern part of India people consider this festival to be a celebration of God Krishna's or Goddess Kali's victory over demon Naraksura, as Narak Chaturdasi or Kali Chaudas. For Jain community, Diwali means awakening of their Lord Mahavira, encouraging people to refrain from eating Tamsik food such as meat, fish, eggs, etc. This festival marks the beginning of a new financial year for businesses. For retailers in India, this is the best time for business as sales increase significantly and profits earned during this period can help small entrepreneurs survive comfortably for the rest of the year without much business. The demand and supply of international goods during this auspicious period in India is extremely high, thereby reflecting a tolerance of the local population towards errors in production and acceptance of sub-standard international products. For example, the deity "God Ganesha" – who is the first in line of prayer for every Hindu and whose statue is used by every Hindu family during Diwali prayers, along with the statue of the mother "Goddess Lakshmi" – was found with his trunk in the opposite direction, i.e., left. The supply of Vaastu Ganesha instead of Dakshin Murti Ganesha was accepted by people in India because of ignorance and knowledge that the position of the trunk was linked to the kundalini. Hence, being ignorant of these complexities, the Indian population has been buying Ganeshas produced in China with the trunk on the wrong side during Diwali. These aspects of the Indian market when combined with the support provided by Rowan Williams, the Archbishop of Canterbury – the spiritual leader of the global Anglican Church with 80 million members – to the acknowledgement of Sharia regulations of the Islamic community in England, reflect on the culture in knowledge or non-knowledge driven economies. The support provided by the Archbishop of Canterbury was opposed by the then British Prime Minister Gordon Brown, who argued that consideration of Sharia would undermine values, weaken the position of women in British culture, and reflect on British law.

CONCLUSION

International businesses have successfully brought the world together not only in commercial sense but also emotional sense by surpassing the restrictions laid down by boundaries of religion or faith. Intercultural activities promoted by international firms leads to stronger integration of different cultures in a market that consists of individuals from diverse cultures. It promotes a concept of global citizens as individuals who have been able to acculturate themselves to the local culture, wish to stay connected with the culture of their home country and learn about other cultures as well.

CASE STUDY 4
The Tomato: Vegetable or Fruit?

By Michael Czinkota

In 1893, the US Supreme Court grappled with an international legal question that continues to confound to this day – does a tomato qualify as a vegetable or a fruit?

Though many associate the tomato with the stews, salads, and sandwiches that are typically the domain of vegetables, any botanist will tell you that the plant meets the scientific definition of a fruit: a seed-bearing structure that develops from the ovary of a flowering plant.

But in the US Supreme Court case *Nix* v. *Hedden*, the judges unanimously arrived at a different definition. They ruled that imported tomatoes should be taxed as vegetables, which had a 10 percent tariff when they arrived on American shores, rather than as fruit, which carried no tariff.

Though the court acknowledged that a tomato is technically a fruit, it went on to write that according to the "common" definition most people use, tomatoes fall under the same category as other vegetables such as lettuce, cabbage, and carrots. In other words, a tomato counts as a vegetable because most people thought it was.

A more recent example of changing definitions in trade policy arose during a trade war between Vietnam and the USA that started in 2001. When cheap imports of Vietnamese catfish threated to put US producers, who had a higher cost, out of business, American lobbyists and lawmakers scrambled to find a way to bar Vietnamese producers from the market.

The coalition persuaded Congress that the word "catfish" only applied to US varieties, not Vietnamese imports, even though there was no biological difference between the fish. Thus, when Congress normalized trade relations with Vietnam, its definition of "catfish" excluded *basa* or *tra*, the names applied to Vietnamese catfish.

DISCUSSION QUESTIONS

1. Even today, the question explored by the *Nix* v. *Hedden* case continues to have implications. What does the Supreme Court case – along with the example of the Vietnamese catfish – tell us about trade policy?
2. Who ultimately defines a product, and how could altering definitions affect trade policy?
3. Do tariffs still play a role in modern-day international trade, and can markets make a difference?

CASE STUDY 5
Mixel Agitators, a French SME Expanding into China

By Noémie Dominguez[1] and Ulrike Mayrhofer[2]

MIXEL AGITATORS, A FRENCH INDUSTRIAL SME

Mixel Agitators is an SME specialized in the design, manufacture, and trading of industrial mixers. These are machines designed to process products in the chemical, food, pharmaceutical, and cosmetic industries, in order to mix liquids, promote reactions of chemical substances, keep homogeneous liquid bulk in storage, or increase heat transfer (Agitators, n.d.) (Exhibit 5.11).

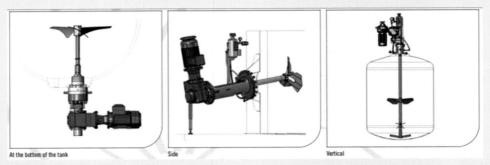

At the bottom of the tank   Side   Vertical

Exhibit 5.11 Examples of industrial agitators
Source: MIXEL – Manufacturer of industrial agitators website: www.mixel.fr/en/agitators/

Created in 1969, the company has established itself as one of the main players in its industry. Recognized for the technical nature of its offer, it also stands out for its proactivity and its strong international orientation. Constrained to develop a new development strategy in the late 1980s, Mixel Agitators did not hesitate to rapidly target international markets, especially emerging markets. In 2018, the company employed 70 people and had a turnover of 10 million euros (of which 60% abroad). It is present in 30 countries, particularly in Asia, Brazil, and Western Europe. With 20% of turnover, China is the main foreign market of the company – Mixel Agitators realizing 35% of its turnover in Asia in 2018 (Exhibit 5.12).

The SME controls its value chain, offering its customers a whole solution from the design to the production and the maintenance of devices, including staff

This case study won first prize in the 2019 Cambridge/Czinkota/Kent International Case Competition
[1] Noémie Dominguez is Associate Professor of International Business at IAE Lyon School of Management, University of Lyon: noemie.dominguez@univ-lyon3.fr
✉1C Avenue Frères Lumière CS 78242 – 69372 Lyon Cedex 08 (France)
[2] Ulrike Mayrhofer is Professor of International Business at IAE Nice Graduate School of Management, Université Côte d'Azur: ulrike.mayrhofer@univ-cotedazur.fr
✉24 Avenue des Diables Bleus, 06300 Nice (France)

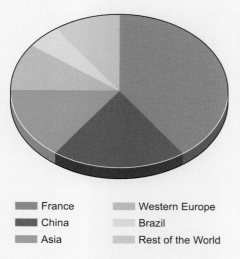

Exhibit 5.12 Mixel Agitators' main geographical markets (2018)
Source: Mixel Agitators: Internal documents.

- France
- China
- Asia
- Western Europe
- Brazil
- Rest of the World

training. It offers a wide range of standard and customized mixers (top entry, bottom entry, static, or magnetic), 50 cm to 25 m in length, for industrial application (Exhibit 5.13). The mixers are mainly used in the environmental, chemical and petrochemical, pharmaceutical, cosmetics, and food processing industries.

As mentioned by the company's CEO, "the environment is a key market for us today. It is the most important one, actually (35% of our total turnover), ahead of the chemical, pharmaceutical/cosmetics, and, finally, the food processing industries. Food processing activities are a bit down compared to the other industries. In these activities, the mitigation process is less critical than in other industries – like chemicals or water treatment – and where the materials are of lower quality and less specific (mitigation is a key issue and the devices highly used)."

The company benefits from its expertise, its partnership with small and multinational companies, as well as from the national and international certifications obtained over the years – notably the ISO 9001 and ATEX (explosive environments). Its product offering is presented in Exhibit 5.13.

Located in the outskirts of Lyon, Mixel Agitators began its activities by opening a design office composed of three engineers. At that time, the SME focused on the design of agitators, intended for the chemical sector, and outsourced the production of equipment to small local boilermakers. The industrialization and the economic growth in France enabled the SME to develop on the national territory (Coviello & Munro, 1997). The year 1989 marked a first turning point in the history of the company. The crisis in the chemistry sector in the late 1980s led to a contraction of the market: competition became more intense and margins decreased (Exhibit 5.14).

Exhibit 5.13 Mixel Agitators' product offering

	AGIMAG	AGIPRO	CONTRAMIX	DIGIMIX	HOMIX	HYDRO-MIX	JET	SEALBOX	SEALMIX	STATMIX
Def.	Magnetically driven agitator for aseptic areas	Standard, economic and practical agitator	Industrial agitator with counter-rotating twin movement	Agitator for sludge digestion and methanization	Rotor-stator type industrial agitator	Efficient and robust top entry Agitator	Agitator with guiding turret for easy maintenance of sealing system	Agitator, with sealing. Designed for small spaces	Agitator with sealing. A simple and economic design	Static mixers for online liquids
Industry	Light chemicals Pharmaceuticals Food processing Cosmetics	Water treatment, Industrial effluents, Food processing, Chemistry Cosmetics	Cosmetics, Food processing, Chemistry, Pharmaceuticals	Treatment of sludge from industries and municipalities	Food processing, Cosmetics, Pharmaceuticals Etc.	Water production and treatment Industrial effluents Chemistry, Paper, paint, Cosmetics ...	Chemistry, Petro-chemistry, Oil & Gas Etc.	Chemical, Pharmaceutical Food-processing industries Cosmetics	Chemical, Pharmaceutical Food-processing industries Cosmetics	Water treatment, food processing, chemistry, petrochemistry
Application	Blending Dispersion Dissolution Heat transfer	Blending Dilution Homogenization Neutralization	Blending, Storage, Dispersion, Dissolution, Suspension, Fermentation Emulsion Chemical reaction	Homogenization Suspension	Immiscible liquid/liquid emulsions Dispersion Homogenization	Homogenization, Coagulation, Storage, Suspension Flocculation, Sludge maturation	Chemical reaction, Heat transfer, Crystallization, Fermentation	Blending Storage Dispersion Dissolution Suspension Fermentation Emulsion	Blending, Storage, Dispersion, Dissolution Suspension, Fermentation Emulsion Chemical reaction	Blending Dilution Homogenization Heat transfer

	AGIMAG	AGIPRO	CONTRAMIX	DIGIMIX	HOMIX	HYDRO-MIX	JET	SEALBOX	SEALMIX	STATMIX
Performance	Up to 16 bars	Viscosity up to 4,000 cps	Product viscosity up to 20,000 cps	30 to 60 mbars	Product viscosity up to 90,000 cps	n.c.	Up to 180 bars	Up to 25 bars	Up to 1.5 bar	Up to 75 bars
Power/velocity	58 to 400 r/m	1.14 to 3.18 m/s	Up to 110 kW	Up to 37 kW	Up to 45 kW	Up to 30 kW	Up to 200 kW	Up to 11 kW	Up to 22 kW	0,77 to 1,49 m/s
Temperature	Up to 150°C	n.c.	Up to 180°C	38°C	n.c.	Ambient	Up to 300°C	Up to 300 °C	Up to 130 °C	n.c.
Length	Up to 25 m									
Materials	Zirconium Silicon FDA approved materials	Stainless steel Galvanized steel	All materials (Stainless Steel, carbon steel, coated steel, Alloy ...)	All materials (Stainless Steel, carbon steel, coated steel, Alloy ...)	Stainless steel Special Alloys Titanium	Steel (Carbon, Stainless, rubber coated carbon, plastic coated carbon) Alloy	FGS400 cast iron Carbon steel Alloy Coated carbon steel	Carbon steel Stainless steel Alloy Plastic Coated steel	Carbon steel Stainless steel Alloy Plastic coated steel	Stainless Steel Special alloys
Tank capacity	Up to 40 m³		Up to 25 m³	Up to 15,000 m³	n.c.	Up to 500 m³	Up to 55,000 m³	Small tanks	–	–

Source: Mixel Agitators: Internal documents.

> ### EXHIBIT 5.14 "Black Monday," the global recession
>
> On October 19, 1987, the world faced a massive financial crash (called "Black Monday"), which was due to the rising national debts and the fluctuation of several currencies, such as the US dollar. Even if this crash had been rapidly contained globally, it deeply affected several industries, including the chemical industry. Constrained by the credit crunch to reduce their costs in order to preserve their margins, many European and American companies decided to relocate their activities to countries with lower labor costs – notably in Asia. These relocations resulted in a strong intensification of the industrial rivalry already existing in Europe and North America. Suppliers were forced to reduce their margins and fight to keep their clients or to relocate their activities to follow their industrial partners.
>
> **Source:** Solomon and Dicker, 1988.

THE ARRIVAL OF A NEW CEO WITH AN INTERNATIONAL VISION

The arrival of Philippe Eyraud, nephew of the founder and current CEO of Mixel Agitators, in 1990 impelled a new dynamic and was accompanied by a change in strategy: manufacturing and maintenance were integrated within the company and the scope of prospecting was expanded to integrate international markets. Philippe Eyraud was a mechanical engineer, who had graduated from the National Institute of Applied Sciences (INSA – *Institut National des Sciences Appliquées*) of Lyon in 1986. He began his career as a commercial attaché at the French Embassy in Singapore in 1988 and 1989. These two years aroused in him a taste for becoming a CEO in international markets.

The industrial recession faced by the SME at the beginning of the 1990s forced the CEO to take some drastic measures so that the company could survive in the challenging market conditions. Although he had the option to reduce the margins to keep his clients on the domestic market, the CEO decided to look for new opportunities abroad and diversify the company's activities to spread the risks. Upon his arrival as head of the company, he rapidly developed export activities for the family business. The aim was to diversify markets and find new sources of growth to mitigate the intensification of competition and the loss of historical customers.

"When I arrived, the company was doing well. We received orders and we did not even remember that we had made a quote! It came back on its own except that, when I took over in 1990, we had a [the] beginning of [a] reversal of trend, for us, but also for our customers: the main market of Mixel Agitators was the [chemical] industry, but when the [chemical] industry goes, we must ask ourselves the question of 'where am I going to go to?' I had a lot of customers in other sectors but [chemicals] was 85% of my turnover so I thought 'I'll follow my clients.' Then there was a saturation of the national market: from the moment when there are a few more actors and a few less customers, we walk on our feet. The competition was ultra-strong, investments decreased sharply, so I had to go elsewhere."

THE DEVELOPMENT OF EXPORTS TO NEARBY MARKETS AND THEN TO ASIA

A proactive expansion strategy was then deployed, initially to Belgium, Morocco, and Switzerland. The choice of these markets can be explained by the obtaining of an equipment contract from a Solvay plant in Belgium (in 1990) following the extension of relationships with the French subsidiary of the Belgian group and the receipt of unsolicited orders from Moroccan pharmaceutical and sugar companies. While these operations attested to the potential of the SME abroad, they also testified to the growing saturation of the nearby markets. Philippe Eyraud explained that "all my competitors, who were in the same situation as me, went to Switzerland, Belgium, Italy, Spain, etc. I found them in the same place and I was fed up with always being faced with the same competitors with, for some, a kind of hate rivalry that was not very pleasant. So I decided to go elsewhere and see other types of competitors with other types of issues. In France, it was not easy to differentiate. There, I arrived in countries where there was investment: when the cake is bigger, we can feed more people ... "

In view of his past experience and his desire to strengthen ties with the most important clients, the CEO quickly decided to target the Asian countries. These dynamic markets offered Mixel Agitators a particularly interesting growth driver. The CEO seized the opportunity proposed by the Interprofessional Group of Suppliers of the Chemical Industry and participated, in 1991, in his first collective mission in China, India, and Japan. This group was reassuring because "these countries are totally inaccessible to a single SME." It was possible to share costs and to increase the visibility and the bargaining power toward the customers, but also to enlighten the entrepreneur about the local realities and specificities. Philippe Eyraud then decided to focus on China to get closer to the company's historical customers and take advantage of the size and strong growth potential of the country. Between 1991 and 1994, he participated in several trade shows that allowed him to develop and consolidate his networks.

The decision to export to Asia, however, exposed the company to a first wave of unanticipated difficulties related to the company's low openness to the outside world. Having focused on the French market until the end of the 1980s, the SME had neither the structure nor the resources and skills to manage the various international operations. In addition, many tensions emanated internally, with employees fearing to see the production of agitators relocated to a country with low labor costs. Philippe Eyraud then made two major decisions. As a first step, he was working to address the concerns of employees by exposing the strategy for Mixel Agitators.

THE ESTABLISHMENT OF AN ORGANIZATIONAL CULTURE ORIENTED TOWARD INTERNATIONAL MARKETS

"I remember, I was traveling in China when one of my colleagues called me to tell me that it heated internally. I asked him to [get everyone together] the next day at noon. I immediately flew to Lyon … I remember, I landed at 11:30, and at noon I took everyone to a good restaurant to explain the plan. The idea was not to relocate production in China but to open a second production site to be more responsive there. They were fairly convinced, but when they saw that the old machines were being sent to China and that we were buying new ones to equip the factory in France, that reassured them. They saw that I had not lied: the opening of the subsidiary in China did not lead to relocation, but it generated a surplus of activity at headquarters. Internal communication is the key. People need to know where you want to go and how you plan to go about it."

Philippe Eyraud used external resources to internationalize the culture of the company as a whole. "At home, everyone has to be international, from the worker to the switchboard operator to the engineer or the salesperson. If they reason from a local perspective, it will not work. You have to be able to understand customers, work with employees abroad, and so on … A device that goes abroad is not the same as a device that stays in France. There are lots of little nuances that make it necessary to internationalize the material so I want everyone to be international."

Both the organizational structure and the management style within Mixel Agitators were influenced by the CEO's personality, his international orientation, and his relentless pursuit of diversity. Having been French Foreign Trade Advisor (CCEF – *Conseiller du Commerce Extérieur de la France*) since 2009, Director of the Axelera Cluster (Lyon & Rhône-Alpes Chemistry-Environment competitiveness cluster), President of the International Commission of the Rhône CCI (*Chambre de Commerce et d'Industrie* between 2010 and 2015), active member of export clubs, etc., Philippe Eyraud advocated both for the internationalization of SMEs and for the promotion of local know-how.

ESTABLISHMENT IN HONG KONG AND CHINA

Between 1995 and 1996, Philippe Eyraud began to set up a representative office abroad (Hong Kong). He joined forces with three metallurgical SMEs to take over a branch of the Federation of Mechanics while retaining the local manager at the head of the structure, the aim being to take advantage of knowledge and networks to quickly penetrate the Chinese market. This operation proved to be a failure owing to the lack of involvement of the local manager in the development of the Chinese business.

Between 1996 and 1999, Mixel Agitators was forced to decrease its international operations to make up for the losses accumulated in Hong Kong. From 1998, however, the SME received many requests from China to equip the future waste-water treatment plants, following the efforts previously made by the CEO to build, develop, and mobilize the various networks to which the SME belongs. That year, Mixel Agitators signed its first two contracts in China: one with Veolia – a major customer of the SME in France – and the other with a Japanese multinational company introduced at a trade show.

The CEO's prospecting efforts allowed Mixel Agitators to intensify its exports between 1998 and 2004. The growing volume of orders from China prompted the CEO to strengthen his level of commitment by setting up, in 2005, the first production and sales subsidiary abroad. The objective was to establish the positioning and strengthen the competitiveness of Mixel Agitators in the country.

Philippe Eyraud explained that "in 2004, I had the opportunity to leave with the Minister of Foreign Trade, whose name was François Loos. I had access to the boss of Veolia who gave me orders and I said 'but why do you order my equipment, a small company of 30 people in Lyon?' He told me 'because we have not found it here yet.' I had two solutions: I could wait for him to find and lose the future market, or I could try to keep this market definitively by being, myself, the first step. That's what I did; that's how I settled in China."

THE SME IS PURSUING AN AMBITIOUS STRATEGY IN ASIA

The Chinese subsidiary employed 12 people in 2017. In addition to the volume of activities provided to the headquarters, it acts as a real growth driver in Asia. Philippe Eyraud indicated that "Mixel was the smallest SME to set up in China, to accompany one of our customers. In this country, it is necessary to start by selling to the Western companies established locally or by joint-venture, which prefer quality over price. Working in China requires a good international culture and a grain of madness. The cultural difference is such that one cannot show amateurism. But the game is worth it: I have never exported so much and I have increased the workforce in France since we [have been] in China. Indeed, we realize all the studies in France and manufacture products which exceed the Chinese know-how."

He concluded: "Today, I think the subsidiary is strong ... Now, I'd like to see what's going on around it. There are some interesting things happening in Vietnam, Thailand, etc. Our know-how is recognized, manufacturers look for our products not because they are 'made in France' or 'made in China' but because they are 'made by Mixel.' We have to go where our customers plan to go and one way to do it is from China." The company implements a bridgehead strategy to develop its activities in other Asian markets (see Exhibit 5.15) and has created a representation office in Ho Chi Minh City (Vietnam) to accelerate its expansion in Asia.

EXHIBIT 5.15 Bridgehead strategies

As a new type of location strategy, bridgehead strategies allow a company to access a foreign market indirectly, by using support from a subsidiary located in a peripheral territory. The first experience in a market can prove to be a real springboard to other neighboring countries. The implementation of this type of strategy is facilitated by the presence of free trade agreements. It can also be explained by the need for a company to work in a transparent, stable, and predictable reaction zone, as well as to reduce its exposure to local risks such as political instability, target market volatility, or currency exchange risk. The use of a bridgehead country therefore makes it possible to penetrate new markets (geographically or culturally more distant) from a familiar environment, thus mitigating the impact of the perceived risk on decision-making.

Source: Dominguez, 2018.

DISCUSSION QUESTIONS

1. How does a French manufacturing SME manage to become a reference supplier in China?
2. To what extent did the CEO's personality, experience, and international orientation influence the expansion trajectory of the firm?
3. What are the main stages of the SME's international development? How can they be explained, especially in terms of market choice?
4. How has the CEO managed to internationalize the culture of an organization strongly rooted in its territory of origin?
5. What do you recommend to the CEO to help him pursue further international development of Mixel Agitators?

FURTHER RESOURCES

Dominguez, N. and Mayrhofer, U. (eds.). (2018). Key Success Factors of SME Internationalisation: A Cross-Country Perspective, Emerald.

Johanson J. and Vahlne J.-E., (2009), The Uppsala internationalization process model revisited: From liability of foreignness to liability of outsidership, Journal of International Business Studies, 40(9), 1411–1431.

CASE STUDY 6
HSBC: Guanxi for Internationalization

By Doane Ye, Suraksha Gupta, and YiChuan Wang

HSBC is one of the largest international financial and banking services group in the world. It has four main businesses internationally: Global Private Banking, Retail Banking and Wealth Management, Global Banking and Markets, and Commercial Banking. The organization has offices in 66 countries and territories with over 39 million customers, as well as 235,000 employees, who speak 144 different languages (Exhibit 6.7) (HSBC-UK Web, 2019).

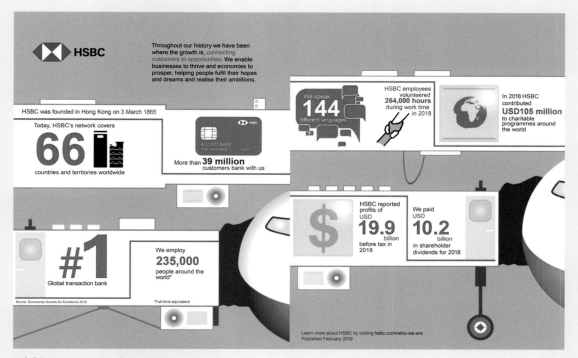

Exhibit 6.7 HSBC Factsheet
(HSBC-UK Web, 2019)

Because of the international financial recession that started in 2008, there was considerable decline in HSBC's revenue from US$68.3 billion in 2012 to US$53.8 billion in 2018. HSBC's stock (LSE) decreased from roughly 470 GBX in 2012 to below 450 GBX in 2016 (see Exhibit 6.8). After that, it increased with fluctuations from below 450 GBX in 2016 to over 650 GBX in June 2019 (Financial Times, 2019). Furthermore, it became the top international transaction bank in the world.

Exhibit 6.8 HSBC's stock

It contributed US$105 million to charities, achieved profits of US$19.9 billion (before tax), and paid US$10.2 billion in shareholder dividends in 2018 (HSBC-UK Web, 2019).

HSBC aims to become the world's largest global bank, connecting business partners, customers, and employees worldwide to maintain organizational sustainability. There are organizations to develop, an economy to grow, and customers seeking to make their financial dreams come true. Facilitating all these aspects requires establishing strong guanxi with all of them.

GUANXI

Guanxi is a concept based on trust developed between two enterprises or individuals. It is significantly built at the interpersonal level among people that represent companies. Guanxi can be understood from various perspectives. It is an answer to the economic reform and the impact of the "bourgeois individualism." Guanxi applies social sanctions to support behavioral norms as an actioning mechanism, and it runs beyond non-individual participation and involves individual favors and influence as part of the way to obtaining business objectives. In the Confucian relationalism, guanxi represents the essential human relationship that exists in everyday engagement between individuals of various positions. Guanxi comprises interactions across multiple dynamic dimensions of reciprocity, self-disclosure, and long-period proportion theory and can be divided into three types:

GANQING

Ganqing is a psychological factor that works with emotional connections, understanding, and the sharing of happiness and fears, by people in a social setting. It is a social connection which defines the understanding, feeling, and quality of a connection between people (Barnes et al., 2011; Yen et al., 2011). In a business environment, ganqing reflects on the relationship and feelings established between two commercial parties. It is usually actioned across various social engagements during both formal commercial encounters and informal social occasions.

RENQING

Renqing represents a different standard of human nepotism emerging from human compassion and benevolence by owing favors. It generates promises by giving gifts or favors and by dining. It is an intricate art to manage petty and offensive occasions and can be considered as bribery. However, compared to ganqing, renqing concentrates on the social obligation that is needed for the social exchange. The reciprocity discusses the fundamental theory of how the exchanges can be perpetuated.

XINREN

Xinren responds to personal trust between people. Kindness and integrity are the commitment. Using Xinren, organizational engagements are implemented and approaches to disputes are dealt with (Yen et al., 2011). Xinren works when the identification of who maintains the agreements in different ways is developed using personal experiences, reputation, and previous success stories of implementation. Therefore, xinren is a measure of benevolence and credibility, which is built fundamentally on the justification of the third party's trustworthiness.

HSBC'S GUANXI

HSBC has consistent guanxi with its internal and external resources. Guanxi helps HSBC to increase its existing stakeholder interactions and make sure that the commercial aspect of business is consistent with its internal established structure. HSBC uses xinren for protecting its customers' and partners' information and data, and offering fair implementation of its policies with high levels of service for long-term success. Simultaneously, managers of HSBC try to understand the feelings of junior employees. They encourage the implementation of their potential by creating a cultural environment where people feel free to speak up. Such behavior is to be demonstrated by participating in behavioral surveys to provide input and feedback. An increase in the workforce of HSBC from 64% in 2017 to 66% in 2018 reflects on its evaluation, illustrated as xinreng in leadership. Xinren helps HSBC to promote career establishment for its employees based on their performance and problem solving skills. The platform thus created is open with a sense of sharing. These kind of Xinreng practices help HSBC to gain employees' trust and deal with issues without the use of power or discrimination.

As a result, today the culture of HSBC is open, dependable, and connected, encouraging its employees to hear their colleagues' voices, to speak up, and to consider the long-term influence of their capability. The diversity of HSBC reflects its history – working in over 60 nations in over 100 languages – and it creates quality business sense, and provides new ideas. Based on the data, 28% of employees have stayed at the bank for ten years or more. It is believed that organizational culture should offer talented employees various approaches to satisfy their potential, and it is essential to allow employees to balance their workload with personal responsibility and flexibility. This is based on the organizational strategies, objectives, sectors, and local culture of the global organization, which can use the current way to build up the corporate culture, and HR strategies to match the needs.

- Ethnocentric – direct transfer of employees from the parent nation to the host nation.
- Polycentric –following the local regulation to recruit people
- Global – imposed strategy all over the local branches
- Hybrid – depending on the circumstances of the host nation to customize the plan.

HSBC focuses on valuing diversity to recruit talented people around the world with regard to working families, race/ethnicity, sexual orientation, faith, gender, disability, and age. HSBC provides opportunities to establish a satisfying career within an assistive and inclusive condition. It aims to be an environment where everyone can reach their full potential. HSBC has been integrating customers to business opportunities for more than 150 years; the distinct culture has established to get growth in the current approach and commit to using the highest levels for the business. The data showed that 49% of employees have work flexibly to complete the tasks, seven international employee networks promote diversity, and employees spent 6.2 m hours on formal training in 2018.

DISCUSSION QUESTIONS

1. Can Guanxi be applied to the context of international business by firms operating in other countries?
2. What are the three dimensions of Guanxi? Please explain each dimension from the perspective of (a) head-office subsidiary relationship and (b) supply chain relationships
3. How can Guanxi be understood when seen through the lens of Geert Hofstede? (Hofstede, 2015)

CASE STUDY 7
The Bell Boeing V-22

By Ilkka A. Ronkainen

The Bell Boeing V-22 Program is a strategic alliance between Bell Helicopter, a Textron company, and the Boeing company. The program announced that the V-22 Osprey tiltrotor (Exhibit 7.9) would be featured at the Dubai International Air Show in the United Arab Emirates. The Dubai Air Show is one of the world's fastest growing aerospace events and it presents an excellent opportunity for Bell Boeing to showcase the tiltrotor Ospreys. The focus will rest on its one-of-a-kind capability, unique value proposition, and outstanding record of operational performance. The V-22 is seen as the right solution for Middle East customers seeking range, speed, payload, and mission flexibility for military and humanitarian operations. The Dubai International Air Show is a biennial show held in Dubai, United Arab Emirates. It is organized jointly by the Government of Dubai, the Department of Civil Aviation, Dubai International Airport, and the UAE Union Defense Forces. Since its start in 1986, the show has been a key international aerospace show (Dubai Airshow, 2019). The flying display demonstrates the technical capabilities of exhibited aircrafts and has included the Airbus A380, A400M, F-16, F/A-18, F-22 Raptor, V-22 Osprey, B-1B, and Eurofighter Typhoon.

Defense and commercial trade offsets are valued in the tens of billions of dollars each year and often accompany the export of advanced technological goods. US defense firms tend to see offsets merely as a reality of the marketplace and part of the competition for international defense sales. The US Government's lack of a proactive policy that addresses the impact of offsets may undermine its economic and national security interests.

The V-22 exceeds current Japan Self-Defense Forces helicopters in terms of range, speed, and payload. Indian Aviation Research Centre (ARC) became interested in acquiring four V-22s for personnel evacuation in hostile conditions, logistic supplies, and deployment of the Special Frontier Force (SFF) in border areas. United Arab Emirates was in the final negotiation stages to purchase several V-22s. It was reported that the UAE intended to use it to support special forces. South Korea is to launch a new version of a large-deck landing ship from which short-takeoff-and-vertical-landing aircraft can operate by the late 2020s. The flight deck was adapted to accommodate two V-22 Osprey tilt-rotor aircraft.

ANALYZING THE EFFECTS OF OFFSETS

Offsets are obligations imposed on the seller in major (most often military hardware) purchases by or for foreign governments. The goal is to minimize any trade imbalance or other adverse economic impact caused by the large outflow of currency

Exhibit 7.9 Boeing V-22 Osprey
Credit: Jon Hobley/MI News/NurPhoto via Getty Images.

required to pay for such purchases. Two basic types of offset arrangements exist: direct and indirect (as seen in Exhibit 7.10). Although offsets have long been associated only with the defense sector, there are now increasing demands for offsets in commercial sales where the government is the purchaser or user.

EXHIBIT 7.10 The offset process

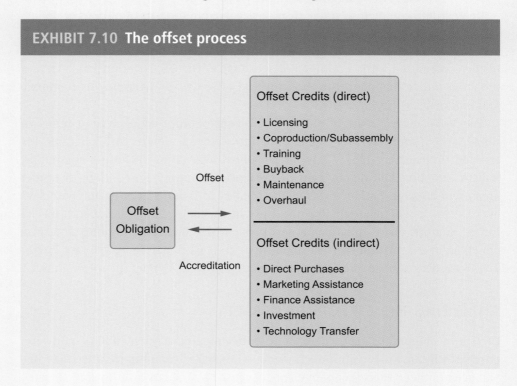

Offset Credits (direct)

- Licensing
- Coproduction/Subassembly
- Training
- Buyback
- Maintenance
- Overhaul

Offset Credits (indirect)

- Direct Purchases
- Marketing Assistance
- Finance Assistance
- Investment
- Technology Transfer

Offset Obligation

Offset →

Accreditation ←

The Bureau of Industry and Security (BIS) collects data annually from US firms involved in defense exports. Information is gathered about offset agreements in order to assess the impact of such requirement on defense trade. In 2017, US defense contractors reported entering into 50 new offset agreements with 12 countries valued at $2.09 billion (BIS, 2019). The value of these agreements equalled 65.32% of the $3.20 billion in reported contracts for sales of defense articles and services to foreign entities. In 2017, US firms reported 543 offset transactions with 29 countries and a value of $4.6 billion. Reported offset agreements ranged from a low of 12% of the defense export sales contract value to a high of 100% (Exhibit 7.11).

EXHIBIT 7.11 Defense export sale contract values

Year	Contract value ($ millions)	Offset agreement value ($ millions)	Percent of offset agreement to contract value	US firms (number)	Agreements (number)	Countries (number)/ Multi-country arrangements
1993	$13,935	$4,784	34.33%	17	28	16
1994	$4,792	$2,049	42.75%	18	49	20
1995	$7,632	$6,204	81.30%	21	48	18
1996	$3,120	$2,432	77.94%	16	53	19
1997	$5,925	$3,826	64.56%	15	60	20
1998	$3,079	$1,786	57.99%	14	42	17
1999	$5,657	$3,457	61.11%	11	45	11
2000	$6,576	$5,705	86.75%	10	43	16
2001	$7,116	$5,550	77.99%	12	35	13
2002	$7,406	$6,095	82.29%	12	41	17
2003	$7,293	$9,110	124.92%	11	31	13
2004	$4,934	$4,331	87.78%	14	41	18
2005	$2,260	$1,464	64.79%	8	25	18
2006	$5,265	$3,655	69.42%	15	48	21
2007	$6,932	$5,469	78.89%	11	45	20
2008	$6,442	$3,835	59.53%	17	56	17
2009	$11,065	$6,847	61.89%	15	65	21
2010	$4,019	$2,451	60.98%	15	34	14

EXHIBIT 7.11 (cont.)

Year	Contract value ($ millions)	Offset agreement value ($ millions)	Percent of offset agreement to contract value	US firms (number)	Agreements (number)	Countries (number)/ Multi-country arrangements
2011	$10,989	$5,665	51.56%	9	63	27
2012	$25,717	$10,425	40.54%	13	50	17
2013	$10,015	$5,182	51.75%	17	69	19
2014	$13,075	$7,709	58.96%	14	46	15
2015	$8,180	$3,183	38.90%	13	40	16
2016	$4,352	$1,491	34.26%	6	33	14
2017	$3,201	$2,091	65.32%	12	50	12
Total or Ave.	$188,976	$114,794	60.75%	64	1,140	51

Note: Due to rounding, totals may not add up exactly. Reported offset-related data for certain previous years have been revised. The values shown have not been adjusted for inflation.

Source: BIS, 2019.

Direct offsets consist of product-related manufacturing or assembly either for the purposes of a project or for a longer-term partnership. Offsets, therefore, enable the purchaser to be involved in the manufacturing process. For example, various Spanish companies produce dorsal covers, rudders, aft fuselage panels, and speed brakes for clients having purchased the F/A-18s. Licensed production is also prominent. Examples include Egypt producing US M1-Al tanks, China producing 719 aircrafts, and South Korea assembling the F-16 fighter. An integral part of these arrangements is the training of the local employees. Training is not only for production/assembly purposes but also for the maintenance and overhaul of the equipment in the longer term. Some offsets have buyback provisions; the seller is obligated to purchase output from the facility or operations it has set up or licensed. For example, Westland takes up an agreed level of parts and components from the South Korean plant that produces Lynx Helicopters under license. In practice, therefore, direct offsets amount to technology transfer.

Indirect offsets are agreements that involve products and investments that are not used in the original sales contract but will satisfy part of the seller's "local" obligation. Direct purchases of raw materials, equipment, or supplies by the seller or its suppliers from the offset customer country present the clearest case of indirect offsets.

Sellers faced with offset obligations work closely with their supplier base, some having goals of increasing supplier participation in excess of 50%. Many governments see offsets as a mechanism to develop their indigenous business and industrial sectors. Training in management techniques may be attractive to both parties. The upgrading of skills may be seen by the government as more critical for improving international competitiveness than efforts focused only on hardware.

Trade development may involve the analysis of business sectors showing the greatest foreign market potential, improving organizational and product readiness or conducting market research. It can also help identify buyers or partners for foreign market development, or assist in the export process.

Sales are often won or lost on the availability of financing and favorable credit terms to the buyer. Financing packages put together by one of the seller's entities can earn offset credits which can be used to reduce an accepted offset burden.

Many nations have signed contracts that call for offsetting the cost of their purchases through investments. Saudi Arabian purchases of military technology have recently been tied to sellers' willingness to invest in manufacturing plants, defense-related industries, or special-interest projects in the country. British Aerospace, for example, has agreed to invest in factories for the production of farm feed and sanitary ware.

No two offset deals are alike. Governments may require "pre-deal counter purchases" as a sign of commitment and ability to deliver. Some companies, such as United Technologies, argue that there is limited advantage in carrying out offset activities in advance of the contract, unless the buyer agrees to a firm commitment. While none of the bidders may like it, buyers' market conditions give them very little choice to argue. Even if a bidder loses the deal, it can always attempt to sell its offset credits to the winner or use the credits in conjunction with other sales that one of its divisions may have. Also the government often wants to direct purchases from certain industries or types of companies (Herrnstadt, 2008).

BELL BOEING V-22

With the speed of a plane and the hovering ability of a helicopter, the V-22 Osprey is a true multitask aircraft (see Exhibit 7.12).

Osprey's unique capabilities
- increased speed; twice as fast as a helicopter
- much longer range resulting in greater mission versatility
- amphibious assault and combat support
- long-range special ops
- infiltration and exfiltration

- search and rescue, and medevac
- future tanker capability

Osprey aircraft particulars
- can transport 24 combat troops, 20,000 pounds of internal, or up to 15,000 pounds of external cargo using its medium lift and vertical takeoff and landing capabilities
- meets US Navy requirements for combat search and rescue, fleet logistics support, and special warfare support
- matches the US Special Operations Command's requirement for a high-speed, long-range, vertical lift aircraft
- can be stored aboard an aircraft carrier or assault ship because the rotors can fold, and the wings rotate
- has air-to-air refueling capability, the cornerstone of the ability to self-deploy

Boeing is responsible for the fuselage and all subsystems, digital avionics, and fly-by-wire flight-control systems. Boeing partner Bell Helicopter Textron, Inc. is responsible for the wing, transmissions, empennage, rotor systems, and engine installation. The V-22 provides a significant increase in operational range over the legacy systems it will replace and is the only vertical platform capable of rapid self-deployment to any theater of operation worldwide.

EXHIBIT 7.12 V-22 Osprey is a true multitask aircraft

General characteristics	
Propulsion	Two Rolls-Royce AE1107C, 6,150 shp (4,586 kW) each
Length	Fuselage: 57.3 ft. (17.48.20 m); Stowed: 63.0 ft. (19.20 m)
Width	Rotors turning: 84.6 ft. (25.78 m); Stowed: 18.4 ft. (5.61 m)
Height	Nacelles vertical: 22.1 ft. (6.73 m); Stabilizer: 17.9 ft. (5.46 m)
Rotor Diameter	38.1 ft (11.6 m)
Vertical Takeoff Max Gross Weight	52,600 lbs. (23,859 kg)
Max Cruise Speed	275 kts (443 km/h) SL
Mission Radius	430 nm (796 km) – MV-22 Blk B with 24 troops, ramp mounted weapon system, SL STD, 15 min loiter time
Cockpit – crew seats	2 MV / 3 CV
Source: Boeing: www.boeing.com/defense/v-22-osprey/	

IMPACTS ON THE US INDUSTRIAL BASE

Offset arrangements and their impacts are largely determined by private sector firms' agreements with foreign nations. So far, the federal government has ceded its authority over offsets to market participants. Yet other governments are not necessarily aligned with US economic and national security interests. Offsets can exacerbate the decline in the defense industrial base or disrupt critical parts of the defense supply chain. Second, offsets may undermine national security if the offsets result in the loss of critical skills in the defense industry's workforce that cannot later be replaced or expanded quickly. And third, while the USA has export licensing requirements, offsets multiply the chances that "leading edge weapons and the technology for producing them" may go to countries that represent a threat to US national security interests.

Despite the risks that are raised by the use of offsets, the US has yet to develop a proactive offsets strategy. Therefore, the Department of Commerce has begun to develop a proactive strategy that addresses the risks posed by defense and commercial trade offsets (Petersen, 2011).

DISCUSSION QUESTIONS

1. Why would the members of Bell Boeing agree to an offset deal rather than insist on a money-based transaction?
2. Why do governments typically take an unsupportive stance on countertrade arrangements?
3. Comment on this statement: "International offsets trade short-term sales for long-term loss of market position."
4. The international market is key for the V-22, which has been named as vulnerable to deep cuts in US defense spending. Where is the market of the future for the Osprey?

CASE STUDY 8
Tao Kae Noi Seaweed Snack: Going Global

Exhibit 8.10 Assortment of Tao Kae Noi seaweed snack products in Tao Kae Noi Land shop
Credit: KYTan/Shutterstock.com.

"My plan is to turn Tao Kae Noi (TKN) into a truly global company by 2024, though it will still focus mainly on the seaweed industry. Our business will expand to hundreds of countries and generate revenue to at least Bt10 billion," said Aitthipat, who founded the seaweed snack business Tao Kae Noi – meaning "young boss" in Thai – in 2003, when he was only 19 years old. TKN headquarters was located on a small plot on the outskirts of Bangkok, Thailand, but the machines to produce the snacks cost almost 10 million baht. Within two years, he had become a millionaire at the tender age of 21 years old, when his trade volume reached 75 million baht. When he was 26 years old, a Thai movie entitled "The Billionaire" was made about his life (see movie trailer with English subtitles: www.youtube .com/watch?v=HxbeZ6WjLCU).

In 2019, after fifteen years in business and having exported TKN seaweed snacks worldwide, Atthipat faced many challenges – such as the rising cost of imported seaweeds, counterfeit products, fluctuating exchange rates, intense competition, and high expenses in diversifying product lines. If these problems could not be resolved, TKN's ability to become a global leader would be out of reach.

BRIEF COUNTRY BACKGROUND

Known previously as Siam, Thailand is in the center of Southeast Asia surrounded by Laos, Myanmar (Burma), Cambodia, and Malaysia. Thailand is about the size of

France, and its total population in 2018 was 69 million. As a tropical country, its temperature ranges from 23 °C to 32 °C.

Thailand's population is relatively homogeneous, with Thais as the majority, followed by Chinese and other ethnic groups. Chinese and other ethnic groups have assimilated into the Thai culture, although the Chinese are more likely to reside in urban areas and engage in business. Thais are predominantly Buddhists.

The country comprises 76 provinces divided into 4 regions: Central, North, Northeast, and South. Situated in the Central region, Bangkok is the capital city and the center of political, commercial, industrial, and financial activities. The unit of currency is the baht, with approximately 32 baht per US dollar in 2019.

BUSINESS INCEPTION

TKN was established in 2003 by Aitthipat Kulapongvanich, nicknamed Tob. His initial capital came from trading characters and points earned from playing online games. He invested part of his money into selling the first product – baked, ready-to-eat Chinese chestnuts, targeting women who did not want to get their hands dirty cracking the chestnut shells. Previously, the only place for people to get Chinese chestnuts was in Chinatown, but his franchise was located in department stores convenient for customers. He named this new venture "Tao Kae Noi" or "Young Boss" because his father teased him that his son was going to be a boss. In just over a year the business had expanded to more than 30 units. In addition to grilled chestnuts, Tob tried to add other product lines, including pickled plums, dried fruit, and fried seaweed, to be sold at his outlets. Since the revenue from selling fried seaweed exceeded that of other products, including chestnuts, his business interest turned to the fried seaweed snack.

His business experienced rapid expansion in 2004 (see Exhibit 8.10) when the 7-Eleven convenience chain, the largest outlet in Thailand for snack items, accepted TKN into the store. Tob expanded his production capacity quickly to serve the huge demand generated from selling at the convenience stores. Since no bank would lend him money for this expansion, he had to sell his roasted chestnut franchise to finance a new factory. Obtaining initial access to the convenience stores seemed to be easier than keeping his snack on the shelf, since the stores would drop any products if their sales volume did not meet expectations. To stimulate an initial product trial, TKN used a low-price strategy of 10 baht (about 35 cents) per unit and allocated 40 percent of total output as free samples distributed at schools, universities, and BTS Sky Trains stations for three months. This tactic turned out to be successful as sales of his snack at the convenience stores increased dramatically. Eventually, his snack was distributed in all major convenience stores and modern trade outlets throughout Thailand.

SCOPE OF BUSINESS

Tao Kae Noi seaweed snacks were made of imported seaweed, mainly from Korea, and were processed using modern production systems similar to those of global brands. Initially, its product line included fried, grilled, baked, crispy, roasted, and tempura seaweed snacks. Later TKN marketed new products, including corn snacks, mini breads, popcorns, potato sticks, and whey protein. Brand building was important to TKN. Working with Ogilvy & Mather in creating its distinctive brand story and DKSH in distributing the snack had helped the company to develop a competitive edge over its competitors (see www.taokaenoi.co.th/product.php for all TKN products).

In addition to market seaweed snacks, TKN broadened its business in many directions. In 2009, "Tao Kae Noi Land", a souvenir store, opened in various tourist locations in Thailand, mainly to target the international tourists. In 2009, TKN acquired Want More Industry Co. Ltd. and later renamed it to Tao Kae Noi Care Co. Ltd., to operate a trading business targeting products for the health market, such as whey protein. In 2011, TKN acquired NCP, a local manufacturer and distributor of seasonings, to be used as its crucial raw material supplier for the seaweed snacks and other products. This acquisition allowed TKN to launch unique flavors such as salted egg seaweed tempura and seaweed chicken satay. In 2017, it took over GIM Factory Inc. in California, USA, to manufacture and distribute processed seaweed in the American region (Tao Kae Noi, 2018).

THE SNACK MARKET IN THAILAND

Thailand's snack foods market was one of the largest and most diverse in the Asia-Pacific region, with the value of 2.9 billion baht (approx. US$ 900 million) in 2018 and a growth rate of 5.4 percent. The market was dominated by potato chips, extruded snacks, and nuts, with a combined share of over 78 percent (USDA Foreign Agricultural Services, 2018). Seaweed snacks controlled another 7 percent share.

Although there were many players in the snack industry, Frito-Lay Thailand Co. Ltd. (owned by Pepsi-Cola Thai Trading Company), the manufacturer of Lay's, Tawan, Doritos, Twisties, and Cheetos, maintained its leadership in 2019. Its Lay's potato chips gained over 75 percent share of retail value sales. However, the increased awareness of health and wellness trends among Thai consumers helped perceived healthier snacks such as seaweed, fish, fruits, and nuts to grow faster than other fried processed snacks. More healthy ingredients and the reduction of salt, sugar and fat content became crucial for manufacturers in this industry.

In the seaweed snack segment, TKN was able to maintain its leading position, but its success spawned competition initially by numerous imitators whose brand names purported to be of the same corporate family – for example, Tao Kae Nie (Woman Boss) and Tee Leek (Younger Brother). Other competing brands such as Taberu, Mtaro, Yuki, Shogune, Slimi, and Khun Film also employed similar strategies to Tao Kae Noi in positioning the product as a Japanese-style seaweed snack and appealing to young consumers. However, in 2008, only Seleco was a real challenge to TKN; it had been in the market long before the entrance of TKN and was backed by a large conglomerate. In 2018, prominent competitors continued to enter the market, including Machita and Onori. In 2011, Singha Corporation, one of the two largest brewers in Thailand, diversified its business by launching Machita seaweed snack market and gained a 17 percent share in 2018. Launched in 2012, Onori brand was owned by Oishi Group Plc., Thailand's leading Japanese restaurant and beverage operator, which was a subsidiary of Thai Beverage Public Company Limited, another large brewer in the country. Nevertheless, the market share of Onori was negligible.

FIRST STEP IN EXPORTING

The first country to which TKN exported was Singapore, followed by Hong Kong and other countries in Pacific Rim.

Singapore

In 2004, after noticing a large volume purchase from a buyer, Tob found that his snack was being shipped to Singapore. He visited traditional trade markets where he had been informed that his snack was being sold. Finding his products prominently displayed in front of a retail store, he was encouraged to see that his snack was selling well; however, it was often out of stock. Having a higher disposable income, Singaporean consumers could afford the seaweed at 80 baht per pack, while it was sold in Thailand at only 30 baht.

Setting up a trading company in Singapore was out of reach since his business in Thailand was growing rapidly and consumed most of his time and effort. He needed a trader to venture into the Singaporean market. Finding potential trading partners through trade shows was impractical because the desired trade show was scheduled or the following year, and he realized that, by then, his product might fall out of favor or the competitors might already have entered the market. After several days and several attempts in making appointments with buyers of large retail stores, he had a meeting with a purchaser of the 7-Eleven Convenience chain, but was told that regulations in Singapore prohibited manufacturers to deal directly with retailers. Finding a distributor in Singapore proved to be difficult because no-one was interested in his business proposal.

Fortunately, in 2005, TKN met San SeSan Global, a smaller distributor that showed some interest in having discussions with him. They were a good match in their long-term orientation toward brand building, and so both worked together in adapting the snack to meet the local needs. For instance, the original label was in Thai, which Singaporeans did not understand, so the package had to use both Chinese and English. No Thai language was shown on the package because, in Singapore, the country image "Made in Thailand" was associated with inferior quality. Also, the Singaporean market preferred tomato sauce flavor and milder flavors than those products offered in Thailand. It took TKN almost nine months to adjust its snack to meet the need of this new market. The trader conducted several field tests before launching a six-month marketing blitz.

This well-planned effort had helped TKN to become a mainstay on convenience store shelves all over the island. Two years after it was launched, TKN was displayed in the front of many shops. Crediting the entry success to his collaboration with his trader, Tod also believed that a superior product was a key factor and that brand building helped to differentiate his brands from others. Tob stressed that "the product must have a story to tell, not just the tangible product itself. Consumers will appreciate the effort that we put in making this snack."

Hong Kong

After the initial success in Singapore, Tob realized the vast opportunity in the export market. The market was more lucrative, and payment was more rapid since buyers sent him a letter of credit before he shipped out the order. By comparison, in Thailand, he had to wait to receive payments and had to follow the strict guidelines of large retail operators.

Thus, in 2006, when a trader supplying Thai food items to Hong Kong approached him to export his snack to this market, Tob was delighted. After sending a few boxes, orders expanded rapidly. Tob went to Hong Kong to investigate the market. Similar to in Singapore, the snack was sold in only one traditional retail shop and was not available in the mainstream market. He employed the same technique in searching and screening local representatives. Once he had found one trader matching his criteria, they developed a marketing plan to launch the snack in Hong Kong.

Finding traders in Hong Kong was easier than in Singapore. The annual sales volume in Thailand had reached over 200 million baht in 2006. That success, combined with the successful market entry in Singapore, had convinced several Hong Kong traders to be interested in representing his snack. After he selected one of the traders, the others approached his competitors in Thailand. Fortunately, the competing Thai companies were more concerned with making an immediate profit and, therefore, were not interested in cooperating with traders in investing in brand building.

Asia Pacific

Byr entering the Hong Kong market, TKN had expanded its exports to countries in the Asia Pacific including Indonesia, Philippines, Taiwan, Malaysia, and Brunei. The company relied on trade shows to meet potential partners because it was more cost effective than visiting individual countries. TKN formed two patterns of trade relationships with these buyers. Overseas distributors were used in those markets where the TKN brand was well established. These distributors operated under the contract to purchase a specific amount in a certain period. They worked closely with TKN to plan strategy in their markets. On the other hand, TKN did not force similar agreements with foreign importers and Thai exporters – that is, they could freely operate their businesses. This latter group was beneficial to TKN in exploring opportunities in new markets. Once the sales volume in a specific market became sufficiently large, TKN would switch to use overseas distributors.

Exporting to more countries required TKN to adapt to the diverse needs and regulations. For instance, Japan has restrictive rules for imported food. One lot of Tao Kae Noi snacks being shipped to Japan contained a food color that was prohibited by the Japanese Government. The Japanese custom informed him that the product would be destroyed or shipped back to Thailand. Another difficulty occurred when dealing with a Chinese trader. The trader did not follow the distribution and marketing rules initially agreed upon, causing some friction in their relationships. Penetrating the Chinese market successfully turned out to be difficult. Tao Kae Noi snacks could reach only a small fraction of the market because, having import duties of 30 percent, his retail price was higher than that of goods produced in China. Building a factory in China was also next to impossible since foreigners could not solely own a factory. Tob had to form a joint investment with a Chinese partner, which led to him losing some control. Finding a suitable partner was also rather difficult because he wanted a partner who was interested in long-term success. Moreover, setting up a factory in China was a very complicated process, since each province had its own set of regulations in addition to those from the central government. Exporting its products from Thailand and employing overseas distributors were the more realistic options to TKN at this stage.

Going Global

After fifteen years in business, TKN snack was available worldwide and accounted for 71 percent of the company's total revenue. The company reported its revenue in 2018 as 5.7 billion baht (US $178 million). However, to achieve 10 billion baht and to be a global player, TKN had to deal with the following challenges.

Diversification

A high concentration on sources of TKN revenue caused concern among TKN management. Ninety-six percent of its revenue was from seaweed product lines. Having diversified to non-seaweed related businesses such as supplementary food and retailer businesses, the company was still incurring losses. Moreover, 90 percent of the seaweeds used as raw material was bought from Korea. Any disruption of the flow of this supply source could be detrimental to the company's survival since finding alternative locations, including farming in Thailand, was still in an early stage.

In addition to its heavy dependence on the seaweed snack business, 40 percent of its total revenue was from the Chinese market. To reduce its dependence on this market, in 2017, TKN acquired a California-incorporated organic seaweed producer, and subsequently offered a roasted seaweed snack product under the "Nora" brand. The company planned to add tempura chips to reach the US mainstream audience which preferred salty snacks. The competition from global competitors, such as PepsiCo, Kellogg's, Mondelēz, and Kraft was expected to be a tough battle since TKN would enter into the market territory of these well-established operators.

Counterfeit Competition

In 2018, TKN terminated one of its two distributors in China after this distributor, who accounted for 50 percent of Chinese sales, counterfeited TKN products and distributed them locally (Vacharawongsith & Khaoeian, 2018). Previously, TKN enjoyed high margins and high sales growth from the Chinese market. This was mainly owing to the sales and marketing expenses being absorbed by these distributors. After the termination, the company had to shift part of its sales process in-house. For instance, TKN launched a flagship store at Tmall, the Chinese-language website for business-to-consumer sales owned by the Alibaba Group. By doing so, higher marketing and sales office expenses were unavoidable. TKN also recruited new Chinese distributors, who required time to adjust to the seaweed snack business. However, the concern on counterfeit problems continues to prevail because the product is easily copied and enforcing its brand patent in China is costly and ineffective.

Volatile Environment

The exchange rate fluctuation turned out to be a regular challenge because its international transaction was done mostly in US dollars. Furthermore, the fluctuation of its domestic revenue was largely due to the instability of international tourist flows to Thailand. Increasingly, its domestic sales came from Chinese tourists. Seventy percent of customer traffic at its Taokaenoi Land retail stores was from Chinese tourists. However, the flow of Chinese visitors to Thailand was sensitive to the country's negative news in the mainland. For example, Chinese tourist arrivals in Thailand were tumbling as a consequence of a tour boat accident off Phuket in July 2018 that had killed dozens of Chinese holidaymakers and raised safety concerns (Thanthong-Knight, 2018).

DISCUSSION QUESTIONS

1. What does it take to make a new SME business a successful exporter? Is it important to be successful in the domestic market before expanding overseas?
2. Discuss the importance of brand building even in the early stage of exporting.
3. Which types of market entry did TKN employ in exporting?
4. In order to encourage more young entrepreneurs to export, how should a government set up its export programs? How should the assistance services from the government reflect different stages in exporting?
5. In 2019, TKN expanded its business beyond selling seaweed snacks in a few countries for many reasons, including to reduce its dependence on specific sources of revenue and to be more competitive. Analyze if these expansions could help TKN to reach its sales revenue goal and be a successful global player.

AN INTERNATIONAL NEW VENTURE
New Zealand's Economic Environment

New Zealand is a small island nation in the South Pacific south-east of Australia. Its landmass of 268 million square kilometers compares with the size of Oregon. With a slightly higher population than Oregon – just over four million (4.36 million in 2010) – New Zealand's domestic market is small. GDP per capita is about US$30.045 per year (2010), slightly more than half of that of the USA, with an annual economic growth rate of 3 percent in 2010. Virtually free access of overseas competitors to New Zealand's home market forces its numerous small and medium enterprises (SME1) to seek and develop international markets. Australia is its most important trading partner, accounting for 22 percent of New Zealand's exports, followed by the USA (11.5 percent) and Japan (9.2 percent). New Zealand relies for its economic viability mainly on the success of its SMEs, since these constitute up to 90.7 percent of all firms and provide about 50 percent of New Zealanders with work and income. A 2002 report initiated by the New Zealand Treasury identified the two major constraints for economic growth in New Zealand: the distant geographic location from international markets and the difficulty of raising sufficient capital.

The Making of Honeyland and its Products

Honeyland is an export business specializing in native New Zealand honeys. It was established in Palmerston North, a small town in the New Zealand Manawatu region, in July 1986. The business started exporting right from its beginnings and has, in effect, never operated in the domestic New Zealand market, focusing on one international market only. The company supplies exclusively to the lucrative Japanese market. The company is, even by New Zealand's standards, very small. It is literally a one woman enterprise. That does not limit the success, though. From modest beginnings the enterprise has grown into a business that turns over more than NZ$500,000 (about US$275,000) operating from a small office in the family home.

New Zealand honey is positioned as a health-promoting product, using New Zealand's clean and green image. The company strategically targets quality-conscious customers, especially those who have been to New Zealand for a holiday and know its spectacular landscape. New Zealand has a reputation for its beautiful and rather unspoilt natural environment, including its exotic plants. The majority of New Zealand's plants are indigenous, found growing naturally only in that part of the world. In particular, New Zealand has many flowering trees, such as the pohutukawa, kamahi, manuka, tawari, and rewarewa. Native bush and forest honey, which is produced in this environment, has a reputation for being healthy and beneficial to human well-being. The honey that bees collect from the flowers of the New Zealand tea or manuka tree is said to have a great taste and very beneficial healing properties.

The owner of Honeyland, Sue, a trained school teacher, became aware of the good reputation and health benefits of New Zealand honey early on. In the 1970s, she raised a young family while keeping bees in a few beehives in the back of her garden around the family home. Sue has always kept a friendly open home and entertained the many international friends of her teenage children and business partners of her husband. "When I look back, our home was always an open home, long before other people actually were in the international world." Many of these visitors were Japanese because Palmerston North has strong links to Japan through its Japanese-based International Pacific College and Massey University. Many young Japanese students complete their high school and university education there. Attracted to the cultivated polite Japanese people, Sue chose her preferred market destination long before she started the company. Her interest in Japan and Japanese culture grew during visits when she accompanied her husband, a successful wool merchant, on his business trips. Soon Sue started looking for a business idea that would enable her to visit Japan on a regular basis without having to depend on her husband. The hobby of producing honey grew into a business idea.

Export Market Japan

The contacts with Japanese friends exposed her to their culture, way of life, and work. While on her trips in Japan she gradually built up an extensive network of friends and business partners. "We had a real network of friends and acquaintances in Japan. I think that probably has been one of the great advantages, because some of them are students, some of them are old, they range from 15 years old to 90 years old. They are all around Japan and they enjoy different sorts of lifestyles. So that is a wonderful way of getting a feel for what a country is like." Additionally, Sue undertook further preparation before starting up the enterprise. She began to learn the Japanese language because she understood the importance of language skills when doing business in Japan. It did not take long before she became convinced that New Zealand specialty honeys would be a suitable export product. Sue applied great care to understanding the specifics of the Japanese market. One major hurdle she had to overcome was gaining access to Japanese distributors and retail businesses. She said that in the 1980s this was not easy for a businesswoman. Speaking the language, and with some support from her friends, she eventually overcame this difficulty. Sue modifies and markets her products to conform with the special Japanese requirements.

Marketing Strategy

Honeyland's market can be categorized into three different segments. One third of the business comes from sales through a supermarket chain that operates a "fixed price" strategy. Quality branded products are sold at a discount: "It is a discount type store. Unbelievable, their whole layout is similar to the one of the 'two dollar' shop. Like 1 dollar, 2 dollar, 3 dollar shop! It is primarily liquor ... So they use good brands to bring people in and sell them cheaply." Another third of her business involves supplying a Japanese honey company with New Zealand comb honey. This company brands the product under its own name. The third and most important segment of Honeyland's business derives from sales to a firm that is associated with Japan Travel Business (JTB). It targets the top range of the gift product industry with high returns selling gifts of various honeys in small gift packaging to returning travelers. Sue says: "The third part of my market is very much a niche market, a very top shelf specialty honey ... The niche market is going through my representative in Japan." Japanese tourists spend their short holidays in New Zealand's surroundings. They experience the great outdoors enjoying the scenery doing bush walks and encountering many exotic plants among New Zealand's wild flora. It is part of Japanese culture that travelers take home a small gift to friends and family. Others like to have a piece of New Zealand as a memory for themselves. Honeyland provides a solution for those tourists who do not want to worry about purchasing presents when holidaying. Honeyland products are available in Japanese airport stores for tourists to pick up upon arrival back in Japan. Packaged in small, beautifully labeled containers, the distinctive New Zealand honeys have become a much appreciated gift in Japan.

Export Barriers

One of the biggest obstacles to Honeyland's growth is sourcing and securing the supply of quality honey. Thus, the New Zealand supply determines the extent of the company's involvement in the international market and limits business expansion. Annual variations in quality and quantity are natural occurrences of the product. Sue solved the supply difficulties by developing and maintaining a very good relationship with her domestic supplier. Its loyal commitment guarantees preferential supply even when overall stocks are low and it cannot deliver to other clients. Another problem is the management of organic export products. New Zealand has entered into an international treaty to protect plants and natural vegetation that requires strict export controls. New Zealand's Ministry of Agriculture and Fisheries (MAF) is the official body that looks after the treaty's enforcement. Export operations are difficult because MAF requires strict compliance with its phyto-sanitary and biosecurity regulations, including the inspection of all exported organic products and detailed documentation. Careful planning and organization on the part of Honeyland is necessary to be able to meet the export deadlines. These problems have been solved through close attention to MAF regulations at the planning and strategy stages. Thus, Honeyland now organizes international trade around these requirements and uses the MAF certificates for quality differentiation.

Logistics

Access to reliable and cost-effective transportation is another issue with which Honeyland has to deal. New Zealand is far off the main shipping routes and transport costs are high compared to countries that are in the center of the world trade network. The large geographical distance between New Zealand and Japan is a big obstacle in itself. The normal shipping time to Japan is ten days on average. However, in reality it takes much longer for a shipment to arrive safely to the customer. Why is this? Honeyland usually ships out of Napier, a small rural town with international harbor facilities. Napier has turned out to be a convenient location since most of the honey is sourced and packaged regionally. The supplier loads the honey into sea containers onsite so transport costs and time inside New Zealand are minimized. However, using a small regional port also has disadvantages. Most of the drawbacks are related to capacity and frequency of transportation services, particularly during times when the general harvest season is underway. Around harvest time a variety of produce exporters usually compete for limited container space and shipping facilities.

There are other problems concerning logistics. The size of Honeyland's export unit is on average just one container load. The shipping of a "20 foot" standard container to Japan costs about NZ$4000 (US$2,200). This price includes the basic paperwork such as customs declaration. There may be times when customers require a more frequent delivery mode and then the size of the shipment can be less than one container. If containers are shared, the projected arrival time is less predictable than normal because a suitable load going to the same destination to fill up the remainder of the container has to be found. When shipping smaller quantities of high-priced niche products, Honeyland employs the services of a reliable international freight forwarder. Although utilizing the services of freight forwarders is more costly than organizing the shipping with the shipping company directly, it has the advantage that professional logistics services take care of all the formalities, including the customs declaration and the documentation of the bio- security requirement. It also ensures the necessary import license that is only valid for one year and has to be renewed in a timely fashion. If need be, it organizes the clearing of customs at port in Japan swiftly, which reduces the order cycle time considerably.

Export Pricing

For the setting of export prices it is important to remember that Honeyland has no domestic sales and that only one export market is involved. Therefore, the price decision is straightforward since the export prices are based on the costs of sourcing the honeys as well as logistics. The prices for the Japanese customers are quoted and paid for in NZ$. Sue acknowledges that sufficiently large profit margins are critical to manage foreign exchange risk. Frequent currency fluctuations of the NZ$ affect profits and in the long term the business itself.

Risk Management

Sue believes in the benefits of maintaining long-term relationships with her clients. One factor that will most certainly upset Japanese clients is the renegotiating of prices. Sue knows this sensitivity. Therefore, she attempts to keep her prices fairly constant in spite of the New Zealand currency volatility. She does so even if that means that sometimes losses occur. Another important aspect of good business relationships is that it minimizes general risks, lowers transaction costs, and helps to avoid lengthy negotiations. For example, Honeyland experiences reliable payments on time and payment to the full amount. The company's excellent networks and culturally appropriate business practices practically guarantee that default situations hardly arise.

For Honeyland, the existing three Japanese business segments are a sufficiently large market because they account for Honeyland's entire export volume. A prerequisite for sustained good business relations with Japanese companies is that size and quality of the export ventures have to match expectations in order to create a good business fit and sustainability. Sue explains: "Just from the beginning I realized three main factors in dealing with Japan: one is quality and guarantee of quality; two is supply ability – you must be able to guarantee supply and that was very important with maintaining this relationship with this catalogue company ... And the third one is stability in price – so you have to take losses sometimes."

International Communications

Over the years, Honeyland has maintained mutually beneficial and trusting relationships with the same networks. Information technology, internet access, and email have allowed Sue to keep in regular contact with her network partners in between her regular visits to Japan. Often she is also busy with answering customers' queries and requests directly. She explains: "There are daily emails from business partners; they have a habit of sending vast numbers of emails with queries, such as potential benefits of treating race horses with NZ Manuka honey to prevent stomach ulcers." These kinds of queries have given Sue food for thought if she ever wanted to expand her business and develop other products. It is not astonishing that Honeyland has its own website for general information and marketing.

Conclusion

Sue says that she is very content with her business. She operates a lean and efficient enterprise with only minimal expenses and overheads. She does so single-handedly (no employees) from a small office room in her own home, and she has no immediate plans to change it. Honeyland is now one of the long-time successful "international new venture" businesses in New Zealand.

DISCUSSION QUESTIONS

1. Imagine that you are in charge of logistics for a small exporting business such as Honeyland. What are the difficulties you need to think about?
2. What are the specific contextual requirements when exporting from New Zealand?
3. Considering that Sue is under a significant time constraint, do you think that outsourcing the entire logistics would be a good move for Honeyland?
4. What would have been an alternative entry strategy for the Japanese market?
5. Do you think the company should expand or diversify?

Additional Resources for Research

General information about New Zealand, including socio-economic details, is supplied by the New Zealand Trade & Enterprise website, which is government sponsored.

CASE STUDY 10
When Diamonds Weep[1]

The ancient Greeks called diamonds the tears of the gods. Today, we know that natural diamonds consist of highly compressed carbon molecules. They have become a symbol of beauty, power, wealth, and love. Nevertheless, diamonds and the diamond trade are plagued by a sad reality: the exploitation of populations for diamond extraction and the use of diamond profits to fund terrorist activity and rebel groups.

Trade in diamonds is highly profitable. They are readily convertible to cash, small and easily transportable, not detectable by dogs, nor do they set off metal detectors. Unfortunately, these virtues also make them an easy target for money laundering activities by terrorist and rebel groups. In addition, their high value encourages some diamond-producing countries to employ means of extraction that may violate human rights. Consider the case in Botswana where a rich diamond deposit was discovered on the land belonging to a tribal group, the Bushmen. The government forcibly resettled the 2,500 Bushmen.

THE DIAMOND PRODUCTION PROCESS: FROM MINE TO MARKET

Diamonds are mined in several different ways: in open pits, underground, in alluvial mines (mines located in ancient creek beds where diamonds were deposited by streams), and in coastal and marine mines. Despite advances in technology, diamond excavation remains a labor-intensive process in most areas of the world. Since 2005, around 142 million carats of diamonds have been mined annually (one carat is the equivalent of 0.2 grams) (Statistica, 2019).

Once diamonds have been excavated, they are sorted, by hand, into grades. While there are thousands of categories and subcategories based on the size, quality, color, and shape of the diamonds, there are two broad categories of diamonds – gem-grade and industrial-grade. Typically, close to 60 percent of the annual production is of gem-quality. In addition to jewelry, gem-quality stones are used for collections, exhibits, and decorative art objects. Industrial diamonds, because of their hardness and abrasive qualities, are often used in the medical field, in space programs, and for diamond tools.

After the diamonds have been sorted, they are transported to one of the world's six main diamond trading centers – Antwerp, Belgium; New York, USA; Tel Aviv, Israel; Shanghai, China; Dubai, United Arab Emirates; and Mumbai, India (Moti Israeli Diamonds, 2015). Around 84 percent of all rough diamonds and 50 percent

---

[1] This case was prepared by Daria Cherepennikova under the supervision of Professor Michael R. Czinkota of Georgetown University.

of all cut diamonds pass through the Antwerp trading center daily (Malathronas, 2018). After they have been purchased, the diamonds are sent off to be cut, polished, and/or otherwise processed. Four countries currently dominate the diamond processing industry – India, which is the largest (processing 9 out of every 10 diamonds); Israel; Belgium; and the United States, which is emerging as a new processing center (Jones, 2016). Finally, the polished diamonds are sold by manufacturers, brokers, and dealers to importers and wholesalers all over the world, who in turn sell to retailers. The total timeframe from the time of extraction to the time at which the diamond is sold to the end consumer is called the "pipeline" and usually takes about 2 years.

THE NOT SO DAZZLING SIDE OF THE DIAMOND TRADE

While women across the world may hope for a diamond on their finger, the industry's sparkling reputation has been tarnished. Reports have shown that profits from the diamond trade have financed deadly conflicts in African nations such as Angola, Sierra Leone, Congo, Cote d'Ivoire, and Liberia. In addition, reports by the *Washington Post* and Global Witness, a key organization in monitoring the global diamond trade, revealed that Al Qaeda used smuggled diamonds from Sierra Leone, most likely obtained via Liberia, to fund its terrorist activities (Duke, 2001; Farah, 2001). Diamonds that have been obtained in regions of the world plagued by war and violence have thus been nicknamed "conflict diamonds" or "blood diamonds" (see Exhibit 10.9).

EXHIBIT 10.9 Conflict diamonds

The use of diamonds for illicit activities has been widespread. During the Bush War of Angola in 1992, Jonas Savimbi, the head of a rebel movement called UNITA (National Union for the Total Independence of Angola), extended his organization into the vast diamond fields of Angola. In less than one year, UNITA's diamond smuggling network became the largest in the world – netting hundreds of million dollars a year with which it purchased weapons (Fowler, 2000). Diamonds were also a useful tool for buying friends and supporters and could be used as a means for stockpiling wealth.

Soon warring groups in other countries such as Sierra Leone, Liberia, and the Democratic Republic of Congo adopted the same strategy. For example, the RUF (Revolutionary United Front) in Sierra Leone, a group that achieved international notoriety for hacking off the arms and legs of civilians and abducting thousands of children and forcing them to fight as soldiers, controlled the country's alluvial diamond fields (United States General Accounting Office, 2002).

According to current diamond industry estimates, conflict diamonds make up between 2 and 4 percent of the annual global production of diamonds (McNamara, 2006). However, human rights advocates disagree with that number. They argue that up to 20 percent of all diamonds on the market could be conflict diamonds (Jha, 2002).

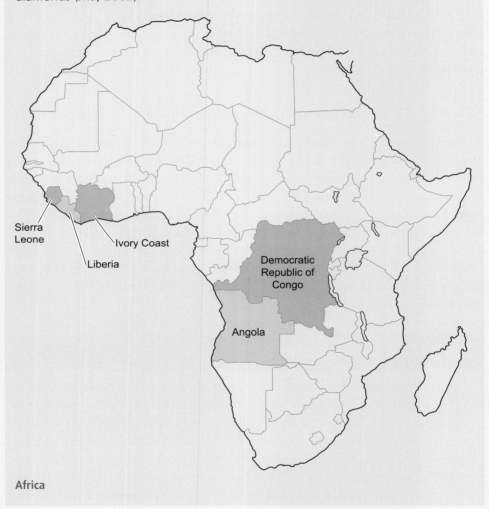

Africa

THE KIMBERLEY PROCESS

Diamonds are generally judged on the "Four Cs": cut, carat, color, and clarity; the international community has recently pushed for the addition of a "fifth C": conflict. On November 5, 2002, representatives from 52 countries along with mining executives, diamond dealers, and members from advocacy groups met in Interlaken,

Switzerland to sign an agreement that they hoped would eliminate conflict diamonds from international trade (Cowell, 2002). The agreement was called the Kimberley Process and took effect on January 1, 2003. As of 2020, the Kimberley Process has 56 participants representing 82 countries (Kimberley Process, 2015).

The Kimberley Process is a United Nations-backed certification plan created to ensure that only legally mined rough diamonds, untainted by conflicts, reach established markets around the world. According to the plan, all rough diamonds passing through or into a participating country must be transported in sealed, tamper-proof containers and accompanied by a government-issued certificate guaranteeing the container's contents and origin (Smillie, 2002). Customs officials in importing countries are required to certify that the containers have not been tampered with and are instructed to seize all diamonds which do not meet the requirements.

The agreement also stipulates that only those countries that subscribe to the new rules will be able to trade legally in rough diamonds. Countries that break the rules will be suspended and their diamond trading privileges will be revoked. Furthermore, individual diamond traders who disobey the rules will be subject to punishment under the laws of their own countries.

CRITICS SPEAK OUT

Several advocacy groups have voiced concerns that the Kimberley Process remains open to abuse, and that it will not be enough to stop the flow of conflict diamonds (Kippenberg, 2018). Many worry that bribery and forgery are inevitable and that corrupt governments officials will render the scheme inoperable (Obale, 2016). Furthermore, even those diamonds with certified histories attached may not be trustworthy. Alex Yearsley of Global Witness, an advocacy group trying to raise global awareness about conflict diamonds, predicts that firms will "be a bit more careful with their invoices" as a result of the implementation of the Kimberley Process, but warns, "if you're determined, you can get around this process" (Global Witness, 2005). A 2005 report published by Global Witness highlighted shortcomings of the Kimberley Process and made specific recommendations for its improvement (Global Witness, 2005). For example, the report urges governments to implement stricter policies of internal control, advocates for the diamond industry to publicize names of individuals in companies found to be involved in conflict trade, and pushes for the United Nations to consider implementing sanctions against diamonds from Cote d'Ivoire.

The General Accountability Office, the investigative arm of the US Congress, also voiced concerns in a 2002 report: "[T]he period after rough diamonds enter the first foreign port until the final point of sale is covered by a system of voluntary industry participation and self-regulated monitoring and enforcement. These and other shortcomings provide significant challenges in creating an effective scheme to deter trade in conflict diamonds" (United States General Accounting Office, 2002).

Government organizations and policy groups are not the only ones bringing the problem of conflict diamonds to light. Rapper Kanye West released a song entitled "Diamonds from Sierra Leone" after hearing about the atrocities of conflict diamonds in Africa. "This ain't Vietnam still/People lose hands, legs, arms for real," he raps. A Hollywood movie "The Blood Diamond," starring Leonardo DiCaprio, also features an ethical dilemma about buying and trading diamonds.

THE DIAMOND INDUSTRY REACTS

Recently, a number of new technologies have emerged which, if adopted by the diamond industry worldwide, could change the way that diamonds are produced, traded, and sold. Several US companies, using machines produced by Russian scientists, have been able to make industrial and gem-grade diamonds artificially since the 1980s (Hoover, 1999), In terms of industrial-grade diamonds, this could mean tremendous cost savings for industries using industrial diamonds and the elimination of conflict diamonds from industrial uses. For gem-grade diamonds the viability of synthetic diamonds is questionable. This is largely due to the success of past diamond marketing campaigns – most consumers see synthetic diamonds as inferior to natural ones.

Another emerging technology is laser engraving. Lasers make it possible to mark diamonds – either in their rough or cut stage – with a symbol, number, or bar code that can help to permanently identify that diamond. Companies that adopt the technology have an interesting marketing opportunity to create diamond brands. For example, Intel, a manufacturer of computer chips, launched a mass marketing campaign "Intel Inside" to create brand awareness in the previously homogenous computer chip market. While consumers don't buy the chips directly, they have positive associations with computers using Intel chips – they may even only consider computers who have "Intel inside." Likewise, establishing brand awareness and building equity in its name could add value to the diamond and help increase consumer confidence.

Processes are being developed to read a diamond's internal fingerprint – its diamond unique sparkle and combination of impurities. The machine used to do this is called a Laser Raman Spectroscope (LRS) (Haubner & Rudigier, 2013). A worldwide database could identify a diamond's origin and track its journey from the mine to end consumer. However, creation of such a database requires large investments for equipment to cope with the volume of diamonds. Such investment will only happen if customers are willing to pay for such identification.

DISCUSSION QUESTIONS

1. In light of the conflict diamond issue, would you buy a diamond? Would you accept one? Why or why not?
2. Do you think the diamond industry as a whole has an ethical responsibility to combat the illicit trade in diamonds?
3. What actions, if any, should the international community take towards nations or corporations found to be trading conflict diamonds?

FURTHER RESOURCES

O'Ferrall. R. M. (2002). De Beers O'Ferrall Calls Kimberley End of Beginning. December 2, 2002. [online], Available at www.diamonds.net (Accessed March 28, 2003).

Olson, D. W. (2001). Diamond, Industrial. US Survey Minerals Yearbook[online]. Available at http://minerals.usgs.gov/minerals/pubs/ (Accessed March 28, 2003).

Olson, D. W. (2001). Gemstones." US Survey Minerals Yearbook [online]. Available at http://minerals.usgs.gov/minerals/pubs/ (Accessed March 28, 2003).

Reeker, P. T. (2003). Implementing the Kimberley Process. January 2, 2003. [online]. Available at www.diamonds.net (Accessed March 28, 2003).

CASE STUDY 11
H-1B Visas: A High-Tech Dilemma

By Susan Ronkainen, Ilkka Ronkainen, Dafina Nikolova, Beverly Reusser

THE DEBATE

The public face of the immigration debate in the USA has typically revolved around illegal workers filling low wage/low skill jobs. Traditional wisdom dictates that some work is so labor intensive and poorly compensated that it can only be performed by desperate foreigners with no option. However, there is another aspect of the immigration debate that generates no less controversy but receives far less public scrutiny. The H-1B temporary worker visa program has long affected US companies looking to attract highly skilled foreign labor. The high-tech industry has particularly sought to liberalize the rules and regulations governing H-1B. Opponents of the program have characterized its current form as the present-day version of indentured servitude. Some domestic labor groups have argued that temporary workers are an unnecessary evil that depresses wages and takes American jobs away from Americans.

The H-1B is a visa program that allows foreign individuals with highly specialized knowledge and skills to work in the USA for a maximum of six years. It was initiated in the 1950s to attract mathematicians, physicists, and engineers from behind the Iron Curtain. H-1B has undergone many revisions since its inception. However, it has not been able to keep pace with the changing needs of American employers. This is well illustrated by estimates where historically robust labor demand is projected to grow 5.2 percent from 2018 to 2028 (Dubina et al., 2019).

Keeping up with legislative changes to the program is a full-time job in itself. In 2020, Congress approved a H-1B allotment 1-Hof 85,000 (H-1B Fiscal Year 2021 Cap Season, 2020; Anderson, 2020b). The bill passed, largely because high-tech lobbyists were successful in positioning the visas as protection to keep the US competitive edge in technology. However, the allotments were scaled back drastically under pressure from domestic interest groups, using the dot-com bubble burst and resulting temporary sector contraction as justification. Currently, there are only 65,000 H-1B visas available, with an additional 20,000 reserved for foreign holders of US advanced degrees. In the H-1B random selection process for FY 2019, there were 190,098 applications filed within five days after the offer date (USCIS, 2018). The Bureau of Citizenship and Immigration Services resorted to a lottery to determine who would get a visa and who would not.

As Exhibit 11.10 demonstrates, demand for H1-B visas has long outpaced supply. Do note that the data include visas given to employers exempt from the cap, such as colleges, universities, and governmental or nonprofit research organizations

EXHIBIT 11.10 H-1B petitions filed and approved by type of petition from FYs 2016 to 2019

	FY 2016	FY 2017	FY 2018	FY 2019
Petitions filed	398,718	403,675	418,799	420,549
Initial employment	144,583	134,348	150,179	148,374
Continuing employment	254,135	269,327	268,620	272,175
Petitions approved	345,262	365,682	332,358	388,403
Initial employment	114,503	108,101	93,615	138,927
Continuing employment	230,759	257,581	238,743	249,476

Source: UCSIS, 2020.

(Gelatt & Pierce, 2018). Even amidst a global downturn, the program has not been able to accommodate demand both from American employers and willing immigrants. This limits the country's human capital growth, and consequently, its productivity and overall economic expansion. Demand for H-1B visas will spike. Simultaneously, growing domestic concerns over unemployment, irrespective of the uneven distribution of job losses across sectors, have already led to accusations of H-1B abuses and calls for increased oversight and more stringent controls.

It is important to recognize that the labor market has indeed managed to find ways of circumventing the stringent H-1B regulations. For example, use of L-1 visas, or short-term visas for intra-company transfer have no annual cap and no requirement to pay holders the prevalent wage (USCIS, 2019). Hence, companies find them less politically sensitive and more user friendly. However, they make it hard to retain the best and the brightest, since L-1s represent only a temporary measure. There also are some flagrant abuses of the system, exemplified by one company that filed numerous H-1B petitions for Iowa, where prevalent wages are lower than the national average, and then transferred approved workers to higher-wage areas.

THE CRITIC'S POSITION

In President Trump's January inaugural address, he promised "Buy American and Hire American." In April 2017, he signed the appropriate executive order (White House, 2017). The H-1B program garnered Trumps attention following reports that US tech workers from Southern California Edison, a utility, and The Walt Disney Company were being terminated and replaced with cheaper H-1B holders (Nellis, 2016). Both companies stated they paid foreign contractors comparably with local staffers. In 2015, Save Jobs USA, an association representing the Southern California Edison US-born tech workers, filed a federal lawsuit against the Department of Homeland Security to challenge the Obama-era rule granting work permission to spouses of the H-1B visa holders (Fuchs, 2019). Four years later under the Trump administration, the US Court of Appeals for the District of Columbia Circuit concluded that the DHS' regulation exposes Save Jobs USA's members to increased competition (United States Court of Appeals for the District of Columbia, 2019).

This critique is predicated on the assumption that employers exaggerate labor shortages. There are some numbers to support such claims. Pew Research shows that temporary foreign workers (H-1B visa holders) have received significant raises over the last decade, while American workers have suffered from relative wage stagnation. The median salary for H-1B visa workers rose from $69,455 to approximately $80,000 per year – a pay raise of almost 16 percent (Krogstad & Ruiz, 2017). By contrast, the wages of domestic workers in similar jobs rose from $73,036 in 2007, to $75,306 today – a 3 percent increase.

However, there are positive effects. The H-1B program is designed to increase the supply of skilled workers. Companies are able to secure lower paid labor, which reduces costs and increases the overall profit potential.

Other critics question whether H-1B attracts the best and the brightest. They argue that truly exceptional workers constitute the minority of the visa holders and point out that the minimum degree requirements for H-1B are rather low – a bachelor's or equivalent experience. The implication is that H-1B is becoming obsolete, given that there are plenty of capable Americans, eager and willing to work, especially in the wake of the global economic collapse and rising unemployment rates. However, this criticism does not take into account long-term processes or current and future differences in labor supply and demand across industries.

There are some key economic and demographic trends. The US Bureau of Labor Statistics projects that the labor force growth will continue to slow due to changing demographic and a lower population growth. The labor force is predicted to grow 0.5 percent annually from 2018 to 2028 (Dubina et al., 2019). At the same time, the traditional age of retirement may well be subjected to change and perhaps encourage people to continue working until age 75. By 2030, the US Census projects that the number of Americans who are in their typical retirement age (65 and older) will take up 20 percent of the population (United States Census Bureau, 2018). One example of the potential impact of an aging workforce is the healthcare industry, which is already grappling with persistent labor shortages. That became particularly evident during the COVID-19 attack. The average registered nurse in the USA is 51 years old (National Council of State Boards of Nursing, 2017). Once baby boomers retire, replacing them would be difficult without the help of qualified foreign workers. Another important concern is the domestic workforce readiness, about four out of ten full-time undergraduate students who seek a bachelor's degree at four-year degree-granting public institutions will not graduate after six years (Undergraduate Retention and Graduation Rates, 2020). Many college-age students in the USA are faced with the triple burden of rising tuition rates, contracting credit, and growing student loans. Of those who do pursue higher education, fewer are entering "hard" science and technology-oriented tracks. Simultaneously, the American economy is gradually shifting away from manufacturing and towards services, as exemplified by the ever-expanding technology sector (Dubina et al., 2019). This trend will increase demand for science, math, and computer skills, which are in increasingly short supply and most frequently taken on by international students.

What would happen if technology companies were unable to find enough skilled workers domestically? The answer lies in importing from abroad, in a word – outsourcing. Expediting the move of America's technology sector overseas is not a desirable outcome, especially from a political point of view. Some policy makers have proposed a comprehensive approach to permanent skilled immigration, similar to the merit-based point systems of Canada and the United Kingdom. This could ensure expedited processing for potential immigrants in needed occupations. However, because of pressures from domestic interest groups, the political will for such a comprehensive overhaul has remained in short supply.

THE VISA HOLDER'S PERSPECTIVE

A political solution to the skilled labor and immigration debate is important. Many analysts operate under the mistaken assumption of "If you build it, they will come." In other words, there will never be a shortage of highly skilled employees, willing to move to America, so immigration reform is not pressing. The incentives for international labor mobility are well-established and straightforward – better wages and standard of living, coupled with job security and possibilities for career advancement. From the immigrant's perspective, the H-1B system fails on almost all counts. The visa represents a temporary work permit, held by the employer and not by the worker. Because the number of available foreign workers has traditionally exceeded the H-1B allotment (refer to Exhibit 11.11), employment-based green card holders have little bargaining power with their employers and can be stuck in a less-than-ideal job for as long as ten years, with no possibility to switch companies or get a promotion.

At the same time, developing countries like China, India, and South Korea have implemented policies aimed at fostering return migration and retaining domestic talent. They have made massive investments in innovation, infrastructure and R&D, with some measurable results. Nearly two out of five international STEM students are undecided about whether to stay in America or return to their home countries after graduation (Applebaum & Han, 2016). More than a third of them

EXHIBIT 11.11 Top 10 H-1B petitions approved by country of birth (FY 2019)

India	278,491
People's Republic of China	50,609
Canada	4,615
South Korea	3,476
Mexico	2,936
Philippines	2,707
Taiwan	2,637
United Kingdom	1,910
Brazil	1,902
Pakistan	1,766

Source: UCSIS, 2020.

are aware of programs designed to lure them back to their country of origin. At the same time, US immigration policy makes it difficult for them to remain.

Indian and Chinese workers who had studied or worked in the USA for a year or more before returning home cited growing demand for their skills and lucrative career opportunities back home as the primary motivator for repatriation. The majority of these individuals were in their early 30s and 62 percent had master's or doctoral degrees (USCIS, 2020). Beyond returning home, in-demand workers also have more opportunities to move to developed countries other than the USA. Over the past decade, many OECD governments have recognized the looming global demographic and skill redistribution trends, and have stepped up efforts to attract skilled foreign employees. For example, Germany has implemented a special visa/incentive program for information technology workers, while Australia and Ireland have adopted fast-track work authorization for in-demand professions. The skilled worker of the future is likely to truly have the world as their oyster, with lucrative employment opportunities across the globe.

THE BALANCE

In order to meet the growing needs of many of its industries, such as information technology and healthcare, the USA will have to completely reevaluate its immigration philosophy. Similar to the "Arms Race" and "Space Race" of the not-so-distant past, the global economic future likely holds an equally challenging and

EXHIBIT 11.12 Top 15 employers of new approved H-1B initial petitioners (FY 2019)

Employer	FY 2019 approved H-1B petitions	FY 2015 approved H-1B petitions	FY 2019 H-1B denial rate	FY 2015 H-1B denial rate	Denial rate change in percentage points FY 2015 to FY 2019
Amazon	3,575	1,070	4%	1%	+3
Google	2,707	849	4%	1%	+3
TCS	1,742	4,771	31%	6%	+25
Microsoft	1,706	970	6%	1%	+5
Deloitte	1,680	1,222	37%	18%	+19
Cognizant	1,598	3,849	56%	8%	+48
Facebook	1,534	422	3%	0%	+3
IBM	1,256	1,934	26%	3%	+23
Apple	1,155	532	2%	2%	+0
Intel	1,014	636	3%	1%	+2
Tech Mahindra	954	1,571	37%	4%	+33
Capgemini	815	556	45%	5%	+40
Larsen & Toubro	773	861	14%	2%	+12
Infosys	767	2,765	35%	2%	+33
Cisco	690	270	7%	1%	+6

Source: Anderson, 2020a; H-1B Employer Data Hub, n.d.

important "Brain Race." The ability to attract and retain skilled foreign workers in key developing industries should not be taken for granted, but fostered through functional immigration policies and incentives (Bach, 2018). The current H-1B system provides a temporary and imperfect fix (Kolakowski, 2018).

On the domestic front, the knowledge base needs to be expanded through increased investment in education and industry-specific career development. Some have suggested that the market might evolve its own measures to combat employment shortages. "Microsoft University" and "The Comcast Institute of Technology" could well be part of the future American academic community. However, without a comprehensive plan to restructure America's workforce, such piecemeal solutions will not guarantee continued economic expansion and prosperity.

In 2019, President Trump has made an announcement via Twitter that he intends to create a path for H-1B holders to gain citizenship (realDonaldTrump, 2019). Here is the memo:

> H1-B holders in the United States can rest assured that changes are soon coming which will bring both simplicity and certainty to your stay, including a potential path to citizenship. We want to encourage talented and highly skilled people to pursue career options in the US.

DISCUSSION QUESTIONS

1. Comment on the following statement: "The firms of the New Economy seem to be awfully fond of the Old Economy of 200 years ago, when indentured servitude was in vogue."
2. Identify some measures that could attract American college students to the technology and "hard sciences" fields. Should companies in these industries bear a greater responsibility for expanding the knowledge base and reinvesting some of their profits in, for example, scholarships and loan-repayment programs?
3. Should the cap for H-1B visas be eliminated altogether? Should no such provision exist at all efforts be directed at domestic supply? What should happen to foreign students with US education to keep the "The Best."

By Michael Czinkota

Classic cases offer perspective deeply rooted in an economy and its citizens. While the numerical specifics may appear to be dated, the relationships have not changed markedly. Use of a classic case communicates business conditions without hibernation information and offers interesting market specific insights.

COMPANY BACKGROUND

Ian J. Ward was an export merchant in difficulty. His company, Ward, Bedas Canadian Ltd., had successfully sold Canadian lumber and salmon to countries in the Persian Gulf. Over time, the company had opened four offices worldwide. However, when the Iran–Iraq war erupted, most of Ward's long-term trading relationships disappeared within a matter of months. In addition, the international lumber market began to collapse. As a result, Ward, Bedas Canadian Ltd. went into a survivalist mode and sent employees all over the world to look for new markets and business opportunities. Late that year, the company received an interesting order. A firm in Korea urgently needed to purchase lumber for the production of chopsticks.

LEARNING ABOUT THE CHOPSTICK MARKET

In discussing the wood deal with the Koreans, Ward learned that in order to produce good chopsticks, more than 60% of the wood fiber would be wasted. Despite the high transportation cost involved and the large degree of wasted materials, Ward's need for new business led him to explore the Korean and Japanese chopstick industry in more detail.

He quickly determined that chopstick making in the Far East is a fragmented industry, working with old technology, and suffering from a lack of natural resources. In Asia, chopsticks are produced in very small quantities, often by family organizations. Even the largest of the 450 chopstick factories in Japan turns out only 5 million chopsticks a month. This compares to an overall market size of 130 million pairs of disposable chopsticks a day. In addition, chopsticks represent a growing market. With increased wealth in Asia, people eat out more often and therefore have a greater demand for disposable chopsticks. The fear of communicable diseases has greatly reduced the use of reusable chopsticks. Renewable plastic chopsticks have been attacked by many groups as too newfangled and as causing future ecological problems.

From his research, Ward concluded that a competitive niche existed in the world chopstick market. He believed that, if he could use low-cost raw materials and ensure that the labor cost component would remain small, he could successfully compete in the world market.

THE FOUNDING OF LAKEWOOD FOREST PRODUCTS

In exploring opportunities afforded by the newly identified international marketing niche for chopsticks, Ward set four criteria for plant location:

1. Access to suitable raw materials
2. Proximity of other wood product users who could make use of the 60% waste for their production purposes
3. Proximity to a port that would facilitate shipment to the Far East
4. Availability of labor

In addition, Ward was aware of the importance of product quality. People use chopsticks on a daily basis and are accustomed to products that are visually inspected one by one, so he would have to live up to high quality expectations to compete successfully. Chopsticks could not be bowed or misshapen, have blemishes in the wood, or splinter.

Ward needed financing to implement his plan. Private lenders were skeptical and slow to provide funds. The skepticism resulted from the unusual direction of Ward's proposal. Far Eastern companies have generally held the cost advantage in a variety of industries, especially those as labor intensive as chopstick manufacturing. US companies rarely have an advantage in producing low-cost items. Further, only a very small domestic market exists for chopsticks.

However, Ward found that the state of Minnesota was willing to participate in his new venture. Since the decline of the mining industry, regional unemployment had been rising rapidly in the state. Unemployment in Minnesota's Iron Range had peaked at 22%. Therefore, state and local officials were anxious to attract new industries that would be independent of mining activities. Of particular help was the enthusiasm of Governor Rudy Perpich. The governor had been boosting Minnesota business on the international scene by traveling abroad and receiving many foreign visitors. He was excited about Ward's plans, which called for the creation of more than 100 new jobs within a year.

Hibbing, Minnesota, turned out to be an ideal location for Ward's project. The area had an abundant supply of aspen wood, which, because it grows in clay soil, tends to be unmarred. The fact that Hibbing was the hometown of the governor also did not hurt. In addition, Hibbing boasted an excellent labor pool, and both the city and the state were willing to make loans totaling $500,000. Further, the Iron Range Resources Rehabilitation Board was willing to sell $3.4 million in industrial revenue bonds for the project. Together with jobs and training wage subsidies, enterprise zone credits, and tax increment financing benefits, the initial public support of the project added up to about 30% of its start-up costs. The potential benefit of the new venture to the region was quite clear. When Lakewood Forest Products advertised its first 30 jobs, more than 3,000 people showed up to apply.

THE PRODUCTION AND SALE OF CHOPSTICKS

Ward insisted that to truly penetrate the international market, he would need to keep his labor cost low. As a result, he decided to automate as much of the production as possible. However, no equipment was readily available to produce chopsticks, because no one had automated the process before.

After much searching, Ward identified a European equipment manufacturer who produced machinery for making popsicle sticks. He purchased equipment from the Danish firm to better carry out the sorting and finishing processes. However, because aspen wood was quite different from the wood for which the machine was designed, as was the final product, substantial design adjustments had to be made. Sophisticated equipment was also purchased to strip the bark from the wood and peel it into long, thin sheets. Finally, a computer vision system was acquired to detect defects in the chopsticks. The system rejected more than 20% of the production, and yet some of the chopsticks that passed inspection were splintering. However, Ward firmly believed that further fine-tuning of the equipment and training of the new work force would gradually take care of the problem.

Given this fully automated process, Lakewood Forest Products was able to develop capacity for up to 7 million chopsticks a day. With a unit manufacturing cost of $0.03 and an anticipated unit selling price of $0.057, Ward expected to earn a pretax profit of $4.7 million in his first full year of operations.

Due to intense marketing efforts in Japan and the fact that Japanese customers were struggling to obtain sufficient supplies of disposable chopsticks, Ward was able to presell the first five years of production quite quickly. Lakewood Forest Products was ready to enter the international market. With an ample supply of raw materials and an almost totally automated plant, Lakewood was positioned as the world's largest and least labor-intensive manufacturer of chopsticks. The first shipment of six containers with a load of 12 million pairs of chopsticks to Japan was ready to be shipped.

Similarly and more recently, a firm in Americus, Georgia began producing chopsticks in 2010. Georgia Chopsticks, founded by Jae Lee, focused on the same niche as Lakewood Forest Products except that their core market was in China, not Japan. Because China was not able to harvest enough wood to create the billions of pairs of chopsticks needed per year, Georgia Chopsticks leveraged their advantage of having more access to wood, much like Lakewood Forest did almost twenty years earlier for the Japanese market.

DISCUSSION QUESTIONS

1. Is Lakewood Forest Products ready for the international playing field? Using the export-readiness framework developed by the US Department of Commerce and available through various sites such as www.tradeport.org (from "Trade Expert" go to "Getting Started" and finally to "Assess Your Export Readiness"), determine whether Lakewood's commitment, resources, and product will pay off in a global context.
2. What are the environmental factors that benefit or burden Lakewood Forest products, both at home in the USA and in the target market, Japan?
3. New-product success is a function of trial and repurchase. How can Lakewood improve customer relations in an international context and maintain satisfaction for chopsticks?
4. Given that proximity to a port was one of Ward's criteria in choosing the location of the plant, why did he choose Minnesota, which is not on either coast of the USA? Generally, what factors determine location choice? Use Michael Porter's Diamond Model to help you in your analysis.
5. CBS reported on Georgia Chopsticks and its mutual benefit for both the small town that it created jobs for, as well as the Chinese market. Watch their report on YouTube (https://youtu.be/RDoMUcHPaQs) and analyze how international business can be leveraged to help both parties involved.

Sources: Michael Czinkota, Georgetown University.

FURTHER RESOURCES

Arndt, Rachel. (2012). Georgia Chopsticks Finds a New Market in China. Fast Company, April 16, 2012. Available at www.fastcompany.com/1826872/georgia-chopsticks-finds-new-market-china. (Accessed April 28, 2020).

Clayton, Mary (1987). Minnesota Chopstick Maker Finds Japanese Eager to Import His Quality Qaribashi. The Christian Science Monitor, October 16, 1987, 11.

The Economist. (1991). Perpich of Croatia. The Economist, April 20, 1991, 27; and personal interview with Ian J. Ward, president, Lakewood Forest Products.

Gill, Mark. (1987). The Great American Chopstick Master. American Way, August 1, 1987, 34, 78–79.

Worthington, Roger. (1988). Improbable Chopstick Capitol of the World. Chicago Tribune, June 5, 1988, 39.

Ecological Cooling: The Fridge from Eastern Germany

By Michael R. Czinkota

In March of 1993, mass production of the world's first refrigerator that works without damaging the earth's vital ozone layer began in Niederschmiedeberg, the hometown of a small eastern German firm.

CFCS AND THE MONTREAL AGREEMENT

For decades, chlorofluorocarbons (CFCs) were the refrigerants of choice worldwide. They were nontoxic, nonflammable, and energy efficient. The price of $.57 per pound in 1980 also made CFCs quite inexpensive. Introduced in the 1930s, by 1985 CFCs represented a worldwide market of $1.5 billion a year. Since 1974, scientists had theorized that CFCs could deplete the earth's ozone layer, which shields the earth from the sun's harmful ultraviolet rays. As a result of these implications, and owing to public pressure, the US Government banned the use of CFCs in aerosol propellants in 1978. Because of the non-availability of reasonable substitutes, however, the use of CFCs in refrigerators and air conditioners continued to be permitted. After scientists observed a hole in the ozone layer over Antarctica, nations from around the world enacted the 1987 Montreal Protocol, which called for a 50 percent cut in CFC use by mid-1988. Given the growing public concern with environmental issues, the protocol was subsequently revised twice: in 1990, it was agreed that the 50 percent reduction in most CFCs was to be achieved by 1995 and the 1992 revision banned all CFC use by 1996. The ban had a chilling effect on the producers of cooling devices since they depended heavily on CFCs. For example, to reduce energy consumption, refrigerators are insulated with polyurethane foam. During manufacture, the foam is saturated with 300 to 600 grams of CFCs. The gas remains in the foam and because it insulates better than air, the gas provides for heat insulation. The disadvantage of CFC-foamed polyurethane is that the CFCs gradually diffuse out of the foam and are replaced by air. The CFC then escapes into the atmosphere and destroys the ozone layer. The energy efficiency of the refrigerators also deteriorates considerably over the years because of the CFC-air exchange. CFCs also contribute to the actual refrigeration process; on account of their thermodynamic properties, CFCs are highly temperature responsive to compression and expansion, therefore allowing an efficient cooling process to take place. Even though hermetically sealed, a leaky pipe or uncontrolled disposal could result in the gradual release of up to 250 grams of CFCs.

DKK SCHARFENSTEIN

Scharfenstein Deutsche Klima und Kraftmaschinen AG was founded in the German state of Saxony in 1927.The firm concentrates on producing heating and cooling devices together with compressors. In the 1950s the East German communist regime took over the firm as state property and renamed it dkk Scharienstein. As the only firm in Eastern Europe producing both refrigerators and compressors, dkk Scharfenstein (DKK) soon achieved a leadership position in the region. By 1989, the firm's 5,200 employees produced more than 1 million refrigerators and 1.5 million compressors. Every apartment built by the East Germany regime had a refrigerator made by DKK. Ten million East German households had a DKK fridge; 80 percent of households had its freezers. With the fall of the Berlin Wall on November 9, 1989, and the collapse of communism in Eastern Europe, DKK's markets collapsed as well. Long-term export contracts were rescinded. At the same time, domestic demand declined precipitously as stylish new products from West Germany became available. By 1992, production had declined to 200,000 refrigerators, and employment had shrunk to 1,000. In light of the continuing decline of its business, dkk Scharfenstein was taken over by Germany's Treuhandanstalt, the German Government's privatization arm.

DEVELOPMENT OF THE ECO-FRIDGE

dkkScharfenstein had been familiar with the ecological problems of CFCs since the mid-eighties. At that time, the firm had considered a switch to hydrofluorocarbon (HFC) IJ4a. This new chemical did not contain chlorine, but still made use of fluor, which contributes to the greenhouse effect and to global warming. However, these plans were abandoned for two reasons. First, the price of HFC IJ4a was far more than that of CFC. Second, unlike its Western counterparts, Scharfenstein was unable to obtain the product from Western markets owing to export control regulations promulgated by the Multilateral Committee For Export Controls (COCOM). While HFC 134a was available in the Soviet Union, only very limited quantities were offered for sale. After 1990, HFC 134a became freely available in eastern Germany. By that time, however, the Scharfenstein staff was already working on a different project. In conjunction with Professor Harry Rosin, head of the Dortmund Institute for Hygiene, Scharfenstein had focused on a mix of butane and propane gases to cool its refrigerators. The ingredients were environmentally friendly and, with newly designed compressors, the equipment operated with less electrical power. Management presented the new product to Treuhand, in an effort to stave off the liquidation of the firm. Treuhand attempted to interest a consortium consisting of the German firms Bosch and Siemens in acquiring Scharfenstein. After a cursory review, however, both firms decided that the new technology was too radical, unproven, and flammable and withdrew from all discussions. They, like major competitors such as Whirlpool and AEG, would continue to concentrate on HFC 134a research and production. Although expensive, HFC l34a was now competitive because new taxes had increased CFC prices to more than $5 per pound. In addition, major investments had already been made into HFC production. For example, in its race against DuPont and ElfAtochem, the British firm Imperial Chemical Industries PLC alone had already invested nearly $500 million into HFC development. To ensure that retailers would share their perspective, major producers of refrigerators supplied leaflets that warned about the dangers of explosion of fridges filled with propane and butane. Treuhand did not approve the production of the new fridge. In light of mounting losses, an additional 360 Scharfenstein employees were laid off and Treuhand announced plans to liquidate the firm. Facing the shutdown of its operations, Scharfenstein's management decided to go public with its new product. Information on the CFC-free fridge was sent to all manufacturers of refrigeration equipment, none of whom showed any interest. However, interest did materialize from unexpected quarters: The leadership of the Greenpeace organization. This worldwide environmental nonprofit group quickly recognized the benefits of the new fridge. It commissioned ten prototype models to be produced, and, after finding them satisfactory, mounted a $300,000 advertising campaign in favor of the production of "greenfreeze." Intense negotiations with retailers brought in orders and options for 70,000 of the refrigerators. The future of Scharfenstein brightened immediately. The German Ministry for the Environment supported a capital infusion of $3 million into the company. Shortly thereafter, Treuhand rescinded the layoffs that had been announced. By 1993, the firm was acquired by a consortium of British, Kuwaiti, and German investors and renamed FORON Household Appliances GmbH. Since then, FORON has received various environmental prizes and labels. The firm was awarded the government's coveted Blue Angel symbol for environmental friendliness. The German Technical Society awarded its safety seal of approval. The business magazine DM named the fridge its product of the year. The giant German appliance manufacturers, which once scorned the new technology as "impossible, dangerous and too energy-consuming," are now scrambling to put out their own green refrigerators. Major efforts for CFC-free refrigerators are also being undertaken by US and Japanese manufacturers. In the USA, a group of utilities offered $30 million to the manufacturer that designed the most energy efficient refrigerator without using CFCs. FORON expects to produce more than 160,000 eco-fridges per year and actively is exploring the possibility of exports. Inquiries have been received from China, Japan, the USA, India, Australia, and New Zealand. Even though the product is priced some 5 to 10 percent more than conventional models, the firm believes that "consumers who are environmentally aware will pay the price."

DISCUSSION QUESTIONS

1. Why is the acceptance of innovation sometimes inhibited by established industry players?
2. Evaluate the role of Greenpeace in promoting the eco-fridge. Is such an activity appropriate for a nonprofit organization?
3. What motivated Scharfenstein's investment in environmentally friendly technology?
4. How can governments encourage the development of environmentally responsive technology

Source: This case was written by Michael R. Czinkota based on discussions with Dr. Juergen Lembke, head of marketing, FORON GmbH, and reports by German and US media. Financial and logistical support from the US Information Agency (USIA) is gratefully acknowledged.

CASE STUDY 14
One Afternoon at the United States International Trade Commission

SOURCE: Excerpts from the Official Transcript Proceedings before the US International Trade Commission, meeting of the commission June 12, 1985, Washington, DC.

Chairwoman Stern, we turn now to investigation TA-201-55 regarding nonrubber footwear. Staff has assembled. Are there any questions? Vice Chairman Liebeler has a question. Please proceed.

Vice Chairman Liebeler: My questions are for the Office of Economics, Mr. Benedick. Do foreign countries have a comparative advantage in producing footwear?

Mr. Benedick: Yes, foreign producers generally have a comparative advantage vis-à-vis the domestic producers in producing footwear. Footwear production generally involves labor-intensive processes that favor the low-wage countries such as Taiwan, Korea, and Brazil, which are the three largest foreign suppliers by volume. For instance, the hourly rate for foreign footwear workers in these countries ranges from about one-twelfth to one-fourth of the rate for US footwear workers.

Vice Chairman Liebeler: Is it likely that this comparative advantage will shift in favor of the domestic industries over the next several years?

Mr. Benedick: It is not very likely. There seems to be little evidence that supports this. The domestic industry's generally poor productivity performance over the last several years, which includes the period 1977 to 1981, roughly corresponding to the period of OMAs (Orderly Marketing Arrangements) for Taiwan and Korea, suggests that US producers must significantly increase their modernization efforts to reduce the competitive advantage of the imported footwear .

Vice Chairman Liebeler: Have you calculated the benefits and costs of import relief using various assumptions about the responsiveness of supply and demand to changes in price?

Mr. Benedick: Yes. On the benefit side, we estimated benefits of import restrictions to US producers, which included both increased domestic production and higher domestic prices. We also estimated the terms of trade benefits resulting from import restrictions. These latter benefits result from an appreciation of the US dollar as a result of the import restrictions.

On the cost side, we estimated cost to consumers of the increase in average prices on total footwear purchases under the import. restrictions and the consumer costs associated with the drop in total consumption due to the higher prices.

Vice Chairman Liebeler: In your work, did you take into account any retaliation by our trading partners?

Mr. Benedick: No.

Vice Chairman Liebeler: What was the 1984 level of imports?

Mr. Benedick: In 1984, imports of nonrubber footwear were approximately 726 million pairs.

Vice Chairman Liebeler: If a six-hundred-million-pair quota were imposed, what would the effect on price of domestic and foreign shoes be, and what would the market share of imports be?

Mr. Benedick: At your request, the Office of Economics estimated the effects of the six-hundredmillion-pair quota. We estimate that prices of domestic footwear would increase by about 11 percent and prices of imported footwear would increase by about 19 percent.

The import share, however, would drop to about 59 percent of the market in the first year of the quota.

Vice Chairman Liebeler: What would aggregate cost to consumers be of that kind of quota?

Mr. Benedick: Total consumer cost would approach $1.3 billion in each year of such a quota.

Vice Chairman Liebeler: What would be the benefit to the domestic industry of this quota?

Mr. Benedick: Domestic footwear production would increase from about 299 million pairs for 1984 to about 367 million pairs, or by about 23 percent. Domestic sales would increase from about $3.8 billion to about $5.2 billion, an increase of about 37 percent.

Vice Chairman Liebeler: How many jobs would be saved?

Mr. Benedick: As a result of this quota, domestic employment would rise by about 26,000 workers over the 1984 level.

Vice Chairman Liebeler: What is the average paid to those workers?

Mr. Benedick: Based on questionnaire responses, each worker would earn approximately $11,900 per year in wages and another $2,100 in fringe benefits, for a total of about $14,000 per year

Vice Chairman Liebeler: So what then would be the cost to consumers of each of these $14,000-a-year jobs?

Mr. Benedick: It would cost consumers approximately $49,800 annually for each of these jobs.

Vice Chairman Liebeler: Thank you very much, Mr. Benedick.

Commissioner Eckes: I have a question for the General Counsel's Representative. I heard an interesting phrase a few moments ago, "comparative advantage." I don't recall seeing that phrase in Section 201. Could you tell me whether it is there and whether it is defined?

Ms. Jacobs: It is not.

Chairwoman Stern: We would like to ask about cost/ benefit analysis. Perhaps the General Counsel's Office again might be the best place to direct this question. It is my understanding that the purpose of Section 201 is to determine whether a domestic industry is being injured, the requisite level for requisite reasons, imports being at least as important a cause of the serious injury as any other cause, and then to recommend a remedy which we are given kind of a short menu to select from to remedy the industry's serious injury.

Are we to take into account the impact on the consumer?

Are we to do a cost/benefit analysis when coming up with the remedy which best relieves the domestic industry's serious injury?

Ms. Jacobs: As the law currently stands, it is the responsibility of the commission to determine that relief which is a duty or import restriction which is necessary to prevent or remedy the injury that the commission has determined to exist. The president is to weigh such considerations as consumer impact, etc. The commission is not necessarily responsible for doing that. Of course, the commission may want to realize that, knowing the president is going to consider those factors, they might want to also consider them, but in fact, that is not the responsibility of the commission. It is the responsibility of the commission only to determine that relief which is necessary to remedy the injury they have found.

Chairwoman Stern: I can understand our reporting to the president other materials which aren't part of our consideration but nevertheless necessary for the president in his consideration, but having that information and providing it to the president is different from its being part. of the commission's consideration in its recommendations.

Ms. Jacobs: That's right. Your roles are quite different in that respect.

Vice Chairman Liebeler: Nations will and should specialize in production of those commodities in which they have a comparative advantage. Fortunately, our country has a large capital stock which tends to provide labor with many productive employments. Our comparative advantage is in the production of goods that use a high ratio of capital to labor. Shoes, however, are produced with a low ratio of capital to labor.

Therefore, American footwear cannot be produced as cheaply as foreign footwear. The availability of inexpensive imports permits consumers to purchase less expensive shoes and it allows the valuable capital and labor used in this footwear industry to shift to more productive pursuits.

This situation is not unique to the footwear industry. The classic example is agriculture, where the share of the labor force engaged in farming declined from 50 percent to 3 percent over the last 100 years. This shift did not produce a 47 percent unemployment rate. It freed that labor to produce cars, housing, and computers.

The decline of the American footwear industry is part of this dynamic process. This process is sometimes very painful. Congress, by only providing for temporary relief, has recognized that our continued prosperity depends on our willingness to accept such adjustments.

The industry has sought this so-called temporary import relief before. The ITC has conducted approximately 170 investigations relating to this industry. This is the fourth footwear case under Section 201, and so far the industry has gotten relief twice. The 1975 petition resulted in adjustment assistance. The 1976 case resulted in orderly marketing agreements with Taiwan and Korea.

In spite of the efforts of the domestic industry to suppress imports, the industry has been shrinking. Between 1981 and 1984, 207 plants closed; 94 of these closings occurred just last year. The closing of unprofitable plants is a necessary adjustment. Import relief at this stage will retard this process and encourage entry into a dying industry.

Because there is no temporary trade restriction that would facilitate the industry's adjustment to foreign competition, I cannot recommend any import. barrier.

Chairwoman Stern: The intent of the General Import Relief law is to allow a seriously injured industry to adjust to global competition. The commission must devise a remedy which corresponds to the industry and the market forces it must face.

No other manufacturing sector of our economy faces stiffer competition from abroad than the US shoe industry. Imports have captured three-fourths of our market. No relief program can change the basic conditions of competition that this industry must ultimately face on its own. The best that we as a commission can do – and under Section 201 that the president can do – is to give the industry a short, predictable period of relief to allow both large and small firms to adjust, coexist, and hopefully prosper.

I am proposing to the president an overall quota on imports of 474 million pairs of shoes in the first year. Shoes with a customs value below $2.50 would not be subject to this quota. The relief would extend for a full five years.

Commissioner Lodwick: Section 201 is designed to afford the domestic industry a temporary respite in order to assist it making an orderly adjustment to import competition. The fact that the law limits import relief to an initial period of up to five years, to be phased out after three years to the extent feasible, indicates that Congress did not intend domestic producers to find permanent shelter from import competition under the statute.

Accordingly, I intend to recommend to the president a five-year quota plan which affords the domestic nonrubber footwear industry ample opportunity to implement feasible adjustment plans which will facilitate, as the case may be, either the orderly transfer of resources to alternative uses or adjustments to new conditions of competition.

Commissioner Rohr: In making my recommendation, I emphasize the two responsibilities which are placed on the commission by statute. First, it must provide a remedy which it believes will effectively remedy the injury which is found to exist.

Secondly, Congress has stated that we, as commissioners, should attempt, to the extent possible, to develop a remedy that can be recommended to the president by a majority of the commission. I have taken seriously my obligation to attempt to fashion a remedy with which at least a majority of my colleagues can agree. Such remedy is a compromise.

I am concurring in the remedy proposal which is being presented today by a majority of the commission. This majority recommendation provides for an overall limit on imports of 474 million pairs; an exclusion from such limitation of shoes entering the United States with a value of less than $2.50 per pair; a growth in such limitation over a five-year period of 0 percent, 3 percent, and 9 percent; and the sale of import licenses through an auctioning system.

Commissioner Eckes: It is my understanding that a majority of the commission has agreed on these points. I subscribe to that and will provide a complete description of my views in my report to the president.

DISCUSSION QUESTIONS

1. What are your views of the ITC recommendation?
2. Should the principle of comparative advantage always dictate trade flows?
3. Why are the consumer costs of quotas so often neglected?
4. Discuss alternative solutions to the problem.
5. How would you structure a "temporary relief program"?

Whiskey to Vietnam: Learning Rapidly

By Michael R. Czinkota

So you're interested in an import/export business. Perhaps you're in the same position I was five months ago and have no previous experience in the field. Where do you begin? In August, I began an independent study on US whiskey exports to Vietnam with Georgetown Professor Michael Czinkota, one of the authors of this book. We decided to keep notes on the process and share some suggestions here so that students could benefit from our work. I'll take you through the process of how in five months I went from knowing absolutely nothing about import/export to obtaining exclusive rights to export Wasmund's, a brand of single malt whiskey, to Vietnam.

PRELIMINARY RESEARCH: SEE WHERE GOOGLE TAKES YOU

The first step is to begin preliminary research on the topic and bridge the information gap. Utilize all of the resources at your disposal, such as websites, books, and personal contacts, to glean introductory information on the subject. Open Google, type in "import export business" and see where the URL links lead you. I found an article by Entrepreneur.com titled, "How to Start an Import/Export Business." The article gave first-timers like me a picture of what life was like in the business, covering topics such as expenses, potential income, and what a typical day might look like. Next, surf Amazon for a related book that interests you. I found *Building an Import/Export Business* by Kenneth Weiss to be a helpful overview of what I was getting myself into. Finally, set up informational interviews with family, friends, and any other contacts familiar with the business. Valuable contacts are oftentimes just an introduction away. I learned that a couple of classmates had family import/export businesses in Columbia and Kenya. I set up meetings with them to ask them questions about their family businesses. After three to four weeks of preliminary research, I had a basic understanding of the key components of an import/export business.

LEVERAGE YOUR SCHOOL

Students should make sure to take advantage of the resources available to them through their schools. There is a wealth of information, resources, and contacts to tap into during this short window of academic life. You will find that courses, students, and professors have much to offer. If your university doesn't specifically have a class on import/export, then find professors that have experience in the field and see if they are interested in doing an independent study with you. It's likely that there are professors at your school who have import/export experience. Do some research and find the professor that best matches your particular area of interest. I sent Professor Czinkota an email saying that I was interested in an independent study on import/export. He replied asking for my résumé and for my thoughts on what it was that I wanted to accomplish with such a study. Through my preliminary research I had a few products in mind and knew that I specifically wanted to work in Asia. After some discussion, we agreed that I would have a two part project. The first part would be research based and would study consumer perception and acceptance of import – specifically in Asia. The second part would involve the study of (and the practical application of) exporting Wasmund's single malt whiskey to Vietnam. Wasmund's is based in northern Virginia and has distribution in the USA and Europe but was not available in Asia. Fellow students are also a great resource and should not be overlooked. Campuses and business schools are becoming increasingly international. Take advantage of the fact that there are people from all over the world studying at your university. Reach out to some of them and build friendships. If you are genuinely interested in them, their country, their culture, and their food, it's a good opportunity to build a mutually beneficial relationship where you can both learn from and help each other.

EXPLORE YOUR CONTACTS

It's important to take some time and give careful thought to your contacts. Spend a few minutes putting together a list of all the relevant contacts you can think of. Doing so may help identify opportunities that you never knew existed. Earlier I stated: "Valuable contacts are oftentimes just an introduction away." For example, through Ambassador Mark Palmer, one of my mentors, I was able to get an introduction to an executive at the Distilled Spirits Council of the United States (DISCUS), the national trade association. Additionally, as I explored my contacts, I found that, through one of my classmates in the Georgetown MBA program, I was one introduction away from the Vietnamese Trade Counselor to Germany. He was formerly the Trade Counselor to Italy and had experience with importing alcohol to Vietnam. Your contacts may not be as strong as mine or they may be better, but the point is to explore them to see where they might lead.

IDENTIFY POTENTIAL PRODUCTS AND COUNTRIES

Now it's time to move beyond the preliminary search and narrow the research. I wanted to start focusing on specific products and countries. Some of my questions were: What products stand out as interesting? Were there any countries that piqued interest? What opportunities seemed to be the most viable? There were a number of products that I was considering, such as seafood, clothing, and sand (used for construction). However, the lowest hanging fruit seemed to be exporting American whiskey to Asia. Wasmund's was interested in exporting to Asia – now I just had to do the market research to see if American whiskey was a good product for Vietnam.

MARKET RESEARCH

Market research is a critical component of import/export. A person cannot succeed until they first understand the consumer and the market. Market research can be done in various ways. It can be done informally, by setting up a format where you can test your product. For example, I did whiskey "tastings" with Vietnamese people in the USA and asked for their thoughts on Wasmund's. I gave samples to Vietnamese classmates, professionals, and even people at the trade office. An even more effective method would be to travel to the country and set up tasting events there to see how consumers respond to the product.

STARTING AN IMPORT/EXPORT BUSINESS

Additionally, market research can be gathered through public data available on-line. An internet search on "distilled spirits Vietnam" brings up relevant reports. I went to the DISCUS website and entered "Vietnam" in the search box and found a number of reports and press releases. A press release titled "Vietnam's WTO Membership Will Significantly Reduce Spirits Tariffs" announced that Vietnam would be reducing tariffs on imported spirits from 65 percent to 45 percent. As a result, it was anticipated that distilled spirits imports would be on the rise. Government resources can also be very helpful when it comes to market research. There are online resources such as email updates on the www.trade.gov website. The Department of Commerce has Country Commercial Guides available that provide detailed information about doing business in a certain country. The 2018 Vietnam Country commercial Guide is over a hundred pages long and has a wealth of country-specific information. The US International Trade Commission also provides valuable data. I was able to obtain data through a report on US distilled spirits exports to Vietnam. I learned that there was US$0 whiskey export in 2006 and 2007. In 2008, there were $300,000 dollars of whiskey exports in the first quarter alone. This increase is due both to Vietnam joining the WTO in 2007 and more favorable consumer perception of American whiskey. Information can also be gathered by meeting with people at the DOC or your government's trade ministry. If you are in the Washington, DC, area, it will be easier to take advantage of government resources. If you are not, this is still possible through the internet, email, and phone. Try to schedule a meeting (in person or over the phone) with the industry specialist for the area you are considering and the desk officer for the country you want to export to. For those that hit a roadblock here, my advice is be persistent and leverage any contacts that might effect an introduction. I sent an email to a Georgetown alumnus that I met in passing. He was a Deputy Assistant Secretary at the DOC and agreed to arrange a meeting between me and the industry specialist for distilled spirits. (It's important to note here that these are very busy people who are overloaded with requests for meetings. Naturally, they want to devote their time to prospects with the most potential. It is important to sell yourself and your business throughout the process.) I put on a suit and tie and went over to the DOC for a meeting with the industry specialist. Three important things happened during that meeting: (1) I gained some industry-specific knowledge about distilled spirits, (2) the specialist gave me reports, such as the 2007 Vietnam Retail Food Sector Report," as well as historical data on the amount of alcohol the USA exports to Vietnam, (3) I received an introduction to the Vietnam desk officer at the DOC. While the specialist gave me great information about the distilled spirits industry, the Vietnam desk officer gave me helpful information about the industry in Vietnam. In our meeting, we discussed specifics such as tariffs and consumption tax related to my product. We also talked about the overall potential for whiskey in Vietnam and the marketing that would be required to launch a new product.

DEFINE YOUR BUSINESS AND CONNECT THE DOTS

The end goal of doing the above-mentioned research is to arrive at a point where you can define your potential business. In order to do so, you need a product, a seller in one country, and a buyer in another country. It is said that the hardest part of import/export is finding a buyer. At this point, I had identified a product and a seller in the USA. Now I had to find a buyer and distributor in Vietnam. There are three ways to find a buyer and distributor: (1) through your government's export assistance activities (e.g., in the USA, the DOC's Export Assistance Center), (2) through the foreign trade office of the country you are trying to export to, (3) through other organizations and individual contacts. In the following section, I'll walk you through how each of these groups can help you identify a distributor.

US EXPORT ASSISTANCE CENTER

The Export Assistance Center (EAC) is the commercial service arm of the DOC designed to help US citizens with their import/export business. There are local EAC offices throughout the country and the nearest office can easily be located through the website. An EAC can help in a variety of ways, but its bread and butter is to help find distributors in the target country. Note that there are fees associated with using EAC's services. To give you all an idea, there is a charge of $700 to set up one day of meetings with four to six potential distributors in the target country.

While the DOC may be the most helpful government agency, don't forget to connect with other groups. The Department of the Treasury has an International Trade Division that can provide information as well. I emailed the program manager at the Alcohol and Tobacco Tax and Trade Bureau and received a response with some information on the industry in Vietnam. In addition, there may be industry-specific organizations. Since I was dealing with distilled spirits, the USDA Foreign Agricultural Service became a valuable contact. If your product is in the food and beverage industry, this will be a helpful group as well.

FOREIGN TRADE OFFICES

Next, I called the Vietnamese trade counselor in Washington, DC. I had a personal introduction and was able to set up a meeting fairly easily. If you are not able to see the trade counselor, it should be feasible to meet with one of the commercial attachés at the office. Vietnam also has an import/export counseling center in New York. These foreign government resources can provide country-specific information and can also suggest distributors. Depending on your product and circumstances, they can most likely recommend several possibilities. For some industries, they will already have a prepared list of distributors. It is probably a good strategy to try and find a distributor through a dual strategy, utilizing both the EAC and the foreign trade office. In a country like Vietnam, the foreign trade office might be biased towards State Owned Enterprise distributors, while the EAC may have stronger relationships with private distributors.

TRADE ASSOCIATIONS AND INDIVIDUAL CONTACTS

Alternative ways to find distributors are through individual contacts or other organizations. For example, as mentioned earlier, DISCUS is the national trade association for distilled spirits. It has an international program for promotional events in places such as China, Vietnam, and South Korea. That is one way to introduce your product to a market and possibly link up with a distributor. Other potentially helpful groups are the American Chamber of Commerce and the Association of Southeast Asian Nations.

NEGOTIATIONS AND LEGAL AGREEMENT

At this point, I wanted to make sure I was in agreement with my business partners regarding pay and any other legal issues, such as exclusivity. The first thing to discuss was how I would be paid. Working as an agent or middle-person, 15–25 percent commission is typical. Another option involves the company selling the product to you at a certain price and letting you decide the retail price in the foreign market. We agreed that I would buy the products at a certain price and whatever margin I sold the products at would constitute my commission. I was shooting for 15 percent. Exclusivity was the next item on the agenda. It was important for me to have exclusive rights for Vietnam. If I was going to put in much of the work up front to create a business there, I wanted to insure an opportunity to be rewarded for my work. Exclusivity for the local distributor is another issue. Some distributors may ask for exclusive rights to distribute the product in a country. Some minimum level of sales typically needs to be reached in order to receive exclusivity. Marketing is the final major piece to discuss. If the distributor has a retail presence it may not require any marketing support. Alternatively, they may say, "We'll take this product but only if you provide us with marketing support. The question is: who will pay this fee?" I am currently suggesting that Wasmund's provide minimal marketing support at first, with the distributor marketing the product in its retail locations.

INTERNATIONAL TRAVEL: MEETING POTENTIAL DISTRIBUTORS

Finally, it's time to travel to the country and meet with the potential distributors. I'll be traveling to Vietnam as soon as I graduate in May. While in the country, I'll be meeting with both the EAC-suggested distributors and those proposed by the Vietnam trade office. When meeting with the distributors, it's important to have an in-depth understanding of pricing. They will want to know the CIF price, which is the price of the products when they arrive at the port in Vietnam (this includes costs such as shipping and insurance). I'll need to have enough of an understanding to know how low I am willing to go during negotiations. In addition, I will need to be prepared to discuss how various shipment sizes will determine the cost per case. I'll also have to decide how to get samples of the product there for the initial trip. This entails researching customs issues so as to make sure samples of the product aren't stuck at entry points. Some of the potential distributors starting an import/export business may be able to help with this process and ensure that the samples get there without any problems.

TRY A SHIPMENT

During your visit, if you are fortunate enough to find a good distributor, the next step is to try a shipment. If my meetings in Vietnam go well, we'll try shipping some cases of Wasmund's single malt whiskey to Asia for the first time. International trade is a fun business. If you have a curiosity about international markets, like to travel internationally, and don't mind risk, this could be the business for you. As with most things, the best way to learn is to get your hands dirty and give it a try. The points outlined above should give you some clarity on how to get started. Good luck!

DISCUSSION QUESTIONS/ACTION POINTS

1. Complete preliminary research on possible import/export activities. What countries and industries catch your interest?
2. Put together a contact list and set up some informational interviews.
3. Define a potential business. Name a potential product, seller, and buyer.
4. Leverage government resources such as the Department of Commerce and the nearest Export Assistance Center for information on the industry and country.
5. Identify some potential distributors through the three methods mentioned in this case study (DOC, EAC, and other organizations).

Source: This case study was contributed by Mike Kim, graduate student of the McDonough School of Business at Georgetown University (2009).

References

Adam, K. (2008). Archbishop Defends Remarks on Islamic Law in Britain, Washington Post, February 12, 2008, A 11; Archbishop of Canterbury: Sharia law unavoidable in Britain, Christian Today, February 7, 2008.

Adamyk, B. (2016). Problems and perspectives of banking regulation in Ukraine during economic crisis in 2014–2016. *Czech Journal of Social Sciences Business and Economics*, *3*, 18–28.

Adelaja, T. (2016). *Capital Budgeting: Capital Investment Decision*. CreateSpace Independent Publishing Platform.

Africa: The Good News. (2011). Increased Investment Rapidly Changing Africa's IT Landscape.

Ahmadinejad, B. and Asli, H. (2017). E-business through social media: A quantitative survey (Case Study: Instagram). *International Journal of Management, Accounting and Economics*, *4*.

Aksoy, L., Allerstorfer, P., Cadet, F., Cook, P., Keiningham, T., and Koser, M. (2020). Building service businesses in Africa: Introducing the business builder model. *Thunderbird International Business Review*, *62*(1), 5–16.

Aleem, Z. (2018). The US-China trade war, explained in under 500 words. *Vox*. [online] Available at www.vox.com/world/2018/7/6/17542482/china-trump-trade-war-tariffs (Accessed Feb. 6, 2020).

Aliber, R. (1979). *Exchange Risk and International Finance*. New York: Wiley.

Altman, R. C. (2009). Globalization in retreat-further geopolitical consequences of the financial crisis. *Foreign Affairs*, *88*, 2.

American Marketing Association. (2020). Definitions of Marketing. *American Market Association* [online]. Available at www.ama.org/the-definition-of-marketing-what-is-marketing/ (Accessed May 13. 2020).

Amiti, M., Dai, M., Feenstra, R., and Romalis, J. (2017). *China's WTO entry benefits US consumers | VOX, CEPR Policy Portal*. [online] Voxeu. org. Available at https://voxeu.org/article/china-s-wto-entry-benefits-us-consumers (Accessed Feb. 7, 2020).

Andersen, T. and Andersson, U. (2017). Multinational Corporate Strategy-Making: Integrating International Business and Strategic Management. In T. Andersen (ed.), *The Responsive Global Organization* (Emerald Studies in Global Strategic Responsiveness, Emerald Publishing Limited. Available at www.emeraldinsight.com) pp. 13–34.

Anderson, R. and Reeb, D. (2003). Founding-family ownership and firm performance: evidence from the S&P 500. *The Journal of Finance*, *58*(3), 1301–1328.

Anderson, S. (2020a, February 26). H-1B Denials Remain High, Especially For IT Services Companies. Forbes [online]. Available at www.forbes.com/sites/stuartanderson/2020/02/26/h-1b-denials-remain-high-especially-for-it-services-companies/#2b6a2927b229 (Accessed May 12, 2020).

Anderson,S. (2020b, April 1). H-1B Visa Selection Completed: Will All Companies Follow Through? Forbes [online]. Available at www.forbes.com/sites/stuartanderson/2020/04/01/h-1b-visa-selection-completed-will-all-companies-follow-through/#178799de2520 (Accessed May 12, 2020).

Ang, S. and Inkpen, A. C. (2008). Cultural intelligence and offshore outsourcing success: A framework of firm-level intercultural capability. *Decision Sciences*, *39*(3), 337–358.

Anto, A. and Nag, A. (2018, April 20). Bloomberg – Are you a robot? www.bloomberg.com [online]. Available at www.bloomberg.com/news/articles/2018–04–20/why-india-is-now-scrambling-to-print-more-currency-quicktake (Accessed April 27, 2020).

Appelbaum, R. and Han, X. (2016). *Will They Stay or Will They Go? International STEM Students Are Up for Grabs*. Ewing Marion Kauffman Foundation [online]. Available at www.kauffman.org/wp-content/uploads/2019/12/STEM_Students_FINAL.pdf

Armstrong, M. (2016, August 11), Google Rules The West, Baidu Top In China. *Statistia*.

Arora, R. (2017). Marketing of agricultural commodities in India. In *Strategic Marketing Management and Tactics in the Service Industry*. IGI Global, pp. 185–212.

Asquith, P. and Weiss, L. (2016). *Lessons in Corporate Finance: A Case Studies Approach to Financial Tools, Financial Policies, and Valuation*. 1st ed. New York: Wiley.

Atlas Van Lines, Inc (2018). *International Assignments*. [online]. Available at www.atlasvanlines.com/corporate-relocation/survey/2018/international-assignments (Accessed Feb. 9, 2020).

Atsmon, Y. and Dixit, V. (2009). Understanding China's Wealthy. *McKinsey Quarterly*, (July), 32–33.

Bach, N. (2018, August 23). Business Leaders Warn of Immigration Policy's "Substantial Harm on US Competitiveness." Fortune [online]. Available at https://fortune.com/2018/08/23/business-roundtable-letter-immigration-policy/?utm_source=twitter.com&utm_medium=social&utm_campaign=social-button-sharing (Accessed May 12, 2020).

Bade, D. (2015). *Export Import: Procedures and Documentation*. New York: American Management Association.

Baldwin, R. E. and Venables, A. J. (1995). Regional economic integration. *Handbook of International Economics*, *3*(1).

Barnes, B., Yen, D., and Zhou, L. (2011). The influence of ganqing, renqing and xinren in the development of Sino-Anglo business relationships.

Industrial Marketing Management,
40(4), 510–521.

Barrad, S. and Valverde, R. (2020).
The Impact of e-Supply Chain
Management Systems on Procurement
Operations and Cost Reduction in the
Electronics Manufacturing Services
Industry.

Bartlett, C., Ghoshal, S., and Beamish, P.,
(2013). *Transnational Management.*
New York: McGraw-Hill Education.

Bartlett, J. (2016). Cypherpunks write
code. (Excerpt from Dark Net: Inside
the Digital Underworld). *American
Scientist*, 104(2),120– 123. Available at
https://doi.org/10.1511/2016.119.120

Bartram, P. (2015). How to ... manage
foreign exchange currency risk.
Director, 70.

Battacharya, A., et al. (2018). Building
the New Global Enterprise: The New
Globalization. *Boston Consulting
Group.* Available at www.bcg.com/
publications/2018/building-new-
global-enterprise.aspx. (Accessed May
21, 2020).

BBC News. (2018). *Panasonic to move Europe
HQ out of UK.* [online]. Available at
www.bbc.com/news/business-45351288
(Accessed Feb. 6, 2020).

Bea.gov. (2017). Expenditures by Foreign
Direct Investors for New Investment
in the United States, 2014–2016 | US
Bureau of Economic Analysis (BEA).
[online] Available at www.bea.gov/
news/2017/expenditures-foreign-
direct-investors-new-investment-
united-states-2014–2016 (Accessed
Feb. 3, 2020).

Beagrie, N., Beagrie, R., and Rowlands, I.
(2009). Research Data Preservation

and Access: The Views of Researchers.
Ariadne, [online] (60). Available at
http://www.ariadne.ac.uk/issue/60/
beagrie-et-al/ (Accessed Feb. 26,
2019).

Beall, A. E. (2017). *Strategic market
research : a guide to conducting
research that drives businesses.*
CreateSpace.

Beaman, K. (2012). 2011–2012 Going
Global Report HCM Trends in
Globalization. In Karen V. Beaman
(p. 14). Jeitosa Group International
[online]. Available at http://
karenvbeaman.com/wp-content/
uploads/2016/01/2012-Beaman-
Going-Global-Report-HCM-Trends-
in-Globalization-FINAL-IHRIMWire-
DEC-2011–1-PGV.pdf

Bernstein, W. (2008). *A Splendid Exchange.*
New York: Grove Press.

Beske-Janssen, P., Schaltegger, S., and
Liedke, S. (2019). Performance
measurement in sustainable supply
chain management: linking research
and practice. In *Handbook on the
Sustainable Supply Chain.* Edward
Elgar Publishing.

Betros, C. (2010). Drinks all round.
Japantoday [online]. Available at
https://japantoday.com/category/
features/executive-impact/1088172
(Accessed May 3, 2020).

Beugelsdijk, S., Kostova, T., and Roth, K.
(2016). An overview of Hofstede-
inspired country-level culture research
in international business since 2006.
*Journal of International Business
Studies, 48*(1), 30–47.

Beugelsdijk, S., Kostova, T., and Roth, K.
(2017). An overview of Hofstede-

inspired country-level culture research in international business since 2006. *Journal of International Business Studies*, *48*(1), 30–47.

BGRS. (2016). Breakthrough to the Future of Global Talent Mobility – 2016 Global Mobility Trends Survey. BGRS [online]. Available at http://globalmobilitytrends.bgrs.com (Accessed April 21, 2020).

Binder, C. (2019). *Agency, Freedom and Choice.* New York: Springer.

BIS. (2019). Offsets in Defense Trade Twenty-Third Study. US Department of Commerce Bureau of Industry and Security. Available at www.bis.doc.gov/index.php/documents/other-areas/strategic-industries-and-economic-security/offsets-in-defense-trade/2387-twenty-third-report-to-congress-4–19/file (Accessed May 4, 2020).

Black, T. and Webb, A. (2017). *Trump's Strong Dollar Means Weaker Sales at Apple, Honeywell.* Bloomberg [online]. Available at www.bloomberg.com/news/articles/2017–02-03/trump-s-stronger-dollar-means-weaker-sales-at-apple-honeywell (Accessed Feb. 7, 2020).

Blackmer, W. (2016, May 5). GDPR: Getting Ready for the New EU General Data Protection Regulation. Info Law Group website [online]. Available at www.infolawgroup.com/insights/2016/05/articles/gdpr/gdpr-getting-ready-for-the-new-eu-general-data-protection-regulation (Accessed April 30, 2020).

Blazyte, A. (2018). Alibaba continues to lead retail e-commerce sales in China. In *Statista* [online]. Available at www.statista.com/chart/14717/alibaba-continues-to-lead-retail-e-commerce-sales-in-china-in–2018/ (Accessed April 6, 2020).

Bloomberg Businessweek. (2019). KFC Aims to Keep Its China Edge With AI Menu, Robot Ice Cream Maker. [online]. Available at www.bloomberg.com/news/articles/2019–03-20/yum-china-is-building-the-kfc-of-the-future (Accessed May 1, 2020).

Bloomenthal, A. (2019). World's Top 10 Internet Companies. [online] *Investopedia*. Available at www.investopedia.com/articles/personal-finance/030415/worlds-top-10-internet-companies.asp (Accessed May 3, 2020).

Blumentritt, T. and Nigh, D. (2002). The integration of subsidiary political activities in multinational corporations. *Journal of International Business Studies*, *33*(1), 57–77.

Bobillo, A., Rodríguez-Sanz, J. and Tejerina-Gaite, F. (2017). Corporate governance drivers of firm innovation capacity. *Review of International Economics*, *26*(3), 721–741.

Bolling, C. (2019). Price and exchange rate transmission. *Elasticities In International Agricultural Trade*, 163.

Bond, D., Murgia, M., and Garrahan, M. (2017, March 21). Financial Times [online]. Available at www.ft.com/content/019e1608-0d88-11e7-a88c-50ba212dce4d (Accessed April 27, 2020).

Bork, J., Gollakota, K., and Gupta, V. (2010). Reaching customers at the base of the pyramid – a two-stage business strategy. *Thunderbird International Business Review*, *52*(5). Available at https://onlinelibrary.wiley.com/doi/abs/10.1002/tie.20361 (Accessed April 5, 2020).

Borlea, S. and Monica Violeta, A. (2013). Theories of corporate governance. *Studia Universitatis Vasile Goldiş, Arad – Seria Ştiinţe Economice*, *23*(1), 117–128.

Bosse, D. and Phillips, R. (2016) "Agency theory and bounded self-interest," *Academy of Management Review*, *41*(2), 276–297.

Boston Consulting Group. (2015). The mobile Internet takes off everywhere, *BCG Perspectives*, March 20. Available at www.bcgperspectives.com

Boudette, N. and Jacobs, A. (2020). Inside G.M.'s Race to Build Ventilators, Before Trump's Attack. In *The New York Times* [online]. Available at www.nytimes.com/2020/03/30/business/gm-ventilators-coronavirus-trump.html (Accessed April 4, 2020).

Boyett, J. (2016). *12 Major World Religions: The Beliefs, Rituals, and Traditions of Humanity's Most Influential Faiths*. Berkeley, CA: Zephyros Press.

Bradsher, K. (2017). For China's Factories, a Weaker Currency Is a Double-Edged Sword. *New York Times*, [online] March 1, 2017. Available at www.nytimes.com (Accessed May 3, 2020).

Braga, V., Correia, A., Braga, A. and Lemos, S. (2017). The innovation and internationalisation processes of family businesses. *Review of International Business and Strategy*, *27*(2), 231–247.

Brake, T. (2002). *Managing Globally*. New York: Dorling Kindersley.

Bramley, E. (2020). Prada the latest fashion brand to make medical face masks. In *The Guardian* [online]. Available at www.theguardian.com/fashion/2020/mar/24/prada-the-latest-fashion-brand-to-make-medical-face-masks (Accessed April 4, 2020).

Brannen, M. Y., Piekkari, R., and Tietze, S. (2017). The multifaceted role of language in international business: Unpacking the forms, functions and features of a critical challenge to MNC theory and performance. *Language in International Business*. Palgrave Macmillan, (pp. 139–162).

Brem, A. and Freitag, F. (2015). Internationalisation of New Product Development and Research & Development. *International Journal of Innovation Management*, *19*(1), 1–32.

Brookfield Global Relocation Services. (2012a). Global Relocation Trends – 2012 Survey Report. *Brookfield Global Relocation Services*. [online]. Available art http://ivemadeit.com/pdf/2012-Brookfield-Global-Relocations-Trends-Survey.pdf

Brookfield Global Relocation Services (2012b). *To Developing Locations Spotlight Report 2012*.

Brunelli, L. (2012). 30 Global Companies That Will Hire You to Work at Home. Balance Careers [online]. Available at www.thebalancecareers.com/global-work-at-home-jobs–3542823 (Accessed April 22, 2020).

Bruner, J. S. (1996). *The Culture of Education*. Harvard University Press.

Buckland, K. and Du, L. (2018). *Why Specter of a No Deal Brexit Is Spooking Asian Companies.* Bloomberg.com [online]. Available at www.bloomberg.com/news/articles/2018–10-02/risk-of-hard-brexit-has-these-asian-companies-on-edge (Accessed Feb. 6, 2020).

Buckley, P. (2017). *International Business.* New York: Routledge.

Buckley, P. J., Doh, J. P., and Benischke, M. H. (2017). Towards a renaissance in international business research? Big questions, grand challenges, and the future of IB scholarship. *Journal of International Business Studies, 48*(9), 1045–1064.

Buckley, P. J., Enderwick, P., and Cross, A. R. (eds.). (2018). *International Business.* Oxford University Press.

Buffie, E. F., Airaudo, M., and Zanna, F. (2018). Inflation targeting and exchange rate management in less developed countries. *Journal of International Money and Finance, 81,* 159–184.

Bughin, J., LaBerge, L., and Mellbye, A. (2017). The case for digital reinvention. *McKinsey Quarterly,* February 2017. Available at www.mckinsey.com

Bughin, J., Lund, S., and Manyika, J. (2015). Harnessing the power of shifting global flows. *McKinsey Quarterly,* February 2015, 1–13.

Bureau of Labor Statistics. (2020). Employment change by industry with confidence intervals, March 2020, seasonally adjusted, in thousands. In *Bureau of Labor Statistics.* Available at www.bls.gov/ces/ (Accessed April 4, 2020).

Burns, A., Veeck, A., and Bush, R. (2017). *Marketing Research.* Pearson Education, Inc.

Burton, F. and Cross, A., (2001). International franchising: Market versus hierarchy. In G. Chryssochoidis, C. Millar, and J. Clegg, (eds.), *Internationalisation Strategies,* New York: St. Martin's Press, pp. 135–152.

Business Insider. (2020). Coronavirus is the "biggest challenge to tourism since World War II." *Business Insider* [online]. Available at www.businessinsider.com/coronavirus-is-biggest-challenge-to-tourism-since-world-war-ii-2020–3 (Accessed May 3, 2020).

Cannizzaro, A. (2019). Social influence and MNE strategic response to political risk: A global network approach. *Journal of International Business Studies* [online]. Available at https://link.springer.com/epdf/10.1057/s41267-019-00246-4?author_access_token=8uM6sN10XAatduhVugwnT1xOt48VBPO10Uv7D6sAgHts5CQWPfDrbcTJyluEtV17CZv9ZYK1WvpiHNrkiosndcCicyLwqLMKD7RyZ4pGqvUQZjqqpTeUAuDFduJDhLjkDP8FQVKz9fQaGNx3emUNnQ%3D%3D (Accessed May 11, 2020).

Cantwell, J. (2017). Innovation and international business. *Industry and Innovation, 24*(1), 41–60.

Carroll, A., Brown, J., and Buchholtz, A. (2018). *Business & Society: Ethics, Sustainability & Stakeholder Management.* Boston: Cengage Learning.

Cartus. (2018). Global Relocation Trends: 2018 Biggest Challenges Survey.

[online]. Available at www.cartus
.com website: www.cartus.com/
en/relocation/resource/biggest-
challenges-survey/ (Accessed April 21,
2020).

Casna, K. (n.d.). *4 Genuine* Examples *of
Good Customer Service.* [online]
Salesforce.com. Available at www
.salesforce.com/hub/service/customer-
service-examples/ (Accessed Feb. 11,
2020).

Caudell, D. (2019). *Amazon's Inventory
Management Secrets.* [online] RFgen.
com. Available at www.rfgen.com/
blog/bid/246924/amazon-s-inventory-
management-secrets (Accessed Feb. 9,
2020).

Cavusgil, T. (1998). International
partnering: A systematic framework
for collaborating with foreign
business partners. *Journal of
International Marketing* 6, 91–107.

Cavusgil, T. and Knight, G. (2015). The
born-global firm: An entrepreneurial
and capabilities perspective on early
and rapid internationalization. *Journal
of International Business Studies*,
46(1), 3–16.

Central Intelligence Agency. (2019). *The
World Factbook 2019*. Washington, DC,
2020. Available at www.cia.gov/library/
publications/resources/the-world-
factbook/index.html

Central Intelligence Agency. (2020). *The
World Factbook.* [online]. Available
at www.cia.gov/library/publications/
the-world-factbook/ (Accessed May 3,
2020).

Chaffey, D., Hemphill, T., and Edmundson-
Bird, D. (2019). *Digital Business and
E-Commerce Management*, New York:
Pearson.

Chakravarthy, B. (2012). MAGGI Noodles
in India: Creating and Growing the
Category. Case no. IMD-3-2296.
IMD [online. Available at www
.thecasecentre.org/educators/products/
view?id=113470 (Accessed May 3,
2020).

Chalaby, J. (2009). *Transnational Television
in Europe*. London: I.B. Tauris & Co.
Ltd.

Chandler, D. (2017). *Strategic Corporate
Social Responsibility: Sustainable
Value Creation*, 4th ed. Thousand
Oaks, CA: Sage.

Chandra, Y. (2017). A time-based process
model of international entrepreneurial
opportunity evaluation. *Journal of
International Business Studies*, 4,
423–451.

Cheng, E. (2019). China's giant middle
class is still growing and companies
from Walmart to start-ups are trying
to cash in. *CNBC* [online]. Available
at www.cnbc.com/2019/09/30/
chinas-giant-middle-class-is-still-
growing-and-companies-want-in.html
(Accessed May 3, 2020).

Chesterman, S. and Fisher, A. (2020). *Private
Security, Public Order: The Outsourcing
of Public Services and Its Limits*,
Oxford: Oxford University Press.

Cheung, J. (2017). Shortcomings in China's
Corporate Governance Regime. *China
Law & Practice,* February 2007(1).

Chew, J. (2016, February 24). Ikea Is Facing
Huge Problems In This Important
Country. Fortune [online]. Available
at https://fortune.com/2016/02/24/
ikea-india-rules/ (Accessed April 21,
2020).

Child, J., Hsieh, L., Elbanna, S.,
Karmowska, J., Marinova, S.,

Puthusserry, P., ... and Zhang, Y. (2017). SME international business models: The role of context and experience. *Journal of World Business*, *52*(5), 664–679.

China Daily. (2014). In Quotes: Deng Xiaoping. China Daily [online]. Available at www.chinadaily.com.cn/china/2014–08/20/content_18453523.htm (Accessed April 20, 2020).

China Internet Watch. (2013). 4 Types of Chinese Consumers by Attitude to Brands. China Internet Watch [online]. Available at www.chinainternetwatch.com/4494/4-types-of-chinese-consumers-by-attitude-to-brands/ (Accessed Feb. 11, 2020).

Chironga, M., De Grandis, H., and Zouaoui, Y. (2017, September 1), "Mobile financial services in Africa: Winning the battle for the customer," McKinsey & Co., www.mckinsey.com/industries/financial-services/our-insights/mobile-financial-services-in-africa-winning-the-battle-for-the-customer

Cho, W., Ke, J. Y. F., and Han, C. (2019). An empirical examination of the use of bargaining power and its impacts on supply chain financial performance. *Journal of Purchasing and Supply Management*, *25*(4), 100550.

Choudhary, A. (2013). Anatomy and impact of bribery on Siemens AG. *Journal of Legal, Ethical & Regulatory Issues*, *16*(2), 131–142.

Christiansen, H. and Koldertsova, A., (2008). *The Role of Stock Exchanges in Corporate Governance*. Paris: Organisation for Economic Co-operation and Development, 2008. Available at www.oecd.org

Cigna Health and Life Insurance Company. (2015). *GLOBALLY VOCAL: Candid insights from employees abroad Results from the Global Mobility Trends Survey 2015*. Available at www.cigna.com/assets/docs/newsroom/886022-global-mobility-exec-summary-final.pdf

Claessens, S., Kose, A., Laeven, L., and Valencia, F. (2014). *Financial Crises: Causes, Consequences, and Policy Responses*, USA: International Monetary Fund. IMF eLibrary [online]. Available at https://doi.org/10.5089/9781475543407.071 (Accessed February 7, 2020).

Clark, D. (2016). *Alibaba: the house that Jack Ma built*. New York: Ecco, an imprint of HarperCollins Publishers.

Clarke, T. (2017). *International Corporate Governance: A Comparative Approach*. New York: Routledge.

Cohn, P. and Caminiti, M. (2011). Corporate Taxes: The Multinational Advantage. *Bloomberg Businessweek*, 31.

Colgate-Palmolive. (2017). Investing for global growth winning with focus. Colgate-Palmolive Company 2017 Annual Report. (2017). *Colgate-Palmolive Company* [online]. Available at https://investor.colgatepalmolive.com/static-files/0f093899-7f24-448f-93b2-c236a3c93d99

Collins, D. (2017, September 26). The Key Factors of Toyota's Success. Bizfluent [online]. Available at https://bizfluent.com/info-8444139-key-factors-toyotas-success.html (Accessed April 21, 2020).

Companik, E., Gravier, M. J., Farris, I. I., and Theodore, M. (2018). Feasibility of warehouse drone adoption and implementation. *Journal of Transportation Management, 28*(2), 5.

Congressional Budget Office (2017). *International Comparisons of Corporate Income Tax Rates.* [online]. Available at www.cbo.gov/system/files/115th-congress-2017–2018/reports/52419-internationaltaxratecomp.pdf (Accessed Feb. 6, 2020).

Contractor, F. (2016). Tax avoidance by multinational companies: Methods, policies, and ethics. *Rutgers Business Review, 1*(1), 27–43.

ControlRisks. (2018). *RiskMap 2018.* [online] Available at www.controlrisks.com/riskmap (Accessed Feb. 6, 2020).

Cook, T. and Raia, K. (2017). *Mastering Import and Export Management.* New York: AMACOM.

Corning, P. (2018). Stakeholder Capitalism: An Idea Whose Time has Come (Again). [Blog] *Institute for the Study of Complex Systems.* Available at: http://complexsystems.org/publications/stakeholder-capitalism-an-idea-whose-time-has-come/ (Accessed Feb. 9, 2020).

Cornwell, B. (2020). *Sponsorship in Marketing.* London: Routledge.

Corominas, A. (2017). *Research into the Area of Supply Chain.* OmniaScience.

Cottrell, R. (2006). Thinking Big: A Survey of International Banking. *The Economist,* May 20, 2006, survey section.

CountryWatch. (2018). *India: Country Review (2018 Edition).* [online] Countrywatch.com. Available at www.countrywatch.com/intelligence/countryreviews?countryid=78 (Accessed Feb. 8, 2020).

Coviello, N. E. and Munro, H. J. (1997). Network relationships and the internationalization process of small software firms, *International Business Review, 6*(4), 361–386.

Cowell, A. (2002, November 6). 40 Nations in Accord on "Conflict Diamonds." *The New York Times* [online]. Available at www.nytimes.com/2002/11/06/world/40-nations-in-accord-on-conflict-diamonds.html

Crane, A. and Matten, D. (2016). *Business Ethics: Managing Corporate Citizenship and Sustainability in the Age of Globalization* Oxford: Oxford University Press.

Cravino, J. and Levchenko, A. A. (2017). Multinational firms and international business cycle transmission. *The Quarterly Journal of Economics, 132*(2), 921–962.

Crawford, D. and Esterl, M. (2007a). Inside Bribery Probe of Siemens. *Wall Street Journal,* October 5, 2007, p. A4.

Crawford, D. and Esterl, M. (2007b). Siemens Ruling Details Bribery Across the Globe. *Wall Street Journal,* November 16, 2007, p. A1.

Crawford, D. and Esterl, M. (2007c). Widening Scandal: At Siemens, Witnesses Cite Pattern of Bribery. *Wall Street Journal,* January 31, 2001, p. A1.

Cuervo-Cazurra, A. (2016). Corruption in international business. *Journal of World Business, 51*(1), 35–49.

Cunningham, L., Young, C., Lee, M., and Ulaga, W. (2006). Customer perceptions of service dimensions: Cross-cultural analysis and perspective. *International Marketing Review*, *23*(2), 192–210.

Czinkota, M. (1991). International information needs for US competitiveness. *Business Horizons*, *34*(6), 86–91.

Czinkota, M. (1997). Russia's transition to a market economy: Learning about business. *Developments in Marketing Science*, 233.

Czinkota, M. (2000). The policy gap in international marketing. *Journal of International Marketing*, *8*(1), 99–111.

Czinkota, M. (2010). A national export development policy for new and growing businesses. In M. Czinkota, I. Ronkainen, and M. Kotabe (eds.), *Emerging Trends, Threats and Opportunities in International Marketing: What Executives Need to Know*. New York: Business Expert Press.

Czinkota, M. (2016). Leadership, Corporate Social Responsibility and Sustainability, Part 7: Curative Marketing. Available at http:// michaelczinkota.com/2016/06/ leadership-corporate-social-responsibility-and-sustainability-part-7-curative-marketing/. (Accessed May 12, 2020).

Czinkota, M. (2016). Are you prepared for a new surge of countertrade? *Sri Lanka Guardian* [online]. Available at www.srilankaguardian.org/2011/08/ are-you-prepared-for-new-surge-of. html (Accessed Feb. 6, 2020).

Czinkota, M. (2017). How Psychic Distance Impacts Trade. *Psychology Today* [online]. Available at www .psychologytoday.com/us/blog/ the-initiative/201703/how-psychic-distance-impacts-trade (Accessed May 13, 2020).

Czinkota, M. (2018). Tariffs Can be Good. Available at http://michaelczinkota. com/2018/03/tariffs-can-be-good/

Czinkota, M. (2019). *In search for the soul of international business.* New York: Business Expert Press, LLC.

Czinkota, M. (2019a). Good souls bring curative marketing. *The Korea Times.* Accessed on May 21, 2020. https://www.pressreader.com/ korea-republic/the-korea-tim es/20190424/281689731217980

Czinkota, M. (2019b). In Search for the Soul of International Business– Foreword. *Business Expert Press.* Available at https://ceoworld. biz/2020/03/20/battling-the-virus-strengthens-education/

Czinkota, M. (2020). Battling the Virus Strengthens Education. *CEOworld.biz.* (Accessed May 21, 2020).

Czinkota, M. and Enke, M. (2014). An International Perspective on Commodity Marketing. Springer Link. April 16, 2014, pp. 405–419.

Czinkota, M. and Horkan, H. (2019). In Search for the Soul of International Business. *Business Expert Press.* pp. 18–26.

Czinkota, M. and Kotabe, M. (1997). A marketing perspective of the US International Trade Commission's antidumping actions: An empirical inquiry." *Journal of World Business*, *32* (Summer), 169–87.

Czinkota, M. and Ronen, D. (1983). Order sourcing and transfer pricing in the multinational corporation. *Journal of Business Logistics*, 4(1), 65–76.

Czinkota, M. and Ronkainen, I. (2003). International Marketing Manifesto. *Journal of International Marketing*. 11(1), 13–27.

Czinkota, M. and Ronkainen, I. (2014). Achieving "glocal" success. *Marketing News*, 48(4). Available at http://search.proquest.com/docview/1519580040/

Czinkota, M. and Ronkainen, I. (2014). *International Marketing*. Boston: Cengage.

Czinkota, M. and Woronoff, J. (1991). *Unlocking Japan's Market*. Chicago: Probus Publishing.

Czinkota, M. and Zeneli, V. (2016). Why the Transatlantic Trade and Investment Partnership is More Important than TPp. The Diplomat, January 30, 2016. Available at http://thediplomat.com/2016/01/why-the-transatlantic-trade-and-investment-partnership-is-more-important-than-tpp (Accessed April 9, 2020).

Czinkota, M. R. and Czinkota, M. L. (2020). Educational innovation in the time of coronavirus. In *Shanghai Daily*. [online]. Available at https://archive.shine.cn/opinion/Educational-innovation-in-the-time-of-coronavirus/shdaily.shtml (Accessed April 3, 2020).

Czinkota, M., Grossman, D., Javalgi, R., and Nugent, N. (2009) Foreign market entry mode of service firms: The case of US MBA programs. *Journal of World Business*, *44*(3), (July), 274–286.

Czinkota, M., Kaufmann, H., and Zakrzewski, M. (2015). B2B and internal relationships and curative international marketing: A polish case study. In *Industrial Marketing Management*. [online] Available at www.sciencedirect.com/science/article/abs/pii/S0019850115001996 (Accessed April 6, 2020).

Czinkota, M., Ronkainen, I., and Donath, B. (2004), *Mastering Global Markets*. Cincinnati: Thomson, p. 362.

D'Arpizio, C., Levato, F., Kamel, M., and de Montgolfier, J. (2017). Luxury Goods Worldwide Market Study, Fall–Winter 2017. Bain & Company [online]. Available at www.bain.com/insights/luxury-goods-worldwide-market-study-fall-winter-2017/ (Accessed May 3, 2020).

Dahad, N. (2018). *Apple Looks to India to Stem Decline in iPhone Sales*. EE Times [online]. Available at www.eetimes.com/apple-looks-to-india-to-stem-decline-in-iphone-sales (Accessed Feb. 8, 2020).

Daniels, J. and VanHoose, D. (2018). *Global Economic Issues and Policies*. 4th ed. New York: Routledge.

Das, N. (2017). Case Study of Starbucks Entry to China with Marketing Strategy! *ilearnalot* [online]. Available at www.ilearnlot.com/ill-3359-starbucks-entry-to-china-with-marketing-strategy/ (Accessed February 8, 2020).

de los Reyes, G., Kim, T. W., and Weaver, G. R., (2017). Teaching ethics in business schools: A conversation on disciplinary differences, academic provincialism, and the case for integrated pedagogy. *Academy of Management Learning & Education 16*(2), 314–336.

Deng, S., Townsend, P., Robert, M., and Quesnel, N. (1996). A guide to intellectual property rights in Southeast Asia and China. *Business Horizons,* (November/December 1996), 43–50.

Deresky, H. (2017). *International Management: Managing Across Borders and Cultures.* New York: Pearson Education.

Dhingra, S., Machin, S., and Overman, H. (2017). Local economic effects of Brexit. *National Institute Economic Review*, 242, R24–R36.

Dholakia R., Dholakia, N., and Chattopadhyay, A. (2018). Indigenous marketing practices and theories in emerging economies: Consumer behavior and retail transformations in India. *Journal of Business Research*, *86* (May), 406–415.

Dimant, E. and Tosato, G. (2018). Causes and effects of corruption: What has past decade's empirical research taught us? A survey. *Journal of Economic Surveys*, *32*(2), 335–356.

Dinlersoz, E. M. and Pereira, P. (2007). On the diffusion of electronic commerce. *International Journal of Industrial Organization*, *25*(3)(June), 541–574.

Diop, M. (2017, October 11), "Africa Can Enjoy Leapfrog Development," World Bank. www.worldbank.org/en/news/opinion/2017/10/11/africa-can-enjoy-leapfrog-development

Doh, J. P. and Stumpf, S. A. (2013, January). Emerging markets and regional patterns in talent management: The challenge of India and China. Available at www.researchgate.net/publication/287783864_Emerging_markets_and_regional_patterns_in_talent_management_The_challenge_of_India_and_China (Accessed April 22, 2020).

Doh, J., Rodrigues, S., Saka-Helmhout, A., and Makhija, M. (2017). International business responses to institutional voids.

Doland, A. (2016, December 2). Pizza Hut's New Concept Restaurant in Shanghai Has Robots on Staff. AdAge [online]. Available at https://adage.com/article/cmo-strategy/pizza-hut-s-concept-restaurant-shanghai-robots-staff/306976 (Accessed April 27, 2020).

Dollinger, P. (1999). *The German Hansa*, London: Psychology Press.

Dominguez, N. (2018). *SME Internationalization Strategies: Innovation to Conquer New Markets*, Wiley-ISTE.

Dou, E. (2017, July 18). China's Stopchat: Censors Can Now Erase Images Mid-Transmission. *Wall Street Journal* [online]. Available at www.wsj.com/articles/chinas-stopchat-censors-can-now-erase-images-mid-transmission-1500363950

Doupnik, T. and Perera, H. (2015). *International Accounting.* 4th ed. New York: McGraw-Hill Education.

Dowlah, C. (2018). *Transformations of Global Prosperity: How Foreign Investment, Multinationals, and Value Chains Are Remaking Modern Economy.* London: Palgrave Macmillan.

Dowling, D. C. (2013, November 20). Global Telecommuting Brings a Host of Issues. SHRM [online]. Available at www.shrm.org/resourcesandtools/hr-topics/global-hr/pages/global-telecommuting-issues.aspx (Accessed April 21, 2020).

Dratler, J. and McJohn, S., (2017). *Licensing of Intellectual Property*. Newark, NJ: Law Journal Press.

Dubai Airshow. (2019). The Future of the Aerospace Industry. Dubai Air Show website. Available at www.dubaiairshow.aero (Accessed May 4, 2020).

Dubberke, S. (2017, August 3). 5 Ways to Develop a Global Mindset – Training Industry. Training Industry [online]. Available at https://trainingindustry.com/articles/strategy-alignment-and-planning/5-ways-to-develop-a-global-mindset/ (Accessed April 22, 2020).

Dubina, K. S., Morisi, T. L., Rieley, M., and Wagoner, A. B. (2019, October). Projections overview and highlights, 2018–28 : Monthly Labor Review. US Bureau of Labor Statistics. [online]. Available at www.bls.gov/opub/mlr/2019/article/projections-overview-and-highlights-2018–28.htm (Accessed May 12, 2020).

Dugger, C. (2007). Brazil Overrides Merck Patent on AIDS Drug. [online] *New York Times*, May 5. Available at www.nytimes.com/2007/05/05/world/americas/05briefs-brazil.html (Accessed May 11, 2020).

Duke, L. (2001, April 29). Diamond Trade's Tragic Flaw. *Washington Post* [online]. Available at www.washingtonpost.com/archive/business/2001/04/29/diamond-trades-tragic-flaw/b4c2c3c4-f5a8-4ba7-9d96-c9a8f80945a1/

Dun & Bradstreet. (2020). *Harley Davidson Corporate Profile*. Dun & Bradstreet [online]. Available at www.dnb.com/business-directory/company-profiles.harley-davidson_inc.95c1d03b3487e3a72ed5bb3c9e74fed6.html (Accessed Feb. 8, 2020).

Dunfee, T. W. and Warren, D. E. (2001). Is guanxi ethical? A normative analysis of doing business in China. *Journal of business ethics*, *32*(3), 191–204.

Edelman (2017). Edelman Trust Barometer Archive [Blog] Available at www.edelman.com/research/2017-edelman-trust-barometer (Accessed Feb. 9, 2020).

Edelman (2019). Edelman Trust Barometer Global Report. [Blog] Available at www.edelman.com/research/2019-edelman-trust-barometer (Accessed Feb. 9, 2020).

eMarketer. (2019). Global Digital Ad Spending. eMarketer [online]. Available at www.emarketer.com/content/global-digital-ad-spending-2019 (Accessed May 3, 2020).

Emerald Insight. (2007). Selecting international business managers effectively. *Human Resource Management International Digest*, *15*(3), 33–35. https://doi.org/10.1108/09670730710744005

Encyclopaedia Britannica. (2019). Cixi: Empress Dowager of China. In *Encyclopaedia Britannica*. Available at www.britannica.com/biography/Cixi (Accessed April 5, 2020).

Enderwick, P. (2011). The Imperative of Global Environmental Scanning. *Insights 11*(1), 12–15.

Erickson, G. (1997). Export controls: Marketing implications of public policy choices. *Journal of Public Policy and Marketing, 16*(1), 83–95.

Erisman, P. (2017). *Six Billion Shoppers: The Companies Winning the Global e-Commerce Boom* (1st US ed.). New York, NY: St. Martin's Press.

Esterl, M. and Crawford, D. (2008). Ex-Siemens Manager Sentenced. *Wall Street Journal*, November 25, 2008, p. B2.

Esty, D., Pangestu, M., and Soesastro, H. (2017). Globalisation and the environment in Asia: Linkages, impacts and policy implications. In *Asia's Clean Revolution*. Routledge, pp. 63–87.

Euromonitor International. (2018a, February 21). Digital Consumer in Brazil.

Euromonitor International. (2018b, February 23). Digital Consumer in China.

Euromonitor International. (2018c, March 21). Digital Consumer in India.

European Commission. (2008). *Television Broadcasting Activities: "Television Without Frontiers" (TVWF) Directive.* Available at www.europa.eu.

European Commission. (2018). Dual-use trade controls. [online]. Available at https://ec.europa.eu/trade/import-and-export-rules/export-from-eu/dual-use-controls/ (Accessed May 11, 2020).

European Commission. (2018). EU data protection rules. European Commission website [online]. Available at https://ec.europa.eu/info/priorities/justice-and-fundamental-rights/data-protection/2018-reform-eu-data-protection-rules/eu-data-protection-rules_en

European Commission. (2020). Audiovisual Media Services Directive (AVMSD). [online]. Available at https://ec.europa.eu/digital-single-market/en/audiovisual-media-services-directive-avmsd (Accessed May 3, 2020).

European Medicines Agency. (2016). The European regulatory system for medicines. [online]. Available at www.ema.europa.eu/en/documents/leaflet/european-regulatory-system-medicines-european-medicines-agency-consistent-approach-medicines_en.pdf (Accessed May 11, 2020).

European Parliament. (2020). Financing of the CAP [online]. Available at www.europarl.europa.eu/factsheets/en/sheet/106/financing-of-the-cap (Accessed April 21, 2020).

Evans, J. and Mavondo, F. (2002). Psychic distance and organizational performance: An empirical examination of international retailing operations. *Journal of International Business Studies, 33*(3), 515–532.

Farah, D. (2001, November 2). Al Qaeda Cash Tied to Diamond Trade. *Washington Post* [online]. Available at www.washingtonpost.com/archive/politics/2001/11/02/al-qaeda-cash-tied-to-diamond-trade/93abd66a-5048-469a-9a87-5d2efb565a62/

Fauver, L., McDonald, M., and Taboada, A. (2018). Does it pay to treat employees well? International evidence on the value of employee-friendly culture. *Journal of Corporate Finance*, 50, 84–108.

Ferraro, G. P. and Briody, E. K. (2017). *The Cultural Dimension of Global Business*. Taylor & Francis.

Fidler, S. (2018). UK Has Two Choices on Brexit Path. *Wall Street Journal*, p. R11.

Financial Times. (2019). *Financial Times* [online]. Available at https://markets.ft.com/data/equities/tearsheet/summary?s=HSBA:LSE(Accessed June 20, 2019).

FINSMES. (2019). The Top 8 Most Popular Sponsor Brands in Sports. [online]. Available at www.finsmes.com/2019/11/the-top-8-most-popular-sponsor-brands-in-sports.html (Accessed April 24, 2020).

Fladmoe-Lindquist, K. (2000). International franchising. In Y. Aharoni and L. Nachum (eds.), *Globalization of Services*. London: Routledge, pp. 197–216.

Foo, P. Y., Lee, V. H., Tan, G. W. H., and Ooi, K. B. (2018). A gateway to realising sustainability performance via green supply chain management practices: A PLS–ANN approach. *Expert Systems with Applications, 107*, 1–14.

Forbes. (2020). Top 100 Digital Companies. *Forbes* [online]. Available at www.forbes.com/top-digital-companies/list/#tab:rank (Accessed May 3, 2020).

Fowler, R. (2000, March 10). Final Report of the UN Panel of Experts. Global Policy Forum [online]. Available at www.globalpolicy.org/global-taxes/41606-final-report-of-the-un-panel-of-experts.html (Accessed May 19, 2020).

Frontier Economics. (2017). The Economic Impacts of Counterfeiting and Piracy. [online]. Available at www.inta.org/Communications/Documents/2017_Frontier_Report.pdf (Accessed May 3, 2020).

Fryer, B. (2009, July 20). The Problem with Short-Term Overseas Assignments. Harvard Business Review [online]. Available at https://hbr.org/2009/07/can-your-family-handle-your-ov (Accessed April 21, 2020).

Fuchs,C. (2019, February 23). After long wait, US moves forward with proposal to end work permits for spouses of H-1B visa holders. NBC News [online]. Available at www.nbcnews.com/news/asian-america/after-long-wait-u-s-moves-forward-proposal-end-work-n974821 (Accessed May 12, 2020).

Fuhrmans, V. (2020). Pressure Tactics Diversify Boards. *Wall Street Journal*, p.B6.

Gartenberg, C. (2018). *Apple will reportedly start assembling its premium iPhone models in India*. The Verge [online]. Available at www.theverge.com/2018/12/27/18157565/apple-expensive-iphone-x-models-assembly-india-tariffs (Accessed Feb. 8, 2020).

Gartner Inc. (2018). *Gartner Supply Chain Top 25 List*. [ebook] © 2018 Gartner, Inc. Available at https://emtemp.gcom.cloud/ngw/globalassets/en/supply-chain/documents/trends-top-25/gartner-supply-chain-top-25.pdf (Accessed Feb. 9, 2020).

Gaybellaev, B., Chen, Su-Chin, and Gaybullaev, D. (2012). Changes in water volume of the Aral Sea after

1960. In *Springer*. Available at https://link.springer.com/article/10.1007/s13201-012-0048-z (Accessed April 3, 2020).

Gelatt, J. and Pierce, S. (2018, March 27). Evolution of the H-1B: Latest Trends in a Program on the Brink of Reform. Migration Policy Institute [online]. Available at www.migrationpolicy.org/research/evolution-h-1b-latest-trends-program-brink-reform (Accessed May 12, 2020).

Georgise, F. B., Heramo, A. H., and Bekele, H. (2020). Improving automotive service through e-logistics: a case of Moenco Hawassa, Ethiopia. *International Journal of Economics and Management Systems*, 5.

Gerber, J. (2018). *International Economics*. 7th ed. London: Pearson Education.

Gereffi, G., Garcia-Johnson, R., and Sasser, E. (2001). The NGO-Industrial Complex. *Foreign Policy*, (July/August), 56–66.

Ghemawat, P. (2017). Globalization in the age of Trump: Protectionism will change how companies do business – but not in the ways you think. *Harvard Business Review*, July/August, 112–123.

Ghislanzoni, G., Penttinen, R., and Turnbull, D., (2008). The multilocal challenge: Managing cross-border functions. *McKinsey Quarterly* [online]. Available at www.mckinseyquarterly.com

Gilbert, N. (2020). *20 Best Order Fulfillment Services & Companies of 2020 – Financesonline.com*. [online] Finances Online. Available at https://financesonline.com/top-20-order-fulfillment-services/ (Accessed Feb. 9, 2020).

Gilmore, D. (2018). *Understanding the Gartner Top 25 Supply Chains 2018*. [online] Scdigest.com. Available at www.scdigest.com/firstthoughts/18–05-24.php?cid=14255 (Accessed Feb. 9, 2020).

Gitman, L. (2018). The State – and Future – of Sustainable Business in 2018. [Blog] *BSR – Our Insights*. Available at www.bsr.org/en/our-insights/blog-view/csr-sustainability-business-trends-now-and-the-future (Accessed Feb. 9, 2020).

Global Witness. (2005). Making it Work: Why the Kimberley Process Must Do More to Stop Conflict Diamonds. Global Witness [online]. Available at www.globalwitness.org/en/archive/making-it-work-why-kimberley-process-must-do-more-stop-conflict-diamonds-0/ (Accessed May 19, 2020).

Globewomen.org. (2020). *GlobeWomen: Linking women in business worldwide*. [online] Available at: http://globewomen.org/index.html (Accessed Feb. 9, 2020).

Gordon, J. N. and Ringe, W. (2018). *The Oxford Handbook of Corporate Law and Governance*. Oxford, UK: Oxford University Press.

Graham, T. (1983). Global trade: War & peace. *Foreign Policy*, 50, 124–127.

Gravier, M. (2013). Challenging or enhancing the EU's legitimacy? The evolution of representative bureaucracy in the Commission's staff policies. *Journal of Public*

Administration Research and Theory, *23*(4), 817–838.

Great Place to Work® Institute (2018). *Fortune 100 Best Companies to Work For 2018*. Great Place To Work United States [online]. Available at www.greatplacetowork.com/best-workplaces/100-best/2018 (Accessed Feb. 9, 2020).

Gronroos, C. (2006). Adopting a service logic for marketing. *Marketing Theory*, *6*(3), 317–333.

Groysberg, B. and Abrahams, R. (2014, February 13). A Successful International Assignment Depends on These Factors. *Harvard Business Review* [online]. Available at https://hbr.org/2014/02/a-successful-international-assignment-depends-on-these-factors (Accessed November 29, 2019).

Guilford, G. (2015). *The most egregious examples from the Chinese government's long, sordid history of data-doctoring.* [online] Quartz, October 29, 2015. Available at https://qz.com/530096/china-data-tricks/ (Accessed Feb. 8, 2020).

Gunther, M. (2013). Unilever's CEO Has a Green Thumb. *Fortune*, pp. 124–128.

Gupta, S. (2019). Role of MNEs in building zero waste communities. In *Socially Responsible International Business.* Edward Elgar Publishing.

Gur, N. (2015). The G20 and the governance of global finance. *The Foundation for Political, Economic and Social Research*, *9*.

H-1B Employer Data Hub. (n.d.). USCIS [online]. Available at www.uscis.gov/h-1b-data-hub (Accessed May 12, 2020).

H-1B Fiscal Year (FY) 2021 Cap Season. (2020, April 13). USCIS [online]. Available at www.uscis.gov/working-united-states/temporary-workers/h-1b-specialty-occupations-and-fashion-models/h-1b-fiscal-year-fy-2021-cap-season (Accessed May 12, 2020).

Hackett, P. (2018). *Quantitative Research Methods in Consumer Psychology: Contemporary and Data Driven Approaches* (1st ed.). Routledge.

Hagerty, J. (2015). Harley-Davidson's Hurdle: Attracting Young Motorcycle Riders. *Wall Street Journal.* [online]. Available at www.wsj.com/articles/can-harley-davidson-spark-a-motorcycle-counterculture-1434706201 (Accessed Feb. 8, 2020).

Hague, P. N., Cupman, J., and Harrison, M. (2016). *Market research in practice: how to get greater insight from your market.* London: Kogan Page.

Hale, D. (2008). International comparisons of labour disputes in 2006.*Economic & Labour Market Review*, *2*(4), 32–39. https://doi.org/10.1057/elmr.2008.56

Hamilton, L. and Webster, P. (2018). *The International Business Environment.* Oxford University Press.

Handley, L. (2018). Sponsorship spending to hit $66 billion worldwide, but most firms don't know if it really works. CNBC [online]. Available at www.cnbc.com/2018/09/25/does-sponsorship-work-deals-value-to-reach-66-billion-in-2018.html (Accessed April 20, 2020).

Harley-Davidson USA. (2020). *Harley-Davidson USA Homepage.* [online]

Available at www.harley-davidson
.com (Accessed Feb. 8, 2020).

Hartley, R. and Claycomb, C. (2014).
Marketing Mistakes and Successes.
12th ed. Hoboken, NJ: Wiley.

Hastig, G. M. and ManMohan, S. S.
(2019). Blockchain for Supply Chain
Traceability: Business Requirements
and Critical Success Factors
(November 25, 2019). SSRN [online].
Available at https://ssrn.com/
abstract=3493418 or http://dx.doi.
org/10.2139/ssrn.3493418

Haubner, R. and Rudigier, M. (2013).
Raman characterisation of diamond
coatings using different laser
wavelengths.*Physics Procedia*, *46*,
71–78. https://doi.org/10.1016/j.
phpro.2013.07.047

Hendrie, A. (2019). Tax reform is
making American companies
more competitive around the
world. *Washington Examiner*
[online]. Available at www
.washingtonexaminer.com/opinion/
tax-reform-is-making-american-
companies-more-competitive-around-
the-world (Accessed Sep. 3, 2019).

Henisz, W. (2017). *Corporate Diplomacy:
Building Reputations and
Relationships with External
Stakeholders.* New York: Routledge.

Herrnstadt, O. E. (2008, April 17). Offsets
and the lack of a comprehensive
US policy: What do other countries
know that we don't? Economic
Policy Institute website. Available
at www.epi.org/publication/bp201/
(Accessed May 4, 2020).

Hewlett, S. A. (2009, August 17). Flex Time:
A Recession Triple Win. *Harvard
Business Review* [online]. Available

at https://hbr.org/2009/08/time-as-
currency (Accessed April 21, 2020).

Hinson, R. E., Adeola, O., and Amartey, A.
F. O. (2018). *Sales Management: A
Primer for Frontier Markets.* IAP.

Hofstede, G. (2003). Culture's
consequences: Comparing values,
behaviors, institutions, and
organizations across nations.
Behaviour Research and Therapy, 41,
861–862.

Hofstede, G. (2015). *Geert Hofstede* [online].
Available at http://geerthofstede.
com/culture-geert-hofstede-gert-
jan-hofstede/6d-model-of-national-
culture/ (Accessed June 7, 2017).

Hofstede, G., Pedersen, P., and Hofstede, G.
(2002). *Exploring culture: exercises,
stories, and synthetic cultures.*
Yarmouth, ME: Intercultural Press.

Holley, P. (2019). Amazon's one-day
delivery service depends on the
work of thousands of robots.
Washington Post [online]. Available
at www.washingtonpost.com/
technology/2019/06/07/amazons-one-
day-delivery-service-depends-work-
thousands-robots/ (Accessed May 3,
2020).

Hoover, A. (1999, August 18). Simply
Brilliant: UF/Russian Team
Makes Gem-Quality Diamonds.
University Of Florida [online].
Available at www.sciencedaily.com/
releases/1999/08/990817092046.htm
(Accessed May 19, 2020).

Hopewell, J. (2018). Europe, Hollywood
Hail Landmark EU Territorial
Licensing Agreement. *Variety* [online].
Available at https://variety.com/2018/
digital/news/europe-hollywood-
landmark-e-u-territorial-licensing-

agreement-1203092594 (Accessed Feb. 8, 2020).

Hovav, A. and D'Arcy, J. (2012). Applying an extended model of deterrence across cultures: An investigation of information systems misuse in the US and South Korea. *Information & Management*, *49*(2), 99–110.

HSBC-UK Web. (2019). *HSBC* [online]. Available at www.about.hsbc.co.uk.

Hu, H. and Wooldridge, P. (2016). International business of banks in China. *BIS Quarterly Review* [online]. Available at www.bis.org/publ/qtrpdf/r_qt1606y.htm. (Accessed April 20, 2020).

Huang, Z. (2017). *The Chinese government finally admitted that its economic data was made up.* [online] Quartz, January 18, 2017. Available at https://qz.com/887709/chinas-liaoning-province-admitted-that-it-inflated-gdp-figures-from-2011-to-2014/ (Accessed 8 Feb. 2020).

Huang, Z. (2018). *Doubtful of China's economic numbers? Satellite data and AI can help.* [online] Quartz, April 16, 2018. Available at https://qz.com/1251912/doubtful-of-chinas-economic-numbers-satellite-data-and-ai-can-help/ (Accessed Feb. 8, 2020).

Hunt, B. (2018, March 7). Hreflang Implementation: The 8 Biggest SEO Misconceptions. *Search Engine Journal* [online]. Available at www.searchenginejournal.com/hreflang-implementation-mistakes/240451/ (Accessed April 27, 2020).

Hutzschenreuter, T., Kleindienst, I., and Lange, S. (2016). The concept of distance in international business research: A review and research agenda. *International Journal of Management Reviews*, *18*(2), 160–179.

IBISWorld. (2018, February). Social Networking in China.

Icon Group International. (2018). *The 2019–2024 World Outlook for Franchising.* San Diego, CA: Icon Group International.

Immelt, J., Trimble, C., and Govindarajan, V. (2009). How GE Is Disrupting Itself. *Harvard Business Review*, *87* (October), 56–63.

In, J., Bradley, R., Bichescu, B. C., and Autry, C. W. (2019). Supply chain information governance: toward a conceptual framework. *The International Journal of Logistics Management*, 30, 506–526.

International Chamber of Commerce. (2017). *Global Impacts of Counterfeiting and Piracy to Reach US$4.2 Trillion by 2022.* [online]. Available at https://iccwbo.org/media-wall/news-speeches/global-impacts-counterfeiting-piracy-reach-us4-2-trillion-2022/ (Accessed May 3, 2020).

International Chamber of Commerce. (2018). ICC announces 2017 figures confirming global reach and leading position for complex, high-value disputes. [online]. Available at https://iccwbo.org/media-wall/news-speeches/icc-announces-2017-figures-confirming-global-reach-leading-position-complex-high-value-disputes/ (Accessed May 11, 2020).

International Chamber of Commerce. (2020). ICC International Court of Arbitration. [online]. Available at https://iccwbo.org/dispute-resolution-services/icc-international-court-arbitration/ (Accessed May 11, 2020).

International Organization for Standardization. (2018). ISO/IEC 27000:2018. (2019, February 4). International Organization for Standardization [online]. Available at www.iso.org/standard/73906.html

International Telecommunications Union. (2017). Measuring the Information Society Report 2017. International Telecommunications Union website [online]. Available at www.itu.int/en/ITU-D/Statistics/Pages/publications/mis2017.aspx (Accessed Nov. 13, 2019).

International Telecommunications Union. (2019). *Measuring the Information Society 2018.* Geneva, Switzerland: International Telecommunications Union.

International Trade Administration. (2016). *Basic Guide to Exporting: The Official Government Resource for Small and Medium-Sized Businesses.* Washington, DC: International Trade Administration.

International Trade Administration. (2018). Finding Foreign Buyers: Choosing a Sales Channel. March 16, 2018. [online]. Available at www.export.gov

International Trade Administration. (2020). Export Pricing Strategy. [online]. Available at www.trade.gov/pricing-strategy (Accessed May 3, 2020).

Internet World Stats. (2020). *World Internet Usage and Population Statistics, June 30, 2018.* [online] Internetworldstats.com. Available at https://internetworldstats.com/stats.htm (Accessed Mar. 1, 2019).

iResearch (2016). *China's Cross-Border Online Shopping Market Will Not Vary Obviously in The Near Future.* [online] Iresearchchina.com. Available at www.iresearchchina.com/content/details7_20812.html (Accessed Feb. 11, 2020).

Isaacson, W. (2014). *The Innovators: How a Group of Hackers, Geniuses, and Geeks Created the Digital Revolution,* New York: Simon & Schuster.

Iyengar, R. (2019). *Apple needs a cheap iPhone to crack India.* [online] CNN. Available at https://www.cnn.com/2019/01/04/tech/india-smartphone-market-iphone-apple/index.html (Accessed Feb. 8, 2020).

Jacobs, W. and Horster, R. (2020). Commodity supply networks as complex adaptive systems: how commodity and freight markets respond to a supply shock. In *Geographies of Maritime Transport.* Edward Elgar Publishing.

Jacobson, R. (2017, April 12). Internet Censorship Is Advancing Under Trump. WIRED [online]. Available at www.wired.com/2017/04/internet-censorship-is-advancing-under-trump/

Jakab, S. (2015). Harley-Davidson's Profitable Road Trip. *Wall Street Journal* [online]. Available at www.wsj.com/articles/harley-davidsons-profitable-road-trip-1429553905 (Accessed Feb. 8, 2020).

Jameson, D. A. (2007). Reconceptualizing cultural identity and its role in intercultural business communication. *The Journal of Business Communication (1973),* 44(3), 199–235.

JETRO. (2012). *Laws & Regulations on Setting Up Business in Japan.*

Japan External Trade Organization [online]. Available at www.jetro.go.jp/en/invest/qa/setting_up/pdf/settingup_201210.pdf (Accessed May 11, 2020).

Jha, A. (2002, December 27). Diamond pact hits Surat cutters. The Times of India [online]. Available at https://timesofindia.indiatimes.com/india/Diamond-pact-hits-Surat-cutters/articleshow/32506011.cms (Accessed May 19, 2020).

Jia, N., Huang, K., and Man Zhang, C. (2019). Public governance, corporate governance, and firm innovation: An examination of state-owned enterprises. *Academy of Management Journal, 62*(1), 220–247.

Johansson, J. and Furick, M. (2017). *The New Global Marketing.* San Diego, CA: Cognella Academic Publishing.

Jones, C. (2016, August 31). Where are Diamonds Cut? The Diamond Gurus [online]. Available at www.dmia.net/where-are-diamonds-cut/

Jones, C. (2019). A value chain approach to support Southeast Asian economic regionalism.*Journal of ASEAN Studies, 7*(1), 40–57.

Jones, D. M. and Mei, S. C. E. (2019). ASEAN's economic community: ASEAN way or Beijing's way? In *Southeast Asia and the ASEAN Economic Community.* Cham, Switzerland: Palgrave Macmillan, pp. 421–453.

Jonnalagadda, D. (2019). Students Endorse Reconciliation Fee in GU272 Referendum. *The Hoya* [online]. Available at https://thehoya.com/students-endorse-reconciliation-fee-gu272-referendum/ (Accessed May 15, 2020).

Jurse, M. and Jager, J. (2017). Marketing channel strategy management in international markets. *International Journal of Innovation and Learning, 21*(2), 127–138.

Kabir, M., Singh, S., and Ferrantino, M. J. (2019). *The Textile-Clothing Value Chain in India and Bangladesh: How Appropriate Policies Can Promote (or Inhibit) Trade and Investment.* The World Bank.

Kache, F. and Seuring, S. (2017). Challenges and opportunities of digital information at the intersection of Big Data Analytics and supply chain management. *International Journal of Operations & Production Management, 37*(1), 10–36.

Kapadia, R. (2012). The Currency Conundrum. *SmartMoney,* pp. 78–82.

Kaufmann, D., Kraay, A., and Mastruzzi, M. (2010). *The Worldwide Governance Indicators: A Summary of Methodology, Data and Analytical Issues.* World Bank Policy Research, Working Paper No. 5430. World Bank.

Kavanagh, M. H. and Ashkanasy, N. M. (2006). The impact of leadership and change management strategy on organizational culture and individual acceptance of change during a merger. *British Journal of Management, 17*(S1), S81–S103.

Kedia, B. L. and Mukherji, A. (1999). Global managers: Developing a mindset for global competitiveness, *Journal of World Business* 34, 230–251.

Keen, M. and Konrad, K. (2013). The theory of international tax competition and coordination. In A. Auerbach, R. Chetty, F. Martin, and E. Saez (eds.), *Handbook of Public Economics, vol. 5.* Amsterdam, the Netherlands: Elsevier, pp. 259–330.

Kemme, D., Parikh, B., and Steigner, T. (2017). Tax havens, tax evasion and tax information exchange agreements in the OECD. *European Financial Management, 23*(3), 519–542.

Kendall, G. (2019). Your Mobile Phone vs. Apollo 11's Guidance Computer. RealClearScience [online]. Available at www.realclearscience.com/articles/2019/07/02/your_mobile_phone_vs_apollo_11s_guidance_computer_111026.html

Kermisch, R. and Burns, D. (2018a). A Survey of 1,700 Companies Reveals Common B2B Pricing Mistakes. *Harvard Business Review* [online]. Available at https://hbr.org/2018/06/a-survey-of-1700-companies-reveals-common-b2b-pricing-mistakes (Accessed May 3, 2020).

Kermisch, R. and Burns, D. (2018b). Is Pricing Killing Your Profits? Bain & Company [online]. Available at www.bain.com/insights/is-pricing-killing-your-profits/ (Accessed Feb. 11, 2020).

Kerr, S. and Kerr, W. (2016). *Immigrant entrepreneurship, Working Paper 17–001.* Cambridge, MA: Harvard Business School.

Kershaw, D. (2018). *The Foundations of Anglo-American Corporate Fiduciary Law.* Cambridge, UK: Cambridge University Press.

Khaitan, R. (2017). China Will Account For Half of Global Luxury Consumption by 2025, Here Are 4 Stocks To Buy. Frontera [online]. Available at https://frontera.net/news/asia/china-will-account-for-half-of-global-luxury-consumption-by-2025-here-are-4-stocks-to-buy/ (Accessed February 15, 2020).

Khan, D. (2017). Indian smartphone market grows 23% to overtake US in Q3; Samsung, Xiaomi drive shipments. *The Economic Times.*

Kimberley Process (2015). About Kimberley Process. Kimberley Process [online]. Available at www.kimberleyprocess.com/en/about (Accessed May 19, 2020).

King, G., Lam, P., and Roberts, M. E. (2017). Computer-assisted keyword and document set discovery from unstructured text. *American Journal of Political Science, 61*(4), 971–988.

Kingiri, A. N. and Fu, X. (2020). Understanding the diffusion and adoption of digital finance innovation in emerging economies: M-Pesa money mobile transfer service in Kenya. *Innovation and Development, 10*(1), 67–87.

Kippenberg, J. (2018, May 10). Diamond Trade Still Fuels Human Suffering. Human Rights Watch [online]. Available at www.hrw.org/news/2018/05/10/diamond-trade-still-fuels-human-suffering (accessed May 19, 2020).

Kluyver, C. (2013). *A Primer on Corporate Governance.* New York: Business Expert Press.

Knight, G. and Liesch, P. (2016). Internationalization: From incremental to born global. *Journal of World Business 51*(1), 93–102.

Kolakowski, N. (2018, August 29). Tech CEOs Issue Open Letter Over H-1B, Immigration Concerns. Dice Insights [online]. Available at https://insights.dice.com/2018/08/29/tech-ceos-issue-open-letter-h-1b-immigration-concerns/ (Accessed May 12, 2020).

Korn Ferry (2020a). *Future of Work.* Kornferry.com. [online]. Available at www.kornferry.com/challenges/future-of-work (Accessed Feb. 9, 2020).

Korn Ferry (2020b). *Women in Boardrooms: One Step Forward, One Step ....* Kornferry.com. [online]. Available at www.kornferry.com/insights/articles/women-leadership-board-directors (Accessed Feb. 9, 2020).

Kotler, P. and Keller, K. L. (2016). *A Framework for Marketing Management, 6th ed.* Boston: Pearson.

Kourula, A., Pisani, N., and Kolk, A. (2017). Corporate sustainability and inclusive development: highlights from international business and management research.*Current Opinion in Environmental Sustainability*, 24, 14–18.

KPMG. (2018, February 23). Corporate Tax Rates Table. [online]. Available at https://home.kpmg/xx/en/home/services/tax/tax-tools-and-resources/tax-rates-online/corporate-tax-rates-table.html (Accessed April 17, 2020).

KPMG. (2019). Balancing rules and flexibility for growth. (2019, September 2). KPMG [online]. Available at https://home.kpmg/ng/en/home/insights/2017/09/balancing-rules-and-flexibility-for-growth.html (Accessed April 21, 2020).

Krippendorff, K. H. (2012). *Content Analysis – 3rd Edition: an Introduction to Its Methodology.* Thousand Oaks: Sage Publications, Inc.

Krogstad, J. M. and Ruiz, N. G. (2017, August 16). Salaries rise for H-1B foreign workers in US. Pew Research Center [online]. Available at www.pewresearch.org/fact-tank/2017/08/16/salaries-have-risen-for-high-skilled-foreign-workers-in-u-s-on-h-1b-visas/ (Accessed May 12, 2020).

Kumar, K. and Muniraju, Y. (2014). Exchange rate fluctuations and its impact on foreign trade: An empirical study. *Finance India*, *28*(3), 973–983.

Kurmanaev, A. and Vyas, K. (2017). GM ceases operation in Venezuela as plant is seized. *Wall Street Journal.* April 20, 2017 [online]. Available at www.wsj.com/articles/gm-ceases-operation-in-venezuela-as-plant-is-expropriated-1492694621 (Accessed May 11, 2020).

Kyd, S. (1793). *A Treatise on the Law of Corporations.* London: J. Butterworth.

Kyle, M. (2011). Strategic responses to parallel trade. *Journal of Economic Analysis & Policy*, *11*(2), 1–32.

Laqueur, W. (2016). *A History of Terrorism.* New Brunswick, NJ: Transaction Publishers.

Laudon, K. C. and Traver, C. G. (2017). *E-Commerce 2017* (13th ed.). Pearson.

Lebedeva, A. (2017, February 15). 75% of Websites Have Hreflang Implementation Mistakes. *Search Engine Journal* [online]. Available at www.searchenginejournal.com/75-multilingual-websites-hreflang-implementation-mistakes/185737/ (Accessed April 27, 2020).

Lee, H., Chung, C. C., and Beamish, P. W. (2019). Configurational characteristics of mandate portfolios and their impact on foreign subsidiary survival. *Journal of World Business*, *54*(5), 100999.

Lee, K. F. (2018). *AI Superpowers: China, Silicon Valley, and the New World Order.* Houghton.

Leonidou, L., Katsikeas, C., Samiee, S., and Aykol, B. (2018). International marketing research: A state-of-the-art review and the way forward. In *Advances in Global Marketing.* New York: Springer, pp. 3–33.

Lester, S. and Manak, I. (2018). The rise of populist nationalism and the renegotiation of NAFTA. *Journal of International Economic Law*, *21*(1), 151–169.

Levy, A. (2018, January 23). 19 Facebook Statistics That Are Hard to Believe. The Motley Fool website [online]. Available at www.fool.com/slideshow/19-facebook-statistics-are-hard-believe/ (Accessed April 30, 2020).

Li, P. (2018). Competing with dragons. Amazon in China. *International Journal of Case Studies in Management*, *16*(1), 1–19.

Liao, S. (2018). *Netflix's European users can access their home catalog throughout the EU.* The Verge. [online]. Aailable at www.theverge.com/2018/4/2/17187910/netflix-european-users-home-catalog-traveling (Accessed Feb. 8, 2020).

Licensing Journal. (2009). History of merchandising. *Licensing Journal*, April, p. 23.

Lieberstein, M., Feingold, S., James, C., and Rosenblatt, P, (2011). Current developments and best practices in trademark licensing (Part I). *Licensing Journal*, (February), 20–28.

Lindblad, C. (2018). Companies give worker training another try. *Bloomberg Businessweek*, 44–45.

Liu, B. (2015). *Sentiment Analysis: Mining Opinions, Sentiments, and Emotions.* Cambridge: Cambridge University Press. doi:10.1017/CBO9781139084789

Liu, C. and Hong, J. (2016). Strategies and service innovations of haitao business in the Chinese market: A comparative case study of Amazon.cn vs Gmarket.co.kr. Asia Pacific Journal of Innovation and Entrepreneurship, 10(1), pp. 101–121.

Livius, T. (2006). *The History of Rome.* Indianapolis, IN: Hackett Publishing.

Loesche, D. (2017). World's Largest B2C E-commerce Markets. In *Statista.* [online]. Available at www.statista.com/chart/7958/worlds-largest-b2c-e-commerce-markets/ (Accessed April 3, 2020).

Loungani, P., Papageorgiou, C., and Wang, K. (2017). Services Exports Open a New Path to Prosperity. *IMF Blog.* [online]. Available at http://blogs.imf.org (Accessed May 1, 2020).

Lund, S., Windhagen, E., Manyika, J., Härle, P., Woetzel, J., and Goldshtein, D. (2017). *The New Dynamics of Financial Globalization.* McKinsey Global Institute, [online]. Available at www.mckinsey.com/industries/financial-services/our-insights/the-new-dynamics-of-financial-globalization (Accessed Feb. 7, 2020).

Lunt, N., Horsfall, D., and Hanefeld, J. (2016). Medical tourism: A snapshot of evidence on treatment abroad. *Maturitas, 88*, 37–44.

Luo, Y. (2007). *Guanxi and Business*, vol. 5. World Scientific.

MacDougall, A., Valley, J., Bettel, C., Param, A., Schmidt, J., Sigurdson, A., Strachan, T., and Suppa, O. (2017). *2017 Diversity Disclosure Practices: Women in leadership roles at TSX-listed companies.* Osler: Hoskin & Harcourt, LLP.

Maffi, L. (2005). Linguistic, cultural, and biological diversity. *Annual Review of Anthropology, 34*, 599–617.

Malathronas, J. (2018, June 12). On the gemstone trail: A tour of Antwerp's diamond district. CNN [online]. Available at https://edition.cnn.com/travel/article/antwerp-diamond-district-belgium/index.html (accessed May 19, 2020).

Malsin, J. (2018, July 18). Throughout Middle East, the Web Is Being Walled Off. *Wall Street Journal* [online]. Available at www.wsj.com/articles/throughout-middle-east-the-web-is-being-walled-off-1531915200

Mangan, J. and Lalwani, C. (2016). *Global logistics and supply chain management.* John Wiley & Sons.

Mankiw, N. (2017). How Best to Tax Business. *New York Times* [online]. Available at www.nytimes.com/2017/04/21/upshot/tax-code-business.html (Accessed Feb. 6, 2020).

Mansfield, E. and Reinhardt, E. (2015). International institutions and the volatility of international trade. *The Political Economy of International Trade*, 46 (August), 65–96.

Martin, S. (2014). *The Economics of Offsets: Defence Procurement and Countertrade.* New York: Routledge.

Matthew, L. (2008). Archbishop Williams Is Wrong to Back Sharia Law, Bloomberg.com, February 28, 2008.

Mattoo, A., Stern, R. M. and Zanini, G. (eds.). (2007). *A Handbook of International Trade in Services.* Oxford, UK: Oxford University Press.

McKinsey & Company. (2010). *The challenges ahead for supply chains: McKinsey Global Survey results.* [online] Available at www.mckinsey.com/business-functions/operations/our-insights/the-challenges-ahead-for-supply-chains-mckinsey-global-survey-results (Accessed Feb. 9, 2020).

McKinsey Global Institute. (2015). [online]. www.mckinsey.com/~/media/McKinsey/Featured%20Insights/Employment%20and%20Growth/How%20a%20private%20sector%20transformation%20could%20revive%20Japan/MGI-Future-of-Japan-Full-report-March%202015-03-2017.pdf (Accessed November 11, 2020).

McKinsey Global Institute. (2016). *Digital Globalization: The New Era of Global Flows.* [online]. Available at www.mckinsey.com/business-functions/mckinsey-digital/our-insights/digital-globalization-the-new-era-of-global-flows. (Accessed April 20, 2020).

McLaren, S. (2018). These Industries Will Face the Biggest Talent Shortages by 2030. [online] *LinkedIn Talent Blog.*

Available at https://business.linkedin.com/talent-solutions/blog/trends-and-research/2018/industries-biggest-talent-shortages-2030 (Accessed May 1, 2020).

McMillan, R. (2017, May 14). How to Protect Yourself From Ransomware. *Wall Street Journal* [online]. Available at www.wsj.com/articles/how-to-protect-yourself-from-ransomware-1494793417

McNamara, M. (2006, December 11). Facts About Blood Diamonds. CBS [online]. Available at www.cbsnews.com/news/facts-about-blood-diamonds/ (Accessed May 19, 2020).

Melvin, M. and Norrbin, S. (2017). *International Money and Finance.* 9th ed. Cambridge, MA: Academic Press.

Mercer. (2019). Vienna tops Mercer's 20th Quality of Living ranking. (March 20, 2019). mercer.com [online]. Available at www.mercer.com/newsroom/2018-quality-of-living-survey.html (Accessed April 22, 2020).

Merrilees, B. (2014). International franchising: Evolution of theory and practice." *Journal of Marketing Channels, 21*(3), 133–142.

Mesquita, L. and Ragozzino, R. (2017). *Collaborative Strategy: Critical Issues for Alliances and Networks.* Cheltenham, UK: Edward Elgar.

Meyer, K. E. (2017). International business in an era of anti-globalization. *Multinational Business Review.*

Miles, Tom. (2018). Antigua "losing all hope" of US payout in gambling dispute. In *Reuters.* Available at www.reuters.com/article/uk-usa-trade-antigua/antigua-losing-all-hope-of-u-s-payout-in-gambling-dispute-idUSKBN1JI0VZ (Accessed April 3, 2020).

Miller, M. (2013). *The Foundations of Modern Terrorism : State, Society and the Dynamics of Political Violence* (New York: Cambridge University Press.

Milne, R. and Scheele, M. (2007). Probe Finds 'General Practice' of Alleged Bribery at Siemens. *Financial Times,* p. 1.

Miroshnik, V. (2002). Culture and international management: A review. *Journal of Management Development,* 21, 521–544.

Mitchell, L. and Myles, W. (2010). Risk Sense: Developing and Managing International Education Activities with Risk in Mind. Centre for International Programs, University of Guelph.

Mobile Ecosystem Forum. (2016). 10 things you need to know about India's mobile market. [Blog] *Mobile Ecosystem Forum Blog.* Available at https://mobileecosystemforum.com/2016/06/07/10-things-you-need-to-know-about-indias-mobile-market/ (Accessed 8 Feb. 8, 2020).

Molnar, M. (2017). Revitalizing China's economy by improved corporate governance and state-owned enterprise reforms. *Journal of International Commerce, Economics and Policy,* 08(03), 1750015.

Mondelez. (2020). Tang: 2017 Fact Sheet. [online]. Available at www.mondelezinternational.com/~/media/MondelezCorporate/Uploads/

downloads/tang_Fact_Sheet.pdf (Accessed May 3, 2020).

Moore, Gordon E. (2006), "Moore's Law at Forty," in David C. Brock, ed., *Understanding Moore's Law: Four Decades of Innovation*, Philadelphia: Chemical Heritage Press.

Morrison, S. and Winston, C. (1995). *The Evolution of the Airline Industry.* Washington, DC: Brookings Institution Press.

Morschett, D., Schramm-Klein, H., and Zentes, J. (2015). *Strategic International Management.* New York: Springer.

Mosley, L. (ed.). (2016, September 15). Opinion: Does globalization hurt poor workers? It's complicated. *The Washington Post* [online]. Available at www.washingtonpost.com/news/ in-theory/wp/2016/09/15/does- globalization-hurt-poor-workers-its- complicated/

Moti Israeli Diamonds. (2015). Top 6 diamond exchanges in the world. (December 14). Moti Israeli Diamonds [online]. Available at www.moti- israeli-diamonds.com/blog/top-6- diamond-exchanges-world (Accessed May 19, 2020).

Mueller, H. and Philippon, T. (2011). Family firms and labor relations. *American Economic Journal: Macroeconomics*, 3(2), 218–245. Available at https://doi. org/10.1257/mac.3.2.218

Mueller, S. (2012). Works councils and establishment productivity. *Industrial and Labor Relations Review.* 65(4), 880–898.

Nagle, T. and Müller, G. (2018). *The Strategy and Tactics of Pricing.* New York: Routledge.

Narayanaswami, C., Nooyi, R., Govindaswamy, S. R., and Viswanathan, R. (2019). Blockchain anchored supply chain automation. *IBM Journal of Research and Development, 63*(2/3), 7–1.

Nath, H. and Liu, L. (2017). Information and communications technology (ICT) and services trade. *Information Economics and Policy*, 41(December), 81–87.

National Council of State Boards of Nursing. (2017). 2017 National Nursing Workforce Study. National Council of State Boards of Nursing [online]. Available at www.ncsbn .org/workforce.htm (Accessed May 12, 2020).

National Research Council (2000). *Surviving Supply Chain Integration: Strategies for Small Manufacturers.* [ebook] Washington, DC: The National Academies Press. Available at https:// doi.org/10.17226/6369 (Accessed Feb. 9, 2020).

NCMA. (2017). *Contract Management Body of Knowledge.* Ashburn, Virginia: National Contract Management Association. Available at www .ncmahq.org

Nellis, S. (2016, November 21). Tech worker visas face uncertain future under Trump, Sessions. *Reuters*. [online]. Available at www.reuters.com/article/ us-trump-immigration-analysis/ tech-worker-visas-face-uncertain- future-under-trump-sessions- idUSKBN13G0J7

Net MarketShare. (2018, September). Search Engine Market Share.

Newzoo. (2019). Number of smartphone users worldwide from 2016 to 2021 (in billions) [Graph] (September 17, 2019). *Statista.* [online]. Available at www-statista-com.proxy.library. georgetown.edu/statistics/330695/ number-of-smartphone-users-worldwide/ (Accessed April 13, 2020).

Nielsen (2018). Was 2018 the Year of the Influential Sustainable Consumer? [Blog] *Insights.* Available at www .nielsen.com/us/en/insights/article/ 2018/was-2018-the-year-of-the-influential-sustainable-consumer/ (Accessed Feb. 9, 2020).

Noland, M. (2018). US trade policy in the Trump administration. *Asian Economic Policy Review*, *13*(2), 262–278.

Nutcase Helmets. (2020). Homepage. Nutcase Helmets [online]. Available at www.nutcasehelmets.com (Accessed Feb. 8, 2020).

Nye, C. W., Roth, M. S., and Shimp, T. A. (2008). Comparative advertising in markets where brands and comparative advertising are novel. *Journal of International Business Studies*, 851–863.

O'Malley, C. (2016). *Bonds Without Borders: A History of the Eurobond Market.* Chichester, UK: Wiley.

Obale, O. (2016). *From Conflict to Illicit: Mapping the Diamond Trade From Central African Republic to Cameroon.* Partnership Africa Canada [online]. Available at https:// impacttransform.org/wp-content/ uploads/2017/09/2016-Dec-From-Conflict-to-Illicit-Mapping-the-diamond-trade-from-Central-African-Republic-to-Cameroon.pdf

OECD (2013). OECD Guidelines on the Protection of Privacy and Transborder Flows of Personal Data. Organization for Economic Cooperation and Development website [online]. Available at www.oecd.org/internet/ ieconomy/oecdguidelinesonthe protectionofprivacyandtrans borderflowsofpersonaldata.htm

OECD. (2015). *OECD Principles of Corporate Governance.* Paris: Organisation for Economic Co-operation and Development.

OECD. (2016). Integrity Framework for Public Investment. Available at www.oecd.org/corruption-integrity/ reports/integrity-framework-for-public-investment-9789264251762-en.html (Accessed May 11, 2020).

OECD. (2017). Economic surveys and country surveillance. Organization for Economic Cooperation and Development website [online]. Available at www.oecd.org/ economy/surveys/

OECD. (2020), Trade in services (indicator). doi: 10.1787/3796b5f0-en (Accessed May 15, 2020).

Owens, J. C. (2018, July 27). Amazon earnings explode to record thanks to surprising e-commerce profit, stock gains. MarketWatch [online]. Available at www.marketwatch.com/story/ amazon-earnings-explode-to-record-thanks-to-surprising-e-commerce-profit-stock-gains-2018-07-26 (Accessed April 27, 2020).

Packaging Europe. (2018). Sustainability a Variable Driver of European Shopper Behaviour. [Blog] Available at https:// packagingeurope.com/sustainability-variable-driver-europe-shopper-behaviour/ (Accessed Feb. 9, 2020).

Palmquist, M. (2018). *Workplace perks: Wasteful indulgence or powerful profit driver?* Strategy and Business [online]. Available at www.strategy-business.com/blog/Workplace-Perks-Wasteful-Indulgence-or-Powerful-Profit-Driver (Accessed Feb. 9, 2020).

Papa, D. and Elliott, L. (2016). *International Trade and the Successful Intermediary.* New York: Routledge.

Patients Beyond Borders. (2020). [online]. Available at www.patientsbeyondborders.com/. (Accessed April 20, 2020).

Patterson, P. and Cicic, M. (1995). A typology of service firms in international markets: An empirical investigation. *Journal of International Marketing 3*(4), 57–83.

Perchard, A., MacKenzie, N. G., Decker, S., and Favero, G. (2017). Clio in the business school: Historical approaches in strategy, international business and entrepreneurship. *Business History, 59*(6), 904–927.

Percy, L. (2018). *Strategic Integrated Marketing Communications.* New York: Routledge.

Perraton, J. (2019). The scope and implications of globalisation. In *The Handbook of Globalisation*, 3rd ed. Edward Elgar Publishing.

Petersen, C. D. (2011). Defense and commercial trade offsets: Impacts on the US industrial base raise economic and national security concerns. *Journal of Economic Issues, 45*(2), 485–491. Available at www.jstor.org/

stable/23071527 (Accessed May 4, 2020).

Peterson, R. (2018). *6 segmentation case studies open up new revenues for brands – BarnRaisers, LLC.* [online] BarnRaisers, LLC. Available at https://barnraisersllc.com/2018/08/segmentation-case-studies-revenues/ (Accessed Feb. 11, 2020).

Philips, D. (1994). Building a "Cultural Index" to World Airline Safety. *The Washington Post*, August 21, 1994, A8.

Picciotto, S. (2017). Rights, responsibilities and regulation of international business. In *Globalization and International Investment*. Routledge, pp. 177–198.

Pierce, J. and Schott, P. (2018). Investment responses to trade liberalization: Evidence from US industries and establishments. *Journal of International Economics, 115*(November), 203–222.

Pinto, A. and Branson, D. (2018). *Understanding Corporate Law.* Durham, NC: Carolina Academic Press.

Prada, P. (2006). Bolivian nationalizes the oil and gas sector. *New York Times,* May 2, 2006 [online]. Available at www.nytimes.com/2006/05/02/world/americas/02bolivia.html (Accessed May 11, 2020).

Premium Official News. (2018). Understanding bots, botnets and trolls. (November 14). *Premium Official News.*

PricewaterhouseCoopers (2017). *International Comparison of Effective Corporate Tax Rates: A Report*

Prepared for Alliance for Competitive Taxation.

PricewaterhouseCoopers. (2018). *Explore the Data: SDG Reporting Challenge 2018.* PricewaterhouseCoopers [online]. Available at: www.pwc .com/gx/en/services/sustainability/ sustainable-development-goals/sdg-reporting-challenge-2018/sdg-data-explorer-2018.html (Accessed Feb. 9, 2020).

PricewaterhouseCoopers (2020). *Talent Mobility 2020.* [online] Available at www.pwc.com/gx/en/managing-tomorrows-people/future-of-work/ pdf/talent-mobility-2020.pdf (Accessed Feb. 9, 2020).

Purnell, N. and Purnell, T, M. (2018). "It's Been a Rout": Apple's iPhones Fall Flat in World's Largest Untapped Market. *Wall Street Journal* [online]. Available at www.wsj.com/articles/ its-been-a-rout-apple-stumbles-in-worlds-largest-untapped-market-11545146399 (Accessed 8 Feb. 2020).

Putsch, R. W. (1985). Cross-cultural communication: the special case of interpreters in health care. *Jama,* *254*(23), 3344–3348.

Radu, S. (2019). Countries the US Sees as Threat to Patents and IP. *US News & World Report*, August 7, 2019 [online]. Available at www.usnews .com/news/best-countries/slideshows/ these-countries-pose-the-biggest-ip-protection-threats-according-to-the-us (Accessed May 11, 2020).

Radu, S. (ed.). (2018). How Soon Will You Be Working From Home? US News & World Report [online]. Available at https://www.usnews.com/news/

best-countries/articles/2018–02-16/ telecommuting-is-growing-but-still-not-unanimously-embraced (Accessed April 21, 2020).

Rai, S. (2016, January 6). India Just Crossed 1 Billion Mobile Subscribers Milestone And The Excitement's Just Beginning. Forbes [online]. Available at www.forbes.com/sites/ saritharai/2016/01/06/india-just-crossed-1-billion-mobile-subscribers-milestone-and-the-excitements-just-beginning/#2c74b0be7db0 (Accessed April 27, 2020).

Rasche, A., Morsing, M., and Moon, J. (2017). *Corporate Social Responsibility: Strategy, Communication, Governance.* New York: Cambridge University Press.

Reagan, C. (2017, April 19). Think running retail stores is more expensive than selling online? Think again. CNBC [online]. Available at www.cnbc .com/2017/04/19/think-running-retail-stores-is-more-expensive-than-selling-online-think-again.html (Accessed April 28, 2020).

realDonaldTrump. (2019, January 11). H1-B holders in the United States can rest assured that changes are soon coming which will bring both simplicity and certainty to your stay, including a potential path to citizenship. We want to encourage talented and highly skilled people to pursue career options in the US [Tweet]. Available at https:// twitter.com/realdonaldtrump/ status/1083705208834834433? lang=en (Accessed May 12, 2020).

Rein, S. (2011, March 7). Why Best Buy Failed in China. CNBC [online].

Available at www.cnbc.com/ id/41882157 (Accessed April 27, 2020).

Reshoring Initiative. (2018). Reshoring Initiative 2017 Data Report: Reshoring Plus FDI Job Announcements Up 2,800% Since 2010. (April 10, 2018). reshorenow.org [online]. Available at http://reshorenow.org/april-10–2018/ (Accessed April 21, 2020).

Richards, G. (2017). *Warehouse management: a complete guide to improving efficiency and minimizing costs in the modern warehouse.* Kogan Page Publishers.

Ritchie, H., Hasell, J., Appel, C., and Roser, M. (2019, November). Terrorism. [online] Our World in Data website. Available at https://ourworldindata. org/terrorism#how-many-people-are-killed-by-terrorists-worldwide (Accessed May 18, 2020).

Robb, Greg. (2018). White House advisor: Foreign investment is skyrocketing, even with Harley-Davidson's move overseas. In *Market Watch*. [online]. Available at www.marketwatch.com/story/white-house-advisor-foreign-investment-is-skyrocketing-even-with-harley-davidsons-move-overseas-2018–06-26 (Accessed April 5, 2020).

Roberts, R. (2019). *Amazon FBA E-commerce Business Model 2019.* Independently published, 2019.

Romanoff, L. (2016). Coffee travels fast – Starbucks' supply chain. [Blog] *Deakin Business School – Marketing Management.* Available at https:// mpk732t12016clusterb.wordpress. com/2016/05/16/coffee-travels-fast-starbucks-supply-chain/ (Accessed Feb. 9, 2020).

Romm, T. (2018). Europe Hits Google With Record $5 Billion Antitrust Fine Over Bundling Of Its Apps On Android. *The Washington Post*; European Commission. (2020). *Antitrust: Commission Opens Formal Investigation Against Google In Relation To Android Mobile Operating System.* [online] Available at https:// ec.europa.eu/commission/presscorner/ detail/en/MEMO_15_4782 (Accessed Feb. 6, 2020).

Ronquillo, E. D. (2017). Trade cluster impacts on southern border transportation costs. *Collection for University of Texas, El Paso.* AAI10608492. Available at https://scholarworks.utep.edu/ dissertations/AAI10608492

Rosenberg, T. (2018). H.I.V. Drugs Cost $75 in Africa, $39,000 in the U.S. Does It Matter? *New York Times* [online]. Available at www.nytimes .com/2018/09/18/opinion/pricing-hiv-drugs-america.html (Accessed Feb. 8, 2020).

Safarian, E. and Bertin, G. (2014). *Multinationals, Governments and International Technology Transfer.* New York: Routledge.

Sakwa, R. (2016). *Frontline Ukraine.* London: I. B. Tauris.

Sampson, T. (2017). Brexit: The economics of international disintegration. *Journal of Economic Perspectives*, *31*(4), 163–184.

Sanders, N. (2017). *Supply Chain Management: A Global Perspective.* 2nd ed. Hoboken, NJ: Wiley.

Sang-Hun, C. (2009). South Koreans Struggle With Race. *The New York Times.* [online]. Available at www

.nytimes.com/2009/11/02/world/ asia/02race.html. (Accessed May 22, 2020).

Sauter, M. B. and Stebbins, S. (2016, April 23). Manufacturers bringing the most jobs back to America. USA TODAY [online]. Available at www.usatoday.com/story/money/ business/2016/04/23/24-7-wallst-economy-manufacturers-jobs-outsourcing/83406518/ (Accessed April 22, 2020).

Schweidel, D., Fader, P., and Bradlow, E. (2008). Understanding service retention within and across cohorts using limited information. *Journal of Marketing*, *72*(1)(January), 82–94.

Sengupta, J. K. (2007). *Dynamics of Entry and Market Evolution*. New York: Palgrave Macmillan.

Seyoum, B. (2013). *Export–Import Theory, Practices, and Procedures*. New York: Routledge.

Shane, D. (2018). *Panasonic is moving its Europe HQ out of the UK ahead of Brexit*. CNNMoney, [online]. Available at https://money.cnn.com/2018/08/30/ news/companies/panasonic-brexit-europe-hq/index.html (Accessed Feb. 6, 2020).

Shimizu, N., Osono, E., and Takeuchi, H. (2014, August). The Contradictions That Drive Toyota's Success. Harvard Business Review [online]. Available at https://hbr.org/2008/06/the-contradictions-that-drive-toyotas-success

Siles-Brügge, G. (2019). Bound by gravity or living in a 'post geography trading world'? Expert knowledge and affective spatial imaginaries in the construction of the UK's post-Brexit trade policy. *New Political Economy*, *24*(3), 422–439.

Silva, G. M., Styles, C., and Lages, L. F. (2017). Breakthrough innovation in international business: The impact of tech-innovation and market-innovation on performance. *International Business Review*, *26*(2), 391–404.

Simmering, M. (2020). Executive Compensation. Reference for Business. Available at www .referenceforbusiness.com/ management/Em-Exp/Executive-Compensation.html (Accessed December 18, 2020).

Singh, K. D. (2017), "The Internet's Next Big User Group," *Wall Street Journal*, Eastern Ed., August 7, www.wsj.com/ video/the-internet-next-big-user-group/06EEBEC5-B170-4FD3-877A-95D0163D939B.html

Singh, N. and Pereira, A. (2005). The Culturally Customized Web site: Customizing Web sites for the Global Marketplace. Burlington, MA: Elsevier Butterworth-Heinemann.

Sitsanis, N. (2019). Top 10 Languages Used On the Internet for 2020. *Speakt*. [online]. Available at https://speakt. com/top-10-languages-used-internet/ (Accessed May 2, 2020).

Smillie, I. (2002). *The Kimberley Process The Case For Proper Monitoring*. [online]. Available at https:// impacttransform.org/wp-content/ uploads/2017/09/2002-Sep-The-Kimberly-Process-The-Case-for-Proper-Monitoring.pdf

Smith, A. (2018). Panasonic agrees to pay US government $280 million for anti-bribery violations. *CNN* [online]. Available at https://money.cnn.com/2018/04/30/news/companies/panasonic-us-government-penalty/index.html (Accessed May 11, 2020).

Smith, C. (2003). Theorizing religious effects among American adolescents. *Journal for the Scientific Study of Religion*, *42*(1), 17–30.

Smith, D. (2020). Trump plays down US-China trade war concerns: 'When you're $500bn down you can't lose'. [online] *The Guardian*. Available at www.theguardian.com/business/2018/apr/04/trump-china-trade-war-concerns-import-taxes-stock-market (Accessed Feb. 6, 2020).

Snow, B. (2019). Construction Giant Skanska Sweden Has Big Plans to Go Completely Digital by 2023. *Redshift*. [online]. Available at www.autodesk.com/redshift/digital-construction/ (Accessed April 29, 2020).

Sokolowski, T. (2020). *Trade wars: US-China tariff battle already impacting industries globally – Outside Insight*. [online] Outside Insight. Available at https://outsideinsight.com/insights/trade-wars-us-china-tariff-battle-already-impacting-industries-globally (Accessed Feb. 3, 2020).

Solomon, L. and Dicker, H. (1988). The Crash of 1987: A Legal and Public Policy Analysis. In *Fordham Law Review* (p. 191). Fordham Law Review website [online]. Available at https://ir.lawnet.fordham.edu/flr/vol57/iss2/2

Sorge, A. and Streeck, W. (2018). Diversified quality production revisited: its contribution to German socio-economic performance over time. *Socio-Economic Review*, *16*(3), 587–612.

Southern, M. (2018, April 13), "Google Releases Tool to Show Off Natural Language Search Capabilities," *Search Engine Journal*, www.searchenginejournal.com/google-releases-tool-show-off-natural-language-search-capabilities/249313/

Sponder,M. and Khan,G. F. (2018a). *Digital Analytics For Marketing*, Routledge. An overview of quantitative benchmarks and metrics that can be used to evaluate the performance of websites and other digital platforms.

Srai, J. S. and Gregory, M. (2008). A supply network configuration perspective on international supply chain development. *International Journal of Operations & Production Management*. 28, 386–411.

StatCounter GlobalStats. (2017, December). Desktop Search Engine Market Share Worldwide, December 2017.

Statistica. (2019). Global production of rough diamonds from 2005 to 2019. (September 2019). Statista [online]. Available at www.statista.com/statistics/274921/worldwide-production-of-rough-diamonds/ (Accessed May 19, 2020).

Steenkamp, J.-B. (2017). *Global Brand Strategy*. London: Palgrave Macmillan.

Sue, D. W. (2001). Multidimensional facets of cultural competence. *The Counseling Psychologist*, *29*(6), 790–821.

Suharyanti, S., Wijaya, B. S., Sutawidjaya, A. H., and Marseila, M. (2016). How the client service department in local advertising agency manages relationships with multinational client: An intercultural business communication perspective. *International Business Management*, *10*(05), 667–675.

Sukar, A. and Hassan, S. (2001). US exports and time-varying volatility of real exchange rate. *Global Finance Journal*, *12*(1), 109–114.

Swanson, A. (2018). Trump's Trade War With China Is Officially Underway. *The New York Times*.

Szabó, L. (2019). In Search of the Soul of International Business – Foreword. *Business Expert Press*. pp. 14–16.

Talay, B., Townsend, J., and Yeniyurt, S. (2015). Global brand architecture position and market-based performance: The moderating role of culture. *Journal of International Marketing*, *23*(2), 55–72.

Talent Mobility. (2020). [online] Available at www.pwc.com/gx/en/managing-tomorrows-people/future-of-work/pdf/talent-mobility-2020.pdf (Accessed Feb. 9, 2020).

Talley, I. and Volz, D. (2019, September 15). US Targets North Korean Hacking as Rising National-Security Threat. *Wall Street Journal* [online]. Available at www.wsj.com/articles/u-s-targets-north-korean-hacking-as-rising-national-security-threat-11568545202

Tallman, S., Luo, Y., and Buckley, P. (2017). Business Models in Global Competition. *Global Strategy Journal*, *7*(5). Available at www.onlinelibrary.wiley.com

Tao Kae Noi. (2018). Investor Relations. Taokaenoi Food & Marketing Public Company Limited. Available at http://investor.taokaenoi.co.th/ar.html.

Tasaki, T., Tojo, N., and Lindhqvist, T. (2019). Differences in perception of extended producer responsibility and product stewardship among stakeholders: an international questionnaire survey and statistical analysis. *Journal of Industrial Ecology*, *23*(2), 438–451.

Tatoglu, E., Glaister, A. J., and Demirbag, M. (2016). Talent management motives and practices in an emerging market: A comparison between MNEs and local firms. *Journal of World Business*, *51*(2), 278–293.

Taylor, C. and Okazaki, S. (2015). Do global brands use similar executional styles across cultures? *Journal of Advertising*, *44*(3), 276–288.

Teagarden, M. B., Von Glinow, M. A., and Mellahi, K. (2018). Contextualizing international business research: Enhancing rigor and relevance. *Journal of World Business*, *53*(3), 303–306.

Thanthong-Knight, R. (2018). Thailand disturbed by sharp decline in Chinese tourists, turned off by series of unfortunate events. *Post Magazine*, October 3, 2018. Available at www.scmp.com/magazines/post-magazine/travel/article/2166804/thailand-disturbed-sharp-decline-chinese-tourists.

The Economist (2008). The Siemens scandal: Bavarian baksheesh. December, 17, 2008, p. 112.

The Economist. (2009). Feast and famine. *The Economist*, vol. 392, no.8651, October 3, 2009, pp. 78–80.

The Institute of Customer Service. (2020). *UK Customer Satisfaction Index*. [online]. Available at https://lp.instituteofcustomerservice.com/hubfs/UKCSI%20Jan%202020/ICS%20UKCSI%20Exec%20Summary_January%202020%20INTERACTIVE_22.01.20_LP-1.pdf (Accessed May 1, 2020).

The Milan City Journal. (2020). Haitao: the Chinese online shopping experience. [online]. Available at https://themilancityjournal.com/haitao-the-chinese-online-shopping-experience/ (Accessed May 2, 2020).

The White House (2018). Statement from President Donald J. Trump on Additional Proposed Section 301 Remedies | The White House. [online] Available at www.whitehouse.gov/briefings-statements/statement-president-donald-j-trump-additional-proposed-section-301-remedies/ (Accessed Feb. 6, 2020).

Thomas, D. C. and Peterson, M. F. (2018). *Cross-Cultural Management* (Thousand Oaks, CA.

Tjemkes, B., Vos, P., and Burgers, K. (2017). *Strategic Alliance Management*. London: Routledge.

Tooze, A. (2018). *Crashed: How a Decade of Financial Crises Changed the World*. New York: Viking.

Topend Sports. (2020). World Sports Timeline. [online]. Available at www.topendsports.com/world/timeline/index.htm (Accessed April 22, 2020).

Toto, D. (2018). EU adopts plastics policy agenda. *Recycling Today* [online]. Available at www.recyclingtoday.com/article/eu-commission-adopts-plastics-recycling-policy/ (Accessed May 3, 2020).

Townsend, J. (2003). Understanding alliances: A review of international aspects in strategic marketing. *Marketing Intelligence & Planning* 21, 143–158.

Transparency International. (2020). *Corruption Perceptions Index 2019*. [online]. Available at www.transparency.org/cpi2019 (Accessed May 11, 2020).

Turban, E., Outland, J., King, D., Lee, J. K., Liang, T.-P., and Turban, D. C. (2018). *Electronic Commerce 2018: A Managerial and Social Networks Perspective*. Springer International.

Tyekiff, P. (2019). 4 Cross Cultural Marketing Flops You Won't Forget in a Hurry. [Blog] *Kwintessential Ltd.* Available at www.kwintessential.co.uk/blog/localisation/cross-cultural-marketing-flops-you-wont-forget-in-a-hurry (Accessed Mar. 1, 2019).

UNCTAD. (2017). *World Investment Report 2017*. Geneva: United Nations Conference on Trade and Development.

UNCTAD. (2018). Handbook of Statistics 2018. United Nations website [online]. Available at https://unctad.org/en/pages/PublicationWebflyer.aspx?publicationid=2297

UNCTAD. (2018). *World Investment Report*. Geneva: UNCTAD. Available at www.unctad.org

UNCTAD. (2019). Global foreign direct investment slides for third consecutive year. Available at https://unctad.org/en/pages/newsdetails.aspx?OriginalVersionID=2118 (Accessed April 5, 2020).

UNCTAD. (2020). *World Investment Report 2019*. New York: United Nations.

Undergraduate Retention and Graduation Rates. (2020, April). National Center for Education Statistics [online]. Available at https://nces.ed.gov/programs/coe/indicator_ctr.asp (Accessed May 12, 2020).

Unilever. (2019). *Unilever Sustainable Living Plan.* Unilever Global Corporate Site [online]. Available at www.unilever.com/sustainable-living/our-strategy/about-our-strategy/ (Accessed Mar. 5, 2019).

United Nations Conference on Trade and Development. (2020). *World Investment Report 2019.* New York: United Nations.

United Nations World Tourism Organization. (2020). *Impact Assessment of the Covid-19 Outbreak on International Tourism.* [online] Available at www.unwto.org/impact-assessment-of-the-covid-19-outbreak-on-international-tourism (Accessed May 3, 2020).

United States Census Bureau. (2018). Older People Projected to Outnumber Children. (December 3). The United States Census Bureau [online]. Available at www.census.gov/newsroom/press-releases/2018/cb18-41-population-projections.html (Accessed May 12, 2020).

United States Commercial Service. (2018). *Doing Business in India: 2018 Country Commercial Guide for U.S. Companies.* [online] 2018.export.gov. Available at https://2016.export.gov/india/doingbusinessinindia/index.asp (Accessed Feb. 8, 2020).

United States Court of Appeals for the District of Columbia Circuit. (2019). Save Jobs USA v. United States Dep't of Homeland Sec., 942 F.3d 504, 2019 U.S. App. LEXIS 33431, 2019 WL 5849503 (United States Court of Appeals for the District of Columbia Circuit November 8, 2019, Decided). [online]. Available at https://advance-lexis-com.proxy.library.georgetown.edu/api/document?collection=cases&id=urn:contentItem:5XFT-6721-JNCK-229 R-00000-00&context=1516831.

United States General Accounting Office. (2002). International Trade: Significant Challenges Remain in Deterring Trade in Conflict Diamonds. [online]. Available at www.gao.gov/assets/110/109096.pdf

UPS. (2020). UPS Fact Sheet. [online]. Available at https://pressroom.ups.com/pressroom/ContentDetailsViewer.page?ConceptType=FactSheets&id=1426321563187-193 (Accessed May 3, 2020).

US Bureau of Labor Statistics. (2019). Union Members Summary. (January 22, 2019). US Bureau of Labor Statistics [online]. Available at www.bls.gov/news.release/union2.nr0.htm (Accessed April 22, 2020).

US Department of Justice. (2017). *A Resource Guide to the US Foreign Corrupt Practices Act (FCPA).* Washington, DC: US Department of Justice.

US Department of State. (2017). *National Consortium for the Study of Terrorism and Responses to Terrorism, Annex of statistical information: Country reports on terrorism 2016.* [online]. Available at www.state.gov/documents/organization/272485.pdf. (Accessed May 11, 2020).

US Department of State. (2017a) Annual Living Quarters Allowance In US Dollars (DSSR 130). (2017, October 29). US Department of State [online]. Available at https://aoprals.state.gov/Web920/lqa_all.asp?MenuHide=1 (Accessed April 21, 2020).

US Department of State. (2017b) Indexes of Living Costs Abroad, Quarters Allowances, and Hardship Differentials – October 2017. US Department of State [online]. Available at https://aoprals.state.gov/content.asp?content_id=186&menu_id=81 (Accessed April 21, 2020).

US Department of State. (2020). Outcomes of Current US Trade Agreements. Available at www.state.gov/trade-agreements/outcomes-of-current-u-s-trade-agreements/ (Accessed April 18, 2020).

US Trade Representative. (2020). Caribbean Basin Initiative. Available at. https://ustr.gov/issue-areas/trade-development/preference-programs/caribbean-basin-initiative-cbi Accessed April 19, 2020).

USCIS. (2018). USCIS Completes the H-1B Cap Random Selection Process for FY 2019. (April 12). USCIS [online]. Available at www.uscis.gov/news/alerts/uscis-completes-h-1b-cap-random-selection-process-fy–2019 (Accessed May 12, 2020).

USCIS. (2019). L-1A Intracompany Transferee Executive or Manager. (April 29). USCIS [online]. Available at https://www.uscis.gov/working-united-states/temporary-workers/l-1a-intracompany-transferee-executive-or-manager (Accessed May 12, 2020).

USCIS. (2020). Characteristics of H-1B Specialty Occupation Workers. *USCIS.* [online]. Available at www.uscis.gov/sites/default/files/reports-studies/Characteristics_of_Specialty_Occupation_Workers_H-1B_Fiscal_Year_2019.pdf

USDA Foreign Agricultural Services. (2018). Thailand Food Processing Ingredients, USDA Foreign Agricultural Services. Available at https://gain.fas.usda.gov/Recent%20GAIN%20Publications/Food%20Processing%20Ingredients_Bangkok_Thailand_4–5-2018.pdf

USIDFC. (2020). US International Development Finance Corporation. [online]. Available at www.dfc.gov (Accessed May 11, 2020).

USTR. (2020). *2019 National Trade Estimate Report on Foreign Trade Barriers.* Washington DC: Office of the United States Trade Representative. [online]. Available at https://ustr.gov/sites/default/files/2019_National_Trade_Estimate_Report.pdf (Accessed May 11, 2020).

Vaccarini, K., Spigarelli, F., et al. (2018). *Cultural Distance in International Ventures: Exploring Perceptions of European and Chinese Managers.* London: Palgrave MacMillan.

Vacharawongsith, V. and Khaoeian, P. (2018). Taokaenoi Food & Marketing: At the cross roads; cut to contrarian sell. RHB Thailand Company Update, December 17, 2018. Available at https://research.rhbtradesmart.com/attachments/87/rhb-report-th_taokaenoi-food-marketing_company-update_20181217_rhb-245486720461440245c16f68393a68.pdf.

Van de Ven, A. H., Gustafson, D. H., and Delbecq, A. (1975). *Group Techniques for Program Planning: A Guide to Nominal Group and Delphi Processes* (p. 83). Glenview, IL: Scott Foresman.

Varma, S. (2017). Nokia is back but is it the same daring, innovative Nokia of old? *India Today* [online]. Available at www.indiatoday.in/technology/talking-points/story/nokia-comeback-is-it-the-same-daring-innovative-nokia-of-old-hmd-global-964816–2017-03-09 (Accessed May 3, 2020).

Veiga, P. D. M. and Rios, S. P. (2019). MERCOSUR experience in regional integration: what could Africa learn from it?

Verbeke, A. and Asmussen, C. Global, (2016). Local, or Regional? The Locus of MNE Strategies. *Journal of Management Studies 53*(6), 1051–1075.

Verschoor, C. (2007). Siemens AG is latest fallen ethics idol. *Strategic Finance*, *89*(5), 11–13.

von Glinow, M. A. V., Shapiro, D. L., and Brett, J. M. (2004). Can we talk, and should we? Managing emotional conflict in multicultural teams.

Academy of Management Review, *29*(4), 578–592.

Vranica, S. (2005). Trends: Advertising; Anywhere, Anytime. *Wall Street Journal*, November 21, 2005, R6.

Walbank, F. (2003). *The Cambridge Ancient History, Vol. 7*. Cambridge: Cambridge University Press.

Walt, V. (2017). Unilever CEO Paul Polman's Plan to Save the World. *Fortune*. [online] Available at https://fortune.com/2017/02/17/unilever-paul-polman-responsibility-growth/ (Accessed Feb. 9, 2020).

Wang, X. (2018, April 2). Walled Garden No More: Digital China Goes Global. Forrester [online]. Available at www.forrester.com/report/Walled+Garden+No+More+Digital+China+Goes+Global/-/E-RES135569 (Accessed April 27, 2020).

WARC (2018, February), "Five Trends That Are Shaping India's e-Commerce Opportunity."

Weisbrot, M. (2019). The IMF is hurting countries it claims to help. In *The Guardian*. Available at www.theguardian.com/commentisfree/2019/aug/27/imf-economics-inequality-trump-ecuador (Accessed April 8, 2020).

Weiß, J. (2018). Globalisierungsreport 2018. Bertelsmann Stiftung. Available at www.bertelsmann-stiftung.de/en/publications/publication/did/globalisierungsreport–2018. (Accessed May 21, 2020).

Wells, T. (2016, June 8). How can HR protect the safety of globally mobile employees? Personnel Today [online]. Available at www.personneltoday

.com/hr/can-hr-protect-safety-globally-mobile-employees/ (Accessed April 22, 2020).

White House. (2017). Presidential Executive Order on Buy American and Hire American. (April 17). The White House [online]. Available at www.whitehouse.gov/presidential-actions/presidential-executive-order-buy-american-hire-american/ (Accessed May 12, 2020).

Whittaker, Z. (2019, May 15). New secret-spilling flaw affects almost every Intel chip since 2011. TechCrunch [online]. Available at https://guce.techcrunch.com/consent?brandType=non EU&done=https%3A%2F%2Ftechcrunch%2Ecom%2F2019%2F05%2F14%2Fzombieload%2Dflaw%2Dintel%2Dprocessors %2F&tg crumb=oD1eEJc= (Accessed April 27, 2020).

Wielaard, R. (2009). Microsoft Loses E.U. Antitrust Case. *The Washington Post*.

Wilkinson, M., Dumontier, M., Aalbersberg, I., Appleton, G., Axton, M., Baak, A., Blomberg, N., Boiten, J., da Silva Santos, L., Bourne, P., Bouwman, J., Brookes, A., Clark, T., Crosas, M., Dillo, I., Dumon, O., Edmunds, S., Evelo, C., Finkers, R., Gonzalez-Beltran, A., Gray, A., Groth, P., Goble, C., Grethe, J., Heringa, J., 't Hoen, P., Hooft, R., Kuhn, T., Kok, R., Kok, J., Lusher, S., Martone, M., Mons, A., Packer, A., Persson, B., Rocca-Serra, P., Roos, M., van Schaik, R., Sansone, S., Schultes, E., Sengstag, T., Slater, T., Strawn, G., Swertz, M., Thompson, M., van der Lei, J., van Mulligen, E., Velterop, J., Waagmeester, A., Wittenburg, P., Wolstencroft, K., Zhao, J., and Mons, B. (2016). The FAIR Guiding Principles for scientific data management and stewardship. *Scientific Data*, 3(1).

Williams, D. (2019). *International Business Blunders: Lessons for Future Managers*. Bingley, UK: Emerald Publishing.

Wilson, A. (2014). *Ukraine Crisis*. New Haven (CT): Yale University Press.

Wisner, J., Tan, K.-C., and Keong Leong, G. (2016). *Principles of Supply Chain Management: A Balanced Approach, 4th ed.* Boston: Cengage Learning.

Wood, J. (2018, February 20). Expats in Mexico: Pros and Cons of Living in Mexico. ExpatExchange [online]. Available at www.expatexchange.com/ctryguide/5014/77/Mexico/Expats-in-Mexico-Pros-and-Cons-of-Living-in-Mexico (Accessed April 21, 2020).

World Bank. (2018). *Combating corruption.* [online]. Available at www.worldbank.org/en/topic/governance/brief/anti-corruption (Accessed May 11, 2020).

World Bank. (2019). *Belt and Road Initiative.* [online] Available at www.worldbank.org/en/topic/regional-integration/brief/belt-and-road-initiative (Accessed Feb. 7, 2020).

World Bank. (2019a). *Listed domestic companies, total.* [online] data.worldbank.org. Available at: http/data.worldbank.org/indicator/

CM.MKT.LDOM.NO?view=chart (Accessed April 17, 2020).

World Bank. (2019b). *Worldwide Governance Indicators, 2019*. World Bank [online]. Available at https://info.worldbank.org/governance/wgi/ (Accessed Feb. 9, 2020).

World Bank. (2020). Bribery incidence (% of firms experiencing at least one bribe payment request). [online]. Available at https://data.worldbank.org/indicator/IC.FRM.BRIB.ZS (Accessed May 11, 2020)].

World Bank. (n.d.). Available at www.worldbank.org/en/topic/regional-integration/brief/belt-and-road-initiative

World Economic Forum (2018). *The Global Risks Report 2018, 12th ed.* Geneva, Switzerland.

World Federation of Exchanges. (2018). 2017 Full Year Market Highlights. Available at www.world-exchanges.org

World Trade Organization (WTO). (2018). World trade statistical review 2017. Downloaded from www.wto.org

World Trade Organization. (2020). Members and Observers. [online]. Available at www.wto.org/english/thewto_e/whatis_e/tif_e/org6_e.htm (Accessed April 9, 2020).

World Trade Organization. (2020). *Trade-Related Aspects of Intellectual Property Rights*. [online]. Available at www.wto.org/english/tratop_e/trips_e/trips_e.htm (Accessed May 11, 2020).

World Trade Organization. (2020). *World Trade Report 2019*. [online]. Available at www.wto.org/english/res_e/booksp_e/03_wtr19_2_e.pdf (Accessed April 24, 2020).

Wright, M. et al., (2013). *The Oxford Handbook of Corporate Governance*. Oxford, UK: Oxford University Press.

WTO Electronic Commerce. (2020). Available at www.wto.org/english/tratop_e/ecom_e/ecom_e.htm (Accessed May, 3 2020).

Wu, Q., Muthuraman, K., and Seshadri, S. (2019). Effect of financing costs and constraints on real investments: The case of inventories. *Production and Operations Management*, *28*(10), 2573–2593.

Wu, W. (2018). China Seeks New Insights On US Trade Strategy As It Plans Next Moves. *South China Morning Post*.

Wu, Z. and Salomon, R. (2017). Deconstructing the liability of foreignness: Regulatory enforcement actions against foreign banks. *Journal of International Business Studies*, *48*(7), 837–861. Available at https://doi.org/10.1057/s41267-017-0092-x

X-Ray Mega Airport (2015) (TV series), Discovery UK, www.discoveryuk.com/series/x-ray-mega-airport/

Yan, A. and Luo, A. (2016). *International Joint Ventures: Theory and Practice*. New York: Routledge.

Yen, D., Barnes, B., and Wang, C. (2011). The measurement of guanxi: Introducing the GRX model. *Industrial Marketing Management*, *40*(1), 97–108.

Yifan, D. (2018). *How Will the BRICS Lead the Global Economy?* China-US Focus [online]. Available at www.chinausfocus.com/finance-economy/how-will-the-brics-lead-the-global-economy (Accessed Feb. 7, 2020).

Yip, G. and Hult, G. T. (2013). *Total Global Strategy*. Upper Saddle River, NJ: Pearson Education.

Zhao, K., Zhao, X., and Deng, J. (2016). An empirical investigation of online gray markets. *Journal of Retailing 92*(4), 397–410.

Zhen, W. (2012). Intercultural conflicts of international marketing activities – from the perspective of Chinese companies. *Review of European Studies*, *4*, 118.

Zhou, N. (2013). New Buying Behavior of Chinese Consumers. China Internet Watch [online]. Available at www .chinainternetwatch.com/2186/new-buying-behavior/ (Accessed February 16, 2020).

Index